ANCIENT SOLSTICE

UNCOVERING THE SPIRITUAL MEANING
OF THE SOLSTICES AND EQUINOXES

MARK ATWOOD
with LARA ATWOOD

Ancient Solstice: Uncovering the Spiritual Meaning of the Solstices and Equinoxes

Copyright © 2011-2021 Mark Atwood and Lara Atwood

All rights reserved. No part of this book may be reproduced, modified, incorporated, or transmitted in any form or by any means, electronic, mechanical, or otherwise, including photocopying, recording, or by any information storage and retrieval system—except by a reviewer who may quote brief passages in a review to be printed in magazine, newspaper, or on the Internet—without permission in writing from the copyright holder. Mark Atwood and Lara Atwood assert their moral right to be identified as the authors of Ancient Solstice.

Updated Fourth Edition, December 2021. Previously published as The Ancient Path of the Sun: Uncovering the Spiritual Meaning of the Solstices and Equinoxes, January 2021

ISBN 978-0-6487565-3-8

Sura Ondrunar Publishing

Requests for permission to reproduce copyrighted material may be emailed to the publisher Sura Ondrunar Publishing, visit suraondrunar.org.

Every reasonable effort has been made by the publisher to locate and acknowledge copyright owners, and obtain any necessary clearances. Please refer to the Copyright Acknowledgments section at the end of this book for the full list of works. If any works requiring clearance have unwittingly been included, or any corrections need to be made, the publisher will be pleased to do so at the earliest opportunity.

The core content of this book was first published in a series of Internet articles between June 2011 and June 2013. All chapters of this book were jointly authored by Mark Atwood, who contributed the esoteric knowledge from his experience of the path of the spiritual sun, and Lara Atwood, who contributed the historical research.

NON-PROFIT PRINCIPLES

The authors do not receive any money for the writing or sale of this book, as they follow the ancient principle that spiritual knowledge should not be profited from. This book is sold by a not-for-profit publisher with the same principles who set its price to cover the cost of production, with any surplus going back into their operating expenses.

DISCLAIMER

This book contains general information on the topic of religion for educational use only. Neither the authors nor the publisher are providing any service or advice to the individual reader.

While we endeavor to keep the information in this book up-to-date and correct, we make no representations or warranties of any kind, express or implied, about the completeness, accuracy, reliability, or suitability for any purpose. Any reliance you place on such information is therefore strictly at your own risk. You need to make your own inquiries to determine if the information is appropriate for your intended use.

The information in the book should not be used to diagnose, prevent, treat, or cure any sickness, disease, health or medical condition and is not meant to substitute medical or health advice or treatment. If you have any mental health concerns, you should consult with a qualified medical professional before acting upon or using any information in the book. Never disregard professional medical advice or delay in seeking it because of something that you have read in this book.

CONTENTS

PREFACE 1

PART I:
••• THE PATH OF THE SUN •••

CHAPTER ONE
The Spiritual Meaning of the Solstices and Equinoxes 13
What Are the Solstices and Equinoxes? 14
As Above, so Below 15
As Within, so Without 16
The Spiritual Sun 17
The Ancient Religion of the Sun 20
The Spiritual Son 26
The Divinity of Fire 31
The Spiritual Nature of Light 38
The Path of the Spiritual Sun 41
Ancient Remnants of Solstice and Equinox Celebrations 46
Spiritual Symbols Found in the Cosmos 48
Cosmic Connections 66
Different Types of Astrological Myths 67
Cross-Quarter Days 67
Looking at the Past with Discernment 70
Connect with the Heavens and the Earth by Celebrating
the Solstices and Equinoxes 78

Autumn Equinox
Death and Descent into Darkness

CHAPTER TWO
The Spiritual Meaning of the Autumn Equinox 83
A Time When Darkness Is Greater Than Light 84
The Rival of the Sun 85
The Death of John and the Wicker Man 89
Inner Death 90
The Descent into the Underworld 92
The Fall into Darkness 97
The Role of Chaos 98
The Quest for Light in Darkness 99

The Sacred Seed	100
The Seven Bodies of the Sun	103
The Nine Regions of the Underworld	108
The Warrior Aspect of the Mother Goddess	112
The Mystery of the Minotaur and the Labyrinth	121
Ancient Rites of Descent	123
The Meaning of the Autumn Equinox in Daily Life	125
The Principles of Inner Death and Descent	125

Winter Solstice
Birth

CHAPTER THREE

The Spiritual Meaning of the Winter Solstice — 129

The Most Celebrated Religious Time in the World	130
The Birth of the Sun	132
The Spiritual Son	134
The Potential of Consciousness	135
The Birth of the Spiritual Sun Within	136
The Creative Power of Sex	141
Spiritual Birth from Alchemical Union	143
The Birth of the World Teacher and Savior	147
The Meaning of the Mound, Cave, Stables, and Prison Where the Son Is Born	153
The Baby Sun	158
Why Christmas Is Celebrated Three Days after the Winter Solstice	159
The Three Steps into the Seven Dimensions	160
The Symbols of the Nativity	162
The Creation of the Four	164
The Meaning of the Winter Solstice in Daily Life	166
Children of the Sun	166

Spring Equinox
Resurrection

CHAPTER FOUR

The Spiritual Meaning of the Spring Equinox — 169

The Churning of the Milky Ocean	170
The Cycle of the Sun	172
Darkness and Light in the Greater Cycles of Life	173
The Struggle between Darkness and Light	174
The Treasures	175
The Poison	175

The Nectar	176
The Necessity of Darkness	177
The Traps	177
Betrayal	179
The Divine Role of Judas	180
Trial	181
The Crucifixion of the Sun	182
The Good Thief and the Bad Thief	188
The Death of Self-Image	189
Self-Sacrifice	191
Anubis, Guardian of the Gateway to Immortality	194
The Return to the Womb	195
The Descent into Hell	202
Resurrection	204
The Meaning of the Spring Equinox in Daily Life	207
The Eternal Life of the Spirit	208

CHAPTER FIVE

Decoding the Ancient Meaning of the Sphinx and Its Origin as Anubis — 209

The Sphinx as Anubis	210
The Sphinx Resurrection Theory	211
Spiritual Truths Later Interpreted Literally	212
Resurrection	213
The God Anubis	214
Anubis and Inner Death	215
The Nine Layers of the Underworld	217
The Tomb	217
The Sacred Lake of Anubis	218
Purification of the Energies and the Four Bodies	218
Return to the Womb	221
Overcoming the Law	223
The Astronomical Alignments of the Sphinx	225
The Resurrection of Osiris in the Stars and on the Ground	229
The Use of Universal Principles in the Giza Design	230
Osiris between the Paws of the Anubis Sphinx	231
The Age of the Sphinx	233
How the Sphinx Was Lost	234
The Gradual Loss of the Spiritual Knowledge of Ancient Egypt	237
Spiritual Knowledge Turned into a Religion of the Afterlife	239
My Out-of-Body Experiences in the Great Pyramid	240
A Site for Spiritual Initiation	241

Summer Solstice
Ascension

CHAPTER SIX
The Spiritual Meaning of the Summer Solstice 245

    The Trinity and the Feathered Serpent   246
    Creation in Reverse   249
    The Three Days and Three Rings   251
    Ascension   254
    Return to the Source of Creation   258
    The Union of Heaven and Earth, and the Tree of Life   259
    The Virgins of the Sun   264
    Dew and Holy Water   268
    Earth Crowned by the Sun   271
    The Meaning of the Summer Solstice in Daily Life   273
    Return to the Light   273

PART II:
··· ANCIENT SITES ···

CHAPTER SEVEN
Introduction 279

CHAPTER EIGHT
Ancient Sacred Sites Aligned to the Autumn Equinox 281

    The Great Pyramid ~ Egypt   281
    Pyramid of Kukulcán, Chichen Itza ~ Mexico   283
    Pyramid of the Sun, Teotihuacán ~ Mexico   284
    Intihuatana Stone, Machu Picchu ~ Peru   286
    The Seven Moai of Ahu Akivi ~ Easter Island   287
    Temple of the Seven Dolls, Dzibilchaltún ~ Mexico   289
    The Palace of Knossos ~ The Greek Island of Crete   289
    More Sites   292

CHAPTER NINE
Ancient Sacred Sites Aligned to the Winter Solstice 293

    Glastonbury Tor ~ England   293
    Pyramid of Kukulcán, Chichen Itza ~ Mexico   294

Goseck Circle ~ Germany	295
Nebra Sky Disk ~ Germany	296
Mynydd Dinas ~ Wales	297
Karnak Temple ~ Egypt	297
Newgrange ~ Ireland	299
Ness of Brodgar ~ Scotland	301
The Four-Handed Moai Statue ~ Easter Island	304
The Great Pyramids ~ Egypt	305
The Sun Gate, Tiwanaku ~ Bolivia	306
Machu Picchu ~ Peru	308
Cerro Pinkuylluna Mountain, Urubamba Sacred Valley ~ Peru	309
Ajanta Caves ~ India	310
Great Zimbabwe ~ Africa	311
Nazca Lines ~ Peru	312
The Monastery, Petra ~ Jordan	314
Angkor Wat ~ Cambodia	315
Arkaim and Surrounding Megalithic Sites ~ Russia	316
More Sites	319

CHAPTER TEN

Ancient Sacred Sites Aligned to the Spring Equinox 323

The Great Sphinx ~ Egypt	323
Angkor Wat ~ Cambodia	325
Tikal ~ Guatemala	328
Cahokia Mounds ~ Illinois, United States	329
Cairn T ~ Ireland	331
Knowth ~ Ireland	332
The Millmount-Croagh Patrick Alignment ~ Ireland	333
Cairnpapple and Arthur's Seat Alignment ~ Scotland	334
Persepolis ~ Iran	335
More Sites	337

CHAPTER ELEVEN

Ancient Sacred Sites Aligned to the Summer Solstice 339

The Great Pyramids and Sphinx ~ Egypt	339
The Osireion ~ Egypt	340
The Essene Monastery, Qumran ~ West Bank	341
Stonehenge ~ England	343
Nabta Playa ~ Egypt	347
Linn Oir Alignment, Mount Seskin ~ Ireland	348
Externsteine ~ Germany	349

Ajanta Caves ~ India	350
Serpent Mound ~ Ohio, United States	352
Chaco Canyon ~ New Mexico, United States	353
Ahu Tongariki ~ Easter Island	355
El Castillo, Tulum ~ Mexico	355
The Pyramid of the Magician, Uxmal ~ Mexico	357
The Lost World Pyramid, Tikal ~ Guatemala	357
The Way of Viracocha ~ Bolivia and Peru	358
Stepped Pyramids ~ Various Islands around the World	359
Ziggurat of Ur ~ Iraq	360
Wurdi Youang Stone Arrangement ~ Australia	361
Lascaux Cave Paintings ~ France	362
More Sites	363

PART III:

··· CEREMONIES ···

CHAPTER TWELVE

A Guide to Celebrating the Solstices and Equinoxes — 369

Why Celebrate the Solstices and Equinoxes?	370
Connect with the Heavens and the Earth by Celebrating the Solstices and Equinoxes	371
Celebrating According to Your Circumstances	372
Working out a Calendar and Preparing in Advance	374
Using a Sacred Space	375
Working out Ceremonies and Activities	381
Ten Tips for Creating Your Own Ceremony	390
The Value of Experience	393

Autumn Equinox

CHAPTER THIRTEEN

Ceremonies to Celebrate the Autumn Equinox — 397

Ceremony Overview	397
A Guide to Creating an Autumn Equinox Ceremony	398
Example Themes	402
Example Solitary or Small Group Ceremony ~ Vedic/Hindu	404
Example Solitary or Small Group Ceremony ~ Germanic/Nordic	413
Example Group Ceremony ~ Minoan/Greek	428

Winter Solstice

CHAPTER FOURTEEN
Ceremonies to Celebrate the Winter Solstice   441
   Ceremony Overview   441
   A Guide to Creating a Winter Solstice Ceremony   442
   Example Themes   446
   Example Group Ceremony ~ Inca (Andean)   448

Spring Equinox

CHAPTER FIFTEEN
Ceremonies to Celebrate the Spring Equinox   463
   Ceremony Overview   463
   A Guide to Creating a Spring Equinox Ceremony   464
   Example Themes   468
   Example Solitary or Small Group Ceremony ~ Maya   469

Summer Solstice

CHAPTER SIXTEEN
Ceremonies to Celebrate the Summer Solstice   483
   Ceremony Overview   483
   A Guide to Creating a Summer Solstice Ceremony   484
   Example Themes   488
   Example Group Ceremony ~ Slavic   489

CHAPTER SEVENTEEN
Conclusion   501
   Applying the Principles of the Sun   501
   More Information   503

REFERENCES   507
   Textual   507
   Images   537

COPYRIGHT ACKNOWLEDGMENTS   559
   Textual   559
   Images   563

Preface

by Lara Atwood

This book uncovers something highly significant, which has the potential to both decode and explain many ancient religious texts, sites, mythologies, and rituals. While numerous researchers focus on lost civilizations and ancient technologies, our focus is on ancient religion. That is, what we feel is most important to understand about ancient peoples are not their scientific or technological achievements, but their spiritual ones.

Researching the past offers us tantalizing snippets and scattered pieces of the religion of a distant golden age, and what this book provides is a way to practice that same religion today. Many focus on a purely academic study of ancient religion, which has almost no bearing on their own lives. Others seek to reconnect with ancient spirituality based on a very loose interpretation of it, which has little grounding in history. My point is not to criticize either approach—I would prefer to live in a world where people are free to choose how to pursue truth, without having to endure the vitriol of others. I only raise them in order to point out the differences. What we aim to do is offer the revival of this ancient religion based on real historical evidence combined with tangible spiritual experience.

What we've uncovered explains why so many ancient sacred sites align to the sun's major annual stages (the solstices and equinoxes), why so much ancient spiritual knowledge shares similarities across cultures, why so many ancient peoples revered the sun even though separated by great distances, and reveals the common roots behind many religions and traditions still practiced today. I will go so far as to say it acts as a virtual Rosetta Stone of ancient religion.

Formerly, my husband and I both believed that much of the great spiritual wisdom of the past, though describing many of the same truths, was not part of the same ancient religion, but had arisen independently of one another.

However, while writing and researching the articles that later became the foundation of this book, we came to realize that there were just too many—often identical—similarities between ancient sites, myths, and texts, and that these similarities could not possibly be coincidental. We traced them across many parts of the world, and as far back into ancient sources as we could, to discover that there had once been a shared religion that spread across much of the world in ancient times, tracing back to a fabled golden age of spirituality in Earth's history. In this religion, the sun was seen as the highest manifestation of the divine, which is why so many ancient cultures venerated the sun, and so we named this religion the Religion of the Sun. For those interested, I have written a detailed history of this religion in my book titled *The Ancient Religion of the Sun*.

Primarily what *Ancient Solstice* reveals is how practitioners of this ancient religion saw in the journey the earth makes annually around the sun a sacred path or way that both men and women could take in life to become a "son of the sun," which was a special title held by great teachers of this religion in ancient times.

Through examining the ancient sites aligned to and traditions celebrated on the solstices and equinoxes—the four major annual stages in this journey—and deciphering their spiritual symbols, Mark (my husband) has been able to correlate the sun's annual journey through the sky with this sacred path. Because he is the first to make this correlation, we have named it "The Sacred Sun Path Theory" and it's this theory my husband elaborates here in this book—using numerous references from ancient sacred texts, and symbols used at the ancient sites and found in the surviving ancient traditions of those who practiced or were influenced by this religion, as supporting evidence.

However, this book is not an encyclopedic style compendium of research on the celebration of the sun—that would be a much bigger book, would serve little real purpose in terms of practical understanding, and would also be very boring! Instead, it ultimately aims to synthesize the deeper meaning behind the celebration of the solstices and equinoxes as something that can be practiced today, just as the ancients did thousands of years ago. It uncovers the lost threads that connect the very process of spiritual transformation with the movement of the heavens and the earth, as well as the remaining fragments of ancient spiritual knowledge we have access to today.

But to the world this knowledge is lost. After thousands of years of persecution, suppression, destruction, and degeneration, the ancient Religion of the Sun in its diverse forms of expression has arrived to us in the present day in fragments that no longer form a coherent whole. Much of it was also kept from public circulation to protect it from persecution and perversion.

Testament to this comes from one of the only known expeditions of its kind. In 1895, the famous twentieth century author and teacher of mystical subjects, George Ivanovich Gurdjieff, helped form a group of around fifteen members called "Seekers of the Truth" who traveled to remote locations in order to find ancient esoteric knowledge, often risking their lives and going through extreme hardships to do so. They are said to have traveled across three continents to places that included Egypt, Ethiopia and the Sudan, Mesopotamia, Central Asia, the Gobi Desert, Northern Siberia, Northern India, Australia, and the Solomon Islands.

> "During their travels the Seekers studied literature, oral tradition, music, dance, sacred art, architecture and esoteric monuments, and they conducted their own experiments and archeological excavations. Their investigations led to many exciting discoveries related to the science of human transformation, including ancient methods of music composition, architecture, and dance choreography which produced exact and predictable alterations in consciousness in the listener, observer or practitioner.
>
> From their journeys and research the Seekers concluded that knowledge of human spiritual potential once existed as a complete teaching, but that only widely scattered fragments remained." [1]
> ~ GURDJIEFF'S SEARCH FOR ESOTERIC KNOWLEDGE, BY THE LEARNING INSTITUTE FOR GROWTH, HEALING AND TRANSFORMATION

In some cases we have access to more of these fragments today, thanks to the discoveries of suppressed texts like those from the Nag Hammadi Library (discovered in 1945 in Egypt and containing never before seen teachings of Jesus). In another sense we also have less, due to the rapid increase of materialism, corporatization, violent strife in the world, the persecution of those who practice this kind of spiritual knowledge today, and the disruption and destruction of many of the cultural traditions and sacred sites that carried spiritual knowledge.

But even having access to more fragments, as in the case of the previously unknown Nag Hammadi Library, many remain obscure due to the fact that they were encoded by their authors in layers of symbology. On top of this, the symbols used by different cultures to express the same message can often be different. So when trying to piece together the fragments of ancient knowledge, not only are they incomplete, but they are often encrypted in an unknown symbolic script, and also use different codes of encryption to one another.

Sometimes the key similarities among this array of fragments stand out—enough to conclude that many of these ancient spiritual peoples accessed the same source of knowledge, and that they did once explain the mysteries of life and its purpose. But mostly questions remain, such as what is this common source, how did they tap into it, what are these mysteries, and most importantly, how can they be experienced again today?

There is one missing key that has the capacity to crack open the codes and answer these questions. Researchers only have access to physical artifacts and texts, which they sometimes try and piece together. It's like putting together a puzzle when you don't know what the image of the puzzle is—in fact, when you've never even seen what the puzzle image is before, and you only have a few of the pieces that are not clear because each piece is encrypted, and each using a different code of encryption. Not only that, but some of the pieces don't even belong to the puzzle because so much of the spiritual knowledge of the past has been distorted and infiltrated over time!

We can theorize what the puzzle image is going to be forever, but we're never going to really know. Unless, that is... we had gone through the same process of spiritual transformation and gained the same spiritual knowledge in the same ways that these ancient peoples did.

Then we would approach the mystery of the puzzle in a completely different way. We could know what the puzzle picture is, even without the pieces, and could see where the few pieces that we had fit together, and could even explain which pieces are missing and which ones are not part of the puzzle at all. And this is exactly what Mark has done.

Anyone can compile information, even in the field of spiritual knowledge, but to synthesize, to get to the essence of it, and to explain it so that other people can transform themselves through it, requires one crucial ingredient found severely lacking in much of religion and spirituality today—and that is firsthand metaphysical experience.

Although both Mark and I are listed as the authors of the book, we both had very different roles in putting it together. Both Mark and I did the writing and researching, but it was Mark's own spiritual and metaphysical experience that is really behind it.

The contents of this book first started coming together in June of 2011 when Mark, having a sense of the connection between the ancient veneration of the sun and the process of spiritual transformation, standing on our verandah with a week to go before the summer solstice, turned and said, "We should do something for the summer solstice." It was then we began first researching the ancient traditions connected with the celebration of midsummer from around the world. Incorporating what we found, Mark created a ceremony to celebrate the summer solstice based on its spiritual meaning, using ancient Vedic mantras and Eastern European traditions, which we then published as a web article.

Some of those who used this ceremony for their solstice celebration were deeply moved by their experience of it, and felt they would never be the same again. We realized there was a lot more to these ancient traditions than first seemed, and continued our research, this time preparing for the coming autumn equinox. Over the course of a year between 2011 and 2012, we released web articles explaining the spiritual meaning of the autumn equinox, winter solstice, and spring equinox. Later, in mid-2013 we released a web article on the meaning of the summer solstice.

We did this by researching a broad range of ancient sites, texts, and traditions, and then used Mark's spiritual knowledge and experience to help decipher them. Based on the symbolic meaning of these times of year, Mark also created ceremonies for each of them.

Mark used his metaphysical experience when looking at how the solstice and equinox had been celebrated throughout the ancient world, to incorporate what most communicated the spiritual meaning of these times of year. At one point, to his surprise, he came across an obscure Greek reference to a winter solstice ceremony celebrated in ancient Egypt which contained virtually the same ritual he'd not long before written into a winter solstice ceremony he'd created for an earlier edition of this book.

And so, we began reconstructing the actual meaning of the solstices and equinoxes, and came to realize that a number of ancient people in the distant past had to have understood their deeper meaning at one time, and had sometimes incorporated these meanings into the sacred sites they aligned to the solstices and equinoxes, and into their rituals and celebrations.

In September of 2013 we compiled our web articles on the solstices and equinoxes, and released them as a free eBook, which was the earliest edition of this book, explaining within it that there had once been a solar religion practiced across large parts of the world in ancient times, which had given rise to the building of many of the world's most enigmatic sacred sites, like the Great Pyramids of Egypt, the statues of Easter Island, Stonehenge in England, and countless others, each of which aligned to the solstices and equinoxes.

We began referring to this religion as "the Religion of the Sun"—a term we coined ourselves, but later discovered had been used in a handful of instances over the last few centuries, most notably by Thomas Paine, who was one of the Founding Fathers of the United States and likely a Freemason. Thomas Paine was the only one to employ it as any kind of formal title, using it to describe the religion that had been practiced from the remotest antiquity before spreading over large parts of the ancient world, and later being preserved in Freemasonry (very partially in my view, with influences from sources diametrically opposed to the Religion of the Sun later added). All other uses (of which I have only found a number that can be counted on one hand) were merely passing and one-off, using it as a descriptive phrase for ancient forms of solar religion—mostly in books dating from over seventy years ago.

By this time I had done a massive amount of research by reading scores of ancient texts from numerous traditions (over one hundred from cover to cover) and researching the alignments of large numbers of ancient sites from around the world. Out of this, we included hundreds of excerpts from ancient texts as well as images of ancient sites and symbols, which you will find in this book as supporting evidence.

Our eBook had been downloaded over thirty thousand times as of January 2016, when it was taken offline, due to it being extensively plagiarized, and was instead first published as a paperback book in September 2016. We had provided the eBook completely free of charge (as well as our articles on the solstices and equinoxes, which were still online at that point), and anyone was able to download it without subscribing or registering for anything. As a paperback book, its price was (and still is) set only to cover publishing costs.[2] We receive no money from the sale of any of our books, as it's against our principles to profit from spiritual knowledge.

Initially I had thought that the many different cultures evidenced as practicing the Religion of the Sun in some form had done so independently of one another. In my research, I had come across numerous similarities between the symbols of ancient cultures (even though they were never meant to have had any contact with one another), and had put this down to people within these ancient cultures coming upon the same spiritual knowledge through mystical experience and encoding it using the same symbols.

The first time I began to doubt this, however, was when I saw a statue of the Aztec goddess Coatlicue looking almost identical to the Hindu goddess Kali. Nevertheless, I pressed on with holding an isolationist viewpoint, as Wikipedia and its repeaters, which had saturated the top layers of Internet search results for just about every term on ancient history, were adamant that everything in prehistory was definitely not connected, in any way, at all, period.

Left: The goddess Kali, a major deity in Hinduism in India. Right: The goddess Coatlicue, a major deity worshiped by the Aztecs in Mexico. The similarities between these images sowed the first seeds of doubt in my mind about my isolationist viewpoint.

Looking back, I can't believe I didn't realize so much earlier how different ancient cultures must have had contact in prehistory. It was staring me in the face, with the exact same pyramid designs, symbols, etc., found from one continent to another. But I had been so indoctrinated to believe that they didn't, that all the glaring similarities were simply hiding in front of me in plain sight.

The penny dropped only later, in March 2016, when researching ancient sites on the Internet (as part of preparing the first print edition of this book), I stumbled across the website of Martin Doutré, http://celticnz.co.nz. In his work, Doutré painstakingly analyzes the measurements used in the building and layout of many ancient sites in different parts of the world, and demonstrates that their builders used the same standard measurement system, and thus were part of or influenced by the same global civilization. Although Doutré does not discuss the Religion of the Sun, he does recognize that the builders of these sites venerated the sun. After reading some of his articles, Mark and I realized that the traces of the ancient Religion of the Sun that we had been researching and studying had originated from the same source in remote times, and had once been the religion of a post Ice Age global culture and civilization now lost. Mark and I named this civilization "the Lost Civilization of the Sun."

Months later, in September of 2016, Mark and I released an updated edition of this book to include a chapter titled "The Lost Civilization of the Sun," in which we shared our findings on this lost civilization. At the time, we traced it as much as we could throughout the world, and sourced its origin in a group of wisdom bringers who are likely to have been survivors of Atlantis. Since then, I've read some of the works of authors such as Thor Heyerdahl, Graham Hancock, and David Frawley, whose research has confirmed and added detail to what we had first realized in 2016 about the existence of such a lost civilization. The chapter on the Lost Civilization of the Sun is no longer included in this book. Instead I have greatly expanded upon it, and included the information from it in my book *The Ancient Religion of the Sun*.

Throughout this time, our original articles on the spiritual meaning of the solstices and equinoxes, which we had first written between 2011 and 2013, still remained freely available online. They were shared a total of over twenty-three thousand times and viewed about half a million times as of March 2018, which is when we took them offline. We withdrew them because they were being plagiarized so much—excerpts from them had been copied and pasted into other people's websites without attribution over one thousand times. Our articles had become a world reference for the meaning of the solstices and equinoxes and ranked among the top results in search engines for terms like "winter solstice meaning," often above reference sites like Wikipedia.

Before releasing our articles, the actual deeper spiritual meanings of the solstices and equinoxes, as far as I'm aware, were not understood. We had searched through much of the material available in English at the time on their meaning

"Big Bang," and that the first few elements which emerged from this sudden burst of creation fused to form stars. These stars then created almost all matter and everything we see, including us, and even now are in a constant process of creation as they produce and eject elements into space.

But life is multidimensional. Mystics have known this throughout time—that there is more to our world than what we perceive with our five senses. With improvements in technology, there are now huge numbers of compelling accounts from near-death experiences of life beyond the physical body in other dimensions, reported by people all over the world, and these numbers are increasing rapidly by the day.

Because the universe is multidimensional, everything within it, including the sun, has other dimensional aspects.

In the ancient text Pistis Sophia, Jesus speaks of the multidimensional nature of the sun:

> "For the light of the sun in its shape in truth is not in this world, for its light pierceth through many veils and regions." [8]
> ~ JESUS IN PISTIS SOPHIA

The sun that exists in the physical world as the fire we see in the sky also exists in the higher dimensions as a spiritual fire and the spiritual source of creation, which is why there is an overlap between natural and supernatural phenomena in accounts of creation in many ancient cultures. The natural phenomenon is the physical, tangible manifestation of the supernatural phenomenon. That is why many spiritual cultures throughout the world venerated the sun—they knew of its spiritual side.

The author and thirty-third degree Freemason, Manly P. Hall, wrote in his extensive study of the esoteric teachings of the world:

> "In the majority of cases, the religions of antiquity agree that the material visible sun was a reflector rather than a source of power. The sun was sometimes represented as a shield carried on the arm of the Sun God, as for example, Frey, the Scandinavian Solar Deity. This sun reflected the light of the invisible spiritual sun, which was the true source of life, light, and truth. The physical nature of the universe is receptive; it is a realm of effects. The invisible causes of these effects belong to the spiritual world. Hence, the spiritual world is the sphere of causation; the material world is the sphere of effects; while the intellectual—or soul—world is the sphere of mediation. Thus Christ, the personified higher intellect and soul nature, is called 'the Mediator' who, by virtue of His position and power, says: 'No man cometh to the Father, but by me.'" [9]
> ~ MANLY P. HALL, THE SECRET TEACHINGS OF ALL AGES

when writing our articles, and found no single source that described what they meant. We were only able to do this ourselves after months of painstaking research into barely preserved ancient traditions, by deciphering the spiritual symbolism encoded into the ancient sites that were built to align to these times of year, and combining this with Mark's spiritual knowledge and experience.

As a result, after our articles were released, the spiritual meanings of the solstices and equinoxes became much more widely understood. Before this they had been fairly mundane seasonal celebrations, interpreted, usually from a modern Wiccan perspective, as to do with letting go of attachments, tuning into the rhythm of the seasons, giving birth to new personal projects, setting goals, etc.

It's important to mention that our research was a journey—we in no way set out with a destination in mind when we first began writing about the solstice back in June of 2011. We had absolutely no idea what we were in for—we instead simply followed the evidence as it led us from one thing to another.

However, there is a difference between our methods of study and those of purely academic researchers. We not only write about the Religion of the Sun and research its evidence throughout history, but first and foremost, we practice it. Many people think you find out about things just by reading, but there is a limit to how much you can find out by reading alone. Ancient mystics discovered their knowledge through experience—one which is inner/metaphysical. The Religion of the Sun is a body of knowledge and a metaphysical practice that is directed toward the transformation of the individual, and thus someone can only truly uncover and understand its practice through practicing it and transforming themselves.

This book comes from the knowledge of one who has tread upon the ancient path of the sun to where the very references to its stages become almost as rare as those who have passed through them. Mark was able to recreate its practice, not just from studying and researching its ancient remnants, but from his actual practice of it. His spiritual experience was essential to reconstructing the ancient meaning of the solstices and equinoxes, as many traditions that had preserved remnants of their practice had lost the deeper meaning of the symbols in their traditions, if they were even still kept alive.

Mark has been a dedicated spiritual practitioner since 1990. Since then he has practiced a broad range of spiritual techniques derived from a number of ancient traditions, which we now know to be remnants of the lost Religion of the Sun. These practices include having out-of-body experiences using the same techniques practitioners of the ancient Religion of the Sun did, and putting into practice those principles that lie at the heart of the profound meaning of the solstices and equinoxes. Likewise, someone can essentially have the same metaphysical experiences these ancient peoples did, and can thus penetrate into the true meaning of the symbols and writings they left behind, even when they are currently obscured or misunderstood.

Modern practitioners of the Religion of the Sun can and have seen many things, while out of the body, that were taught as part of the religion. This includes experiences of being shown and visiting such places as hell, called Xibalbá, Narakam, and Helheim/Nifel-heim, etc., in different ancient traditions, meeting the beings now called gods who founded the Religion of the Sun in ancient times, and, like my husband, seeing some of these beings in higher dimensions still using the ancient sites they built while alive on Earth, such as the Great Pyramid of Egypt, to initiate those worthy into deeper knowledge.

What we have put together in terms of the sacred sites, texts, and traditions is by no means exhaustive. Firstly, there are a huge number of examples we could have included (with sites still being discovered), but we felt it was only necessary to include enough in order to clearly make a point. Secondly, there was a limit to the time we had before the next solstice or equinox came around, and therefore to the breadth of what we could include. And thirdly, there are no doubt many other sites, texts, and traditions linked with the solar year that are largely unwritten about in English, and which were therefore much more difficult and time consuming to find. We hope, however, to add some of these to later editions as we have the time so that even more people can understand the path of the spiritual sun through their own cultural heritage.

One final note: because so much spiritual knowledge is esoteric (meaning it requires grades of spiritual wisdom and experience to understand), some parts of this book may seem obscure. Additionally, some of the information about spiritual subjects is stated in a matter of fact way. This is because Mark is writing from his own experience of them, which he's corroborated with ancient sources, rather than solely drawing upon research as with the historical aspects of this book. Many of these spiritual topics are only briefly touched upon, as they would require lengthy explanations in themselves; Mark will explain them in more depth in forthcoming books. Despite the difficulty these things may present while reading, it's worth persisting, as what you can gain at the very least is an understanding of the meanings behind many ancient sites, texts, and traditions—how much more beyond this depends entirely upon how much you can personally spiritually experience.

Lara Atwood

PART I
THE PATH OF THE SUN

CHAPTER ONE

The Spiritual Meaning of the Solstices and Equinoxes

Tens of thousands gather at Stonehenge to witness its alignment to the summer solstice sunrise again in modern times.

The ancient veneration of the sun is one of the greatest celebrations in history. It has been encoded in sacred sites and texts for thousands of years by peoples separated by vast distances across the world—all the way from the Great Pyramids of Egypt, to the megaliths of Stonehenge, and the huge stone statues of Easter Island. The sun is one of the oldest and most universal themes connecting the ancient wisdom traditions of the world.

Ancient cultures built at least hundreds of megalithic structures, stone circles, temples, and secret inner rooms that aligned with the sun at its major annual stages—the solstices and equinoxes—in Europe; Africa; Russia; North, Central, and South America; Easter Island; Australia; Asia; and other parts of the world.

Most today see these sites as being based upon a simpleminded form of agriculture and nature worship—and yet some of them have endured as the most enigmatic and mystical places in the world, and remain some of the most advanced sites astronomically, mathematically, architecturally, and spiritually even to this day. Down through the ages they have echoed messages from a golden age of spirituality, that have largely been misinterpreted as primitive by a modern world that has become so distanced from natural principles that it has failed to recognize what is hidden in plain sight.

The sun and stars, source of all light and life in the universe, are central to a religion that spread across large parts of the world in ancient times, which saw the sun as the most revealed manifestation of the divine. This religion, which my wife Lara and I call the Religion of the Sun, is both ancient and timeless—and the truths it preserved are as ever-present as always. Its principles have formed the basis of many of the world's ancient religions—unknown even to many of their adherents—and are just as relevant to people searching for spirituality today.

This book delves into the profound spiritual significance of the veneration of the sun, pulling together the sites, texts, traditions, and symbols from around the world that were based on the sun's cycle, to reveal the common thread of spirituality running through all of them. This knowledge has then been used to form a practical guide to celebrate the spiritual sun just as it was in ancient times, with examples from many ancient cultures, for people to re-enliven and experience it again today.

WHAT ARE THE SOLSTICES AND EQUINOXES?

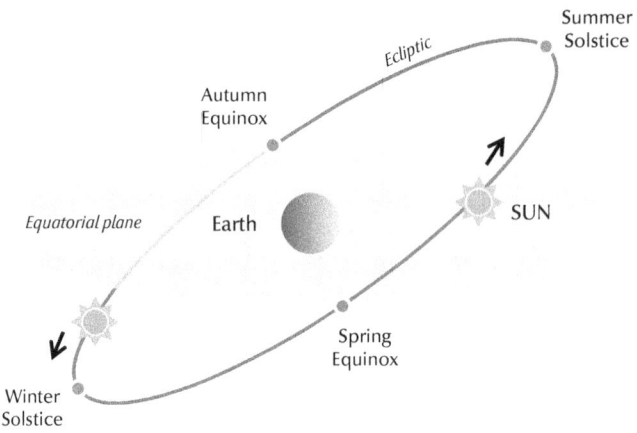

A diagram of the solstices and equinoxes from the viewer's perspective of the sun from the earth.

The journey of the sun through the sky (or rather our planet's journey around it) goes through four distinct stages every year, with each occurring approximately three months apart from the other. These are the autumn/fall equinox, winter solstice, spring/vernal equinox, and summer solstice, which together form "the wheel of the year."

The winter solstice is the time of greatest darkness in the year, when the hours of night are longest. The summer solstice is the opposite, being the time of greatest light in the year, when the hours of daylight are longest. Between each is a crossing point, or equinox, when the length of day and night are exactly equal.

These points mark the main stages in the movement of the earth around the sun and the sun's varying influence over light and darkness, day and night, and the passage of the seasons. But they also hold a greater spiritual significance.

AS ABOVE, SO BELOW

Here the alchemist draws our attention to the relationship between the world contained in the smaller circle in which we find ourselves, and the world contained in the larger circle—that is, between the microcosmic and the macrocosmic, as well as the mathematical principles that apply to both. The alchemist looks above, while the figure of the man in the drawing, points below.

It's easy to write off ancient spiritual people as simpleminded nature worshipers. But there is a reason why natural principles are found throughout many sacred texts and ancient sites—this is because there are universal principles that govern all of creation, including all life at the largest to smallest of scales. Thus we can see the same principles of the macrocosmic movement of the planets, in the microcosmic structure of an atom. Mathematically, in the spiral of a galaxy, we see the spiral of a shell, and the unfolding of a fern.

The principles that govern all life above us, also govern life here below on Earth—which is why an ancient maxim of wisdom was, "as above, so below."

> "As large as the universe outside, even so large is the universe within the lotus of the heart. Within it are heaven and earth, the sun, the moon, the lightning, and all the stars. What is in the macrocosm is in this microcosm." [1]
>
> ~ CHANDOGYA UPANISHAD

> "Man takes his law from the Earth; the Earth takes its law from Heaven; Heaven takes its law from Tao; but the law of Tao is its own spontaneity." [2]
>
> ~ LAO-TZU IN TAO TE CHING

> "The sages of old studied living things to a point of realization that God is most perfectly understood through a knowledge of His supreme handiwork—animate and inanimate Nature. Every existing creature manifests some aspect of the intelligence or power of the Eternal One, who can never be known save through a study and appreciation of His numbered but inconceivable parts. When a creature is chosen, therefore, to symbolize to the concrete human mind some concealed abstract principle it is because its characteristics demonstrate this invisible principle in visible action." [3]
>
> ~ MANLY P. HALL, THE SECRET TEACHINGS OF ALL AGES

AS WITHIN, SO WITHOUT

Going further, not only do the principles of life and creation govern the outer world, but they also govern the inner, spiritual world. Spirituality exists in the very fabric of the universe. Thus when someone studies creation, they find spirituality and the supernatural. This is why scientists are now theorizing about the existence of other dimensions, parallel universes, and the inexplicable realm of possibilities, energy, and matter, from the study of the behavior and structure of minute particles.[4]

Today, these properties of the universe, in which the same principles apply at the largest to the smallest scales, and both to the inner and outer world, have been described as fractal and holographic. Fractal in that the same fundamental pattern appears at all scales, and holographic in that wholeness is found everywhere and in everything, essentially making the same observations as the ancient maxims of wisdom "as above, so below," and "as within, so without."

> "I tell you truly, the kingdom of our Heavenly Father is vast, so vast that no man can know its limits, for there are none. Yet the whole of his kingdom may be found in the smallest drop of dew on a wild

flower, or in the scent of newly-cut grass in the fields under the summer sun. Truly, there are no words to describe the kingdom of the Heavenly Father." [5]

~ JESUS IN THE ESSENE GOSPEL OF PEACE

"Recognize what is in your sight, and that which is hidden from you will become plain to you. For there is nothing hidden which will not become manifest." [6]

~ JESUS IN THE GOSPEL OF THOMAS

"What is within us is also without. What is without is also within. He who sees difference between what is within and what is without goes evermore from death to death." [7]

~ KATHA UPANISHAD

The sun in its movement throughout the course of the year then becomes a symbol of something much, much greater than a physical object bringing the change of seasons.

THE SPIRITUAL SUN

Ancient Egyptian painting of the ankh,
symbol of eternal life, holding up the sun.

The physical sun, in essence, is a blazing fire—it gives light and life to all material things. From the physical sun, all creation comes into being. Literally, science generally believes that the universe came from a fiery burst of light called the

Because creation of physical matter comes from the physical aspect of stars, then the higher dimensional parts of matter are likewise created by the stars in higher dimensions. We find references to this in ancient texts. In the Taoist texts of ancient China for instance, creation is described as moving from the subtle and unseen realms (which are higher dimensional), into physical manifestation. The source of these subtle energies is said to be the stars, and the sun is the star with which we share our closest relationship.

> "Trees and animals, humans and insects, flowers and birds: These are active images of the subtle energies that flow from the stars throughout the universe. Meeting and combining with each other and the elements of the earth, they give rise to all living things." [10]
> ~ LAO-TZU IN HUA HU CHING

In The Vision of Hermes, a text attributed to Hermes Trismegistus and believed to have originated in Egypt prior to Christianity, the spirits of the stars are said to control the universe and have their origin in the "One Fire," which is the spiritual source of creation.

> "At the Word of the Dragon the heavens opened and the innumerable Light Powers were revealed, soaring through Cosmos on pinions of streaming fire. Hermes beheld the spirits of the stars, the celestials controlling the universe, and all those Powers which shine with the radiance of the One Fire—the glory of the Sovereign Mind." [11]
> ~ THE VISION OF HERMES

Going further, not only does both physical and other dimensional matter have its source in the stars—so too does our own inner spiritual light, called consciousness. The light of the sun and stars is the spiritual source of creation, and gives rise both to matter and the spirit.

> "These two things, the spiritual and the material, though we call them by different names, in their origin are one and the same. This sameness is a mystery—the mystery of mysteries. It is the gate of all spirituality." [12]
> ~ TAO TE CHING

The ancient Mayans and the Hermetic writers saw the Milky Way as the place where our souls were born.

> "Behold, O Hermes, there is a great mystery in the Eighth Sphere, for the Milky Way is the seed-ground of souls..." [13]
> ~ POIMANDRES (THE MIND OF THE UNIVERSE) TO HERMES IN THE VISION OF HERMES

Is it little wonder then, that often when pondering the meaning of life and the question of where we came from, we tend to raise our eyes to the stars or gaze at the sun, and likewise when calling for spiritual guidance or help. This intuitive sense of home has been with humankind throughout the ages. From a scientific perspective, the elements that created our bodies, and all that exists materially, came from the stars. From a spiritual perspective, our consciousness—the spark of divinity within us—also originated in the stars, in higher dimensions, from the greatest source of life and light in creation.

> "He [Atman] who is in the fire, and he who is here in the heart, and he who is yonder in the sun—he is one." [14]
> ~ TAITTIRIYA UPANISHAD

This is one of the reasons why so many ancient peoples, such as the Aryans, Sumerians, Egyptians, Gnostics, and Maya, all referred to themselves as the "Children of the Sun" or "Children of Light." The Inca royal family was literally believed to be the offspring of the sun, and their spiritual lineage was celebrated at the winter solstice.

The sun worship of the past in the more advanced societies was really the worship of the spiritual sun, not the physical sun.

Paracelsus, the great alchemist of the Renaissance, wrote in the 1500s:

> "There is an earthly sun, which is the cause of all heat, and all who are able to see may see the sun; and those who are blind and cannot see him may feel his heat. There is an Eternal Sun, which is the source of all wisdom, and those whose spiritual senses have awakened to life will see that sun and be conscious of His existence; but those who have not attained spiritual consciousness may yet feel His power by an inner faculty which is called Intuition." [15]
> ~ PARACELSUS

There are hundreds of ancient sites aligned to the solstices and equinoxes, some of the most famous sacred texts encode solar events and venerate the sun, and supreme deities in many ancient spiritual teachings are associated with the sun and its attributes. Both the Druids and mystery schools of Greece conducted their initiation rituals and mysteries on the equinoxes and solstices. Throughout the world we see evidence of an ancient religion of the sun.

THE ANCIENT RELIGION OF THE SUN

In ancient times there once existed what I call the Religion of the Sun. It was a major religion of the ancient world in which the sun was used as the supreme symbol of divinity. Following is a short summary, taken from my wife's book *The Ancient Religion of the Sun*.

A solar religion existing from ancient times is well known in academia. For example, the Encyclopaedia Britannica entry on "sun worship" says:

> "Although sun worship has been used frequently as a term for "pagan" religion, it is, in fact, relatively rare. Though almost every culture uses solar motifs, only a relatively few cultures (Egyptian, Indo-European, and Meso-American) developed solar religions. All of these groups had in common a well-developed urban civilization with a strong ideology of sacred kingship. [...]
>
> The sun is the bestower of light and life to the totality of the cosmos; with his [...] all-seeing eye, he is the stern guarantor of justice; with the almost universal connection of light with enlightenment or illumination, the sun is the source of wisdom." [16]

Essentially, it is well known within academia that three major branches of ancient civilization practiced solar religions—namely those of the ancient Egyptians, Indo-Europeans, and Mesoamericans—although it also influenced and was practiced by numerous other cultures too, as I explain below.

Indo-European is a broad term that includes a vast set of religious traditions that branched off over time. They include the Armenians in the Caucasus region where some theorize the Indo-Europeans originally migrated from; those in the steppe regions to the north of the Caucasus like the Yamnaya and Scythian; those of the east, which are the Vedic/Hindu traditions found today in India and extending into Indonesia, Thailand, Cambodia, and China; those in the south, which include Zoroastrianism in Persia (what is now Iran); the Hittites and Luwians of Anatolia; the Euphratic speakers of Mesopotamia who influenced the later religions of the region, such as that of the Sumerians and surviving among the Yazidi; and those that spread westward into Europe, such as the Thracian, Slavic, Baltic, Germanic (including Scandinavian), Celtic, Minoan, Mycenaean/Greek/Hellene, and later Roman pre-Christian religions like Mithraism. At one time, Indo-European traditions stretched all the way from Ireland in the west to at least as far east as western China (from at least as early as 1,800 BC).

Solar religions in the Americas stretched over an equally vast area, and include those in Central America, like the Olmec, Aztec, and Maya—but also those in North America, among pre-Columbian peoples such as the Hopi and Zuni of the southwest and the stone and mound builders of the east, as well as in South America, among peoples such as the Inca, Chimú, Chachapoya, Moche, Tiwanaku, Muisca (and possibly Chinchorro), and others. Following the ocean currents, this solar religion also spread west to Easter Island, New Zealand, and the Pacific Islands.

The Egyptian branch of the Religion of the Sun likely extended much further than Egypt itself: south into parts of Africa, across to the Canary Islands, and following the ocean currents west of Egypt, connecting into the traditions of the Americas. Furthermore, all three traditions of solar religion enumerated by Encyclopaedia Britannica—the Egyptian, Indo-European, and Mesoamerican—are connected to one another, and many of the overlaps between them will become apparent in the ancient texts, sites, and symbols explored in this book.

But there was also a manifestation of this great religion in more recent history. When looking at what survives of what Jesus taught, including those texts not included in the Bible, it becomes clear he also taught the Religion of the Sun.

It has been well noted that there are large numbers of similarities between the events of Jesus' life and those of other pre-Christian deities, and between his teachings and other pre-Christian pagan religions—specifically ancient Egyptian and Indo-European religions (like Hinduism, Zoroastrianism, Mithraism, and Hellenism). Some believe this was solely because the early Church subsumed these pagan practices and incorporated them into Jesus' life in order to placate the pagans they were converting. However, caches of early Christian texts have been discovered in the last couple of centuries that were banned by the early Church for the very reason that they contain teachings, including many attributed to Jesus, that were considered "pagan" and heretical. These texts, such as the Nag Hammadi Library and Pistis Sophia, are real ancient texts that contain Jesus' teachings about concepts like a great Mother Goddess and reincarnation. They reveal that Jesus and his early followers already had "pagan" worldviews central to the Religion of the Sun before the formation of the Church.

A number of texts also record how Jesus spent time during his "lost years" with different spiritual groups before he turned thirty. One such text belongs to an ancient Gnostic sect called the Mandaeans who still survive today in Iraq and Iran. The Mandaeans believe they are the inheritors of knowledge from the Indo-Iranian/Zoroastrian and ancient Egyptian religions (themselves both remnants of the ancient Religion of the Sun), and that Jesus and John the Baptist became priests of the Mandaeans. These priests are called Naṣuraiia (Naṣoreans), which indicated someone who was a knower of esoteric knowledge and white magic and who observed the stars and omens.[17] This is very likely the basis of the references to Jesus being a Nazarene in the New Testament, as there are no references to a town called Nazareth existing until 200 AD.[18] Jesus became learned in the ancient Religion of the Sun from at least this source, and the events of his life were divinely planned in order to reveal its mysteries—renewing much of the ancient knowledge of the Religion of the Sun that had become lost and obscured.

While many of his teachings were excluded from the Bible, and at the same time many other texts were included that Jesus did not write or condone, the events of his life as recorded in the Gospels have continued to encode and carry the message of the ancient path of the spiritual sun for around two thousand years.

Although these solar religious traditions are seen as disconnected and as having arisen organically out of the same instinctual impulse to deify those important natural elements necessary to survival, my wife Lara and I have found much evidence to show that they are in fact very much connected and derive from the same body of profound knowledge in the very ancient past, and even from the same great spiritual teachers who traveled the world with the mission to spread it. This body of knowledge, we call the ancient Religion of the Sun, and I explain much of the body of knowledge that was preserved by this ancient religion here in this book.

Legends preserved in the ancient texts of the Religion of the Sun, like those of ancient Egypt, Iran, and India, state that this religion was from a spiritual "golden age," and was practiced by a prior global civilization destroyed by a great worldwide catastrophe (likely to have been the civilization most famously called Atlantis), probably around 9,700 BC. After this catastrophe, great teachers of this religion are recorded as setting out to different parts of the world to reseed it and to reinitiate civilization. I call these teachers the wisdom bringers; some of them possibly included Osiris of ancient Egypt, Viracocha of the Inca in Peru, Quetzalcoatl and Kukulkan of the Aztec and Maya respectively, Maasaw of the Hopi of North America, and Manu of India. These teachers were real people that were later deified as gods. They established what became a global civilization, which I call the Lost Civilization of the Sun, in places like Egypt, Mesopotamia, India, and the Americas, where often identical symbols, sacred sites, and ancient legends exist. Over time however, this civilization collapsed and was lost to history—with the Religion of the Sun they had once carried surviving only in scattered fragments.

If our civilization collapsed tomorrow and the world entered a dark age where its technology and literacy was extinguished, and thousands of years later the people of the future were archeologically investigating it, they would find identical symbols, building styles, legends, remnants of similar sacred texts, etc., all over the world, and possibly wonder why. In the case of Christianity for example, either identical or near identical churches, crucifixes, and statues of Jesus, would be unearthed in almost every continent and region. The people of the future would rightly conclude that there had once existed a lost global civilization that had, for the most part, shared a common religion.

When looking back at ancient history we see exactly the same thing. We find the same pyramid and megalith designs orientated to the sun, using the same geometric principles and standard measurements, as well as building styles and techniques. Stepped pyramids, for example, can be found in a huge number of locations—in ancient Egypt, the Canary Islands, Mauritius, the Azores, the Maldives, Sicily, Sardinia, Russia, Central America, South America, Cambodia, and some of the Polynesian islands. In Sumer they were built as ziggurats, and in India and other parts of Asia they are known as stupas.

We also find identical symbols in use throughout the ancient world. One of the most prolific of these is the swastika, an ancient solar symbol, which has been found in such widespread places as the Americas (North, Central, and South), the whole of Europe, Russia, the Middle East, and large parts of Asia (including India and China).

Other symbols found in different parts of the world dating from ancient times include the solar disk, solar cross, double spiral, the lotus, the "Master of Animals," feathered serpent, and third eye, which are all symbols related to the sun.

Not only that, but legends of the same great teachers and preachers of an ancient solar religion, who were associated with these symbols and the building of many of these sacred sites, like stepped pyramids, can be found in disparate parts of the world. Dressed in robes and described as similar in appearance, with supernatural abilities, they were the equivalent of Jesus in their day, and as with the image of Jesus, similar images and descriptions of them are found across continents.

When looking at the evidence of ancient history, it starts to become obvious that there was once a global civilization in ancient times that shared a common religion, which has been all but lost to history.

THE SPIRITUAL SON

Central to the ancient Religion of the Sun was always a solar hero or sun god, whom I call the Spiritual Son.

Many of the great teachers of the Religion of the Sun, such as Osiris (ancient Egyptian), Jesus (Gnostic Christian), Krishna (Hindu), Quetzalcoatl (Aztec), Kukulkan (Mayan), and Viracocha (Andean), identified themselves with the sun and its fire and light—indicating the connection between their incredibly profound spiritual teachings, and the sun, stars, and cosmos.

> "Thou shinest in the horizon, thou sendest forth thy light into the darkness, thou makest the darkness light with thy double plume, and thou floodest the world with light like the Disk at break of day. Thy diadem pierceth heaven and becometh a brother unto the stars, O thou form of every god." [19]
>
> ~ HYMN TO OSIRIS

> "[Osiris said to his disciples] The light that is with me was kindled at The Supreme Source, which is the God of Gods. Therefore, my light shines with such brilliance that it must be veiled in part, lest it blind you. It is even as the sun be seen through a veil of cloud, it may be gazed upon for as long as desired." [20]
>
> ~ THE TEACHINGS OF YOSIRA [OSIRIS], THE KOLBRIN

> "It is I who am the light which is above them all. It is I who am the all. From me did the all come forth, and unto me did the all extend." [21]
>
> ~ JESUS IN THE GOSPEL OF THOMAS

> "After six days Jesus took with him Peter, James and John the brother of James, and led them up a high mountain by themselves. There he was transfigured before them. His face shone like the sun, and his clothes became as white as the light." [22]
>
> ~ MATTHEW 17:1-2

> "The light which, residing in the sun illumines the whole world, that which is in the moon and in the fire—know that light to be Mine." [23]
> ~ KRISHNA IN THE BHAGAVAD GITA

> "We learn from various narratives that the 'preaching', 'teaching', and 'instructions' of Viracocha were of a religious as well as of a practical nature. He was anxious that the Indians should consider him the representative of the sun, a divine being in spite of his human appearance [...]. It is interesting to note from various accounts how anxious this legendary preacher was to teach the tribes that he and his followers were god-men, connected with the sun [...]." [24]
> ~ THOR HEYERDAHL, AMERICAN INDIANS IN THE PACIFIC

Remarkably, the lives of these teachers and many other spiritual figures of the ancient world, like Odin/Wotan (Germanic), Mithra (Indo-Iranian), Dionysus (Greek), Horus (Egyptian), Svarog and Kolyada (Slavic), etc., share numerous similarities—not only with one another, but also with the annual journey of the sun. For example, they are often remembered as being born at the winter solstice and as resurrecting at the spring equinox. Even today, people still celebrate the birthday of these deities at the winter solstice—the birth of Mithra is celebrated at the winter solstice in Iran as Yalda, in Germanic tradition Yule (the winter solstice) is celebrated in connection with Odin, the birth of the sun god Kolyada is celebrated by Slavs at the winter solstice, the birth of the sun god Inti at the winter solstice festival of Inti Raymi in Peru, and the birth of Jesus at Christmas.

Some have argued that the reason for these similarities is that none of these figures ever existed, but were all simply made-up to symbolize the sun and its annual journey, and that the mythology surrounding them was recycled across cultures in ancient times. However, this overlooks the overwhelming evidence that at least some of these teachers were real historical people. For example, the accounts of the Spanish historians and explorers who recorded the oral histories of the indigenous peoples of Central and South America (like the Inca, Maya, and Aztec), consistently state that these peoples had previously been visited by bearded men of Caucasian appearance in the distant past who had arrived by boat and taught them their solar religion and the arts of civilization.[25] The accounts of these indigenous peoples are nearly identical despite many of them having had no contact with one another. The famous Egyptologist, E. A. Wallis Budge, who was knighted in 1920 for his service to Egyptology and the British Museum, concluded that Osiris at one time had been a real person who entered Egypt, teaching religion and the arts of civilization, as did some of the classical Greek historians.[26]

Also overlooked are the profound truths that were encoded into these mythologies, which formed a central part of the ancient Religion of the Sun.

These truths were so important to convey that there is evidence that the events of Jesus' life were divinely planned and were timed with the major stages of the sun. For example, the ancient text the Gospel of Judas reveals that Jesus chose Judas to take the role of his betrayer as his most advanced disciple so that the events of his crucifixion would occur.

The reason many of the lives of these solar deities share similarities is because they all have the Spiritual Son in common, which has been allegorized by or has been present within different people numerous times throughout history, each who have represented the same kinds of events in their lives based on the same spiritual principles. These principles were taught as part of the Religion of the Sun in ancient times, and were spread and passed down, albeit often in fragmented form, from one culture and civilization to another.

Some of the most ancient texts and myths of the Religion of the Sun explain that creation arises from the union of a Father and Mother who represent the masculine and feminine halves of the creator, and that their union produces a Son who is identified with the sun, and who proceeds to make creation.

This is described in possibly one of the most ancient preserved stories of creation in the world—found in the Stanzas of Dzyan, which Helena Petrovna Blavatsky, author and founder of Theosophy, claimed to have read and translated while at the Tashilhunpo Monastery in Tibet.[27] This text is the likely source of similar creation stories found in China, in the Rig Veda of India, and Genesis of the Bible.

> "The root of life was in every drop of the ocean of immortality, and the ocean was radiant light, which was fire, and heat, and motion. Darkness vanished and was no more; it disappeared in its own essence, the body of fire and water, or father and mother. Behold, oh Lanoo! The radiant Child of the two, the unparalleled refulgent Glory: Bright Space Son of Dark Space, which emerges from the depths of the great Dark Waters. It is Oeaohoo the younger [...]. He shines forth as the Sun; he is the blazing Divine Dragon of Wisdom [...]. Behold him lifting the Veil and unfurling it from East to West. He shuts out the above, and leaves the below to be seen as the great Illusion. He marks the places for the shining ones [the stars], and turns the upper into a shoreless Sea of Fire, and the One manifested into the Great Waters."[28]
>
> ~ THE STANZAS OF DZYAN

This Spiritual Son is both a cosmic and personal force. At a universal level, the Son is the spiritual force produced from the union of the cosmic Father and Mother in creation. In the Vedas of India, this Spiritual Son is described as the golden child who arises at the dawn of creation.

> "In the beginning there arose the Golden Child (Hiranya-garbha); as soon as born, he alone was the lord of all that is. He established the earth and this heaven [...]. He who gives breath, he who gives strength, whose command all the bright gods revere, whose shadow is immortality, whose shadow is death [...]. He who through his might became the sole king of the breathing and twinkling world, who governs all this, man and beast [...]." [29]
> ~ FROM THE HYMN TO THE UNKNOWN GOD IN THE RIG VEDA

As the process of creation at a universal level also applies to the creation of the spiritual within us, following the principle of "as above, so below," the Son at a personal level is an aspect of each person's higher Being produced from the union of each person's Spiritual Father and Mother in higher dimensions.

> "The rejected Son is One [the energy of the cosmic Son in creation]. The "Son-Suns" are countless [the individual Sons are as numerous as there are individual beings]." [30]
> ~ THE STANZAS OF DZYAN

Like all things, our Being has its origins in the stars in higher dimensions—the source of all creation. When our consciousness was first created from the higher dimensional stars, it descended through the dimensions into matter, and as it did, left higher parts of itself behind in higher dimensions. The Spiritual Son, also known as the Christ in the teachings of Jesus, is one part of this Being, which is of the same nature as the stars and sun—as a much higher frequency of spiritual energy and light—which is why the Spiritual Son is symbolized by the sun. Through their lives and teachings, those who had their own Spiritual Son within or who were representing it, showed how someone can incarnate this higher part of their Being themselves, calling this process liberation, salvation, immortality, etc. Those who incarnated this part of their Being were referred to as "Sons of the Sun" in ancient times (both men and women can become sons of the sun).[31] The final destination of this journey was always described as the heavens, sky, sun, and stars, as it is ultimately about the return to the divine source of creation and to each person's own higher Being, which has its origin in the stars.

The ancient Christian Gnostics, who followed the esoteric side of Jesus' teachings, describe this in their ancient texts, stating that Christ—a higher part of each person's Being—illuminates the psyche of each person, just as the sun illuminates the earth and a lamp lights up a place.

> "Live with Christ and he will save you. For he is the true light and the sun of life. For just as the sun which is visible and makes light for the eyes of the flesh, so Christ illuminates every mind and the heart. [...]

> For everything which is visible is a copy of that which is hidden. For as a fire which burns in a place without being confined to it, so it is with the sun which is in the sky, all of whose rays extend to places on the earth. Similarly, Christ has a single being, and he gives light to every place. This is also the way in which he speaks of our mind, as if it were a lamp which burns and lights up the place. (Being) in a part of the soul, it gives light to all the parts." [32]
> ~ THE TEACHINGS OF SILVANUS

Both the fire of the sun and earthly fire give light and life, and are what allow us to see in the physical world. Likewise, on a spiritual level, the Son within brings spiritual light and life to our own inner darkness, which is the darkness of the human personality and subconscious.

In the West there were many traditions that the orthodox called pagan and suppressed as Christianity took hold, but Christianity itself has many similarities with those pagan traditions, which also appear in many other cultures.

People argue that the winter solstice was a pagan tradition which was simply used by the Church as Jesus' birthday and that the celebration actually has nothing to do with Jesus, and even that Christians adapted pagan myths and symbols to create the story of Jesus' life. Others argue that the pagan people of Europe were simple people whose celebration was little more than a form of nature worship, which they personified into gods. But both ignore the role of the Spiritual Son and the shared principles contained in their religion's forms.

Many people of the past did not have this dismissive attitude. Instead, there is evidence that people in the different traditions that derived from or were influenced by the Religion of the Sun recognized the same principles as existing in each other's traditions. As one example, an ancient text preserved by the Celts records how some of the followers of Jesus, who fled to Britain for safety with Joseph of Arimathea, joined their teachings together with those of the Druids, as both saw the light of truth in each. This is one of the ways Christianity came to share traditions in common with the Druids.

> "When Elyid [Joseph of Arimathea], our father in the faith, came in full flight from afar, seeking refuge beyond the confines of his persecutors' dominion, he set his kolistone in Lanavalok [Glastonbury in Britain]. Here, when he spoke to them, the Druthin [Druids] said, 'We have never been without the light of Truth, yet you seek to bring another light, strange to us, which seems less bright than ours.'
>
> Then Elyid said, 'Let us not argue as to whose light, lit at the fount of Truth, burns brightest, but let us put our two lights together so they may jointly give more illumination and dispel more darkness.' The

Druthin said, 'The light of your teachings was always foreshadowed and He [Jesus] of who you bring tidings is not unknown to us. The origin of Truth is immaterial, for it stands alone on its merits and should always be welcomed, being unlike men who have to be supported by their lineage.'" [33]
~ THE GOSPEL OF THE KAILEDY

In the ancient Religion of the Sun, and all those traditions influenced and derived from it, the solstices and equinoxes are a celebration of the Spiritual Son. This is why the Spiritual Son was born at the winter solstice, and died and resurrected at the spring equinox in sacred myths throughout the world. What is described by the name "Christ" is not unique to Christianity—Jesus portrayed events that occur on the path of the Spiritual Son in his life, just as Osiris did hundreds and thousands of years earlier, and Quetzalcoatl and Hun Hunahpu did vast distances away.

Symbolized by the sun, the Spiritual Son is present in many ancient spiritual practices where people were in touch with the divine, given different names, but naturally having key aspects in common.

THE DIVINITY OF FIRE

Zoroastrian fire temple in Azerbaijan. The Zoroastrians see fire as being divine, in continuation of an ancient Indo-European religious tradition that originated in the ancient Religion of the Sun.

The Spiritual Son has not only been associated with the sun, but also with fire, as when we look at the sun, we are essentially watching a blazing fire.

But this begs the question, what is fire?

Fire is not just the result of combustion as many believe. Instead, matter contains fire; when we witness a fire, we are seeing an object's fiery energy released. When the fire is burned out, the object once full of color, texture, shape, and substance, has now disappeared and all that remains is grey dust. Thus, it stands to reason that fire is what gives everything its color, texture, shape, and substance.

> "O fire, thy force which is present in metals like gold, in all the spheres like the sun and in lightning; is vast and deep. [...] That force is present in every object." [34]
> ~ YAJUR VEDA

Fire destroys things, but few realize that it is also what creates. It is well known in science that literally everything in our universe, all that we see around us, including our own bodies down to the very atoms, originated from within the fiery furnace of the stars.[35][36] When we look around then, we can begin to see that all we are looking at are forms of fire. It has been said that all that separates us from the burning stars above is time.

Fire is also what sustains us. Without the light and heat of the sun's fire, and the continual outpouring of its energy, no life could exist—the universe would be nothing but an utterly dark and freezing void. When the sun has set, its light reflected on the moon, the shining fire of the stars, and the fire released from wood that has absorbed and stored the fiery energy of the sun through photosynthesis, are what give us light and warmth. Even electricity is a form of fire, and may even be the source of it—a recent theory called "the electric universe" proposes that the sun and stars are powered by currents of electric energy flowing throughout the cosmos that are invisible to the human eye.[37] The shared origin of sun, electricity (seen as lightning to ancient people), and fire was known in the ancient Slavic religion, where they were seen as the three faces of the one supreme god.[38]

The fiery energy of the sun that is absorbed by plants is suddenly released when they are burned, and this fire ascends upward as if returning to the sun and stars from where it came. This is why ancient Vedic and Mayan rituals use fire as a messenger to carry offerings and prayers from earth to heaven.

> "Oh Ajaw!
> Oh, you, sacred fire, purifying fire.
> You who sleep in the *pom* [incense]
> who rise up in brilliant flames above the altar
> You are the heart of the sacrifice
> the daring flight of prayer
> the hidden spark in all things
> You are the glorious soul of the Sun." [39]
> ~ MAYA PRAYER OF THE GROUP OF KI'CHE DAY KEEPERS KOMON TOHIL IN ZUNIL, GUATEMALA

> "[...] the Immortals all rejoice in thee, O Agni [fire]. Centre art thou [...] of the people, sustaining men like a deep-founded pillar. The forehead of the sky, earth's centre, Agni became the messenger of earth and heaven. [...] As in the Sun firm rays are set for ever,

treasures are in [...] Agni. Of all the riches in the hills, the waters, the herbs, among mankind, thou art the [Sovereign]." [40]

~ THE RIG VEDA

An ancient Vedic ritual called "yajna" being performed, in which fire is central, and symbolizes the sun. The element of fire is believed to be divine and thus able to convey messages between our physical world and the otherworldly, spiritual realms. Similar rituals called "yasna" are performed by Zoroastrians. These rituals share the same root, which traces back to the Indo-European religion both the Vedic and Zoroastrian traditions originated from. Mayans also practice similar rituals, which I believe were influenced by the same ancient religion.

Eventually, billions of years from now, the entirety of Earth and its life will be engulfed by the sun when it expands into a "red giant." And so the fiery light of the sun will fulfill its role as the universe's creator, sustainer, and destroyer.

This was already understood in ancient Hindu texts where the sun and fire are described as creator, sustainer, and destroyer. The following excerpt is taken from a Hindu text attributed to Krishna's son named Samba, and in it the sun is not only seen as the source and return destination of all creation, but also the destination of those who obtain salvation.

"During the period of the creation the entire universe is created from the Sun while at the time of dissolution everything merges into that splendorous Sun. All the Yogis and the followers of the Samkhya (philosophy) leaving their old bodies and having become totally pure enter into this splendorous Sun. The saints who have obtained the siddhis live with the gods taking shelter of the thousand rays of the Sun as the birds live on slender branches of the trees." [41]

~ THE SAMBA PURANA

The sun (and stars), so associated with the Son/Christ (as Jesus, Viracocha, Osiris, and Horus, etc.), is a raging fire and that which creates, sustains, and ultimately destroys all of creation. This is why Krishna, who was associated with the sun in India, says that he contains the Eternal Spirit (his higher Being) from whom this universe proceeds, in whom it subsists, and to whom, in the end, it returns.

> "[Krishna said] I will speak to thee now of that great Truth which man ought to know, since by its means he will win immortal bliss— that which is without beginning, the Eternal Spirit which dwells in Me, neither with form, nor yet without it. [...] It is the upholder of all, Creator and Destroyer alike; It is the Light of lights, beyond the reach of darkness; the Wisdom, the only thing that is worth knowing or that wisdom can teach [...]." [42]
> ~ KRISHNA IN THE BHAGAVAD GITA

The Son, born of the union of masculine and feminine forces at the dawn of creation, is the light of the first day, the sun, which is fire.

As life is multidimensional it follows that while there is physical fire that appears from within matter, this fire also exists in higher dimensions even when we don't see it, as every physical form has its corresponding multidimensional aspect. Fire's origins trace back into the very highest of dimensions, where it is the force that sustains all life, and even beyond the dimensions into the unknowable, where it becomes impossible to see beyond it to where it came from. This is the realm of Brahman, the Absolute, the Self-Generated, and the Tao—the incomprehensible, immeasurable creator of all things.

Fire has played an essential part of sacred rituals and ceremonies, and has held a central place on altars and shrines that honor the divine throughout the world since the beginning of history. This knowledge of the spiritual nature of fire has come down, at least in part, from the ancient sacred teachings that originated from the lost global civilization that practiced the Religion of the Sun, and influenced or gave rise to the religion of ancient Egypt, the Vedic and Hindu religion of India, Indo-Iranian Zoroastrianism in Iran, the Inca religion of South America, the Druidism of the British Isles, the religion of the Baltic people of Europe, and a number of others in which the sun and fire were seen as manifestations of the divine.

In the pre-Christian religion of the Baltic region in Europe fire is also held sacred. This is because it is another branch of ancient Indo-European religion, like Hinduism and Zoroastrianism. This ceremony is being conducted by the Romuvans in Lithuania.

The opening hymn of the Rig Veda (one of the four Vedas, the foundational texts of Vedic/Hindu religion, and one of the most ancient known sacred texts in the world) speaks of the divinity of fire:

> "I worship the Sacred Fire (Agni), the chosen Priest, God, minister of sacrifice, the invoker [...]. Worthy is Agni to be praised by living as by ancient seers. [...] To you, dispeller of the night, O Agni, day by day with prayer bringing you reverence, we come, ruler of sacrifices, guard of Law eternal, radiant One, increasing in your own abode." [43]
>
> ~ THE RIG VEDA

The Atharva Veda (another of the four Vedas) in its "Hymn to the Earth" states that divine fire exists within everything—within all the elements, in all life, and in the sun:

> "There is a Divine fire in the Earth and in the plants. The Waters carry the fire and the same fire dwells in the rocks. There is a fire within human beings, within the cows and the horses are sacred fires. The Divine fire shines from heaven as the Sun. The Divine fire extends the wide atmosphere through the wind. Mortals enkindle the Fire that carries their prayers, which loves clarity." [44]
>
> ~ THE ATHARVA VEDA

In the ancient scriptures of Zoroastrianism, both fire and the sun are attributed to God as the greatest sources of light, and in particular fire is worshiped as "the son of God."

> "We attribute to you, O Mazda Ahura [God], the most beautiful body among bodies, these lights here (the fire) (as well as) yonder (light), the highest among the high since it was given the name 'sun'." [45]
>
> ~ YASNA HAPTANHAITI

> "Yes, we worship the Creator Ahura Mazda and the Fire, Ahura Mazda's son [...]. We worship the Fire, the son of God, the holy lord of the ritual order." [46]
>
> ~ YASNA IN THE ZEND AVESTA

Illustration of Zoroaster (the founder of Zoroastrianism) worshiping fire and the sun.

In the Hermetic text The Vision of Hermes, the divine mind of the universe (who appears as a dragon) reveals to Hermes Trismegistus the mysteries of creation. In the vision, the Son of God appears as a pillar of flame:

> "I Thy God am the Light and the Mind which were before substance was divided from spirit and darkness from Light. And the Word which appeared as a pillar of flame out of the darkness is the Son of God, born of the mystery of the Mind." [47]
> ~ POIMANDRES (THE MIND OF THE UNIVERSE) TO HERMES IN THE VISION OF HERMES

In the ancient Egyptian Book of the Dead, Osiris identifies himself as the son of God and as fire:

> "I am the great One, the son of the great One. I am Fire, the son of Fire [...]. I have made myself whole and sound. I have become young once more. I am Osiris, the Lord of Eternity." [48]
> ~ OSIRIS IN THE BOOK OF THE DEAD

In an ancient Gnostic text, the Gospel of Thomas, Jesus equates himself with fire and says that he is the origin of everything and is everywhere, just as the Vedic texts describe fire as existing in everything:

> "He who is near me is near the fire, and he who is far from me is far from the kingdom. [...] It is I who am the light which is above them all. It is I who am the all. From me did the all come forth, and unto me did the all extend. Split a piece of wood, and I am there. Lift up the stone, and you will find me there." [49]
> ~ JESUS IN THE GOSPEL OF THOMAS

In the Bhagavad Gita, Arjuna sees Krishna as a blaze of light and fire, and as pervading the entirety of creation:

> "Arjuna said: [...] I see Thee [Krishna], infinite in form, with, as it were, faces, eyes and limbs everywhere; no beginning, no middle, no end; O Thou Lord of the Universe, Whose Form is universal! I see thee with the crown, the sceptre and the discus; a blaze of splendor. Scarce can I gaze on thee, so radiant thou art, glowing like the blazing fire, brilliant as the sun, immeasurable. Imperishable art Thou, the Sole One worthy to be known, the priceless Treasure-house of the universe, the immortal Guardian of the Life Eternal, the Spirit Everlasting. Without beginning, without middle and without end, infinite in power, Thine arms all-embracing, the sun and moon

Thine eyes, Thy face beaming with the fire of sacrifice, flooding the whole universe with light." [50]

~ THE BHAGAVAD GITA

Krishna himself says to Arjuna:

"Remember that the Light which, proceeding from the sun, illumines the whole world, and the Light which is in the moon, and That which is in the fire also, all are born of Me. I enter this world and animate all My creatures with My vitality; and by My cool moonbeams I nourish the plants. Becoming the fire of life, I pass into their bodies and, uniting with the vital streams of Prana and Apana, I digest the various kinds of food. I am enthroned in the hearts of all [...]." [51]

~ THE BHAGAVAD GITA

In a famous passage of the Yajur Veda (one of the four Vedas), the supreme creator called Narayana is described as a great flame of fire that is said to reside within the heart of every being.

"Whatever all this universe is, seen or heard of—pervading all this, from inside and outside alike, stands supreme the Eternal Divine Being (Narayana).

He is the Limitless, Imperishable, Omniscient, residing in the ocean of the heart, the Cause of the happiness of the universe, the Supreme End of all striving, (manifesting Himself) in the ether of the heart which is comparable to an inverted bud of the lotus flower.

Below the Adam's apple, at a distance of a span, and above the navel (i.e., the heart which is the relative seat of the manifestation of Pure Consciousness in the human being), effulges the Great Abode of the universe, as if adorned with garlands of flames.

Surrounded on all sides by nerve-currents (or arteries), the lotus-bud of the heart is suspended in an inverted position. In it is a subtle space (a narrow aperture, the sushumna-nadi), and therein is to be found the Substratum of all things.

In that space within the heart resides the Great Flaming Fire, undecaying, all-knowing, with tongues spread out in all directions, with faces turned everywhere, consuming all food presented before it, and assimilating it into itself.

His rays, spreading all round, sideways as well as above and below, warm up the whole body from head to foot. In the centre of That (Flame) abides the Tongue of Fire as the topmost among all subtle things.

Brilliant like a streak of lightning set in the midst of the blue rain-bearing clouds, slender like the awn of a paddy grain, yellow (like gold) in colour, in subtlety comparable to the minute atom, (this Tongue of Fire) glows splendid.

In the middle of that Flame, the Supreme Self dwells. This (Self) is Brahma (the Creator), Siva (the Destroyer), Hari (the Protector), Indra (the Ruler), the Imperishable, the Absolute, the Autonomous Being." 52

~ THE NARAYANA SUKTAM FROM THE YAJUR VEDA

The fire of the material sun, the fire of the spiritual sun, the fire within matter, and the flame of our Being within, are all connected. This is why the sun and fire have been seen as living representations of the divine, and so often associated with divinity.

THE SPIRITUAL NATURE OF LIGHT

The sun was seen as the greatest source of light physically, and also spiritually in higher dimensions. Although we see the sun as a distant object, its light pervades Earth's atmosphere—and so we live in an environment illuminated by light, either from the sun, stars, or reflected by the moon, and from the same elements on Earth, such as fire and electrical light. Manifesting as fire, light is not only what illuminates creation, but also what gives everything its color, life, and energy—shining from the greatness of the sun, and from within the smallness of every atom.

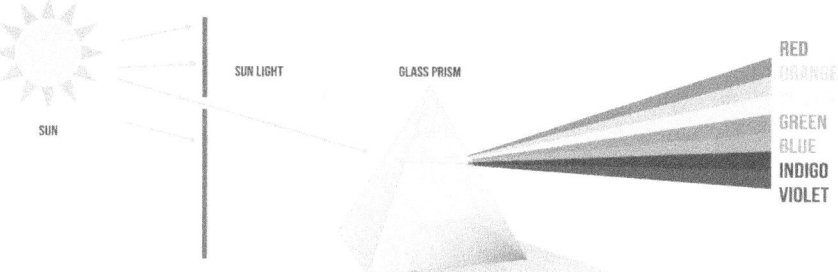

White light, like that from the sun, contains all colors, as seen when it shines through a prism or water droplets to make a rainbow. Light is what gives everything its color.

This is one of the reasons why ancient peoples saw the sun as the great outpouring of the limitless, eternal, and all-pervading creator—who is both small and great, and at the same time both near and far away.

"Sun illumines all objects. God is self-Resplendent. This is the manifestation of His Glory." 53

~ YAJUR VEDA

> "In the highest golden sheath
> Is Brahma, without stain, without parts.
> Brilliant is It, the light of lights—
> That which knowers of the Soul (Atman) do know!
> The sun shines not there, nor the moon and stars;
> These lightnings shine not, much less this [earthly] fire!
> After Him, as He shines, doth everything shine.
> This whole world is illumined with His light.
> Brahma, indeed, is this immortal. Brahma before,
> Brahma behind, to right and to left.
> Stretched forth below and above,
> Brahma, indeed, is this whole world, this widest extent.
> [...] Truly, it is Life (Prana) that shines forth in all things!" [54]
> ~ MUNDAKA UPANISHAD

Light in its higher dimensional aspect is spiritual in its nature and contains everything that is spiritual within it, including love, inner peace, wisdom, joy, divine happiness, etc. Each person's Being is essentially a quality of light that comes from the great light of the creator. This is why the Spiritual Son is described as a child of light and identified with the light of the sun, stars, and fire.

In the ancient Religion of the Sun, heavenly realms were always located in the region of the sun and stars above, which are the regions of light. This is because the dimensions become less dense and material—that is less composed of the substance of darkness—and less subject to the laws of matter, the higher they are. Thus, as they ascend, the more they're comprised of unconstrained light—making them increasingly vivid, alive, and beautiful.

These higher dimensions, or "heavens," have been described by numerous people who've visited them in near-death experiences.

> "[I] began in a primitive, coarse, unresponsive realm [...] from which I was rescued by a slowly spinning clear white light associated with a musical melody, that served as a portal up into rich and ultrareal realms [...]. It was as if the blinders came off and the reality there was much more crisp, real, and interactive and fresh than any reality I've ever known in this earthly existence. [...] Higher than the clouds—immeasurably higher—flocks of transparent, shimmering beings arced across the sky [...]. Everything was distinct, yet everything was also a part of everything else. [...] The chants and hymns thundering down from those angelic choirs provided yet another portal to higher realms, eventually ushering my awareness into the Core [...] whom many might label as God." [55]
> ~ DR. EBEN ALEXANDER

Their descriptions are essentially the same as those of people who've visited these higher realms in out-of-body experiences, like the following account of an initiate's experience from ancient Egypt.

> "He hears the music of the sacred spheres and sees the throbbing pulsations of life heaving about him, like waves upon the great seas. He becomes aware of an inflowing of unspoken knowledge from a surrounding power. It does not come from any one point, but appears to flow out of all things and to penetrate all things. Material objects lose their density and become visible within, they become as though compounded of ten thousand whirling spheres of brightness. Colours are no longer dull and restricted, they become infinite in depth and number. The spirit becomes lost in adoration and wonder at the beauty revealed in everything. The soul is aware of something glorious within all this and knows it for the spirit outflowing from its source." [56]
> ~ THE HIBSATHY, THE KOLBRIN

Those who go on to reach the heavenly realms are said to live more fully there than they do here.

> "He lives over there, lives more fully than he ever lived. He lives in splendor, he lives in beauty, he lives in knowledge and in the waters of life." [57]
> ~ THE SACRED REGISTERS - PART 1, THE KOLBRIN

As explained further in the following chapters, beings have come into the world of form where there is a duality of light and darkness like individual flames descending from the sun into the darkness of matter.

> "Imperishable is the Lord of Love.
> As from a blazing fire thousands of sparks
> Leap forth, so millions of beings arise
> From the Lord of Love..." [58]
> ~ MUNDAKA UPANISHAD

On the return ascent, someone unlocks the spiritual fire found within the dark sheath of matter and their subconscious, gradually returning to their own Spiritual Son/sun, and transforming themselves into a being of light as they do. In Egypt, this being of light was known as the "akh," and in India as Atman.

This journey of transformation and return to the light I call the path of the spiritual sun.

THE PATH OF THE SPIRITUAL SUN

The Spiritual Son as the Egyptian god Horus.

In traditions that were influenced by or descended from the ancient Religion of the Sun, there are references to a path of the sun leading to salvation, immortality, and liberation—and at the same time to the heavenly realm of the sun and stars. The major stages on this path were celebrated as occurring on the solstices and equinoxes. This is because the annual journey of the sun is symbolic of the journey of consciousness in its return to source, to the spiritual light of the stars—a journey which is eternal and lies at the heart of existence. The correlation between spiritual transformation and the movements of the cosmos is no coincidence, but part of the greater design of the universe, revealing the process of spiritual awakening to humanity.

The great teachers of the Religion of the Sun understood this profound message that literally comes from above, and knew that the movement of the heavens and Earth was intimately linked to the process of a human reuniting with the spiritual, with the sun representing the Spiritual Son that a person on the path of the sun reunites with. For those who journey on this path, the sun can be shown in dreams and out-of-body experiences in this spiritual context.

Some believe that the correlation of heavenly movements to the lives of different deities only indicates that different religions borrowed from one another, basing their stories on the pagan traditions of sun worship. But to mystics, this correlation is the result of something hidden and profound—the path of the spiritual sun.

This path is one that is mirrored in the heavens with the movements of the celestial bodies and is found imbued in the very fabric of life. It has been enacted by those who had made themselves Sons of the Sun throughout time, and who became great teachers of the Religion of the Sun. At the solstices and equinoxes many ancient people celebrated its stages in tune with the natural rhythms of the sun and seasons, which are permeated by its principles.

Krishna, in the famous text the Bhagavad Gita, actually refers to the path of the sun, which takes one to the Supreme Primeval Abode beyond birth and death—as being related to the summer solstice, also saying that this path has always existed, and elsewhere in this text that it is "the supreme secret" that was preserved by the ancient divine kings of the ancient solar dynasty in India.

> "Now I will tell thee, O Arjuna, of the times which, if the mystics go forth, they do not return, and at which they go forth only to return. If knowing the Supreme Spirit the sage goes forth with fire and light, in the daytime, in the fortnight of the waxing moon and in the six months before the Northern summer solstice, he will attain the Supreme. But if he departs in gloom, at night, during the fortnight of the waning moon and in the six months before the Southern solstice [winter solstice], then he reaches but lunar light and he will be born again. These bright and dark paths out of the world have always existed. Whoso takes the former, returns not; he who chooses the latter, returns. The sage who knows this passes beyond all merit that comes from the study of the scriptures, from sacrifice, from austerities and charity, and reaches the Supreme Primeval Abode." [59]
> ~ KRISHNA IN THE BHAGAVAD GITA

References to this path trace back even further to more ancient Hindu texts, in the Upanishads:

> "That which is Brahman is light; that which is light is the Sun. [...] The king named after the wind, having made his obeisance to him and duly offered his homage, went, with his aim attained, to the northern path. There is here no going by any by-way. This is the path to Brahman. Bursting open the door of the sun, he departed by the upward path. On this point the sages declare;
>
> Endless are the rays of that soul which abides like a lamp in the heart [...]. One of these rises upward which pierces the orb of the sun; by this, having passed beyond the world of Brahman, they attain to the supreme abode. [...]
>
> Therefore yonder adorable Sun is the cause of creation, of heaven, and of emancipation." [60]
> ~ THE MAITRĀYAṆĪYA UPANISHAD

> "The sun gives light and life to all who live,
> East and west, north and south, above, below;
> It is the prana of the universe.
> The wise see the Lord of Love in the sun,
> Rising in all its golden radiance
> To give its warmth and light and life to all.
> The wise see the Lord of Love in the year,
> Which has two paths, the northern and the southern.
> Those who observe outward forms of worship
> And are content with personal pleasures
> Travel after death by the southern path,
> The path of the ancestors and of rayi,
> To the lunar world, and are born again.
> But those who seek the Self through meditation,
> Self-discipline, wisdom, and faith in God
> Travel after death by the northern path,
> The path of prana, to the solar world,
> Supreme refuge, beyond the reach of fear
> And free from the cycle of birth and death." [61]
>
> ~ THE PRASHNA UPANISHAD

These same paths in and out of the world, connected to the winter and summer solstices, can be found in Mithraism. An author describes the design of the secret caves of Mithras as follows:

> "But this cave was adorned with the signs of the zodiac, Cancer and Capricorn. The summer and winter solstices were chiefly conspicuous, as the gates of souls descending into this life, or passing out of it in their ascent to the Gods; Cancer being the gate of descent, and Capricorn of ascent. These are the two avenues of the immortals passing up and down from earth to heaven, and from heaven to earth." [62]
>
> ~ JOHN P. LUNDY, MONUMENTAL CHRISTIANITY

Records preserved in ancient Egypt state that before the historically accepted beginning of Egyptian civilization, in 3,000 BC, there was a period of civilization ruled by those called the Shemsu Hor, said to have lasted over thirteen thousand years.[63] The term Shemsu Hor is loosely interpreted as "the followers of Horus"—but a more precise and literal translation of their name is "'those who follow the path of Horus,' that is, the 'Horian way,' also called the solar way..."[64] It could also be translated as "those who follow the path of the Spiritual Son/sun."

In the Stanzas of Dzyan—a very ancient text that was preserved for thousands of years in Tibet—the Spiritual Son is described as making a pilgrimage upon a wheel.

> "Darkness alone filled the boundless all, for father, mother and son were once more one, and the son had not awakened yet for the new wheel, and his pilgrimage thereon." [65]
> ~ THE STANZAS OF DZYAN

This wheel is that of creation and time, and at a more microcosmic scale correlates to the wheel of the year—the annual journey of the sun. The Spiritual Son, symbolized by and manifest as the sun, enacts the events on the path of the spiritual sun each year as a kind of pilgrimage to the sacred destination symbolized by the summer solstice. This is why so many sun gods who represented the Spiritual Son were celebrated as being born at the winter solstice, resurrecting at the spring equinox, and ascending at the summer solstice.

This intrinsic relationship between spirituality and the natural world is one of the reasons why so many ancient sacred sites, texts, and celebrations combined spiritual and natural phenomena. Spiritual principles can be read in the natural world around us just as they were by ancient spiritual peoples, as they are timeless and ever-present.

FOLLOWING THE SUMMER SOLSTICE

Around three days following the summer solstice, the sun begins to descend in the sky, and darkness begins to increase as the nights begin to lengthen toward winter. This symbolizes consciousness, the eternal spark of light within each person, the seed of inner potential, coming out from the spiritual sun and stars, and descending into the darkness of matter and the material world (from heaven to Earth), to learn and awaken through the process of life like the seed which is produced from the tree at summer. On a personal spiritual level it also symbolizes the beginning of a new journey on the path of the spiritual sun.

AUTUMN EQUINOX

At the autumn equinox, day and night are equal, but from the autumn equinox onward there is more darkness than light—this is the time of descent into the underworld to face and overcome one's own inner darkness, just as the sun descends in its annual journey. In nature, it is a time of death, when the old is shed in preparation for the new life of spring. Likewise, spiritually it is a time when one's false self and ego must die in preparation for the coming life of the Spiritual Son/sun within. Many deities died and descended into the underworld/hades/hell at this time of year, as the seed of inner potential remains dormant indefinitely, and does not germinate, unless it descends into the darkness of the earth. As the course of the sun throughout the year can also be found in its course through one day, the autumn equinox corresponds to the time of sunset and the cardinal direction of west.

WINTER SOLSTICE

At the winter solstice, darkness is at its maximum, but there is hope in the winter sunrise from which the light gradually increases—this is the time of the birth of the Spiritual Son/sun within, and is the reason why so many solar deities were born at the winter solstice. The winter solstice finds its parallel with the cardinal direction of south in the Northern Hemisphere, and north in the Southern Hemisphere, and the time of midnight, which is why Christmas Mass is traditionally held at midnight. It is a celebration of the birth of light at the time of greatest darkness. The seeds that have gone into the earth now germinate in darkness beneath the ground, and life is born. Similarly, the influence of the Spiritual Son within starts as something small like a child or tiny seed that gradually increases/grows—just as the sun's influence does from the winter to summer solstice, transforming someone spiritually as it does.

SPRING EQUINOX

At the spring equinox day and night are once again equal, but from this time onward light is greater than darkness. This is the time of resurrection, the triumph over darkness, and attainment of eternal spiritual life, which is why so many deities die at the autumn equinox and later come back to life to live eternally at the spring equinox, when the life of spring bursts forth from within the earth to overcome the forces of darkness and death in the light of the triumphant sun. The spring equinox corresponds to the time of dawn and the direction of east.

SUMMER SOLSTICE

At the summer solstice, the sun has ascended to its highest point in the sky and the light is at its greatest, symbolizing the return to one's higher Being symbolized by the sun—this is the time of the ascension from Earth to heaven, the return to wholeness of Being and the spiritual source from which consciousness originated. Like the flowers and fruits of summer, the life of the spirit is at full bloom and corresponds to midday in the sun's daily journey and the direction north in the Northern Hemisphere, and south in the Southern Hemisphere. From the ending of the summer solstice, the sun descends once more to begin the eternal cycle again.

Some of those who incarnated the Spiritual Son, and who made themselves Sons of the Sun, enacted these events in their lives to demonstrate the process of spiritual transformation, and those who go through this process will also go through these same events in their lives. It is a process that has taken place within a number of men and women throughout history, and is continuously repeated in the cycles of the sun.

This correlation between the path to reunite with the Spiritual Son and higher Being symbolized by the sun, and the annual journey of the sun, I put forward as "The Sacred Sun Path Theory."

ANCIENT REMNANTS OF SOLSTICE AND EQUINOX CELEBRATIONS

The Great Sphinx of Egypt gazes precisely at the rising sun on the equinox.

Thousands of years ago, using highly advanced knowledge, ancient peoples built huge megalithic structures and temples that aligned with the sun at the equinoxes and solstices. And some—such as the Great Pyramids, Angkor Wat, and Easter Island—even align with each other from across the world. A few traditions of celebrating the solstice and equinox still survive today, although many others passed into history.

While traditions often change or lose their meaning through time, these stone monuments have stood for thousands of years. They were purposefully built as giant symbols and have thus kept a knowledge of the path of the spiritual sun, and the spiritual meaning of the solstice and equinox, encoded into their structures that can still be read today.

Here are just some of the ancient markers that align to the solstices and equinoxes:

- The Great Pyramid of Egypt has multiple alignments to the solstices and equinoxes, functioning as an enormous sundial. Its shadow to the north, and its reflected sunlight to the south, accurately mark the annual dates of both the solstices and the equinoxes. Two of its faces are orientated precisely due east and west respectively, which are the exact points of the rising and setting sun on the spring and autumn equinoxes, and on the winter solstice a shadow cast on one of its outer sides is at the same angle as the descending and ascending passages inside.

- The Great Sphinx of Egypt gazes precisely at the equinox sunrise and is crowned by the setting summer solstice sun.

- The first rays of the rising sun on the summer solstice pass through stone markers to hit the altar stone in the center of Stonehenge in England.

- Newgrange in Ireland is a giant one acre mound which receives a shaft of sunlight into a central chamber shaped like a cross at dawn on the winter solstice.

- At the ancient city of Angkor Wat in Cambodia, the spire of its central tower aligns with the sun on the equinox.

- The giant Serpent Mound in Ohio in the United States faces the summer solstice sunset.

- On Easter Island, seven of the giant stone statues called moai face the equinox sunset, while on another part of the island, fifteen face the summer solstice sunset.

- The "Sun Dagger" in Chaco Canyon in the United States is a stone structure which uses shadow and sunlight to mark the equinoxes and solstices. The nearby ancient city also has various alignments to the solstices and equinoxes.

- On the equinox at the pyramid of Chichen Itza in Mexico, the light creates the effect of the feathered serpent slithering down the side of the pyramid.

- Two of the thirty rock-cut caves at Ajanta in India capture the sunlight on the solstices so that the sacred statues of Buddha they contain are illuminated.

- The ancient city of Arkaim in the Ural Mountains of Russia aligns to the solstices and equinoxes.

- A number of temples in Egypt are aligned with the winter solstice sunrise. At the temple of Amun in Karnak, which is the largest temple complex in the world, the sun's rays flood an inner sanctuary of the god Amun with light, and are funneled along a giant temple causeway lined with massive pillars.

An understanding of the symbols used in these ancient sites reveals that many were representing the same spiritual principles around the same celestial events.

The knowledge encoded into their designs tells us that what happens above is related to our world below, and most importantly, to ourselves. They show the great link between the human and divine, the personal and the cosmic, and the inner and outer world, and were centered around the path of the spiritual sun.

SPIRITUAL SYMBOLS FOUND IN THE COSMOS

Some of the world's most ancient and well known spiritual symbols also encode spiritual principles that are found in the movements of the planets, sun, and stars.

Symbols operate on different levels, only being able to be interpreted according to the understanding of the observer. If we understand something, it can become apparently visible in the symbol, but that which is out of our reach will remain hidden and invisible.

While many will be familiar with the following symbols, most will be unaware of what these symbols describe. These examples reveal how symbols can actually describe universal principles that operate on different levels. They encode information about the movement of the earth around the sun, yet at the same time, also reveal how these principles are connected to the journey of consciousness and operate within the human psyche.

This is why the great maxim of wisdom states, "as above, so below." These symbols reveal how physical, cosmic phenomena are related to inner, spiritual ones, and why the progress of the sun throughout the year was so important to ancient spiritual cultures. As a microcosm of the universe, we are connected to creation in ways we cannot possibly imagine. To someone who understands how to perceive the universe in this way, the outer world becomes a magnificent reflection of our own personal journey through eternity.

YIN AND YANG

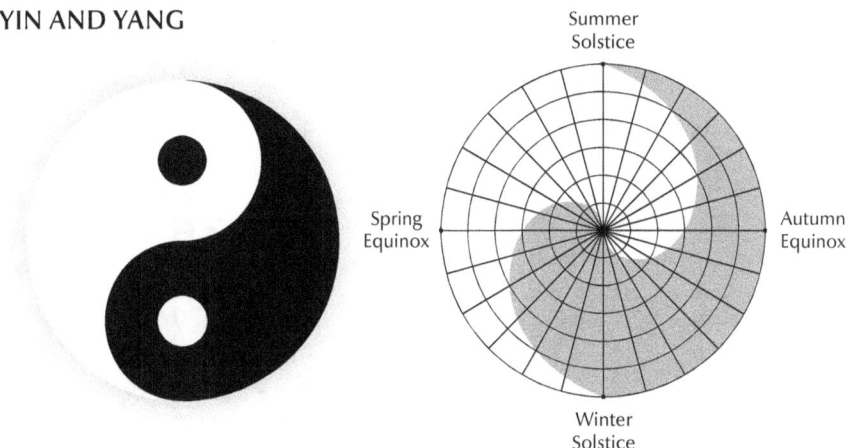

Left: The yin and yang symbol. Right: The yin and yang symbol found when mapping the duration of light and darkness throughout the year.[66] Image based on diagram by Allen Tsai.

The ancient symbol of yin and yang, most famously used in China, can be seen in the annual cycle of the sun. The most ancient depiction of the yin-yang symbol was found in southeastern Europe, dating to between 5,500-2,750 BC.[67]

This symbol expresses the principle of duality and polarity, which forms the bounds of all manifest creation. It also represents the cycles of light and darkness that everything, including our consciousness, progresses through.

The ancient Aztec symbol known as the Hunab Ku from the sixteenth century Aztec Codex Magliabechiano is a variation of yin-yang symbol.

TRINITY

A holy family of three was central to traditions around the world that derived from the ancient Religion of the Sun. The most famous examples are the ancient Egyptian family of Osiris, Isis, and Horus, and the Christian holy family of Joseph, Mary, and Jesus.

This trinity is symbolic of the three fundamental forces of creation—of positive, negative, and neutral, which are also found expressed in the cycles of the earth and sun each year.

The Christian holy family of Joseph, Mary, and Jesus—representing Father, Mother, and Son. The trinity of creation is a very ancient symbol, representing the three fundamental forces of creation, which underlie and give rise to it, and the three stations of the sun at the solstices and equinoxes. This painting illustrates it beautifully, with Father standing above at summer solstice position (his ladder ascending to heaven), Mother seated on the earth at winter solstice position, and the Son standing upon his Mother Earth rising toward his Father, though exactly in the middle at equinox. Each are crowned with a halo as the three stations of the sun.

The extreme ascent of the sun at the summer solstice, and the light half of the year, represents the masculine/positive force of creation. While the extreme descent at the winter solstice, and the dark half of the year, represents the feminine/negative force of creation. The sun at the equinox, which is midway between these two extremes (both autumn and spring), represents the neutral force of creation—which is the child of the two, who is both human and divine, being created of both spirit (light) and matter (darkness).

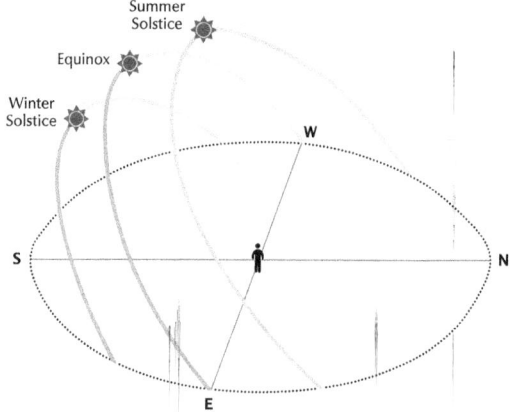

Diagram illustrating the three main stations of the sun—at winter solstice on the lower extreme, summer solstice on the higher extreme, and equinox in the middle.[68] It is based on an observer being at a mid-northern latitude. Diagram based on illustration by Professor Judith Young, UMASS Sunwheel Project.

The main symbol used by modern Druids that shows the triple aspect of the creator, known also as the "Triad of the Sunrises"—represented as three dots, or three suns rising at the solstices and equinoxes. The three lines or rays emanating from them symbolize "awen," described as "flowing spirit," within the surrounding circles of creation.[69]

A number of ancient symbols and sites of the Religion of the Sun express this trinity—such as the Master of Animals and feathered serpent symbols, and the triptych style entrances used at ancient sites.[70]

CROSS

The cross is one of the most prolific religious symbols in the world, both ancient and modern. Its origins stretch back into prehistory where variations of it have been used for thousands of years—for example as the ankh of ancient Egypt, the flared cross of ancient Mesopotamia, and the cruciform chambers of the megalithic mounds of the British Isles.

The vertical arm can represent the line drawn between the directions of north and south, and the horizontal arm the line drawn between due east and west, which coincides the with sunrise and sunset on the equinoxes.

This is illustrated in the image below, which is a diagram of an ancient wood-henge (sacred circle made of wooden posts) at the site of Cahokia Mounds in Illinois, United States (which has solstice and equinox alignments).

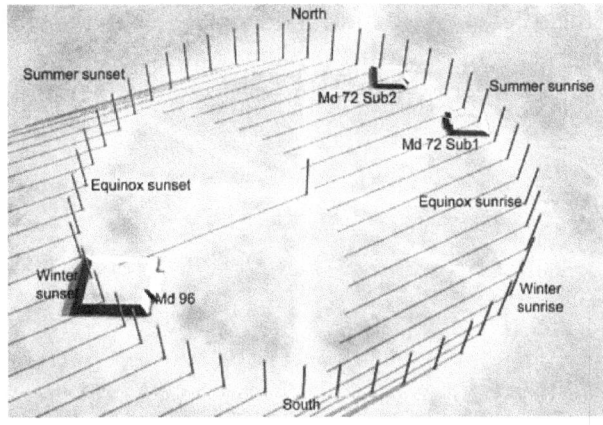

Diagram of an ancient woodhenge aligned to the solstices and equinoxes in North America.

The summer and winter solstice sunrise and sunsets create a further four arms, making eight in total.

The cross can also symbolize the intersection of the dual forces of creation—of vertical and horizontal, space and time, sky and earth, positive and negative, masculine and feminine, light and dark, day and night, Father and Mother—which give birth to a third neutral force: the fire of the divine Son/sun, which is often represented at the center of the cross.

Left: Ancient stone engraving of a "solar cross" within a winged sun disk, from the Assyrian city of Nimrud in Iraq. Right: Symbol of the cross used by the Knights Templar. Both are identical to the appearance of a single photon of light.

The symbol of the cross can be found macrocosmically, in the path of the sun through the solstices and equinoxes, and can be sometimes seen when looking at the sun as its rays extend in four directions. Likewise it is found at a microcosmic level, as a single packet of light (called a photon) takes the shape of a cross. This was discovered by Polish physicists in a study led by Radoslaw Chrapkiewicz, when they created a hologram of a photon to see what it looked like.[71] The image they produced was a red cross, nearly identical to that used by the Knights Templar.

SOLAR CROSS

The symbol of the solar cross is a further development of the cross; it encloses the cross within a circle. It is another prolific symbol of the ancient world, and reveals the religious importance of the solstices and equinoxes to ancient peoples.

Left: Ancient rock carving of people worshiping the sun as a solar cross in Sweden.

It can represent the sun at the solstices and equinoxes with the earth at the center. The vertical arm is the line drawn between the summer solstice at the top, and the winter solstice at the bottom, while the horizontal arm represents the line drawn between the autumn equinox on the left, and the spring equinox on the right. The circle represents the plane of the ecliptic— the path of the sun—as it journeys through the four points of the year (the solstices and equinoxes) as viewed from Earth.

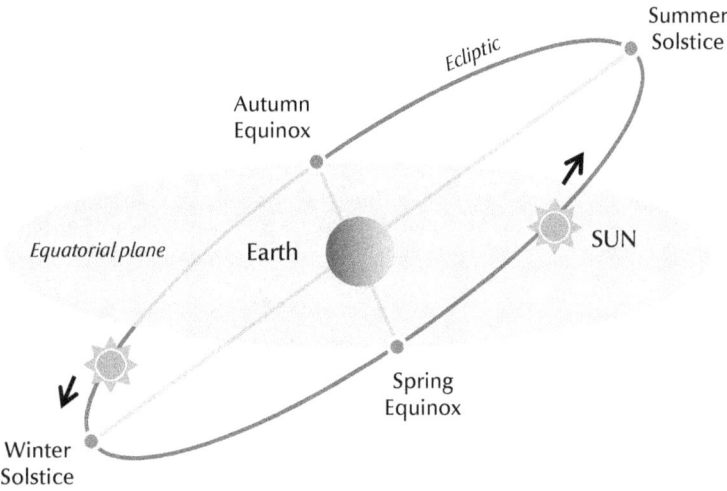

Diagram illustrating the solar cross when the earth is in the center.

It can also represent the earth at the solstices and equinoxes, with the sun in the center. In this case, the circle represents the annual journey of the earth around the sun, with the four arms intersecting the times of year when it passes through either a solstice or equinox.

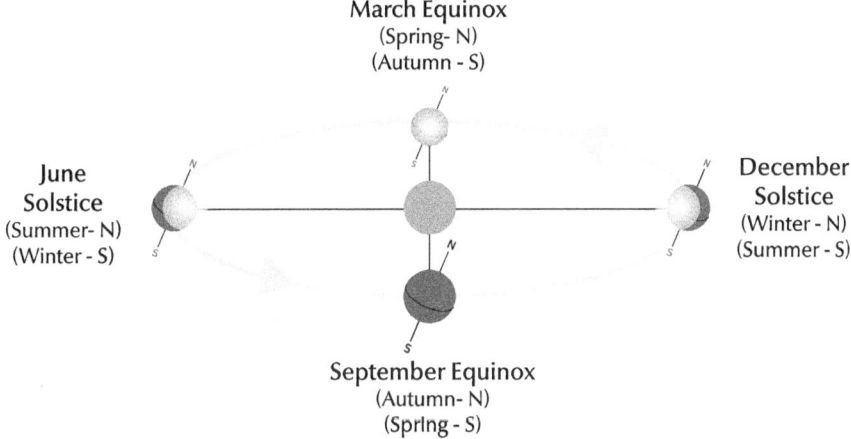

Diagram illustrating the solar cross when the sun is in the center.

LATIN CROSS/CRUCIFORM

The Latin cross is a variation of the cross. Instead of having arms of equal length, its lower arm extends further than its upper. It is the most central symbol of Christianity, as it represents the cross that Jesus was crucified on. Astrologically, it is even more accurate than the equilateral armed cross, as it takes into account the elliptical orbit of the earth around the sun (although to be completely accurate its right arm would need to extend slightly further than its left).

The famous image of Jesus being crucified. The cross symbolizes the solstices and equinoxes, and Jesus at the center represents the Son/sun. Note that I avoid images of Jesus depicted as dead on the cross, as these essentially celebrate his death.

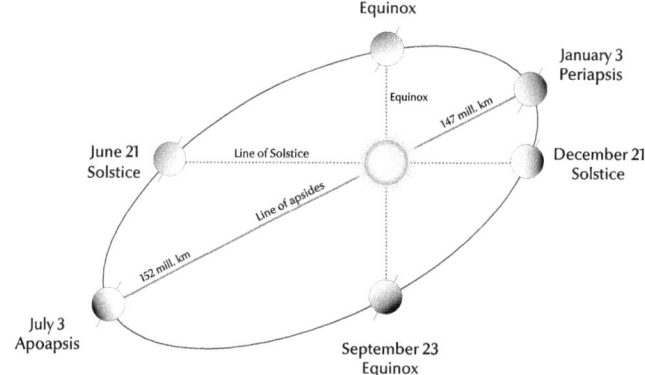

Diagram showing the elliptical orbit of the earth around the sun, which causes two arms of the cross that intersect the solstice and equinoxes to be longer than the others, creating an approximate Latin cross.

A traditional Celtic cross, which is a variation of the Latin cross as it includes a ring or circle like a solar cross does, denoting the path of the sun or orbit of the earth. This one even has spherical planet and sun shaped engravings where the main stations of the sun and Earth would be approximately. This same basic symbol can be found in the British Isles dating back thousands of years before the advent of Christianity.

THE SPIRITUAL MEANING OF THE SOLSTICES AND EQUINOXES

Illustration of the Maya sacred world tree, which is cruciform in shape. In Maya cosmology it stretches out in the four cardinal directions, corresponding to the solstices and equinoxes.

SWASTIKA

The symbol of the swastika is a further development of the solar cross. The circle of the solar cross is broken into arms that indicate the direction the sun appears to travel on its path along the ecliptic.

The swastika is one of the most prevalent ancient symbols of all time, and is found across the ancient world where it was used as a symbol of the sun. The most ancient swastika that has been found to date was carved into the tusk of a woolly mammoth in Ukraine and is dated to 10,000 BC.[72]

It represents the eternal sun, and the manifestation of divinity (as the sun) within material creation and the flow of time.

Its arms can also symbolize the spiritual sun's influence and light reaching into creation, which is illustrated more clearly in yet another variation of the solar cross called "the hands of God," and "the hands of Svarog" (who is the Slavic god of sun, fire, and heaven). Each arm of the cross terminates in a hand instead, as if they are reaching out in the four directions.

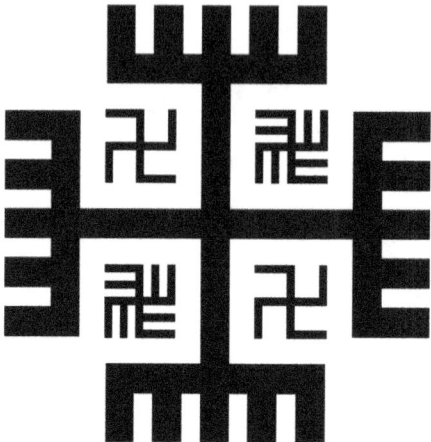

This design was found on an ancient burial urn discovered in Poland that is over two thousand years old. Each arm of the cross ends in a symbolic hand, with the five prongs representing the five fingers.

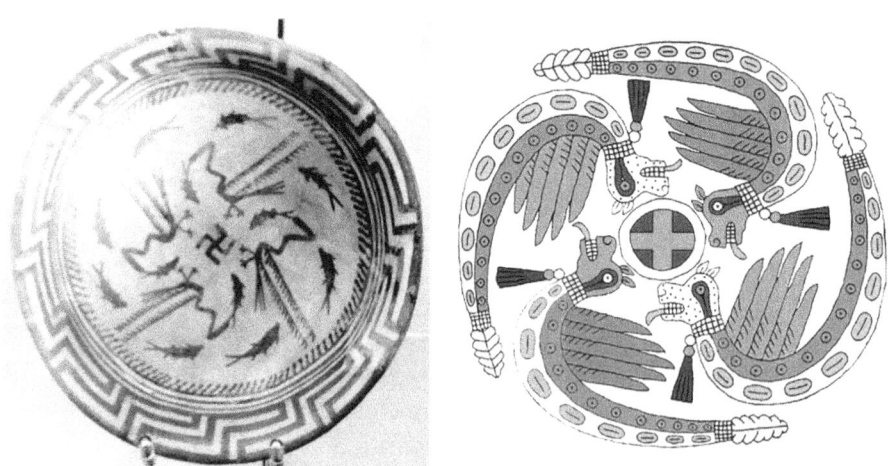

Left: An ancient bowl dated to 4,000 BC discovered in Iraq with a swastika in the center. Cleverly placed animals surrounding it reveal its motion. Right: The same swastika concept found in the art of the pre-Columbian North American peoples who depicted it in connection with their Spiritual Son deity, the feathered serpent.

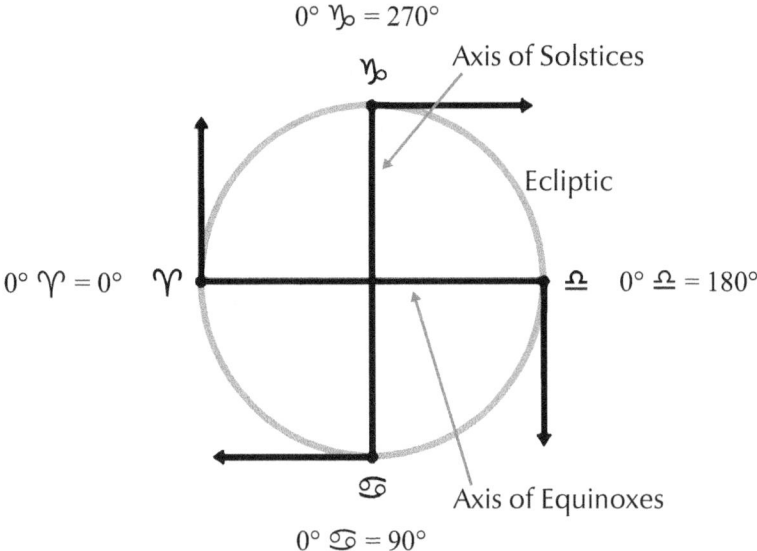

The precession of the equinoxes rotating along the plane of the ecliptic viewed as if one were looking down while directly above the North Pole. This movement can be illustrated by a swastika.[73]

INFINITY

The symbol of infinity as a figure eight has been in use at least as early as Roman times. Astronomically, this figure has a reality, as it can be found in the relationship between the sun and the earth in a phenomenon called the analemma, described as follows.

If someone were to locate the position of the sun in the sky at the same time every day, while standing in exactly the same spot, the location of the sun would change, and the different positions it occupies in the sky plot out a figure eight in a continuous loop every year—just like the symbol of infinity. The sun's shifting position in the sky occurs because of the slightly altered way we view it from Earth throughout the year, which is due to the elliptical shaped orbit of the earth around the sun, along with the slight wobble of the earth's axis.[74]

At the extreme end of one loop is the winter solstice (greatest darkness), and at the extreme end of the other is the summer solstice (greatest light). Where the two loops cross is the equinox, which is the point of rotation toward either light or darkness.

The symbol represents the eternally cycling nature of life and the cosmos, and the axis of ascent and descent that is found within us, either into light or darkness.

ANCIENT SOLSTICE

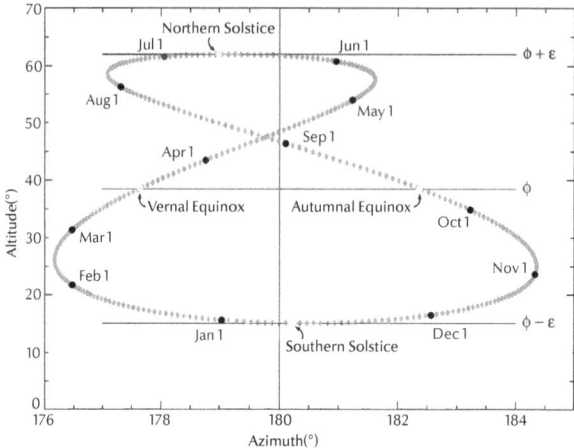

A plot of the position of the sun at 12:00 noon made from the Royal Observatory in Greenwich.

DOUBLE SPIRAL

Closely related to the symbol of infinity and the phenomenon of the analemma is the double spiral, one of the most prolific symbols of ancient Ireland, where it's found adorning megalithic sites aligned to the solstices and equinoxes.

It has also been found at the site of the ancient solar calendar called the Sun Dagger at Chaco Canyon in North America, and in the facial markings of those who practiced the ancient Religion of the Sun.

The symbol of the double spiral has cosmological origins, as it can be found in the relationship between the sun and the earth. It is a symbol of the solstices and equinoxes, which is why it was used in the artwork of those who practiced the Religion of the Sun.

It appears in the pattern the sun's light and shadow traces on the earth over the course of one year.

> "If the shadows of the sun are correlated over the period of one year in chronological order following their curvature they form a double spiral. In winter the spiral is counter-clockwise and the coils are wide. The shadows begin to straighten as equinox approaches, and after equinox they begin to wind into a clockwise spiral and tighten. They contract until the summer solstice, straighten again at equinox and return to a left-handed spiral again in winter to continue the process perpetually." [75]
>
> ~ MARTIN BRENNAN, THE STARS AND THE STONES: ANCIENT ART AND ASTRONOMY IN IRELAND

THE SPIRITUAL MEANING OF THE SOLSTICES AND EQUINOXES

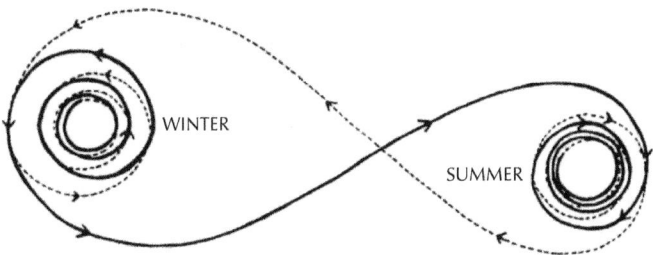

Diagram illustrating the changing shadow of the sun over the course of a year, spiraling clockwise toward summer, and counter-clockwise toward winter, and back again—winding and unwinding in a never-ending double spiral.

The artist Charlie Ross also inadvertently discovered this same ancient symbol when in 1971 he created his work for the exhibition titled *Sunlight Convergence/Solar Burn*.

> "Rather than dispersing sunlight through a prism he decided to focus it into a single point of raw power to create a solar burn. Each day for one year he burned the path of the sun through a large lens into a wooden plank. [...] Each of the 366 planks captured one day of sunlight, a portrait of sunlight drawn by the sun itself. In 1971 Ross discovered that the solar burns traced a double spiral when laid end-to-end." [76]
> ~ CHARLES ROSS, BIOGRAPHY

The double spiral is a symbol of the solstices and equinoxes. It has the same meaning and essentially illustrates the same principles as that of the symbol of infinity and the yin and yang.

Left: Artist's rendition of the spirals painted across the face of a mummy discovered in China. She was an ancient Indo-European woman who appears to have venerated the sun and is believed to have lived around 1,000 BC.[77] Right: Facial tattoo of a Maori chief in New Zealand. Similar double spirals are tattooed across his cheeks and nose, representing the sun winding and unwinding through the solstices and equinoxes. "Note the use of the double spirals, in miniature, on each side of the nose and larger spirals on each cheek. The cheek spirals are marked by double lines, which track the Sun's movement inward to the center of the spiral (Solstice) where it turns and moves toward the Equinox (marked by the bridge of the nose). The Sun then continues its journey to the other Solstice position on the opposite side of the face." [78] ~ Martin Doutré.

SPIRALS

The entrance stone to the ancient megalithic temple of Newgrange, which aligns to the winter solstice sunrise, and is covered in the symbol of the spiral.

The spiral is often found in the spiritual symbology of the ancient Europeans and Britons. At the ancient site of Newgrange in Ireland, the light of the rising sun on the winter solstice enters its innermost chamber. This ancient site is decorated with the symbol of the spiral.

While we often think of the earth's rotation around the sun as being an ellipse on a flat plane, it is really rotating in a spiral around the sun as the sun itself moves at great speed throughout space (at around 450,000 miles per hour) in its own rotation around a greater sun, in an even greater rotation around the center of the galaxy—dragging the planets of the solar system with it in a great whirling spiral. Recent evidence from NASA shows our solar system actually has a tail much like a comet because of its movement through space.[79]

The spin of the earth, rotating around the sun, which is rotating around the galactic center, is a small spiral within larger and larger spirals, producing cycles within cycles within cycles, and demonstrating the fractal nature of reality.

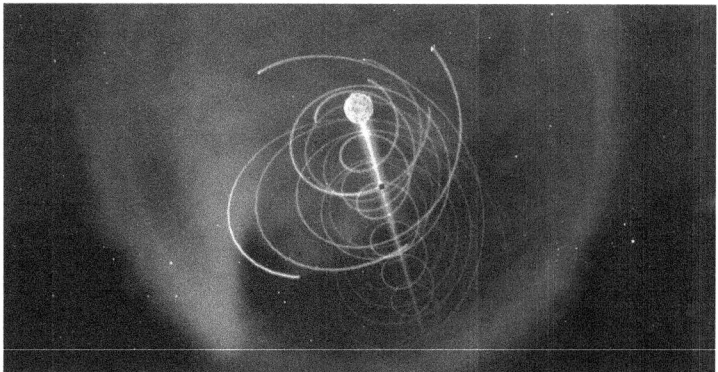

An illustration of the spiraling rotation of the planets of our solar system around the sun as it moves through the galaxy at great speed.

PENTAGRAM

The symbol of the pentagram has been used for thousands of years, dating back to at least 6,000 BC in Mesopotamia. It is used pointed both upward and downward. When pointed with one apex upward, it is a symbol of ascent—as its one point above the other four represents spirit over matter. It has been used in this position as a symbol of protection against evil. When pointing downward, it is a symbol of descent, as its four points above the one represents consciousness trapped in and dominated by matter. It has been used like this to attract evil forces.

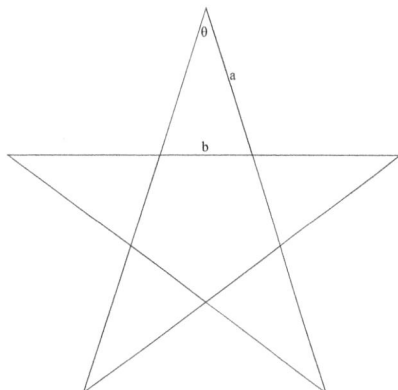

The symbol of the pentagram. Each of its five arms are a golden triangle.

Incredibly, the pentagram is found in the natural world, and related to cosmic cycles of time. It also contains numbers and angles that were considered sacred by ancient people.

The planet Venus actually traces a pentagram in its orbit around the sun in its relation to Earth every eight years.[80] Both Jesus and Quetzalcoatl were associated with Venus as the morning star.

Each apex of a pentagram is a golden triangle; golden numbers and ratios are found throughout nature and were used prolifically throughout ancient Egyptian art and architecture, as well as in sacred sites in at least Europe and North America where people had practiced the Religion of the Sun.

The angle of 108 degrees, as well as 36 and 72 (which added together equal 108), occur throughout the pentagram. The number 108 is considered sacred in Hinduism and Buddhism, and is found in the proportions of the sun in relation to the earth, and in the cycle of the earth through its "Great Year," which is a larger cycle of time known as the precession of the equinoxes.

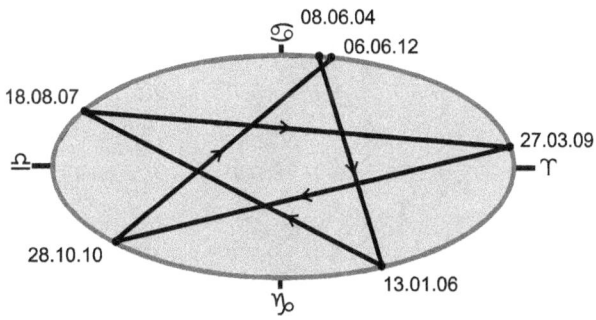

The positions of Venus at its lower conjunctions with Earth between the two transits of 2004 and 2012. Venus' orbit as viewed from Earth assumes a near perfect pentagram shape, due to the approximate 13:8 ratio between the orbital periods of Earth and Venus.

SERPENT

Serpents were often used by peoples in the ancient Religion of the Sun to symbolize the cycles of time and nature. When the hours of daylight are plotted out on a graph, they produce a line that moves in a continuous wave, like the slithering of a serpent.

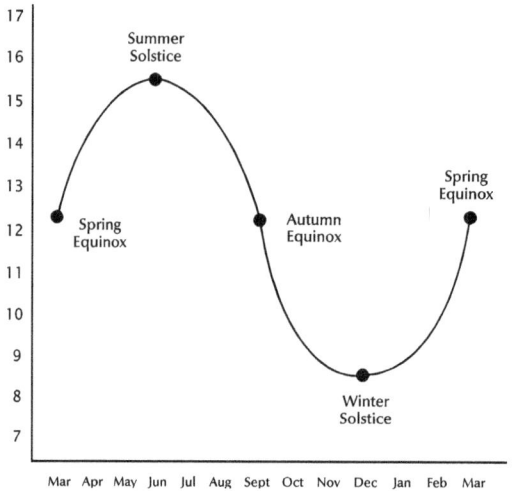

Additionally, because the sun is not stationary, but is moving through the galaxy, Earth rotates in a corkscrew spiral around it, tracing what looks like the coils of a serpent.

It's no coincidence, then, that a serpent was used to symbolize the cycle of the earth around the sun as it progressed through the solstices and equinoxes.

The most well-known of these is called the ouroboros, which is a serpent swallowing its tail, symbolizing the never-ending orbit of Earth around the sun, and the continuous renewal of nature through the death and birth of life throughout the seasons.

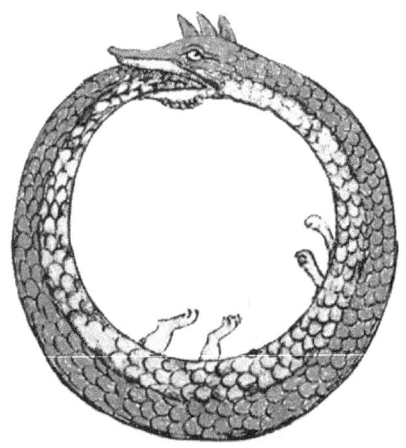

The symbol of the serpent swallowing its tail, called the ouroboros. This is a medieval depiction of it, but the earliest depiction has been found in ancient Egypt.

THE SPIRITUAL MEANING OF THE SOLSTICES AND EQUINOXES

Left: Illustration of an ouroboros/serpent in ancient Egypt encircling the infant sun god Horus, just as the earth cycles around the sun. Right: Illustration of an Aztec sun calendar, with the sun encircled by a serpent, much like an ouroboros, but with knots at the four solstices and equinoxes.

Another variation of the ouroboros. This is a swastika in which each of its four arms are a serpent. This symbol is based on ancient archaeological finds in Northern Europe and is used by the pagan group Romuva in Lithuania.

A serpent was also used to symbolize the annual progress of the earth through the solstices and equinoxes in the ancient Hindu story called the Churning of the Milky Ocean, which was carved into a mural at the ancient site of Angkor Wat in Cambodia—a site which aligns to the spring equinox.

A painting of the famous Hindu story called the Churning of the Milky Ocean. A serpent is wrapped around a central pole (symbolizing the North Pole), and is used just like a rope in a tug of war. Two teams pull back and forth on the serpent from the winter solstice on one extreme, to the summer solstice at the other, with the equinox in the center.

This mural symbolizes the cycles of light and darkness the earth progresses through each year as it rotates around the sun, pivoting upon the equinox, with the winter solstice at the darkest extreme, and the summer solstice at the lightest. Numbers of the annual cycle of the sun were encoded into Angkor Wat, as well as those of The Great Year which the earth cycles through approximately every twenty-six thousand years, and even those of a greater cosmic cycles, including huge epochs of time known as Yugas in Hinduism[81]—with the Churning of the Milky Ocean expressing the underlying principle behind the motion of the cycles of the cosmos from the microcosmic scale to the macrocosmic, as well as those related to the journey of consciousness.

It's important to note however, that serpents can symbolize a number of different things.

Two serpents coiled into spirals to create a double spiral, symbolizing the annual cycle of the earth and sun—carved into the ancient city of Kuélap, high up in the Andean mountains of Peru.

THE HORNS OF THE SOLSTICES

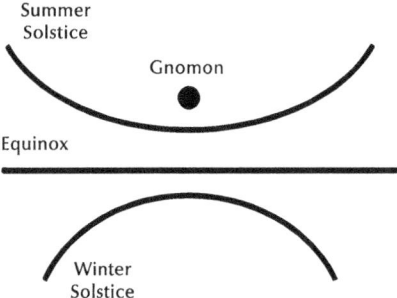

When the shadows cast by a gnomon (a form of sundial) are measured throughout the day on the summer solstice, winter solstice, and equinox, they plot what are called the "horns of the solstices." The summer solstice shadow positions plot an arc, the equinox a straight line, and the winter solstice another arc but opposite in shape to the one plotted in summer.

These "horns" were used as symbols in traditions of the ancient Religion of the Sun—in one of the oldest civilizations in Europe, called the Cucuteni-Trypillia (existing between 5,500 to 2,750 BC); by the ancient Egyptians; and by the Minoans of Crete whose religion was clearly influenced by both the Cucuteni-Trypillia and ancient Egyptian.

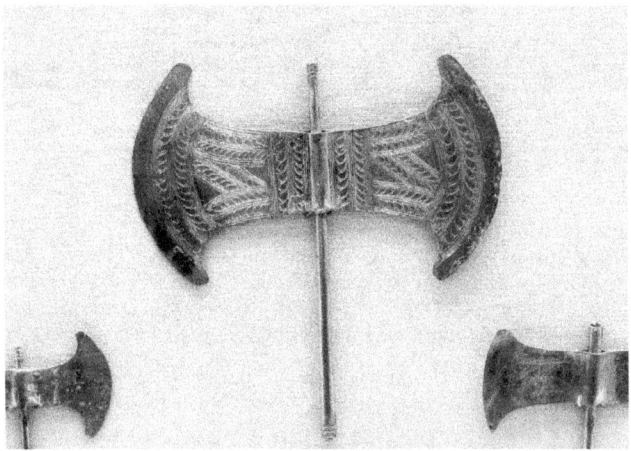

An ancient ceremonial Minoan labrys that looks very similar in shape to that produced by the "horns of the solstices."

In all three of these cultures, these horns could be represented by cow/bull horns, or as an actual bull or cow with the sun between its horns. In other instances these horns adorned the top of temples.

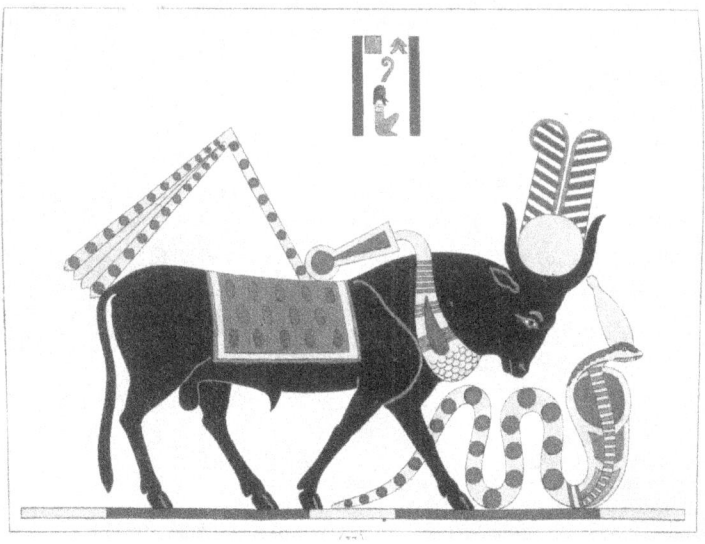

The bull and cow were used as spiritual symbols in ancient Egypt—with the sun shown as sitting between its horns. The sacred bull was commemorated as dying and then later resurrecting as sun gods often were in association with the solstices and equinoxes.

ANCIENT SOLSTICE

CT civilization, Nebelivka temple. 4000 BC

A recreation of an ancient temple of the Cucuteni-Trypillia civilization in Ukraine. It's adorned with a host of solar symbols, including those detailed in this section—the yin-yang, double spiral, and swastika. At the apex of the temple are the horns of the solstice, and the axis of the temple was aligned to equinox sunrise. These symbols would appear in later European cultures, such as the Minoan and Western European megalithic culture.

The continued use of this symbol across ancient cultures over thousands of years is yet another example of the knowledge of the Religion of the Sun being passed across people and time.

COSMIC CONNECTIONS

The knowledge encoded in ancient sacred sites and texts is not just shared on a planetary level, but also on a cosmic one, as however different the cultural expressions may seem, the knowledge is that of the universal principles governing all of creation and is shared even by inhabitants of other planets and solar systems.

Many spiritual principles and symbols we are familiar with have been found integrated into the unique geometric designs of crop circles, and interactions with extraterrestrials have revealed they are deeply spiritual beings.[82]

This crop circle appeared on the summer solstice 2001 in a field in Wiltshire, England, which is significant as Wiltshire is home to Stonehenge—an ancient site aligned to the summer solstice. The symbol in the crop circle correlates with the spiritual meaning of the summer solstice—the sun at the pinnacle of the pyramid represents ascension and the return to the light, which is represented by the summer solstice as the day of most light in the year. If this crop circle is genuine, it indicates the knowledge of the spiritual sun has been shared not just by some here on Earth, but even by those who inhabit other planets, as it is the knowledge of creation.

DIFFERENT TYPES OF ASTROLOGICAL MYTHS

When looking into ancient texts, it can be startling to discover just how many of them were encoded with astronomical data, and how often characters of the myths and religious stories of old correlate with celestial bodies, such as the sun, moon, stars, and constellations, and enact their cycles and movements.

These kinds of astrological correlations can be found in ancient Egyptian, Vedic, Germanic/Nordic, Mesopotamian, and Christian religious texts to name just a few. But given that ancient people lived in quite a different world to our own, maybe it's not so surprising. Without electric lights, television, books, computers, or movies, the sky was perhaps the most accessible canvas that could be read by all no matter what their culture or language.

Having physical objects, such as the sun and stars to point to, these myths could easily be remembered and transmitted down through time, making celestial objects a great way to convey ideas. And conversely, dramatic stories were a memorable way to pass on otherwise fairly technical astronomical data, and ensure the knowledge of it survived.

Because the sky is so accessible, and it was used by so many different people over time, as far as I can see, there are essentially two kinds of astrological myths.

The first kind describes inherent spiritual principles that are expressed through the very same celestial bodies used, as nature is imbued with these spiritual principles on a macrocosmic and microcosmic scale, both fractally and holographically. These myths impart profound and objectively real truths through allegory.

The second uses celestial bodies as religious and storytelling devices. These stories may have a moral and historical value, but are otherwise profane. Celestial bodies are used as actors on the stage of the sky to express not inherent truths, but the creative imagination of the playwright.

These two types, profound and profane, are often intermixed and interwoven within traditions. Studying the profound can be of value spiritually, whereas studying the profane offers little to none. In this book, I focus on the profound.

CROSS-QUARTER DAYS

There are other seasonal celebrations that are often associated with the solstices and equinoxes, called cross-quarter days, which have been celebrated since ancient times. I'll address them here, since many may wonder about them.

They are commonly described as being produced when the year is divided equally into eight instead of four. To my knowledge, their observance has only survived in European pagan traditions. The term cross-quarter derives from their use in Celtic paganism where they are individually named Samhain, Imbolc, Beltane, and Lughnasadh, but are called different names in other European traditions. For example, the cross-quarter day between the spring equinox and summer solstice is popularly called May Day and is celebrated in many European countries today. Like the solstices and equinoxes, these cross-quarter days were also subsumed by the Church, but given Christian meanings, and are still part of Christian ritual calendars.

It seems, however, that they are not the simple result of dividing the year into eight—but are the result of the year being divided into two crosses.[83] The solstices and equinoxes are the cross of the sun, and mark the major transitions of the sun's light. The cross-quarter days on the other hand are the cross of the earth, and mark the major changes in the earth's climate and temperature.[84]

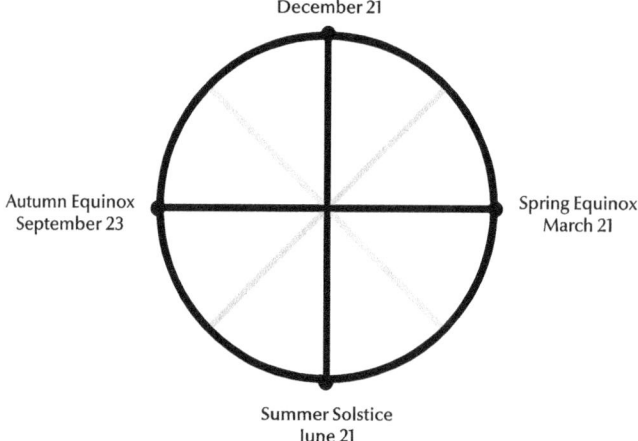

The cross of the sun. Dates are approximate.

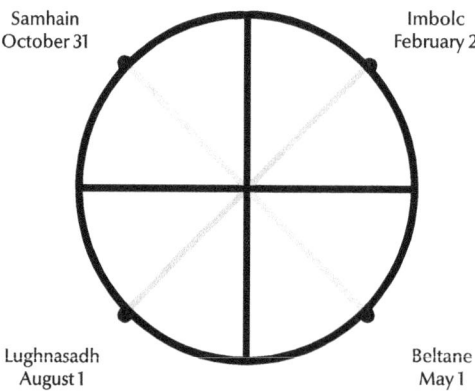

The cross of the earth. Dates are approximate.

So for example, in the Northern Hemisphere the winter solstice is when the hours of daylight first begin to increase, and the sun's journey in the sky reverses its course from a southward to northward direction. However, even though it's midwinter at the winter solstice, the earth still hasn't stopped getting colder (due to what's called seasonal lag)—this will only happen at the cross-quarter day following it, called Imbolc, considered the first day of spring when the earth starts to warm up again.

There are ancient sites aligned to the cross-quarter days. Almost all of them are located in Europe (as far as I'm aware), particularly in Ireland, which is not surprising considering that's where traditions of their celebration have been maintained. There is evidence their observance also spread with the migration of Europeans to North America in ancient times. For example, Mystery Hill in New Hampshire in the United States is an ancient site dated to around 2,000 BC that has alignments to the cross-quarter days, and also has inscriptions in Phoenician, Iberian, and Ogham script (an ancient form of Irish writing).[85] Another cross-quarter day alignment is found at the ancient site called Mesa Verde in Colorado—again, along with Ogham script.[86]

It seems likely that the cross-quarter days were part of a cycle of eight festivals, which were brought to Europe during the Neolithic age with some of the first farmers that migrated there.[87] These farmers venerated the spiritual sun as their supreme deity. Maintaining a calendar of these eight times of year had a very practical agricultural value for farmers, but they also clearly held a religious significance for them too.[88]

However, the evidence shows that even among European Neolithic farmers, and certainly everywhere else in the world, the solstices and equinoxes were the more ancient and important celebrations. The oldest, most advanced, most important, and most used ancient sites in the world align to the solstices and equinoxes. The swastika, which is a symbol of the solstices and equinoxes and one of the most prolific in the ancient world, is also the oldest—found in Ukraine dated to 10,000 BC.

I personally don't celebrate cross-quarter days, as I don't feel they have the profound spiritual meaning that the solstices and equinoxes do, and it seems neither did most ancient peoples.

The cross-quarter days are often used by people in the dark occult for the celebration of dark rituals—particularly Samhain (known commonly as Halloween). Irish legends record that in ancient times Samhain especially was a time of mass human sacrifice.[89] That's not to say that everyone who celebrates cross-quarter days is doing something dark—not at all. Almost all people who celebrate these days do so harmlessly, and with good intentions.

It's just that in my experience, dark forces do all they can to avoid celebrating the sun and light—worshiping instead at night, based on a lunar calendar, particularly even without the light of the reflected sun on the moon during what is called a dark or new moon, and at times that have nothing, or as little to do as possible with the sun.

The longest night at the winter solstice is another example of this, as it is the time of greatest darkness in the year. Zoroaster, an ancient teacher and reformer in the Indo-Iranian tradition, taught that the forces of evil were at their peak on this "dark night," and so people were advised to stay awake during it to avoid falling prey to their influence. Iranians and Zoroastrians still gather together with friends and family to stay up on Yalda night—some maintaining the tradition of lighting candles to keep the darkness at bay.[90]

The cross-quarter days certainly don't have the same direct connection with the clear turning points of the sun and its major stages, and are the days furthest from each of them. This is why emphasis may have shifted toward them in the Celtic tradition of the British Isles during times when rites of human sacrifice seemed to have increased as well as the worship of demons like Moloch and Baal, whose veneration came from the Levant.[91]

There are many celestial objects and dates that are associated with their cycles, so it's important to note that the Religion of the Sun is just as its name says—a religion centered primarily around the spiritual light that emanates from the sun (and stars).

LOOKING AT THE PAST WITH DISCERNMENT

People often wonder why ancient builders went to such great lengths to create such incredible structures. What many overlook is that these buildings were primarily religious in their function, and that the ancient peoples who built them often understood that spirituality was the most important aspect of life.

However, over time the knowledge of many ancient builders became distorted and lost. What were originally spiritual celebrations either degenerated or were inverted to include human and animal sacrifice and all manner of debauchery, such as found in the mad parties of Sol Invictus in Rome and the blood revelry of the Aztecs. When this happens civilizations are no longer able to hold themselves together, having turned on the very principles that allow them to do so, and thus fall into barbarism and ruin, and can eventually totally collapse and disappear or succumb to invaders. This degeneration, which happened in some cases over hundreds to thousands of years in different cultures, has unfortunately, in many instances, associated the celebration of the spiritual sun with the worst of human behavior, as when we look back we tend to see civilizations as a whole, rather than being able to distinguish different groups and movements within them, as well as a civilization's periods of spiritual decline.

And so when looking back into the past in search of the traces of spiritual knowledge, it is not possible to do so without confronting the darker aspects of society and human behavior, and the resulting degeneration of spiritual traditions. And while this may be uncomfortable to face, it's important to do so now that we are about to delve into the past, to be able to clearly distinguish the different influences that have affected the spiritual knowledge of the world.

DOGMATIC BELIEFS AND RELIGIOUS PERSECUTION

The arrival of the Spiritual Son into the world is an incredible event; the Son brings a profound message to the earth that often inspires huge movements of people. Over time these coalesce into religions. However, the mass religions that take root often bear little resemblance to the original wisdom that inspired them (if they were even based on true spiritual knowledge in the first place), as over time, people who co-opt spiritual knowledge, but don't have the spiritual level of the original source, incorporate their own interpretations and cultures into them. And so while these religions can carry spiritual symbols and teachings, they can also incorporate degenerate and barbaric things that were never part of the original message, and are the very opposite of the spirituality of the Son.

Those who had a spiritual level capable of comprehending the mysteries of the spiritual sun were always in the minority, and therefore usually became marginalized and even persecuted by the mass religions that formed, just as the Gnostics (those who followed the more profound side of Jesus' teachings) were by the early Christians. Their texts were banned as heretical by the early Church, which suppressed and destroyed them en masse, and excluded them from the Bible. This suppression and distortion of the message of Jesus had already started even within the lifetime of Jesus' disciple Peter, who had been given the role of teaching Jesus' message in the West. After Jesus' death, Peter was faced with large numbers of people misappropriating not only Jesus' message, but also his own.

> "But these men, professing, I know not how, to know my mind, undertake to explain my words, which they have heard of me, more intelligently than I who spoke them, telling their catechumens that this is my meaning, which indeed I never thought of. But if, while I am still alive, they dare thus to misrepresent me, how much more will those who shall come after me dare to do so!" [92]
> ~ PETER TO JAMES IN THE CLEMENTINE HOMILIES

Peter then attempts to address the issue by only passing his books on through a process of initiation to ensure they would not fall into the wrong hands. This is an example of how secret schools were formed out of necessity in response to various social pressures.

> "[...] give the books of my preachings to our brethren, with the like mystery of initiation, that they may indoctrinate those who wish to take part in teaching; for if it be not so done, our word of truth will be rent into many opinions. And this I know, not as being a prophet, but as already seeing the beginning of this very evil. For some from

among the Gentiles have rejected my legal preaching, attaching themselves to certain lawless and trifling preaching of the man who is my enemy [Paul]." [93]

~ PETER TO JAMES IN THE CLEMENTINE HOMILIES

"Hear me, brethren and fellow-servants. If we should give the books to all indiscriminately, and they should be corrupted by any daring men, or be perverted by interpretations, as you have heard that some have already done, it will remain even for those who really seek the truth, always to wander in error. Wherefore it is better that they should be with us, and that we should communicate them with all the fore-mentioned care to those who wish to live piously, and to save others." [94]

~ JAMES IN THE CLEMENTINE HOMILIES

It was actually Paul's version of Christianity (someone who had never met Jesus and whom the disciples were opposed to) that became widely accepted and popular, while the deeper interpretation of Jesus' message eventually became persecuted, even though Jesus had given it his own authority in appointing his disciple Peter as its teacher. Paul added many of his own interpretations to the message of Jesus, including statements promoting the suppression of women, which a number of banned texts reveal was something that Jesus was profoundly against.

A study of the teachings of Jesus, including those that were suppressed and banned from the Bible, reveals a message that shares more in common with the spiritual knowledge of Egypt, the East, and the Druids, than it does with orthodox Christianity, and yet it was often Christianity that suppressed these beliefs as "pagan."

Throughout history, dogmatic believers have ripped people from their cultures in blindly enforcing their doctrines, when the many cultural expressions of spiritual principles form part of the diverse tapestry of nature expressing the same inherent truths and the perpetual creativity of human consciousness. They are cause for mutual celebration and should be preserved and allowed to naturally develop. Whether someone chooses to connect with the spiritual sun through the solar deity of one culture or another generally makes little or no difference, if what is being connected with is the same.

Symbolism, iconography, and parables are simply a means of illustrating principles and imparting knowledge, which is why they can take so many different forms. Through them, mystics have been able to communicate higher spiritual truths. However, an icon is not an absolute truth in itself, and this is where many religious believers get stuck. An icon or symbol is not the spiritual principle; it is a representation of it, just as our reflection in a mirror is not us, but allows us to see and understand ourselves.

Due to their amassed influence and size, religions and not the actual spiritual practitioners tend to become the public carriers of spiritual symbols and sacred texts into the future. However, usually not having an inner spiritual level, religious believers are unable to comprehend higher truths nor distinguish between what's really spiritual and what's not, and thus exclude the complete body of spiritual knowledge and the deeper meaning of their religious symbols. As has happened so many times in history, while an outer shell remains, this complete body of knowledge and the original meaning behind religious traditions then becomes lost, either because it has to be encoded and veiled in symbolism for its protection, or because it is forced underground.

Genuine spiritual practitioners then have to function under the banners of accepted religions in order to survive, while teaching real knowledge apart from them and often in secret. So when searching into the past, although certain ancient religions carry many spiritual truths, you'll find those who were actually getting knowledge and practicing it were often operating on the edges of society in remote places, and in secret mystery schools. They were not generally large groups of people, but individuals and small groups who emerge in traces here and there, carrying a remarkable wisdom.

THE INFILTRATION OF DARK FORCES

Apart from dogmatism, there is also another influence at work against the expression of the genuinely spiritual. It is impossible to look at spirituality throughout history without finding and having to confront the opposite of the practitioners of the Religion of the Sun, which are instead the practitioners of darkness. These are people who, knowingly or unknowingly, have sought their awakening in darkness, rather than in light, and part of their goal has always been to suppress human spiritual potential.

These people have likewise operated in secrecy throughout history to avoid detection, which has made looking back into the past a very muddied and murky affair, as wherever you find people attempting to awaken in light, the forces of darkness follow, often attacking them from the shadows. This has caused a real mixing of very different influences and forces within the same scenes on the stage of history—with both those attempting to awaken in light and in darkness operating largely in secrecy at the same time, and both working in opposition to each other.

It is possible, however, to separate out their influence once you become more familiar with spiritual principles. But this is difficult for most, as those seeking to awaken in darkness use deception as one of their main methods. Working by stealth and infiltration, they have often taken over, subverted, hijacked, and distorted much of the spiritual knowledge of humanity, even taking over entire spiritual schools and religions. Thus they have often maintained the outward shell of a spiritual teaching, but beneath the surface worked to distort it in order to lead people away from the light, even while using the highest sounding of ideals. This makes it even more important and pressing for all sincere people to really understand the spiritual principles of life and creation as much as they possibly can.

There are however, tell-tale signs of the presence of practitioners of dark knowledge, and looking back in history, there are some stark signs of their existence. Some examples include the tendency to use the number four in their rituals and ceremonies to strengthen the darkness of materialism; the goal of subjugating and controlling others through force and by stealth; inverting the symbols of light (like the inverted pentagram and cross); mocking and persecuting the Spiritual Son; the use of animal and human sacrifice; taking multiple partners and engaging in all manner of sexual deviancies; advocating adultery and fornication; taking pleasure in hurting and persecuting others; and looking to develop occult powers for their own benefit, which they use to impress and mislead people with.

Taken on their own, these things don't necessarily indicate the presence of the dark occult. They can also be indicators of degeneracy, as they are precisely the things that dark practitioners introduce into societies in order to degenerate them. That's why sometimes their mass practice can be found in civilizations throughout history, including at ancient sites, and in many so-called sacred texts.

ANIMAL AND HUMAN SACRIFICE

One of the most horrific practices of the dark occult is ritual animal and human sacrifice, evidence for which can be found in many parts of the world.

Perhaps most infamously was its widespread practice by the Maya and the Aztecs of Central America. The level it was taken to has shocked the world for centuries, and sadly now many associate the ancient knowledge found at these sites entirely with its practice.

However, there is evidence that their knowledge originated far back in antiquity as their legends speak of bearded fair skinned peoples who came from across the ocean and taught their ancestors a solar religion and built many of their sacred sites aligned to the solstices and equinoxes; remnants of this earlier time came down through a veneration of these great teachers and wisdom bringers called Quetzalcoatl, Kukulkan, and Viracocha, who were remembered as forbidding human and animal sacrifice, as well as violence. Many of these Central American sites were built over multiple times, indicating that successive cultures took over and built upon the sacred sites of those they conquered or assimilated—eventually the cultures that took over had adopted the savage practice of human and animal sacrifice.

Perhaps nowhere is the evidence clearer for this than in the surviving written legends of the Maya themselves, recorded in their text Popol Vuh.

It recounts how "the nations" were taken over by a small group of people who came under the influence of "gods" who at first asked for animal sacrifice, and then human. The text is written from this group's point of view, and they actually refer to themselves as "bloodletters and sacrificers" as though it were a sacred title. Through sorcery and violence it describes how they subjugated these surrounding nations. Many of the passages are too disturbing to reproduce here, but these excerpts give a glimpse of what has happened similarly in other parts of the world when religious groups have come under the influence of dark forces.

> "But do not reveal yourselves. Do this now and your existence shall become great. You shall conquer all the nations." [95]
> ~ THE "GODS" WHO ARE CONSULTED IN POPOL VUH

> "There they multiplied and became many. They had daughters and they had sons on top of Hacavitz. They rejoiced then, for they had defeated all the nations there on top of the mountain. Thus they had done this. They had surely defeated the nations, indeed all the nations. [...]
>
> There they put down roots at Chi Izmachi, and there also their bloodletting god increased in greatness. And all the nations, the small and the great, became afraid. They witnessed the arrival of captive people to be sacrificed and killed by the glory and sovereignty of Lord Co Tuha and Lord Iztayul, in alliance with the Nihaib and Ahau Quichés." [96]
> ~ POPOL VUH

Rather than promote it, some of the greatest teachers of the Religion of the Sun around the world actually tried to outlaw human and animal sacrifice, including Osiris, Quetzalcoatl, and Jesus, but their message was ignored by many at the time.

Osiris, who became revered as the most important god of ancient Egypt, even risked his own life to save a man from being sacrificed. In this account from *The Kolbrin*, he draws fire from out of the air in order to protect himself from being attacked by those who were just about to perform a human sacrifice.

> "When Yosira [Osiris] came to Kambusis he found there a man of the Hestabwis bound and prepared for sacrifice, and he cried out against the deed but none gave ear to his word. So, standing off, Yosira placed a staff of power upright into the ground and danced around it, singing the song for drawing forth the spirit. When they

saw this, the people were wroth against him and called upon their charmers to curse him so he departed from the Earth. Their curses were ineffective and when one charmer approached the dance ring of Yosira, Yosira called forth a tongue of flame which consumed the charmer. Then the people became afraid and fled. So Yosira released the man who was bound upon the place of sacrifice, but he was not yet whole. Yosira also cursed all those who offered the Hestabwis as a sacrifice to their gods; since that day no man of the Hestabwis was ever slain upon the altars." [97]

~ THE RULE OF YOSIRA, THE KOLBRIN

"Thus, when Yosira cried out against those who, while not permitting the slaying of men and women in their daily lives, nevertheless allowed a child to be slain as sacrifice, or buried beneath the pillars they raised up, he was condemned as an enemy of the gods." [98]

~ THE TRIBULATIONS OF YOSIRA, THE KOLBRIN

Similarly, Quetzalcoatl, the teacher of the Religion of the Sun remembered by the Aztec of Central America, also attempted to abolish the practice.

"In his study of aboriginal American religions (1882, p. 140), Brinton comments: He [Quezalcoatl] forbade the sacrifice of human beings and animals, teaching that bread, flowers, and incense were all that the gods demanded. And he prohibited wars, fighting, robbery, and other forms of violence to such an extent that he was held in affectionate veneration, not only by his own people but by distant nations as well, who made pilgrimages to his capital. The fact that the Aztecs, who excelled in human sacrifice at their pyramids and temples, still recollected a benevolent, pacifist culture-bringer whose teachings closely paralleled the Biblical Commandments so impressed the Spanish friars that they identified Quetzalcoatl with the Apostle Thomas—an exact analogy to the confusion of Viracocha with St Bartholomew in Peru." [99]

~ THOR HEYERDAHL, THE BEARDED GODS SPEAK

These quotes show that the people Quetzalcoatl and Osiris tried to teach were already practicing human sacrifice and that Quetzalcoatl and Osiris tried to dissuade them from it. Unfortunately, they were ultimately unsuccessful, and these barbaric practices either persisted or were later revived.

Similarly Jesus could not have been clearer when he said:

"I came to destroy the sacrifices, and if ye cease not from sacrificing, the wrath *of God* will not cease from you." [100]

~ JESUS IN THE GOSPEL OF THE EBIONITES

> "And to those who supposed that God is pleased with sacrifices, He [Jesus] said, 'God wishes mercy, and not sacrifices'—the knowledge of Himself, and not holocausts." [101]
> ~ PETER IN THE CLEMENTINE HOMILIES

Ancient texts from Egypt and Britain, preserved in the book called *The Kolbrin*, explain some of the reasons why human and animal sacrifice is unnecessary and wrong, and what sacrifice in a spiritual sense really means.

> "There is nothing on Earth that man can give God which could add to God's glory or increase what He has. The only acceptable sacrifice man can offer is service to the will of God, and God's will is that man should spiritualise himself and improve the Earth. To offer goods or money as a sacrifice is an insult to God, it is shirking the needful effort, evading the necessary duty and obligation; it is the easy way and not acceptable." [102]
> ~ ELOMA, THE KOLBRIN

> "These are the only sacrifices to bring: Bodily lusts and passions, evil thoughts, lies, deceit, slander and all forms of wickedness. To offer the blood of harmless creatures is easy and cowardly, and an insult to He who created them. These are the offerings to dedicate to His service: Diligent study of the Good Books, wisdom, courage, moral purity and steadfastness, together with all things serving the purpose of good." [103]
> ~ THE LAST FOREST TEACHINGS (OF ELIDOR), THE KOLBRIN

> "My desire is for love rather than futile sacrifices of burnt offerings, but it should not be a passive love but one expressing service in My Cause. A certain knowledge of right and wrong, with free choice of the former, is of greater value in My sight than pointless ritualistic worship. I derive no pleasure from the wasteful shedding of blood from bulls and lambs. I gain nothing from the fat of sheep and the flesh of goats. I am the Creator of All, so what can men give that would increase My greatness? Men are misled if they believe that their sins can be purged by vain rituals. Only active goodness can obliterate the stain of sin. [...] The ultimate in goodness is to actively combat all the root causes of evil. Those who are my true followers live a life of service and goodness. They live in harmony with their neighbours, harm none and do not shirk the burdens and obligations of earthly existence. [...] They who devote their lives to My service must do more than love and worship Me, for such service entails the elevation of mankind, the spreading of good and the combating of evil. They must not only

fight against the ungodly, but also overcome the wickedness welling up in their own thoughts. They who love Me desire the wellbeing of all men, and their souls are filled with harmony and peace. Dearer to Me than their love for Me is the labour and tribulations of those who serve Me. I am their end. I am never the God of Inertia but the God of Effort; if you offer no more than deeds done in My service or in conformity with My design, then you serve Me adequately." [104]
~ THE VOICE OF GOD, THE KOLBRIN

SOME OF THE ORIGINAL KNOWLEDGE SURVIVED

Thankfully, not all spiritual knowledge has been destroyed by dark forces and oppression. Due to the tireless efforts of many brave men and women, there do exist fragments of knowledge that have been kept safe. By looking back today with the same shared knowledge as the original practitioners, someone can recognize the Religion of the Sun in their ruins and preserved texts, which preceded and survived all the degeneration and persecution—allowing someone familiar with this knowledge to understand ancient mysteries where archeologists and academics remain baffled.

Despite the passing of these ancient cultures into history, this knowledge is never truly lost, as it is palpitating throughout the universe, waiting to be rediscovered by those who make themselves "sons of the sun."

What I explore in the following chapters are many of the remnants of spiritual knowledge left over from the once great global ancient Religion of the Sun—found in ancient sites, sacred texts, and spiritual traditions. To my knowledge, this is the first time anyone has ever pieced together these remnants to recreate this ancient religion.

CONNECT WITH THE HEAVENS AND THE EARTH BY CELEBRATING THE SOLSTICES AND EQUINOXES

Solstices and equinoxes are a time of connection between the heavens and the earth, the personal and the divine, the inner and the outer, the material and the spiritual, and even a time when contact through mystical experiences is made more possible. It is a beautiful time, which unfortunately most people today have lost touch with, as did other civilizations who degenerated in the past and lost their spiritual orientation.

By taking part in ceremonies to celebrate the solstices and equinoxes, one is able to use the event for its higher purpose just as the ancients did—to connect with the cosmos, to understand eternal principles through intuitive experience and the cycles of nature, and to take spiritual nourishment. This is not simply the revival of something past, but the partaking in something eternal that permeates our lives, even if we pay little attention to it.

The whole of creation has been formed to imbue the principles of spirituality, and thus these principles can not only be found all around us, but also within us, allowing us to understand our origins and the true purpose of life. This has allowed people throughout the ages to tap into the same spiritual knowledge.

> "In everything that is life is the law written. You find it in the grass, in the tree, in the river, in the mountain, in the birds of heaven, in the fishes of the sea; but seek it chiefly in yourselves. For I tell you truly, all living things are nearer to God than the scripture which is without life. God so made life and all living things that they might by the everlasting word teach the laws of the true God to man. God wrote not the laws in the pages of books, but in your heart and in your spirit. They are in your breath, your blood, your bone; in your flesh, your bowels, your eyes, your ears, and in every little part of your body. They are present in the air, in the water, in the earth, in the plants, in the sunbeams, in the depths and in the heights. They all speak to you that you may understand the tongue and the will of the living God. But you shut your eyes that you may not see, and you shut your ears that you may not hear. I tell you truly, that the scripture is the work of man, but life and all its hosts are the work of our God. Wherefore do you not listen to the words of God which are written in His works? And wherefore do you study the dead scriptures which are the work of the hands of men?" [105]
> ~ JESUS IN THE ESSENE GOSPEL OF PEACE

The message of the spiritual sun transcends both time and culture and forms a cosmic book for all who can read it.

Autumn Equinox
Death and Descent into Darkness

CHAPTER TWO

The Spiritual Meaning of the Autumn Equinox

The path of the spiritual sun—the sacred way of the solstices and equinoxes—starts as darkness begins to increase, three days after the summer solstice. This is when the sun begins its annual descent, after having reached its apex at the summer solstice, and the days gradually begin to shorten toward the cold and darkness of winter.

The annual descent of the sun into darkness is symbolic of the consciousness descending from its heavenly abode into the darkness of matter, of it coming into a body, into the darkness of the subconscious of the psyche, to join the process of life (referred to as the Wheel of Life in Hinduism and Buddhism). This darkness is necessary, as without darkness we would not know light, and it is from darkness (the subconscious) that light (consciousness) is extracted, giving us the knowledge gained from experience.

In the beginning of creation this unique spark of light comes down into matter to learn from life in the universe of duality between darkness and light which gives rise to form. Experience, learning, and suffering propel it in a quest to return to the spiritual source from which it first emanated: from darkness to the birth of light at the winter solstice, culminating at the summer solstice, when light is at its maximum.

After the sun's descent following the summer solstice, the next stage in the sun's journey is the autumn equinox, when darkness becomes greater than light.

A TIME WHEN DARKNESS IS GREATER THAN LIGHT

The autumn equinox is a mysterious time. It marks an essential passage on the path of the spiritual sun that is often overlooked, misunderstood, and mistaken as dark and heretical.

Equinoxes occur twice a year—in spring and autumn—when day and night are approximately equal lengths, which is when the sun crosses the earth's celestial equator.

Interestingly, in the Northern Hemisphere, the sun enters the astrological sign of Libra at the autumn equinox, which is the sign of the scales and of balance. The glyph for Libra represents the sun setting/rising, expressing the balance between night and day.

The symbol of the star sign of Libra, which expresses the principles of equinox.

The autumn equinox marks a turning point in the earth's annual journey around the sun, as immediately following it the nights become longer than the days, bringing the coming winter—a time of darkness and death.

Remnants of the spiritual meaning of the autumn equinox can barely be found in the few lasting traditions from ancient peoples who celebrated it and knew of its real significance. To discover the spiritual meaning by looking at rituals and traditions is not easy. There are traditions which have been passed down today, but which have strayed from their root meanings. Different civilizations and cultures have added their own veneer, altering and losing much of the original meaning as they themselves lost the understanding of it.

Its meaning has been obscured with time, much more than the other three events in the wheel of the year. As the understanding of spiritual knowledge was lost, its meaning became vague and must have seemed to represent sinister, evil forces. Thus the symbols were given different meanings and turned into other things in the way that Santa Claus now largely symbolizes Christmas.

Parts of autumn equinox celebrations moved to cross-quarter days and meanings changed into celebrations of the dead, of evil spirits, harvest festivals, sacrifices, drunkenness, and debauchery.

So you have to start with the understanding of the path of the spiritual sun, to have a basis upon which you can search and piece together the jigsaw. Fortunately the builders of ancient sites, such as the Great Pyramids, left the message of the real meaning in their architecture, which mirrored the meanings found in the cosmos and survived in sketchy details in ancient myths and traditions.

Traditionally, the autumn equinox is a celebration of the harvest, as it is when summer has finished giving its fruits, which are collected in preparation for winter. But there are other indicators given by the most ancient sacred sites that align to the autumn equinox: a descending passage into a subterranean chamber beneath the Great Pyramid of Egypt, a seven-scaled feathered serpent of light descending a pyramid in Mexico, an ancient palace associated with legends of a labyrinth built to contain a half-man, half-beast, and seven massive stone statues facing the equinox sunset on Easter Island.

What was known to the practitioners of the ancient Religion of the Sun is the part darkness plays in the work of spiritual transformation. Those in the orthodox superstitiously fear it, and many in the New Age almost completely ignore it, but at the autumn equinox it can be found in the cycles of the sun— and traces of it can be found here and there in ancient legends and myths that have become distorted over time.

The message contained in the autumn equinox tells us that all things must die before they can be born, all spiritual ascent requires descent first, and all those who long for light must firstly face their own inner darkness and overcome it.

THE RIVAL OF THE SUN

An Egyptian statue with the rival gods Horus on one side (the god of light), and Seth on the other (the god of darkness). Notice how their opposite arms form a pyramid of ascent and descent.

In the ancient myths of Britain the sun god has a rival. He is known as "the god of darkness," whose dominion is the night and dark half of the year, which begins at the autumn equinox when he overcomes "the god of light." This opposition between light and darkness has been depicted in the rivalry between the Oak King and the Holly King, the Welsh hero and sun god Llew and his rival Goronwy, and their equivalents in Irish mythology Lugh and Balor.[1]

In ancient Egypt the god Seth was the dark antithesis of the sun god Horus, and like the Welsh and Irish rivals above, these two also fought battles against one another. In Norse mythology, Höder is the god of darkness and blind brother of Baldr, the god of the summer sun, whom Höder kills. In Aztec mythology Quetzalcoatl has a twin brother called Xolotl, who was the dark aspect of Venus as the evening star, while Quetzalcoatl was Venus as the morning star.

Baldr—Germanic god of the summer sun depicted with a flaming sun as his shield.

"Balder the beautiful was the most noble and pious of the gods in Asgard. The whitest flower upon earth is called Balder's brow, because the countenance of the god was snow-white and shining. Like fine gold was his hair, and his eyes were radiant and blue. He was well loved by all the gods, save evil Loke, who cunningly devised his death. Balder, the summer sun-god, was Odin's fairest son; his mother was Frigg, goddess of fruitful earth and sister of Njord. His brother was blind Hodur. On Balder's tongue were runes graven, so that he had great eloquence. He rode a brightly shining horse, and his ships, which men called 'billow falcons,' were the sunbeams that sailed through the drifting cloudways." [2]
~ DONALD A. MACKENZIE, TEUTONIC MYTH AND LEGEND

The god of light of pagan tradition is born three days after the winter solstice as the Spiritual Son in many traditions (including the birth of Jesus at Christmas), because the sun, having reached its lowest and weakest point in the sky for the year, then begins its ascent as it gains strength toward summer. The god of darkness in pagan tradition, however, is born three days after the summer solstice, as this is when the nights and darkness begin to increase toward winter.[3]

Some have confused John the Baptist, whose birthday is celebrated on June 24 (three days after the summer solstice in the Northern Hemisphere) as the equivalent of the god of darkness. John, however, represents something else. He can be seen as symbolic of the one who starts the path of the spiritual sun, which begins in the darkness of one's own subconscious.

This rivalry between the god of light and god of darkness, which was part of the pagan autumn equinox traditions of Western Europe, later became incorporated into the Christian celebration known as "Michaelmas," which was timed by some Western Churches to coincide with the autumn equinox when Europe was Christianized. For Christians it celebrates the Archangel Michael's victory over Satan, and like other pagan celebrations of the solstices and equinoxes that became Christianized, it likely echoes some of the earlier pagan traditions.

The Archangel Michael slaying Satan while holding a set of scales. Scales can symbolize the balance between light and darkness, and thus can be a symbol of the equinox.

The Archangel Michael is typically identified with the sun, and is often depicted holding a set of scales (which symbolize justice, but are also a symbol of the equinox), while slaying a dragon/serpent (symbolizing the demon Satan as the head of darkness) with a sword or lance. Here the god of light defeats the god of darkness at the autumn equinox, instead of vice versa as in the former pagan celebrations. And so it seems the Christians reversed the meaning of the autumn equinox, while also associating the god of darkness with the Christian concept of Satan. The god of darkness was never meant to represent Satan however, but is the personification of darkness itself—of the forces of chaos, disease, decay, and death, which reign in nature during the dark half of the year. This is what the sun god, or Spiritual Son, will eventually overcome at the spring equinox, when the image of Michael becomes more relevant.

Interestingly, in Germany, Michael was used by Christians to replace the Germanic god Wotan (who is known in Nordic countries as Odin), with the mountains held sacred to Wotan in Germany later being topped with chapels of St. Michael instead.[4] Like Michael, and other sun gods such as Lugh of Irish legend, Wotan was known for carrying a spear, and in Norse mythology chaos was symbolized by the serpent Jörmungandr, like the serpent representing Satan in Christian iconography. This shared symbology between Michael and Wotan may be the reason why Michaelmas was chosen by the Church as the festival to replace the Indo-European autumn equinox celebrations. Thus, Michael and Wotan have been interpreted as symbolizing the will to face and overcome the impending forces of darkness at the autumn equinox.[5]

The Germanic god Wotan/Odin holding the spear he has been associated with for thousands of years.

The god of darkness can symbolize many different things, as darkness itself has many aspects to understand. He has typically been associated with the Christian idea of "the Devil" and "Satan," however, this pagan symbol predates Christianity.

Light and darkness are both substances; they are not good and evil in themselves, but become the realms inhabited by divine and evil beings respectively. Darkness only carries evil and light only carries good. Darkness is a necessary and intrinsic part of creation, however evil beings (most commonly called demons) exist in and use it. This is illustrated in the death of the Germanic sun god Baldr. In Nordic mythology he is killed by his blind brother Höder, who represents darkness, Baldr's opposite. However, Höder neither wished to kill Baldr, nor was able to, since he is blind (representing darkness), but is deceived into firing an arrow of mistletoe (symbolic of winter) at Baldr by the malicious character Loki—who represents evil, and how it uses darkness.

The blind brother of Baldr stands with his eyes shut in the foreground. Loki stands beside him, and gives him an arrow of mistletoe (symbolic of winter) to fire at the shining summer sun god Baldr.

The "god of darkness" so associated with the autumn equinox and found in ancient myths that predate Christianity, can be seen then as a symbol of the darkness that is found in creation, in the cycles of the sun throughout the day and the year, which also exists within us as a microcosm of the universe. The darkness within us is the psychological darkness of our subconscious, which is inhabited by our egos, and is the antithesis of our own inner light, which is our consciousness, and of the aspect of our higher Being represented by the sun.

THE DEATH OF JOHN AND THE WICKER MAN

A person starts the path of the spiritual sun where they are, which is in the darkness of the subconscious and the world of matter, and why John the Baptist is born when darkness begins to increase in the sun's annual cycle, and light decreases—symbolizing the descent of the light of consciousness into the darkness of matter.

John represents the person who takes the path of the spiritual sun. He begins the path by descending into darkness, into chaos. Having gone into darkness, the Son is later born within him, symbolized by the birth of the Son at the winter solstice. As the Son, symbolized by the sun, grows and increases, the darkness of the egos and the subconscious within the person must decrease. This reference is found in the Gospels:

> "A man can receive nothing unless it has been given him from heaven. You yourselves are my witnesses that I said, 'I am not the Christ,' but, 'I have been sent ahead of Him.' He who has the bride is the bridegroom; but the friend of the bridegroom, who stands and hears him, rejoices greatly because of the bridegroom's voice. So this joy of mine has been made full. He must increase, but I must decrease." [6]
> ~ JOHN 3:27-30

In Celtic traditions of the autumn equinox that still survive today, a figure is made from the stems of cut seed and is burnt by fire, representing John Barleycorn, the spirit of the fields, as it was said he must die in order to become a man. John the Baptist is said to have died six months before Jesus whose death was at the time of the spring equinox, making John the Baptist's death at the time of the autumn equinox—the same time as the symbolic death of John Barleycorn.[7]

The Celts were said to have burnt a wicker man at the autumn equinox. Photo is of the same practice still performed today.

The autumn equinox is a time of death, as just as in nature at this time of year the seeds produced at summer fall to the earth and appear to die before they germinate, and the old must die to make way for the next season of new life, so too must the inferior within us die and be shed to make way for the new life of the spirit within.

> "Jesus replied, 'The hour has come for the Son of Man to be glorified. Very truly I tell you, unless a kernel of wheat falls to the ground and dies, it remains only a single seed. But if it dies, it produces many seeds.'" [8]
> ~ JOHN 12:23-24

The one who walks the path of the sun must die inwardly to make way for the Spiritual Son whose presence within transforms someone from being an animal—created by the egos which are animalistic in nature, and symbolized by John dressed in animal hair and crying out in the wilderness—into a "true human." This death is an inner one. It is the death of the egos and darkness of the subconscious, which is part of preparing the way for the birth of the spiritual within. John refers to this preparation as "making straight the way for the Lord."

> "John replied [...], 'I am the voice of one calling in the wilderness, 'Make straight the way for the Lord.''" [9]
> ~ JOHN 1:23

INNER DEATH

Death features prominently in the lives of those who symbolized the path of the spiritual sun, as death is an important principle of creation and therefore of spiritual transformation. In the cycle of the wheel of the year, it corresponds to the autumn equinox—when the life of summer dies and its seeds go into the ground to conceive new life. Death is just as important to spiritual transformation as birth, as the old and inferior must die to make way for the birth of the new and superior.

Most are familiar only with physical death, when the material bodies of living things die. But death is a phenomenon that happens to things in other dimensions too. Death occurs when that which gives life to matter withdraws from it permanently, and matter returns to an inert state.

The egos that we have can be put to death, which is a form of inner death in which we don't physically die, but these parts of our psyche in other dimensions do. This is sometimes symbolized as death itself.

In the following excerpt, a famous ancient Hindu sage says he will attain to his true Being, not in the afterlife, when he physically dies, but in this life, when his ego dies.

> "This Self who gives rise to all works, all desires, all odors, all tastes, who pervades the universe, who is beyond words, who is joy abiding, who is ever present in my heart, is Brahman indeed. To him I shall attain when my ego dies." [10]
> ~ THE CHANDOGYA UPANISHAD

In initiations on the path of the spiritual sun, someone also goes through the death of their self-image before they can resurrect, which I explain in the chapter on the meaning of the spring equinox.

Stone sarcophagus/coffin within the King's Chamber of the Great Pyramid of Egypt—discovered completely empty.

One of the great mysteries of the ancient world is why the chambers of the Great Pyramids contained stone sarcophaguses (coffins that are usually made of stone and above-ground) that were found empty of burials (though later intrusive burials were found in the smaller two pyramids). It's because they were used for initiatory rites, with the chamber and coffin symbolizing the initiation of death preceding resurrection.

This is supported by an expansive set of writings called *The Kolbrin*, which was published in 1994 claiming to be a collection of ancient Egyptian texts that had been brought to Britain by refugees from Egypt and then added to by ancient Britons, who contributed a number of their own books. It's said to have been passed down for centuries in secrecy in Britain, until being handed over for publication by an elderly man from Wales who'd attended a Druid organization and been member of a Hermetic one.[11] Excerpts from some of the Egyptian books indicate that the tomb of the Great Pyramid was used for a ritual of spiritual (not physical) death and rebirth, and that the most famous funerary text of Egypt, known as the Book of the Dead, encodes its hidden meaning, which was later misinterpreted as being for those who physically died:

> "Now the Great House of the Hidden Places [the Great Pyramid] stands in Kahemu [Egypt]. It is built to last forever and stands up

strongly towards Heaven, high above the heads of men. It is covered with white stones [...] and above it is topped with copper. It is not the copper of men, but the copper of God. Within it lies the Womb of Rebirth [likely the King's Chamber] used by the Twice Born of the Enlightened Ones. Men enter its portals to die and come out restored to life, reborn as gods." [12]

~ THE SCROLL OF THOTIS, THE KOLBRIN

"Men read the Great Book of the Master of the Hidden Temple [likely the Book of the Dead]. They die and take it with them, but there is no power in their words, and who but we, the Enlightened Ones, know the hidden meanings? It is not for those dead to the Earth, who step forth in the Netherworld, but for those who died and remain with us." [13]

~ THE SCROLL OF HERAKAT, THE KOLBRIN

"O priests and priestesses. Stamp on wickedness. Stamp on hypocrisy. Stamp your feet on malice and hatred. [...] Come, stamp on the head of pride, stamp on the Foul Fiend of Lust. [...] I am pure, I am pure, I am pure. [...] Before the Sacred Shrine I renew my strength. I free myself from all earthly desire, from all bodily passions, of all soul-eating lusts, of all soul-destroying vices. [...] Before the Place of Awe I stand unafraid [...]." [14]

~ THE HYMN OF REWA, THE KOLBRIN

THE DESCENT INTO THE UNDERWORLD

In the Great Pyramid of Egypt there is a descending passage that leads to an underground chamber directly beneath it. Over certain time periods during the third and fourth millennium BC, the North/Pole Star, which was the brightest star in the constellation Draco at the time, aligned with the passage and could be seen from within it.[15] This star is known as Alpha Draconis and Thuban, meaning "head of the serpent."[16]

Looking down the descending passage of the Great Pyramid.

The circumpolar stars had different connotations in Egyptian religion. Primarily, they were seen as the ultimate destination of those who attained immortality (and became an "akh" or being of light) because of their constancy in the sky. However, they were also the location of the constellation of Seth (god of chaos and antithesis of the sun god Horus), as well as constellations depicted as crocodiles (in Egyptian religion, the jaws of a goddess with the head of a crocodile was said to be the entrance to the underworld). Greek mythology also saw a reptile in the constellation Draco in the northern stars, as it was portrayed as a dragon that was an enemy of the gods. It was also associated with the most deadly monster of Greek mythology—the serpentine creature Typhon,[17] symbolic of darkness and chaos, who became associated with the Egyptian Seth.[18]

There is an explanation for this seeming contradiction in the symbology of the circumpolar stars, which my wife realized, and which unlocks the meaning of the Great Pyramid's passageway alignment to Alpha Draconis. One of the most central themes of ancient Egyptian religion that persisted for thousands of years was the journey of the sun god Ra through the Duat or underworld—variations are recorded in Egypt's most famous religious texts, such as the Book of the Dead and Coffin Texts. As the sun set in the west, Ra was shown descending into the underworld where he had to encounter various obstacles and dangerous entities (symbolizing the egos) during the twelve hours of the night, passing through a gate for each hour, before he could be born again at dawn in the east.[19] There are only two times in the year when there are twelve hours of night, which is at the equinoxes, indicating that this is when Ra descended and ascended—descent most associated with autumn, and ascent with spring. The greatest obstacle Ra had to confront was the giant serpent Apep (also sometimes depicted as a crocodile), who personified evil and chaos itself, and whose titles included "Enemy of Ra," "Lord of Chaos," "Eater of Souls," and even "Evil Dragon." My wife believes the Egyptians originally saw Apep in the constellation Draco, which appears to wrap around the center of the circle that the North Pole traces through the sky in its precessional cycle, essentially guarding or standing in the way of the region of immortality, and thus the obstacle of all those who wished to attain it.

It's likely that the correlation between Apep and Draconis was passed down in ancient Greece, where it became symbolized as Typhon and the memory of the constellation Draconis as a dragon/serpent was preserved.

It's interesting to note that Apep was considered to have come into being from Ra himself, possibly symbolizing the entire embodiment of the egos/evil each one has given rise to within themselves.[20] Apep also finds a counterpart in the serpent of Norse mythology called Jörmungandr, battled by Odin and his son Thor, which as discussed earlier, is connected to the dragon slain by St. Michael. Thus the Spiritual Son (Ra, Odin/Thor, Michael) must confront and defeat the egos and evil within (Apep, Jörmungandr, the dragon) before immortality can be attained.

This became symbolized in Norse initiation ritual by a serpent that guarded the gold of divine wisdom in the underworld, and had to be slain to obtain it.[21] In the Celtic version of this same initiation, the bard (and sage) Taliesin confronts a dragon that guards the drink of knowledge held in cups of gold in the underworld.[22] This serpent/dragon became the treasure-guarding dragon, and the dragon slain by the hero to free the damsel in distress (symbolizing the ego that is destroyed to free consciousness as I explain in chapter 3) in European mythology.

Top left: The ancient Egyptian god Ra seated in his boat with the serpent Apep being speared before him. Top center: The Norse god Thor battling Jörmungandr. Top right: St. Michael slaying the dragon. Bottom left: The Greek god Zeus battling Typhon.

The alignment to Alpha Draconis also coincided with another stellar and solar alignment, further associating the descending passageway with the equinox. At midnight on the autumn equinox around 2,170 BC, while the descending passage aligned with Alpha Draconis/Thuban, the passage was perpendicular (at a right angle) to the star Alcyone, the brightest star in the Pleiades star cluster.[23]

In ancient Egypt, the Pleiades represented the mother goddesses Hathor[24] and Neith,[25] who were associated with the sky below the horizon from which the sun is born, and whom they gave birth to. Neith was known as the opener of the pathways of the underworld, particularly as the "opener of the sun's paths."[26] And so it may have been she who symbolically opened the pathway into and out of the Great Pyramid's subterranean chamber, as it was the goddess who swallowed Ra into her underworld womb, guided him through it, subdued his enemies there, and finally gave him birth in the twelfth and final hour. Along the various stages of Ra's journey she is called by various names including, "She who is great in her power," "Mistress of the deep night," and "Smashing the foreheads of the enemies of Ra." She was the warrior aspect of the Mother Goddess, whom I explain more about later in this chapter.

However midnight was also a spiritually significant time, as it was when the "ultimate mystery" occurred in Ra's journey, which is likely why it was incorporated into the pyramid's alignments. It was the time of greatest darkness, called "thick darkness"—representing the primordial feminine matrix of creation from which the light is born.[27]

The subterranean chamber seems to have represented some aspect of the Duat/underworld, which included "mysterious caverns" and "hidden chambers."[28] There is possibly even evidence that water from the Nile, brought in using canals, flowed through it,[29] just as it flows through the Duat. Indeed, my wife and I suspect that the descriptions and drawings of the Duat symbolically depict the various regions of the Great Pyramids and Giza Plateau, which had originally been used for initiatory rites.

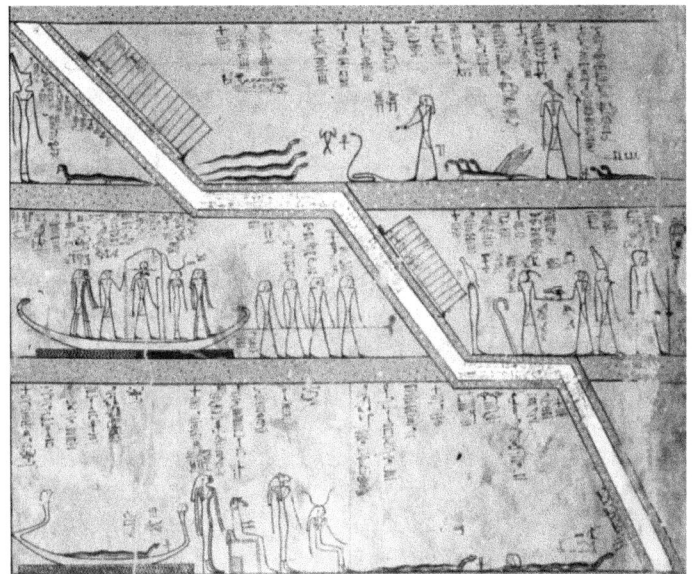

What looks like some kind of descending passage or ramp in the illustration of the fourth hour of Ra's journeys through the Duat, from the text known as Amduat.

"The course of Ra in the West,
  the secret plans which this god brings forth in it,
  the excellent guide, the secret writing of the Duat,
  which is not known by any person, save a few.
  This image is done like this,
  in the secrecy of the Duat,
  unseen and unperceived.
  Whoever knows this mysterious image will
  be a well-provided Akh-spirit [being of light].
  [...] A true remedy, (proven) a million times!"[30]
  ~ BOOK OF THE HIDDEN CHAMBER (AKA AMDUAT)

The dimensions of the descending passage have even been calculated as representing the time period of twelve hours, linking it to the twelve hours of Ra's journey and to the equinox, while the height of the Great Pyramid has been shown to mathematically correspond to the sun's mean distance from Earth (the sun being symbolically positioned at its summit), and the perimeter of its base to the sun's annual cycle.[31] [32] And so the chamber was located beneath the earth, within the symbolic underworld, from which the sun, Ra, is reborn, "becoming an akh [being of light] rising toward the imperishable, circumpolar stars."[33]

Altogether, this layout and its alignments may have symbolically represented the descent into the underworld/womb of the Mother (represented by the Pleiades and the chamber within the earth) at the autumn equinox to face one's egos and inner darkness (represented by Draco and the time of midnight) with her help, in preparation for the birth of the Spiritual Son/sun (Ra). This same initiatory pattern survived among the ancient mystery schools of Egypt, Greece, and Northern Europe, as I explain further on. That their basic principles may be found in the design and alignments of the Great Pyramid indicates that their origins are very ancient.

A similar design can be found at the Pyramid of the Sun at Teotihuacán in Mexico, which has almost the same footprint as the Great Pyramid of Egypt. This pyramid faces the setting sun on August 13 (an important day in the Maya calendar), and viewed from its summit the equinox sun rises from behind a nearby mountain. It was built over a man-made cave just as the Great Pyramid was built over a subterranean chamber. The cave is shaped like a four-leaf clover, perhaps representing the flower of four petals that was used as the Maya glyph for the sun. The local Maya people saw caves as earthly wombs and gateways to the underworld, and a "Great Goddess" associated with the underworld was worshiped at this site. And so, like the Great Pyramid of Egypt, we find a similar theme of descent into the underworld and womb of the Mother who gives birth to the sun. Teotihuacán was known as "the birthplace of the gods," while the threshold/gate of the last hour of the Duat was called "that which raises the gods" and was where Ra was born.[34]

Another strange site that shares similarities is the mysterious Ratapignata Pyramid in France. It aligns to the equinox, and contains a descending stairwell that leads into a subterranean chamber.[35] No one knows who built it, but many believe it was the Knights Templar, an order of warrior monks founded in 1119 AD, that are said to have had people within their ranks that carried the knowledge of many of the secret mystery schools of Europe and the East.

Many sacred sites which encode the symbols of descent at the equinox face the cardinal direction of west, which is the direction of the setting sun and is associated specifically with the autumn equinox. These sites include Chichen Itza and statues on Easter Island. The fact that these ancient sites have alignments with the sunset on the equinox is an important clue to their meaning. The direction of west, as the place where the sun sets, was associated with death and the descent into the underworld by the Maya, ancient Greeks, and ancient Egyptians.

THE FALL INTO DARKNESS

The descent into the underworld is related to a universal principle—the fall into darkness, where someone must first descend before they can ascend, as light is extracted from darkness.

Each of us has fallen—from the heavenly realm where we were created, into the darkness of matter—in order to gain the knowledge of our own existence. It is here in matter that we learn and are tested by the many challenges, difficulties, and rewards we face in life. This same principle applies to the path, where we must descend into darkness, difficulties, and the depths of our own subconscious, in order to learn and be tested before being able to reunite with our divine Being and ascend to the heavenly realm from where we first came.

This is why ancient myths and monuments symbolize the descent into the underworld (down steps, descending passageways, into caves and subterranean chambers, etc.), and spiritual ascents (up flights of stairs, ascending passageways, leading to the apexes of pyramids, etc.).

The underworld occupies a place in the cosmology of nearly all ancient peoples. And numerous people who've had out-of-body and near-death experiences have seen and visited an underworld, and their accounts share many similarities with one another, as well as with those of ancient peoples. This underworld exists as a place in other dimensions, but is also connected to the human psyche. The regions of the underworld correspond to the interior regions of the subconscious, which interpenetrate our body and psyche in the present moment.

The autumn equinox expresses the principle of descent, which occurs throughout the path of the spiritual sun. The darkness and underworld is that of the psyche, which someone descends into while out of the body in dreams and in out-of-body experiences, and also in the difficult circumstances that arise in their daily life, in order to suffer, learn, and be tempted and tested, which reveals what is truly within them.

> "John [the Baptist] said, 'Worthy teachers, you dress in white proclaiming your purity yet fear to put this to the test. Is your flesh so weak that it must be kept continually under restraint? Is the imprisoned malefactor good by his own desire or by his circumstances? Is not the world a place of temptation so each may discover his own strength or weakness? Untested you can know neither and must always remain in a state of doubt. The fire hidden in wood gives warmth only when released, it also provides light and is useful, but while hidden away it is of little value.'" [36]
> ~ THE GOSPEL OF THE KAILEDY

It is never guaranteed that someone will emerge from a descent, as it is only through overcoming their internal obstacles that they can ascend from out of the darkness back into the light, but this time with more light than they had before.

One of the earliest known representations of the equinox, found at an ancient megalithic site in Ireland—showing the eternal winding and unwinding, or rotation of the earth, from winter solstice, through the equinox, to the summer solstice, and back again.

THE ROLE OF CHAOS

The fall into darkness is related to chaos, as to fall is to plunge into it. Chaos is a very important aspect of creation, as all of creation emerges from it. The ancient text called the Rig Veda, which was written in India, contains one of the oldest and most famous accounts of creation in the world, and says that creation emerged from darkness, void, and water indiscriminate.

> "At first was neither Being nor Nonbeing.
> There was not air nor yet sky beyond.
> What was wrapping? Where? In whose protection?
> Was Water there, unfathomable deep?
> There was no death then, nor yet deathlessness;
> of night or day there was not any sign.
> The One breathed without breath by its own impulse.
> Other than that was nothing at all.
> Darkness was there, all wrapped around by darkness,
> and all was Water indiscriminate." [37]
> ~ THE RIG VEDA

Likewise, matter is in chaos after creation in the most widely held theory of creation called the "Big Bang," which many scientists believe was the origin of our universe. Then, as matter crystallized, it gradually organized into forms, structure, and order.

This same principle, which is at work on a macrocosmic scale in creation, is also at work when creating the spiritual within—the old and inferior must firstly dissolve into chaos in order to be reduced back into basic elements, which are then refined and purified to create the new and superior. The old, decrepit, and decayed is shed, like the leaves and chaff of autumn, to make way for the new and provide the chance to start again.

The descent into the darkness of chaos at the autumn equinox is the descent into psychological chaos, represented by the dark and chaotic forces of winter. It's in our darkest times that the egos come to the surface, like when under pressure, unwell, abandoned, attacked, unjustly treated, etc. A person has to fight their way out of this psychological chaos by seeing and removing the dark inner states (egos) that arise, rather than being overcome by them, and in doing so, gradually establishes order within themselves. As they do, they emerge with greater understanding, and more consciousness, and therefore come out with something superior, different, and new to what they had before.

This same principle is found in a study of sound called cymatics. It was discovered that as sound moved to higher and higher frequencies, the patterns it formed became more complex, but that the pattern would firstly dissolve into chaos before reforming to create the next more complex pattern.[38]

THE QUEST FOR LIGHT IN DARKNESS

Contained within the darkness, and the dark half of the year, is the seed of light of the coming summer, just as within the dormant seed at autumn lies the germ of new life. It is from darkness that light is extracted, as darkness is light inverted and vice versa.

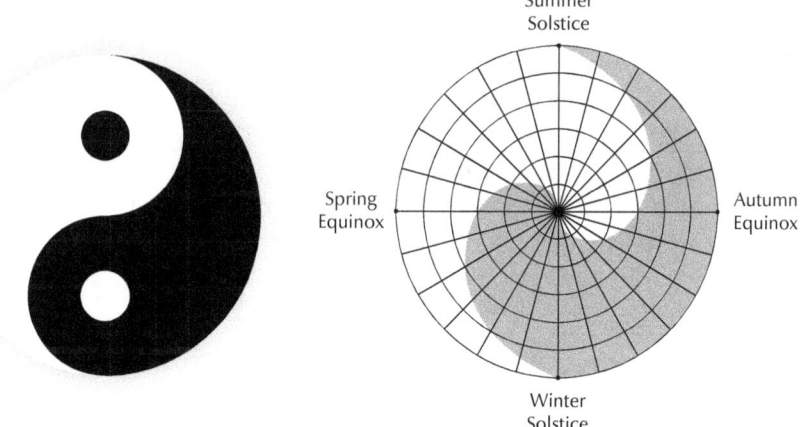

This is illustrated in the symbol of yin and yang, which is a depiction of one year's cycle of light and shadow. The dark half of the symbol carries the seed of light, while the light half carries the seed of darkness. Each one transforms into and takes the place of the other, as there is only either day or night, light or darkness, male or female, dry or wet, and hot or cold, in this universe of duality.

Although darkness is often feared and stigmatized, without darkness there would be no shadow, and it is shadow that allows us to see just as much as light does. Without shadow we could not see form, and there would be no recognition that light even exists.

> "If one does not stand in the darkness, he will not be able to see the light [...]. And to someone who will not know the [root] of all things, they remain hidden. Someone who will not know the root of wickedness is no stranger to it." [39]
> ~ JESUS IN THE DIALOGUE OF THE SAVIOR

In the work of inner transformation on the path of the spiritual sun, light is extracted from darkness. The subconscious, which is given by nature, is the darkness, and on the path of the spiritual sun, the light of consciousness is extracted from the dark multidimensional elements (egos) within the subconscious, gradually increasing consciousness within a person until the subconscious is illuminated and there is total light. This consciousness, once extracted, then contains the knowledge of light, but also the knowledge of the darkness that once trapped it, which has been referred to as "the knowledge of good and evil." This is how all the qualities of light, such as knowledge, wisdom, honesty, courage, and love, are attained on the path of the sun.

Each person starts this path in the darkness of the subconscious, and then must go through much learning and suffering in their life to understand and be able to overcome it, and through a spiritual process transmute it to become the light with the knowledge of that light and the darkness that contained it.

Just as in the wheel of the year, winter is transformed into summer, so must the dark side of ourselves be transformed into light.

> "Those who sow in winter reap in summer. The winter is the world, the summer the other Aeon (eternal realm). Let us sow in the world that we may reap in the summer." [40]
> ~ THE GOSPEL OF PHILIP

THE SACRED SEED

In nature during autumn, the seeds produced at summer fall and are buried beneath the ground, returning to the earth as all things that die do.

Seed was central to the Eleusinian Mysteries of ancient Greece, as were the equinoxes and seasons. They were used to symbolize the process of death and descent (with the planting of seeds at autumn), and the birth of the Spiritual Son and later resurrection to eternal life (at spring). Inscriptions at Eleusis describe a ritual in which people looking to both the earth (mother) and sky (father) sung out "rain and conceive." The ritual then enacted a divine son being born from a sacred fire. The climax of the celebration was when an ear of grain was cut in silence, symbolizing new life and immortality.⁴¹

It's not just plants that contain seeds, as we also contain seeds that have the power to create new life in the conception of children. But our seed not only has the potential to create material things; in higher dimensions it also contains the potential to create spiritual things too, which the Mysteries of Eleusis ultimately symbolized.

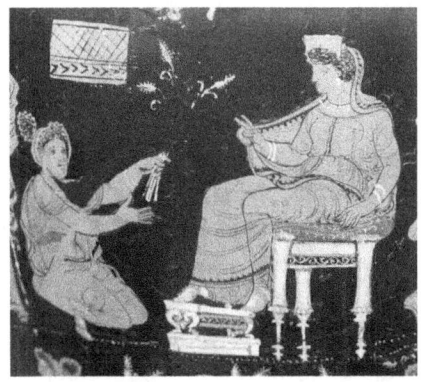

A queen of Eleusis offering a triune of wheat to the goddess Demeter from a Greek vase dated to 340 BC.

The seed was considered sacred, as it symbolizes the latent inner seed within each person that has the power of creation.

> "We invoke the bright and glorious Stars
> To which the Heavenly Father
> Hath given a thousand senses,
> The glorious Stars that have within themselves
> The Seed of Life and of Water." ⁴²
> ~ THE ESSENE GOSPEL OF PEACE

> "Know, O Arjuna, that I am the eternal Seed of being." ⁴³
> ~ KRISHNA IN THE BHAGAVAD GITA

Veiled references to this appear in some of the earliest texts of Hinduism, called the Upanishads, which talk about the use of sex and seed for spiritual purposes.

> "Those who use their days for sexual pleasure
> Consume prana, the very stuff of life;
> But mastered, sex becomes a spiritual force.
> The wise see the Lord of Love in all food;
> From food comes seed, and from seed all creatures.
> They take the lunar path who live for sex;
> But those who are self-controlled and truthful
> Will go to the bright regions of the sun." ⁴⁴
> ~ THE PRASHNA UPANISHAD

When used within the practice of sexual alchemy, the sexual seed is used inwardly in its energetic form, rather than expelled outwardly in its material one.

When the opposite charges of positive and negative, of male and female, are united in sex, scientifically measurable electricity is generated. Electricity is a form of fire, but because all matter has higher dimensional aspects, this sexual electrical fire in higher dimensions is a spiritual inner fire. Fire, like that found in the sun and stars, reduces matter back into energy and light, which can then be used to form new elements.

Likewise, this spiritual inner fire can be used to incinerate the dark energetic substance of the egos, to cleanse one's energies, and give birth to the spiritual within by forming new elements that crystalize into higher spiritual parts. This practice has been referred to as Maithuna (as a practice found within some Tantric traditions) in the East, alchemy in medieval and Renaissance Europe, the practice of HeQi in Taoism, and the bridal chamber of the Gnostics.

Through an alchemical process of transmutation, light is extracted from darkness and someone is "born again"—not of flesh, but of the spirit.

> "Flesh gives birth to flesh, but the Spirit gives birth to spirit. You should not be surprised at my saying, 'You must be born again.'" [45]
> ~ JESUS IN THE GOSPEL OF JOHN 3:6-7

Mayan sculpture of the maize god emerging from within a cob of maize.

However, to be able to create higher spiritual parts using one's sexual energies, these energies need to be purified so that they are of a suitable frequency. As the egos are put to death, one's energies become increasingly cleansed in the purifying inner flames, in preparation for the birth of the Son within. This is the spiritual meaning behind the symbolic transmutation of base metals into gold in alchemy, and the ritual purification, and spiritual cleansing, given by John the Baptist (baptism).

Like the practitioners of the Eleusinian Mysteries, the Maya also considered their staple seed corn (also known as maize) to be sacred. It was associated with their Spiritual Son, called Hun Hunahpu, who was known as the maize god, and the cakes they made of maize were used to symbolize the sun. It was also said to be the substance that humans were made of, revealing a connection between sun, Spiritual Son, seed, and humans.

THE SEVEN BODIES OF THE SUN

The energy of the sun and stars is a creative energy; the stars create almost all the elements of the universe. We too contain creative energy, as man and woman united can create children. But this creative energy is not limited to creating physical things. Ancient practitioners of the Religion of the Sun state that when this energy is directed inwardly rather than outwardly, in a practice often called "alchemy," it can create spiritual things within instead.[46]

There is a need to create these spiritual things within if someone wishes to reunite with their higher Being. This is because higher parts of the Being, like the Spiritual Son, are of a higher frequency of energy and light—like that found in the blinding light of the sun—and for these higher parts to be able to manifest within, someone needs to have the vessels to contain them.

Our physical body acts as a vessel for our consciousness, as well as for other parts of our psyche, and allows us to be here in this physical dimension. We have vessels in other dimensions too, like for example an astral body that allows us to travel out of our physical bodies in the fifth dimension (in what's often referred to as the astral plane) during out-of-body experiences, while we dream, and in near-death experiences. These bodies interpenetrate one another, across multidimensional reality, allowing us to exist as multidimensional beings in the here and now.

The bodies that most people start off with, however, are only suitable to carry a basic frequency of energy, and are not able to withstand the higher frequency of energy of the Spiritual Son. The same principle is at work with electricity, as without the proper cable to carry an electrical charge, the cable will be overloaded and burn out.

> "For I maintain that the eyes of mortals cannot see the incorporeal form of the Father or Son, because it is illumined by exceeding great light. Wherefore it is not because God envies, but because He pities, that He cannot be seen by man who has been turned into flesh. For he who sees God cannot live. For the excess of light dissolves the flesh of him who sees; unless by the secret power of God the flesh be changed into the nature of light, so that it can see light, or the substance of light be changed into flesh, so that it can be seen by flesh. For the power to see the Father, without undergoing any change, belongs to the Son alone. But the just shall also in like manner behold God; for in the resurrection of the dead, when they have been changed, as far as their bodies are concerned, into light, and become like the angels, they shall be able to see Him." [47]
> ~ PETER IN THE CLEMENTINE HOMILIES

Jesus alluded to this same principle when he spoke about not putting new wine in old wine skins.

> "[...] no one pours new wine into old wineskins. Otherwise, the wine will burst the skins, and both the wine and the wineskins will be ruined. No, they pour new wine into new wineskins." [48]
> ~ MARK 2:22

These spiritual vessels have been symbolized in the ancient Religion of the Sun in a number of different ways. They are usually associated with the sun, as they are the vehicles of the Spiritual Son created with the sexual/creative energies that have been purified into a higher type of energy, and have been called bodies of gold, spiritual bodies, and solar bodies.

Unlike physical bodies, these spiritual bodies do not decay with time, which is why creating them is part of the path that leads to immortality.

> "The visible body born of nature is far different from that of spiritual birth. For the one can be dissolved and the other cannot; the one is mortal and the other immortal. Do you not know that you have become divine and that you are a son of the One? So also am I." [49]
> ~ CORPUS HERMETICUM

> "The body of the dead is of gold like that of a god and so it consists of imperishable material. 'Rise on your bones of bronze and on your limbs of gold, for this body of yours belongs to a god. It does not perish. It does not decompose, it does not consume.'" [50]
> ~ THE PYRAMID TEXTS OF QUEEN NEITH

> "The bones of the king are firm (or, copper), and the limbs of the king are like the stars, the imperishable stars." [51]
> ~ THE PYRAMID TEXTS, UTTERANCE 684

> "Heaven is not the wide blue sky but the place where corporeality is begotten in the house of the Creative. If one keeps this up for a long time there develops quite naturally, in addition to the body, yet another spirit-body." [52]
> ~ THE SECRET OF THE GOLDEN FLOWER

Jesus referred to these bodies as spiritual garments, as they clothe one's Being. In ancient Gnostic texts they are also called "the children of the bride-chamber."

> "[Jesus said] But if ye be persuaded and keep your souls chaste before God, there will come unto you living children whom these blemishes touch not, and ye shall be without care, leading a tranquil life without grief or anxiety, looking to receive that incorruptible and

true marriage, and ye shall be therein groomsmen entering into that bride-chamber which is full of immortality and light." 53

~ THE ACTS OF THOMAS

The Taoist sages called the energy the bodies are created with the "golden elixir," and the ancient Egyptians called the bodies it creates the "bodies of gold," like the gold of the resplendent sun; it is the same refined gold many alchemists symbolically sought in their chemical experiments for hundreds of years.

> "The common householder, husband and wife, are endowed with *ch'i* blood, *ching* and spirit, and are not different from the great *tao*. Each and every one of them is capable of perfection. The blazing "golden elixir" can be consumed by any man." 54
>
> ~ TRUE TRANSMISSION OF THE GOLDEN ELIXIR BY SUN JU-CHUNG

There are seven solar bodies, as there are seven dimensions, and a vehicle needed for the Being in each.

> "In the Roman Mystery cult of Mithras, seven degrees of initiation enabled the neophyte to proceed through the seven celestial bodies, allowing a reversal of the descent of the human soul into the world at birth." 55
>
> ~ PAYAM NABARAZ, THE MYSTERIES OF MITHRAS

The ancient Gnostics wrote that there were seven spheres, which are a reference to these seven dimensions, placing above them an eighth, which were the fixed stars as the source of creation and all its dimensions. In the excerpt below, these seven dimensions are referred to as "seven houses"—and the eighth as the place of rest, the sun and stars, and source of creation.

An illustration of the celestial spheres, with the seven lower spheres assigned to planets, and the eighth to the region of the fixed stars.

> "Come, compassionate mother.
> Come, communion of the male.
> Come, she that revealeth the hidden mysteries.
> Come, mother of the seven houses, that thy rest may be in the eighth house." 56
>
> ~ THE ACTS OF THOMAS

On Easter Island there are seven statues that face sunset on the autumn equinox and the setting/descent of the constellation Orion (which in ancient Egypt represented Osiris), which occurs at the same time,[57] representing the descent into the underworld. These statues symbolize the seven solar bodies that someone needs to have prepared before the descent into the darkness symbolized by the autumn equinox, ready for the birth of the Spiritual Son within.

The seven moai facing the equinox sunset at Ahu Akivi on Easter Island may represent the seven spiritual bodies in the seven dimensions (and/or the seven wisdom bringers who founded the Religion of the Sun).

The energy referred to as kundalini in Hinduism also needs to be raised up the spinal column in each body. The kundalini is usually symbolized as a serpent of solar light (depicted with a sun disk or made of gold) because a slithering snake moves like the waves of energy and light, and because a human spine in profile looks like a risen serpent. The energy of kundalini is a higher frequency energy, produced from the purified sexual energies, which travels up the spinal column as the main conduit of the central nervous system (which runs on electrical energy). This creates and transforms the nervous system in each of the seven bodies so that each body has its electrical system of movement to move within its dimension, just as the physical body does.

At the pyramid of Kukulcán (the feathered serpent) in Mexico, on the autumn equinox, a serpent made of seven triangles of light representing Kukulcán descends the pyramid—likely symbolizing his seven bodies and awakened serpentine energy (kundalini), and the descent into the underworld.

The pharaohs of Egypt were laid to rest totally covered in gold with a serpent on their forehead to symbolize the golden bodies and the risen kundalini.

THE SPIRITUAL MEANING OF THE AUTUMN EQUINOX

Left: The Egyptian god Sokar, who later became associated with Osiris, beneath a mound with the seven solar serpents raised. These seven serpents correspond to the seven solar bodies. Center: The Hindu sun god Vishnu depicted as floating upon the cosmos on a serpent with seven heads, symbolizing the seven risen serpents/kundalini in the seven bodies. Right: Buddha seated upon a serpent with seven heads, like the Hindu god Vishnu.

In the ancient Gnostic text called the Acts of Thomas, Jesus' disciple Thomas sings about the consciousness as the daughter of light, and that she has seven groomsmen and seven bridesmaids, which symbolize the seven bodies and the seven serpents. The participants of a wedding are used as the symbols because these bodies are created in the symbolic "bridal chamber."

> "The damsel is the daughter of light [...]. And surrounding her, her groomsmen keep her, the number of whom is seven, whom she herself hath chosen. And her bridesmaids are seven, and they dance before her." 58
> ~ THE ACTS OF THOMAS

The groomsmen "surround" and "keep her" because the solar bodies are the vessels and vehicles for consciousness, and the bridesmaids "dance before her" because they are the central nervous systems of each body, which allow the bodies, and thus the consciousness that inhabits them, movement.

The baptism of John the Baptist is a symbolic reference to the secret practice of alchemy; John's ritual purification of the body through clean water is symbolic of the spiritual purification of the sexual energies, and the use of this purified energy to create the seven solar bodies and raise the seven serpents of light.

In the following quote attributed to Jesus, the number seven appears again symbolically in connection with the purification of a person's inner energies.

> "[Jesus said] For only the pure water can mirror forth the light of the sun; and that water which has become dank with filth and murk can reflect nothing. And when the body and the spirit of the Son of Man have walked with the angels of the Earthly Mother and the Heavenly Father for seven years, then is he like the running river under the noonday sun, mirroring forth dazzling lights of brilliant jewels." [59]
> ~ THE ESSENE GOSPEL OF PEACE

This is how John, the initiate, makes "straight the way of the Lord" to prepare for the coming of the Son within, as these bodies will become the vehicles for the Spiritual Son in all the dimensions of creation. This completed state was symbolized in India by the sun god Surya, representing the Spiritual Son, whose chariot was pulled by seven horses, representing the seven bodies of the sun.

The Hindu sun god Surya riding in his chariot drawn by seven horses across the sky, which can represent the Spiritual Son using his seven bodies.

THE NINE REGIONS OF THE UNDERWORLD

The underworld is a place described by ancient peoples all over the world. In their explanation of creation, the Maya divided the underworld, which they called Xibalba, into nine regions, as did the Aztec. In Norse mythology they also described hell as having nine regions.

> "Below cold and darksome Nifel-heim are the nine divisions of torture in which the souls of the wicked are punished [...]. Then they enter the Na-gates and die the second death. Punishment is given in the nine realms of torture according to the sins that were committed." [60]
> ~ DONALD A. MACKENZIE, TEUTONIC MYTH AND LEGEND

In the Eleusinian Mysteries of ancient Greece there were nine spheres, and the Taoists described a "nine-fold heaven." Hell and heaven are lower and higher dimensions respectively; each consists of nine regions, and each region of the underworld corresponds to a region of heaven. They are the regions of both lower and higher frequency light and energy that are invisible to the human eye, as they are outside the spectrum of visible light.

On the autumn equinox at the pyramid of the feathered serpent Kukulcán, the Maya symbolized the descent of the feathered serpent with the risen kundalini (serpent energy) through the nine layers of the underworld as a serpent of light that descends the nine terraces of the pyramid.

 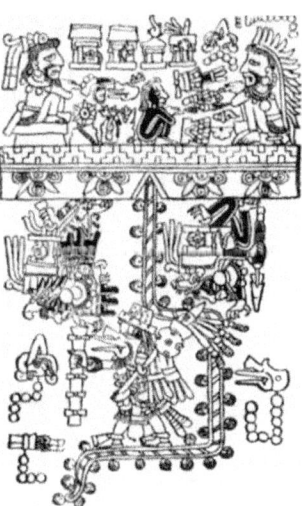

Left: The pyramid of the feathered serpent Kukulkan at the site of Chichen Itza in Mexico. Its nine terraces symbolize the nine regions of the underworld. At sunset on the equinox it appears as if a serpent of light descends the nine terraces—see chapter 8 for details. Right: Illustration of the descent of Quetzalcoatl into the underworld from an Aztec codex. Quetzalcoatl is the Aztec equivalent of the Maya deity Kukulkan, who was depicted as descending into the underworld at the ancient Maya site of Chichen Itza on the equinox.

Each of the nine regions of both the lower and higher dimensions also correspond to the nine regions within the human psyche, as everything, including us, is multidimensional. All matter is energy in vibration, and so these regions exist in the present moment, interpenetrating our psyche, but without us seeing them since their vibrations are outside of this dimension and the band of frequency the physical eye can perceive. These other dimensional worlds, regions, and realities have been experienced by many people in lucid dreams, out-of-body experiences, and near-death experiences since ancient times.

The ninth region of the underworld is the center of the earth in another dimension, which is the location of the earth's central fire in this physical one. Likewise, in another dimension, fire exists in abundance in the lower anatomy of a human, in the sexual organs. The ninth region, located in the sexual organs, and in the womb of the earth, is also the womb in which the Son gestates. At autumn, the seeds produced at summer descend into the earth; the nine layers of the underworld symbolize the gestation of the Son in the womb of the earth over nine months.

The earth is like a womb and corresponds to the human body on a microcosmic scale.

Earth's electromagnetic field moves through and around the earth in the shape of a torus, which is based on the same principle as the symbol of infinity. The central axis of the torus is found within the center of the earth.

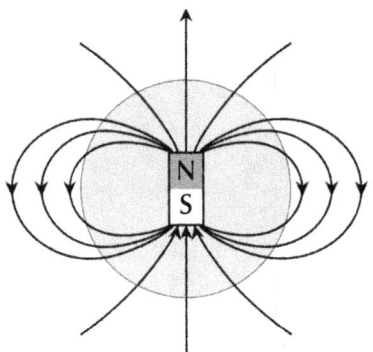

Diagram of Earth's magnetic field. N is for the north magnetic pole, and S for south. When drawn two-dimensionally like this, it takes the shape of the symbol for infinity.

This same central axis that exists within the earth also exists within each person, and the forces within a person all revolve from it, both into superior regions (heavens), or into inferior ones (hells). The direction we take all depends on the way the central fire found at the equinoctial axis, our inner creative energy, is used—whether to create the spiritual and imperishable, or material and transitory.

In the figure of infinity, the equinox is the crossing point—to reach the birth of the light, the Spiritual Son at the winter solstice, which is the extreme of darkness at one end of the figure, one must descend. As mentioned earlier, there are nine regions of the underworld, and for each of these underworld regions there are nine corresponding heavens. Someone must descend through each of the nine layers of the underworld to reach each of the nine heavens (and each layer of the underworld is suffering), as it is only by overcoming the egos and darkness, found in each region of the subconscious, that we reach to the light of consciousness and its heavenly qualities and feelings found in each corresponding heavenly region.

The symbol for infinity (like the number eight turned on its side).

For each region of both heaven and hell there is a gate/door to pass through to reach to the next level. Someone can only enter through a heavenly gate if they pass the required internal examination, which tests their spiritual level. Gaining the right to pass through these gates has been called initiation (these initiations don't happen in the physical world, but take place in out-of-body experiences). These gates are detailed extensively in ancient Egyptian sacred texts, and are symbolically illustrated by the sun god Ra's journey through the underworld as I explained earlier.

> "I stretched out my hands and my arms unto Osiris. I have passed on to judgment [...]. I enter in, having been judged; I come out at the door of Neb-er-tcher magnified and glorified. I am found pure at the Great place of passage [of souls]. I have put away my faults. I have done away mine offences. I have cast out the sins which were a part of me. I, even I, am pure, I, even I, am mighty. O ye doorkeepers, I have made my way [unto you]. I am like unto you. I have come forth by day.
>
> [...] may Anubis make my legs firm that I may stand upon them May the goddess Sekhet make me to rise so that I may ascend unto heaven [...]. I know my heart, I have gotten the mastery over my heart, I have gotten the mastery over my two hands and arms, I have gotten the mastery over my feet, and I have gained the power to do whatsoever my ka pleaseth. My soul shall not be shut off from my body at the gates of the underworld; but I shall enter in peace, and I shall come forth in peace." [61]
>
> ~ THE EGYPTIAN BOOK OF THE DEAD

These gates correspond to the nine chambers of initiation in the Norse mysteries of Odin, the nine days of initiation in the Eleusinian Mysteries, and the nine stages of cultivating immortality in Taoism.

> "The nine days are typical of the death journey in Norse myths, as it is of the initiation journey. Hel rules nine spheres, the number of days it takes to reach her High Hall is nine, and Odin hung for nine nights before he reached his illumination. [...] The nine nights probably indicate a journey through all nine worlds [...]." [62]
>
> ~ MARIA KVILHAUG, THE SEED OF YGGDRASILL

Nine regions have been described by both Jesus and Krishna as existing within the body, as both heaven and hell are not only external places, but also exist within. In the following excerpts, they are referred to as "the city of nine gates," "the house of nine bushes," and "the nine-storied pagoda."

> "I [Peter] replied, asking him, 'What is the name of the place to which you go, your city?' He [Jesus] said to me, **'This is the name of my city, "Nine Gates."** Let us praise God as we are mindful that the tenth is the head.'" [63]
> ~ THE ACTS OF PETER AND THE TWELVE APOSTLES

> "He [the Self] resides in **the city of nine gates**, which is the body." [64]
> ~ SHVESTASHVATARA UPANISHAD

> "Mentally renouncing all actions, the self-controlled soul enjoys bliss in this body, **the city of the nine gates**, neither doing anything himself nor causing anything to be done." [65]
> ~ KRISHNA IN THE BHAGAVAD GITA

> "Ahau spread his feet apart. Then it was that the word of Bolon cacab descended to the tip of his tongue. Then the charge of the katun was sought; nine was its charge when it descended from heaven. Kan was the day when its burden was bound to it. Then the water descended, it came from the heart of the sky for the baptism of **the House of Nine Bushes**." [66]
> ~ THE BOOK OF CHILAM BALAM OF CHUMAYEL

> "Mysteriously floating in space hangs a 'precious pearl,' the size of a millet grain, which is variously called the 'great Mahayana prajna (wisdom of the Great Vehicle),' **the 'nine-storied pagoda,'** the **'Buddha body,'** 'cintamani (talisman-pearl),' 'saddharma (wonderful law),' or the 'marvellous Muni pearl.'" When the adept consumes it, his body sprouts wings and he joins the ranks of the immortals." [67]
> ~ TRUE TRANSMISSION OF THE GOLDEN ELIXIR BY SUN JU-CHUNG

THE WARRIOR ASPECT OF THE MOTHER GODDESS

The Mother Goddess has been depicted as a warrior by different traditions derived from the ancient Religion of the Sun, and her worship has been associated with the autumn equinox since ancient times.

In India the autumn equinox is celebrated with the Hindu festival of Durga Puja (meaning ritual prayer to the goddess Durga), also called Navaratri. It is dedicated to the Mother of the Universe—the warrior goddess Durga, and is the largest celebration of the Spiritual Mother in the world today. It commemorates Durga's defeat of the buffalo demon called Mahishasura—who is symbolic of the egos.

Starting at the autumn equinox, the celebration lasts for nine nights and ten days, and Durga is celebrated through nine plants associated with her nine aspects.[68] This symbolizes the nine layers of the underworld and psyche she is intimately related to, as the earth and underworld is her womb.

The Mother Goddess, symbolized as a female of great power, is the feminine aspect of each person's own higher Being. While she has loving qualities, she also has powerful, punishing, and destructive ones, represented by the many warrior goddesses around the world. The war that she fights is against the forces of darkness and evil—in Hinduism, the goddess Durga is said to have the power to protect someone from evil and misery through her ability to destroy its cause, which are the egos.

The Hindu goddess Durga riding upon her tiger (often a lion instead) while slaying the buffalo demon Mahishasura, symbolic of the egos.

> "[The goddess Durga is] always decked in celestial garlands and attired in celestial robes—who is armed with sword and shield, and always rescues the worshiper sunk in sin, like a cow in the mire, who in the hours of distress calls upon that eternal giver of blessings for relieving him of their burdens." [69]
> ~ THE MAHABHARATA

As part of Durga Puja, traditional songs are sung to Durga, like this one, which describes how the Mother Goddess destroys a person's egos.

> "O Mother! Severe afflictions distress me
> and no one except Your Honoured Self can provide relief,
> please end my afflictions.
> Hopes and longings ever torture me.
> All sorts of passions and lust ever torment my heart.
> O Goddess [Durga]! I meditate only upon you
> Please kill my enemies O Queen!" [70]
> ~ DURGA CHALISA

A similar traditional song describes the same thing, though is dedicated to Durga in her aspect as Kali.

> "I am in a perilous predicament, O Mother, and know not whom [else] to call for help.
>
> I am being pursued on the rough roads of life by four robbers who are bent upon turning me against the lord [...] Rama.
>
> These are my prime enemies, the sovereign lords of all the deadly evils; lust, anger, infatuation and avarice.
>
> If you overthrow them (and abandon me not to my troubles), I would be blessed with devotion to [...] Lord Krsna [Krishna]." [71]
>
> ~ SRI KALI CHALISA

It's in this context that the celebration of Durga Puja was said to have originated. It's drawn from a section of one of the oldest Hindu epics, called the Ramayana, where the hero Rama (the higher Self/Being) fights to save his wife Sita (symbolic of consciousness/the individual Self) from the demon Ravana (symbolic of the egos).[72] In the oldest version of this story Rama was said to have called upon the sun god for aid, while in another he calls upon Durga, and offers her 107 blue lotuses and one of his blue eyes to make 108 in total, in order to gain her help. He was said to have done this around the time of the autumn equinox, which is why Durga Puja is still held at the autumn equinox today.[73] Rama's ritual prayer to Durga is considered the most ancient reference to a Durga Puja, and seems likely to have been based on an existing ancient tradition.

This is indicated by a hymn praising the feminine nature of the supreme creator, as it appears in the oldest sacred text in India, the Rig Veda. In its verses the Spiritual Mother is associated with the battle against evil, and is said to reside within all.

> "I am the Queen [...].
>
> Through me alone all eat the food that feeds them—each man who sees, breathes, hears the words outspoken.
>
> They know it not, but yet they dwell beside me. [...]
>
> I make the man I love exceedingly mighty, make him nourished, a sage, and one who knows Brahman.
>
> I bend the bow for Rudra [Shiva], that his arrow may strike, and slay the hater of devotion.
>
> I rouse and order battle for the people, I created Earth and Heaven and reside as their Inner Controller.
>
> On the world's summit I bring forth sky the Father: my home is in the waters, in the ocean as Mother.

> Thence I pervade all existing creatures, as their Inner Supreme Self, and manifest them with my body.
>
> I created all worlds at my will, without any higher being, and permeate and dwell within them.
>
> The eternal and infinite consciousness is I, it is my greatness dwelling in everything." [74]
>
> ~ DEVI SUKTA, RIG VEDA

Durga is symbolically depicted as fighting huge supernatural battles against legions of asuras (demons). The battleground is said to be our consciousness, and the demons symbolic of our egos. The following excerpt comes from a text that is recited as part of Durga Puja celebrations.

> "She [Durga] filled the entire sky with her terrible roar, and from the immeasurable din a great echo roared. All the worlds shook and the ocean churned. The earth quaked and the mountains heaved. In joy the gods exclaimed 'Victory!' to the lion-mounted Devi; and with bodies bowed in devotion, the sages praised her. [...]
>
> 'Aha! What is this?' Mahishasura bellowed in wrath. Surrounded by countless asuras [demons], he rushed toward the sound and then beheld the Devi, who pervaded the three worlds with her radiance, bending the earth under her tread, scraping the sky with her diadem, shaking all the nether regions with the resonance of her bowstring, and standing there, penetrating every direction with her thousand arms.
>
> Thereupon, the battle began between the Devi and the enemies of the gods. Swords and missiles, hurled in every direction, lit up the quarters of the sky [...].
>
> Amid chariots, elephants, and horses, myriads of other great asuras battled with the Devi [...]. Some hurled spears while others threw nooses; intent on killing her, they began an assault with their swords. But she, the Devi Candika, showered down all manner of weapons and cut through their armaments as if in play.
>
> Praised by gods and seers, she remained serene, even while unleashing her weapons at the asuras' bodies.
>
> Her lion-mount, shaking its mane in fury, stalked among the demon throngs as fire rages through a forest [...].
>
> Then the Devi, with her trident, club, and volleys of spears, with her swords and other weapons, slew great asuras by the hundreds and brought down still more with the confounding din of her bell." [75]
>
> ~ THE DEVIMAHATMYA

This war against the ego is most clearly portrayed in depictions of the Hindu goddess Kali which means "she who is death" (not to be confused with the demon Kali, whose name is written/pronounced differently in Sanskrit). Kali is an even more ferocious aspect of the goddess Durga. She brandishes a weapon in her hands which beheads numerous demons. Her hands are bloodied and the heads of her enemies hang around her neck. Her enemies are the egos, and she fights them within the person working to change. Kali is said to inhabit a cremation ground,[76] which is the place where the egos are killed and destroyed in the inner sexual fire.

Like Kali, the Aztec goddess Coatlicue is a mother goddess with her destructive side emphasized. She bears an astonishing resemblance to Kali, with tongues sticking out, and wearing a necklace made of hearts, hands, and skulls. It is said that in her both the grave and womb exist,[77] as the Mother has power over life and death both in a physical and spiritual sense.

In Egypt, Sekhmet is the Mother Goddess in her destructive aspect. She has the head of a lion and dresses in red like the Hindu goddess Durga, the color of blood, the earth, and underworld. She is said to be the fiercest of all goddesses—her name means "powerful one," but she also had titles such as the "one before whom evil trembles,"[78] "the flame," "lady of terror," and "the one who loves Ma'at [cosmic order] and who detests evil."[79]

In Buddhism, the warrior aspect of the goddess also bears a resemblance to the Egyptian Sekhmet, Aztec Coatlicue, and Hindu Kali. She is Senge Dongma (Simhamukha in Sanskrit), who was created to destroy demons, and like Sekhmet,

The goddess Kali portrayed in her aspect as Dakshina Kali, which is when she has her right foot forward as a protector. Dakshina can be taken to mean "south," as Kali is traditionally seen as facing south in the same direction as the souls who are heading south toward hell, so that she can rescue them. The word Dakshina also has connections to the transit of the sun as it travels south after crossing the celestial equator at the autumn equinox (in the Northern Hemisphere). The southern transit of the sun is also connected to the "night of the gods," so she may also be said to be facing the night.

Left: The Aztec goddess Coatlicue with an astonishingly similar necklace, skirt, and appearance to the Hindu goddess Kali. Right: The lion-headed Egyptian warrior goddess Sekhmet.

she has the head of a lion and can be the color red. Again, like Kali, Senge Dongma is also associated with cremation grounds, her eyes are wide open, her tongue is bared, she wears a skirt made of tiger skin, and a long necklace made of bones and severed heads, which are symbolic of the egos as the various self-centered states, "moods," and "personas," she destroys within a person.

The Sumerian goddess Inanna was known as the Queen of Heaven and was a powerful warrior whose chariot was drawn by lions; she was even sometimes symbolized as a lioness in battle. Likewise in Hinduism, the goddess Durga is depicted as a warrior mounted on a lion or tiger. Sekhmet and Senge Dongma were both portrayed with the head of a lion. These mother goddesses were each associated with lions or tigers as they are such powerful animals, that all are their prey. They are symbolic of the spirit which has the power to defeat all evil.

The Sumerian goddess Inanna and her lion. The mace in her left hand and the weapons sprouting from her shoulders indicate her war-like nature (from a cylinder seal found in Iraq from the Akkadian Period, circa 2,254–2,193 BC).

These goddesses were not only associated with the war against evil, but also with sex, Tantra, and fire. Inanna was a goddess of sexual love. Senge Dongma is known as the "Guardian of the Secret Tantric Teachings," and is depicted as circled by flames, with mythological links to a cremation ground. Kali is primarily a tantric goddess who inhabits a cremation ground. Durga is "Keeper of the Flame" and Sekhmet is known as "the flame."

The warrior aspect of the goddess is so intimately related to Tantrism, sex, and fire, because it is in the sexual fire that she destroys the egos, and also why she is linked to cremation grounds—symbolic of the incineration of the egos in the inner sexual fire.

"As the heat destroys the bad qualities of the metals of the mountains so the defects of the body created by the senses should be burnt down by the control of the mind. [...] By becoming unattached and egoless, he gets supreme position. [...] Endowed with the Omkara (Pranava) [the mantra Om], the Yogins destroy the sins by meditation [...]." [80]
~ THE SAMBA PURANA

There are even traditions in Christianity that depict the Virgin Mary as a warrior and in a similar way to the Hindu goddess Kali, as like Kali, Mary is sometimes portrayed as standing upon an evil demon with a club raised in combat against it. This is symbolic of the Spiritual Mother destroying the egos.

Left: Goddess Kali destroying the egos in the fire of sacred sexuality (painting is from the 19th century). Right: The Virgin Mary armed with a club to protect her children against evil, as she was sometimes depicted. The painting is titled *Our Lady of Succor* by Giovanni da Monte Rubiano.

The Carmelite Order is a Christian order that was founded around 1206 AD on the sacred site of Mount Carmel. Their patron is the Virgin Mary whom they see as their Spiritual Mother and protector. A Catholic priest, inspired by their traditions, wrote of Mary as a warrior, saying:

"How strange it seems to think of Mary as a warrior.

The gentle maid of Nazareth, the Virginal Mother, the Mother of the Prince of Peace, is still called—and properly called—"More terrible than army in battle array."

And so she is....

Mary, conqueror of heresies

> Mary, triumphant always in the battle with sin.
>
> When then we put on the scapular, which is Mary's uniform, we join in a special way the regiment of which Mary is the queen and honorary colonel.
>
> We pledge ourselves to do battle against the enemy of the human race.
>
> We will be victorious as Mary is victorious, and conquering as Christ is conquering." [81]
>
> ~ NOVENA TO OUR LADY OF MOUNT CARMEL

In the ancient Religion of the Sun, the feminine is associated with the cycles of nature and the cosmos, and all that is transitory and impermanent in creation, which is why in Hinduism she was described as Maya—as all that is illusory and passing.

> "The one absolute, impersonal Existence, together with his inscrutable Maya, appears as the divine Lord, the personal God, endowed with manifold glories. [...] With Maya uniting, thou hast brought forth the universe. [...] At Thy bidding Maya, thy power divine, projects this visible universe, projects name and form." [82]
>
> ~ THE SVETASVATARA UPANISHAD

This indicates that feminine energy is the basis of all manifest nature, found expressed on a microcosmic scale in the dynamic cycling of electrons (feminine, negatively charged) around the stable nucleus of protons (masculine, positively charged) in atoms, and on a macrocosmic level in the cycling of the earth around the sun, the changing of the seasons, the waxing and waning of the moon, and even greater galactic and stellar cycles. The Mother is the giver of nature, the physical body, matter, and the subconscious, symbolized by the growing darkness following the summer solstice, which the consciousness enters into when joining the process of life. Her womb is the earth, and so even the underworld forms part of the learning she provides in the cycles of life and nature.

In many ancient teachings, the goddess is associated with the autumn equinox because this time begins the dark half of the year, which is connected with the feminine—as darkness, matter, earth, and underworld. It is a time of entering her realm of knowledge, which she provides through the darkness of matter.

It is also these energies of Maya, of matter, that form our egos, and so because these energies ultimately derive from the feminine aspect of creation, it is the Spiritual Mother that has the power to destroy them, having the ability to transform our energies (and matter), and use them to build spiritual parts within a person instead.

While this world of Maya places limitations on our ability to perceive spiritual realities, without it there would be no darkness, no duality, no sense of separation, and therefore no knowledge of light. Thus, the Mother provides the incredible world of learning we go into, while also having the power to free us from it.

> "She creates all this universe, moving and unmoving, and it is she who graciously bestows liberation on humanity. She is the supreme knowledge and the eternal cause of liberation, even as she is the cause of bondage to this transitory existence. [...]
>
> You are Savitri, the source of all purity and protection; you are the supreme mother of the gods. By you is this universe supported, of you is this world born, by you it is protected, O Devi, and you always consume it at the end.
>
> You are the creative force at the world's birth and its sustenance for as long as it endures. So even at the end of this world, you appear as its dissolution, you who encompass it all.
>
> Armed with sword and spear, and with club and discus, waging war with conch, bow and arrows, sling and iron mace, you inspire dread. Yet, you are pleasing, more pleasing than all else that is pleasing, and exceedingly beautiful. Transcending both highest and lowest, you are indeed the supreme sovereign. [...]
>
> You are this entire, manifold world and you are primordial matter, supreme and untransformed. [...]
>
> O Devi, who are the cause of liberation and great, inconceivable austerities: sages yearning for liberation contemplate you with sense restrained, intent upon truth, with all faults cast off, for you are the blessed, supreme knowledge. [...]
>
> O Devi, who remove the sufferings of those who take refuge in you, be gracious. Be gracious, mother of the entire world. Be gracious, ruler of all. Protect the universe, O Devi, who are the ruler of the moving and unmoving.
>
> You alone are the sustaining power of the world, for you abide in the form of the earth. By you, who exist in the form of water, all this universe prospers, O Devi of unsurpassable strength.
>
> Of boundless might, you are Vishnu's power, the source of all, the supreme maya. Deluded, O Devi, is all this universe. In this world, you alone, when pleased, are the cause of liberation.
>
> May your terrible, flaming trident, exceedingly sharp and destroying all asuras, protect us from dread. [...]

May your bell that destroys the daityas' life-force and fills the world with its ringing protect us from all evils, O Devi, even as a mother protects her children. [...]

O ruler of the universe, you protect the universe. You are the essence of all things, and you support all that is. All kings must praise you, O revered one, and those who bow to you in devotion become the refuge of all."[83]

~ THE SEER IN THE DEVIMAHATMYA

In nature, we see transformation continuously taking place, which ultimately has its root in the mysterious properties of electricity and fire, which in higher dimensions have spiritually transformative properties and are related to the sexual energies, which is why mother goddesses from around the world are associated with birth, death, sex, and transformation.

THE MYSTERY OF THE MINOTAUR AND THE LABYRINTH

The ancient Minoans aligned a number of their ancient sites on the island of Crete to the autumn equinox. The central religious area of their palace at Knossos aligns with the equinox sunrise and has been theorized as being the actual location of, or the inspiration for, the legendary labyrinth of King Minos that contained the Minotaur.[84] Myth has it that the wife of King Minos gave birth to the savage beast called the Minotaur—a half man, half bull creature. King Minos was said to have built a labyrinth on Crete in order to imprison it. Later, King Minos' son was killed in Athens; to avert the plague caused by his death, King Minos demanded that seven men and women were sent from Athens every nine years to be fed to the Minotaur. The son of the King of Athens, named Theseus, went as one of them, and, with the help of King Minos's daughter Ariadne, slew the Minotaur.

This myth has a symbolic meaning. The autumn equinox is the time of descent into the underworld to overcome the animalistic egos with the aid of the Mother Goddess. The labyrinth represents the underworld, as it was said to be a treacherous place that no one could ever find their way out of, just as hell has been described as a place that once people enter, they cannot escape. The Minotaur is a symbol of the ego—of a person turned into a beast by the animalistic egos within.

A half-man, half-beast (in this case a centaur in place of the Minotaur) pictured at the center of a labyrinth, symbolic of the egos that inhabit our psychological underworld.

This Minotaur inhabits the labyrinth as our psychological underworld is the place where our egos reside.

In the legend, the Minotaur was the offspring of the Queen of Knossos, the wife of King Minos, as it is the energies of the Mother that are used to create the egos. However, it was also symbolically a royal woman, the king's daughter Ariadne, who then assisted the hero Theseus to kill the Minotaur, as the divine feminine also has the power to defeat the ego. It appears the Minoans understood this, as it was the goddess who was worshiped primarily at this site. An inscription at the palace reads, "Mistress of the Labyrinth,"[85] as the underworld is the realm of the Mother.

In Minoan religion, this mistress was the great goddess of nature, who gave birth to a divine son each year[86]—symbolized at the winter solstice.

The symbol of the labyrinth of Crete is also used by the Hopi people of the southwest of North America; it appears in petroglyphs near their ancient settlements and is used in their ceremonies. It's likely to have been taken to North America by ancient travelers. The Hopi have preserved its meaning; they call it the Mother Earth, and Mother and Child symbol. The enfolding lines represent the fetal membranes within the womb, and the straight line, from within the labyrinth to the outside, the path of emergence or birth canal.[87][88] Thus the labyrinth represents the womb of the Mother, which is also the underworld, and as explained in the next chapter, is the place from which the divine child is born at the winter solstice.

Symbol of the labyrinth found in ancient Crete and the North American southwest.

Theseus battling the Minotaur in the dark passageways of the labyrinth, symbolic of the one who battles their egos within their own psychological underworld—the subconscious.

There are cave complexes on Crete that were very likely used ceremoniously to enact the descent into the labyrinth of the underworld on the autumn equinox, where someone symbolically had to confront the beast of the ego they carry within.

Remarkably, the bull Minotaur slain by Theseus is similar to that of the buffalo demon slain by the Hindu goddess Durga. This may be because there is evidence that the Minoans of Crete and the Indus Valley Civilization in India were related to one another.[89]

ANCIENT RITES OF DESCENT

Painting of an ancient ritual of the goddess Isis.

The same themes expressed in the legend of the Minotaur and in the celebrations of the goddess Durga in India are also found elsewhere in Europe and in Egypt, as they were an important part of the ancient Religion of the Sun.

The themes of descent into the underworld, having to battle obstacles symbolizing the egos to reach wisdom and resurrection, under the guidance of a goddess, are found repeatedly in the Norse texts called the Eddas.[90] The author and expert in Old Norse mythology Maria Kvilhaug believes that these stories in the Eddas were based on an ancient Nordic initiation ritual. She describes the basic storyline as involving a hero who seeks the guidance of a goddess of the underworld, which she says "would point out the path that he must follow. Then follows a descent, where the hero moves into the Underworld. There he is faced with various trials."[91] He "would encounter obstacles in the form of dangerous entities, usually representing fear, hatred, greed and oblivion, or a guardian who challenges him so that he must prove his knowledge, his eloquence and wisdom."[92] Then follows a consecration, which "involves the embrace of the goddess and the imparting of her wisdom" at which time he reaches "a bright golden realm of resurrection where he is restored and transformed [...]."[93] The initiate then resurrects and returns to the world—often as a sage or king, and later at death experiences Salvation.[94]

As with initiations of rebirth and resurrection in ancient Egypt and Greece, the sequence of events in the Nordic ritual correlate with the path of the sun.

Kvilhaug has also identified a number of other important elements in Nordic spiritual initiation. In the stories of the Eddas, these rituals would often involve dreams—particularly in order to communicate with the goddess of the underworld, who would appear to the initiate in their dreams.[95] In fact, one initiation ritual takes place in dreams entirely.[96] This is because in the ancient Religion of the Sun, initiations take place in the dimension where we dream, as they are administered by divine Beings, and any physical initiation is intended only to be a physical replica of what occurs while out of the body in higher dimensions.

Another element identified by Kvilhaug is the both personal and cosmic nature of the goddess, as the goddess sought by the initiate was individual to each person, but at the same time associated with the goddesses of Norse religion (each themselves aspects of the one great goddess).[97] This is because each person has their own individual divine Being that follows the same fundamental patterns found in the universe, which I explain about further in the following chapters.

As Kvilhaug points out, many of these same elements and themes are also found in the Mysteries of Eleusis in Greece (believed to have been established by Minoans) and in a surviving account of an initiation ritual from ancient Egypt.[98] This Egyptian ritual was recorded in the second century, but is likely to have been passed down over thousands of years as its prototype was encoded in some of Egypt's most ancient texts, and possibly traces back to the design of the Great Pyramid as I explained earlier. It was written down by Apuleius—a Berber who lived under the Roman Empire and was initiated into the Egyptian mysteries at the time—in his book Metamorphoses (also called The Golden Ass). It is a fictional story that incorporates real details of his initiations, offering one of the few surviving accounts of them.

In the story, the protagonist is turned into an ass/donkey—symbolizing the state of humanity as animals that are completely subject to circumstance, as well as being turned into an animal by the animalistic egos within. This is illustrated in the first parts of the story in which the ass is subjected to one terrible event after another, often caused by its own impulses, all of which are beyond its control. Finally, not being able to take it anymore, the ass washes himself in the ocean seven times in order to purify himself, and begs "the mother of the universe" to make him human again. The goddess, who is described as the divine feminine power of creation worshiped as many different goddesses, appears to him in his dreams as the Egyptian goddess Isis, and instructs him on what he needs to do. After becoming human, he undergoes a ritual at the temple of Isis, which Apuleius describes as follows:

> "I came to the boundary of death and after treading Proserpine's [the goddess of the underworld's] threshold I returned having traversed

all the elements; at midnight I saw the sun shining with brilliant light; I approached the gods below and the gods above face to face and worshiped them in their actual presence. [...] In my right hand I held a flaming torch and my head was encircled with a beautiful crown of palm, its bright leaves projecting like rays. Equipped thus in the image of the Sun [...] I celebrated my rebirth as an initiate [...]. For the keys of hell and the guarantee of salvation were in the hands of the goddess, and the initiation ceremony itself took the form of a kind of voluntary death and salvation through divine grace." [99]

~ LUCIUS IN METAMORPHOSES

THE MEANING OF THE AUTUMN EQUINOX IN DAILY LIFE

The principles expressed in the autumn equinox are found on many levels. They exist not only on the path of the spiritual sun, but also in daily life, just as the autumn equinox that occurs each year corresponds to sunset each day.

Facing one's inner darkness, extracting the light of consciousness and knowledge from within it, and eliminating one's egos by calling upon one's Spiritual Mother, forms part of the spiritual practice that leads someone along the path of the spiritual sun.

Yet everyone goes through difficult times in their lives, whether they are on the path or not, and this principle of extracting light from darkness is at work whenever someone chooses to apply it. It is especially relevant when going through difficult circumstances, as going through these can be a form of descent in one's own life. Facing hardships can cause someone to descend into the chaos and darkness of their psyche, as reactions and turbulent emotions arise in response, such as rage, depression, anxiety, etc., which don't manifest in ordinary circumstances. If instead of giving in to these states, someone confronts them, they can learn and understand themselves and ascend out of their inner darkness with greater consciousness (light) and wisdom than they had before. In fact, this kind of descent is necessary for gaining knowledge and transforming oneself within.

THE PRINCIPLES OF INNER DEATH AND DESCENT

The autumn equinox symbolizes the principles of inner death and descent. It reveals that in order to attain light, one must firstly face the darkness and chaos of one's own inner underworld/subconscious, and descend with the aid of the divine feminine, their Spiritual Mother, to fight their egos, and extract the light of consciousness from within it. And from the deepest depths of darkness, in the womb of the earth, to establish the beginnings of order amidst the raging chaos of winter, and germinate the spiritual seed that will become the newborn sun.

Winter Solstice
Birth

CHAPTER THREE

The Spiritual Meaning of the Winter Solstice

The ancient Neolithic temple of Newgrange in Ireland, which has an inner chamber in the shape of a cruciform that aligns to sunrise on the winter solstice, the birthday of Jesus, though Newgrange was constructed thousands of years before Jesus was born.

The birth of a divine child and savior at the winter solstice formed a central part of the ancient Religion of the Sun across much of the world since the beginning of history—in ancient Egypt as the birth of Horus, the birth of Mithra in Iran, the birth of Kolyada in Slavic traditions, the birth of the Spiritual Son at Alban Arthan of the Druids, the birth of Inti to the Inca, and the birth of Jesus at Christmas, etc. These celebrations have expressed a profound spiritual truth that is just as relevant now as it was then.

They speak of a deep and mysterious understanding of spiritual transformation. All things which come into being must first be born. Even as creation was borne by the great Mother of the universe, so too must we be born of the spirit to become spirit. The winter solstice is a celebration of being "born again"—not of flesh, but of the spirit. It's a celebration of the birth of the Spiritual Son within a person's consciousness on the path of the spiritual sun.

Symbolized as a child just as the winter sun is at its weakest, it will grow until reaching its full strength at the summer solstice—just as the influence of the spirit grows within a prepared individual to transform them from inner darkness into light.

THE MOST CELEBRATED RELIGIOUS TIME IN THE WORLD

People in India ritually bathe and offer prayers to the sun at a winter solstice festival in one of the largest religious pilgrimages in the world—attended by up to 100 million people.

The winter solstice is the most celebrated annual religious occasion in the world. It is the time of Christmas, which is celebrated by an estimated two billion Christians as well as many non-Christians (accounting for around a third of the world's population). It is celebrated as an indigenous festival of the sun by hundreds of thousands of people in South America, by European pagans that celebrate the birth of the sun, and by Iranians and Zoroastrians as one of their most ancient and important festivals called Yalda—meaning "birth," as it celebrates the birth of the sun god Mithra.[1] In India, the winter solstice is celebrated with a festival called Makar Sankranti attended every twelve years by one of the world's largest pilgrimages—made by an estimated forty to one hundred million people—who travel to a river to bathe and pray to the sun.[2]

The celebration of the winter solstice stretches far back into ancient times, and is also possibly the oldest known religious occasion in the world—evidenced by caves in Europe aligned to the winter solstice containing rock art dating back to the Stone Age.[3] I believe that most of the celebrations of the winter solstice derive from the same ancient Religion of the Sun that originated far back in prehistory.

Records of ancient winter solstice ceremonies held in ancient Egypt, at the ancient city of Petra in Jordan, and at Eleusis in Greece, were all noted as celebrating the same thing—described as the birth of an only-begotten aeon (a great divine power) from a virginal mother goddess.

These celebrations were recorded by a bishop called Epiphanius in Cyprus at the end of the fourth century when writing about practices considered heretical by the Christian orthodoxy. In the following passages Epiphanius is quoted by G. R. S. Mead, who was a translator of important ancient Gnostic Christian texts. They reveal that the birth of the spiritual sun was already celebrated around the winter solstice on December 25 (the birthday of Jesus) by a number of ancient civilizations, and would have been from ancient times. As Mead points out, these ancient pagan ceremonies are very similar to those of early Christianity—as all of them, including the birth of Jesus, celebrate the birth of a divine Son from the dark womb of the Spiritual Mother at the time of the winter solstice, revealing that they symbolize something far greater and more mysterious than the birth of one person or deity alone.

> "'This day *[of the solstice]* the Greeks, I mean the Idolaters, celebrate on the twenty-fifth day of December, a feast called Saturnalia among the Romans, Kronia among the Egyptians, and Kikellia among the Alexandrians. *[Epiphanius presumably means that it was called Kronia by the Greeks, Saturnalia by the Romans, and Kikellia by the Egyptians, or, at any rate, by the Alexandrians.]* For on the twenty-fifth day of December the division takes place which is the solstice, and the day begins to lengthen its light, receiving an increase [...].
>
> For instance, at Alexandria, in the Koreion *[That is the temple of Kore. This can hardly be the temple of Persephone, as Dindorf (iii. 729) suggests, but is rather the temple of Isis, who in one of the treatises of the Trismegistic literature I called the World-Maiden.]* as it is called— an immense temple—that is to say, the Precinct of the Virgin; after they have kept all-night vigil with songs and music, chanting to their idol, when the vigil is over, at cockcrow, they descend with lights into an underground crypt, and carry up a wooden image lying naked on a litter, with the seal of a cross made in gold on its forehead, and on either hand two other similar seals, and on both knees two others, all five seals being similarly made in gold. And they carry round the image itself, circumambulating seven times the innermost temple, to the accompaniment of pipes, tabors and hymns, and with merry-making they carry it down again underground. And if they are asked the meaning of this mystery, they answer and say: 'To-day at this hour the Maiden (Kore), that is, the Virgin, gave birth to the aeon.'
>
> In the city of Petra also—the metropolis of Arabia [...]—the same is done, and they sing the praises of the Virgin in the Arab tongue,

calling her in Arabic Chaamou, that is, Maiden (Kore), and the Virgin, and him who is born from her Dusares, that is, Alone-begotten (monogenes) of the Lord. This also takes place in the city of Elousa *[? Eleusis]* on the same night just as at Petra and at Alexandria.'

Ancient depiction of the god Dusares, whose birth at the winter solstice was celebrated in the ancient city of Petra in Jordan.

This symbolic rite represented a macrocosmic mystery, Epiphanius tells us; but was there not also an analogous microcosmic mystery? And if so, must it not have been familiar to all those mystic schools and communities, Essene, Therapeut, Hermetic and Gnostic, which are so inextricably interwoven with nascent Christianity? [...] Do we not further possess the ritual of a very early Christian mystery-drama, or form of initiation, in which "the things done" closely resembled that of the passion-the crucifixion?" [4]

~ G. R. S. MEAD QUOTING EPIPHANIUS

THE BIRTH OF THE SUN

The meaning of the winter solstice operates on a number of levels. At its core is the birth of the sun—both personally and universally.

The rising of the sun on the winter solstice, out of the darkest time of the year, echoes the birth of the light from out of darkness during the creation of the universe.

> "The Eternal Parent (Space) wrapped in her ever-invisible robes, had slumbered once again for seven eternities.
>
> Time was not, for it lay asleep in the infinite bosom of duration.
>
> Universal mind was not, for there were no Ah-hi to contain it.
>
> The seven ways to bliss were not. The great causes of misery were not, for there was no one to produce and get ensnared by them.
>
> Darkness alone filled the boundless all, for father, mother and son were once more one, and the son had not awakened yet for the new wheel, and his pilgrimage thereon. [...]
>
> Alone the one form of existence stretched boundless, infinite, causeless, in dreamless sleep; and life pulsated unconscious in universal space [...].
>
> Darkness alone was Father-Mother [...].
>
> These two are the Germ, and the Germ is one. The Universe was still concealed in the Divine Thought and the Divine Bosom.... [...]
>
> "Darkness" radiates light, and light drops one solitary ray into the waters, into the mother-deep. The ray shoots through the virgin egg; the ray causes the eternal egg to thrill, and drop the non-eternal germ, which condenses into the world-egg. [...]
>
> Behold, oh Lanoo! The radiant Child of the two, the unparalleled refulgent Glory: Bright Space Son of Dark Space, which emerges from the depths of the great Dark Waters. It is Oeaohoo the younger [...]. He shines forth as the Sun; he is the blazing Divine Dragon of Wisdom [...]. Behold him lifting the Veil and unfurling it from East to West. [...]
>
> Where was the germ and where was now darkness? Where is the spirit of the flame that burns in thy lamp, O Lanoo? The germ is that, and that is light, the white brilliant son of the dark hidden father." [5]
>
> ~ THE STANZAS OF DZYAN

The ancient Egyptians understood the connection between creation and the winter solstice, as they aligned their Karnak Temple Complex, the largest in the world, to the winter solstice sunrise and dedicated one of its central temples to creation and their supreme creator god Amun. This temple complex was never completed, as successive pharaohs kept making additions to it as a living example of the process of creation and its continuous unfoldment. These additions were even built according to the Fibonacci sequence—a key mathematical principle found in the growth and expansion of life—and the temple was called the "House of Life."[6]

Looking down the central axis of the Karnak Temple Complex in Egypt—the largest in the world—which aligns to the winter solstice sunrise. It was here, and at the nearby Luxor Temple, that the ancient Egyptians celebrated the birth of the Spiritual Son.

The spiritual sun is a living and divine fire, and the source of creation, as explained in ancient sacred texts of the Religion of the Sun. However, as creation follows universal principles, the birth of the sun as the light of the first day also represents the birth of the light of our own spiritual sun within us. On Earth, it is born into the time of most darkness in the year, while in the individual, into the darkness of the human psyche and body—the physical sun gives life to the external world; the spiritual sun gives spiritual life to the individual.

THE SPIRITUAL SON

Many ancient traditions that were influenced by or derived from the ancient Religion of the Sun still have remnants of a divine savior connected to the sun, and associated the birth of this savior with the winter solstice. This divine savior is often remembered as teaching people how to become a "son of the sun" or "Son of God," and return to the spiritual source awakened.

Although Christmas is now largely about shopping, the birth of the savior was intended to bring to Earth a profound spiritual message for the whole of humankind. This message has been brought to Earth anew at different times as previous teachings became old, obscure, and locked within religious dogma.

An ancient depiction of the Madonna and Child in Egypt, with Isis/Hathor as the Spiritual Mother nursing her son Horus.

The teaching of these divine saviors often had a dual aspect—they taught through what they said, but also through the events of their lives.

A study of the events of the lives of the divine saviors who were part of the Religion of the Sun in different times, such as Jesus (Christian Gnostic), Mithra (Indo-Iranian), and Osiris (Egyptian), reveal that events of their lives match the progress of the sun throughout the year.

Some theorize this happened because the different religions borrowed from one another. Others point to the fact that each of these deities was closely associated with the sun, and therefore were merely representing the astrological worship of the sun to simpleminded sun worshipers, waiting for their crops to grow, etc.

But there is another explanation for this incredible similarity. Often this explanation was only known by the initiates of mystery schools who encoded the knowledge of it in the symbols of sacred sites. To the public these often complex symbols look obscure and even nonsensical, therefore protecting the knowledge from those who would deride and destroy it. This mechanism has helped to preserve much of the knowledge found in sacred sites up until this day.

Each of these deities was known as a savior of mankind, and a beloved and sacred divine child. Each of these deities was associated with the sun, and all of them born at the time of the winter solstice in a miraculous birth. The lives and stories of these deities tell us of a great mystery, which in the case of Jesus, he came to Earth with a mission to reveal both in the events of his life and his teachings.

THE POTENTIAL OF CONSCIOUSNESS

Every human being is a latent spiritual potential that lies dormant like a seed. We live asleep to the greater realities of existence, but whether we choose to realize it or not, each of us has the potential to become an awakened being. This is why sacred texts of the Religion of the Sun point toward spiritual transformation as the ultimate goal of life.

Literally, the work of spiritual transformation is found written in the cosmos in the movement of the sun and stars, which is why practitioners of the Religion of the Sun incorporated celestial movements into their spiritual monuments and sacred texts. This is what life is created for, so no wonder we find it reflected to us from the heavens, and intrinsic to everything around us. This is so we can always discover our true purpose for being here and realize our own spiritual potential—whenever we choose to search for it.

The creative process which gives birth to the universe also gives birth to the spiritual within a human. Thus the divine savior is not just born into the world, they can be born within us—into the symbolic stables, prison, or cave, which is the spirit entering into the humble and limited personality and body.

> "When you come to know yourselves, then you will become known, and you will realize that it is you who are the sons of the living father. But if you will not know yourselves, you dwell in poverty and it is you who are that poverty." [7]
> ~ JESUS IN THE GOSPEL OF THOMAS

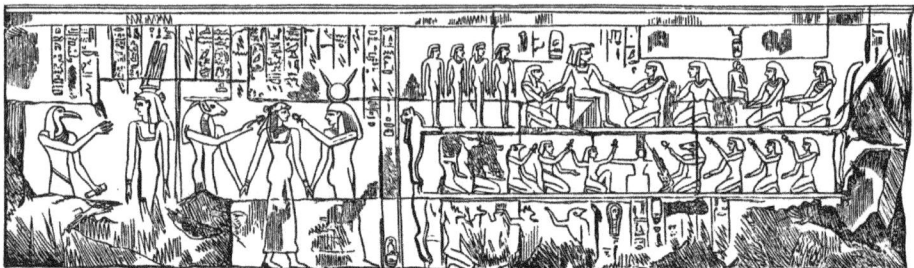

This scene portrays the annunciation, divine conception, birth, and adoration of the divine son as the king/pharaoh, at the Luxor Temple in Egypt (also given the name the Temple of Man by the Egyptologist Schwaller de Lubicz, as its proportions seem to correlate with those of the human body, thus the divine son is born into a person). Firstly the queen, who is seen as the earthly embodiment of the Mother Goddess Isis, is told by Thoth that she will become pregnant with the divine son of the Father God Amun. The goddesses Kneph and Hathor impregnate the queen using the ankh, the breath of life, and thus the queen spiritually conceives and remains "ever virgin." She gives birth to the child king, seen as the earthly embodiment of Horus, the Spiritual Son/sun, who is praised by the gods. This Egyptian depiction of the birth of the divine son shares remarkable similarities with the birth of Jesus.

THE BIRTH OF THE SPIRITUAL SUN WITHIN

We are born as physical beings, but in order to become spiritual we must be born as spiritual beings. This particular spiritual birth is the birth of the Son—the spiritual sun—within. The process of creation in the universe is the same process that creates everything, including both the physical aspect of our being, but also the inner, spiritual aspect of our higher Being. Each person's consciousness is a spark of the great spiritual light found in the sun and stars, which is why the Milky Way has been described in ancient texts of the Religion of the Sun as the birth place of souls.

> "Behold, O Hermes, there is a great mystery in the Eighth Sphere, for the Milky Way is the seed-ground of souls..." [8]
> ~ POIMANDRES (THE MIND OF THE UNIVERSE) TO HERMES IN THE VISION OF HERMES

The Inca celebration of Inti Raymi—meaning "solemn festival of the sun"—is one of the most famous winter solstice celebrations in the world, and is attended by over one hundred thousand people each year in Peru. The sixteenth century chronicler Garcilaso de la Vega wrote:

> "The festival was dedicated to the Sun in recognition of their worship of it as the sole, supreme, and universal god, who created and

sustained everything in the earth with his light and virtue. Out of regard for the fact that the Sun was the natural father of the first Inca Manco Cápac and of [his wife] the Coya Mama Ocllo Huaco and of all the kings and their children and descendants sent down to earth for the universal benefit of mankind, the feast was a very solemn one.." [9]

We are, literally, the offspring of the sun—created from the stars both physically and spiritually. This is why ancient cultures, such as the Sumerians, Egyptians, Gnostics, Inca, and Maya, all referred to themselves as the "Children of the Sun" or "Children of the Light."

> "Believe in the light while you have the light, so that you may become children of light." [10]
> ~ JESUS IN THE GOSPEL OF JOHN 12:36

As our consciousness descends from the source into the darkness of matter, it divides and leaves behind parts of itself in higher dimensions, just like the sun's light and power diminishes after the summer solstice, as it descends toward the darkness of autumn.

The ancient text sometimes referred to as The Hymn of the Pearl, allegorically describes this descent of consciousness (the child) from the spiritual source into the world of matter (referred to symbolically as Egypt), parting from its Father, Mother, and Son (higher parts of our Being), in order to rescue a symbolic pearl in the depths of the ocean (light and wisdom extracted from the depths of darkness and the subconscious), and return with it to the source.

> "When, a quite little child, I was dwelling
> In the House of my Father's Kingdom,
> And in the wealth and the glories
> Of my Up-bringers I was delighting,
> From the East [the direction of the sun], our Home, my Parents [Father and Mother]
> Forth-sent me with journey-provision.
> Indeed from the wealth of our Treasure,
> They bound up for me a load.
> Large was it, yet was it so light
> That all alone I could bear it. [...]
> My Glorious Robe they took off me
> Which in their love they had wrought me [...].
> And with me They (then) made a compact;
> In my heart wrote it, not to forget it:

> "If thou goest down into Egypt,
> And thence thou bring'st the one Pearl —
> (The Pearl) that lies in the Sea,
> Hard by the loud-breathing Serpent —
> (Then) shalt Thou put on thy Robe [...]
> And with thy Brother [the Son], Our Second,
> Shalt thou be Heir in our Kingdom." [11]
> ~ THE ACTS OF THOMAS

The trinity of Father, Mother, and Son, found so often in ancient teachings, represents parts of each person's higher Being. It is through the birth of the Son within, the spiritual fire and light represented by the sun, that our spiritual potential can be realized, like a seed that finally germinates. This is what Jesus referred to when he said we must be "born again."

> "Now there was a Pharisee, a man named Nicodemus who was a member of the Jewish ruling council. He came to Jesus at night and said, 'Rabbi, we know that you are a teacher who has come from God. For no one could perform the signs you are doing if God were not with him.' Jesus replied, 'Very truly I tell you, no one can see the kingdom of God unless they are born again.' 'How can someone be born when they are old?' Nicodemus asked. 'Surely they cannot enter a second time into their mother's womb to be born!' Jesus answered, 'Very truly I tell you, no one can enter the kingdom of God unless they are born of water and the Spirit. Flesh gives birth to flesh, but the Spirit gives birth to spirit. You should not be surprised at my saying, 'You must be born again.''" [12]
> ~ JOHN 3:1-7

This need to be "born again" was also taught in the Eleusinian mystery schools of ancient Greece in which the human condition was seen as a tomb, and why the Spiritual Son in different cultures (as Viracocha, Jesus, Mithras, Hu Gadarn, etc.) was symbolized as being born into a cave:

> "The soul of man—often called Psyche, and in the Eleusinian Mysteries symbolized by Persephone—is essentially a spiritual thing. Its true home is in the higher worlds, where, free from the bondage of material form and material concepts, it is said to be truly alive and self-expressive. The human, or physical, nature of man, according to this doctrine, is a tomb, a quagmire, a false and impermanent thing, the source of all sorrow and suffering. Plato describes the body as the sepulcher of the soul; and by this he means not only the human form but also the human nature.

> The gloom and depression of the Lesser Mysteries represented the agony of the spiritual soul unable to express itself because it has accepted the limitations and illusions of the human environment. The crux of the Eleusinian argument was that man is neither better nor wiser after death than during life. If he does not rise above ignorance during his sojourn here, man goes at death into eternity to wander about forever, making the same mistakes which he made here. If he does not outgrow the desire for material possessions here, he will carry it with him into the invisible world, where, because he can never gratify the desire, he will continue in endless agony. Dante's Inferno is symbolically descriptive of the sufferings of those who never freed their spiritual natures from the cravings, habits, viewpoints, and limitations of their Plutonic personalities. Those who made no endeavor to improve themselves (whose souls have slept) during their physical lives, passed at death into Hades, where, lying in rows, they slept through all eternity as they had slept through life.
>
> To the Eleusinian philosophers, birth into the physical world was death in the fullest sense of the word, and **the only true birth was that of the spiritual soul of man rising out of the womb of his own fleshly nature.** 'The soul is dead that slumbers,' says Longfellow, and in this he strikes the keynote of the Eleusinian Mysteries. Just as Narcissus, gazing at himself in the water (the ancients used this mobile element to symbolize the transitory, illusionary, material universe) lost his life trying to embrace a reflection, so man, gazing into the mirror of Nature and accepting as his real self the senseless clay that he sees reflected, loses the opportunity afforded by physical life to unfold his immortal, invisible Self." [13]
>
> ~ MANLY P. HALL, THE SECRET TEACHINGS OF ALL AGES

To be born of the spirit is not a matter of adopting or changing beliefs—for anything to be born, it must follow the same process of creation which we see from the largest of scales, right to the very smallest, throughout the whole of creation.

In the previous quote from the Gospel of John, Jesus refers to being born of water and Spirit. The waters are the feminine aspect of creation, found symbolized in numerous Mother goddesses, and the Spirit is the masculine aspect, symbolized by various Father gods.

These dual creative forces can be found within every atom as negatively polarized particles called electrons and positively polarized particles called protons, and have been symbolized in ancient creation myths of the Religion of the Sun found throughout the world as a great Mother and Father who come together to make creation.

They are the dual masculine and feminine aspects of the creator that underlie and give rise to everything in the universe.

In ancient Chinese texts they were called yin (feminine) and yang (masculine).

> "One yin and one yang is called the tao... male and female mingle their ching and all creatures are born." [14]
> ~ I CHING (THE OLDEST KNOWN BOOK OF CHINA)

> "All things are brought forth from the subtle realm into the manifest world by the mystical intercourse of yin and yang. The dynamic river yang pushes forward, the still valley yin is receptive, and through their integration things come into existence." [15]
> ~ LAO-TZU IN HUA HU CHING

In ancient India, the supreme creator assumed a dual nature in order to create, called Prana/Purusha, which is masculine, and Rayi/Prakriti, which is feminine.

> "The Lord of Beings [...] meditated and produced Prana, the primal energy, and Rayi, the giver of form, desiring that they, male and female, should in manifold ways produce creatures for him." [16]
> ~ PRASHNA UPANISHAD

Similarly, the first being in Egypt that emerged from the unknowable source was called Atum, and the first gods this being created were the male god Shu and female goddess Tefnut.

Ancient surviving Welsh mythology indicates the Druids believed that the sap of the cauldron of the Mother goddess Ceridwen was fertilized by three drops of dew from the Father god Celu, and gave birth to a son called Taliesin who was associated with the sun.[17]

In an ancient Chinese story of creation there existed a cosmic egg that floated in the void. The egg was the opposites of yin and yang totally mingled; as they were mingled, creation was not yet able to come into being. Then within this egg grew the primordial man, P'an Ku, who broke out of the egg and split yin and yang into opposites, creating the sky and the earth. Later, P'an Ku entered a holy virgin as a ray of light, and was born into the world as T'ien-Tsun, the first principle of the universe.[18]

In a Maya account, creation also comes into being from the union of Mother and Father, who give birth to a son of light:

> "Great is its performance and its account of the completion and germination of all the sky and earth—its four corners and its four sides. All then was measured and staked out into four divisions,

> doubling over and stretching the measuring cords of the womb of sky and the womb of earth. Thus were established the four corners, the four sides, as it is said, by the Framer and the Shaper, the Mother and the Father of life and all creation, the giver of breath and the giver of heart, they who give birth and give heart to the light everlasting, the child of light born of woman and the son of light born of man, they who are compassionate and wise in all things—all that exists in the sky and on the earth, in the lakes and in the sea." [19]
> ~ POPOL VUH

In ancient Gnostic Christian texts that were excluded from the Bible, there are accounts of a Spiritual Mother and Father giving birth to a divine Son, many of which are attributed to Jesus.

> "[Jesus said] in joy did the Earthly Mother and the Heavenly Father give birth to the Son of Man. [...] the spirit of the Son of Man was created from the spirit of the Heavenly Father, and his body from the body of the Earthly Mother." [20]
> ~ THE ESSENE GOSPEL OF PEACE

Male and female energies united give birth to all life. At the dawn of creation, their union gave birth to the sun—the light of the first day—and the entirety of creation. This birth of the sun, at a spiritual level, is the birth of the spiritual sun—the birth of the life, love, wisdom, and power of the Son within.

THE CREATIVE POWER OF SEX

Sex is the foundation of life. Human life is created from the union of male and female in the birth of a child. In the ancient Hindu text the Brihadaranyaka Upanishad, the primordial being, after realizing it was alone, created a woman from its body. From their union humans were born. After this, the woman hid from the man by taking the form of a cow. But he came as a bull and from their union, cattle were born. She then hid as a mare, but he came as a stallion, and from their union all hoofed animals were born. This went on for each of the various animals for which there is a male and female, right down to the ants. This teaching illustrates the creative power of sex found throughout life and the universe, and that the union of male and female forces (called yang and yin in Taoism) gives birth to and creates all life at the largest of scales, right down to the smallest.

> "In the beginning this was Self alone, in the shape of a person. He looking round saw nothing but his Self. [...] But he felt no delight. [...] He wished for a second. [...] He then made this his Self to fall in two,

and thence arose husband and wife. Therefore Yagnavalkya said: 'We two are thus (each of us) like half a shell.' Therefore the void which was there, is filled by the wife. He embraced her, and men were born. [...] She then became a cow, the other became a bull and embraced her, and hence cows were born. The one became a mare, the other a stallion; the one a male ass, the other a female ass. He embraced her, and hence one-hoofed animals were born. [...] And thus he created everything that exists in pairs, down to the ants. He knew, 'I indeed am this creation, for I created all this.' Hence he became the creation, and he who knows this lives in this his creation." [21]

~ THE BRIHADARANYAKA UPANISHAD

A Buddhist depiction of the practice called Maithuna in Hinduism (more commonly referred to as Tantrism in the West).

Some people treat sex as ungodly and taboo, as if it was something separate from spirituality. But spirituality is not separate from life, and thus sex is not separate from spirituality either. Sex is part of the great mystery of creation. Deified in a number of ancient texts, man and woman are seen as god and goddess with the powers of creation. This is also why in these texts the sexual relationship between a man and woman is viewed as sacred, as in essence it belongs to the processes of divinity unlike any other human relationship. Within this relationship is the potential and power of the divine if used properly.

"The Master said: '(The trigrams) *Kh*ien and Khwăn may be regarded as the gate of the Yî.' *Kh*ien represents what is of the yang nature (bright and active); Khwăn what is of the yin nature (shaded and inactive). These two unite according to their qualities [...]. In this way we have the phenomena of heaven and earth visibly exhibited, and can comprehend the operation of the spiritual intelligence. [...] The yang originates a shadowy outline which the yin fills up with a definite substance. So actually in nature Heaven (*Kh*ien) and Earth (*Kh*wăn) operate together in the production of all material things and beings. [...] Heaven and earth existing, all (material) things then got their existence. All (material) things having existence, afterwards there came male and female. From the existence of male and female there came afterwards husband and wife [...]." [22]

~ I CHING

Ancient practitioners of the Religion of the Sun knew that creation is a process which is universal and which is found from the very largest scale, to the most microscopic. Therefore, they knew that the forces of male and female united give birth on Earth, give birth to the universe, and give birth to the spiritual within.

"Join the male to the female in their own proper humidity, because there is no birth without union of male and female." [23]

~ HERMES (QUOTED IN THE TEXT THE STONE OF THE PHILOSOPHERS)

SPIRITUAL BIRTH FROM ALCHEMICAL UNION

Physically, we know that sex between a man and a woman can create a child. Out of a tiny egg, an unmanifested potential springs forth almost miraculously becoming an entirely new human being that grows just as a plant from out of a tiny little seed. Thus we see within man and woman the primordial forces of the Egyptian father god Amun and his wife, the mother goddess Mut, which give rise to all creation. These three forces have been symbolized time and again, as the creative trinities of Osiris, Isis, and their son Horus (Egyptian); Father, Mary, and Jesus (Christian); Vishnu, Lakshmi, and Brahma (Hindu); Celu, Ceridwen, and Hu/Taliesin (of the Druids); Svarog, Lada and Dazhbog (Slavic); and others.

"In this trinity is hidden the wisdom of the whole world." [24]

~ HERMES TRISMEGISTUS IN THE EMERALD TABLET

This creative potential we each have is mentioned in a number of texts, which say that we are a microcosm of the universe and made in the image of the creator:

> "Eternity [...] is an image of god; the cosmos is an image of eternity; and the sun is an image of the cosmos. The human is an image of the sun." [25]
> ~ CORPUS HERMETICUM

> "For the sun and moon and all planets, as well as all the stars and whole chaos, are in man... [...] For man was created from heaven and earth, and is therefore like them! Consider how great and noble man was created, and what greatness must be attributed to his structure! No brain can fully encompass the structure of man's body and the extent of his virtues; he can be understood only as an image of the macrocosm, of the Great Creature. Only then does it become manifest what is in him. For what is outside is also inside; and what is not outside man is not inside. The outer and the inner are *one* thing, *one* constellation, *one* influence, *one* concordance, *one* duration... *one* fruit." [26]
> ~ PARACELSUS

But the power we have to create is not limited to the creation of a physical child. Within the human being we also find the materials of spiritual creation. From this union of male and female, not only can children be born, but also the Son within, just as the spiritual sun/Son is born from the union of these forces at the dawning of creation.

> "The seed of your body need not enter the body of woman to create life; for the power of the angel of Earth can create the life of the spiritual within, as well as the life of the body without." [27]
> ~ JESUS IN THE ESSENE GOSPEL OF PEACE

> "Within the great cosmic process, the two ch'i—Ch'ien the father and K'un the mother—blend harmoniously and give birth to all creation. Therefore, it is said that in all creation only man is also thus. Man possesses a prenatal and postnatal nature. The prenatal is the spiritual father and divine mother; the postnatal is the mundane father and mundane mother. When the mundane father and mother have intercourse, the mercury arrives and is projected into the lead. When yang bestows and yin receives, this is called "the natural course." When the natural course is followed, then the human fetus is formed and sons and daughters are born. When the spiritual father and mother have intercourse, the lead arrives and is projected into the mercury. When yin bestows and yang receives, this is called "contrary to the natural course." If carried out contrary to the natural course, the holy fetus forms and birth is given to Buddhas

and immortals. The principle of forming the holy and the human fetus is one and without distinction. The difference is simply one of following the natural course or going against it." [28]
~ TRUE TRANSMISSION OF THE GOLDEN ELIXIR BY SUN JU-CHUNG

The joining of husband and wife together in sexual union within a fully committed and loving marriage was given as a key spiritual practice (though usually in a veiled and coded way) in the ancient Religion of the Sun, and has been called Maithuna (a practice found within some Tantric traditions) in the East, the bridal chamber of the Gnostic/esoteric Christians, HeQi in Taoism, and alchemy in the Middle Ages, in which man and woman in sexual union are depicted as spiritual co-creators. Within the practice, each partner can use the forces of creation to gradually transform themselves inwardly, until reaching the spiritual level required for the Son to be born within.

Crowned as king and queen in nature, man and woman are co-creators in this seventeenth century illustration, giving birth to the divine child from out of the sexual waters/energies.

> "Great is the mystery of marriage! For without it, the world would not exist. [...] No one can know when the husband and the wife have intercourse with one another, except the two of them. Indeed, marriage in the world is a mystery. [...] If there is a hidden quality to the marriage of defilement, how much more is the undefiled marriage a true mystery! It is not fleshly, but pure. It belongs not to desire, but to the will. It belongs not to the darkness or the night, but to the day and the light. [...] It is from water and fire that the soul and the spirit came into being. It is from water and fire and light that the son of the bridal chamber (came into being). The fire is the chrism, the light is the fire. [...] 'The Holy of the Holies' is the bridal chamber." [29]
> ~ THE GOSPEL OF PHILIP

This sacred sexual practice (which only works within a fully committed and loving marriage), involves the purification of the waters, which are the sexual energies, in preparation for creation; the awakening of the sacred fiery energy called kundalini symbolized as the serpent rising up the spine in ancient India, and crowning the forehead in Egypt; the creation of spiritual bodies in higher dimensions, referred to as the wedding garments by Jesus, and as the imperishable bodies of gold by the ancient Egyptians and Hindus; and other spiritual processes which must be gone through, until someone has reached a level of spiritual preparedness and purity for the Son to be born within—referred to as "the son of the bridal chamber" in the previous quote.

> "The first integration of yin and yang is the union of seed and egg within the womb. The second integration of yin and yang is the sexual union of the mature male and female. Both of these are concerned with flesh and blood, and all that is conceived in this realm must one day disintegrate and pass away. It is only the third integration which gives birth to something immortal. In this integration, a highly evolved individual joins the subtle inner energies of yin and yang under the light of spiritual understanding. Through the practices of the Integral Way he refines his gross, heavy energy into something ethereal and light. This divine light has the capability of penetrating into the mighty ocean of spiritual energy and complete wisdom that is the Tao." [30]
> ~ LAO TZU IN HUA HU CHING

> "When one begins to apply this magic it is as if, in the middle of being, there were non-being. When in the course of time the work is completed, and beyond the body there is a body, it is as if, in the middle of non-being, there were being. Only after concentrated work of a hundred days will the light be genuine, then only will it become spirit-fire. After a hundred days there develops by itself in the midst of the light a point of the true light-pole (yang). Then suddenly there develops the seed pearl. It is as if man and woman embraced and a conception took place. Then one must be quite still and wait. The circulation of the light is the epoch of fire.
>
> In the midst of primal transformation, the radiance of the light (yang-kuang), is the determining thing. In the physical world it is the sun; in man, the eye. The radiation and dissipation of spiritual consciousness is chiefly brought about by this energy when it is directed outward (flows downward). Therefore the Way of the Golden Flower depends wholly on the backward-flowing method."[31]
> ~ THE SECRET OF THE GOLDEN FLOWER

We run on electric energy, which travels throughout the nervous system of our body. This means we are each electrically charged, and electrically charged matter creates an electromagnetic field, which is why we have a measurable electromagnetic field around our body. Feminine energies are polarized negatively and have a negative charge, while masculine energies are polarized positively and have a positive charge. This is the basis of sexual attraction, as positively and negatively charged particles are attracted to one another. When a couple unite sexually, their union creates measurable electricity and initiates an electrochemical reaction, which turns their energies into a form of inner fire.

Just as physical fire has the ability to destroy and create things, as does the spiritual fire that creates and ultimately destroys the universe, so does this inner sexual fire have the same ability to create spiritual things within us and destroy the negative aspects of ourselves—allowing us to be "born again" spiritually, and return to the source of creation, the Absolute (the Brahman of ancient India), as a "Son of the Sun" and "Son of God."

> "But as many as received him [Christ], to them gave he power to become the sons of God, even to them that believe on his name: Which were born, not of blood, nor of the will of the flesh, nor of the will of man, but of God." [32]
> ~ JOHN 1:12-13

This is not a matter of adopting or changing beliefs—for anything to be born, it must follow the same process of creation which operates on the largest of scales, right to the very smallest.

The male and female forces are what give birth to all life. At the dawn of creation, their union gave birth to the sun and the entirety of creation. This birth of the sun, on a spiritual level, is the birth of the spiritual sun—the birth of the force of the Son within.

Without understanding this process of creation and harnessing it, ancient teachings state that any spiritual practice, no matter how rigorous, is ultimately futile in creating the spiritual within.

> "This is the reason that all the sages began their work at the germinal vesicle in which outflowing [of sexual energy/orgasm] had ceased. If one does not establish this path, but sets up other things, it is of no avail. Therefore all the schools and sects which do not know that the ruling principle of consciousness and life is in this germinal vesicle, and which therefore seek it in the outer world, can accomplish nothing despite all their efforts to find it outside." [33]
> ~ THE SECRET OF THE GOLDEN FLOWER

THE BIRTH OF THE WORLD TEACHER AND SAVIOR

Christmas is not only the celebration of the birth of the Spiritual Son into a human being—it is also a celebration of the birth of the Son into the world as a great sage and teacher. Jesus, Horus, and Mithras were each referred to as a "divine savior." The title of divine savior has a dual meaning—the Son/Christ both saves the individual by entering into and transforming them spiritually, and also works to save humanity by teaching how to become a Son of the Sun through the individual that is entered into. The mission of the Son within a person, and thus in the world, is to save.

The pre-Inca and Inca creator and sun god Viracocha, who is said to have come disguised as a beggar to teach people and perform miracles.

> "For God so loved the world that he gave his one and only Son, that whoever believes in him shall not perish but have eternal life. For God did not send his Son into the world to condemn the world, but to save the world through him." [34]
> ~ JOHN 3:16-17

The aspect of each person's Being, the Son, descends into a spiritually prepared person, and is born into the symbolic cave, which is the darkness of the psyche and physical body, to join with the consciousness and raise it back up to the divine source. This is what it means to be saved and why the consciousness has been symbolized as a beautiful damsel in need of rescuing in the Religion of the Sun.

The story of a hero slaying a dragon or serpent, sometimes in order to rescue a woman, is one of the oldest surviving and most common Indo-European religious allegories—found from India to Western Europe. This same symbolism was later used in Christianity in the famous scenes of Saint George slaying the dragon, which became romanticized in medieval legends.

Saint George and the Dragon by Paolo Uccello. Saint George represents the Son who rescues the consciousness (the damsel) from the cave, which is the darkness of matter and the subconscious. The cave is also the dwelling place of the dragon, which is the embodiment of the egos. On the hill is the kingdom of heaven, which the rescued consciousness returns to.

This same story is found in the ancient Gnostic text Pistis Sophia, which records the teachings Jesus gives his disciples after his ascension. The story revolves around a divine female in distress called Pistis Sophia, who symbolizes consciousness. In the text, Jesus explains how the Son must save Pistis Sophia from the "depth of the chaos" and "the dragon of outer darkness" as, like the hapless damsel, consciousness doesn't have the power to do this itself. Only the Spiritual Son has the power to raise up consciousness, which is why the sun gods who represented the Spiritual Son were often called saviors and depicted as divine heroes:

> "It came to pass then after all this, that I [Jesus] took Pistis Sophia and led her into the thirteenth aeon, shining most exceedingly, there being no measure for the light which was about me. [...] It came to pass then, when Pistis Sophia saw her fellows, the invisibles, that she rejoiced in great joy and exulted exceedingly and desired to proclaim the wonders which I had wrought on her below in the earth of mankind, until I saved her. She came into the midst of the invisibles, and in their midst sang praises unto me, saying: 'I will give thanks unto thee, O Light, for thou art a savior; thou art a deliverer for all time. I will utter this song to the Light, for it hath saved me and saved me out of the hand of the rulers, my foes.' [...] And when I was come out of the Height, I wandered round in regions in which is no light, and I could not return to the thirteenth aeon, my dwelling-place. For there was no light in me nor power. My power was utterly weakened. And the Light saved me in all my afflictions. I sang praises

unto the Light, and it hearkened unto me, when I was constrained. It guided me in the creation of the aeons to lead me up into the thirteenth aeon, my dwelling-place. I will give thanks unto thee, O Light, that thou hast saved me, and for thy wondrous works unto the race of men. When I failed of my power, thou hast given me power; and when I failed of my light, thou didst fill me with purified light. I was in the darkness and in the shadow of the chaos, bound with the mighty fetters of the chaos, and no light was in me. For I have provoked the commandment of the Light and have transgressed, and I have made wroth the commandment of the Light, because I had gone out of my region. And when I had gone down, I failed of my light and became without light, and no one had helped me. And in my affliction I sang praises unto the Light, and it saved me out of my afflictions.'" [35]

~ PISTIS SOPHIA

The influence of the Spiritual Son within a person's psyche gradually develops as the person progresses along the path of the spiritual sun—just as the sun's influence upon the earth does from the winter to summer solstice, until eventually fully merging with the consciousness of an individual. Then he is the world teacher, a light unto the world, and the teacher of teachers.

The Indo-Iranian sun god Mithra was known as "the Mediator."[36] This is because the Son acts within a person to reconcile, return, and reconnect them with their Spiritual Father; and as the world teacher, acts as the intermediary between humanity and divinity, becoming a vital link between heaven and earth.

> "For the ancient Magi, Mithra was [...] the god of light, and as the light is borne by the air he was thought to inhabit the Middle Zone between Heaven and Hell [...] When he was identified with Shamash [the Mesopotamian god of the sun], his priests in investing him with the appellation of "intermediary" doubtless had in mind the fact that, according to the Chaldean doctrines, the sun occupied the middle place in the planetary choir. But this middle position was not exclusively a position in space; it was also invested with an important moral significance. Mithra was the "mediator" between the unapproachable and unknowable god that reigned in the ethereal spheres and the human race that struggled and suffered here below." [37]

~ THE MYSTERIES OF MITHRA BY FRANZ CUMONT

"Now the Prophet of the truth is He who always knows all things—things past as they were, things present as they are, things future as they shall be; sinless, merciful, alone entrusted with the declaration

of the truth. Read, and you shall find that those were deceived who thought that they had found the truth of themselves. For this is peculiar to the Prophet, to declare the truth, even as it is peculiar to the sun to bring the day." [38]
~ PETER IN THE CLEMENTINE HOMILIES

"This awakening you have known comes not through logic and scholarship, but from close association with a realized teacher." [39]
~ THE KATHA UPANISHAD

Many people become attached to a particular religion, denouncing others as untrue. But much of the world's spiritual knowledge sprouted from eternal spiritual truths given by those who had the Son within. Once a person who has the Son within is rejected by that religion and leaves it, the religion loses much of its vital connection with the heavens, becoming something barren and static, like an empty vessel that retains its shell but is no longer filled and renewed with the living knowledge and guidance from above.

And so the Son must come again to give spiritual truth anew through another spiritually prepared person. The aim of a true seeker is to always find the living Son to receive the direct living wisdom of the divine—cosmic, omnipresent, and beyond all dogmatism.

This divine savior is always said to come again. Local oral history recalls that Viracocha promised to one day return, and it's still believed he will reappear in times of difficulty; the same is believed of Quetzalcoatl. The ancient Indian creator and sun god Vishnu is said to incarnate in different avatars (the most famous of which are Rama and Krishna) throughout various ages.

"Whenever spirituality decays and materialism is rampant, then O Arjuna, I reincarnate Myself! To protect the righteous, to destroy the wicked and to establish the kingdom of God, I am reborn from age to age." [40]
~ KRISHNA IN THE BHAGAVAD GITA

This is the return of the Spiritual Son within an individual to teach humanity. Unfortunately however, each time the Spiritual Son comes their message eventually becomes a religion where people await the literal return of Jesus, Krishna, etc. Very often, people in these religions are then unable to recognize the Spiritual Son when he incarnates within a person, as this person may not conform to their religious ideals or expectations. And so, rather than being celebrated, someone who has the Spiritual Son within is usually rejected by the world and society, teaching living wisdom unbeknownst to and even hated by many religious believers who lack the understanding of the deeper meaning of the knowledge that formed the basis of their religion.

There are numerous men and women, most of whom are probably unknown to history, who have incarnated the Son on the path of the spiritual sun in their lifetime and taught others. However, there are others, like Jesus, who were more advanced and were born with a mission to show the path of the spiritual sun in the events of their lives.

In the legends of the Inca, Viracocha is said to have risen from Lake Titicaca (or in some sources the cave Paqariq Tampu, which means "to dawn/to be born" in the Quechua language) in order to manifest light at a time of great darkness, and is said to have then created everything.[41] According to Wikipedia, he is said to have "wandered the earth disguised as a beggar, teaching his new creations the basics of civilization, as well as working numerous miracles" (just as Jesus did, who had the Son within), and to have "wept when he saw the plight of the creatures he had created."[42]

Expressing himself through the ordinary personality of an individual, the Son brings his wisdom to share, as he has done so many times in the past among those who have incarnated him. Viracocha was said to appear as a beggar, as the Spiritual Son is born into a humble person, disguised and unable to be seen by the ordinary observer because of the rags the Spiritual Son is clothed in, which is the personality of the individual.

> "Foolish men, without an understanding of My higher nature as the Supreme Lord of all that exists, disregard Me manifested in the human body." [43]
>
> ~ KRISHNA IN THE BHAGAVAD GITA

In the Gnostic Christian text the Acts of Peter and the Twelve Apostles from the Nag Hammadi Library, Jesus disguises himself and gives pearls away to the poor of the city (the poor are those who recognize their inner poverty; the pearls are the "pearls of wisdom" and the spiritual treasures of the path), while the rich of the city reject him (those who are proud and vain). The apostles meet him as fellow "strangers" as none of them belong to worldly, mundane society.

> "A man came out wearing a cloth bound around his waist, and a gold belt girded it. Also a napkin was tied over his chest, extending over his shoulders and covering his head and his hands.
>
> I was staring at the man, because he was beautiful in his form and stature. There were four parts of his body that I saw: the soles of his feet and a part of his chest and the palms of his hands and his visage. These things I was able to see. A book cover like (those of) my books was in his left hand. A staff of styrax wood was in his right hand. His voice was resounding as he slowly spoke, crying out in the city, 'Pearls! Pearls!'

I, indeed, thought he was a man of that city. I said to him, 'My brother and my friend!' He answered me, then, saying, 'Rightly did you say, 'My brother and my friend.' What is it you seek from me?' I said to him, 'I ask you about lodging for me and the brothers also, because we are strangers here.' He said to me, 'For this reason have I myself just said, 'My brother and my friend,' because I also am a fellow stranger like you.'

And having said these things, he cried out, 'Pearls! Pearls!' The rich men of that city heard his voice. They came out of their hidden storerooms. And some were looking out from the storerooms of their houses. Others looked out from their upper windows. And they did not see (that they could gain) anything from him, because there was no pouch on his back nor bundle inside his cloth and napkin. And because of their disdain they did not even acknowledge him. He, for his part, did not reveal himself to them. They returned to their storerooms, saying, 'This man is mocking us.'

And the poor of that city heard his voice, and they came to the man who sells this pearl. They said, 'Please take the trouble to show us the pearl so that we may, then, see it with our (own) eyes. For we are the poor. And we do not have this [...] price to pay for it. But show us that we might say to our friends that we saw a pearl with our (own) eyes.' He answered, saying to them, 'If it is possible, come to my city, so that I may not only show it before your (very) eyes, but give it to you for nothing.'" 44

~ PETER IN THE ACTS OF PETER AND THE TWELVE APOSTLES

THE MEANING OF THE MOUND, CAVE, STABLES, AND PRISON WHERE THE SON IS BORN

A depiction of the birth of Jesus as a baby into a cave. Although it is unlikely the creator of this image knew of the deeper symbolism it represents, the symbols given in the teachings of Jesus have been passed on and retain their meaning nevertheless.

The winter solstice sun is "born" at the darkest time of the year. The spark of life ignites within the darkness of the womb and the earth. All creation takes place from out of darkness, as it did in the most famous ancient creation stories in the world, like that found in Egyptian mythology, and in the verses of the ancient Vedic text the Rig Veda.

This was symbolized in the life of a number of sun gods who were said to have been born in caves at the winter solstice, as a cave can symbolize the dark womb from which creation emerges.

Jesus was said to have been born in a cave in the Gospel of James. Mithras was symbolized as being born from a rock representing the world cave. Viracocha was also said to have been born in a cave to bring light into the darkness.

At the Dinas Mountain in Wales there is a nearby cave that goes by a Welsh name meaning "Voice of God" where the Druids enacted the birth of their solar god Hu Gadarn (as the Mabyn Taliesin/baby sun) at the winter solstice. The Druid priest acting as Hu gave a loud musical shout from within the cave to which the gathered crowds would reply "Ein Hoes," meaning "Our Life!" [45]

At the ancient Neolithic site of Newgrange in Ireland, the winter solstice sunlight enters an otherwise dark giant mound at sunrise. The Gaelic/Irish name for Newgrange is Brú na Bóinne, which can be translated as "the womb of the goddess Boann" or "womb of the white cow/milky way," as the Celtic goddess Boann, who was said to have lived at the site, was also known as the white cow and was associated with the milky way.[46] Researchers have noted that the design of Newgrange resembles a womb. In Irish mythology Boann conceived a son by the god Dagda, owner of the mound. In another the sun god Lugh conceived the hero Cúchulainn by visiting his mother in a dream as she slept at the mound.[47] Clearly this mound was associated with the birth of a son. The ray of dawning light illuminates the chamber, which is in the shape of a cross—the cross symbolizing the union of masculine and feminine, of phallus and uterus, which gives birth to all creation and the Son. Here the cross is associated with the Spiritual Son on the winter solstice, thousands of years before Jesus. The Son is born as the sun into the mound, which acts as the womb. Also inside the chamber are found spiral designs, showing the spiraling nature of creation.

The ancient passage mounds of Europe had the same design—a round mound of earth containing an inner chamber often aligned to the winter solstice sunrise (or the equinoxes or summer solstice). The oldest passage mound in Europe, which is aligned nearly exactly to the winter solstice, is located at the ancient site of Carnac in France, and is dated to 4,700 BC. The inner chambers of a number of passage mounds in the British Isles, including Newgrange, are laid out in cruciform shape. The ancient temples of Malta, some of which are aligned to the solstices and equinoxes, share a similar design (though their chambers were larger and rounded, believed to resemble the figure of the Mother Goddess).[48]

My wife realized the design of these mounds resembles the symbol of the labyrinth of Crete, used also by the Hopi of the North American southwest, as mentioned in the previous chapter. Remarkably, the Hopi have preserved its meaning, which can help unlock the meaning of the ancient mounds of Europe.

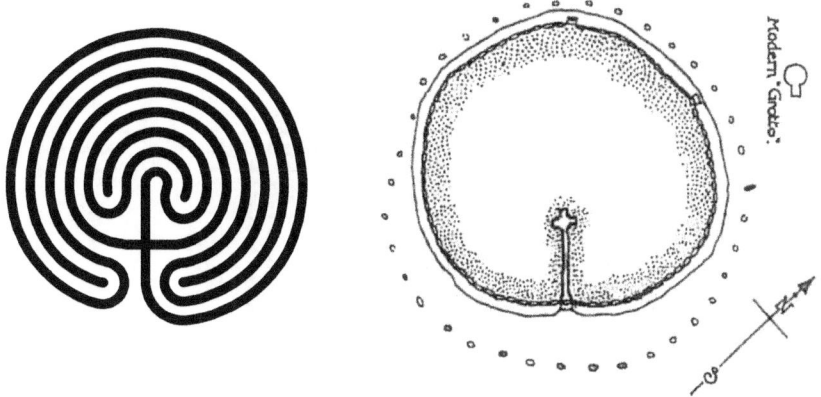

Left: Labyrinth symbol found in ancient Crete, and in the southwest of North America. Right: Plan of Newgrange, looking from above, showing its cruciform chamber. Like the labyrinth, it is rounded, and its entrance passage is laid out in the form of a cross.

Model of the Mnajdra temples in Malta, one of which aligns to the solstices and equinoxes. They used to be covered in earth like the mounds of Europe, and share a similar design.

In Hopi tradition, the labyrinth symbol is called "tapuat" and symbolizes the womb of the Mother Earth. The inside lines represent the fetal membranes, which enfold the unborn child. The line that leads from within the labyrinth to the outside, and which is straight for part of its length, represents the birth canal. The point at which the other line intersects it to form a cross symbolizes the Father Sun, who gives life.[49] Thus, it can be inferred that the cruciform chambered mounds of the British Isles, and possibly the passage mounds of Europe, were aligned to allow the light of the Father Sun to enter the chamber within the womb of Mother Earth, particularly at the solstices, to conceive the Divine Son.

Left: Callanish Stones. Right: Diagram showing the layout of the Callanish Stones from above. They form an approximate Celtic cross.

The standing stones of Callanish in Scotland, which date to between 2,900-2,600 BC, are laid out in the approximate shape of a Celtic cross, with its longest arm flanked by stones on either side creating an avenue. A legend states "that early on midsummer morning an entity known as the 'Shining One' walks the length of the avenue."[50] There is a phallic shaped stone near the center of its stone circle; similar phallic stones were placed within the chambers of passage mounds or near them where they sometimes received the solstice or equinox sunlight, likely symbolizing the Shining One or Father Sun. Phallic/masculine and rounded/feminine shaped stones have also been found within and near passage mounds like Newgrange, and again indicate the meaning of the mound as the union of Father and Mother, who give birth to a child.

The labyrinth/tapuat symbol was also known among other indigenous peoples of the Americas—to the Guna people of Panama the cross inside it represents the tree of life.[51] The cross and tree of life essentially symbolize the same thing, which is the union of masculine and feminine, of Father and Mother, and I discuss their meaning in chapter 6.

Passage mounds in the British Isles with cruciform chambers were also aligned to the equinox sunrise, where they were not connected to birth, as those aligned to the winter solstice are, but to rebirth and resurrection, as I explain in the next chapter.

In the nativity scene of the Gospels, Jesus is also said to be born at midnight in a stable among animals. The stable symbolizes the physical body. Midnight at the winter solstice is the darkest time of the year, representing the darkness of the subconscious. The animals represent the egos that inhabit the body and subconscious, which are animalistic in nature, such as anger, pride, envy, hatred, etc. This illustrates that, although someone has reached a certain spiritual level for the Son to be born within, they are still in darkness and have many egos. The Son is born into this darkness, and works within to destroy these egos and spiritually transform someone as he grows. This is why the Son was often depicted as a hero that battled evil and monstrous animals, as in the Greek legends of Hercules.

Mithras being born from a rock holding a flaming torch and dagger.

The Roman god Mithras, who was based on the ancient Indo-Iranian sun god Mithra, was said to have been born from a rock on December 25, three days following the winter solstice (the same day celebrated as Jesus' birthday).[52] The rock is said to represent the earth and world cave.[53] He is depicted as emerging holding a flaming torch and dagger. The torch represents the light and purification by fire that he brings, and the dagger is the one he uses to symbolically slay a bull, representing the old and possibly the ego (like the buffalo demon of Hinduism, and the Minotaur of the Minoans), that must make way so that life can spring forth from death. Mithras later ascends to heaven, where he is given a solar crown and takes his place beside the sun.[54]

Krishna was born at midnight into a prison,[55] which symbolizes the birth of the Son into the darkness of the physical body and psyche, which to the divine is likened to a prison because of its constraints and material nature.

At a pyramid of Chichen Itza in Mexico, the rising winter solstice sun appears to ascend the nine terraces of the pyramid before shining momentarily at the temple atop the pyramid's peak.[56] This illustrates the birth of the sun/Son, which appears from the lowest point, the womb of the earth, and rises through the nine terraces, which symbolize the nine layers of the underworld, the nine heavens, and nine initiations, which the Spiritual Son goes through before reaching resurrection.

Glastonbury Tor with its ancient clearly man-made terraces topped by a more modern Christian tower.

Similarly, at the site of Glastonbury Tor in England, on the winter solstice the sun appears at the base of the mound, rises up its terraces, and clips the pinnacle of the tower[57]—symbolizing the birth of the Spiritual Son from within the earth and his rising toward resurrection. The terraces form a continuous path from the base of the mound to reach its summit and resemble the winding lines of the labyrinth symbol, connecting this ancient site to the passage mounds of Europe and the religious beliefs of their builders.[58]

At the winter solstice—in the womb of the earth, in the midst of darkness and chaos—the Spiritual Son is born.

THE BABY SUN

The Son is born as a baby at the winter solstice as all things that are born must start small and grow. The winter sun appears small and weak as a baby, and so Horus and Jesus were depicted at this time as babies nursed by their mothers.

At the winter solstice the Druids would gather in Wales to watch the sun rise over the sacred mountain of Mynydd Dinas, and believed the sun represented the birth of a divine baby Son who grew as the year progressed toward the summer solstice.[59]

This mirrors the birth of the spiritual within, because just as a baby is born as something that feels and perceives but is not able to do much, the birth of the Son within someone brings a new feeling and way of perceiving, but is yet to develop.

In reality, the actual physical sun at the winter solstice is no different to the sun at any other time—instead it's our orientation to it on Earth that changes. At winter, the sun radiates faintly at a distance through the dark gloom of winter, just as the Spiritual Son does through the darkness of one's subconscious and egos. The Son is born as a baby, and its influence within the psyche begins weakly—this influence grows just as a child does, and as the darkness of the egos is destroyed.

Although the light is born at the winter solstice, giving hope, it is still born into the peak of darkness and has yet to grow.

WHY CHRISTMAS IS CELEBRATED THREE DAYS AFTER THE WINTER SOLSTICE

The word solstice literally means "sun stands still." After the winter solstice, the sun for the first time will appear to "increase" as the duration of sunlight will gradually lengthen each day and the sun will ascend in its position in the sky. However, for three days the sun does not visibly appear to ascend, thus looking as though it's "standing still" in its path.

Interestingly, the birth of Jesus, celebrated as Christmas, is celebrated not on the date of the winter solstice itself (which is around December 22 in the Northern Hemisphere), but only once the three days of standstill have passed and the sun begins to visibly ascend (which usually occurs on December 25).

Not only Jesus, but a number of other solar deities were celebrated as having been born on December 25.

There is a spiritual significance to this. The birth of the spiritual sun on the winter solstice is the birth of the cosmic Son at the dawning of creation. From the Son comes all of creation, just as in ancient India the golden womb created from the male and female forces at the dawning of creation gives birth to Brahma, the creator god, and the entire universe called Brahm-anda.

In the Vedas of ancient India, the supreme creator and sun god Vishnu was known as the triple-strider (as Tri-vikrama and as Uru-krama). It is said that he created the universe, making the dwelling of humanity possible, by taking three steps—one encompassing the earth, the other the air, and the third the heights of heaven, which is his supreme abode.[60] This illustrates how creation takes place in three steps, and the number three is therefore also found in the process of creating the spiritual within.

Temple relief of Vishnu with his legs outstretched as he takes three steps in order to traverse the realms of creation.

The number three is a number of completion and crystallization—of bringing things into realization. In rituals it is common that phrases are said three times as an act of crystalizing them.

There are three primary forces in creation, which are symbolized as Father, Mother, and Son.

The three Great Pyramids of Egypt.

On the path of the spiritual sun, there are three series of nine initiations, and then three steps to merge oneself with the trinity of creation—each time repeating the same events symbolized by the solstices and equinoxes, but at progressively higher levels. These initiations and steps are themselves grouped into three major stages on this path, which have been called three mountains. They were represented in ancient Egypt as the three Great Pyramids that align to the three stars in the constellation Orion called Orion's Belt. The Egyptians associated the constellation Orion with the god Osiris, whose life represented the path of the spiritual sun.

This act of going through things three times, each time at a higher level/octave, crystallizes the spiritual within, and allows us to reach from the lower realms of matter where we are, to the brilliant regions of light, like steps that allow our legs to traverse a great height.

This underlying principle of three correlates with the three days of standstill at each extreme of the year—both at winter and summer solstice, as the cycle of the sun pauses in its symbolic creation from the source at the winter solstice, and return back to it at the summer solstice.

THE THREE STEPS INTO THE SEVEN DIMENSIONS

The three primary forces of Mother, Father, and Son, which are negative, positive, and neutral, give rise to all of creation.

> "Tao produced Unity; Unity produced Duality; Duality produced Trinity; and Trinity produced all existing objects." [61]
> ~ THE TAO TE CHING

> "[...] among the things that were created the monad is first, the dyad follows it, and the triad [...]. This is the pattern <among the> immortals." [62]
>
> ~ EUGNOSTOS THE BLESSED

But creation, which is in three forces, needs organization, and so it unfolds through the number seven, which is the number through which creation is organized, and is found in the seven colors of the spectrum, and the seven notes of the musical scale. On the path of the spiritual sun there are seven serpents of light to raise in the seven solar bodies. These bodies correspond to the seven dimensions, and representations of them can be found in ancient Egypt, India, and Easter Island.

As we are multidimensional, in order to incarnate and be born into a person, the Son (like Vishnu) is said to take three steps through the seven dimensions, entering into the body and psyche of a person as he does.

Our consciousness resides in a higher dimension, which is where the Son is first born from the Mother and Father, and is symbolized by the "birth" of the sun on the winter solstice.

The Son firstly enters the plane of our mind and thoughts (the mental plane of the fifth dimension), secondly he enters the plane of our emotions (the astral plane of the fifth dimension), and finally is able to be present in the four dimensions of space-time where we are awake in the physical body.

In the following excerpt, Jesus enters a realm of darkness three times. This realm of darkness is the psyche and body, which are also described as a "chaos" and "prison." This is because within each person's psyche exists their own inner underworld, which is inhabited by their egos and which the higher parts of their Being, such as the Son, bring spiritual light to and destroy.

> "And I went into the realm of darkness and I endured till I entered the middle of the prison. And the foundations of chaos shook. And I hid myself from them because of their wickedness, and they did not recognize me.
>
> Again I returned for the second time, and I went about. I came forth from those who belong to the light, which is I, the remembrance of the Pronoia. I entered into the midst of darkness and the inside of Hades, since I was seeking (to accomplish) my task. And the foundations of chaos shook, that they might fall down upon those who are in chaos and might destroy them. And again I ran up to my root of light, lest they be destroyed before the time.
>
> Still for a third time I went—I am the light which exists in the light, I am the remembrance of the Pronoia—that I might enter into the midst of darkness and the inside of Hades. And I filled my face with the light of the completion of their aeon. And I entered into the

midst of their prison, which is the prison of the body. And I said, 'He who hears, let him get up from the deep sleep.' And he wept and shed tears. Bitter tears he wiped from himself and he said, 'Who is it that calls my name, and from where has this hope come to me, while I am in the chains of the prison?' And I said, 'I am the Pronoia of the pure light; I am the thinking of the virginal Spirit, who raised you up to the honored place. Arise and remember that it is you who hearkened, and follow your root, which is I, the merciful one, and guard yourself against the angels of poverty and the demons of chaos and all those who ensnare you, and beware of the deep sleep and the enclosure of the inside of Hades.

And I raised him up, and sealed him in the light of the water with five seals, in order that death might not have power over him from this time on." [63]

~ JESUS IN THE APOCRYPHON OF JOHN

The deep sleep, mentioned in the excerpt above, is the psychological sleep of the subconscious.

In each of the three steps, the Son enters into the inferior dimensional regions of the mind and inner structure of the human being. Upon entering the physical body on the third step, the Son is "born" within. This is the real Christmas—a personal, sacred, and spiritual event, which is celebrated three days following the winter solstice on Christmas day.

THE SYMBOLS OF THE NATIVITY

The birth of Jesus symbolizes the
manifestation of the Spiritual Son within.

Billions of people are familiar with the events of Jesus' birth, called the nativity. Few realize, however, that each has a deeper spiritual significance. They relate specifically to a stage on the path of the sun when the Son is born within a person and the preparation leading up to it. Although we can't be sure of what the actual events at Jesus' birth were, the account of it in the Gospels is full of symbolism.

For example, Jesus was born in a cave/stables where animals were kept, which represents the Son's birth in an individual among their animal egos. The Son comes into a person in whom the animal egos live. He works within to destroy those egos. The cave represents the womb of creation, but because of the multidimensional structure of creation, the cave exists at the center of the inferior regions inside the earth, and also within our body and psyche in other dimensions.

He was born as a baby, and helpless, because the Son when incarnated is small and needs to grow to maturity.

He was wrapped in basic clothes, as the inner bodies that hold him are in a basic state. These bodies will be developed to an even higher frequency of energy as he grows and develops. He was placed in a manger, which is an animal's feeding trough, as this symbolizes the psyche of the person he comes into, which the animalistic egos are feeding from.

At the time of his birth there were shepherds nearby watching their flock. They represent the walkers of the path who are also teachers; their flock is the public. An angel of the Lord appeared to them and the glory of the Lord shone around them and announced the birth of Jesus. A heavenly host appeared with the angel saying, "Peace on Earth to people He favors." The people whom he favors are the initiates who are prepared inwardly to receive him. They visited him just after his birth, meaning that they achieve the birth of the Son within themselves.

The star that shone over the newborn Jesus represents the higher Being and its guidance. It is the light of each one's own Being they aspire to attain to one day.

A number of Magi visited the baby Jesus (traditionally believed to have been three). The term magi denotes someone who is a Zoroastrian priest[64] (as mentioned in the first chapter, Zoroastrianism is an ancient Indo-Iranian religion derived from the ancient Religion of the Sun); these were known as great astrologers, which is why they follow the star that shone over Jesus to find him. They were said to have come "from the rising of the sun," which is the east. The rising sun symbolizes the birth of the Son. They represent those who are on the path of the spiritual sun, worshiping the baby Jesus, showing that they

The Magi visit Jesus.

recognized the Son. Through the sacrifice of their journey they brought gifts fit for a king, demonstrating their understanding of the Son as a divine king to be honored.

THE CREATION OF THE FOUR

The number four is related to the process of creation, which is connected to the time of the winter solstice.

The ancient Maya sometimes depicted the sun as "Ah Kin," which is "He of the Sun." He is represented as a man carrying the glyph of the sun, which is a flower with four petals.

> "Thereupon the heart of the flower came forth to set itself in motion. Four-fold was the plate of the flower, and Ah Kin Xocbiltun was set in the center." [65]
> ~ THE BOOK OF CHILAM BALAM OF CHUMAYEL

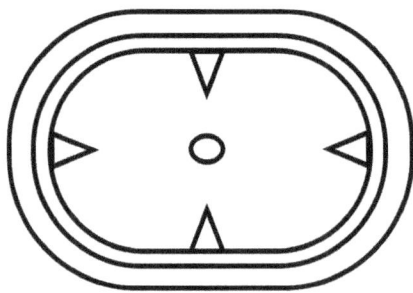

The Mayan glyph/sign for the sun as a flower with four petals.

Likewise, ancient Vedic texts describe the sun as a lotus flower with four petals.

> "Now that which dwelling within the lotus of the heart devours food, the same, dwelling as the solar fire in the sky, being called Time, and invisible, devours all beings as its food. [...] the four quarters and the four intermediate points are its petals." [66]
> ~ THE MAITRĀYAṆĪYA UPANISHAD

The ancient Maya believed that the great Father and Mother created the world with four sides. The Egyptian god Horus was said to have four solar sons who came forth from a lotus blossom and were associated with creation. Similarly, the Hindu creator god Brahma was born from a lotus and was depicted with four faces.

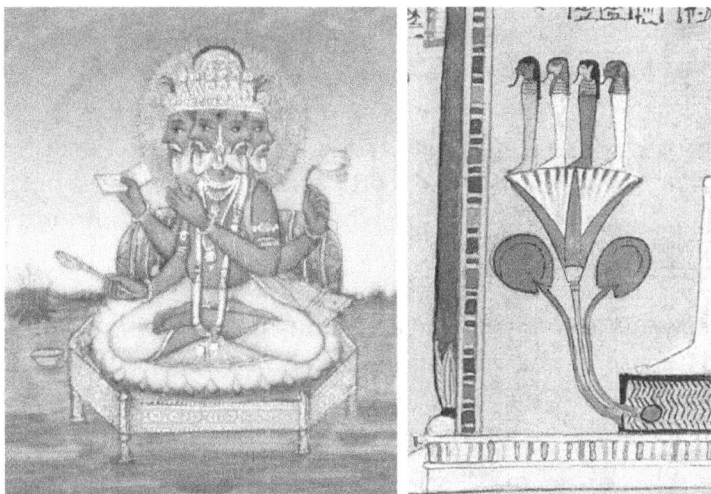

Left: The Hindu creator god Brahma with four faces, seated on the lotus he emerged from. Right: The four solar sons of the ancient Egyptian god Horus who helped make creation, standing upon the lotus they emerged from. The similarities between these two mythologies reveals there is a connection between them.

Four forms the foundation of life and encompasses the bounds of creation. It is found in the four cardinal directions; the four points of the cross of the year, which are the solstices and equinoxes; the four elements; the dimensions of our physical world which are length, width, height, and time; and the four material bodies each person has: physical, vital, astral, and mental.

The birth of stars, which then produce the rest of matter, parallels the birth of the Son/sun who brings the light of the first day, and proceeds to make the rest of creation. In Hindu accounts of creation, the sun god splits everything into three and stretches it out to make both earth and sky; this is like the expansion of three-dimensional space, as well as the fourth dimension, which is time, and is needed for beings to be able to become conscious of their existence. Within our three-dimensional world, we find life manifest in form and substance in the flow of time. Thus, in creation, the Son who is one of the three forces of creation establishes the four, creating the space-time continuum in which space and time are joined together to create the four-dimensional object we all live within, which is the foundation of life and is found in the movement of the sun, forming a cross of four arms and the rotating swastika.

While providing opportunity for learning and awakening, matter also forms a prison that restricts consciousness, as the number four establishes bounds and limits, just like the four walls of a room. While the Son is born into the prison of the material world, he comes to free us from it—liberating a person eventually into the realms of the spirit where they attain immortality beyond the constraints of time and matter.

THE MEANING OF THE WINTER SOLSTICE IN DAILY LIFE

We have the wonderful ability to create in many aspects of our lives; being able to create things that never existed before, sometimes even in times of extreme darkness and difficulty. Additionally, the good and the spiritual may be born into darkness in the world and within ourselves, but they have the potential to grow and develop when given the right opportunities and conditions.

The winter solstice expresses the principles of spiritual birth and creation. Alchemically, it is a principle that can be put into practice between every husband and wife, as they have the ability to unite essentially the same masculine and feminine energies that are found in creation, and that gave rise to it. This practice of creating—of giving birth to spiritual things within—is another of the principles/practices that leads one along the path of the spiritual sun.

CHILDREN OF THE SUN

The winter solstice symbolizes the principle of spiritual birth, which, just as it is found in the universe, so too is it found within us as a microcosm of creation.

Each person can realize their enormous spiritual potential like a seed that lies dormant within the dark womb of the earth.

The dark half of the year and the chaotic forces of winter represent the darkness of the human body and psyche, and the underworld of the subconscious. Like the "newborn" winter solstice sun, the Son brings spiritual light and life to the darkness of our material existence, eventually returning us to the divinity of our own higher nature.

This knowledge is written in the stars, and in the universe. Celebrating the winter solstice offers us the time to reflect on the greatest mysteries of all—of where we came from, why we are here, and how we can attain the truly spiritual—for those who wish to be "born again" as sons of the sun.

Spring Equinox
Resurrection

CHAPTER FOUR

The Spiritual Meaning of the Spring Equinox

The spring equinox (also known as the vernal equinox) is the time in the earth's annual cycle around the sun in which day and night are equal in length, before the days finally become longer than the nights after the dominance of darkness during winter, and life springs forth from death. Its deeper spiritual significance reveals the mysteries of spiritual resurrection.

It is the time when many sun gods resurrected. In Christianity, the spring equinox is the time of the Passion, crucifixion, and resurrection of Jesus. Likewise, the ancient Egyptians celebrated it as the time when the god Osiris resurrected, the Thracians celebrated the resurrection of their god Orpheus, the Greeks celebrated the resurrection of Dionysus, and the Maya celebrated the resurrection of Hun Hunahpu. The Great Sphinx of Giza in Egypt gazes precisely at the rising of the spring equinox sun as a symbol of resurrection. The temple of Angkor Wat in Cambodia aligns to the spring equinox, and depicts the scene of the Churning of the Milky Ocean—the great struggle between the forces of light and darkness that takes place before the Vedic god Indra can return to heaven.

Around the world, the spring equinox is a time of great confrontation between light and darkness, in the death and resurrection of the central deities of sacred teachings. It symbolizes a stage on the path of the spiritual sun, where the struggle between darkness and light creates the opposition needed to attain immortality. This is symbolized by the dark half of the year on one side of the spring equinox sun, and the light half of the year on the other.

THE CHURNING OF THE MILKY OCEAN

The equinox is the point of balance, upon which everything pivots in its motion, in the universe, in the cycles of the seasons, and within ourselves. On one side of the equinox is the dark half of the year, and on the other the light half, representing the duality of darkness (death, descent, and decay) and light (birth, ascent, and life). The dynamic fluctuation between these forces gives motion to all cycles in the universe, and is likewise found on the path of the spiritual sun. This is why Jesus and Osiris faced their greatest confrontation with darkness to attain the light at the equinox.

Painting of the Hindu story called the Churning of the Milky Ocean.

This principle is illustrated at the temple of Angkor Wat in Cambodia, which aligns to the spring equinox. It portrays the ancient sacred Hindu teaching from the epic called the Mahabharata of the Churning of the Milky Ocean in a giant representation on its walls, and in the design of its temple complex which incorporates the sun and the stars as celestial counterparts of the story. In the story, various cosmic and spiritual forces are personified using symbols. Understanding the symbolic meaning of this story reveals much about the meaning of the spring equinox.

In the story, the asuras (demons) and devas (gods) are in a tug of war against each other. They each hold one end of a giant serpent that is wrapped around the sacred world mountain called Mount Meru (specifically its spur Mount Mandara), representing the axis of the earth at the North Pole. This mountain is balanced on a turtle, which represents the earth, swimming through the great milky ocean of the cosmos—and thus depicts the earth cycling through the year, the constellations, and the Milky Way. As the demons (the dark half of nature's cycles) and gods (the light half) pull back and forth, they rotate the mountain (the North Pole) which churns the milky ocean below (which is the view of the sun and stars from Earth).

The central segment of the mural of the Churning of the Milky Ocean at Angkor Wat. Vishnu is the large central figure. Above him is Indra, below him the turtle in the ocean, and on either side the demons and gods pulling.

In the story, this churning produces Amrita, the nectar of immortality, which is eventually consumed by the devas and allows the god Indra to return to his abode as the King of Heaven—who in this mural appears above in the sky.

On the spring equinox, the sun rises to crown the pinnacle of the main tower of Angkor Wat, representing Indra as the sun returning to his abode as the King of Heaven. In Hinduism, Mount Meru is the location of heaven as the home of the gods, and is said to be located at the North Pole, which is why Indra as the sun appearing at its peak signals his return to heaven. The Hindus, ancient Egyptians, and Druids all viewed the regions of the sky around the North/Pole Star as the location of heaven and as the place of the fixed and therefore "eternal" region of the stars, as they never set below the horizon.

Angkor Wat and a number of surrounding temples are laid out in the positions of the stars in the constellation Draco, which is depicted as a dragon or serpent. The constellation of Draco appears in the region of the circumpolar stars, where it literally wraps around the center of the circle that the North Pole traces through the sky in its processional cycle. The constellation of Draco is therefore the celestial depiction of the great serpent of the story, wrapped around the tower of Angkor Wat as the North Pole, with the stars that make its constellation mirrored in the temples on the ground.

The rising spring equinox sun crowning the main tower of the ancient temple complex of Angkor Wat in Cambodia.

Incredibly, as at other related ancient sites, we find the same practice of mirroring and incorporating the cosmos into sacred sites, the use of advanced astronomical observations, and the knowledge of spiritual symbols and principles.

The story of the Churning of the Milky Ocean encodes a principle that underlies all cycles in the cosmos, which is why extensive research at Angkor Wat has uncovered numerous encoded numbers related to the annual cycle of the sun, the precession of Earth through the constellations, and the huge epochs of time known as Yugas in Hinduism.

THE CYCLE OF THE SUN

Scholar of South-East Asian studies, Eleanor Mannikka, has researched the numbers encoded into the design of Angkor Wat, including those found in the mural of the Churning of the Milky Ocean. She discovered that the mural encodes the numbers of the annual cycle of the sun:

> "In the bas-reliefs at Angkor Wat, the position of the churning pivot would correspond to the position of the spring equinox. The 91 asuras in the south represent the 91 days from equinox to winter solstice, and the 88 northern devas represent the 88 days from equinox to summer solstice. In fact, there are either 88 or 89 devas

in the scene; 89 is the Deva atop mount Mandara and is counted with the others. There are 88 or 89 days from the spring equinox, counted from the first day of the new year, to the summer solstice. In Cambodia, the spring lasted for 3 or 4 days [...]. Mount Mandara as the churning pivot would symbolize the 3 or 4 days of the equinox period, the northernmost Deva would represent the summer solstice day, and the southernmost asura would correspond with the winter solstice day. In other words, the scene is a calendar. It positions the two solstice days at the extreme north and south, and counts the days between them [...]."[1]

~ ELEANOR MANNIKKA, ANGKOR WAT: TIME, SPACE, AND KINGSHIP

The design of the mural also depicts greater cosmic cycles which Earth progresses through, as it encodes some of the numbers involved in the precession of the equinoxes along Earth's ecliptic around the sun, which takes approximately twenty-six thousand years to complete. As in the annual cycle of the sun, in this cycle the equinox is also the point of rotation.

The Churning of the Milky Ocean scene also encodes the number 108, as each side occupied by the asuras and devas measures 54 cubits, which added together is a total of 108 cubits. In other parts of the complex there are stone statues of the scene, with 54 asuras and 54 devas.

The number 108 is a mysterious number, which is considered sacred in Buddhism and Hinduism. The 108 beads of Buddha's necklace used in meditation practices, where someone slowly passes each bead through their fingers, is sometimes said to represent the cycle of the sun from summer to winter solstice. By pausing at the end of the necklace before changing direction, the practice symbolizes the period where the sun stands still at the solstice, before reversing its direction.[2]

Hindus also divide the ecliptic of the sun, which is the great circle representing the path of the sun through the sky each year, into 27 sections of 4 parts, making a total of 108 steps the sun takes in its journey. And while this may seem arbitrary, the diameter of the sun is approximately 108 times that of the earth, and the average distance from the sun to the earth is 108 times the sun's diameter. There are other occurrences of the number 108 in the cosmos and its cycles, too numerous to detail here.

What is clear is that the site of Angkor Wat was designed to illustrate the principle underlying the cosmic cycles found in the design of the universe.

DARKNESS AND LIGHT IN THE GREATER CYCLES OF LIFE

Consciousness also progresses through cycles, just as the earth does, with stages of light and ascent (like the waxing of the sun from winter solstice to summer solstice), as well as darkness and descent (like the waning of the sun from summer solstice to winter solstice). These cycles are first known to have been explained in Hindu literature and were later illustrated by Buddha as the Wheel of Life, which shows consciousness reincarnating over different lifetimes through periods of light and evolution, as well as darkness and devolution. Jesus also described this cycle of reincarnation, referring to it as a circuit.

> "Strive thereafter that ye may receive the mysteries of the Light in this time of affliction and enter into the Light-kingdom. Join not one day to another, or one circuit to another, hoping that ye may succeed in receiving the mysteries if ye come into the world in another circuit." [3]
> ~ JESUS IN PISTIS SOPHIA

This same rotation is found in the cycles known as Yugas, which were also encoded in the temple of Angkor Wat, in which human civilization goes through periods of spirituality and progress, as well as decline and degeneration.

A painting of the Wheel of Life in the Sera Monastery of Tibet. Notice the light and dark halves of the middle of the wheel, through which life rotates.

THE STRUGGLE BETWEEN DARKNESS AND LIGHT

This pulling back and forth between light and darkness symbolizes an underpinning principle in creation found in the cycles of cosmic time and human life. It reveals the role of darkness and light in creating movement through their struggle and opposition, and likewise shows the role of darkness and light within ourselves and our lives.

This same struggle between the forces of good and evil takes place within the world. In life, one is either taking part in this struggle or they are simply the unconscious victims of it. If one is in the struggle, they are either pulling for light or for darkness. Those who do neither, who do not participate, and do not struggle against darkness, are like the creatures of the ocean of existence that become unconsciously churned around by forces they are completely unaware of.

THE TREASURES

In the Churning of the Milky Ocean, the struggle between darkness and light causes multiple spiritual treasures to emerge from the ocean, a poison that has the power to destroy the universe, and finally Amrita—the nectar of immortality. Without the opposition that darkness brings there would be no movement and no struggle, and it is from the struggle that the spiritual treasures are produced. The spiritual treasures symbolize the spiritual faculties and virtues which someone gains through the struggle against evil within themselves and the world.

THE POISON

Shiva at the top of the Churning of the Milky Ocean, swallowing the poison. Beneath him various treasures emerge from the ocean.

The poison that the churning produces is called Kalakuta—it is so terrible that it threatens to destroy creation. Before the nectar can be recovered in the story, this terrible poison must firstly be dealt with.

The opposition found in life not only brings out the best in people, but also the very worst, and thus opposition also creates poison.

As this is a key principle, it works on many levels. For example, poison emerges in society as the negative actions and psychological reactions of people, in the practice of sexual alchemy as lustful desire, and within the individual as the responses of their many egos and the harmful actions that they cause them to take.

The poison within, all the hatred, violence, greed, etc., is brought to the surface from the struggle, both within the individual's psyche and externally in the world.

As terrible as the poison is, however, its extraction is of great benefit, as the act of churning separates the poison from the nectar. The ocean that is churned is life, the human energies, the psyche, humanity, and all of creation; to have the poison extracted and separated from the nectar in all these things is of great value, as it allows a process of purification to take place. On the path of the spiritual sun, one must constantly struggle to purify oneself—to remove what is inferior and cultivate what is superior—and it is the struggle that opposition produces which allows this to happen.

As a universal principle, the separation of the poison from the nectar also effectively takes place among groups of people. When the events of life are churned, the nature of people becomes apparent and those who prefer evil and the ego are revealed—this "churning" can uncover negative people within groups, organizations, and projects of all kinds, who would have otherwise continued influencing things for the worse unnoticed.

A person walking the path of the spiritual sun has to face what is within the depths of their subconscious. When the psyche is churned by the agitation created by opposition, they get to see what is really within them: all the egos that were previously hidden beneath the surface of the ocean (the psyche and subconscious), but which can now be seen, understood, and removed.

THE NECTAR

Finally the nectar, the positive results of the struggle, emerges. Out of opposition comes the nectar of knowledge, understanding, wisdom, information, right action, good events, and what is of value in life to those who are working for greater consciousness.

This struggle to acquire the nectar shows the important role that darkness plays in the awakening of the individual. It is in the opposition to darkness that one is tested, one develops strength, self-knowledge, will, wisdom, and many other qualities, and why before Jesus and Osiris resurrect and attain eternal life at the spring equinox, they must firstly face darkness in their betrayal and death.

THE NECESSITY OF DARKNESS

The forces of darkness, evil, death, and decay are found throughout all of creation, in our lives, and within ourselves, and so are the forces of light, goodness, birth, and growth. All form that we see is made perceptible through the combination of both light and shadow—if there were only darkness, or only light, we could not see. Dark and light both form a necessary part of creation, and also a necessary part of the path of the spiritual sun.

The work to awaken consciousness is a fight to overcome the darkness within ourselves, both in our own subconscious and in the events we face in the world, so that the light of the spirit increases within us. This great struggle was depicted in the life of Jesus, Osiris, and many others at the time of the spring equinox—symbolic of the battle between light and darkness.

Numerous teachings and philosophies today, however, wish to focus only on the positive and the "feel good." Darkness and evil are either ignored, or worse, embraced. When what "feels good" is used as the measure for what is spiritual, then there is a tendency to avoid the truth whenever it is uncomfortable or challenging to face. Thus, things like hell, which have been taught about in many ancient sacred teachings, are virtually a subject of taboo. Many religions on the other hand, have turned what were esoteric teachings intended for individuals to use to attain the divine, into idols of worship, dogma, and belief.

Between the spiritual merchants of today and the world's religions, the understanding of the processes involved in spiritual awakening is virtually lost. Reuniting with divinity is not done as some today would suggest—simply by realizing it. Nor is it done simply through holding a belief at the time of death, as many religions teach. The spirit within, which gives eternal life, is reached by those who are prepared to go through great trials, tests, and suffering—to give up all earthly pleasures, riches, fame, etc., for the treasures of the spirit, which are everlasting. This is demonstrated in the teachings of betrayal, death, and resurrection found in the Religion of the Sun.

THE TRAPS

In order for the betrayal and death to occur, and thus resurrection, a series of traps are laid to ensnare the one walking the path of the spiritual sun. The traps are set in multiple circumstances in the person's life and come at no fault of their own to ensure the necessary events in their life will unfold—these traps are set by divine beings, who move the circumstances and people in their life for them to be tested.

> "Keeping a close watch on him, they [the Pharisees] sent spies, who pretended to be sincere. They hoped to catch Jesus in something he

said, so that they might hand him over to the power and authority of the governor." [4]

~ LUKE 20:20

"Then the Pharisees went out and laid plans to trap him [Jesus] in his words." [5]

~ MATTHEW 22:15

Crowds take up rocks to stone Jesus.

In the life of Jesus, the religious authorities (the Pharisees) conspire to trap Jesus from early on, and he is betrayed through deceit. The Mayan Lords of Xibalba (of death and darkness) kill Hun Hunahpu using cunning and deceit. Osiris' jealous brother, Seth, makes a coffin and tricks Osiris into lying in it to see if he will fit, then once Osiris is inside seals it shut with molten metal so Osiris can't get out. The god Loki uses deception to kill the Germanic god of the sun Baldr. In the Hindu story of the Churning of the Milky Ocean, the demons steal the elixir of immortality using deceit.

The force of the Son is love. It comes into the world through a spiritually prepared person, and each time it does, its antithesis, hatred, rises to meet it. Inevitably, the one who has the Son within has to face the hatred and evil of the world.

> "[Jesus said] This is the verdict: Light has come into the world, but people loved darkness instead of light because their deeds were evil. Everyone who does evil hates the light, and will not come into the light for fear that their deeds will be exposed. But whoever lives by the truth comes into the light, so that it may be seen plainly that what they have done has been done in the sight of God." [6]
>
> ~ JOHN 3:19-21

BETRAYAL

Judas leaving the last supper to betray Jesus.

Osiris was betrayed by his brother—someone who was a trusted part of his family. Jesus was betrayed by Judas—someone he taught and trusted as one of his closest disciples. It's possible that Joan of Arc had attained a certain spiritual stage, and as part of her mission came here to complete a part of it—that stage would have been the betrayal. In her life she was betrayed by the King of France, the very person whom she had helped to put on the throne, who left her to be captured by their common enemy the English, leading to her trial and execution based on false allegations.

Another person who was similarly betrayed by the King of France on false charges and burnt at the stake, almost one hundred years earlier, was Jacques de Molay, the last Grand Master of the Knights Templar, along with a number of others in the order. Records were discovered in 2001 in the Vatican Secret Archives that reveal the Pope at the time dropped the accusations against them, but that despite this, the King of France persisted with their execution.

The Templars are believed to have had connections to Freemasonry, with its great wealth of spiritual knowledge; many of the Templars are said to have fled persecution taking their spiritual knowledge with them to the safe haven of Scotland where it is believed the oldest Lodge of the Masons was founded. The name Freemason has been said to possibly derive from the Egyptian words for sun, "Phre," and child, "Mas," meaning "children of the sun," or "sons of light"—titles also used by the Egyptians and Incas. Tragically, Freemasonry was later infiltrated by those with malevolent agendas, as evidenced in the letters of the first President of the United States, George Washington.[7]

The stage of betrayal tests someone's faith in the divine, as all the authorities of the world will turn against them, and those who they thought were with them will desert them completely. When Jesus is seized, the disciples flee. All the students of the Son, who like Peter, even declare they will do anything for Jesus, when the time comes to stand by their teacher, hide and deny that they even know them for fear of being attacked themselves. Apart from a few disciples, the crowds who once massed around Jesus crying "Hosanna!" completely abandon him. Weak, vulnerable, and almost completely alone, they must go through the betrayal, an excruciating stage in which they are handed over to people who hate them, who ruthlessly destroy their image and reputation with lies and falsity, and face the condemnation, insults, and scourging of the world.

THE DIVINE ROLE OF JUDAS

Judas betrays Jesus with a kiss, and hands him over to the soldiers.

Jesus was someone who had already achieved a highly advanced spiritual stage and who was born on Earth with a mission—to bring to Earth the message of the Spiritual Son both in what he taught and through the events of his life. Those around him, both consciously and unconsciously, played a role in Jesus' life that would help to demonstrate this message. The events of Jesus' life were divinely planned, and Judas was given the most difficult role as one of his most advanced disciples—as has now been revealed in the discovery of the ancient text called the Gospel of Judas.

Judas symbolizes the traitor which exists within every person, who betrays the force of the Son—all the love, wisdom, happiness, and treasures of the spirit—in return for thirty pieces of silver, which are symbolic of the desires of the egos and the pleasures of the material world, which seem a pittance by comparison.

TRIAL

Joan of Arc is interrogated in prison.

Defenseless, the one walking the path is symbolically taken captive and treated as a criminal after all they have done to help others. Joan of Arc, who was the savior of a nation, was kept as a common prisoner, and almost completely abandoned.

Jesus is left defenseless, and remains silent at the false accusations made against him to signify how someone is made incapable of defending themselves in the face of their own demise, just like Osiris who was sealed in a coffin. Many of those whom they knew and helped instead emerge to give false testimony against them.

> "The chief priests and the whole Sanhedrin were looking for evidence against Jesus so that they could put him to death, but they did not find any. Many testified falsely against him, but their statements did not agree.
>
> Then some stood up and gave this false testimony against him: 'We heard him say, "I will destroy this temple made with human hands and in three days will build another, not made with hands."' Yet even then their testimony did not agree.
>
> Then the high priest stood up before them and asked Jesus, 'Are you not going to answer? What is this testimony that these men are bringing against you?' But Jesus remained silent and gave no answer. Again the high priest asked him, 'Are you the Messiah, the Son of the Blessed One?'
>
> 'I am,' said Jesus. 'And you will see the Son of Man sitting at the right hand of the Mighty One and coming on the clouds of heaven.'

The high priest tore his clothes. 'Why do we need any more witnesses?' he asked. 'You have heard the blasphemy. What do you think?'

They all condemned him as worthy of death. Then some began to spit at him; they blindfolded him, struck him with their fists, and said, 'Prophesy!' And the guards took him and beat him." [8]

~ MARK 14:55-65

Jesus before Pilate.

Both Jesus and Joan of Arc are put on trial by the religious establishment. This signifies how someone is rejected by their own religion, and in rejecting the Son (the real source of spiritual knowledge in the world), the religion defines itself as that which opposes light no matter what they preach.

Despite all the false evidence, the religious pharisees are unable to find any charge against Jesus or Joan as they did no wrong. However, both are finally accused of blasphemy/heresy as they dared to declare their relationship with divinity, which they had only done for the good of helping others. The Son incarnates within someone as the world teacher, and has done so throughout time to bring the message of awakening to humanity—and for this they are persecuted, attacked, mocked, and hated by many, many people.

Through the trial of the Son, the true nature of society is uncovered. The institutions, dogmas, traditions, and laws, which present themselves as the moral good, are often instead the vehicles of persecution, which are used to suppress the awakening of consciousness—in their persecution of the Son, their true position is revealed. The crowds call for the release of Barabbas, a real criminal who is symbolic of all the degeneration of the ego, instead of Jesus, thereby choosing the ego over the love of the Son.

THE CRUCIFIXION OF THE SUN

At the equinoxes, the sun crosses the celestial equator (which is Earth's equator projected into space). Because of the meaning of this event, a number of sun gods were crucified or depicted on crosses in association with the equinox.

THE SPIRITUAL MEANING OF THE SPRING EQUINOX

Jesus was crucified on a cross at the spring equinox. Quetzalcoatl was depicted on a cross. Hun Hunahpu was decapitated and his head hung on a sacred tree. After his death, Osiris floated down the river Nile until washing ashore and merging with a tree. Odin strung himself upon the world tree as an act of self-sacrifice.

Left: Odin hanging in a tree, piercing his side with a spear. Center: Jesus crucified on a cross and his side being pierced by a spear. Right: The Aztec god Xolotl, the twin brother of Quetzalcoatl, is illustrated as being on a cross. Other images show Quetzalcoatl himself on the cross—a vast distance away from where Jesus was crucified.

The cross and tree can symbolize the same thing, which is why they sometimes appear interchangeably.

The horizontal arms of the cross, which extend east and west, can represent the horizon of the earth from which the sun appears to rise and set each day, as well as the equator which runs east-west, and the spring and autumn equinoxes, which correspond to sunrise (the direction of east) and sunset (the direction of west) respectively. Going further, symbolically the horizontal line of the cross (or horizon) can represent life (east) and death (west).

The vertical line of the cross represents the progression of the sun north and south of the equator—with the light half of the year (from the spring to autumn equinox), representing the upper, heavenly realms of light; and the dark half of the year (from the autumn to spring equinox), representing the underworld, the lower regions of darkness. These realms lie on either side of the horizontal line of the cross, the earthly world.

The Druids are said to have viewed the stations of the sun in the same way:

> "[...] the Druids supposed the godly enter heaven in the northern sky, and that the first entrance into life is from the southern point. [...] On the northern side of the equinoctial line on which human existence is stationed in this life, is the Gwynvyd, or Heaven, of the Druids. When the sun has ascended northwards of the celestial equinoctial line in spring, he gradually increases in glory, power,

and majesty, and the earth under his influence blooms, and scatters fragrance, and is a veritable garden of the Lord!" 9

~ MORIEN O. MORGAN, THE LIGHT OF BRITANNIA

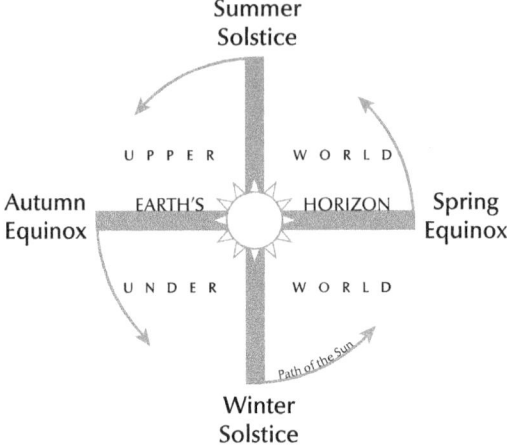

Because of the symbolic relationship between the equinox and the path of the spiritual sun, many "dying and resurrecting gods" were depicted as dying and descending into the underworld at the autumn equinox where they spent six months before resurrecting at the spring equinox. At the autumn equinox the sun descends into the dark half of the year—symbolic of the womb, tomb, and underworld, which the Spiritual Son descends into after their death. While at the spring equinox the sun symbolically emerges from the underworld and darkness of winter to ascend into the eternal spiritual realms of light.

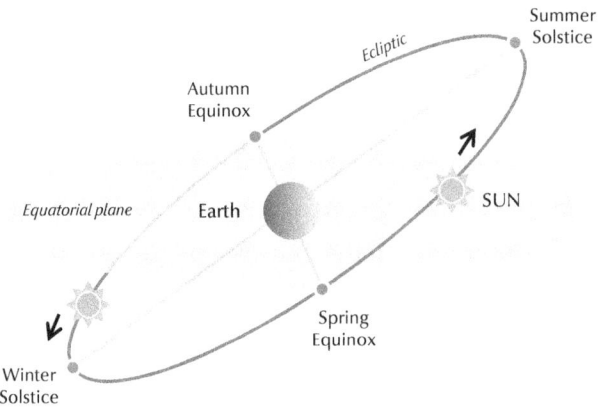

The sun crosses the plane of the earth's celestial equator at the autumn and spring equinoxes. At autumn it descends, and in spring it ascends. Note that this diagram is from the perspective of someone in the Northern Hemisphere.

Most today are familiar with the crucifixion of Jesus as being commemorated at the time of Easter, which occurs around the spring equinox in the Northern Hemisphere. However, astrologically, the crucifixion is most accurately symbolized by the sun's crossing the celestial equator at the autumn equinox. The symbolism of Jesus' entire crucifixion and resurrection likely occurred all at the spring equinox because he had to represent these things within a human lifetime and within the bounds of what was physically possible to demonstrate and do.

The sun descending across the celestial equator at the autumn equinox is the cross on which the Son is symbolically crucified. Jesus is stripped of his clothes and possessions, and the sun darkens, representing the loss of the powers of the Spiritual Son. The nails he is bound to the cross with symbolize the painful things of life that hold him within the confines of three-dimensional matter and time, represented by the cross. The Spiritual Son/sun descends into matter, and suffers within it, in order to save and raise the person he descends into back up to heaven.

> "[Jesus said] For I have come down from heaven not to do my will but to do the will of him who sent me. And this is the will of him who sent me, that I shall lose none of all those he has given me, but raise them up at the last day. For my Father's will is that everyone who looks to the Son and believes in him shall have eternal life, and I will raise them up at the last day." [10]
>
> ~ JOHN 6:38-40

> "[Jesus said] No one has ever gone into heaven except the one who came from heaven—the Son of Man." [11]
>
> ~ JOHN 3:13

> "For God did not send his Son into the world to condemn the world, but to save the world through him." [12]
>
> ~ JOHN 3:17

Jesus is said to have descended into the underworld following his crucifixion for three days.

> "For as Jonah was three days and three nights in the belly of a huge fish, so the Son of Man will be three days and three nights in the heart of the earth." [13]
>
> ~ JESUS IN THE GOSPEL OF MATTHEW 12:40

These three days correspond to the three days when the sun appears to stand still at the winter solstice, as this is when the sun is in the maximum amount of darkness, symbolic of the Son being in the very center or heart of the earth, the subconscious, and matter.

The sun ascending across the celestial equator at the spring equinox creates the cross of resurrection in which no bindings are used, as instead the trappings of material existence are broken. It is a symbol of the rising sun, of the eternal Spiritual Son, resurrecting from within material existence.

> "I will call unto Him with all my heart, I will praise and exalt Him with all my members.
>
> For from the East and unto the West is His praise;
>
> Also from the South and unto the North is His thanksgiving. [...] I extended my hands and hallowed my Lord,
>
> For the expansion of my hands is His sign.
>
> And my extension is the upright cross. [...]
>
> I extended my hands and approached my Lord, for the expansion of my hands is His sign.
>
> And my extension is the upright cross, that was lifted up on the way of the Righteous One. [...]
>
> All my persecutors have died, and they sought me, they who declared against me, because I am living. [...]
>
> I was not rejected although I was considered to be so, and I did not perish although they thought it of me.
>
> Sheol saw me and was shattered, and Death ejected me and many with me.
>
> I have been vinegar and bitterness to it, and I went down with it as far as its depth.
>
> Then the feet and the head it released, because it was not able to endure my face. [...]
>
> My chains were cut off by His hands, I received the face and likeness of a new person, and I walked in Him and was saved. [...]
>
> And from there He gave me the way of His steps, and I opened the doors which were closed.
>
> And I shattered the bars of iron, for my own shackles had grown hot and melted before me.
>
> And nothing appeared closed to me, because I was the opening of everything.
>
> And I went toward all my bound ones in order to loose them; that I might not leave anyone bound or binding.

And I gave my knowledge generously, and my resurrection through my love." [14]

~ THE ODES OF SOLOMON

"Wherever life is seen in things movable or immovable, it is the joint product of Matter and Spirit. He who can see the Supreme Lord in all beings, the Imperishable amidst the perishable, he it is who really sees. Beholding the Lord in all things equally, his actions do not mar his spiritual life but lead him to the height of Bliss. [...] He who sees the diverse forms of life all rooted in One, and growing forth from Him, he shall indeed find the Absolute. [...] As space, though present everywhere, remains by reason of its subtlety unaffected, so the Self, though present in all forms, retains its purity unalloyed. As the one Sun illuminates the whole earth, so the Lord illumines the whole universe. Those who with the eyes of wisdom thus see the difference between Matter and Spirit, and know how to liberate Life from the Law of Nature, they attain the Supreme." [15]

~ KRISHNA IN THE BHAGAVAD GITA

The symbol of the solar cross is a symbol of the Spiritual Son/sun manifest within creation, the suffering the Son/sun goes through when subject to the limitations and darkness of matter, and the mission this aspect of the Being has to descend into the body as a microcosm of creation in order to save consciousness, and enable it to ascend.

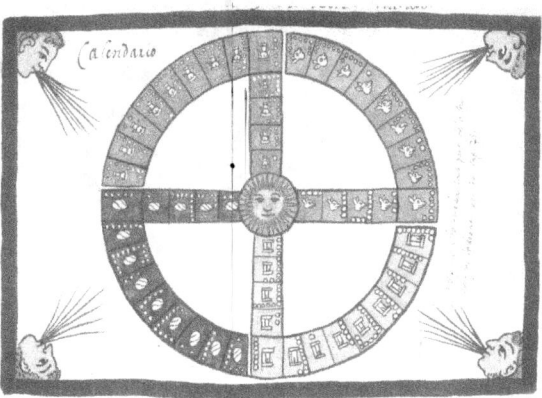

An Aztec solar cross (which is actually a swastika if you look carefully), with the sun at the center.

The potential for immortality comes into a person by the Son incarnating into their mortal body—like a seed that contains the potential for life—firstly going into the earth (the body), before sprouting the life of the eternal spirit within. This is a profound mystery, as just as the earth is empty and lifeless without the seed, so the seed needs the earth to sprout.

> "Jesus said, "If the flesh came into being because of spirit, it is a wonder. But if spirit came into being because of the body, it is a wonder of wonders. Indeed, I am amazed at how this great wealth has made its home in this poverty." [16]
> ~ THE GOSPEL OF THOMAS

On a microcosmic scale, the autumn equinox, winter solstice, and spring equinox can represent the whole process of resurrection, while on a more macrocosmic one, it can represent the path of the spiritual sun when the summer solstice is included, as the principles contained in the annual cycle of the sun operate like fractals in which the principles are the same whatever the scale.

Both the cross and tree can symbolize the union of feminine/earthly and masculine/heavenly forces—of the human with the divine. The masculine principle is represented by the vertical line of the cross and branches of the tree, and the feminine by the horizontal line and roots.

Similar symbols are also found at the Neolithic temple mound Knowth, whose cruciform chamber aligns closely to the equinox. Outside the mound is a tall stone beside a short rounded one, representing the masculine and feminine principles.

A tall stone and round stone at the Neolithic temple mound Knowth, symbolic of the male and female principles and sexual organs.

THE GOOD THIEF AND THE BAD THIEF

The thieves crucified next to Jesus can represent the dark half of the year (the bad thief), and the light half of the year (the good thief) on either side of the equinox, which is when Jesus was crucified.

But they also have other meanings and can be read as alchemical symbols. The cross for example, as a symbol of the union of masculine and feminine, can represent the practice of alchemy. In alchemy, the good thief represents the one who "steals" or takes the sexual energy to use it for spiritual purposes, and the bad thief the one who steals this energy to use it to feed desire. They represent how sexual energy can be used for different purposes.

Jesus crucified between the good thief and the bad thief. Both the practice of alchemy and inner death are alluded to in this painting with the position of Mary Magdalene at the base of the cross, as well as the symbol of the skull. A pyramid even appears on the horizon.

The symbol of the struggle between the good thief and the bad thief is also portrayed in the Hindu story of the Churning of the Milky Ocean, explained earlier in this chapter. The ocean that is churned represents the Milky Way, but also the sexual waters/energies, which need to be controlled so that the spiritual treasures and the elixir of immortality emerge. One must struggle between the pull of sexual desire as the demons on one side, representing the bad thief, and that of the spirit, symbolized as the gods, on the other, representing the good thief. The gods and demons pull back and forth on a giant serpent, which is also a symbol of the sexual energies.

THE DEATH OF SELF-IMAGE

The death of crucifixion represents a stage on the path in which someone goes through the death of their self-image. For most, this does not involve actual physical death, but instead the destruction of virtually everything else they have in the world, such as the work they have created in their lives, their reputation, and their standing in society. Only those doing a higher, more advanced work, like Jesus, go through actual physical death, but Jesus also firstly had his reputation destroyed by lies.

Someone's self-image must die to make way for the full expression of the Spiritual Son within. The destruction of one's self-image, through lies and treachery, tests their attachment to the things of worldly and material existence. It also tests the level of inner death of the egos they have been able to achieve up until this time, and so the death of crucifixion also symbolizes the culmination of someone's inner death.

The cross of crucifixion symbolizes the Spiritual Son who is trapped within materiality and in the self-image of the person, illustrated by Jesus suffering as he is nailed to the four arms of the cross—representing the four material elements, and the four dimensions of the physical world. The worldly must die so that the Spiritual Son can fully manifest within and live as the person, so that he is no longer constrained by it. The box coffin of four sides, like the stone sarcophagus within the chamber of the Great Pyramid of Egypt, again symbolizes the confines of materiality and of all that is worldly, mortal, and passing. At resurrection these trappings are transformed and overcome by the imperishable and immortal Son.

Jesus resurrecting from within the stone
coffin of four sides, and the cave of the earth.

Jesus was crucified at the time of the spring equinox on the "Skull Place," as a symbol of this death. The site of the Great Pyramids where the Great Sphinx aligns to the equinox was also associated with death, as its ancient name was the Necropolis, which means graveyard. The chambers of the Great Pyramids contained stone sarcophaguses that were empty of burials, as they were used for initiatory rites in which the death preceding resurrection was symbolized. The Great Pyramids align with the three stars of Orion's Belt—the symbol of

Osiris in the sky, whose death and resurrection was the most central event of his life. Incredibly, the three great pyramids of Teotihuacán in Mexico align just as the Great Pyramids of Giza do—to the three stars of Orion's Belt. The largest, called The Pyramid of the Sun, shares almost exactly the same base area as the Great Pyramid in Egypt. These pyramids are built along what is called the Avenue of the Dead, which is another reference to death, and the site itself was known as "birthplace of the gods," which is a reference to the spiritual transformation of resurrection. These principles later became horribly misinterpreted in the practice of human sacrifice.

SELF-SACRIFICE

The crucifixion of the Spiritual Son at the equinox is also a symbol of sacrifice. This kind of sacrifice, which symbolizes a key principle in the universe and on the path of the spiritual sun, is not the horrific kind that involves violence and the sacrifice of others, but is the inner kind in which we sacrifice what is inferior within ourselves to gain what is superior (the spiritual within), and make sacrifices in our life out of love for others. This has been called self-sacrifice and is based entirely on selflessness and love.

This principle of self-sacrifice has been symbolized in the lives of a number of great spiritual figures. Both Jesus and Joan of Arc allowed themselves to be betrayed and handed over to execution as an act of self-sacrifice in pursuit of a higher cause. In the Churning of the Milky Ocean, the god Shiva comes forward to swallow the terrible poison that emerges as an act of self-sacrifice to save creation and allow the churning to continue. The Aztec god Quetzalcoatl created human beings from an act of self-sacrifice. The Norse god Odin hung on a tree as an act of self-sacrifice, in order to gain and give the wisdom of his sacred runes to humanity.

Odin's self-sacrifice.

"I know that I hung on a windy tree nine long nights,

wounded with a spear, dedicated to Odin, myself to myself,

on that tree of which no man knows from where its roots run.

No bread did they give me nor a drink from a horn, downwards I peered;

I took up the runes, screaming I took them, then I fell back from there." [17]

~ HÁVAMÁL

The principle of sacrifice exists throughout creation. Energy and materials have to be taken from somewhere in order to create something else. We see this principle at work when creating anything new. Many materials are sacrificed in order to build a house for example. Plants of all kinds, as well as animals, are surrendered too so that other plants and animals can survive. A whole cycle of sacrifice, and of give and take, exists throughout the universe.

> "In this world people are fettered by action, unless it is performed as a sacrifice. Therefore, O Arjuna, let thy acts be done without attachment, as sacrifice only.
>
> In the beginning, when God created all beings by the sacrifice of Himself, He said unto them: 'Through sacrifice you can procreate, and it shall satisfy all your desires. Worship the Powers of Nature thereby, and let them nourish you in return; thus supporting each other, you shall attain your highest welfare. For, fed, on sacrifice, nature will give you all the enjoyment you can desire. But he who enjoys what she gives without returning is, indeed, a robber.'
>
> The sages who enjoy the food that remains after the sacrifice is made are freed from all sin; but the selfish who spread their feast only for themselves feed on sin only.
>
> All creatures are the product of food, food is the product of rain, rain comes by sacrifice, and sacrifice is the noblest form of action.
>
> All action originates in the Supreme Spirit, which is Imperishable, and in sacrificial action the all-pervading Spirit is consciously present.
>
> Thus he who does not help the revolving wheel of sacrifice, but instead leads a sinful life, rejoicing in the gratification of his senses, O Arjuna, he breathes in vain." [18]
>
> ~ KRISHNA IN THE BHAGAVAD GITA

This same principle applies when creating the spiritual; in order to have the materials to be able to create spiritual things within, sacrifices must be made within ourselves to be able to provide these materials. These materials are the quintessential energies and elements within a person, and they become the prima materia of the alchemists—the symbolic base substance that is used to create the golden energies of the sun within. For those working toward becoming a Son of the sun, the dark energetic substances of the egos, and the energies we use to feed them, are sacrificed so that our energies can be put toward creating things of light within us instead. So for example, selfish pleasures are sacrificed in order to gain love. Low states of all kinds, like aggression and anxiety, are sacrificed to have inner peace. Negative behaviors and addictions are given up in order to bring about mystical experiences and spiritual states. What is lower then, is sacrificed, or given up, in order to gain what is of a higher nature.

Likewise, this principle applies when creating things for the greater good in the world. For example, we can sacrifice our time and effort voluntarily to create something that will not just benefit ourselves, but many others. In giving charity, we give up things that we could have kept to ourselves, to instead help those in need. Those things which confer a smaller benefit are given up so that those things which bring a greater benefit can take place.

> "O Ye men, increase the store of goods acquired by honest and fair means to be used in the service of humanity. May your life, be constantly dedicated to this principle. May the spiritually minded people, also, not give up this humanitarian work." [19]
> ~ THE YAJUR VEDA

This same principle applies to spreading spiritual knowledge, as to do this we give up things in our life in order that fellow beings have the opportunity to find out about spiritual awakening.

> "Those who see themselves in all and all in them, help others through spiritual Osmosis to realize the Self themselves." [20]
> ~ THE KATHA UPANISHAD

The spring equinox expresses the principle of sacrifice. It's by giving up the things of darkness within that we gain the light, just as the sun after the spring equinox increases toward the summer solstice.

The sacrifice of the spring equinox also symbolizes giving up everything someone believes themselves to be—the ideals they hold about themselves, their achievements in life, the place they hold in the opinions of others, etc.—all of which constitute someone's own self-image. This is given up in the process of betrayal and crucifixion, where someone's image is destroyed with lies and falsity, and exists on the path of the spiritual sun, in part, so that someone sacrifices their attachment to their own self-image and their status in society, as they cannot pass this stage if they don't let it go. Our image is crucial to our acceptance in society and yet it belongs to the lower nature of the personality and the things of the world, and as such, has to be given up to gain that which belongs to one's eternal Being.

> "But you will exceed all of them. For you will sacrifice the man that clothes me." [21]
> ~ JESUS TO JUDAS IN THE GOSPEL OF JUDAS

It is through the death of one's sense of "self" that someone reaches the self-less and yet unique nature of their higher Being—that which is not of this world and which brings a new life. It is where someone gives up their own self-centric will, so that their will becomes as one with the selfless will of the divine Spirit whom they can then truly serve—and that will is love.

> "Father, if you are willing, take this cup from me; yet not my will, but yours be done." [22]
> ~ JESUS IN THE GOSPEL OF LUKE 22:42

> "There are two selves, the separate ego
> And the indivisible Atman. When
> One rises above *I* and *me* and *mine*,
> The Atman is revealed as one's real Self." [23]
> ~ THE KATHA UPANISHAD

ANUBIS, GUARDIAN OF THE GATEWAY TO IMMORTALITY

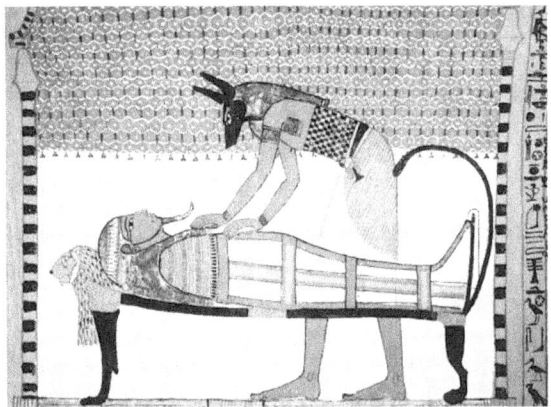

Anubis attending to the dead.

At the spring equinox, the ancient Egyptian god Anubis plays a central role in spiritual resurrection. In the story of the life of Osiris, the god Anpu (Anubis in Greek) receives the dead body of Osiris and places it in a tomb, and along with the goddesses Isis and Nephthys, resurrects him. This reflects a real role that the Being Anubis has in the higher dimensions, which the ancient Egyptians depicted, as someone must pass through Anubis, the guardian between the realm of earthly and spiritual existence, to attain immortal life.

Anubis' role in resurrection was symbolically designed into the ancient site of the Great Sphinx and Pyramids of Egypt—the most famous and enigmatic ancient site in the world—and one which aligns to sunrise on the equinox. Thousands of years ago, this giant statue of Anubis would have also gazed directly at the constellation we now know of as Leo, but looks just like the recumbent Anubis. This constellation of Anubis appeared in the sky just before the rising of the sun as Osiris, standing between the path of the sun as it appeared over the horizon and its ascent into the sky, thereby enacting the role Anubis has as gatekeeper between the realm of earthly and immortal existence, and symbolizing Anubis' role in facilitating the resurrection of Osiris, on the spring equinox, the time of Osiris' resurrection. This incredible alignment and its meaning is explored in detail in the following chapter "Decoding the Ancient Meaning of the Sphinx and Its Origin as Anubis."

An artist's impression of what the Great Pyramids and Sphinx of Giza may have once looked like.

THE RETURN TO THE WOMB

In ancient myths from the Religion of the Sun, creation emerges from water, symbolic of the eternal feminine and the womb. In Egypt, creation is depicted as emerging from out of the primordial waters, and in Druidic myth, creation emerges from the cauldron of sap of the goddess Ceridwen. Similarly, creation emerges from the primordial waters in the ancient Vedas of the Hindus. These primordial waters are those of the eternal feminine womb, the cosmic Mother, which gives birth to the Spiritual Son/sun, and from which all of creation unfolds.

The death of the Spiritual Son is a return to the primordial waters of the Mother, which is a return to her womb. This return to the womb and the resurrection that follows it is found symbolized in sacred teachings and at ancient sites around the world aligned to the spring equinox.

To resurrect and attain eternal life, the Son must be reabsorbed by the Mother, as by returning to the Mother someone returns to the imperishable source of creation—as she was not born of any, but arose from the creator dividing into male and female. Unlike the Son, because she is not born of any, she is not subject to death, and so by merging with this higher feminine part of someone's Being, a person attains eternal life.

References to the great Mother Goddess as not being born of any are found in ancient Egypt. Perhaps the most ancient and supreme goddess recorded in ancient Egypt is Neith/Net. A high priest of hers at a very ancient temple in Egypt, now lost, was recorded as saying this about her:

"Utchat-Heru was an official of very high rank in Saïs, and he was high-priest of Net, and as such bore the official title of Ur-sun [meaning] "great one of knowledge." He [...] explained to him the antiquity and greatness of the goddess Net, and conducted him through the various sanctuaries which were grouped together in her temple. In the course of his conversation with the king he told him that it was Net, the mighty mother, who had given birth to Rā [the sun god], and that she was the first to give birth to anything, and that she had done so when nothing else had been born, and that she had never herself been born." [24]

~ E. A. WALLIS BUDGE, THE GODS OF THE EGYPTIANS VOL 1

The famous Egyptologist Budge goes on to say:

"[...] the Egyptians regarded Net as the "Being" par excellence, i.e., the Being who was eternal and infinite, and was the creative and ruling power of heaven, earth, and the underworld, and of every creature and thing in them. [...] The statements of Greek writers, taken together with the evidence derived from the hieroglyphic texts, prove that in very early times Net was the personification of the eternal female principle of life which was self-sustaining and self-existent, and was secret, and unknown, and all-pervading [...]." [25]

~ E. A. WALLIS BUDGE, THE GODS OF THE EGYPTIANS VOL 1

She and the later Egyptian goddesses identified with her, such as Isis and Hathor, were described as the lady of heaven, the mother of all the gods who came into being in the beginning, and the mighty mother (and also great cow) which gave birth to Rā (the sun).[26] The Egyptians were said to call her Athene, meaning "I have come from myself." [27]

In the earliest records of her, she was considered "a personification of a form of the great, inert, primeval watery mass out of which sprang the Sun-god Rā." [28]

This is perhaps the oldest and clearest reference to the feminine aspect of the creator who is not born but is a division of the original creative androgyny—the great primordial waters, who gave birth to the Spiritual Son, and the universe.

The Son came from the womb of the great Mother, and so to return to the source of creation, the Son must return to his Mother's womb. But a return to the womb is also a time of death, as it is a return to the state that precedes birth.

This return to the womb is symbolized by Jesus' placement in a cave-like tomb, which no one had been placed in before—signifying the return to the womb of the pure and undefiled Spiritual Mother. In the Gospel of James, Jesus was also said to be born into a cave, which is a symbol of the womb, and his placement back inside a cave at his death completes the return to the womb. These few symbolic clues are part of the little of what remains of the

Spiritual Mother in early Christian writings. Jesus' teachings about the Spiritual Mother were almost entirely censored by the orthodoxy, and this has become increasingly apparent as many other early Christian writings have come to light over the last century or so where the Mother is described as part of the Trinity of creation.

The body of the crucified Jesus being placed in a cave-like stone tomb.

In the story of Osiris, he is betrayed by Seth (just as Jesus was by Judas). Seth seals Osiris in a coffin, and then throws the coffin into the Nile River, symbolic of the Milky Way and eternal Mother, which flows out to the sea—this is again symbolic of the return to the womb of the Spiritual Mother, the primordial waters of creation.

Hathor is one of the most prominent mother goddesses of ancient Egypt, being a later form of the goddess Neith. She was depicted as a cow, sometimes with a face shaped like a uterus to reflect her role of sacred birth. Both she and the Egyptian goddess Nut were associated with the Milky Way. This has an actual basis, as it is now known that the center of the Milky Way is a birthplace of stars—hence the Mother as the Milky Way giving birth to "suns." The goddess Nut is depicted as stretching across the sky with a body of stars to show her as the Milky Way, giving birth to and then swallowing the

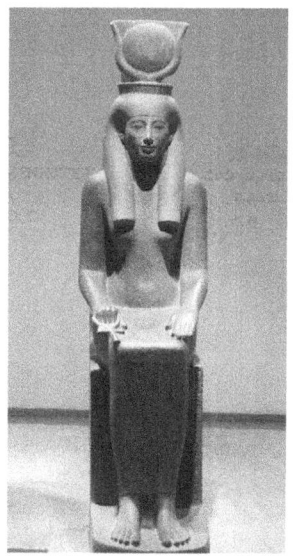

The Egyptian goddess Hathor, wearing a headdress of cow horns holding the sun, symbolizing her giving birth to the sun.

sun in an eternal cycle of birth, death, and rebirth. Death for ancient Egyptians was a return to the womb by being swallowed by the goddess.

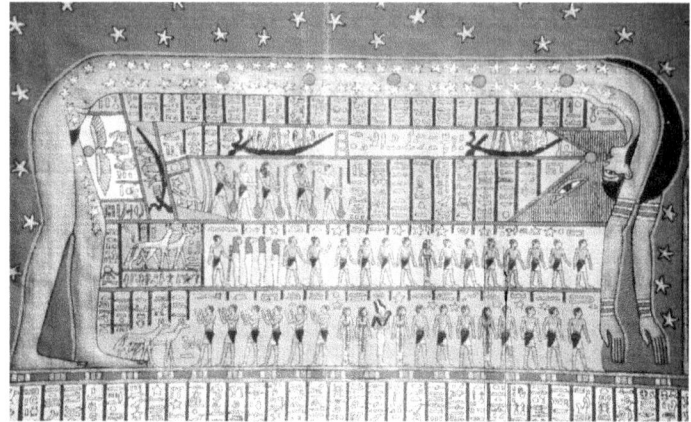

The Egyptian goddess Nut who was symbolized by the Milky Way and who swallowed and gave birth to the sun in a continuous cycle of death and rebirth.

The chambers of the pyramids of Egypt were intended to symbolize both the womb of the goddess Nut and the underworld. This is described in the oldest surviving texts of Egypt (the Pyramid Texts), which detail the function and meaning of the pyramids they were inscribed into.[29] The chambers of the different pyramids of Egypt follow a similar layout that was developed and standardized over time.[30] The layout matches the descriptions of the burial ritual of the pharaoh detailed in the Pyramid Texts, and corresponds to ancient Egyptian religious beliefs, as explained by the Egyptologist James P. Allen, a specialist in ancient Egyptian language, texts, and religion.

Allen describes that after death the pharaoh was believed to be reborn to new life like the rising sun after its journey through the darkness of night. This night was both the womb of the goddess Nut, and the netherworld (called the Duat), which the sun entered at sunset. In the middle of the night it was believed one merged with Osiris, receiving from him the mysterious force of new life—like that found in the growth of plants from dormant seeds. This gave someone the ability to be reborn like the sun from the womb of Nut.[31] As Allen explains, this whole process can be read in the layout of the pyramids.

> "The stone sarcophagus in the west end of the burial chamber was an analogue of Nut's womb. Within it, the king's mummy was both a fetus and an analogue of the mummy of Osiris lying in the Duat. The Pyramid Texts refer to the burial chamber itself as the Duat [...].
>
> As the sun united with Osiris's mummy in the Duat, the king's spirit was thought to join with his own mummy in the Duat of his tomb and, like the sun, receive through this union the power of new life.

[...] Finally, as Nut gave birth to the morning sun, the king's akh [spiritual self] left his tomb. In the earliest pyramids it was apparently thought to do so through the long corridor connecting the antechamber to the outside on the north of the pyramid, an analogue of the birth canal.[32]

[...] The result was an evocative metaphor of rebirth: beneath the pyramid, the king's mummy lay like a seed planted in a mound of earth, waiting each night to transmit Osiris's power of new life to his spirit. Pyramids were not merely monumental tombs erected to perpetuate the memory of Egypt's kings: they were also—and more fundamentally—resurrection machines, designed to produce and ensure eternal life." [33]

~ WHY A PYRAMID? PYRAMID RELIGION BY JAMES P. ALLEN

I believe (based on my experience) that the oldest of these "resurrection machines" were originally used for rituals of spiritual resurrection, which is a spiritual stage attained in life, not through physical death, but became interpreted as such by those who were uninitiated into their mysteries. This is why the stone sarcophagus of the Great Pyramid was found empty of any burial. The spiritual knowledge of ancient Egypt became a religion of the afterlife, similar to how Christianity did.

The ancient mounds of Europe share similarities with the pyramids of Egypt—as while there were ancient mounds that were used as tombs, there were some also found empty of burials (or are known to have been used for long periods before later intrusive burials), as they were instead probably used for initiation rituals of resurrection.

Like the ancient Egyptians, the Neolithic peoples of Ireland, who built sacred mounds like Newgrange, also associated the Milky Way with the Mother Goddess—in Irish it is called "Bealach na Bó Finne," which means the way of the white cow.[34]

Some of the smaller mounds surrounding the
larger ancient mound of Knowth in Ireland.

In Neolithic Ireland, as in Egypt, they also aligned their sacred sites to the spring equinox using symbols of resurrection, and associated the Milky Way with the river around which they built them, just as the ancient Egyptians did around the river Nile—both associating it with a Mother Goddess represented as a cow.

At the ancient mound site of Knowth in Ireland, the symbols of the womb of the Mother, resurrection, and cross all come together at the spring equinox. Knowth was constructed as a mound with a passageway leading to an inner chamber, much like the pyramids of Egypt. The mound's eastern passage is laid out in a cruciform shape and aligns with sunrise on the sixth day following the equinox[35]—it's the longest megalithic passage in Europe and leads to the largest megalithic chamber in Ireland.[36] Within a recess off the chamber there is a large stone cauldron shaped basin, engraved with a symbol of the sun.[37] It's been associated with the Dagda Cauldron of Irish mythology, which is said to have had the power to regenerate life so that dead bodies could be placed into the cauldron and drawn out alive and whole again[38]—symbolizing resurrection from the womb of the Mother Goddess. The mound itself also represents the earth as the womb.

> "It is highly probable that these chambers were viewed as wombs, and that rebirth and reincarnation beliefs were a fundamental part of the rituals that went on here." [39]
>
> ~ MARTIN BYRNE, TOUR GUIDE AND RESEARCHER OF ANCIENT IRISH MEGALITHIC SITES

Records of these rituals survive in European mythology. In Welsh mythology, the bard Taliesin (whose name is one of the Druidic titles of the sun[40]) is swallowed by the goddess, and spends nine months (in another version of the myth nine nights) in her womb where he drinks from her cauldron before being reborn.[41]

> "[...] for nine nights I rested
> At peace in her womb.
> [...] I was dead and alive.
> [...] I am Taliesin, I sing of one true-born." [42]
>
> ~ THE BOOK OF TALIESIN

In Norse mythology, a great cauldron lies in the depths of Hel/the underworld, realm of the goddess. It was not only the place of the dead, but also where with the help of the sun goddess, one resurrected.[43]

> "Son! As your father, I have counselled you, as have the sons of Sun Cauldron Woman, toward the Horn of the Heart that he brought from the death-mound [...]." [44]
>
> ~ SONG OF THE SUN (AN OLD NORSE POEM)

It seems likely that ceremonies symbolizing resurrection were enacted inside the mound of Knowth on the spring equinox, just as they were inside the chambers of the Great Pyramids of Egypt, and incorporated the stone cauldron, which was used as a symbol of the womb just as the sarcophagus of the Great Pyramid was.

An ancient ceremonial Celtic cauldron, called the Gundestrup cauldron, which is one of the most beautiful Celtic artifacts ever found.

One of the scenes on the Gundestrup cauldron. It shows warriors fallen in battle walking in the underworld toward a large god or goddess, who dunks them in "the cauldron of rebirth"[45] to resurrect them into the heavenly realm of the afterlife. Resurrected warriors ride to the right, toward the light.[46]

Pyramids and mounds are also found across the Americas, and many show evidence of being used like those in Egypt and Europe were.

For example, the Mayan god Hun Hunahpu was depicted as resurrecting as the rising sun (and simultaneously as the maize plant) from within a turtle,[47] which was known as the tomb of the earth in Maya religion—another symbol of the womb. This same enactment is found at the pre-Columbian site of

Monks Mound in the United States, where the spring equinox sun appears to rise (or resurrect) from out the giant mound that appears to have been built in the form of a turtle.[48]

The Maya maize god Hun Hunahpu resurrecting from a turtle, on a plate found at a temple at the ancient city of Palenque in Mexico.

The mound, cauldron, tomb, turtle, and waters are all symbols of the womb, which deities symbolically entered after their death, before later resurrecting. It symbolizes the reabsorption of the Son into the Mother.

The womb is also the receptacle in which sexual activity takes place. Therefore, the Son's return to the womb also represents the practice of spiritual birth/alchemy in which someone works together with their Mother to harness the forces of life and death—in the death of the ego, and the creation of the imperishability of the spirit. In returning to the womb, the person with the Son within works alchemically to transform themselves in order to resurrect.

THE DESCENT INTO HELL

The return to the womb is also to enter into the primordial chaos of creation, into darkness, and the underworld.

After Jesus' death around the time of the spring equinox, he descended into hell. After Odin's self-sacrifice on the world tree, he descended into the underworld to find the runes carved into its roots. Baldr also descends into the underworld after his betrayal and death. Osiris descended to the underworld after his betrayal and death. Quetzalcoatl, the feathered serpent, was symbolized as descending the nine regions of the underworld at the equinox.

This is the descent into hellish psychological regions in which someone faces the sufferings like those found in hell itself, in order to destroy their egos and gain knowledge of themselves. It is a time of death, as the underworld is the realm of the dead who are in hell.

Jesus enters the underworld, which also symbolizes his entrance into the subconscious to do battle with the egos within it.

Numerous traditions that were influenced by the ancient Religion of the Sun speak of an underworld. It is the place where those who have not attained immortality undergo the process of the death and decay of their egos. To the ancient Egyptians it was the habitation of the evil dead called the Place of Annihilation. To the Maya it was Xibalba, meaning Place of Fright. The Hindus and Buddhists call it Naraka. To the Norse it was Hel. In Christianity it is Hell, and in Greek mythology it is Hades, etc. In ancient Egypt the underworld was entered through the jaws of the goddess Ammit, and to the Norse hell was overseen by a queen called Hel. This is symbolic of the Mother who destroys the egos of the dead. Either the Mother works with us in the underworld to destroy our egos during life, or the Mother destroys them in the underworld as we suffer the consequences of our egos after death.

After their betrayal and symbolic crucifixion, someone descends into the hellish regions of their own psyche, and then needs to work to rise back out in order to resurrect. This descent is into the darkness of the subconscious, as the light of consciousness is trapped within the darkness of the egos and can only be freed through their dissolution.

The Temple of the Great Jaguar in Tikal has nine terraces to its pyramid, which the rising spring equinox sun ascends to crown the pinnacle. As a symbol, the jaguar was considered the night sun—the form the sun takes in its journey through the underworld—so this site symbolizes the ascent of the Son (as the jaguar and sun) from out of the nine layers of the underworld to resurrect.

Looking up at the Temple of the Great Jaguar in Tikal (Guatemala), which aligns to the spring equinox sunrise.

In the mystery schools of Odin, an initiate had to pass through nine chambers in which they were subjected to various trials before being called "resurrected." In Odin's act of self-sacrifice, he hangs on a tree for "nine long nights." Jesus was crucified at nine in the morning and darkness covered the land until "the ninth hour." This is symbolic of the trials an initiate goes through psychologically in the nine regions of hell and their corresponding regions in the subconscious, in order to resurrect.

RESURRECTION

Resurrection is the attainment of eternal life, immortality, and imperishability referred to in ancient texts of the Religion of the Sun and symbolized by the rising sun on the spring equinox. This is why many sacred sites were built to align with sunrise on the equinox—like the Great Sphinx of Egypt, Monks Mound in North America, and Knowth in Ireland—and were associated with resurrection. It's also why Jesus' resurrection occurs at "the rising of the sun" around the time of the spring equinox—and he is described as being risen, just like the sun.

> "Very early in the morning [...] they came unto the sepulcher at the rising of the sun. [...] And when they looked, they saw that the stone was rolled away [...]. And entering into the sepulcher, they saw a young man sitting on the right side, clothed in a long white garment [...]. And he saith unto them [...] Ye seek Jesus [...] which was crucified: he is risen [...]." [49]
> ~ MARK 16:2-6

Anubis resurrecting the pharaoh in the presence of the mother goddesses Isis and Nephthys, who pour the waters of life onto the body to restore it.

Life and creation emerged from the womb of the great Mother of the universe as described in creation stories throughout the ancient world. That which is eternal is that which never dies—and only that which is never born does not die. In creation myths from the Religion of the Sun a divine androgynous being emerges from the great unmanifest and unknowable source. This being divides into male and female in order to create and gives birth to a Son, and the rest of creation. The Mother Goddess is one half of the eternal first being, and therefore is not born of any. When the Son returns to and becomes one with the Mother, the Son becomes immortal, thus resurrecting and attaining eternal life.

> "He [Jesus] called out, saying: 'Whoever has ears to hear about the infinities, let him hear!'; and 'I have addressed those who are awake.' Still he continued and said: 'Everything that came from the perishable will perish, since it came from the perishable. But whatever came from imperishableness does not perish but becomes imperishable.'" [50]
> ~ THE WISDOM OF JESUS CHRIST

> "I [Jesus] tell you truly, the Book of Nature is a Holy Scroll, and if you would have the Sons of Men save themselves and find everlasting life, teach them how once again to read from the living pages of the Earthly Mother. For in everything that is life is the law written. It is written in the grass, in the trees, in rivers, mountains, birds of the sky and fishes of the sea; and most of all within the Son of Man. Only when he returns to the bosom of his Earthly Mother will he find everlasting life

and the Stream of Life which leads to his Heavenly Father; only then may the dark vision of the future come not to pass." ⁵¹
~ THE ESSENE GOSPEL OF PEACE

"Father-Mother spin a web whose upper end is fastened to Spirit (Puruṣa)—the light of the one Darkness—and the lower one to Matter (Prakṛti), its shadowy end; and this web is the Universe spun out of the two substances made in one, which is Svabhavat. It expands when the breath of fire (the Father) is upon it; it contracts when the breath of the mother (the root of Matter) touches it. Then the sons dissociate and scatter, to return into their mother's bosom at the end of the "great day", and re-become one with her." ⁵²
~ THE STANZAS OF DZYAN

To achieve full self-realization and return to the source of creation, the Absolute, where all is one, the Son must reunite with the Mother and then with the Father, becoming whole again as one Being. The different parts of the Being that were divided in creation need to unite to form one whole, as it is not possible to enter the Source divided.

"For truly, no one can reach the Heavenly Father unless through the Earthly Mother." ⁵³
~ JESUS IN THE ESSENE GOSPEL OF PEACE

In the great cycles of nature, death always precedes birth, and life feeds from sacrifice. In the process of spiritual resurrection, that death is of the ego, and the sacrifice is that of the inferior within the psyche. The life that springs forth is not the perishable kind subject to ensuing death, but is eternal, no longer bound by the recurring cycles of material nature.

These principles of resurrection are so central to life that they are found in the natural world, which is why nature was used so often to symbolize them. For example, both the Egyptian god Osiris and the Mayan god Hun Hunahpu died and resurrected, and were associated with the cycles of the sun and corn.

"The cults of Osiris and Re [the sun god] shared the concept of survival after death—the daily rebirth of the sun after a night-time in the underworld, and the annual loss and subsequent renewal of vegetation after the inundation which was reflected in the death and resurrection of the god in the Osiris Myth. In both cases, the god's life, death and re-birth were reflected in the cycles of the natural world, a pattern that formed one of Egypt's most important religious concepts." ⁵⁴
~ ROSALIE DAVID, RELIGION AND MAGIC IN ANCIENT EGYPT

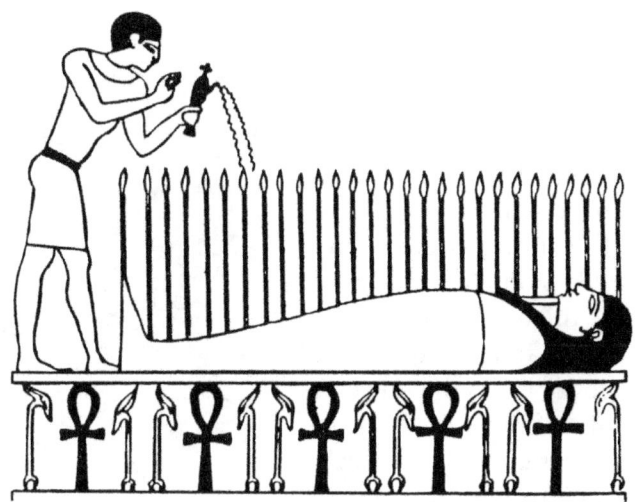

At the ancient Egyptian Khoiak festival, effigies of Osiris were made out of corn and barley seeds, which were sprouted to symbolize his resurrection.

Osiris was the most popular god of ancient Egypt, and great festivals were held every year to celebrate his resurrection across Egypt in many of its greatest temples. These were attended by the public, pilgrims, priests, and rulers—all who hoped to attain resurrection through him. The resurrection of Osiris offered all people the hope of resurrection, as it is the potential the Spiritual Son offers every person.

THE MEANING OF THE SPRING EQUINOX IN DAILY LIFE

The spring equinox expresses the principle of sacrifice, which operates throughout the universe. It is a principle that permeates the whole of creation, as all things live upon the sacrifice of others. This principle can be applied in one's own daily life through giving up those things that are inferior for those that are superior. This means giving up inferior thoughts, feelings, and emotions, such as hatred, anger, and depression, for those that are superior, such as wisdom, clarity, and peacefulness. It also means choosing superior ways of acting over those that are inferior—living selflessly, instead of selfishly.

The darkness preceding the rising spring equinox sun serves its purpose—providing us with the choice between darkness and light of our own free will. Darkness also provides the opposition and resistance needed to forge one's eternal character and being.

Personal sacrifice is another of the key principles/practices that leads someone along the path of the spiritual sun.

THE ETERNAL LIFE OF THE SPIRIT

While the evil of the world celebrated the death of the Son as Jesus, Osiris, Baldr, etc., it is the Son who truly triumphs in the defeat of darkness and in his resurrection, symbolized by the rising of the spring equinox sun. Although the Passion and death of the Son is a tale of human tragedy, the darkness of death and winter has its role in the cycles of life in the universe and on the path of the spiritual sun— and that darkness is overcome by light at the spring equinox and the spiritual resurrection of the individual.

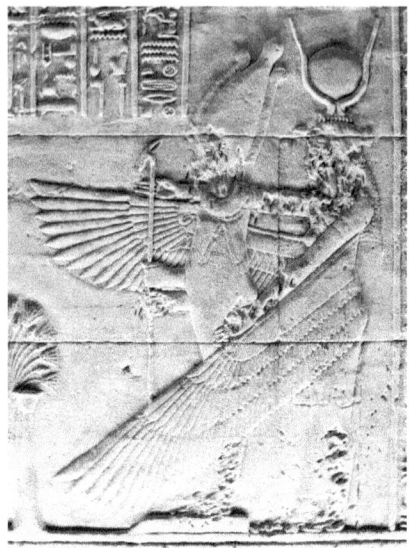

The resurrected Osiris under the protection of the great mother goddess Isis.

Like the new shoots that emerge from within the earth at spring, the eternal life of the spirit resurrects from within the womb of dark matter, which in a human being is the material body and psyche. At winter, seeds germinate beneath the ground, and life begins, but that life is still in darkness. Only at spring does the plant push past its material trappings into the light.

The spring equinox symbolizes the return of the Son to the eternal Mother, and his reintegration with her, to attain immortality.

The work from here is to ascend to the great Father, symbolized at the summer solstice.

> "To say: It is beautiful to see, it is peaceful to hear that Osiris stands at the door of the gods.
>
> Thy sanctuary, King, is to thee as a heart of secret places; it opens for thee the double doors of heaven, it opens for thee the double doors of the way; it makes for thee a way, that thou mayest enter there among the gods, that thou mayest live as thy soul.
>
> O King, thou art not like the dead, who art dead, thou art living, thou art alive, together with them, the spirits, the imperishable stars." [55]
>
> ~ THE PYRAMID TEXTS, UTTERANCE 667

CHAPTER FIVE

Decoding the Ancient Meaning of the Sphinx and Its Origin as Anubis

An artist's impression of what the Great Pyramids and Sphinx of Giza may have once looked like. Note that the Sphinx may have been partly submerged by a small, man-made lake.[1]

The meaning of the Great Sphinx and Pyramids at Giza, Egypt, has eluded the many attempts to understand it using archeology alone. Most academics believe its head is that of a pharaoh called Khafre, others believe it was originally a lion's head, but I'll give some reasons why I believe the Sphinx was likely to have been originally carved as the deity Anubis.

The people who built the Giza site were obviously deeply interested in spirituality. The culture that followed in ancient Egypt, perhaps more than any other, used the intuitive language of symbolism to convey profound spiritual truths—those who had enough inner wisdom could speak this language, while those who did not were rendered incapable of deciphering it. This is why the site at Giza has remained a mystery to most, even though it is one of the most studied sites in the world.

To discover the meaning of the Giza site, it helps to have some understanding of the meaning of the spiritual symbols used in its design. The spiritual knowledge which the builders of the Great Pyramids and Sphinx possessed is timeless, and thus it is possible to unlock this site's meaning through the understanding of this same knowledge today.

The enigmatic and mysterious Sphinx, great centerpiece to this site's design, holds much of the answer. In this chapter, I'll go back as far as possible into the origins of the Sphinx to explore its meaning, using a shared understanding of the spiritual knowledge its ancient builders possessed.

THE SPHINX AS ANUBIS

The Great Sphinx being excavated, starting in AD 1817. Its paws are already covered in restoration stones from Roman times and its head is obviously too small in relation to the size of the body, indicating it was re-carved at least once.

To understand the meaning of the Sphinx, we need to firstly uncover its original form, as the form it takes today is the result of multiple restorations dating from at least 1,400 BC.

Anyone who looks closely at the Sphinx can see that it's obviously out of proportion. Its head is much too small for its body, and is far less weathered than the rest of the body and surrounding enclosure. The head has clearly been re-carved, perhaps numerous times, or is even a purpose made one rejoined to the body after its original head was destroyed. Furthermore, its body has been covered with restoration stones dating from thousands of years ago right up until today, giving the Sphinx its leonine shape while masking how it was originally carved. So to find the clues as to what it originally was, we have to look further than the Sphinx alone.

Evidence for what the Sphinx originally may have looked like can be found in some of the most ancient surviving texts of Egypt, is indicated by the astronomical alignments of the Sphinx and surrounding pyramids, can be seen in the archeological features of the site, and in the spiritual knowledge the site was designed to encode. This evidence all points to the Sphinx originally being sculpted as the ancient wolf (previously thought to be a jackal) deity Anubis, facilitator of the process from death to resurrection, agent of cosmic law, and gatekeeper of the passage to immortality.

A photograph of an African golden wolf, the animal which Anubis is associated with. Until recently, this animal was believed to be a jackal before genetic testing revealed it is actually a wolf. Translations of ancient Egyptian texts still refer to it as a jackal.

In their book *The Sphinx Mystery*, researchers Robert and Olivia Temple have done an immensely detailed and thorough work of investigating and bringing together the archeological, textual, and historical evidence to discover the oldest known form of the Sphinx. Their investigation led them to believe that the Sphinx was originally carved as Anubis in his form as a recumbent jackal/wolf.

THE SPHINX RESURRECTION THEORY

But not only does the archeological evidence point to Anubis being the original form of the Great Sphinx, so too does the spiritual meaning of what the Sphinx was built to symbolize.

Although recognized by millions, the Sphinx has remained an enigma; but by bringing together the references to it in ancient Egyptian texts with my experience of spiritual resurrection, I've put together a theory of what it symbolizes. Aligned to precise cosmic events, lying atop of hidden chambers, surrounded by a sacred lake, and part of an incredible master plan that incorporates the Great Pyramids using advanced geometry, the Sphinx is a monument of magnificent wisdom and scale that I believe symbolizes the attainment of imperishability through resurrection.

The Great Sphinx aligns to the spring equinox, a time of spiritual resurrection as found in the design of other ancient sites aligned to this solar event, and also the time of the death and resurrection of many solar deities, including Jesus. Perhaps the most central spiritual teaching of ancient Egypt was the death and resurrection of Osiris, whose life symbolically encoded the process of attaining immortality, or imperishability as it is called in Egyptian texts. It is the god Anubis who resurrects Osiris, and who thus formed a central symbolic part of the design of the Giza Plateau and the statue dedicated to this momentous spiritual event.

This idea, that the Sphinx symbolizes spiritual resurrection, and was therefore carved as Anubis, possibly with Osiris at his chest (which I explain further on)—the two gods central to the teachings on resurrection in ancient Egypt—I put forward as the "Sphinx Resurrection Theory." I'll now elaborate on how I came to this idea, which explains the form, function, and meaning of the Sphinx—perhaps providing an answer to one of the greatest riddles and mysteries of the ancient world.

In this photo the restoration blockwork on the body of the Sphinx can be seen clearly, in multiple layers, revealing beneath it a very weathered original stone. Modern concrete has been used to fill in the headdress as well as deep rivets in the body.

SPIRITUAL TRUTHS LATER INTERPRETED LITERALLY

Some of the earliest references to the Great Sphinx and Pyramids of Egypt are found in the Pyramid Texts, which are carved into the stone walls of the pyramids at Saqqara in Egypt, and date from around 2,400 BC. By mainstream standards, these texts are currently the oldest officially dated sacred texts in the world. Later versions of them are known as the Coffin Texts, and most famously the Book of the Dead. Together they constitute much of the religious literature of ancient Egypt.

The Pyramid Texts specifically describe an elaborate funeral ritual that was conducted at the Great Sphinx for the pharaohs at the time. Deceased pharaohs were prepared for their afterlife journey at the Sphinx and in the temples surrounding it, where they were ritually "resurrected." At the time of the writing of the Pyramid Texts, and at least hundreds of years prior, the Great Sphinx was a supremely important religious site. The various areas around the Sphinx are mentioned, as well as how they are used for the ritual, and the pharaoh is even identified with the Sphinx whose form is explicitly described.

By the time these texts were written, however, it's clear that the original spiritual knowledge of the site had become misinterpreted, and inner, spiritual processes had become interpreted literally. This has happened in many religions, and the religion of ancient Egypt was no exception.

The pharaoh took the place of the initiate (who symbolically imitated Osiris), and instead of going through the spiritual mysteries of resurrection in life, undertook a vast physical preparation for resurrection in the afterlife. However, even though the meaning of the original symbols is largely lost, the symbols themselves are still preserved by these texts and in the site of Giza itself—enough to allow initiates to recover their meaning. Following, I explore the meaning of some of the rituals conducted at the Sphinx based on passages from the Pyramid Texts, as well as the meaning of the Sphinx itself.

RESURRECTION

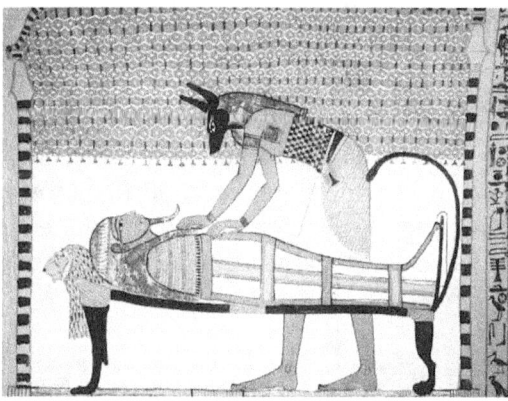

Anubis attending the pharaoh (who took the role of Osiris) to resurrect him.

In the sacred mysteries of ancient Egypt, a person had to undergo a defined spiritual process to pass from mortality to immortality, which led from death to resurrection. Resurrection as a spiritual process can be found in sacred teachings of the ancient Religion of the Sun and is associated with the time of the spring equinox—the most dominant solar alignment of the Giza Plateau, which the Sphinx gazes precisely toward.

Resurrection was central to the life of the Egyptian god Osiris, just as it was in the lives of Jesus and the maize god Hun Hunahpu of the Maya, who resurrected at the time of the spring equinox. The lives of these deities, although appearing in different cultures and times, symbolized the same spiritual process also symbolized at the site of the Great Pyramids. Each of these deities showed the events and processes involved in the path of the spiritual sun and derive from the ancient Religion of the Sun, which is why they contain similarities.

THE GOD ANUBIS

Anpu (Anubis in Greek) is one of the most ancient gods of Egypt—the record of his veneration predates that even of Osiris. He was depicted as a black recumbent African wolf, or as a man with the head of a wolf, and presiding over the process of death. The wolf head is a sacred headdress Anubis wears in his role in the spiritual realms.

In Egypt, Anubis most famously appears in the scene of the weighing of the heart, illustrating events that occur just after someone dies. The heart of the deceased is weighed by Anubis on the scales of divine law (called Maat, which is cosmic order) against a feather to determine how they lived their life, and based on that, what region they would be assigned to in the afterlife. The following illustration is of Anubis in his role as the head judge of cosmic law, which he administers along with forty-two judges, known as "The Assessors of Maat," and the ibis god Thoth. In my experience this reflects a real role that the Being Anubis has in the higher dimensions, which the ancient Egyptians depicted.

Interestingly, the scales Anubis tends are a symbol of the equinoxes, illustrating the balance between night and day—further associating him with the equinox and Great Sphinx which gazes directly toward it. Only when these scales were completely balanced could someone resurrect and attain immortality,[2] further revealing that the equinox was seen as the symbolic time of spiritual resurrection.

The god Anubis weighs the heart of the dead in the presence of the god Thoth and the forty-two judges of divine law, before Osiris who becomes judge of the dead after his resurrection.

ANUBIS AND INNER DEATH

However, few experience firsthand Anubis' role in presiding over inner death on the path to immortality, as few ever meet the requirements. Anubis not only presides over the process of physical death, but also of spiritual, inner death. It is Anubis who has the role in the spiritual dimensions to administer someone upon the stage of death preceding resurrection on the path of the spiritual sun–this death is not a physical one, it is an inner one that involves the death of that which is evil, inferior, and dark within oneself, such as hatred, anger, jealousy, lust, etc., and of one's self-image.

In Egypt this turned into a religious belief (as has happened in other religions) and was misinterpreted by later people who had lost the ability to understand the esoteric meaning of Egypt's sacred texts. Pharaohs believed instead that their physical death would be followed by resurrection in the afterlife, and surrounded themselves with items and spells that would apparently assure them safe passage in the journey to reach immortality. However, the death before resurrection is achieved in life through a spiritual and alchemical work, and the Great Sphinx and the life of Osiris, along with the life of other solar deities, symbolize how it takes place.

In ancient times the site of the Great Pyramids, where the Sphinx lies, was called Ro-Setawe, the Sacred Land, and the Necropolis (meaning graveyard). Coupled with this, the Pyramid Texts refer to Anubis as "Lord of Ro-Setawe," "Anubis who presides over the Sacred Land" (and also Pure Land, and Secluded Land), and "he at the Head of the Necropolis," which are all ancient references to Anubis as the Sphinx, god of death, presiding over the Giza Plateau, which was known as the place of the dead.[3] This is both a physical and spiritual reference, as the Giza site was designed to symbolize spiritual truths and processes.

Physically the Sphinx does indeed stand at the main entrance to the site of the Great Pyramids.

In ancient times, the Giza site would have been entered by boat as the river Nile reached right up to the Sphinx. Boat quays were discovered protruding from the Valley Temple beside the Sphinx (which was built out of the stones excavated from

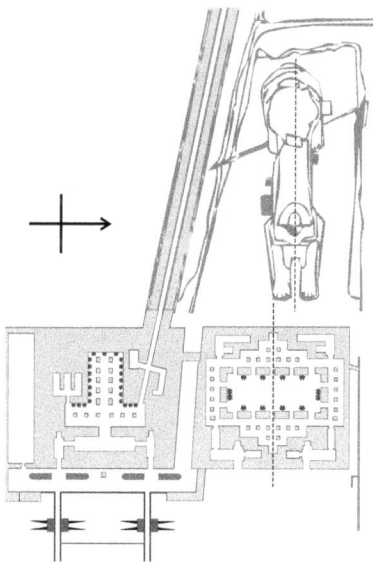

This diagram shows the Sphinx from above. Directly in front of it is the Sphinx Temple, and to its right is the Valley Temple, which has two quays protruding from it (with the spikes protruding left and right) which would have brought people into the Giza site by boat and formed the main entrance to the entire Giza Plateau.

around the Sphinx when it was first created). Anyone who entered the Giza site through this main entrance passed by the great statue as they walked along a grand causeway leading to the pyramids.

The reference to the site of Giza being the place of the dead is not a reference to it being an actual graveyard (although the inhabitants of the site later interpreted it this way), but as a place of those who achieve an inner, psychological death. This finds its parallel in the "Place of Skull" where Jesus was crucified, and the "Avenue of the Dead" at the Pyramids of Teotihuacán in Mexico where it was said "men become Gods"—a site which also shares other similarities with the Pyramids of Giza.

Little wonder that Anubis, the god with a central role in death and resurrection, stood guard over the site of Giza, dedicated to the spiritual process of attaining imperishability, in which inner death and resurrection were essential.

Left: Anubis in his recumbent form lying atop a coffin. This statue was found among the treasures inside the tomb of Tutankhamun.

Right: Ancient Egyptian pyramidion with Anubis sitting atop the coffin of Osiris.

Anubis was often depicted as a dog recumbent on a coffin. On an ancient Egyptian pyramidion, Anubis is illustrated in this way with the gates of heaven above, which he is said to be guarding, while the coffin he sits upon is called the box of Orion[4]—Orion being the constellation of Osiris. That is, Anubis lies atop the coffin of Osiris, and stands guard between Osiris and the gates of heaven. This is the same configuration symbolized by the Sphinx, as it does guard the gates of the starry heavens (as I explain further on), and below it lies the symbolic coffin of Osiris, as well as nine chambers symbolizing the underworld.

THE NINE LAYERS OF THE UNDERWORLD

In 1996 a team of researchers discovered that nine underground chambers lie beneath the Great Sphinx.[5] These likely symbolize the nine layers of the underworld, which are also found symbolized at other ancient sites, such as the nine terraces of the pyramid of Chichen Itza in Mexico. Both the Maya and Norse assigned nine regions to the underworld.

Someone enters these underworld regions after the stage of death preceding resurrection, which is why Osiris is cast into the underworld after being killed by Seth. Like Osiris, Jesus descends into hell after his crucifixion, and Odin descends into the underworld after his self-sacrifice on the world tree. This hell is one experienced internally, where someone suffers hellish psychological states, and must achieve the death of these states in order to surface back from out of the underworld and resurrect, which is why in the quote below Osiris is said to be "weary of the Nine" (the nine regions of the underworld), but now has "no more time there."

> "He comes indeed, Osiris, weary of the Nine, an Imperishable spirit, he that bore more than you, he that suffered more than you, he that is more weary than you, he that became greater than you, he who will be happier than you, he who roars louder than you. You have no more time there!" [6]
> ~ THE PYRAMID TEXTS, UTTERANCE 218

THE TOMB

Both Jesus and Osiris are placed in stone tombs, from which they resurrect. In the life of Jesus, Joseph of Arimathea wraps the body of the crucified Jesus in linen before he places it in his own tomb, just as in the life of Osiris, Anubis conceals Osiris' body in a tomb. Joseph was a member of the Sanhedrin, which was a council of judges, paralleling Anubis who was seen as a spiritual judge in ancient Egypt. The two Marys bring spices and perfumes to anoint the body of Jesus, just as Isis and Nephthys do to Osiris.

> "The secret ways of Ro-Setawe [the ancient site of Giza], The gate of the gods. Only one whose voice is heard May pass them... The secret way to which (only) Anubis has access in order to conceal the body of Osiris." [7]
> ~ THE BOOK OF THE ONE IN THE NETHERWORLD

It seems the tombs of the Great Pyramids were never designed for deceased bodies, but were used for initiatory rites to symbolize the process of inner death. Additionally, few know that beneath the Giza Plateau, in a chamber at a depth of at least 114 feet, is a huge stone sarcophagus on a small island surrounded by water—known as "the Tomb of Osiris." Like the tombs of the Great Pyramids, it too was found empty, as it is a replica of the mythical Tomb of Osiris, from which he rose from the dead, and is meant to symbolize the site of his spiritual resurrection.[8]

Thus, the Sphinx as Anubis does indeed sit over the coffin of Osiris.

It is in the stone tomb (symbol of the womb of the Great Mother), which in Egypt was built into chambers of the pyramids and beneath the Giza Plateau, where the initiate, lying in the stone sarcophagus, is concealed and attended to by Anubis and resurrects to emerge as an immortal spiritual being.

THE SACRED LAKE OF ANUBIS

The researchers Robert and Olivia Temple discovered evidence that the statue of Anubis as the Great Sphinx may have once been surrounded by a sacred lake—in ancient texts it was referred to as the Jackal Lake, Lake of Fire, Lake of Dawn, Canal of the God, Canal of Anubis, Winding Waterway, Lake of Cool Water, Lake of the Netherworld, and Lake of Life.[9] The recumbent body of Anubis as the Sphinx would have been submerged beneath water, which was done for a symbolic reason, as I explain further on.

Looking at a topographical map of the Giza Plateau, the Sphinx can be seen as set down in an area where the waters of the river Nile would have reached in ancient times during the annual inundation of the Nile, which could have been used to fill the Sphinx enclosure. Strange markings around the Sphinx enclosure may have been the location of sluice gates that retained water around the Sphinx to create a lake.[10] A channel is also carved along the causeway that leads to the Sphinx. It empties into the Sphinx enclosure, and would have collected rain water runoff from the Giza Plateau that could have also filled the lake.[11]

PURIFICATION OF THE ENERGIES AND THE FOUR BODIES

The lake around the Great Sphinx may have been a symbol of the sexual waters/energies, which are purified alchemically on the path of the spiritual sun, and used to create the imperishable bodies of gold, which are the vessels of the consciousness in the different dimensions. It is the feminine aspect of someone's higher Being that works within the sexual energies, and is sometimes symbolized as Isis and also as a serpent (the kundalini).

> "O King [pharaoh], your sister the Celestial Serpent has cleansed you upon the causeway in the meadow, you having appeared to them as a jackal... May you govern the spirits, may you control the Imperishable Stars." [12]
>
> ~ THE PYRAMID TEXTS, UTTERANCE 690

This extract refers to the cleansing of the body of the pharaoh (as Osiris) in the sacred lake of Anubis, which surrounded the Sphinx. The causeway referred to runs from the Sphinx to the second largest of the Great Pyramids, and is described as being in a meadow, as thousands of years ago the Giza Plateau was a green and fertile place.

These are a complete set of four canopic jars, which were used by the Egyptians in the process of mummification and preparation for the afterlife. Each jar held a different organ, and each was guarded by a different god, which also corresponded to the four cardinal directions. On a spiritual level, these four jars may represent the four different bodies consciousness uses across different dimensions, which are physical, vital, astral, and mental.

Four gods and four jars are involved. These may have symbolized the four bodies that are cleansed and purified alchemically: they are the physical, vital, astral, and mental bodies. These bodies need cleansing because they are the bodies through which the egos (inferior psychological states) manifest, and the sexual energies permeate. In the process of cleansing, the egos are destroyed and the sexual energies purified.

Anubis carries out the process of mummification. Notice the four jars beneath the table, which represent the four bodies that are purified alchemically.

> "I travel the Winding Waterway . . . because I am pure, the son of a pure one, and I am purified with these four nemeset-jars of mine which are filled to the brim from the Canal of the God in Iseion [sanctuary of Isis], which possesses the breath of Isis the Great, and Isis the Great dries me as Horus. 'Let him come, for he is pure:' so says the priest of Rē [the sun] concerning me to the door-keeper of the firmament, and he announces me to those four gods who are upon the Canal of Kenzet [Land Beyond]." [13]
> ~ THE PYRAMID TEXTS, UTTERANCE 510

This lake in which the symbolic cleansing takes place may have been referred to as the Lake of the Netherworld because the lake is a symbol of the sexual energies/waters within the human being, and these energies permeate through the netherworld/underworld region of our subconscious. Our egos exist in this subconscious underworld and are created from sexual energies (which are the fundamental creative energies within us). The underworld is a real place which we are intimately connected to through our psyche. Being cleansed in the Lake of the Netherworld (also known as Jackal Lake) is to purify the sexual energies/waters from the contamination of the egos through sexual alchemy.

It was common in Greece and Rome for Egyptian deities to be adopted or merged with Greek and Roman ones. In Greece Anubis became the god Hermes, and even merged to form the god Hermanubis, while in Rome he became the god Mercury. Both Hermes and Mercury were also associated with death like Anubis, were both believed to be guides of the dead, and were each depicted with wings. In an experience I had out of the body I lay symbolically dead in the sarcophagus of the Great Pyramid, before the stage of resurrection, and saw Anubis enter the door of the chamber with the wings of Mercury on his head.

The god Hermanubis, who was a merger of the Greek god Hermes with the Egyptian god Anubis. Resting on his left shoulder is the Caduceus of Mercury, which is an alchemical symbol of two serpents entwined around a winged staff.

The netherworld, which both Anubis and Mercury guide the initiate through, is the place in which the process of alchemical purification needs to take place preceding resurrection. The Caduceus of Mercury, which the god Hermanubis also holds, is an alchemical symbol.

> "My father has remade his heart, the other having been removed for him because it objected to his ascending to the sky when he had waded in the waters of the Winding Waterway. Anubis comes and

meets you! And Geb [the Earth] gives you his hand, O my father, (even) he who guards the earth and rules the spirits. I weep deeply, O my father. Oho! Raise yourself, my father, receive these your four pleasant nemeset jars; bathe in the Jackal Lake, be cleansed in the Lake of the Netherworld, be purified." [14]

~ THE PYRAMID TEXTS, UTTERANCE 512

RETURN TO THE WOMB

The sacred lake was also a symbol of the primordial waters, the womb of the eternal Mother, to which the Son (the person with the Spiritual Son within) must return in order to pass beyond death and rebirth. All that is born dies, and so to achieve immortality the Son must go back to the origin of life and death, and merge with the Mother (who is not born and thus does not die), by returning to the womb of creation. From there the Son ascends to become one with the eternal Father. This is a going back to the first instance of creation and a return to wholeness in which the Father, Mother, and Son become one; in Egypt, this complete state of being was symbolized by the god Atum.

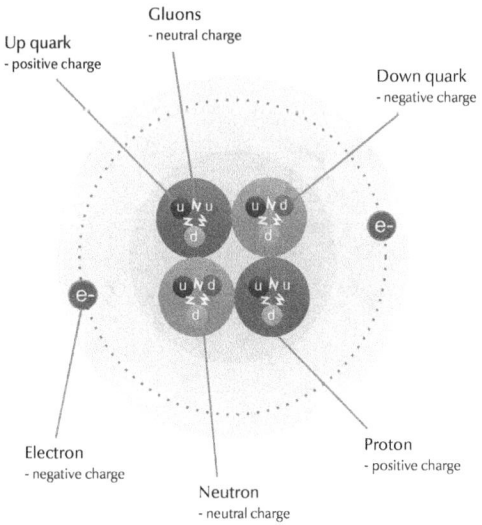

A diagram of an atom which illustrates the three primary forces of creation, as positive (protons), negative (electrons), and neutral (neutrons), which have been symbolized as a spiritual trinity in ancient teachings as Father, Mother, and Son.

The name Atum is very similar to the word "atom," the basic unit of creation which contains the three primary forces of creation. Atoms are comprised of subatomic particles called protons, the positive force of creation (the Father); electrons, the negative force in creation (the Mother); and neutrons, the neutral force in creation (the Son). Subatomic particles themselves are made up of even smaller elementary particles called "up quarks" (which are positively charged), "down quarks" (negatively charged), and "gluons" (the neutral force that binds these quarks together), revealing the same three primary forces that create an atom, but at an even smaller scale. This is an example of the fractal nature of creation.

Ancient Egyptian texts state that Atum permeates all of creation. He was the name of the first god that came into existence. He was self-engendered, and from him all other gods came into being. His name is interpreted as meaning "complete one," "lord of totality," "finisher of the world," "the Being of the Being," and "the Great He-She." Atum symbolizes the Monad, the Being that emerged from the source before it divides into different parts and goes into the different dimensions. The spiritual work is to merge the different parts of one's Being together as a complete whole again, which is a return to the state Atum symbolizes—a state of oneness and completion, but with full consciousness and knowledge gained from the experience of life in matter.

In Egypt, creation is said to have begun when the god Atum emerged as a mound from out of the primordial waters. These primordial waters are those of the eternal feminine womb, which gives birth to all of creation. It is following this same process in reverse through which we return to the spirit who conceived us. At death, Osiris is said to return to the heart of Atum, and Atum is said to return all living beings and creation back into the primordial waters from which it came. However, both Atum and Osiris are said to live on in this realm beyond existence in the form of serpents;[15] when all else passes, only those who resurrect and reach the state of imperishability as Atum will remain. Those who don't awaken are submerged back into the ocean of nonexistence at the end of the great cycle of their lives.

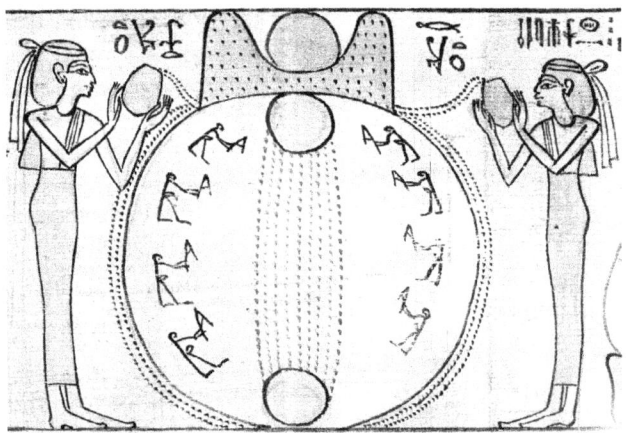

Egyptian painting of the first sunrise at the dawning of creation from the primeval mound that arose from out of the waters.

"Osiris: But how long shall I live?

Atum: You will live more than millions of years, an era of millions, but in the end I will destroy everything that I have created, the earth will become again part of the Primeval Ocean, like the Abyss of waters in their original state. Then I will be what will remain, just I and Osiris, when I will have changed myself back into the Old Serpent who knew no man and saw no god." [16]

~ THE BOOK OF THE DEAD, THE CHAPTER OF NOT DYING A SECOND TIME

With its body set down in the lake, the Sphinx would have appeared as a mound, just like the one that emerged from the primordial waters at the beginning of creation,[17] which is why the deceased pharaoh is said to have the body of Atum and the face of Anubis in the Pyramid Texts, as he takes the form of the Sphinx.

"Thine arm is like that of Atum; thy shoulders are like those of Atum; thy body is like that of Atum; thy back is like that of Atum; thy seat is like that of Atum; thy legs are like those of Atum; thy face is like that of Anubis." [18]

~ THE PYRAMID TEXTS, UTTERANCE 213

The Sphinx therefore symbolizes the return to a complete and imperishable state of being, in which the Son, Mother, and Father unite to become Atum. Atum is said to be a god of post-existence and pre-existence, being that which is both before and after existence. Those who resurrect (becoming one with the Great Mother), and later ascend (becoming one with the Great Father), conquer back their state of wholeness as Atum, being beyond birth and death, as one who is eternal.

"You come into being with your father Atum, you are high with your father Atum, you rise with your father Atum. The wants (of the Netherworld) are severed from you, your head (is held) by the nurse of Heliopolis [the city of the sun]. [...] You have come into being, you have become high, you have become a spirit! [...] Atum! Elevate to you Osiris, enfold him in your embrace! This is your son of your body, eternally." [19]

~ THE PYRAMID TEXTS, UTTERANCE 222

OVERCOMING THE LAW

As head of the divine law, Anubis stands as gatekeeper between the realm of earthly mortality and spiritual imperishability, letting only those who meet the spiritual requirements pass. On the Giza Plateau as the original form of the Sphinx, Anubis stood at the mystical gateway between the earthly and eternal realm, found in the moment of transition between winter and spring on the dawning of the spring equinox.

An example of the hauntingly beautiful walls inside the Pyramid of Teti I in Saqqara. They are inscribed with a version of the Pyramid Texts—containing spiritual knowledge from a far more ancient time.

"The earth speaks: The doors of the earth-god are opened for you, the doors of Geb are thrown open for you, you come forth at the voice of Anubis, he makes a spirit of you." [20]
~ THE PYRAMID TEXTS, UTTERANCE 437

"Anubis, the counter of hearts, deducts Osiris from the gods who belong to the earth, (and assigns him) to the gods who are in heaven." [21]
~ THE PYRAMID TEXTS, UTTERANCE 577

As someone progresses on the path of the spiritual sun, they fulfill and thus overcome the different cosmic laws that are upon them and the world, administered by Anubis. The whole of nature and creation is ordered by and exists under laws, which govern the way things grow, move, etc., and are studied in physics, biology, genetics, geology, and other sciences. It is said that in the beginning, Atum first created "life" and "order" and that they were not separate; this order is the laws that are intrinsic to life. However, there are not just laws that govern the physical and natural world, but also those that govern the matters of other dimensions, which include energetic, psychological, and spiritual principles. These laws include those that apply to human interaction, behavior, and spiritual development.

At the stage just preceding resurrection, there are only three laws remaining, which correspond to the three universal principles of creation, which are Father, Mother, and Son. When someone resurrects, the Mother and Son become one. From here is the ascension where someone then becomes one with the Father, and is when the male and female aspects of the being are made whole again. This is a going back to the first instance of creation and the original unified being Atum, which exists under only one law and is therefore no longer under the rule of Anubis. In order to reach this, the walker of the path must pay all their karma and fulfill all divine laws to pass beyond the laws which Anubis administers.

In the Coffin Texts, the king states "I have come . . . to enter the secret gateway By which Anubis is initiated. I have come to Ro-Setawe In order to know the Mysteries of the Netherworld into which Anubis is initiated." And also, "I have come in order to enter the gateway that is protected by Anubis." [22]

Anubis is the one who must be satisfied that someone has fulfilled everything they need to in terms of the law, before releasing them to become as the Pyramid Texts state—one who is no longer judged, but who fulfills and judges the law themselves.

> "Horus, hurry! Announce to the gods of the East and their spirits: He comes indeed, Osiris, an Imperishable Spirit! Whom he wills that he live, he lives. Whom he will that he die, he dies.
>
> [...] Osiris comes indeed, weary of the Nine, an Imperishable Spirit, to reckon hearts, to take kas, to grant kas. His every appointment obliges one (to do his duty), him who he has elevated, and him who applied to him.
>
> Atum, this your son is here, Osiris, whom you have preserved alive. He lives! He lives! Osiris lives! He is not dead, Osiris is not dead! He is not gone down, Osiris is not gone down! He has not been Judged, Osiris has not been judged! He judges, Osiris judges! [...]" [23]
> ~ THE PYRAMID TEXTS, UTTERANCES 217-219

After his resurrection, Osiris becomes the judge of the dead, just as Anubis had been. The one who has spiritually resurrected receives their jackal face, which is to achieve the state of existing under the one law of heaven (which is love).

> "O King, your shape is hidden like that of Anubis on his belly; receive your jackal-face and raise yourself, stand up." [24]
> ~ THE PYRAMID TEXTS, UTTERANCE 677

THE ASTRONOMICAL ALIGNMENTS OF THE SPHINX

THE SPRING EQUINOX

Today, the Sphinx still gazes due east, precisely aligned to the rising sun on the spring equinox—a time intimately connected to resurrection not only in Egypt, but in remnants of the Religion of the Sun throughout the world.

The spring equinox is when the days first begin to grow longer than the nights, and thus life emerges from the death of winter. In its deeper spiritual meaning, the sun, cosmic symbol of the Spiritual Son, breaks free of the mortal sheath of darkness.

THE CONSTELLATION OF LEO

For a period lasting just over 2,000 years, recurring approximately every 26,000 years, the Sphinx would have also gazed directly at the constellation of what we now call Leo just before sunrise on the spring equinox.[25] The last time this alignment occurred was from approximately 10,960 to 8,800 BC, which was during the astrological age of Leo.[26] The constellation of Leo is depicted as a recumbent lion, which matches the form of the Sphinx, and therefore the Sphinx would have gazed at its own counterpart in the sky during these epochs.[27]

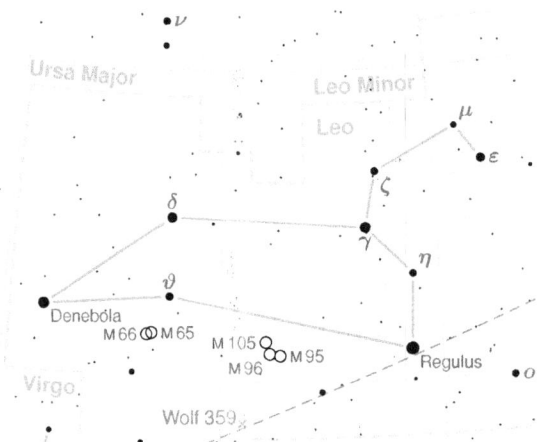

A diagram outlining the constellation of what we now know as Leo. Regulus, the king star, is the largest in the constellation, and is positioned at the heart.

The first currently accepted record of the constellation of Leo appears in 1,530 BC in Babylonia and was later adopted in Egypt. However, the Sphinx predates this time by thousands, and possibly by tens of thousands, of years. The Paleolithic cave painters of France viewed the constellation of Leo as a horse.[28] Therefore it's possible that the builders of the Sphinx didn't see the constellation of Leo as a lion either, but as the celestial representation of Anubis in his form as a recumbent wolf. The long flat back, curved head, protruding snout, and long outstretched paws match the form of the Sphinx and the hieroglyphic representation of the recumbent Anubis in his wolf/dog form in the Pyramid Texts.

The ancient site of Abydos in Egypt further connects Anubis to the constellation of Leo. At this site lies the mysterious temple known as the Osireion where a deity with the head of a wolf and later a dog, who shares many characteristics with Anubis and was later associated with him, was worshiped.[29] It is called the Osireion because it is speculated to be the final resting place of Osiris. The Osireion temple was unearthed during the construction of the temple of the Pharaoh Seti I around 1,280 BC, and later again when excavated along with the temple of Seti I in AD 1902, after both had become covered in sand.

Left: The Osireion at Abydos in Egypt. It shares many architectural similarities with the Valley Temple beside the Sphinx, as well as a connection to the deity Anubis as head of the underworld in alignment with the sun and constellation of Leo. Right: The Valley Temple.

The Osireion temple closely resembles the unique architecture of the Valley Temple which is located next to the Sphinx—both are made out of huge unadorned granite blocks, which also look similar to Stonehenge. The granite blockwork of the Valley Temple, however, was part of later renovations to the much older original limestone temple that was built from blocks quarried from around the Sphinx during its construction.[30] The Sphinx Temple, Valley Temple, and the Osireion, are so old that they were covered in sand and forgotten thousands of years ago, being rediscovered even by the pharaohs of Egypt themselves who renovated them.

On the summer solstice, the light of the setting sun shines through a nearby gap in the Libyan Hills, which intersects the Osireion temple. During the era of 4,400 BC, the summer solstice occurred in the constellation of Leo and a deity called Khent-Amenty was worshiped as a central figure at this site.[31]

Khent-Amenty was depicted with the head of a dog, but was also a variant of a lion deity, and later became associated with Anubis. He was known as "the head of the west" which was a reference to him as the guardian of the underworld, the land of the dead, the entrance to which was seen as being in the direction of west as the place of the setting sun. The underworld was believed to be accessed through the gap in the Libyan Hills, which lay to the west of Abydos, and which the solstice sun shone through in alignment with the Osireion temple.[32]

"Equally curious is that Khent-Amenty, a dog-like deity shown recumbent on a black standard, may in fact reflect an earlier understanding of the zodiac. The guardian of the west suggests a match for that guardian of the east, the Sphinx, and both can be related to the same constellation, that of Leo. Primitive cultures have often seen Leo as a dog-like creature, and it has even been suggested that the Sphinx originally depicted a dog. At the time of the earliest pre-dynastic cultures at Abydos, the ancestors of the Thinites around the turn of the fifth millennium BCE, the summer solstice sun was in Leo. So, standing in the sacred grove on top of the Osireion mound, one would have seen the sun set, and there, sparkling in the night sky, would have been Khent-Amenty, the black dog of Leo, guarding the path of eternal life." [33]

~ VINCENT BRIDGES, ABYDOS, THE OSIREION AND EGYPTIAN SACRED SCIENCE

ALIGNMENT WITH LEO AROUND 10,500 BC AND 36,500 BC

The Sphinx is set low down in the Giza Plateau. Researchers Graham Hancock and Robert Bauval discovered that this lowering of the Sphinx mirrored the constellation of Leo as it rose above the horizon at dawn on the spring equinox during the era around 10,500.[34]

When looking toward the Sphinx and the rising sun, one would have witnessed the constellation of what we now know as Leo rising in the sky before dawn—appearing head first, as if its body was submerged by the horizon, before emerging fully in its recumbent position. At this moment, one could look across to the Sphinx and see only its head, as if it were submerged in the horizon just like the constellation, with both of them aligned to one another.[35]

The rising of the constellation of Leo preceding the sun mirrors the role Anubis has in the resurrection of the Spiritual Son. Anubis, symbolized by the constellation of Leo, appears at the horizon where the sun will rise. The sun must pass through this constellation and the gaze of Anubis (as the Sphinx), to leave the earth and ascend into the sky, the realm of imperishability. At dawn, the sun emerges from the horizon, symbolizing the emergence of the person with the Son within from out of the underworld (which is also symbolized by the nine chambers beneath the Sphinx that represent the nine layers of hell/ the underworld). As the sun rises, it passes through the symbolic gateway created by the gaze and constellation of Anubis, thus overcoming the divine laws which Anubis administers and passing through the gateway of heaven he guards.

Additionally, Bauval discovered that at around 10,500 BC, the Great Pyramids also aligned with the three stars of Orion's Belt.[36] He and Hancock argue that the monuments of the Giza Plateau all had their most dominant alignments around this time,[37] which along with other evidence, indicates they may have been built as part of a master plan.

However, although the date of 10,500 BC is one of the most popularly discussed, due to the precession of the equinoxes, it's possible that these alignments also occurred at an earlier time, around 36,500 BC. According to the researcher Armando Mei, the alignments were even more accurate at this date—and the most accurate they could be anywhere in the period between 100,000 BC to AD 2,000. The date of 36,500 BC also coincides more closely with the beginning of the king lists in Egypt, when it is said that the gods lived on earth.

THE RESURRECTION OF OSIRIS IN THE STARS AND ON THE GROUND

The three Great Pyramids of Egypt superimposed over the three stars of Orion's Belt, showing their correlation as discovered by Robert Bauval.

Remarkably, the story of the resurrection of Osiris is enacted by the stars, which was mirrored on the ground by the Great Pyramids and Sphinx at around 10,500 BC and 36,500 BC.

The Great Pyramids align to the three stars of Orion's Belt. To the ancient Egyptians, Orion was the constellation of Osiris, in whose life story the process of attaining imperishability was symbolized.

> "Behold, he has come (again) as Orion; behold, Osiris has come as Orion." [38]
> ~ THE PYRAMID TEXTS, UTTERANCE 442

The Milky Way corresponds to the Nile and the eternal divine feminine, and Leo with Anubis who resurrects Osiris and is symbolized by the Sphinx. The rising sun on the spring equinox symbolizes the resurrected Osiris as his son Horus.

THE USE OF UNIVERSAL PRINCIPLES IN THE GIZA DESIGN

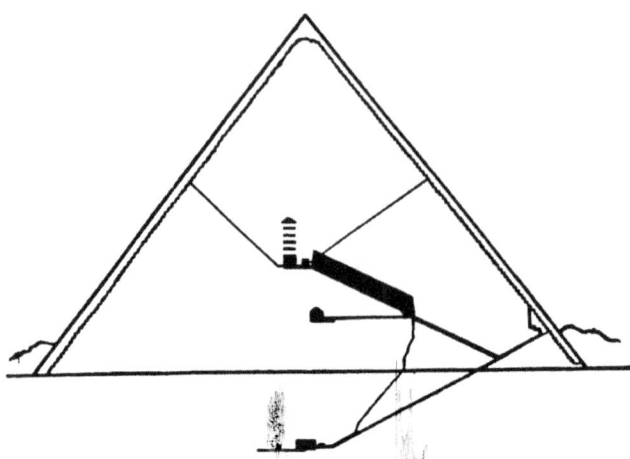

Diagram of the Great Pyramid of Egypt showing its interior passages and chambers. Both the ascending passage (leading to what is called the "King's Chamber") and the descending passage (leading down into the subterranean chamber) are at an angle of 26° 33' 54", which is an angle found in a "golden triangle."[39]

As above, so below—the principles of life exist in everything, which is why the same mathematical logarithmic spiral is found in the shape of a shell, and the spiral of a galaxy. The same principles that govern the movement of the heavens, the formation and structure of life, and the cycles of growth and decay, etc., also govern the spiritual development of consciousness. The whole of life is created for beings to awaken, and is intrinsically imbued with the principles of this process so that we can remember who we truly are and find our way back home.

This is one of the reasons why the builders of the Great Pyramids and Sphinx aligned their sacred structures to the movements of the heavens using sacred geometry, with a precision that is unmatched even today. A study of fifty Egyptian temples revealed that the builders had used highly advanced sacred mathematics in their construction—specifically the Fibonacci series,[40] which is a series of numbers that create a mathematical pattern found throughout nature. Another proved that "the golden section was mandated for use in every sacred building and every royal work of art throughout the whole of Egyptian history."[41]

A universal principle manifests in numbers, sound, color, natural cycles, the formation of life, astronomy, etc., which are studied in separate and distinct disciplines. However, these are all expressions of the same inherent truths. By using the expression of particular principles, whether it be astronomical or mathematical, the builders of the Great Pyramids and Sphinx were able to create places that harnessed these principles energetically and multi-dimensionally, and could be experienced, felt, and understood beyond just an intellectual appreciation of them.

Researcher Robert Temple discovered that throughout the Giza site, the angle of 26 degrees, 33 minutes, and 54 seconds had been used, stating, "this odd angle of slightly more than 26 degrees is the only acute angle possible for a right triangle to be formed that is known as 'the golden triangle,' because it embodies the famous Golden Mean Proportion."[42] Temple found it has been used in both two and three dimensions, between all the pyramids, between the pyramids and sphinx, as well as in the slope of the passages inside the pyramids.[43] The incredible "invisible" three-dimensional layout of the Giza Plateau reveals that the Sphinx and pyramids may have been built and laid out according to a master plan.

Pharaohs were depicted as resurrecting at this angle, which Temple explains is because "the golden angle was viewed by the Egyptians as symbolizing resurrection, and that it represented the transformation of the dead Osiris into his living son Horus in the person of the rising sun"[44]—revealing why the ancient builders wished to harness the energetic power found in this mathematical truth at the site of the Great Sphinx and Pyramids so dedicated to the process of resurrection.

OSIRIS BETWEEN THE PAWS OF THE ANUBIS SPHINX

Left: Ram-headed sphinx at the Temple Complex of Karnak with the figure of a pharaoh between its paws. Right: Photo of an actual Egyptian Anubis sphinx with a pharaoh between its paws. It was built as part of the Ramesseum between 1,279–1,212 BC.

Critics of the theory that the Sphinx was originally carved as Anubis state that the head of the Sphinx is made of a harder and heavier stone than the body, and that because of this, the body would not have been able to support the weight of Anubis' head without it falling off.

However, the ancient Egyptians were master builders. Their statues were built taking into account the fragility of protruding parts like hands and heads, and they incorporated reinforcements into the design to ensure they would last.

My wife noticed that there is a large bulge on the chest of the Sphinx. She realized that this bulge, now almost completely weathered away, could once have been the image of Osiris, Horus, or equivalent deity, which could have supported the head of Anubis. Sphinx statues in Egypt often have the figure of a pharaoh between their paws, and this may have been a symbolic design which carried through thousands of years even though the original form of the Great Sphinx did not.

As further evidence for this, the brightest star in the constellation of Leo (which the Sphinx was likely built to mirror) is situated at its heart, and is known as the King Star (officially called Regulus)—indicating that the bulge on the chest of the Great Sphinx could have been the "King," represented by Osiris.

Regulus also lay along the ecliptic, which is the sun's path through the sky, on the spring equinox during the eras of 10,500 BC and 36,500 BC. As the sun rose shortly after dawn, it crossed over Regulus, enacting Osiris passing through the arms of Anubis to resurrect.

In the Book of the Caverns it refers to "those who are between his [Anubis'] arms,"[45] which may have been symbolized by the Sphinx with Osiris between its "arms." In the Book of the Dead, Anubis is depicted laying his hands upon Osiris, saying "I have come to protect Osiris."[46] Sphinxes later had statues of pharaohs between their paws as they were said to protect the pharaoh. This may show that although the knowledge was lost of what the Sphinx originally was, the idea of the pharaoh being protected between its paws continued.

As the spring equinox sun rose, signaling the resurrection of Osiris as his son Horus, the sun would have emerged from the watery horizon, and created a path of light across the river Nile that could have reached the Sphinx and possibly the statue of Osiris between its paws, creating a path of light across the water uniting Osiris with the sun.

> "Run your course, row over your waterway like Rē [the sun god] on the banks of the sky. O my father, raise yourself, go in your spirit-state." [47]
>
> ~ THE PYRAMID TEXTS, UTTERANCE 512

However, the Sphinx Temple, which stands directly in front of the Sphinx, is in the way—and makes me wonder whether it was built by reusing blocks of an older, ruined temple nearby. The statue of Osiris would have had its lower body beneath the water, symbolizing his rising from out of the underworld and emergence from the primordial waters of the womb to attain eternal life. Images of Osiris actually illustrate him rising from the horizon, with his lower body below the horizon, and his upper body above it.[48]

My wife's theory that the bulge at the heart of the Sphinx was once a statue of Osiris (or equivalent deity) we have called "The Sphinx Osiris Theory."

THE AGE OF THE SPHINX

Following is some information on the age of the Sphinx taken from my wife's book *The Ancient Religion of the Sun*. The age of the Sphinx is a hotly contested topic, as it is one of the few ancient sites in the world that clearly shows evidence of extreme antiquity.

Public debate about it got going in the early 1990s when the researcher John Anthony West and archeologist Robert Schoch put forward the theory that the Sphinx and its surrounding enclosure show signs of heavy weathering from rainwater. They argue that deep rivets in the stone, which have almost entirely eroded away the original form of the Sphinx, were created by a long period of heavy rainfall. Today, Egypt is mostly desert—the last time the Giza Plateau experienced heavy rainfall was during the period called the Nabtian Pluvial, which lasted from 10,000–3,000 BC. This means the Sphinx must have existed during this time, but could also have been built earlier. Schoch places the age of the Sphinx at around 10,000 BC.[49]

However, another prominent researcher in the field, Randall Carlson, believes the erosion is so great that the Sphinx could be at least 20,000–40,000 years old.[50] He came to this conclusion by looking at a number of studies that had measured the rate limestone erodes when subjected to weathering from water (including rainfall), as the Sphinx and surrounding enclosure is carved into the limestone bedrock of the Giza Plateau.[51] The results of his comparative analysis are stunning. One study showed that a coastal limestone cliff-face subjected to the constant action of ocean waves had eroded at the rate of just 1mm per year, which is approximately 0.039 inches.[52] Limestone tombstones in the south-eastern United States eroded at one inch in five hundred years.[53]

Additionally, he looked at the rate of weathering on a number of limestone quarries in Egypt, which have been definitively dated to the period between 1,200–2,000 BC—which is around 500–1,300 years after the Sphinx was apparently carved, and yet the pick marks on them are still clearly visible today, while the enclosure surrounding the Sphinx is weathered approximately seven feet in places.

These extreme signs of weathering combined with the most accurate celestial alignments of the Giza monuments and beginning of Egyptian king lists, all being of comparable date, indicates that the Sphinx, and at least the bases of the Great Pyramids, may have been constructed around 36,500 BC.

This seems to be contradicted by dates obtained from the Sphinx Temple using a technique called "surface luminesce," which found that the limestone blockwork used to build the Sphinx Temple must have been laid between 2,850–2,500 BC.[54] However, Randall Carlson points to a study showing that at around 10,500 BC the Nile experienced massive flooding, which he proposes would have swept away all but the stone blocks heavier than one hundred tonnes[55]—and this is the estimated weight of the largest limestone blocks in the Sphinx and Valley Temples.[56]

My wife and I suspect the Sphinx Temple and Valley Temple were built using the ancient blocks quarried from around the sphinx that had been part of a much older structure ruined during these floods—which is why there seems to be such a contradiction between the dating and evidence of weathering, why the Sphinx Temple blockwork looks haphazard, why the temple itself seems oddly positioned "in the way" of the Sphinx, and is believed to be unfinished. It may be giving the appearance of being "unfinished" because it was built using only the original blocks that remained after cataclysmic flooding.

As research continues, it's looking possible that the Sphinx, and at least the bases of the Great Pyramids, were built tens of thousands of years ago by a people seen as "gods" by the surrounding population. This is when the ancient Religion of the Sun first identifiably appears in prehistory, being the religion of a distant golden age taught by a people remembered as divine—an idea my wife and I have come to, and which is put forward and explored in my wife's book *The Ancient Religion of the Sun*.

HOW THE SPHINX WAS LOST

A partially cleared Sphinx buried in sand up to its shoulders, after having been buried up to its neck. This photo was taken around 1889, but the Sphinx had been buried like this at least once before in the time preceding 1,400 BC.

The knowledge of the original form of the Sphinx was lost thousands of years ago, as it was abandoned, vandalized, re-carved, and restored.

Using circumstantial evidence, mainstream Egyptology has promoted the idea that the Pharaoh Khafre built the Sphinx and the second largest of the Great Pyramids at around 2,500 BC, even though there are no references to

Khafre building either. Restoration blockwork on the Sphinx, as well as the Sphinx and Valley Temples, is believed to date to as early as this time—which would indicate that they were already weathered and in need of restoration by then.

The Pyramid Texts have been dated to soon after Khafre's reign (around 2,400 to 2,300 BC), and were discovered on the walls of a number of pyramids at a site called Saqqara. They contain the oldest references to the Sphinx and Great Pyramids, in which they speak of Anpu/Anubis surrounded by a sacred lake at the Giza Plateau. This reveals that at this time, the Sphinx may have still retained its original form. However, they do not contain references as to who built the Sphinx or Great Pyramids, leaving the time before around 3,000 BC as a veritable blackout in the history of Egypt.

A few hundred years after Khafre's reign, Egypt was hit with droughts, floods, and plagues for around 150 years.[57] During this time (around 2,150 to 2,040 BC) social order broke down and mobs plundered and vandalized the Giza site.[58] The Sphinx may have been severely damaged during these riots (causing such a disfigurement to the head that the knowledge of what it was may have been lost, also giving cause for later pharaohs to restore the face with their own image), and many artifacts and texts looted and destroyed.[59] All that survives is what is set in stone and was too large to destroy: the core structures of the Great Pyramids and Sphinx with their encoded mathematical, astronomical, and spiritual knowledge.

Human-headed sphinxes line a causeway at the Luxor Temple in Egypt. These were a later addition to the temple. Human-headed sphinxes such as these did not start appearing in Egypt until around 1,800 BC.

Social order returned to Egypt in around 2,000 BC. After this, the head of the Sphinx was re-carved at least once, leaving what is likely to be the final image of Pharaoh Amenemhet II (not Khafre or Khufu, who have been attributed with building it, and look nothing like it) who reigned from 1,876 to 1,842 BC.[60] By this time, sphinxes with lions' bodies and the heads of pharaohs or rams were appearing as statues. It is clear that the knowledge of what the Sphinx had been was already lost at large by the Egyptians themselves.

Then, the Sphinx itself was nearly totally lost. Today the area around the Sphinx and pyramids is a parched, sandy desert. In fact, periodically for hundreds and thousands of years at a time, the Sphinx has been covered up to its neck in sand. The famous Dream Stele between the Sphinx's paws records how the Pharaoh Thutmose IV, in around 1,400 BC, had a dream beneath the head of the Sphinx that at the time protruded above the sand. In the dream the Sphinx spoke to Thutmose IV saying that if he restored the Sphinx, in return the Sphinx would make him king.

This reveals that by 1,400 BC the Sphinx had already been long neglected to the sands of time. Rain and the once lush surrounds had long since departed the area, as well as the original civilization of Giza. The focus of Egyptian culture had moved elsewhere.

By the time Thutmose IV had his dream, the Sphinx's head had already been altered and made into the face of a pharaoh, and from at least that time onward it was interpreted as having the body of a lion. Anyone who views the Sphinx today can see the incredible disproportion between the tiny head of the Sphinx with its large, elongated body. This disproportion was created through one, re-carving the head, possibly numerous times, making it smaller each time; and two, adding blockwork casing to parts of the Sphinx's body which had the effect of enlarging it.

Images and statues of Anubis/Anpu in his wolf/dog form, associated with death and resurrection continued however, even though his association with the Sphinx had been severed. This knowledge survived through sacred texts that were passed down over thousands of years, with older texts becoming reincorporated into newer ones.

According to a historical account, the Sphinx was vandalized once more by a local Muslim sheik, who hacked off its nose. Around the same time in AD 1300 after an earthquake shook Cairo, the Great Pyramids were stripped of their outer casing to rebuild the city.

From at least 2,500 BC, successive restorations have been done on the Sphinx, right up until the present day. Ancient Egyptian blockwork which covers the lower part of the Sphinx's body, including the tail and paws, was later added to by the Greeks and Romans who used the Sphinx as a place of worship during their occupations of Egypt. This has been further added to by modern stones. The addition of all these restoration stones has had the effect of widening the torso, massively enlarging the paws, and adding the curled up tail, to create a leonine form instead. It is now impossible to pull back these stones (permission would not be given) to reveal the original form of the torso, paws, and tail. The Sphinx has also been concreted, lengthening the pharaoh's headdress, smoothing the neck, and filling in huge gaping rivets in the body.

It seems likely to me that the Great Sphinx had once been Anubis, as recorded in the oldest preserved texts in ancient Egypt, but after suffering severe damage and the site having been abandoned for hundreds of years, it was re-carved or reinterpreted possibly firstly as a lion, and then later as a lion with a man's head, as the profound understanding of the symbolic significance of the site had been lost by that time (from at least 1,800 BC).

The famous pharaoh of ancient Egypt called Akhenaten—here depicted as the sphinx, worshiping the sun. He reigned around 1,330 BC. He had tried to reinstate the ancient Religion of the Sun, but lacked sufficient knowledge of it, and by that time the Egyptians had also lost the knowledge of the original form of the Great Sphinx [even the Sphinx Temple directly in front of the Sphinx (and possibly also the Valley Temple) was completely buried in sand and unknown to them at that time, and for around seven hundred years prior[01]].

In our times the Sphinx is no longer a site of sacred reverence, but has morphed into a star attraction, replicated in Las Vegas, completely detached from its original spiritual origins. However, through the experience of the same sacred knowledge of the original builders, the Sphinx can once again be understood.

THE GRADUAL LOSS OF THE SPIRITUAL KNOWLEDGE OF ANCIENT EGYPT

There is little evidence to suggest that the Great Pyramids were originally intended as the tombs of pharaohs, although later pyramids were, but there is evidence they served a spiritual purpose as temples of initiation and beacons of knowledge. What happened to Egypt, probably a number of times, is that the spiritual knowledge there became lost to people. While many of the ancient sites themselves preserve the original knowledge of spirituality, the people who inhabit them invariably come and go or lose it as the cycles of nature dictate.

The pyramids at Saqqara in Egypt which contain the oldest known sacred texts in the world, the Pyramid Texts. These pyramids appear to be poor imitations of the Great Pyramids, and so the texts they contain are also likely to be handed down from a much more ancient and pristine source.

Ancient Egypt was also subject to different invasions, population replacements, and was home to opposing peoples living in parallel civilizations for long periods.[62] Most tend to think of ancient Egypt as a homogenous entity, but it was not, and I think this is partly why trying to work out a chronology for it becomes so confounding, as so many different additions and renovations were made by different people to its ancient sites over vast periods. Where the most continuity does seem to have been maintained is in the records kept in some of its oldest temples, which allowed echoes of an incredibly ancient past to reach us. But even that lineage has gone down into dust.

Ancient Egypt was undoubtedly once inhabited by a spiritually advanced and intelligent people; its greatest achievements are its oldest. There is also no doubt that it eventually was home to a religion ruled by megalomaniac elites—scenes at temples even came to depict festivals of drunkenness. Originally the Great Pyramids of Egypt were built free of any attribution and were dedicated to the sacred initiatory rites. Later, lavish tombs were created only for pharaohs and nobles to assure them safe passage in the afterlife, laden with riches, and inscribed with various parts of spiritual teachings.

People's ability to understand this knowledge properly was lost and was eventually interpreted by the public; mass moral decline and degeneration set in. Excavations have uncovered caches of millions of slaughtered and mummified animals (including newborn puppies) used to appease the gods. One dating from the fourth century BC was dedicated to the worship of Anubis in which dogs were bred specifically to be killed and mummified only moments after being born.[63] Obviously this was a totally abhorrent practice and has nothing to do with Anubis in any real sense—revealing just how far society in Egypt had strayed from the original knowledge.

This kind of behavior illustrates why esoteric knowledge was always kept so secret—to maintain its sanctity, and ensure its use for good and rightful purposes. As Jesus would say, "don't throw your pearls before swine lest they trample them underfoot." Not only does the knowledge get trampled upon, but also its practitioners when placed before uncomprehending people.

SPIRITUAL KNOWLEDGE TURNED INTO A RELIGION OF THE AFTERLIFE

The history of Egypt spans many thousands of years during which time the esoteric teachings became a religion merely of the afterlife. Sacred initiatory texts which explain the passage of the initiate in life, through the tests and trials of the path of the spiritual sun, became interpreted as the passage of the soul only after death, as inner death became confused with physical death.

Ancient Egyptian texts describe that unless one attains a certain spiritual level, a person does not have immortality, and after death enters the jaws of the Egyptian crocodile goddess Ammit known as "the eater of the dead," to be given over to eventual destruction in the underworld, or hell, which the Egyptians called the "Place of Annihilation." This was the fate of the evil dead described by the Egyptians as it is in many other remnants of the Religion of the Sun.

The way to avoid this annihilation changed over time. It was originally through spiritual inner transformation, but it was later supposedly reached through repeating spells, by being buried with charms, and inside lavish tombs.

> "I have passed by the roads of Rosetau [ancient name for Giza Plateau] by water and on land; these roads are those of Osiris; they are in the sky. If a man knows the Spell for going down into them, he will be like a god directed by the followers of Thoth. He will indeed go down to every heaven to which he desires to descend. But if he knows not this Spell for passing on these roads, he will fall a prey to the tribunal of the dead, his destiny being that of one who has nothing, and is without (his) justification eternally." [64]
>
> ~ THE BOOK OF THE TWO WAYS

Instead the focus of the religion became a lavish preparation for the journey in the afterlife, rather than making the journey to attain immortality within life itself. For this, material tombs and riches are useless as we only take what we have within ourselves beyond death, and that depends on what we create spiritually within ourselves in life. There is no doubt the Egyptians inherited an incredible knowledge of the realm of the afterlife, but the original builders recognized that this realm did not belong only to death but could be accessed in life, and explored through having out-of-body experiences.

However, there is evidence that later peoples living in Egypt used hallucinogenic plants[65] and would therefore have been influenced by projections of the subconscious mind and even dark forces, rather than receiving dependably clear and meaningful teachings from divine Beings in conscious and natural out-of-body experiences. Hallucinogens were used by other cultures around the world too, as the original spiritual knowledge became diluted.

Although the spiritual knowledge preserved in Egypt became a religion that had steered away from the esoteric toward the mundane, the legacy of ancient Egypt is so great that the knowledge contained in its structures and teachings has remained a source of guidance for those seeking to walk the path of the spiritual sun throughout the ages.

MY OUT-OF-BODY EXPERIENCES IN THE GREAT PYRAMID

My interest in the Sphinx and Great Pyramids of Egypt, as well as the knowledge preserved in ancient Egypt, is not due to an academic curiosity or even an interest in solving ancient mysteries.

Some look for hidden records and chambers, for mathematical and astronomical codes, for building techniques, and artefacts. All of this has merit, as it contributes to our understanding of this incredibly important site. But what I'm interested in is the spiritual knowledge of the builders, and its practical relevance for people today. I'm particularly interested in the pyramids because of the part they have played and still play in the initiations we go through out of the body on the path of the spiritual sun.

I've had a number of out-of-body experiences in the Great Pyramid of Egypt that have revealed their function to me.

In one early experience, I found myself in walking in a corridor made of stone lined with life-sized Egyptian statues. A figure wearing a ceremonial headdress opened a door and I entered a stone room where there were people wearing Egyptian ceremonial outfits. Many of them were sitting around the edge of the room with their knees upright—the same position the "Assessors of Maat" are seated in—and I recognized some of them from ancient Egyptian artwork. I was led to a pedestal holding a granite bowl filled with water, and one of the people gestured to a nearby shaft, which went up a long way through the wall, opening out into the stars. These stars were reflected in the pool of water, which I was shown I should meditate upon. After the experience I learned about the so-called star/air shafts in the Great Pyramid, which I had no prior knowledge of. While these shafts do not open to the stars in the physical world, it was my experience out of the body that one did. This particular experience was my initiation into the path of the spiritual sun.

Years later, in another experience, I found myself lying in the sarcophagus of the King's Chamber in the Great Pyramid. It was cold, dark, and eerily silent in the stone chamber, but I could see a light coming in through the door, and the figure of Anubis was silhouetted against it. As well as the wolf/dog headdress he is portrayed as wearing, he also wore the wings of Mercury on his head; it's interesting that he and Mercury have often been associated. This experience occurred when I was going through the stage of death before resurrection on the path of the spiritual sun. It's because of this experience, of seeing the role Anubis has in resurrection, that I was able to understand the symbolism of the Sphinx.

Through his research, Manly P. Hall also discovered that the King's Chamber had been used for initiations to do with resurrection, writing:

> "In the King's Chamber was enacted the drama of the "second death." Here the candidate, after being crucified upon the cross of the solstices and the equinoxes, was buried in the great coffer. There is a profound mystery to the atmosphere and temperature of the King's Chamber: it is of a peculiar deathlike cold which cuts to the marrow of the bone. This room was a doorway between the material world and the transcendental spheres of Nature. While his body lay in the coffer, the soul of the neophyte soured as a human headed hawk through the celestial realms, there to discover firsthand the eternity of Life, Light, and Truth, as well as the illusion of Death, Darkness, and Sin. [...] The modern world knows little of these ancient rites." [66]
> ~ MANLY P. HALL, THE SECRET TEACHINGS OF ALL AGES

The English word *pyramids* is derived from the Greek *pyramís*, as it is the name they were given by Greeks—they were instead called *Mer* by the ancient Egyptians, meaning "Place of Ascension."[67] This name likely harks back to an earlier understanding of them as places of spiritual ascension.

My experiences have revealed to me that the Great Pyramids were used as places of spiritual initiation, were possibly built for this purpose, and still serve this function in higher dimensions today.

A SITE FOR SPIRITUAL INITIATION

Sun at the pinnacle of the Great Pyramid of Egypt.

What is generally known about the Sphinx and the pyramids has been colored by thousands upon thousands of years of culture, multiple restorations, additions, and changes in form and function. But the Sphinx isn't what some have come to believe—a bizarre statue dedicated to a megalomaniac pharaoh.

It now re-emerges as a sacred symbol of one of the most significant stages in spiritual transformation, and an integral part of a message left in the Giza complex by an advanced people long ago.

I believe that the Great Pyramids and Sphinx weren't intended as monuments dedicated to pharaohs, but as purpose-built places for spiritual initiation and knowledge—with each area of the site having a special form and function related to a stage of the path of the spiritual sun. The design of the various chambers, passageways, subterranean crypts, and alignments are related to various stages of the spiritual path, with its ascents and descents, times of inner death, resurrection, and ascension to the realms of light, etc., and could be used in initiatory rites that correspond to these stages.

In ancient times, it would have been possible for these initiations to take place within the various areas of the site in the physical world. Using the site physically in this way today is clearly not possible, and hasn't been for thousands of years. However, even though today the site is dilapidated and open to a continuous stream of tourists, the structures of the pyramids still exist in the higher dimensions, as everything that is physical has its multidimensional aspect. The builders of the pyramids knew this, and so left a legacy behind not just of physical structures, but of structures that also existed in higher dimensions that would serve as places of initiations out of the body for those going through the path of the spiritual sun well into the future.

> "Do you not know, Asclepius, that Egypt is an image of heaven or, to be more precise, that everything governed and moved in heaven came down to Egypt and was transferred there? If truth were told, our land is the temple of the whole world." [68]
> ~ CORPUS HERMETICUM

As the ancient form of the Sphinx, Anubis guards the entrance of the site as the protector of secrets, allowing only those who are initiated to penetrate its mysteries. He guards the gateway that separates those belonging to the physical, earthly realm, and those who are released into the higher, imperishable spiritual realms, making sure that only those who meet the requirements of resurrection pass through. For potentially a few today, the process of spiritual resurrection is as relevant and important as ever to the purpose of life; Anubis and the deities of ancient Egypt still watch over the sacred process in the higher dimensions, while the Giza Plateau still serves as a site for rites of initiation and spiritual resurrection—a part of human experience that is hidden to the uninitiated, and which takes place beyond the body.

Summer Solstice
Ascension

CHAPTER SIX

The Spiritual Meaning of the Summer Solstice

The summer solstice is a time to celebrate the light of consciousness within ourselves and within each and every person, and to reflect upon the potential for consciousness to awaken.

The progress of the sun throughout the year symbolizes the path of the spiritual sun, and the summer solstice is the climax of this journey as the day of most light in the year. It symbolizes the ascension found in traditions and texts of the Religion of the Sun, and celebrates not only the life-giving power of the sun, but also the reunion with the divine sun. At the spring equinox, the resurrection and return to the Mother is celebrated. Following this, the summer solstice symbolizes the return/ascension to the Father. It is a time to celebrate the triumph of light over darkness in the individual, and the return to wholeness in which the Son, Mother Goddess, and Father God, become one great unified consciousness—a whole and powerful light that enlightens the individual.

The ancient Egyptians, Britons, Maya, Romans, and others aligned their sacred sites to the summer solstice and conducted ceremonies on this day. At the Great Pyramids of Egypt, the summer solstice sun crowns the head of the Sphinx; European pagans celebrated the union of heaven and Earth; the Druids saw the sun as reaching the entrance to heaven in the northern region of the sky;[1] in Rome, the festival of Vestalia continued a Druid tradition of guarding the sacred fire; and the Maya depicted the emergence into heaven in alignment with the summer solstice.

ANCIENT SOLSTICE

The ancient site of Stonehenge in England, which has multiple alignments to the summer solstice.

Light is spiritual in its nature, and so the sun and stars have a spiritual significance that has its root in higher dimensions—in the ancient Religion of the Sun they are described as the source of creation. The summer solstice is therefore a highly spiritual time. The summer solstice is said to be the gate of ascent out of this world into the realm of spirit by both Krishna in the famous text the Bhagavad Gita, and in the designs of the secret caves of Mithras.

THE TRINITY AND THE FEATHERED SERPENT

Hindu painting symbolizing the principle of the feathered serpent. The god Vishnu (center) rides his mount Garuda, which is an eagle. His wife, the goddess Lakshmi, is on either side of him in her dual aspect as material energy, and spiritual energy. The eagle holds the serpent; the eagle represents the masculine aspect of the creator (Vishnu), and the serpent, the feminine aspect (Lakshmi). Behind them is the sun.

246

In ancient teachings of the Religion of the Sun there are incredible similarities—a divine Son who is born to a virgin Mother Goddess and great hidden Father, goes through a series of trials before being betrayed and killed, then resurrects, and later ascends. The events in the life of this Spiritual Son and savior nearly always correspond to the solar year and other astrological events.

These famous trinities of Father, Mother, and Son actually symbolize the fundamental energies and forces that exist within creation—found in atoms, the basic building blocks of all matter, as the three forces of positive, negative, and neutral. Paracelsus, the great alchemist of the Renaissance, saw the cosmos as being fashioned from three spiritual substances or principles called *tria prima*, which the alchemical substances of salt, sulfur, and mercury signified—salt as substance and solidity, mercury as that which is transformative and fusible, and sulfur as binding these two.

As what is above relates to what is below, these three primary forces of the universe are also central to the awakening of consciousness and this explains why the stories of Mother Goddess, Great Father, and Divine Son also contained messages about the process of spiritual transformation. The Mother, Father, and Son exist not only as universal forces, but also as higher parts of each individual's consciousness that exist in more spiritual dimensions and which someone reunites with on the path of the spiritual sun.

Full self-realization is a return to the source of creation, the final ring of the Absolute, where all is one. To do that the different parts of someone's Being that were divided as they came into creation reunite to form one whole, as it is not possible to enter the innermost ring of the Absolute divided; we must return as one, just as we did when we left, but with self-consciousness from the experience of duality in the world of matter.

> "Darkness alone filled the boundless all, for father, mother and son were once more one [...]." [2]
> ~ THE STANZAS OF DZYAN

When the three forces of creation—Father, Mother, and Son—are one and have returned to the divine source, a person has gone through the process of creation in reverse and re-absorbed the principles of life and divinity.

> "It is by love, that the Heavenly Father and the Earthly Mother and the Son of Man become one. For the spirit of the Son of Man was created from the spirit of the Heavenly Father, and his body from the body of the Earthly Mother. Become, therefore, perfect as the spirit of your Heavenly Father and the body of your Earthly Mother are perfect." [3]
> ~ JESUS IN THE ESSENE GOSPEL OF PEACE

This fusion of Mother, Father, and Son has been symbolized as the feathered serpent—it can be found as the Maya and Aztec gods Kukulkan and Quetzalcoatl, the Iranian and Roman god Mithra/Mithras, and prolifically throughout Egypt. The gods Kukulkan/Quetzalcoatl, Mithras, and Horus are the Son; the serpent is a symbol of the Mother; and the feathers symbolic of the Father—it is from the union of Father, Mother, and Son that Quetzalcoatl/Mithras/Horus becomes the feathered serpent.

Left: The feathered serpent in Rome. The Son as Mithras is depicted in the center of the zodiac with the sun atop his head, a serpent wrapped around his body, and wings on his back. Drawing is based on a first century AD Roman white marble relief in the Estense Museum in Modena, Italy. Right: The feathered serpent in Central America. The Son as the sun god Quetzalcoatl who looks out from the mouth of a serpent that is covered in feathers.

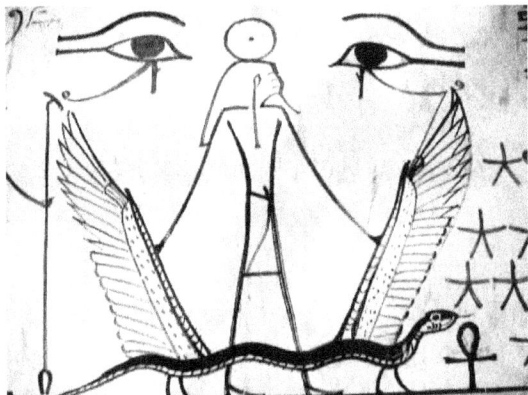

The feathered serpent in Egypt. The sun god in Egypt has the symbol of the sun atop his head and holds out the wings of a feathered serpent. Taken from the illustration of "the 11th hour" from a tomb in the Valley of the Kings.

The serpent is a symbol of the earth (which is substance), and the Earthly Mother, as it is an animal that is at all times in contact with the earth. The feathers are those of an eagle, which is a symbol of the heavens (which is spirit) and the Heavenly Father, as the eagle is an animal that flies and lives above all others and is thus associated with higher realms. The Son/sun, symbolized by Jesus, Quetzalcoatl, Mithras, etc., is the force that unites the earthly human with its higher, heavenly Being.

> "[...] I [Christ] came here, that they might be joined with that Spirit and Breath, and might from two become one, just as from the first, that you might yield much fruit and go up to Him Who Is from the Beginning, in ineffable joy and glory and honor and grace of the Father of the Universe. Whoever, then, knows the Father in pure knowledge will depart to the Father and repose in Unbegotten Father." [4]
> ~ JESUS IN THE WISDOM OF JESUS CHRIST

The Indo-Iranian sun god Mithra was known as "the Mediator," as the Son is the conciliatory force (who, on the path of the spiritual sun, reunites/reconciles us with divinity). The Son is the miraculous reconciliatory aspect of each person's Being that is both personal and cosmic—the light of the spirit manifest in substance that acts within to unite and integrate the earthly human with heavenly divinity, joining the serpent with the feathers so it can fly. This is why the Son has been referred to as the light and savior of humanity in sacred teachings.

> "Dear friends, let us love one another, for love comes from God. Everyone who loves has been born of God and knows God. Whoever does not love does not know God, because God is love. This is how God showed his love among us: He sent his one and only Son into the world that we might live through him." [5]
> ~ 1 JOHN 4:7-9

> "That solar orb is said to be salvation of the human beings. That place is the separator of the human beings from the world." [6]
> ~ THE SAMBA PURANA

CREATION IN REVERSE

The process of creation at the beginning of the universe that gave rise to everything, including what we consist of both physically and spiritually, is one of the greatest of mysteries. Yet understanding some of its basic principles is important for understanding spiritual liberation/salvation, as it is the return to our higher Being and the divine source of creation from where we first came.

"Know what came before time, and the beginning of wisdom is yours." [7]
~ LAO-TZU IN TAO TE CHING

In the ancient Vedic texts, the name given both to the source of creation and to our higher Being is Brahman, who is described as both our originator and our final sanctuary.

"Brahman is the First Cause, and last refuge." [8]
~ THE KATHA UPANISHAD

"The perfection which is the Self is the goal of all beings. [...] This universe, before it was created, existed as Brahman. 'I am Brahman': thus did Brahman know himself. Knowing himself he became the Self of all beings. Among the gods, he who awakened to the knowledge of the Self became Brahman; and the same was true among the seers. [...] Now if a man depart this life without knowing the kingdom of the Self, he, because of that ignorance, does not enjoy the bliss of liberation. He dies without reaching his goal." [9]
~ BRIHADARANYAKA UPANISHAD

In the famous Hindu text the Bhagavad Gita, Krishna urges his disciple Arjuna to search for the first cause of the universe, as he says it is also the eternal goal.

"Seek That, the First Cause, from which the universe came long ago. Not deluded by pride, free from selfish attachment and selfish desire, beyond the duality of pleasure and pain, ever aware of the Self, the wise go forward to that eternal goal." [10]
~ KRISHNA IN THE BHAGAVAD GITA

Enlightenment is the process of creation in the universe in reverse, as it is the return of the individual to the divine source we were created from. In creation myths, a divine androgynous being firstly emerges from the great unmanifest and unknowable source. This being divides into the duality of masculine and feminine, of Father and Mother, in order to create and give birth to a Son, who then makes the rest of creation. These myths not only describe the creation of the universe—as the process of creation is the same on a macrocosmic and microcosmic level, and a cosmic and personal level—but also, they describe the creation of our own unique Being which emerged from the source of creation and divided into its various parts as it came into the dimensions of life.

To follow this process in reverse a person firstly reintegrates with the Son of their higher Being (symbolized at the winter solstice), then the Son returns to and reintegrates with the Mother (symbolized at the spring equinox), then the Son-Mother returns to and reintegrates with the Father (symbolized at the summer solstice). The feathered serpent—the three forces of creation, as Mother, Father, and Son—a unified self-realized androgynous being, which is now whole, then returns on the wings of spirit from the earth to the spiritual realm, the divine source of creation called the Absolute.

> "I am the one who is with you always. I am the Father, I am the Mother, I am the Son. I am the undefiled and incorruptible one." [11]
> ~ JESUS IN THE APOCRYPHON OF JOHN

> "It is imperative that not a single thought remain and that the tiniest speck of dust be transformed. There must be no perceived distinction of self and other; enmity and kindness must be seen as one; far and near, intimate and distant must be united as one body; birds and beasts, insects and fish are all of the same ch'i. One's lofty tao and weighty te are equal to heaven's. Following this, in the midst of obscurity and utter silence, the blessing is received and the 'mysterious pearl' presented in all its splendor and brilliance, more precious than words can tell. When the 'pearl' is consumed, the body sprouts feathered wings, and 'disappearing from Mount Wu-I' flies to the paradise of the immortals." [12]
> ~ TRUE TRANSMISSION OF THE GOLDEN ELIXIR BY SUN JU-CHUNG

THE THREE DAYS AND THREE RINGS

At the winter solstice, the sun appears to stand still in its journey for three days. This likewise happens at the summer solstice when the sun stands still at the climax of light for three days following the solstice before reversing its course to begin its annual cycle again.

The three days of standstill at the winter solstice can be seen to symbolize the process of creation, with each day corresponding to the three forces of creation as Father, Mother, and Son emanating from the unmanifest source. The three days also correspond to the Spiritual Son being born into creation and likewise within a person, taking three symbolic strides to do so.

At the summer solstice, this process happens in reverse, as the Spiritual Son now returns to the unmanifest source, having fully integrated within the consciousness of a person. The three days of standstill can be seen to represent him retracing his steps on the way to the source, and reuniting with the higher parts of consciousness, of Mother and Father.

These three days find a parallel with the symbol of the divine source of creation sometimes called the Absolute, which consists of three concentric rings. These rings represent the three primary forces that emerged from the unmanifest source of creation, as the Trinity of Father, Mother, and Son. The outer ring is reached when someone merges with the Son, which they need to do before they can reach the second inner ring where they merge with the Mother. It is only by reaching the second ring that they can then reach to the third and innermost ring where they merge with the Father. From there a person's consciousness has become whole again, which is represented by the dot of the innermost ring, symbolizing unity. From unity they can return to the unmanifest source of creation, which is not symbolized by anything, to show that it is beyond any form that is perceivable from within our universe of duality.

The three rings of the Absolute were depicted in this illustration of Dante's vision of the source of creation.

In the final climax of Dante Alighieri's *Divine Comedy*, he describes his vision of the "Living Light," the source of creation, appearing to him as three circles, which are the three concentric rings of the Absolute.

> "In the deep and bright essence of that exalted Light, three circles appeared to me; they had three different colors, but all of them were of the same dimension; one circle seemed reflected by the second, as rainbow is by rainbow, and the third seemed fire breathed equally by those two circles." [13]
>
> ~ DANTE ALIGHIERI, THE DIVINE COMEDY, PARADISO CANTO 33

This three-ringed pattern appears in some remarkable places.

Scientists have measured the cosmic microwave background, which is the microwave glow, present everywhere all at once, left over from the creation of the universe. Incredibly, it was the symbol of the Absolute, the three concentric rings, which appeared in it.

The same symbol of the Absolute also appears in connection with the mantra Om from the ancient Vedic texts of India—perhaps the most famous mantra in the world—which is said to represent the Absolute and the sound present at the creation of the universe, which begs the question: how did the authors of the Vedas know? When a recording of this ancient Sanskrit mantra (which was made inside the King's Chamber of the Great Pyramid of Egypt) was played using a CymaScope (created by John Stuart Reid and Erik Larson), it created the three ring symbol of the Absolute.[14] This field of study is called cymatics, which demonstrates the visual effects of sound upon matter and the geometric shapes and patterns it creates.

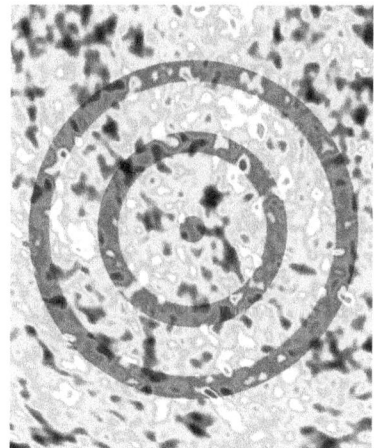 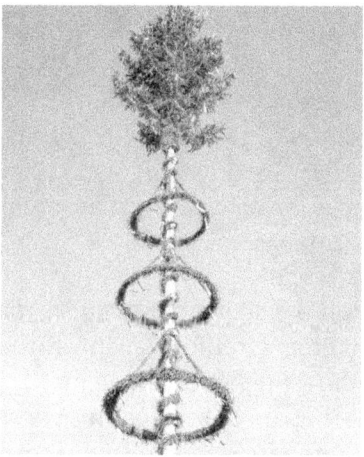

Three concentric rings were discovered in the cosmic microwave background of the universe.[15] Right: A maypole in Germany topped with three rings.

The pattern of concentric rings is also found in a number of sacred sites around the world aligned to the solstice, including Arkaim in Russia, Stonehenge in England, and Goseck Circle in Germany (which each lie along the same line of latitude); the lost island of Atlantis was also described by Plato as having its major city laid out in three concentric rings.[16]

Three rings often top the maypole used at celebrations of midsummer in Germany. References to their meaning may be found in the texts called the Eddas, which are surviving records of pre-Christian Germanic religion. They describe three upper, heavenly realms of immortality that shine like the sun, and which those who have attained immortality, and who are "associated with the splendor of the sun," ascend to.[17] They are at the top of the maypole, which represents the sacred Germanic world tree called Irminsul/Yggdrasil, whose branches reach up into heaven.

ASCENSION

"Jesus said, 'Do not hold on to me, for I have not yet ascended to the Father. Go instead to my brothers and tell them, "I am ascending to my Father and your Father, to my God and your God."'" [18]
~ JOHN 20:17

Ascension is a stage that occurs on the path of the spiritual sun—it is when the Son returns to the heavenly Father and is symbolized by the summer solstice. Interestingly, it's the elements the sun is comprised of—hydrogen and helium—that are light enough to escape the force of the earth, and leave its atmosphere[19] to ascend into the cosmos.

In the life of Jesus his ascension occurred sometime after the spring equinox, the time of his resurrection. In the quote above, Jesus appears first to Mary Magdalene after he resurrects but tells her he has not yet ascended, as at this stage he has become one with the great Mother but not yet with the Father.

References to Jesus' ascension in the Bible are extremely brief and vague—often being only a line in length. At least one of these references is believed to have been added to the Gospels later,[20] so in looking for more extensive and perhaps more authentic references to the ascension, we have to look elsewhere.

There were many early Christian texts that were excluded from the Bible and which contain secret and advanced teachings Jesus gave directly to the disciples. Many of these texts have only resurfaced in the last century or so after remaining hidden or lost for over a thousand years.

In one of these texts called Pistis Sophia, the ascension of Jesus is witnessed by the disciples in great detail, and explained by Jesus himself who returns to the disciples after his ascension to relate it to them.

> "It came to pass then, when the sun had risen in the east, that a great light-power came down, in which was my Vesture, which I had left behind in the four-and-twentieth mystery, as I have said unto you. And I found a mystery in my Vesture, written in five words of those from the height: *zama zama ōzza rachama ōzai*—whose solution is this: 'O Mystery, which is without in the world, for whose sake the universe hath arisen—this is the total outgoing and the total ascent, which hath emanated all emanations and all that is therein and for whose sake all mysteries and all their regions have arisen—come hither unto us, for we are thy fellow-members. We are all with thyself; we are one and the same. Thou art the First Mystery, which existed from the beginning in the Ineffable before it came forth; and the name thereof are we all. Now, therefore, are we all come to meet thee at the last limit, which also is the last mystery from within; itself is a portion of us. Now, therefore, have we sent thee thy Vesture, which hath belonged to thee from the beginning, which thou hast left behind in the last limit, which also is the last mystery from within, until its time should be completed, according to the commandment of the First Mystery. Lo, its time is completed; put it on [thee].'" [21]
>
> ~ JESUS IN PISTIS SOPHIA

The ascension is described in association with the rising sun in the east—the spiritual sun, which is referred to as the last limit, and the place that all emanations have emanated from, being the source of creation. The Mystery of Jesus' garment, which he had left behind—in the twenty-fourth mystery, like the twenty-four hours of the day—comes to him at his ascent, and is described as the reason why the whole of the universe with all its regions was created, making it the purpose of existence. Incredibly, the word *zama* on Jesus' vesture is also an ancient Mayan word, which means "dawn."[22]

The text goes on to describe the vesture of light that Jesus is clothed in as being three-fold, and producing three different types of light. These three lights correspond to the three rings of the Absolute and the three primary forces of creation (Father, Mother, and Son). After Jesus ascends, these three lights and vestures are one in him, as the Father, Mother, and Son of the Being are now unified.

> "[...] the heavens opened, and they saw Jesus descend, shining most exceedingly, and there was no measure for his light in which he was. For he shone more [radiantly] than at the hour when he had ascended to the heavens, so that men in the world cannot describe the light which was on him; and it shot forth light-rays in great abundance, and there was no measure for its rays, and its light was not alike together, but it was of diverse kind and of diverse type,

some [rays] being more excellent than others; and the whole light consisted together. It was of threefold kind, and the one [kind] was more excellent than the other... The second, that in the midst, was more excellent than the first which was below, and the third, which was above them all, was more excellent than the two which were below. And the first glory, which was placed below them all, was like to the light which had come over Jesus before he had ascended into the heavens, and was like only itself in its light. And the three light-modes were of diverse light-kinds, and they were of diverse type, one being more excellent than the other..." [23]

~ PISTIS SOPHIA

In Pistis Sophia, Jesus narrates the story of the journey of consciousness (called Sophia) through many perils in the world of matter until its final return to the divine source from which it came. At the end of its journey, he describes its final ascension after which it becomes one with the Ineffable, called "the One and Only." This One and Only is the Being of each person before it divided into creation; in the story Sophia ascends and returns to this wholeness of Being.

"And the soul which receiveth the mystery of the Ineffable, will soar into the height, being a great light-stream [...] and goeth to the region of the inheritance of the mystery which it hath received, that is to the mystery of the One and Only, the Ineffable, and until it becometh one with its Limbs." [24]

~ JESUS IN PISTIS SOPHIA

This ascension doesn't happen physically, but in higher dimensions, which is why in the excerpt above Jesus describes the soul and not a physical person as ascending, and describes it ascending into a higher region—a region that is clearly not in the physical plane. Outwardly then, a person who ascends appears the same, but inwardly they are changed.

This is possible because all the dimensions of life are here and now. When someone's consciousness ascends in the higher dimensions and is reunited with the higher parts of its Being, they are then able to feel the emanations of their Being within them.

Most people only have basic consciousness within, which only gives its own basic level of emanations, whereas the higher aspects of someone's Being—which are the Son, Mother, and Father—give their own much higher spiritual emanations. It is only once the consciousness of someone reunites with the higher spiritual parts of their Being on the path of the spiritual sun that they then contain the spiritual emanations of that higher part permanently. This gives them a much clearer perception of reality, imbued with the emanations of their Being. Thus, they have greater capacity to feel higher states such as peace and love far more than anyone who has not reunited with these parts is able to.

This is the meaning behind some of the sayings of Jesus.

> "His disciples said to him, 'When will the kingdom come?' [Jesus said] 'It will not come by watching for it. It will not be said, "Look, here!" or "Look, there!" Rather, the Father's kingdom is spread out upon the earth, and people don't see it.'" [25]
> ~ THE GOSPEL OF THOMAS

> "He who will receive that light will not be seen, nor can he be detained. And none shall be able to torment a person like this, even while he dwells in the world. And again when he leaves the world, he has already received the truth in the images. The world has become the Aeon (eternal realm), for the Aeon is fullness for him." [26]
> ~ THE GOSPEL OF PHILIP

> "Jesus said, 'If your leaders say to you, "Look, the (Father's) kingdom is in the sky," then the birds of the sky will precede you. If they say to you, "It is in the sea," then the fish will precede you. Rather, the (Father's) kingdom is within you and it is outside you. When you know yourselves, then you will be known, and you will understand that you are children of the living Father. But if you do not know yourselves, then you live in poverty, and you are the poverty.'" [27]
> ~ THE GOSPEL OF THOMAS

Jesus further explains that someone who fuses with the Ineffable is of an unimaginable spiritual stature, and yet is a "man in the world."

> "Now, therefore, amēn, I say unto you: Every man who will receive that mystery of the Ineffable and accomplish it in all its types and all its figures, he is a man in the world, but he towereth above all angels and will tower still more above them all...
> He is a man in the world, but he will rule with me in my kingdom.
> He is a man in the world, but he is king in the Light.
> He is a man in the world, but he is not one of the world.
> And amēn, I say unto you: That man is I and I am that man." [28]
> ~ JESUS IN PISTIS SOPHIA

This same understanding also appears in Taoist texts:

> "Those with determination must find true teachers to instruct them on the 'three stages' and 'three gates'; transmit the 'nine zithers' and

'nine swords'; explain the order of 'obtaining the medicine,' the 'elixir,' and the 'mysterious pearl'; and detail the attainments of the 'earthly and heavenly immortals.' For these, the 'feathered wheels' are not needed to convey them to the Jade Pool 20,000 miles distant, for it is just feet away. One need not mount the celestial winds to the brilliance of the 'ninefold heaven.' Suddenly opening my eyes, the immortals Chang, Ko, Chun, and Lu become my comrades, and the serenity of heaven is my home." [29]
~ TRUE TRANSMISSION OF THE GOLDEN ELIXIR BY SUN JU-CHUNG

And in Hindu texts:

"The Self is hidden in the lotus of the heart. Those who see themselves in all creatures go day by day into the world of Brahman hidden in the heart. Established in peace, they rise above body-consciousness to the supreme light of the Self. Immortal, free from fear, this Self is Brahman, called the True. Beyond the mortal and the immortal, he binds both worlds together. Those who know this live day after day in heaven in this very life." [30]
~ THE CHANDOGYA UPANISHAD

RETURN TO THE SOURCE OF CREATION

This fusion of consciousness with the great, ineffable source of creation described by Jesus can be found symbolized at the Great Pyramids of Egypt at the summer solstice.

On the summer solstice, the sun sets between the second largest of the pyramids and the Great Pyramid. As it does, it creates the Egyptian hieroglyph for the first act of creation—the two pyramids act as the mountains on either side of the sun as it rose for the first time. However, in this case the sun is setting not rising, indicating that this is a process of creation, but in reverse, with the sun returning to the source of creation.

An artist's rendition of the summer solstice sun setting between the two largest Great Pyramids of Egypt, crowning the Sphinx in the foreground.

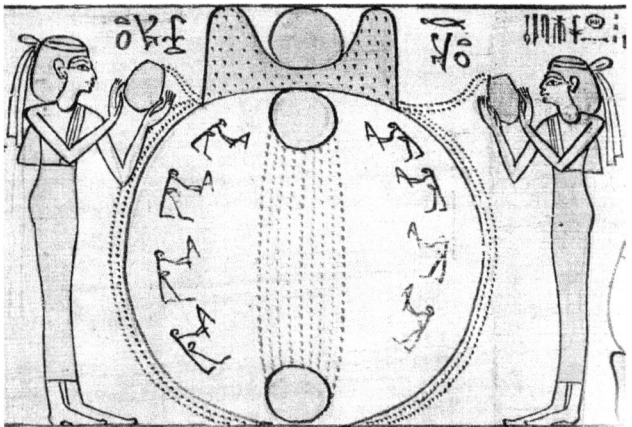

Egyptian painting of the first sunrise at the dawning of creation from the primeval mound that arose from out of the waters. At the top is the "horizon" hieroglyph with the sun appearing between two mountains, which looks like the setting summer solstice sun at the Great Pyramids.

In Pistis Sophia, Jesus teaches his disciples that there are twenty-four mysteries, and that the first mystery is also the last mystery—that is, from where everything came, is also where it returns, just as the sun returns to its point of origin each day after twenty-four hours, and also every year.

> "And Jesus said to his disciples: 'I am come forth out of that First Mystery, which is the last mystery, that is the four-and-twentieth mystery.' And his disciples have not known nor understood that anything existeth within that mystery; but they thought of that mystery, that it is the head of the universe and the head of all existence; and they thought it is the completion of all completions [...]." [31]
> ~ PISTIS SOPHIA

This completion of all completions applies not just to everything that exists, but also to the development of consciousness.

THE UNION OF HEAVEN AND EARTH, AND THE TREE OF LIFE

Summer solstice celebrations in Europe today still echo some of the midsummer celebrations from ancient times. Many Druids see the summer solstice as the time of union between heaven and earth.[32] Slavic pagans celebrated the marriage of god and goddess.[33] The pagan maypole still used in dances at midsummer is a symbol of this union. It represents the tree of life, world tree, and axis mundi found in sacred teachings of the ancient Religion of the Sun with its roots in the earth (feminine) and branches in the heavens (masculine), forming a connection between these two realms.

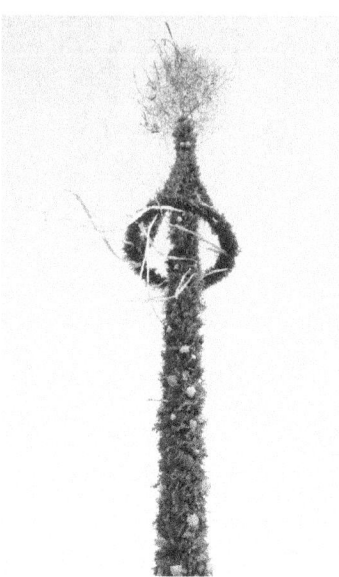

A maypole in Germany with the ring pierced by the pole, symbol of the united masculine and feminine forces, of heaven united with earth.

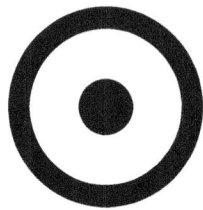

When the maypole is viewed from below or above, it creates the ancient symbol of the sun, in which the circle represents the feminine and the central dot the masculine. These also correspond to the inner two rings of the Absolute, which correspond to the Mother and Father.

Through the unification of these two forces within a person, they become a connection between heaven and earth, and are able to bring heavenly forces, teachings, messages, etc., to the earth, serving as a vital link for humanity by bringing knowledge of otherwise inaccessible divine realms and beings to the world.

This is why Odin is able to bring the knowledge of runes to humanity after his self-sacrifice on the world tree, and after his subsequent journey to its root in the underworld where he sacrifices his eye to be able to drink from the well of "remembrance."

The Old Norse texts called the Eddas describe how nine worlds form part of the sacred tree that stretches throughout creation; these worlds correspond to the nine regions of the psyche, and the nine heavens and hells. On a microcosmic level this tree is symbolic of the structure of divinity within us (consisting of the spiritual bodies and different parts of our higher Being), which when created, connect what is above with what is below.

> "I remember yet the giants of yore,
> Who gave me bread in the days gone by;
> Nine worlds I knew, the nine in the tree
> With mighty roots beneath the mold." [34]
> ~ VÖLUSPÁ, THE POETIC EDDA

The ancient Egyptian symbol of Osiris as the *djed* pillar, with the feathers of the Heavenly Father and serpent of the Earthly Mother crowning his head, united through the Son/sun, is also a symbol of the tree of life. This symbolism was encoded into the events of Osiris' life, as after his death he becomes one with a sacred tree that becomes a great pillar of a king's palace (symbolic of the kingdom of heaven). It symbolized the spine of Osiris, and at the same time, the axis or "spine" of the earth.

The Egyptian symbol of the *djed* pillar which represents the god Osiris as the symbolic pillar of the temple, the world tree, and axis mundi. The four notches on the pillar correspond to the four notches of the sacrum bone at the base of the spine, and also to the four material bodies—physical, vital, astral, and mental. The spirit sits upon these as the double feather plume, serpents, and sun disk. The serpents represent the Mother, the feathers the Father, and the sun the Son, making up the three forces of creation as the symbol of the feathered serpent. The four bodies plus the three forces (of the trinity) correspond to the seven bodies (called physical, vital, astral, mental, causal, buddhic, atmic) and seven dimensions.

The Germanic world tree known as the Irminsul (called Yggdrasil in Northern Germanic/Norse religion) is often depicted with two wing-like branches and serpents entwined at its roots, and can also have a solar cross or eagle atop it. Odin was said to have hung on this tree, which would bring together the same elements of the symbol of the feathered serpent—with Son (Odin), Mother (serpent), and Father (feathers/eagle). The Irminsul also bears a resemblance to the ancient symbol of the caduceus,[35] which has two entwined serpents around a winged staff (symbolizing the spine) and is sometimes topped by a sphere, sun disk, or pine cone, representing the pineal gland as the seat of consciousness. Both the Irminsul and caduceus resemble the *djed* pillar, and each of them appear to be variations of one ancient feathered sun serpent and world tree symbol that expressed the same principles.

The Germanic world tree also shares similarities with the sacred world tree of the Maya, which likewise represents the axis that unites heaven and earth.

> "The ceiba was the most sacred tree for the ancient Maya, and according to Maya mythology, it was the symbol of the universe. The tree signified a route of communication between the three levels of earth. Its roots were said to reach down into the underworld, its trunk represented the middle world where the humans live, and its canopy of branches arched high in the sky symbolized the upper world and the thirteen levels in which the Maya heaven was divided."[36]
>
> ~ NICOLETTA MAESTRI

ANCIENT SOLSTICE

Left: The Germanic Irminsul tree with the solar cross above it. Center: The sacred Mayan world tree. Right: Symbol of the Caduceus. These symbols share similarities, and probably had similar meanings and the same origin.

Some of the beliefs surrounding the Maya world tree are revealed at the ancient city of Palenque in Mexico. Here, the king Pacal (also known as "Sun Shield") was laid to rest in a stone sarcophagus within the chamber of a pyramid,[37] just as some of the pharaohs of ancient Egypt were. His sarcophagus was engraved with an image of him dressed as the Maize god united with the world tree.[38] On the summer solstice, the setting sun aligns with his tomb and the pyramid temple it lies within[39]—symbolizing his rebirth and emergence into heaven.

Oral histories of the local people state that Palenque was first established and built by the wisdom bringer Votan.[40] There is much evidence that indicates the Maya wisdom bringer Votan (pronounced Uotan) was the same person as Odin (called Wuotan in old German), and that Germanic, Maya, and Egyptian religion (as well as many others) have their root in the ancient Religion of the Sun, which was founded by the same wisdom bringers.[41]

It appears that Pacal's afterlife journey symbolized one that others could take, and was based on the path of the spiritual sun, with the site of Palenque being used for spiritual initiations. After likely undergoing a symbolic death and rebirth in the underworld enacted within the underground chambers of the temple, initiates would emerge at its south end—with the noonday summer solstice sun above.[42]

> "And just as the roots of the tree
> Sink into the earth and are nourished,
> And the branches of the tree
> Raise their arms to heaven,
> So is man like the trunk of the tree,
> With his roots deep
> In the breast of his Earthly Mother,
> And his soul ascending
> To the bright stars of his Heavenly Father.
> And the roots of the tree

> Are the Angels of the Earthly Mother,
> And the branches of the tree
> Are the Angels of the Heavenly Father.
> And this is the sacred Tree of Life
> Which stands in the Sea of Eternity." [43]
>
> ~ THE ESSENE GOSPEL OF PEACE

> "See, oh Sons of Light, the branches of the Tree of Life reaching toward the kingdom of the Heavenly Father. And see the roots of the Tree of Life descending into the bosom of the Earthly Mother. And the Son of Man is raised to an eternal height and walks in the wonders of the plain; for only the Son of Man carries in his body the roots of the Tree of Life; the same roots that suckle from the bosom of the Earthly Mother; and only the Son of Man carries in his spirit the branches of the Tree of Life; the same branches that reach to the sky, even so to the kingdom of the Heavenly Father." [44]
>
> ~ JESUS IN THE ESSENE GOSPEL OF PEACE

The union of heaven and earth is symbolic of the union between the feminine and masculine parts of someone's higher Being.

The first being that emerges from the Absolute source of creation at the dawn of time, in creation stories from the Religion of the Sun, is androgynous, and divides into male and female in order to create—just as supreme androgynous creator god Atum in Egypt first creates the male Shu and female Tefnut, and likewise in India Brahman creates through the masculine Purusha and feminine Prakriti, etc.

In order to return to the source of creation, we retrace the steps we took when we left, and undergo this process in reverse. We emerged as an androgynous being, and so we can only return as an androgynous being. This is not a physical or biological change, but an inner spiritual one—references to which can be found in ancient texts of the Religion of the Sun.

> "[...] it will lead your souls into the Light of lights, into the regions of Truth and Goodness, into the region of the Holy of all holies, into the region **which there is neither female nor male**, nor are there forms in that region, but a perpetual indescribable Light." [45]
>
> ~ JESUS IN PISTIS SOPHIA

> "Jesus said to them, 'When you make the two one, and when you make the inside like the outside and the outside like the inside, and the above like the below, and **when you make the male and the female one and the same**, so that the male not be male nor the female female; and when you fashion eyes in the place of an eye, and

a hand in place of a hand, and a foot in place of a foot, and a likeness in place of a likeness; then will you enter the kingdom.'" 46
~ THE GOSPEL OF THOMAS

"Of the Immortal Man it should be said that He is hermaphrodite, or male and female, and eternally watchful." 47
~ HERMES TRISMEGISTUS IN THE VISION OF HERMES

"The perfect Savior said: 'I want you to know that he who appeared before the universe in infinity, Self-grown, Self-constructed Father, being full of shining light and ineffable, in the beginning, when he decided to have his likeness become a great power, immediately **the principle (or beginning) of that Light appeared as Immortal Androgynous Man**, that through that Immortal Androgynous Man they might attain their salvation and awake from forgetfulness through the interpreter who was sent, who is with you until the end of the poverty of the robbers.'" 48
~ THE WISDOM OF JESUS CHRIST

This reunion of the masculine and feminine parts of someone's Being has been symbolized as a marriage, because when separate, a man and woman are seen as incomplete, but when united together in marriage, they become as one, just as masculine and feminine are the dual aspects of the one supreme creator. Marriage and sex are extremely sacred, as they contain the powers and principles of divinity. The marriage of heaven and earth, of god and goddess, celebrated at the summer solstice is symbolic of the fusion between spirit and human.

THE VIRGINS OF THE SUN

The consciousness as a bride of divinity was celebrated in Rome at the summer solstice, and was based on ancient Indo-European tradition.

In Rome, the summer solstice was celebrated at the festival of Vestalia. It was the time of year when ordinary women were allowed to enter the sacred temple of the goddess Vesta, who was protector of the sacred flame, and of chastity and marriage. The temple was kept by Vestal Virgins who were always dressed as brides and tended a sacred fire that continuously burned in a shrine. No men were allowed to enter the temple of Vesta, not even the head of the Roman

Statue of a Vestal Virgin of Rome.

Empire—only the pontifex maximus (the chief high priest of the Roman religion) could enter, but even he was barred from the holy of holies.[49]

This practice shares similarities with a Druidic one: at Kildare in Ireland there was a sacred sanctuary of the Celtic goddess Brighid (an Indo-European goddess of the dawn and fire), which nineteen virgin Druidesses guarded, and which no man was allowed to enter nor even look upon. The priestesses had the duty of attending the sacred fire of the goddess Brighid that continuously burned, just as the Vestal Virgins did in Rome. This role was eventually assumed by nuns when the site became Christian, who themselves were called "Brides of Christ." The original Druidic priestesses were called "Inghean au dagha," which means "the daughters of fire," and were believed to symbolize the virgin daughters of the flame.[50] They were said to have sung the following song,[51] in which they ask to be taken to heaven by the sun:

> "Bride [Brighid], excellent woman, sudden flame, may the fiery, bright sun take us to the lasting kingdom." [52]

Interestingly, there were thousands of women in the Inca Empire who similarly were called "the Virgins of the Sun" and were considered the wives of the sun.[53] Like the Vestal Virgins of Rome, they tended a sacred fire and were committed to vows of celibacy. The female priestesses of the Guanches, the ancient inhabitants of the Canary Islands, also share similarities.

> "In addition to male Shamans, the Spanish priests had also documented the existence of a spiritual order of Guanche holy women called "*Harmagadas*," who were like vestal virgins. Parallels are noted between them and the priestesses on the banks of the Nile in ancient Egypt. They lived together in stone temples called "*Tamoganteen Acoran*" (house of God) [...]. These holy women were distinguished from other women by their long white garments. [...] The Harmagadas never married, but served as midwives, performed rites of baptism, rain ceremonies and various other sacred functions. Historians and anthropologists agree that these women formed a very important component of the Guanche spiritual order and their theocratic government." [54]
>
> ~ GORDON KENNEDY, THE WHITE INDIANS OF NIVARIA

The Romans, Incas, Druids, and Guanches all followed a form of solar religion, and so it is likely that the tradition of the order of the Harmagadas, the Virgins of the Sun, Druidesses, and Vestal Virgins, have some common influence, and that it was a practice that traveled to different parts of the world with the spread of the ancient Religion of the Sun. Unfortunately however, at least the Romans and Inca distorted and added barbaric practices into this tradition, including punishment by death for any violation of the code of virginity.

In Rome, the Vestal Virgins had to commit to thirty years of virginity. These vows of celibacy in Rome and elsewhere however, appear to have been based on a literal interpretation of virginity, which is a distortion of the spiritual meaning of the virginity of consciousness. The priestesses of the temple were symbols of the consciousness, which is feminine in nature; virginity is symbolic of an inward energetic state of purity in which the sexual energies are undefiled by the egos, and in which consciousness, like a holy bride, is faithfully committed to reuniting with the higher aspects of its Being.

> "Wise men of old gave the soul a feminine name. Indeed she is female in her nature as well. She even has her womb. As long as she was alone with the father, she was virgin and in form androgynous. But when she fell down into a body and came to this life, then she fell into the hands of many robbers. And the wanton creatures passed her from one to another and [...] her. Some made use of her by force, while others did so by seducing her with a gift. In short, they defiled her, and she [...] her virginity." [55]
> ~ THE EXEGESIS ON THE SOUL

The sacred fire the priestesses tend to is the flame of the spirit within, and also the sexual fire, which they symbolically protect from defilement—that is from the lower and polluted energies of the egos, and from adultery, lust, and fornication. This is not done through sexual abstinence, but within marriage through a sacred alchemical practice that purifies the internal energies in sex itself—called the bridal chamber in Gnostic Christianity, Maithuna/Tantrism in the East, HeQi in the Taoism of ancient China, and symbolized as the alchemical transformation of lead into gold.

Ancient Gnostic texts, such as the Exegesis on the Soul quoted above, tell the incredible story of consciousness—its fall into matter, perilous trials against darkness, and ultimate goal to ascend to heaven. The quote states that we were originally androgynous—a state we lost as we came into creation as our consciousness split into various parts that stayed above in the different dimensions, until an aspect of it came down to inhabit a physical body. This aspect of consciousness then became defiled by the various ego states that were created, such as lust, greed, anger, hatred, violence, envy, etc., which are referred to as robbers because they steal the light and powers of consciousness.

The summer solstice signifies the regaining of the powers and pure state of consciousness—an inner state gained through the practice of energetic purification in alchemy and the death of the egos—and its ascent to the place it originally descended from, but with the knowledge gained from its experience in matter.

In the life of Jesus, Mary Magdalene played the symbolic role of the aspect of consciousness that descends into matter and falls into spiritual destitution. In his casting out of the seven demons from Mary and redeeming her, Jesus enacted how consciousness is saved by the higher aspect of the Being called the Spiritual Son/Christ and how these two parts of someone's Being become joined on the path of the spiritual sun, so that the consciousness becomes as the "bride of Christ." This is why in Gnostic texts Mary Magdalene was often referred to as the consort of Jesus, and bride-like priestesses sang of being taken up to heaven by the sun.

Below, Jesus refers to consciousness as a drop from the Light, whom he, as representing the Great Savior, saves from "the robbers," awakens, and joins with.

> "All who come into the world, like a drop from the Light, are sent by him to the world of Almighty, that they might be guarded by him. And the bond of his forgetfulness bound him by the will of Sophia, that the matter might be <revealed> through it to the whole world in poverty, concerning his (Almighty's) arrogance and blindness and the ignorance that he was named. But I came from the places above by the will of the great Light, (I) who escaped from that bond; I have cut off the work of the robbers; I have awakened that drop that was sent from Sophia, that it might bear much fruit through me, and be perfected and not again be defective, but be <joined> through me, the Great Savior, that his glory might be revealed [...]." [56]
> ~ JESUS IN THE WISDOM OF JESUS CHRIST

"Now it is fitting that the soul regenerates herself and become again as she formerly was. The soul then moves of her own accord. And she received the divine nature from the father for her rejuvenation, so that she might be restored to the place where originally she had been. This is the resurrection that is from the dead. This is the ransom from captivity. This is the upward journey of ascent to heaven. This is the way of ascent to the father. [...]

From heaven the father sent her her man, who is her brother, the firstborn. Then the bridegroom came down to the bride. She gave up her former prostitution and cleansed herself of the pollutions of the adulterers, and she was renewed so as to be a bride. She cleansed herself in the bridal chamber; she filled it with perfume; she sat in it waiting for the true bridegroom." [57]

~ THE EXEGESIS ON THE SOUL

While the Spiritual Son/Christ represents the masculine child of the Spiritual Mother and Father, the "Virgin of the Sun," "Daughter of the Flame," and "Bride of Christ," represents their daughter, the feminine child, which is called consciousness. In some of the texts that record the teachings of Jesus, but which were excluded from the Bible, consciousness is often called Sophia, and the Spiritual Son/Christ is referred to as her consort and brother. This consciousness is the spiritual part of a much greater Being that exists within each person, and which gradually reunites with the other parts of its Being—the Son, Mother and Father—on the path of the spiritual sun.

DEW AND HOLY WATER

The priestesses of the Romans and Druids that tended the sacred fire in the temple of the goddess also kept sacred waters—the Vestal Virgins of Rome gathered sacred water from a holy spring for summer solstice ceremonial purposes which they did not allow to ever touch the ground lest it be defiled,[58] and the Druid priestesses kept a holy well at their sanctuary which was said to have special healing properties.[59] In pagan traditions, these holy waters are meant to be especially magical and powerful at the summer solstice. Both the Osireion temple in Egypt, and an ancient site on Tallaght Hill in Ireland, align to the summer solstice and incorporate water.

The significance of water on the summer solstice in Druid traditions can be traced back to ancient celebrations that took place on midsummer.

Ancient surviving Welsh mythology indicates the Druids believed that the sap of the cauldron of the Mother goddess Ceridwen was fertilized by three drops of dew from the Father god Celu—the dew containing the warmth of the sun.[60] From the action of these masculine and feminine principles everything came into being. These drops of dew also symbolized "awen"—the "flowing spirit" emanating from the creator.

There is record that in Wales the Druids may have celebrated the summer solstice using holy water from a holy well.[61] This ancient Welsh festival is called Gwyl, meaning something like "dew place."[62] In Lithuania where pagan traditions are still celebrated, midsummer is called Rasos, which means "dew holiday." On the morning of the summer solstice, there are some young women in Lithuania who still wash their faces in dew to this day. As part of summer solstice celebrations in Russia, called Kupala, people also still wash their faces in morning dew.

Dew itself is formed by a natural process of distillation in which water is released from the earth that has been warmed by the sun, cools in the atmosphere, and condenses on surfaces. Distillation is a method of purifying water; it also occurs in the process of inner energetic purification in sexual alchemy. The use of dew symbolizes the purified energies (the sexual waters) separated from the earth (the material world) and united with the sun (the light of the spirit). It also represents the pure emanations of the Spiritual Father.

> "God's influence, from above, through the sun, was supposed to be exercised by the agency of warm dew or humidity. This agent of the Father was personified by the Druids [...]." [63]
> ~ MORIEN O. MORGAN, THE LIGHT OF BRITANNIA

> "Thou purifiest thyself in the dew of the stars." [64]
> ~ THE PYRAMID TEXTS, UTTERANCE 214

The Druids are said to have performed baptismal rites on the summer solstice—a day they called Dydd Syl Gwyn, or Holy Sun Day—using holy water. On a deeper level, baptism symbolizes the purification and cleansing of the internal energies in alchemy. Baptism later became incorporated into the celebration of the Christian Pentecost (celebrated between a month to a week before midsummer)—known also as "White Sunday" in Britain, likely due to its absorption of Druidic customs in which worshipers wore white as the color of the pure light of the sun.

Two Druids, one with an oaken wreath on his head.

> "Whitesuntide is called in Welsh Sal Gwyn or Holy Sun. It was believed by the Druids that when the sun had attained his highest northern ascension all the power of the Almighty was focused in him, and that it was by the exercise of that power the produce of the earth was then being garnished, and the souls of the good perfected through the agency of the sun [...]." [65]
> ~ MORIEN O. MORGAN, THE LIGHT OF BRITANNIA

> "The form in which you created the sun, <in which> you created the earth! The form of the moisture of heaven, the substance of heaven, the yellow blossom of heaven! How did I create your sun? <How did I> create your moon? How did I create your precious stones? I created you. When you were sprinkled with water, you remembered the force of the sun." [66]
> ~ THE BOOK OF CHILAM BALAM OF CHUMAYEL

The following excerpt from the Odes of Solomon—which is a text that the disciples of Jesus studied—contains a reference to someone receiving dew upon their face, like the midsummer practices of ancient European pagans. The imagery of summer is associated with the eternal realm of light, beauty, and fragrance one ascends to.

> "And I abandoned the folly cast upon the earth,
> And stripped it off and cast it from me.
> And the Lord renewed me with His garment,
> And possessed me by His light.
> And from above He gave me immortal rest;
> And I became like the land which blossoms and rejoices in its fruits.
> And the Lord is like the sun
> Upon the face of the land.
> My eyes were enlightened,
> **And my face received the dew;**
> And my breath was refreshed
> By the pleasant fragrance of the Lord.
> And He took me to His Paradise,
> Wherein is the wealth of the Lord's pleasure.
> I contemplated blooming and fruit-bearing trees,
> And self-grown was their wreathed-crown.
> Their branches were flourishing
> And their fruits were shining;
> Their roots were from an immortal land.
> And a river of gladness was irrigating them,
> And the region around them in the land of eternal life." [67]
>
> ~ THE ODES OF SOLOMON

Greenery and flowers are used in pagan celebrations of the summer solstice that have survived throughout Europe today, and are used in the Christian celebration of Pentecost to decorate churches. This is an example of the Christian tradition incorporating pagan symbolism in its celebrations—the greenery and flowers symbolize the realm of the spirit, as a place of eternal summer and light.

> "The Druids saw that flowers and their sweet perfume were not provided to supply nourishment to build up carnal bodies, but were provided by the tender eternal Author of the Universe to gratify the sense of the beautiful in human souls. They, therefore regarded flowers and hues of landscapes, as harbingers of a world of beauty, and eternal summer, beyond this life." [68]
>
> ~ MORIEN O. MORGAN, THE ROYAL WINGED SON OF STONEHENGE AND AVEBURY

"Those who sow in winter reap in summer. The winter is the world, the summer the other Aeon (eternal realm). Let us sow in the world that we may reap in the summer." [69]
~ THE GOSPEL OF PHILIP

EARTH CROWNED BY THE SUN

Little girl wearing a wreath of flowers at a celebration of the summer solstice.

Wreaths form a large part of midsummer celebrations in Europe which originated in ancient times. Women wear wreaths of flowers and men wear wreaths of oak leaves. Wreaths of flowers and greenery are floated upon the waters of lakes and streams, and also adorn the maypole, which is danced around on the summer solstice.

Symbolic references to the wreath can be found in the ancient texts of Gnostic Christianity, and at the Sphinx which is aligned to the summer solstice in Egypt.

In Slavic tradition the wreath represents the sun during spring and summer.[70] It is the eternal crown of the spirit, the awakened pineal gland and third eye, which creates the halo famously depicted in artwork of the Religion of the Sun. At the summer solstice, the Druids celebrate the crowning of the solar god,[71] and in Slavic tradition the sun-god becomes a powerful ruler.[72]

On the summer solstice, the day of most light in the year, the sun sets precisely between the two largest Great Pyramids of Egypt, creating a halo of light around the head of the Sphinx.

In the text Pistis Sophia, Jesus sends down a light stream which forms a wreath around the head of the ascending Sophia—the central character of the story, who symbolizes consciousness.

"And moreover by commandment of myself, the First Mystery which looketh without, the light-stream which surrounded Pistis Sophia on all her sides, shone most exceedingly, and Pistis Sophia abode in the midst of the light, a great light being on her left and on her right, and on all her sides, **forming a wreath round her head.**" [73]
~ JESUS IN PISTIS SOPHIA

In interpreting the above passage, Mary the mother of Jesus refers to another ancient Gnostic Christian text called the Odes of Solomon—quoting the following passage, which explains that the wreath is the Father, referred to as the Lord.

"**Like a wreathed-crown on my head is the Lord**,
And never shall I be without Him.
The wreathed-crown of truth is plaited for me,
Causing Your branches to blossom within me,
For it is not like a parched crown
That fails to blossom.
But You have lived upon my head,
And You have blossomed upon me.
Your fruits are full, even complete;
They are full of Your salvation." [74]
~ THE ODES OF SOLOMON

The halo these divine figures are often portrayed with is a depiction of the sun crowning someone's head, also symbolized by the wreaths of midsummer.

At the summer solstice, the Son who is one with their Mother is crowned by the Father (who is as a king in the spiritual realms—hence the crown).

This same symbolism can be found at the most famous ancient site in the world with a summer solstice alignment. The temple of Stonehenge appears to have been built as a replica of planet Earth, as its inner circle of bluestones mathematically encodes the diameter of Earth, and outer circle of Sarsen stones encodes the radius of the moon as if orbiting around it.[75] Stonehenge aligns to the summer solstice sun at sunrise, when its inner sanctuary receives the rays of the sun.

> "At Sunrise on June 21—anciently 25—the sun, as designed by the arrangements of the venerable structure [Stonehenge], is represented crowning the earth with radiant glory, for then there is a flashing into the sanctuary of sunshine on White Sun-day, or the old British Pentecost." [76]
> ~ MORIEN O. MORGAN, THE ROYAL WINGED SON OF STONEHENGE AND AVEBURY

THE MEANING OF THE SUMMER SOLSTICE IN DAILY LIFE

The summer solstice expresses the principle of ascension, in which things of life and light will naturally grow and rise whenever there are the right conditions, as it is of the nature of the spiritual to ascend, just as the flame of fire always rises toward heaven. This is another reason why fire is a central symbol of divinity in the Religion of the Sun, as its upward rising was seen as its perpetual and natural return to its heavenly source.

These same forces can also be harnessed and expressed within us whenever we fulfil the conditions that cultivate them. Ascension is achieved by employing the other principles of the cross of the year—namely by shedding that which is dark and heavy within us, by giving birth to and cultivating that which is spiritual, and by continuously sacrificing that which is lower for what is higher.

Ascension is not a physical location, but an energetic change, and there are many practices that can temporarily ascend our energetic frequency, which helps to give the incentive and insight to take the path of the spiritual sun, along which permanent changes are made. In the ancient Religion of the Sun, different types of practices like this have been given, such as forms of meditation and mantras. Applying the principles of the solar cross of the year, including these types of practices, gives someone tools they can apply in life toward their own ascension.

RETURN TO THE LIGHT

On the path of the spiritual sun, the sun at the summer solstice represents the ascension and the return to the divine source as a "feathered sun serpent." It is the culmination of the individual's inward spiritual journey that has been represented by the solstices and equinoxes of the year.

For those wishing to gain further knowledge and ascend higher, this journey continues at higher and higher levels, like the octaves of the musical scale, that are potentially endless due to the infinite nature of creation. Although at a higher level, the principles are the same and repeat due to the fractal nature of creation. And so there are Beings who have already achieved a high spiritual level, but choose to descend into the darkness of this world by being born here and completing a special mission, gaining knowledge in the depths of darkness as they do, and thus are able to ascend higher than they were before. At least some of these Beings were great teachers of the Religion of the Sun, like Jesus, Osiris, and Viracocha, who were born on Earth with a mission and to advance their own spiritual journey.

The celebration of the summer solstice is the celebration not only of the life-giving power of the sun, but is the celebration of the reunification of consciousness with its higher parts, symbolized by the physical sun. After the end of the summer solstice, the cycle of the year in its symbolic depiction of the path of the spiritual sun begins again, as the sun starts to descend in its annual journey.

Around three days after the summer solstice in the Northern Hemisphere, the birth of John the Baptist is celebrated as St. John's Day. This is no coincidence, as following the summer solstice is the "birth" of darkness in the wheel of the year when the sun's light begins to decrease, which is a return to the beginning of the descent of consciousness into matter.

And so completes the cycle of the sun in its journey each year; and as it completes it begins again, repeatedly teaching its sacred wisdom through creation to the individual sparks of consciousness that each contain creation's wondrous potential—and that like the seed that goes into the earth at autumn, can have the life of the spirit born within at the winter solstice, overcome its material sheath at spring, and grow to magnificent full bloom at summer.

In Welsh tradition, the Oak King, god of light, departed at the summer solstice to the northern circumpolar stars, which are the stars that rotate around the celestial North Pole.[77]

> "[...] the Druids beheved the entrance to Gwynva or Gwynvyd, their names for the Abode of the Blessed, was in the northern heavens, at, apparently, the point attained by the sun at the summer solstice [...]."[78]
> ~ MORIEN O. MORGAN, THE LIGHT OF BRITANNIA

The ancient Egyptians called these stars, "the ones not knowing destruction," and believed that this was the place those who had become immortal ascended to as these stars are always visible and never set below the horizon. A number of Egyptian pyramids had passageways that were directed toward these stars. This symbolizes the ascent into the eternal realms of divine light, which have their source within the stars in the higher dimensions.

> "The door of heaven is open, the door of earth is open,
> apertures of the (heavenly) windows are open,
> the steps of Nun are open,
> the steps of light are revealed
> by that one who endures always.
> I say this to myself when I ascend to heaven,
> that I may anoint myself with the best ointment and clothe myself with the best linen,
> and seat myself upon (the throne) of "Truth which makes alive";
> while my side is against the side of those gods who are in the north of the sky,
> the imperishable stars, and I will not set [...]." [79]
> ~ THE PYRAMID TEXTS, UTTERANCE 503

Without the birth of the Son within, at death we leave by the gate of the winter solstice in the darkness preceding the birth of the sun, having not realized our true potential, only to return to this material world again. The summer solstice is the gateway for those who have actualized the light of the sun within, and are leaving this world for the realms of imperishability and divine light. For those wishing to return to their Being, the spiritual sun—our own star—is waiting for us.

> "'Come, my child,' says Atum, 'come to us,' say they, say the gods to thee, Osiris. 'Our brother is come to us, the eldest, the first begotten of his father, the first born of his mother,' say they, say the gods." [80]
> ~ THE PYRAMID TEXTS, UTTERANCE 577

> "May you open your place in heaven amongst the stars of heaven! You are indeed the unique star [...]." [81]
> ~ THE PYRAMID TEXTS, UTTERANCE 245

> "Jesus said to them, 'Stop struggling with me. Each of you has his own star [...].'" [82]
> ~ THE GOSPEL OF JUDAS

> "The path to immortality is hard, and only a few find it. The rest await the Great Day when the wheels of the universe shall be stopped and the immortal sparks shall escape from the sheaths of substance. Woe unto those who wait, for they must return again, unconscious and unknowing, to the seed-ground of stars, and await a new beginning. Those who are saved by the light of the mystery which I have revealed unto you, O Hermes, and which I now bid you to

establish among men, shall return again to the Father who dwelleth in the White Light, and shall deliver themselves up to the Light and shall be absorbed into the Light, and in the Light they shall become Powers in God. This is the Way of Good and is revealed only to them that have wisdom. [...] Thus preached Hermes: 'O people of the earth, men born and made of the elements, but with the spirit of the Divine Man within you, rise from your sleep of ignorance! Be sober and thoughtful. Realize that your home is not in the earth but in the Light. Why have you delivered yourselves over unto death, having power to partake of immortality? Repent, and change your minds. Depart from the dark light and forsake corruption forever. Prepare yourselves to climb through the Seven Rings and to blend your souls with the eternal Light.'" [83]

~ THE VISION OF HERMES

"Arising from the surrounding darkness, seeing the higher light, we have reached the Godhead, the Divine Sun, the supreme light." [84]

~ THE RIG VEDA

PART II
ANCIENT SITES

CHAPTER SEVEN

Introduction

The following chapters look at some of the ancient sacred sites across the world that align to the solstices and equinoxes. Many of them are also the most famous. This is just a small sample, as there are at least hundreds of them.

What becomes apparent when studying these sites is just how many of them are directly connected to one another, even though separated by oceans, having been built by the same seafaring cultures. And how all of them are connected to a great ancient body of knowledge called the Religion of the Sun, which they were influenced by as it filtered down through the passage of thousands of years. Because of this common influence, many share common symbols which were used to convey the same meanings. Many were also centered around the same themes—associating the autumn equinox with descent into the underworld, and the spring equinox with spiritual resurrection, etc.

Some not only align to the same astrological phenomena—using the same practice of mirroring constellations on the ground using sacred structures aligned to the solstice or equinox, and encoding the same astrological data—but also align to each other across the earth.

Quite a number of these sites were built so that a line can be traced across the earth intersecting them, some at mathematically symbolic degrees from one another, indicating they were built to align with each other by a seafaring civilization at some time in prehistory. Note that many of these sites were progressively renovated by later peoples over pre-established and extremely ancient sacred places.

"The Great Pyramid is aligned with Machu Picchu, the Nazca lines and Easter Island along a straight line around the center of the Earth, within a margin of error of less than one tenth of one degree of latitude. Other sites of ancient construction that are also within one tenth of one degree of this line include:

Persepolis, the capital city of ancient Persia; Mohenjo Daro, the ancient capital city of the Indus Valley; and the lost city of Petra. The Ancient Sumerian city of Ur and the temples at Angkor Wat are within one degree of latitude of this line. [...]

Many similarities between these sites have been well documented, including the use of perfectly cut and precisely placed monolithic stones, exact orientations to the cardinal points and astronomical orientations." [1]

~ JIM ALISON, EXPLORING GEOGRAPHIC AND GEOMETRIC RELATIONSHIPS ALONG A LINE OF ANCIENT SITES AROUND THE WORLD

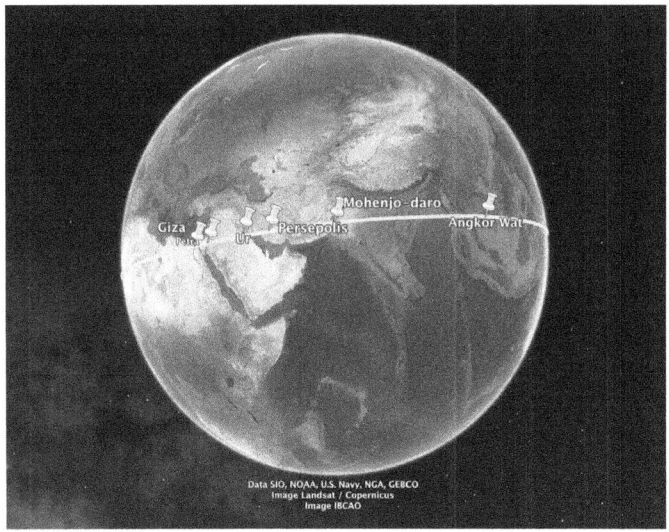

You'll find that some of the information about these ancient sites has already been covered in the previous chapters, but I have included it again under each corresponding site for completeness, as it's nice to be able to pick up this book and read about each site as a reference.

The following chapters give some sense of how there once existed a vast interconnected ancient world that shared many of the same religious principles. You can read much more about this in my wife's book *The Ancient Religion of the Sun*.

CHAPTER EIGHT

Ancient Sacred Sites Aligned to the Autumn Equinox

A careful study of mathematics, astronomy, and sacred symbolism reveals that many sites encode within them very ancient, timeless, and universal messages. Intended to stand the test of time, they have delivered their messages to people searching for truth ever since. Among them include messages about our planet, the nature of reality, the interconnectedness of creation, and the purpose of life. This is why studying how and why these ancient monuments mark certain astrological events, and the symbols they used, can reveal hidden information about their greater significance and meaning.

Here are a few of the most extraordinary cases in relation to the meaning of the autumn equinox (however, any site which aligns to the autumn equinox also aligns to the spring equinox, so you can find more sites aligned to the equinox in the chapter "Ancient Sacred Sites Aligned to the Spring Equinox").

THE GREAT PYRAMID ~ EGYPT

In 3,350 BC and 2,170 BC (and several years either side of those dates), the brightest star of the constellation Draco and the North/Pole Star at the time, called Alpha Draconis/Thuban, aligned with the descending passage of the Great Pyramid so that it could be seen from within it.[1] Also around 2,170 BC, at midnight on the autumn equinox, Alcyone—the brightest star in the Pleiades cluster—was perpendicular (at a right angle) to the descending passage.[2] This alignment appears to have been marked by lines scored into the stone of the descending passage at an exact right angle to its slope. Similar scored lines had been uncovered in the foundation of the pyramid, indicating that those in the descending passageway were not likely to have been later additions, but made by the original builders.[3]

Looking down the descending passage of the Great Pyramid.

The descending passageways of the two other Great Pyramids, as well as those of a number of other Egyptian pyramids, were also angled toward the circumpolar stars, revealing this was an important design feature.[4] Another important feature shared between the three Great Pyramids is that they are each slightly rotated counterclockwise off the cardinal points; this peculiar alignment indicated to the engineer Glen Dash in 2016 that they were orientated using the sun on the day of the autumn equinox.[5] In his book *The Great Pyramid*, Richard A. Proctor gave a detailed analysis over one hundred years earlier of how the pyramid builders could have used the North Star and the sun on the equinox to orientate the pyramid and its descending passageway (which is also its entrance) with such precision.[6]

The Pleiades was known to the Babylonians as Temennu, meaning "The Foundation,"[7] and in Egypt the goddess Hathor was associated with both the Pleiades and "the goddess of the laying of the foundation."[8] This goddess is pictured in ancient Egypt as taking part in the "stretching of the cord," a very ancient ceremony in which a cord was stretched out in alignment to a particular star in order to orientate the foundation of a building (generally temples) to it. This indicates that the Pleiades was used (among other stars) to lay the foundations of buildings, as they appear to have been in the Great Pyramid. Thus, the alignments of the Great Pyramid to the autumn equinox, the North Star, and Alcyone concurrently, would have served a very practical purpose. However, these alignments likely also have a spiritual significance, which served as an initiatory pattern that was passed down through Egyptian and European mystery schools, as I explain in chapter 2.

The Great Pyramid is known to have been built before 2,170 BC, and so the alignments at this date would seem to be coincidental. However, it's possible that similar alignments occurred much earlier, yet as far as I know, this has not been explored as those who identified them only looked for alignments around the time when the Great Pyramid is believed to have been built. Another possibility is that they were coincidental, but the Egyptians at the time noticed them and saw them as extremely spiritually significant.

The Great Pyramid itself functions as an enormous sundial. Its shadow to the north, and its reflected sunlight to the south, accurately mark the annual dates of both the solstices and the equinoxes.[9] Two of its faces are oriented precisely due east and west respectively, which are the exact points of the rising and setting sun only on the spring and autumn equinoxes.

PYRAMID OF KUKULCÁN, CHICHEN ITZA ~ MEXICO

The seven-scaled serpent at Chichen Itza descending the nine terraces of the pyramid at the equinox.

At an ancient site called Chichen Itza, there is a pyramid known as El Castillo dedicated to Kukulcán, the feathered serpent. At the equinoxes, the sun creates an undulating pattern of light on the nine terraces of the pyramid to display seven triangles of light which link up with a stone serpent head at its base. As the sun sets, the scales undulate and eventually disappear, giving the visual effect of the serpent descending the nine terraces of the pyramid.

The pyramid itself is a complex annual astronomical calendar. Its four sides each have ninety-one steps (the number of days between each of the solstices and equinoxes of the year).

The nine terraces depict the nine layers of the underworld, which were recorded in Maya cosmology. The descent of the feathered serpent down these nine terraces enacts the symbolic descent into the underworld on the path of the spiritual sun.

I have seen it stated that at sunrise on the equinox, the effect is the opposite on the other side of the pyramid so that the serpent would appear to ascend—which would symbolize the ascent and resurrection of the feathered serpent from out of the underworld. However, the opposite side of the pyramid has not been fully restored, making any phenomena like this more difficult to observe.

Central American cultures, such as the Maya and Aztec, periodically built over temples and pyramids in layers of renovation—in some cases five successive times. In the 1930s, excavations revealed an earlier temple inside the pyramid of Kukulcán/El Castillo, which had been built over, revealing that this site has much more ancient roots, like many of the ancient sites of the Americas.[10]

Oral traditions state that the site of Chichen Itza is at least as old as the legends of Kukulcán himself, who is recorded as being a real person that founded and oversaw the building of a number of ancient sites in what is now Mexico. He is what I call a wisdom bringer and one of the founders of the Religion of the Sun in ancient times.

> "'The natives affirmed, says Las Casas, that in ancient times there came to that land twenty men, the chief of whom was called 'Cocolcan,'... They wore flowing robes and sandals on their feet, they had long beards, and their heads were bare.' [Brinton, American Hero-Myths] [...] He [Kukulcan] instructed the people in the arts of peace, and caused various important edifices to be built at Chichen Itza. He also founded and named the city of Mayapan. It is at least interesting to note that Kukulcan is simply a translation of Quetzalcoatl. *Kukul* is the Maya term for the *Quetzal*-bird, and *kan* is a serpent."[11]
> ~ THOR HEYERDAHL, AMERICAN INDIANS IN THE PACIFIC

Note that while Kukulcán was described as bringing a message of peace, unfortunately at some time in its history this site became known for the practice of human sacrifice and bloodletting (along with other Central American sites)—thousands of people were sacrificed at this site. The original spiritual knowledge encoded into this site became overlaid by barbarity, giving it a terrible name. It is even recorded in legend that the great teacher Quetzalcoatl (which is a variant of the name Kukulcán) was opposed to human sacrifice. Tragically, his real message was turned away from and distorted as has happened with the message of true love and compassion of so many other great spiritual teachers throughout history.

PYRAMID OF THE SUN, TEOTIHUACÁN ~ MEXICO

Every year at the spring equinox thousands of people visit the Pyramid of the Sun at the ancient city of Teotihuacán in Mexico, with many climbing it to take in the sun's energy. The pyramid faces sunset on August 13 and April 30, and viewed from its summit the sun rises from behind the Cerro Colorado (or Tipayo) Mountain on the equinoxes.[12] These dates in August and April are 260 days apart, which connect them to the ancient ritual calendar of 260 days used in Mesoamerica. In the Maya calendar, our current age is said to have started, following a cataclysm, on August 13, 3114 BC,[13] when the wisdom bringer Itzamna placed three hearth-stones on the ground to establish a new home for humanity. These stones are associated with the three stars of Orion's Belt, and likely represent the three pyramids at Teotihuacán, which appear to be laid out in the same pattern as these stars.[14] The Aztecs believed Teotihuacán was the place where the gods created the universe,[15] and thus Teotihuacán is connected to the start of our current age in Mesoamerican cosmology.

Although dated to around AD 100, archeologists have found even older structures within the Pyramid of the Sun, which the pyramid was built over,[16] and a man-made cave beneath it in the shape of a flower with four petals. In ancient Mexico, caves were seen as earthly wombs and passageways to the underworld,[17] the period of 260 days is approximately that of the gestation of a child within the womb, a "Great Goddess" associated with the underworld was worshiped at this site,[18] and a flower of four petals was used as the Maya glyph for the sun. Thus, the Pyramid of the Sun appears to connect the descent of the sun at sunset with the descent into the underworld and womb of the Mother, and its rebirth or resurrection at sunrise on the equinoxes. The Aztec name Teotihuacán means "birthplace of the gods," and it's likely that rituals of rebirth were performed at the Pyramid of the Sun.[19]

This site shares many similarities with the Great Pyramids of Egypt. The Great Pyramid is the largest pyramid in the world, while the Pyramid of the Sun is the third largest.[20] The base area of the Pyramid of the Sun is almost the same as that of the Great Pyramid. Both were built over man-made caves accessed by a passageway, and were likely used for religious purposes in which they symbolized the underworld and womb. The three pyramids at Teotihuacán, including the Pyramid of the Sun, are laid out in almost the same footprint as the three Great Pyramids of Egypt—a footprint that mirrors the three stars in the belt of the constellation of Orion.[21] There is evidence that the Avenue of the Dead, which the Pyramid of the Sun is located along, was filled with water at certain times to symbolically represent and reflect the Milky Way,[22] while in Egypt, the Milky Way was associated with the river Nile, which the Great Pyramids were built beside. Given these and other similarities, it seems highly likely that the site of Teotihuacán was established by people who carried the same knowledge and Religion of the Sun that once existed in Egypt.

Teotihuacán had been abandoned for around a thousand years before the Aztecs moved into it. It was used for human sacrifice, sadly associating Teotihuacán with this horrific practice, which appears to have been based on "a grotesque misunderstanding" of "an ancient system of purely spiritual initiation, linked to a quest for immortal life"[23] like that found in ancient Egypt. The Aztecs said that Teotihuacán was built by an ancient race of giants,[24] and seemed to have preserved some of the spiritual knowledge from these original builders which had been handed down in the region, but had horribly distorted it.[25]

INTIHUATANA STONE, MACHU PICCHU ~ PERU

The Intihuatana stone at the city of Machu Picchu.

At the ancient city of Machu Picchu in Peru there is a stone called the Intihuatana stone (meaning "Hitching Post of the Sun"), which is a precise indicator of the spring and autumn equinoxes, as at midday on the equinoxes "the sun stands almost directly above the pillar, creating no shadow at all."[26] It is said that the Incas held ceremonies at the stone during these times.[27] The stone also aligns with the summer solstice sun as it sets behind the sacred mountain called Pumasillo (meaning the Puma's claw).[28] Intihuatana stones were held sacred by the peoples of the Inca Empire, and were most probably established much earlier as part of the spread of the Religion of the Sun.

THE SEVEN MOAI OF AHU AKIVI ~ EASTER ISLAND

On Easter Island, the most remote inhabited island in the world, there are numerous megaliths with astronomical alignments. Seven giant statues called moai at the site called Ahu Akivi look out to the ocean. They face the sunset during the autumn (and spring) equinox. They also faced the heliacal setting of the constellation of Orion at the autumn equinox (heliacal describes the conjunction of a star or constellation with the sun as it rises or sets). This alignment was most exact between the fourteenth and fifteenth centuries AD, but is still perceptible today.[29] Conversely, shortly before dawn on the spring equinox, the constellation of Orion rises behind the central moai.[30] Alignments to the constellation of Orion, as well as to the solstices and equinoxes, are found at connected ancient sites throughout the world, including at the Great Pyramids of Egypt.

In Egyptian religion, the constellation Orion corresponded to the god Osiris, whose life events, like those of Jesus, followed the path of the spiritual sun. The descent of Orion beneath the horizon is likely to have symbolized the descent into the underworld, which is represented in ancient traditions of the Religion of the Sun at the time of the autumn equinox. While the ascent of Orion before dawn on the spring equinox likely symbolized the reemergence from the underworld, represented in these traditions at the spring equinox.

The moai facing the equinox sunset at Ahu Akivi.

These statues are connected to Viracocha, the ancient wisdom bringer who was recorded as being fair skinned, red-bearded, having elongated earlobes, and arriving from across the ocean teaching the Religion of the Sun, as these statues all have elongated ear lobes, possibly stylized beards, and some were topped with red lava stone to represent red hair; carvings of Viracocha as the sun god were also found on Easter Island.[31]

They were built by a pre-Polynesian culture that also built many of the ancient sites in South and Central America, including the Nazca Lines, as part of the spread of the Religion of the Sun throughout the world in ancient times. The statues of Easter Island, and the ancient sites of Machu Picchu and the Nazca Lines in Peru, all align to one another, and to the Great Pyramids of Egypt, revealing their shared connection.

Like Viracocha and his followers, the earliest inhabitants of Easter Island were described as fair skinned and red-haired people who practiced ear elongation, and because of this were actually nicknamed the "Long Ears."[32] The earliest evidence for ear elongation is found in the Indus Valley in northern India, and the ancient hieroglyphic writing of the Indus Valley culture and that used on Easter Island (called Rongorongo) shares numerous identical similarities, revealing a connection between these two places.[33] These fair skinned and red-haired people even got as far as New Zealand, where they built numerous megalithic sites aligned to the solstice and equinox.[34]

The hands of the statues point toward the reproductive region—the source of creative sexual energy—which can be used for procreation or for spiritual purposes. Statues with the same hand position are found at the ancient site of Tiwanaku in Bolivia, which Viracocha was said to have been involved in building, and where oral histories of Easter Island say the "Long Ears" came from, and at the ancient site of Göbekli Tepe in Turkey, dated to around 9,600 BC, as well as other parts of the world.[35]

Collage left: Almost the same design of statue found on Easter Island, at the site of Göbekli Tepe (dating back to 9,600 BC), in the remote Hindu Kush mountains among the surviving Indo-European Kalash people, in Indonesia, and on Tahiti.

Image right: Statues built by the Chachapoya culture in Peru, which look very similar to the statues of Easter Island.

TEMPLE OF THE SEVEN DOLLS, DZIBILCHALTÚN ~ MEXICO

The "Temple of the Seven Dolls" at Dzibilchaltún.
At the equinox, the sun shines through the central doorway.

At the ancient site of Dzibilchaltún there is a temple called the "Temple of the Seven Dolls," so named because seven small clay human figures were found buried in the ground there. The temple has openings in the form of arches at each of the four cardinal points. The rising sun on the equinoxes shines through the central doorway of the temple in a beautiful display of light toward a single erect stone.

The seven dolls found here parallel the seven moai on Easter Island that face the autumn equinox sunset, and the seven-scaled serpent of sunlight that descends the Pyramid of Kukulcán/El Castillo at equinox sunset. Perhaps they too were meant to symbolize the descent into the underworld at the time of the autumn equinox with the seven solar bodies and risen serpents, as the dolls were found buried in the ground.

THE PALACE OF KNOSSOS ~ THE GREEK ISLAND OF CRETE

The ancient settlement of Knossos on the Greek island of Crete is believed to be one of Europe's oldest cities. It was first established by Neolithic peoples around 7,000 BC. Later, sometime before 2,000 BC, the ancient Minoan culture began building their central complex there, consisting of 1,300 rooms over 6 acres.

The central palace of this city was known as the legendary home of King Minos. Greek myths recount how King Minos built a labyrinth to imprison the Minotaur—a horrific beast that was half man, half bull. Many are said to have entered this labyrinth, never to come out. Some believe that the palace at Knossos is the fabled labyrinth, while others believe the Labyrinthos Caves at Gortyn twenty miles from the palace were used instead.[36] The Minotaur and labyrinth have a special symbolic meaning, and formed a central part of the spiritual ceremonies of the Minoans that were likely conducted on the autumn equinox.

Studies done by Blomberg and Henriksson reveal that the central religious area of the palace aligns with the autumn equinox sunrise. Evidence shows that this area was built over an earlier Neolithic site, perhaps indicating that the religious practices of the Minoans have more ancient roots. At sunrise on the equinox, the light travels up the corridor of the so-called house of tablets, which contains a bowl that would have been filled with water, and a wall inscribed with the symbol of the labrys, or double-headed axe.

> "On the morning of the equinoxes the rays of the sun strike the middle of the water-filled bowl, and a reflection occurs on the western wall of the sanctuary. At the same time the shadow on the southern wall just touches the tip of the double axe inscribed there." [37]
> ~ G. HENRIKSSON AND M. BLOMBERG, THE EVIDENCE FROM KNOSSOS ON THE MINOAN CALENDAR

The symbol of the double-headed axe was very much connected with the autumn equinox in Minoan iconography, explained as follows.

> "We have found that our constellation Orion could have played an important part in connection with the Minoan new year at the autumn equinox. In the Middle Bronze Age it dominated the southeastern sky at Knossos in the evening on the autumn equinox and would have done so for a very long time. If a line is drawn connecting the eastern most star in Orion's belt (ζ Orionis) and Sirius, then the figure formed and the inclination of the handle is very like that of the double axe touched by the shadow on the southern wall of the corridor. The double axe seems to have been the most important Minoan symbol. There are large numbers of them carved into the walls and pillars of the central palace sanctuary and they occur in other parts of the palace, in other Minoan buildings, and on

objects of all kinds. [...] The bright star Betelgeuse in Orion rose in the evening of the autumn equinox in the middle of the doorway of the corridor in the Middle Bronze Age, also over a very long period of time." [38]

~ G. HENRIKSSON AND M. BLOMBERG, THE EVIDENCE FROM KNOSSOS ON THE MINOAN CALENDAR

As well as at the palace of Knossos, the Minoans also aligned other structures to the autumn equinox.

"At the peak sanctuary on Mt. Juktas, which lies about 15 kilometres southwest of Knossos, we had discovered orientations to equinoctial sunrise and to sunrise eleven days after the autumn equinox, both marked by natural foresights (Blomberg, Henriksson and Papathanassiou 2002). At the peak sanctuary on Petsophas, which is just above the Minoan town Palaikastro on the east coast of Crete, sunset at the equinoxes was marked by a natural foresight, the conical peak of Modi, and there are walls oriented to the heliacal rising and setting, in the Middle Bronze Age, of the bright star Arcturus. Its rising occurred one synodic month before the autumn equinox (Henriksson and Blomberg 1996)." [39]

~ G. HENRIKSSON AND M. BLOMBERG, THE EVIDENCE FROM KNOSSOS ON THE MINOAN CALENDAR

The double-headed axe, called a labrys, is a symbol of the equinox, much like the infinity symbol as the figure eight, as its symmetrically curved blades protruding from a central handle like an axis form the same fundamental shape—each blade represents the solstices with the equinox in the center as the handle. The mother goddess of the Minoans held a labrys, and they were used ceremonially on Crete by Minoan priestesses. An inscription at the palace of Knossos reads "Mistress of the Labyrinth"[40] as it was the goddess who presided over this site so associated with the autumn equinox.

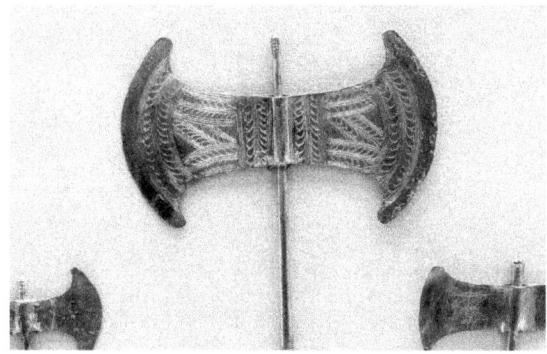

An ancient ceremonial Minoan labrys, symbol of the equinox.

MORE SITES

Here are some more sites that align to the autumn equinox:

Ales Stenar Megalithic "Stone Ship" in Sweden
On the equinox the sun rises and sets over the twelfth stones near the middle of the "ship."[41]

Harman Kaya Observatory in Bulgaria
The sun can be seen through specific notches in the rock formation on the equinox.[42]

Omahk Sacred Landscape and the Majorville Medicine Wheel, Alberta, Canada
The V Rocks at Omahk precisely measure the moment when day and night are of equal length (equinox time) on all four years of the leap-year cycle, as well as which stage of the four-year cycle we are on.[43]

Swansea Petroglyphs in Eastern California, USA
At the Swansea Petroglyphs, there are six vertical bars pecked into the rock that can be used to predict the time of the equinox relative to sunset within a few hours.[44]

CHAPTER NINE

Ancient Sacred Sites Aligned to the Winter Solstice

There are almost countless ancient sites that align to the winter solstice—just a few of these are included here. They have encoded a profound knowledge that can still be grasped even in our modern world—outlasting books and texts, which are easily lost and destroyed. These monuments speak to us through thousands of years about the true spiritual significance of the winter solstice.

Someone who understands the symbolic language used to build these sites can see that their builders knew that the winter solstice expresses the principles of creation and the birth of the Spiritual Son. This knowledge predates Christianity, which reveals that spiritual deities born at the winter solstice, such as Jesus, Horus, Mithras, Kolyada, Hu Gadarn/Taliesin, etc., symbolize something much greater than one event in history.

GLASTONBURY TOR ~ ENGLAND

This ancient site is undated and unexcavated, and is believed by many to be the mysterious Isle of Avalon from the legend of King Arthur. It is a giant seven-terraced mound, which was once surrounded by water. Today it is topped by a church tower, which was built in place of a much older sacred site.

From what appears to be an ancient man-made observation mound on nearby Windmill Hill, someone can watch the winter solstice sun appear at the bottom of the terraces of Glastonbury Tor, and "roll" up the northern side of the terraces until clipping the top of the tower.[1]

Glastonbury Tor rising out of the mist.

The builders of the mound on Windmill Hill are believed to have been the "Windmill Hill people" who are also those most likely to have constructed the first phase of Stonehenge (the earthen ditch and bank)[2] and I suspect are also related to the builders of Goseck Circle in Germany. Both Stonehenge and Goseck Circle have alignments to the winter solstice.

The rising sun on the winter solstice at the base of the terraces is a symbol of the Spiritual Son, which is born in the darkness of the earth (matter), from where it rises through the terraces to reach resurrection. This same design has been used at the next site, which is found in a very different part of the world.

PYRAMID OF KUKULCÁN, CHICHEN ITZA ~ MEXICO

The pyramid of the feathered serpent at Chichen Itza.

At an ancient sacred site called Chichen Itza in Mexico, there is a pyramid dedicated to Kukulcán, the feathered serpent.

On the winter solstice the interaction between the sun and the temple is very similar to that of Glastonbury Tor. When one stands looking at the western face of the pyramid, the rising sun appears to climb up the terraces until it rests momentarily directly above the pyramid on the pinnacle of the temple room that sits on top of the pyramid.[3] Like Glastonbury Tor, it enacts the same theme of the sun being born at the lowest level of the mound or pyramid, before rising to crown its tower and peak. Here at Chichen Itza, the Spiritual Son—who is born at the base of the nine terraces, symbolizing the nine regions of the psyche, underworld, and heavens—will gradually grow and ascend through them.

GOSECK CIRCLE ~ GERMANY

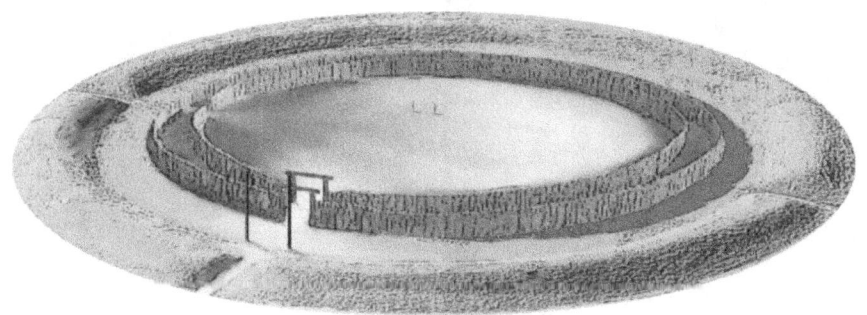

Goseck Circle is an ancient Neolithic henge in Germany, and lies on the same latitude as Stonehenge in England and Arkaim in Russia. Each of these sites have prominent alignments to the solstices.

Goseck Circle is dated to 5,000 BC and was a series of concentric circles constructed out of wooden posts and an earthen ditch. Two of the openings to the circle aligned to the sunrise and sunset on the winter solstice, funneling the rays of sunlight through wooden posts into the center of the circle.

Hundreds of similar ring ditches have been found in Germany, Austria, Croatia, Slovenia, and Czechia, although they are mostly uninvestigated. Very little is known about the

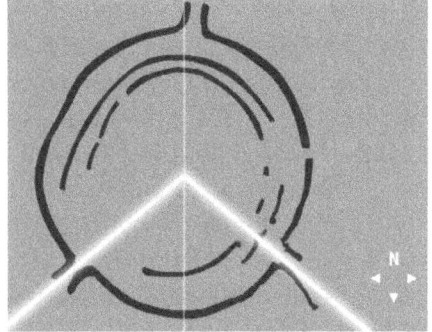

A diagram of Goseck Circle from above. The two white lines show the alignment of the winter solstice sunrise and sunset through openings in the circle to reach its center.

people who built Goseck Circle, although the circle itself is believed to have been a religious site—making it clear that the winter solstice was an important religious date.

With its position on the same latitude as Stonehenge, and similarities between its construction and the earliest stage of Stonehenge—as a circular earthen ditch with an opening to the winter solstice—the builders of the two sites may have originated from the same culture and religion. Stonehenge is included in the chapter on 'Ancient Sacred Sites Aligned to the Summer Solstice'.

NEBRA SKY DISK ~ GERMANY

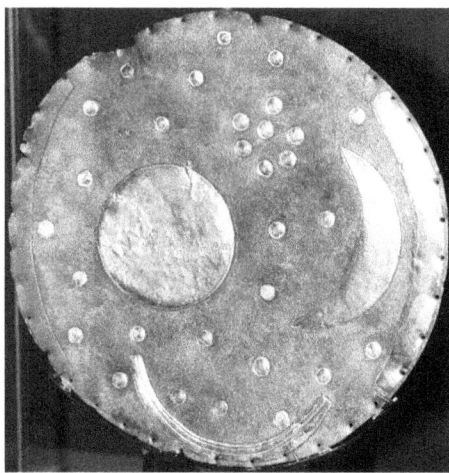

The Nebra sky disk. The outer gold rim on the right was also matched by one on the left, which is now missing. These marked the sunsets and sunrises of the winter and summer solstice. The moon and sun are represented in the middle, and are surrounded by stars, which are believed to represent a number of star formations, including possibly the Pleiades.

The Nebra sky disk is a handheld device for determining the solstice and equinox, made out of bronze with a diagram of the stars, sun, and moon embossed on it in gold. It is dated to 1,600 BC, and was discovered on the hilltop of Mittelberg, which is just twenty-five kilometers away from the location of Goseck Circle in Germany just mentioned.

Goseck Circle and the Nebra disk may be related, as the angle between the two arcs on the disk is the same as that between the two openings of Goseck Circle—marking the rising and setting positions of the sun on the winter solstice in the area at the time.[4]

As well as the winter solstice, the two arcs which run along either side of the Nebra disk mark the sun's position at sunrise and sunset on the summer solstice from Mittelberg, where it was discovered. Additionally, if the Nebra disk is laid flat on this hilltop and oriented north, one of these arcs points to Brocken mountain, the highest peak of the Harz mountain range. When viewed from Mittelberg, the sun sets on the summer solstice precisely behind Brocken mountain.[5]

MYNYDD DINAS ~ WALES

The mountain of Mynydd Dinas, held as sacred by the Druids, who would watch the sun rise over its peak at the winter solstice.

According to local legend, the ancient Druids used to gather every winter solstice to watch the sunrise over the mountain Mynydd Dinas. They believed the sun god Hu Gadarn was born as a baby boy as the winter solstice sun, and would grow as the year progressed toward the summer solstice.[6] Later, the Romans celebrated the birth of Mithras and Christians the birth of Jesus at the winter solstice, and yet both played a part in destroying the religion of the Druids.

Also nearby the Dinas Mountain in Wales there is a cave that goes by a Welsh name meaning "Voice of God" where the Druids enacted the birth of their solar god Hu Gadarn (the Mabyn Taliesin) from within the cave. The Druid priest acting as Hu Gadarn was said to have given a loud musical shout to which the gathered crowds would reply "Ein Hoes," meaning "Our Life!"[7]

KARNAK TEMPLE ~ EGYPT

The Temple of Amun-Ra located within the Karnak Temple Complex was known to the ancient Egyptians as the most hallowed of places, and the very center of the world dedicated to the supreme creator god Amun, where he first brought forth creation. Karnak is the largest temple complex in the world, and houses the largest room of any religious building in the world. Its construction is said to have begun during Egypt's Middle Kingdom, dated between 2,055–1,650 BC.

On the morning of the winter solstice, the light of the rising sun enters the temple's most inner sanctuary dedicated to the creator god Amun.[8] It shines through the doors of this sanctuary along the main axis of the temple complex, out through its entrance and along a great causeway lined with ram-headed sphinxes toward the river Nile[9]—in a spectacular display.

Looking down the central axis of the Karnak Temple Complex in Egypt—
the largest in the world—which aligns to the winter solstice sunrise.

The sanctuary of Amun is a small stone room, and is reminiscent of a womb that is penetrated by the creative force to give birth to the Spiritual Son. Interestingly, this sanctuary aligns to the Temple of Luxor nearby, which the French mystic R. A. Schwaller de Lubicz discovered is laid out in proportions corresponding to a human body. The Luxor Temple depicts an annunciation scene in which the God Amun announces to the mother goddess Mut that she will give birth to a divine child.

The goddess Mut has a dedicated temple as part of the Karnak complex, in probably one of the most ancient areas of it. Enclosed in her precinct is a sacred lake in the shape of a crescent, symbolizing the waters of creation and the womb. Here we have the presence of the father god Amun and mother goddess Mut at a temple complex aligned to the winter solstice sunrise, which is the time of the birth of the Son.

Pylon architecture was used for the main entrance to the temple complex, which the rising winter solstice sun shone through. A pylon is a huge entrance wall which appears to be divided in two, with a winged solar disk over the doorway. Pylons were seen as symbols of first creation and of rebirth, which is central to the spiritual meaning of the winter solstice. Pylons depict in architecture the hieroglyph of the sun rising over the horizon between two mountains as it was said to have done on the first day.

The golden number and the Fibonacci sequence were used at the Karnak and Luxor Temples. These sacred numbers are key to the growth and development of all life. In fact, the Karnak Temple Complex was built upon and expanded over hundreds of years according to the Fibonacci sequence. The entrance to the complex is flanked by rows of giant ram-headed sphinxes that symbolized Amun, and the Fibonacci sequence can be found in the growth of a ram's horns, just as it is found in a nautilus shell. This temple complex was dedicated to life, its growth, the birth of the Son, and creation—and was specifically aligned to the winter solstice.

Left: An example of pylon architecture from the Temple of Horus; at the Temple of Karnak the winter solstice sun shines out of the doorway in a spectacular depiction of first creation. Right: Ram-headed sphinx at the Karnak Temple Complex.

NEWGRANGE ~ IRELAND

Newgrange is a giant one acre, grass-topped mound, and has been carbon dated to 3,200 BC. The builders of Newgrange are unknown, but it is most closely connected to the people in Irish mythology called the Tuatha Dé Danann (known as the people of the mounds), who are said have built Newgrange as a tomb for their chief.[10] They are recorded as coming to Ireland on three hundred ships thousands of years ago, with magical abilities and bearing magical items. While the ancient history of Ireland turned into legends and myth passed on verbally over thousands of years, what is known as set in stone is that Ireland was once inhabited by a highly astronomically advanced people who had knowledge of spiritual principles, which they incorporated into the design of their megalithic sites.

The same spiraling designs found engraved onto the rocks adorning the entrance to Newgrange can also be found adorning those of the ancient megalithic temples on the island of Malta in the Mediterranean dated to a similar time (around 3,150 to 2,500 BC), and which also have solstice and equinox alignments. Other design similarities can be seen between the temples on Malta, Newgrange, Stonehenge in England, as well as the ancient sites on the Orkney Islands of Scotland—and all of them with alignments to the solstices and equinoxes. It appears that Newgrange, and other megalithic mound sites across Ireland, were part of an ancient, seafaring, megalith building culture that stretched from the Mediterranean, through North Africa, and up along the coast of Western Europe. There is evidence that this seafaring culture also spread overseas, as near identical megalithic carvings have been found both at the ancient sites on Malta and Tiwanaku in Bolivia (which also has a solstice alignment).[11]

It is said in Irish mythology that the Tuatha Dé Danann visited four mythical cities located on islands to the north of Ireland before their arrival, where they acquired mystical knowledge,[12] and these are very likely the Orkney Islands of Scotland.[13] All this indicates that there were shared religious beliefs among these ancient megalithic builders.

Although the name Tuatha Dé Danann has become widely interpreted as meaning something like "the people of the goddess Danu," the Irish writer David Halpin has pointed out that the earliest renditions of their name did not include "Danann" (as in Danu). Instead, based on a comparison with Egyptian words, Halpin has suggested that their name may actually mean something more like "Thoth's journey by boat"—Thoth being the name of one of the wisdom bringers of ancient Egypt.[14]

At the winter solstice, the rising sun enters Newgrange mound through a specially built stone box above the main entrance and shines directly along the nineteen-meter-long passage, gradually widening until illuminating the inner chamber for about seventeen minutes. Today the first light enters about four minutes after sunrise, but calculations based on the precession of the earth show that five thousand years ago the first light would have entered exactly at sunrise.[15]

The inner chamber of the mound is laid out in the shape of a cruciform, and beautiful Neolithic artwork can be found etched into the stone both on the inside and outside of the mound. Particularly prevalent are spiral designs, including the famous tri-spiral design found inside the chamber.

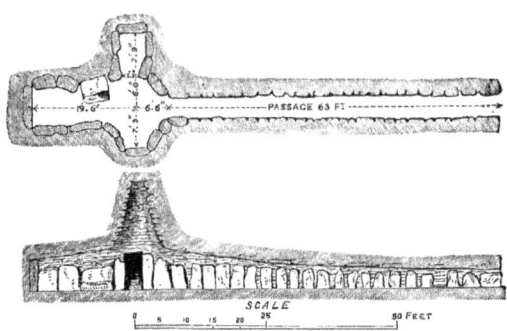

A diagram of the passage and chamber inside Newgrange showing its cruciform shape—a shape fundamental to the solstices and equinoxes as explained in Chapter 1, with the longest arm representing the winter solstice in the Northern Hemisphere, which this chamber aligns to.

The Gaelic/Irish name for Newgrange is Brú na Bóinne, which can be translated as "the womb of the goddess Boann" or "womb of the white cow/milky way," as the Celtic goddess Boann, who was said to have lived at the site, was also known as the white cow and was associated with the milky way.[16] Researchers have noted that the design of Newgrange resembles a womb. In Irish mythology Boann conceived a son by the god Dagda, owner of the mound. In another the sun god Lugh conceived the hero Cúchulainn by visiting his mother in a dream as she slept at the mound.[17] Clearly this mound was associated with the birth of a son. The ray of dawning light illuminates the chamber, which is in the shape of a cross—the cross symbolizing the union of masculine and feminine, which give birth to all creation and the Spiritual Son. Here the cross is associated with the Spiritual Son on the winter solstice, thousands of years before Jesus.

Just as the births of Jesus, Mithras, and Viracocha were said to have taken place in a cave, so too at Newgrange the birth of the sun is enacted inside the dark chamber of the mound.

NESS OF BRODGAR ~ SCOTLAND

The giant standing stones of the Ring of Brodgar.

The Ness of Brodgar is an ancient megalithic complex located in the Orkney Islands of Scotland. It includes numerous standing stones and stone circles, as well as a chambered cairn, all believed to have been built around 3,000 to 2,500 BC. A number of the structures at this site align to the solstices and equinoxes.

One of the stone circles is called the Ring of Brodgar, which has also been referred to as a Temple of the Sun.[18] It is 104 meters in diameter (making it the third largest stone circle in the British Isles), but of the original 60 stones, only 27 remain standing. From the circle someone can view various alignments between the solstice sun, stones, and surrounding hills in the landscape.

The site also includes a chambered cairn called Maeshowe—a canonical man-made mound incorporating massive thirty ton stone blocks—aligned to the winter solstice sunset. Its passage and inner corbeled roof has been compared to the design of the King's Chamber of the Great Pyramid, with its huge stones placed with similar precision so that a knife blade cannot be inserted between them.[19] Like the site of Newgrange mentioned previously, the sun on the winter solstice illuminates its inner chamber and lights up its back wall—again perhaps signifying the birth of the sun within the womb of the earth. Similar chambered mounds aligned to the winter solstice (as well as to the summer solstice and equinoxes) are found elsewhere in Europe, particularly along its coast, dating to as far back as 4,700 BC in France.

Looking out from the large inner chamber of Maeshowe to its entrance, which aligns to the winter solstice.

Early Scandinavian chroniclers described two types of inhabitants of the Orkney Islands which they found on their arrival: the Peti, described as very short people, and the Papae, a type of priestly class who dressed in white.[20]

The Ness of Brodgar obviously served as a spiritual center of some kind, and there is even evidence that it was a staging post on journeys to the Americas in ancient times. For example, sites incorporating woodhenges and man-made mounds that align to the solstices and equinoxes—near identical to those found in Scotland and elsewhere in the British Isles—are also found in North America (see Serpent Mound and Cahokia later in this book).

> "The advanced mathematical principles, found encoded into precisely positioned, purpose-built surveying markers around Ring o' Brodgar and the greater Orkney Islands, tell us the following facts with indisputable clarity:
>
> By about 3000 BC the cousin Caucasoid nations living around the Mediterranean and throughout Continental Europe, were making ocean traversals to the Americas in their very seaworthy, large, planked sailing ships. For this otherwise dangerous undertaking they used Britain as a main staging area and had established several expansive open-air universities for teaching mathematical principles of navigation and cyclic astronomy. In the British Isles great sprawling

schools, offering intensive-comprehensive courses, were laboriously built at Avebury Henge and Durrington Walls Henge in Wiltshire, England, as elsewhere.

This European preoccupation with exploration would go a long way toward explaining why such a high percentage of the Algonquain Indian language of North America, extending to the Great Lakes region and almost across the entire continent, contains many clearly identifiable ancient Basque words (the same word used for elbow, foot, head, breast, shoulder, guts, lake, river, louse, birch bark, ocean, boat, snow (falling), snow (on ground) etc.). Moreover, it's a very ancient form of the Basque tongue, uninfluenced by Indo-Aryan admixtures that crept into the Basque language at later epochs.

[...] Also, ancient European structures, cultural-symbolism and writing are found in profusion up and down the Eastern seaboard of the United States [...]. A very high percentage [of] North American Indians carry the European "Y" chromosome and many tribes in both North and South America have oral traditions of the white tribes that their ancestors vanquished. The same measurement & angle standards employed to build ancient Mediterranean-European structures were used to build the huge geometric earthmound complexes of Ohio and Pennsylvania [...]." [21]

~ MARTIN DOUTRÉ, RING O' BRODGAR, ORKNEY ISLANDS: GATEWAY TO THE AMERICAS

There are thousands of stoneworks, cairns, dolmens, and chambered passage mounds in the northeast of the United States. Three counties in the states of New York, Connecticut, and Vermont have the highest known density of them. Chambered stone mounds in the area are built just like those found on the other side of the Atlantic along Europe's west coast, and like their European counterparts, many have openings to allow beams of light to penetrate them at the solstices and equinoxes. Over two hundred of these ancient stone solar temples have been identified in New England.[22] For example, the so-called calendar chamber in Connecticut has an opening that allows a beam of light to enter on the equinoxes, while chambers in Maine and Massachusetts are similarly designed to allow the light of the sun in on the summer solstice.[23] A number of the stone chambers in North America were found to have inscriptions in them, and artifacts with inscriptions were also discovered in association with them. Dr. Barry Fell, Professor Emeritus at Harvard University, identified the scripts they were written in as Ogham, Iberian, and Phoenician, and was able to translate them as dedications to the sun god of the Celts called Bel and that of the Phoenicians called Baal. Many also include solar symbols, like the eye of the sun god and solar cross, as also found in Europe.[24] A journalist and archaeologist have independently found hundreds of Ogham inscriptions across the Mississippi River Valley and the South West, where many ancient sites aligned to the solstices and equinoxes are found, and which are remarkably similar to those in Britain.[25] Many other artifacts, language similarities, oral traditions, and ancient sites, too countless to list here, link ancient North America to Britain.[26]

We have been contacted by the owners of a site in Clay County, Kentucky in the United States about a natural cave they discovered on their property that aligns to the winter solstice sunrise, and which is inscribed with petroglyphs.[27] The presence of the petroglyphs clearly indicates that the alignment of this site was recognized by ancient people. The use of this site potentially connects it in some way to the same people who built Maeshowe (and other European chambered mounds), as the same theme appears at each of these sites, in which a mound or cave receives the rays of the winter solstice sun to its interior.

THE FOUR-HANDED MOAI STATUE ~ EASTER ISLAND

The four-handed moai on Easter Island.

A lone moai statue in the center of Easter Island, at a site called Ahu Huri A Urenga, faces the rising sun on the winter solstice.[28] Unlike any other statue on the island, it has four hands instead of the usual two, which is interesting, as the number four was often linked to the sun in the ancient Religion of the Sun. This moai is seen as one of the most important astronomical observatories on the island, as it appears that the altar together with five cupules etched on a nearby rock functioned as a "solar-ranging device" which marked the winter solstice and possibly the equinoxes.[29]

THE GREAT PYRAMIDS ~ EGYPT

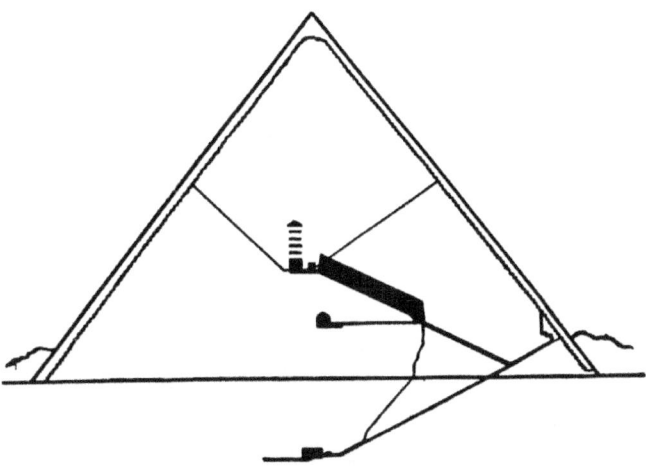

Diagram of the Great Pyramid of Egypt showing its interior passages and chambers. Both the ascending passage (leading to the King's Chamber) and the descending passage (leading down into the subterranean chamber) are at an angle of 26° 33′ 54″.

As the sun set on the winter solstice, researcher Professor Robert Temple noticed that the second largest of the three Great Pyramids of Giza cast a shadow on the southern face of the Great Pyramid beside it at the same angles as the ascending and descending passages inside the Great Pyramid—therefore alluding to what was inside. The angle of the shadow and the passages in the Great Pyramid is 26° 33′ 54″.

> "It just so happens that this odd angle of slightly more than 26 degrees is the only acute angle possible for a right triangle to be formed that is known as 'the golden triangle,' because it embodies the famous Golden Mean Proportion. And it also just so happens that the Golden Mean Proportion is at the basis of the entire canon of ancient Egyptian art and architecture [...]. And in fact, the shadow if truncated by a vertical line running up the middle of the south face of the Great Pyramid, does actually form a golden triangle, which once again is mirrored on the inside, because it is a similar golden triangle which determines the precise point of commencement of the Grand Gallery on the interior of the pyramid [...]. And as for the vertical line running up the pyramid, that too is real, and has been shown from an aerial photograph, although it is invisible to the naked eye or by any perceptual means at ground level. There is actually a purposeful slight indentation of a few inches in the construction of the side of the pyramid, discovered in measurements

made by Petrie. This 'apothegm,' as geometers call such vertical lines, forms the right angle to transform the solstice shadow into a perfect golden triangle." [30]

~ PROFESSOR ROBERT TEMPLE

This golden angle was used throughout the design of the site of the Great Pyramids and in Egyptian artwork in relation to spiritual resurrection.

THE SUN GATE, TIWANAKU ~ BOLIVIA

The Sun Gate at Tiwanaku, with the wisdom bringer and sun god Viracocha featured in the center.

At the ancient sacred city of Tiwanaku (also written Tiahuanaco), the rays of the rising sun on the winter solstice pass through a stone entrance called "the Sun Gate" and hit an obelisk directly behind it. The wisdom bringer and sun god Viracocha is carved into the center of the gate and is surrounded by winged beings. On it are also believed to be the instructions for interpreting a nearby megalithic solar calendar.[31]

Although the gate is said to have been placed speculatively in its position as part of the site's modern restoration, the carving of Viracocha on it depicts him as a baby, linking the gate to the Inca winter solstice celebration called "Wawa Inti Raymi" meaning "festival of the baby sun," and indicating that the gate is likely in its correct position.

Although settlements around Tiwanaku have been dated back as far as 1,500 BC, the dating of Tiwanaku's ancient ruins is debated and remains surrounded in controversy. Arthur Posnansky, a respected avocational archeologist, and the archeoastronomer Rolf Müller, have argued that Tiwanaku was first established at approximately 15,000 BC based upon studies of its astronomical alignments.[32]

Additionally, there are other mysteries surrounding Tiwanaku that seem to indicate the site was established at a much earlier date than is currently accepted. Among these are the ancient myths from throughout the Andean region that tell of its founding and use before a great flood. When the Spanish arrived in South America, the Andean people told them that they did not build these ancient cities, but only moved into them. They stated that they were built by giants and by Viracocha himself. The local people of Tiwanaku believed that Viracocha created giants to move the massive stones, but grew unhappy with them and created a flood to destroy them. This myth parallels others around the world, which also say that a great flood ended a prior civilization on Earth.

Viracocha was also said to have been a real person who arrived to this site by sea and organized the construction of megaliths there to commemorate those who survived the flood, and those nations he intended to create.[33] It's possible that Viracocha knew of the site at Tiwanaku and came to re-establish civilization there after a cataclysmic flood.

Viracocha is described as a man with long beard, fair skin, green/blue eyes, dressed in a long robe, and holding a staff, who arrived from across the sea to teach the Religion of the Sun and the arts of civilization. The clearly bearded image of Viracocha is carved into a stone monolith at this site. Local legends state that he used Tiwanaku as his capital from which he travelled to establish other sacred sites in South America.

> "During the first generations after the Conquest, however, the myths and traditions of the legendary pre-Incas were still alive in Peru, and when the famous historian Prescott began to analyze the early Spanish documents and manuscripts in the archives of the Royal Academy of History at Madrid, he came to the following conclusion concerning the early Inca beliefs (1847, Vol. I, p. 9): 'The story of the bearded white men finds its place in most of their legends.' he also wrote (*Ibid.*): 'Another legend speaks of certain white and bearded men, who, advancing from the shores of Lake Titicaca, established an ascendancy over the natives, and imparted to them the blessings of civilization. It may remind us of the tradition existing among the Aztecs in respect to Quetzalcoatl, the good deity, who with a similar garb and aspect came up the great plateau from the east on a like benevolent mission to the natives. The analogy is more remarkable, as there is no trace of any communication with, or even knowledge of, each other to be found in the two nations.'
>
> [...] Here [on Lake Titicaca] Viracocha is remembered as having made his first appearance among the Indians, and here he built his first abode, from which he spread his culture and benefits all over Peru." [34]
>
> ~ THOR HEYERDAHL, AMERICAN INDIANS IN THE PACIFIC

> "[...] highland legend that says that Viracocha 'was very shrewd and wise and said he was a child of the sun.' All the highland traditions

agree that his first place of residence was on Titicaca Island, before he set forth with a fleet of reed boats to a site on the south shore of the lake, where he built the megalithic city of Tiahuanaco. He and his white and bearded followers were expressly referred to as Mitimas, the Inca word for colonist or settlers. They introduced cultivated crops and taught the Indians how to grow them in irrigated terraces; they showed the Indians how to build stone houses and live in organized communities with law and order; they introduced cotton clothing, sun worship, and megalithic carving; they built step-pyramids and erected monolithic statues [...]. After instructing the Indians of Cuzco in how to behave after his departure, he descended to the Pacific coast and gathered with his Viracocha followers near the port of Manta in Equador, from whence these sun worshipers sailed westward into the Pacific [...]." [35]

~ THOR HEYERDAHL, THE BEARDED GODS SPEAK

"When the Spaniards came to Lake Titicaca, up in the Andes, they found the mightiest ruins in South America—Tiahuanaco. They saw a hill reshaped by man into a stepped pyramid, classical masonry of enormous blocks beautifully dressed and fitted together, and numerous large stone statues in human form. They asked the Indians to tell them who had left these enormous ruins. The well-known chronicler Cieza de Leon was told in reply that these things had been made long before the Incas came to power. They were made by white and bearded men like the Spaniards themselves. The white men finally had abandoned their statues and gone with their leader, Con-Ticci Viracocha, first up to Cusco, and then down to the Pacific. They were given the Inca name of viracocha, or 'sea foam' because they were white of skin and vanished like foam over the sea. [...] When the Spaniards reached the shores of Lake Titicaca, they heard from the Indians there too that Con-Ticci Viracocha had been chief of a long-eared people who sailed on Lake Titicaca in reed boats. [...] The Indians added that it was these long-ears who helped Con-Ticci Viracocha transport and raise the colossal stone blocks weighing over a hundred tons which lay abandoned at Tiahuanaco." [36]

~ THOR HEYERDAHL, AKU-AKU: THE SECRET OF EASTER ISLAND

MACHU PICCHU ~ PERU

At the ancient mountaintop city of Machu Picchu in Peru there is a semi-circular structure called the Temple of the Sun that was constructed around a large boulder. During the winter solstice, the sun shines through the central window and strikes the stone boulder within while also aligning with the tip of a nearby mountain peak.[37]

The Temple of the Sun at Machu Picchu, which is the circular building that encases a large stone boulder that aligns to the winter solstice sunrise.

Machu Picchu, like other ancient megalithic sites in Central and South America, shares striking architectural similarities to ancient megalithic sites in Egypt (both have huge, precision fitted polygonal stones), revealing a connection between their ancient cultures and solar religions. And like other ancient megalithic sites in Central and South America, it clearly had a number of phases of building—with the first phase being the most ancient and sophisticated, later being added to in a much more rudimentary style.[38] Clearly it was an ancient place that was held sacred over a long period of time. It is also one of the sites that lies along the same line around the earth that other ancient sites aligned to the sun do, like the Great Pyramids of Egypt.

Machu Picchu is also home to the Intihuatana stone, which aligns to the equinoxes, and the city is situated on a mountain ridge above the Urubamba Valley, which also has a winter solstice alignment as described below.

CERRO PINKUYLLUNA MOUNTAIN, URUBAMBA SACRED VALLEY ~ PERU

In the Urubamba Valley in the Andes, facing the ancient ruins of Ollantaytambo, there is a mountain sacred to the Andean people called Cerro Pinkuylluna, believed to have the profile of the wisdom bringer Viracocha. The formation is 140 meters high and is made up of indentations that form the eyes and mouth, while protruding rocks make his nose and beard.[39] Ruins built on top of the face are considered to represent a crown on his head. When the sun strikes the profile of Viracocha during the winter solstice, the mineral content of the mountain reflects its rays.[40]

ANCIENT SOLSTICE

In the legends of the Inca, Viracocha, who is depicted with a crown of the sun, is said to have risen from Lake Titicaca (or in some sources the cave Paqariq Tampu, which means "to dawn/to be born" in the Quechua language) "during the time of darkness to bring forth light,"[41] and is said to have then created everything.[42] This ties in with the spiritual meaning of the winter solstice as the time of the birth of the Spiritual Son, and his bringing forth of creation, which is why at the sites of Tiwanaku and the Urubamba Sacred Valley, his image aligns to the winter solstice sunrise.

Photo taken looking over the shoulder of the bearded wisdom bringer Viracocha at his face in the side of the Ollantaytambo mountain. If you look closely you can see the ruins built on top of his head, forming the crown.

AJANTA CAVES ~ INDIA

Cave nineteen at Ajanta, which aligns with the winter solstice sunrise.

The Ajanta Caves are an extraordinary group of around thirty elaborate man-made shrines and temples cut into the side of a sheer cliff face that is naturally U-shaped and located in a remote jungle in India. The caves are believed to have been built by Buddhist monks who carved them into the cliff face between 200 BC and AD 480-650, as they contain sculptures and artwork centered around the life of Buddha.

Two of the caves align to celestial events. Cave nineteen aligns to the winter solstice sunrise. It contains a statue of Buddha standing within a stupa, which is illuminated by the rays of the rising sun on the winter solstice.[43]

A stupa is a symbolic monument which it is said Buddha uses to ascend and descend, and the winter solstice is a time when the Spiritual Son descends into a spiritually prepared person.

GREAT ZIMBABWE ~ AFRICA

The ruins of Great Zimbabwe. The large circular structure is called the Great Enclosure, which is surrounded by various other ruins in the landscape.

In sub-Saharan Africa lie the stone ruins of an abandoned ancient city. Oral histories of the local Bantu people state that their ancestors did not build this site, but attribute it to a fair skinned people they call the Ma-iti.[44] In another Bantu account they were known as Amakalanga, meaning "people of the sun." Their artifacts and building styles are most similar to those of the Phoenicians,[45] who are well known to have been seafarers that venerated the sun.

> "For the opinion of the Phoenicians—wise and possessed of knowledge in respect of divine matters—stated that the sunlight sent forth everywhere is the immaculate action of pure mind itself." [46]
> ~ ROMAN EMPEROR JULIAN, HYMN TO KING HELIOS

A number of stone monoliths at the site line up with certain bright stars in the constellation Orion as they rise on the morning of the winter solstice.[47] Perhaps this was intended to signify the birth of the Spiritual Son, as the Egyptians (whom the Phoenicians had contact with) saw the constellation of Orion as a representation of the god Osiris.

Incredibly, the same lozenge style patterns built into the walls of this circular fortressed city appear in another that looks just like it, built by people also described as fair skinned (called the Chachapoya), at the ancient fortressed city of Kuélap in Peru. These patterns were also used by the megalith builders, who built structures aligned to the solstices and equinoxes in North Africa, the Mediterranean, and along the west coast of Europe. A round tower within the Great Enclosure of Great Zimbabwe looks very similar to those built by the Anasazi in the Four Corners region of the United States, who also aligned their ancient sites to Orion and the solstices and equinoxes, and were described as worshiping the sun.

Great Zimbabwe is just one of a number of ancient sites with alignments to both Orion and to the solstices and equinoxes, which appear to have been built to encode the same spiritual knowledge by a seafaring culture in prehistory.

NAZCA LINES ~ PERU

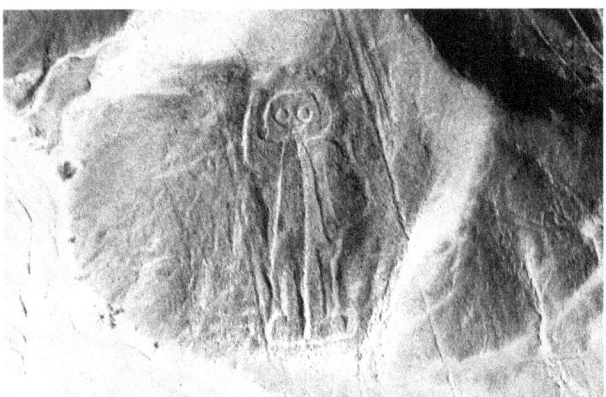

The giant figure known as the astronaut on the side of a mountain as seen from the air at the site known as the Nazca Lines.

In the Nazca Desert in southern Peru, hundreds of giant lines and figures were drawn into the ground by removing the layers of red desert pebbles to expose the white soil beneath. The figures are best viewed from the sky, and one figure has been called an astronaut because of how similar it looks to one. This has led some to theorize that the builders of the lines could have been in contact with extraterrestrials.

Research by Dr. Paul Kosok and Maria Reiche revealed that a number of the lines align to the winter and summer solstices, along with other figures that could have aligned to the constellation of Orion.[48] The lines themselves are not able to be dated, so it is difficult to determine when they aligned to celestial movements, as these alignments shift over time. However, on the winter solstice the sun used to set over one line, exactly between the sixth and first century BC.

The builders of the oldest of the Nazca Lines are the Paracas culture.[49] Genetic tests done on the skulls of the Paracas nobility, organized by biologist Brien Foerster and researcher L. A. Marzulli, revealed in 2018 that they were genetically Caucasian, having haplogroups found only in Europeans.[50] Additionally, numerous mummies found at the site are clearly Caucasian in appearance—having fine, light colored hair. The Paracas people were invaded by a culture whom they taught their arts and sciences, but who later slaughtered and drove them out. This invading culture became known as the Nazca culture, though they were not the builders of the oldest Nazca Lines, but took over and continued to build upon the site.[51]

The original builders were very different people however; evidence for their earlier occupation of the area is found in the tens of thousands of fair-haired European-featured mummies unearthed at the edge of the Nazca valley.

> "According to our experts, the Nazca builders were very superstitious and, as recently as AD 550, built the lines for the purpose of appeasing and stroking the egos of the "gods," in an attempt to get them to send rain during an extended drought of 40-years duration. The fact that Nazca is about the driest place on earth, where a small rain every few years causes a sensation when it happens, or that there has been no significant rainfall there since the end of the last ice-age, tends to make such a hypothesis laughable in the extreme. As it turns out, the expansive sprawl of the Andes mountain ranges just inland, offer a huge catchment area and the Nazca desert region is fed by a multitude of subterranean springs and wells, making water sources, for the most part, eternally abundant.
>
> Before [the] Nazca desert region could be made habitable, to sustain the sizeable population that settled there several thousand years ago, over 93-miles (150-kilometers) of mostly subterranean aqueducts had to be dug. Along with these, there were 28 filtration galleries, some of which penetrate underground over two thirds of a mile into the hard conglomerate deposits and bring out 25 liters of water per second.
>
> The trussed mummy, with the very fine, auburn-red hair [...] is typical of the tens of thousands of mummies that have been found in the region. This reddish hair color is found on only a very small percentage of the world's population (about 1-2 percent). The largest, present-day concentration of redheads in the world is in the United Kingdom, where 13-percent of the population has red hair and 40-percent carry the recessive red gene. The gene is strongly represented in England, Ireland, Wales, Scotland or among the Germanic and Scandinavian tribes, Finns, Russians, Basques and extending to the most ancient occupants of Egypt in the Eastern

Mediterranean (where the early mummies have red, blond, or other European hues of hair color) to the former population of the Canary Islands in the Atlantic (the Guanche ... where the early mummified people found were ethnic Europeans).

Red hair was very prominent in the ancient Pacific, from Easter Island (where the giant, long faced statues had "red" top-knot stones placed on their heads) to New Zealand. In fact, the earliest cave burials of New Zealand (at the very ends of the Earth) were observed to be Caucasoid people with red hair. These most ancient New Zealanders also buried their dead in a trussed, sitting position, alongside personal possessions, in much the same manner as is found with the Nazca mummies. A huge amount of artefact, flora and cultural evidence shows a direct link between ancient New Zealand and Peru.

Well watered, fertile pockets of farmland sit adjacent or very near to the Nazca lines and ancient people, etching or using the lines, could return a reasonably short distance each evening to locations offering hospitable conditions of shelter and sustenance. In essence, the Nazca region would have been an exceptional center for an "open-air university" if the lines were set out for the purpose of offering tutorials, of some sort, to initiate students.

Based upon the mummy evidence of the region, these tall stature, Caucasoid, dolichocephalic-cranium, long thin faced people with typical European hues of multicolored hair, built the Nazca aqueducts, settled the area and made the farms productive. They then undertook the huge task of etching 800 lines and other geometric shapes and glyphs into the desert to indelibly encode their ages-old sciences, brought with them to the region from the Mediterranean and Europe." [52]

~ MARTIN DOUTRÉ, NAZCA

Dr. Paul Kosok, who first discovered their astronomical link, called the Nazca Lines "the largest astronomy book in the world."[53] The native name for the site is "Intiwatana," which means "the place to where the sun is tied," indicating its cosmological link. Just as the builders of the Great Pyramids wished to mirror the stars in the layout of their ancient sites, so too did the creators of this site who carried with them the knowledge of ancient Egypt. Incredibly, the Nazca Lines lie along the same line around the earth as the Great Pyramids of Egypt and a number of other sacred sites.

THE MONASTERY, PETRA ~ JORDAN

Petra is an ancient city located in Jordan. It's famous for its beautiful Assyrian and Hellenistic style buildings, which are carved into the sandstone cliff faces. It is said to have been built by the Nabateans around the third to first centuries BC. A number of its buildings align to the solstices and equinoxes.[54]

The largest building in Petra is called the Monastery (or Al Deir in Arabic), and aligns to the winter solstice sunset. On the winter solstice (and around a week before and after), the light of the setting sun enters the doorway of the temple and illuminates the sacred area deep within its interior (which would have held some sacred object or objects).[55] It was built by the Nabateans, who venerated the sun, as a place where they held religious ceremonies. The Nabateans are recorded as celebrating the birth of the deity Dusares (likely representing the Spiritual Son/sun) from a virgin mother goddess on the winter solstice in Petra,[56] and so it is very likely this celebration occurred within the Monastery.

ANGKOR WAT ~ CAMBODIA

A model of the temple of Angkor Wat, with its layout incorporating cruciform shapes. The center of the temple receives shafts of light on the winter solstice.

Angkor Wat in Cambodia is one of the largest temple complexes in the world. It was built between AD 1113 and 1150 based on the cosmology of the ancient Hindu texts of India, which are some of the most complete remnants of the Indo-European branch of the Religion of the Sun. The entire temple is dedicated to the sun god Vishnu.

On the winter solstice, shafts of light shine on the exact geometric center of the section called the Preau Cruciforme.[57] This section is laid out in a cruciform shape—a shape that is incredibly significant to the time of the winter solstice and the birth of the Spiritual Son/sun.

The union of male (vertical) and female (horizontal) forces gives spiritual birth to the divine child within. At Angkor Wat the light of the sun shines on the cross on the winter solstice, just as it does within the cruciform chamber of Newgrange in Ireland.

There are numerous other alignments to the solstices and equinoxes throughout the temple, which the author Eleanor Mannikka identifies in her book *Angkor Wat: Time, Space, and Kinship*, some of which are explored in other chapters of this book. The temple was built using an ancient unit of measurement called the cubit, believed to have originated in Egypt, and to encode cycles of time from the Vedas using a system tracing back to ancient Mesopotamia.

> "All the measurements of Angkor Wat occur in systems which take the visitor through time cycles that, believe it or not, trace their origins to the Mesopotamian area several thousand years B.C. People may not be aware that our 60-second, 60-minute basis for measuring time (hours) and space (degrees), along with our 24-hour days come from pre-Babylonian astronomy. This data is recorded at Angkor Wat." [58]
>
> ~ ELEANOR MANNIKKA

Although the temples at Angkor Wat were constructed by the Khmer people under the reign of the Khmer King Suryavarman II less than one thousand years ago, its main structures mirrored a key constellation found in the Hindu mythology it encodes in 10,500 BC.[59] The name Suryavarman means something like "protector of the sun,"[60] and with the building of Angkor Wat the king wished to initiate a new golden age as well as revive its ancient religion.[61]

Putting all of this together, it's clear that Angkor Wat was built using astronomical, mathematical, and spiritual knowledge originating from far more ancient times over the ground plan of a far more ancient site.

Angkor also aligns to the spring equinox, and so more information about it is detailed in the chapter dedicated to ancient sites that align to the spring equinox that follows.

ARKAIM AND SURROUNDING MEGALITHIC SITES ~ RUSSIA

Arkaim was an ancient city located on the southern steppe of the Ural Mountains region of Russia, just north of the border with Kazakhstan, and is said to have been built sometime between 2,000 to 1,700 BC, although, as with many ancient sites, further dating has suggested it may be even older.[62]

It is one of at least twenty similar settlements in the region (it's believed there are another fifty in addition to this that are still buried) that were possibly each home to approximately 1,500 people. It is believed to have been built by ancient Indo-European peoples (specifically the Proto-Indo-Iranians, known as the Aryans) who were the source of the sacred texts the Rig Veda and Avesta.[63]

Illustration of what Arkaim may have
looked like based on archeological evidence.

It has been called "Russia's Stonehenge" as it is located at the same latitude as Stonehenge in England as well as Goseck Circle in Germany. This latitude is a very special one for a number of reasons. It is "the exact latitude at which the midsummer sunrise and sunsets are at 90 degrees to the Moon's northerly setting and southerly rising. This particular phenomenon is only possible within a band of less than one degree of which Stonehenge and Goseck lies in the middle-third."[64] It is also "one of two unique latitudes in the world where the full Moon passes directly overhead on its maximum zeniths."[65] It can be no coincidence that each of these sites lie on this latitude, are laid out in concentric circles, and have multiple astronomical alignments, providing strong evidence that they are connected to each other.

According to the research of Konstantin Bystrushkin, Arkaim's alignments include the sunrises and sunsets on the solstices and equinoxes.[66]

Little remains of Arkaim, as it was burned to the ground at some time in history. However, archeologists have been able to reconstruct what Arkaim would have looked like. The ancient city has been called "Swastika City" as the layout of the structure resembles a swastika; the city itself is round and has four entrances that are laid out in the four cardinal directions.[67] According to Wikipedia:

> "Scholars have identified the structure of Arkaim as the cities built "reproducing the model of the universe" described in ancient Aryan/Iranian spiritual literature, the Vedas and the Avesta. The structure consists of three concentric rings of walls and three radial streets,

reflecting the city of King Yima described in the Rigveda. The foundation walls and the dwellings of the second ring are built according to swastika-like patterns; the same symbol is found on various artefacts." [68]

The swastika is a symbol illustrating the movement of the sun, and the solstices and equinoxes, and is one of the oldest and most widely used symbols in the ancient world. It's also interesting to note that Arkaim is laid out in the same three-ring concentric pattern as the main city of Atlantis described by Plato—and Yima was a king who survived a great catastrophe and went on to re-establish civilization afterwards.

"The truth is that Arkaim was a troy town, so-called after the city in Asia Minor that the Greek king Agammenon destroyed during the Trojan Wars. Built on the same circular principle as Troy, as described in Homer's Iliad, but at least six hundred years older, Arkaim finds its prototype in Plato's Atlantis with its three concentric circles of canals; in legendary Electris, the Hyperborean city some said was built under the Pole Star by the sea-god Poseidon; and in Asgard, the sacred city dedicated to the Norse god Odin that is described in the Icelandic saga, the Edda. All these legendary troy towns have the same circular ground plan. They have gone down in history as neolithic Wisdom centers and the seats of ancient god-kings [...]. Built in the unique architectural mould of nordic Asgard, the most sacred shrine of the Aesir of which the Prose Edda relates that 'men call it Troy,' **Arkaim may have been a shrine dedicated to the Aryan Sun religion [...]. Troy towns like Electris – and Arkaim – were built as stellar observatories. Their function was to unite earth to the starry cosmos above according to the principle of 'as above so below'** by means of a central axis symbolized by a stone pillar. Thus Diodorus Siculus of the first century BCE, quoting the historian Hecataeus, described the sanctuary of Electris as a troy town after the pattern of the spheres, by which he meant an astronomical design similar to that of Stonehenge and other ancient sun temples, in which the scheme of the heavenly spheres or astral shells surrounding the earth was represented diagrammatically by a series of concentric circles marked by walls, ditches or moats around a central pillar-stone." [69]

~ VICTORIA LEPAGE, NEW DAWN MAGAZINE

The city of Arkaim provides further evidence of an ancient Religion of the Sun. There is evidence that the Aryans migrated to different parts of the world, including India and Europe, taking their ancient knowledge and sacred symbols, such as the swastika, with them, which emerged at other ancient sites.

Arkaim is located in the Southern Ural region in Russia; in the Central and Southern Ural regions there are also hundreds of megalithic and standing stone sites, most of which have been termed dolmens and menhirs, and some of which have been found to align to the solstices and equinoxes. The largest megalithic complex in the Ural region is located on Vera Island.

A megalith on Vera Island, which has portals that may have been built to allow shafts of sunlight into it.

"Among the most interesting monuments of the isle are its megaliths, similar to the famous megaliths of the Western Europe and Middle East. The largest of them is about 18 meters long, and weighs about 17 tons. Most likely, it is a temple complex related to the sun calendar cult. These megaliths are at average six thousand years old. Their further study may possibly change the history of the mountain forest zone of the Urals in the end of the Stone Age." [70]

~ STANISLAV GRIGORYEV, SENIOR RESEARCH SCIENTIST OF THE CHELYABINSK RESEARCH CENTER OF THE INSTITUTE FOR HISTORY AND ARCHEOLOGY OF THE URALS

MORE SITES

Here are some more sites that align to the winter solstice:

Ales Stenar Megalithic "Stone Ship" in Sweden
On the morning of the winter solstice the sun rises in alignment with the "stern stone," which is at the very rear of the "ship."[71]

Bryn Celli Ddu in Wales
A white standing stone pillar within the inner chamber of the mound was used to determine the solstices and equinoxes; the entrance stones are positioned so that the sun's light is directed at the pillar and moves up and down it over

the course of the year. On the winter solstice a dagger of sunlight would have reached the top of the pillar (this has been obscured by modern renovations to the site).[72]

Cahokia Woodhenge in Illinois, USA
Posts at the Cahokia Woodhenge align to sunrise on the winter solstice.[73]

Chaco Canyon in New Mexico, USA
There are a series of petroglyphs, including two spirals, carved into the cliffs of the Fajada Butte in Chaco Canyon. On the solstices and equinoxes at noon, three large slabs of rock positioned near the spirals direct the sunlight to make patterns of light that mark the time of year. On the winter solstice, two bands of light frame the large spiral at noon.[74]

Harman Kaya Observatory in Bulgaria
The sun shines through specific notches in the rock formation on the winter solstice.[75]

Kanayama Megaliths in Japan
The Higashinoyama megalithic group located east of the Iwaya valley in Japan consists of two nine-meter-long megaliths lying on the ground that are aligned to winter solstice sunrise over the mountain.[76] [77]

Kokino Megalithic Observatory & Sacred Site in Macedonia
The Megalithic Observatory at Kokino has markers pointing directly to the winter solstice sunrise.[78]

Mesa Verde Sun Temple and Cliff Palace Settlement, Colorado USA
At the ancient settlements of Mesa Verde the winter solstice sun sets over the Sun Temple when observed from a viewing site at Cliff Palace, while a ceremonial fire pit at the base of the canyon aligns to the winter solstice sunrise.[79]

Omahk Sacred Landscape and the Majorville Medicine Wheel, Alberta, Canada
On the morning of the winter solstice, the sun rises from the position where the Bow River is closest to the "sun ring" hill at the Omahk Sacred Landscape, intimately linking the sun, the Bow River, and the sun ring.[80]

Oyu Stone Circles in Japan
The four-thousand-year-old Oyu stone circles on the left bank of the Oyu river (in the northeastern Akita Prefecture) include a sundial which marks sunrise on the winter solstice.[81]

Punkri Burwadih in India
The azimuth of the "M1" menhir is oriented directly toward the winter solstice sunrise.[82]

Rego Grande Stone Circle in Brazil (Known as "Stonehenge of the Amazon")
The shadow of one of the blocks completely disappears at the winter solstice as the sun shines above it.[83]

Ancient Stone Structure in Sicily, Italy
On the top of a hill on the southern coast of Sicily, Italian archeologists discovered an ancient stone structure with a large opening that precisely marks the sun on the winter solstice.[84]

The Wolf Rock Dolmens Group of the Lazarevskoye Region, Russia
On the winter solstice the sunrise aligns with the "real" entrance and the sunset aligns with the "false" entrance of one of the twenty dolmens in the area.[85]

Yazilikaya and Hattusa in Turkey
Ancient sites of the Hittites were aligned to the solstices. One of the walls of their Yazilikaya rock sanctuary is illuminated by the winter solstice sunset, as is a chamber at their capital city Hattusa, and one of the corners of the megalithic construction of Yerkapı also in Hattusa.[86] It has been suggested that they held a divine assembly at the winter solstice in Yazilikaya.[87]

CHAPTER TEN

Ancient Sacred Sites Aligned to the Spring Equinox

This chapter brings together ancient sacred sites from around the world that align to the spring equinox. Even though they are separated by vast distances and time, they share a knowledge of the symbolic spiritual significance of the spring equinox as a time of resurrection and attainment of eternal life.

THE GREAT SPHINX ~ EGYPT

One of the most dominant alignments (as there are many both solar and stellar) of the Giza Plateau, home to the Sphinx and the Great Pyramids, occurs at the spring equinox.

The Sphinx gazes due east to where the sun rises on the morning of the equinox. In addition to this, authors Graham Hancock and Robert Bauval realized that during the era of 10,970 to 8,810 BC (but also prior to this at approximately 36,500 BC) it would have also gazed directly toward the rising of its own celestial image (known today as the constellation of Leo in the form of a recumbent lion), which would have preceded the sun at dawn on the spring equinox, because at that time the spring equinox sun rose in the constellation of Leo.[1] This indicates, along with other evidence, that the Sphinx is much older than mainstream Egyptologists say, who date it to around 2,500 BC, while researchers like Graham Hancock, John Anthony West, and Robert Schoch date it to at least 10,000 BC.

The Great Sphinx, which gazes precisely at sunrise on the equinox.

The design of the Sphinx interwoven with the spring equinox and the constellations has an important spiritual meaning. It pinpoints the celestial parts while integrating them into an earthly design, which symbolically re-enacts the process of the resurrection of Osiris as found in the ancient Pyramid Texts—the oldest surviving sacred texts in the world.

As further support for this, the Sphinx Mapping Project (run by AERA) discovered an alignment with the equinox running through the axis of the Sphinx Temple (which stands in front of the Sphinx), through a box that was found with a statue of Osiris in it (although damaged), to the south side of the second of the largest pyramids.

> "The alignment and iconography of the Khafre monuments suggest a strong connection to the cult of the sun god, Re.
>
> One of the significant alignments discovered during the Sphinx mapping project is that a line can be drawn from the Sphinx Temple's east-west axis through an enigmatic box [in which a statue of Osiris had been found, albeit shattered] [...] along the right side of the Sphinx. The line continues to the apparent south side of Khafre's pyramid as it appears on the horizon when viewed from the Sphinx Temple.
>
> Twice a year, on the equinoxes, the sun sets on this alignment and would have illuminated the Sphinx Temple sanctuary and cult statue if the builders had finished the temple interior. The setting sun would renew the power of the dead king and like him, enter the underworld where Re and Osiris are united.
>
> The Sphinx's alignment with the other Khafre monuments indicates a building program linked to beliefs around a solar cult." [2]
>
> ~ ANCIENT EGYPT RESEARCH ASSOCIATION (AERA)

ANGKOR WAT ~ CAMBODIA

The spring equinox sun rising to crown the pinnacle of Angkor Wat in Cambodia.

Angkor is an ancient city with a massive complex of stone temples in the jungle of Cambodia. The temple of Angkor Wat is the most famous and aligns to the rising sun on the spring equinox.

The axis of the temple is offset to give a three-day anticipation of the coming spring equinox alignment. On the morning of the spring equinox, the sun rises up the side of the central tower (mountain peak) of the temple and crowns its pinnacle. What many people don't realize, however, is that Angkor Wat actually brings together the components of an ancient astrological myth, using the earth, sun, and stars.

This astrological myth is called "the Churning of the Milky Ocean" and is found carved into a mural at Angkor Wat. In this myth, the asuras (demons) and devas (gods) are in a giant tug of war using a serpent wrapped around a mountain resting on the back of a turtle, which churns the great milky ocean as they pull back and forth. This churning

The central segment of the mural of the Churning of the Milky Ocean at Angkor Wat. Vishnu is the large central figure—above him is Indra, below him the turtle in the ocean, and on either side the asuras and devas pulling.

produces Amrita, the nectar of immortality, which is eventually consumed by the devas and allows the god Indra to return to his abode as the King of Heaven.

This giant relief is found carved into an eastern wall, and is associated with the spring equinox (part of it is illuminated by the sun on the equinox[3]), while other reliefs are associated with the other solstices and equinoxes.

Graham Hancock, Santha Faiia, and John Grigsby, discovered that Angkor Wat and a number of surrounding temples (around fifteen) mirror the constellation of Draco as it would have appeared in the sky at the time of the spring equinox in the year 10,500 BC, thousands of years before it is said to have been built.[4] It's most likely that Angkor Wat as we see it today was built over a far more ancient sacred site connected in some way to ancient Egypt, as Angkor Wat lies along the same line around the earth as other ancient sites with solar alignments, including the Great Pyramids. It's even located seventy-two symbolic degrees from the Great Pyramids—and seventy-two is a key number in the cycle of the precession of the equinoxes that both sites encode, as the earth cycles through one degree in its precession every seventy-two years.

The main temple of Angkor Wat is said to be a representation of Mount Meru, the ancient Hindu home of the gods, and the North Pole. The five central towers symbolize the five peaks of Mount Meru, and the walls and moat the surrounding mountain ranges and ocean, forming a replica of the universe.[5]

Due to the approximately twenty-six-thousand-year cycle of precession of the equinoxes, the star (called the Pole Star) that the North Pole points toward changes very slowly—tracing an almost perfect circle in the sky as it does.

The constellation of Draco (which is depicted as a dragon or serpent) appears in the region of the circumpolar stars, where it literally wraps around the center of the circle that the North Pole traces through the sky in its processional cycle. The constellation of Draco is therefore the celestial depiction of the great serpent of the Churning of the Milky Ocean, wrapped around the tower of Angkor Wat as the North Pole, with the stars that make its constellation mirrored in the temples on the ground.

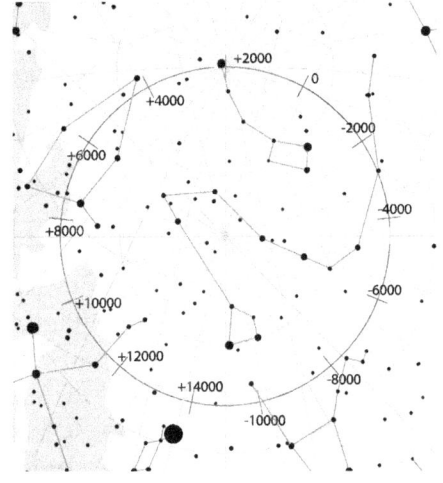

The path of the north celestial pole among the stars due to precession. Draco is the central constellation that appears to wind around the very center of the picture.

In the mural depicting this scene, the number of demons on the left represents the days between the winter solstice and the spring equinox, and the number of gods on the right represents the number of days from the spring equinox to the summer solstice. Each side of either demons or gods measures 54 cubits—which correlates to the average maximum annual arcs of the sun and moon.[6] Together, it adds to 108, the most sacred number in Hinduism and Buddhism, and found in the dimensions of the sun in relation to Earth.

The numbers 108 and 54, along with 72 and 36, have been incorporated into the design of Angkor Wat and surrounding temples. These numbers are part of the mathematics of the phenomenon known as "the precession of the equinoxes," a cosmic cycle of the earth related to the spring equinox, which the Churning of the Milky Ocean is also said to symbolize.

> "At the temple of Phnom Bakheng there are 108 surrounding towers. The number 108, considered sacred in both Hindu and Buddhist cosmologies, is the sum of 72 plus 36 (36 being ½ of 72). The number 72 is a primary number in the sequence of numbers linked to the earth's axial precession, which causes the apparent alteration in the position of the constellations over the period of 25,920 years, or one degree every 72 years. Another mysterious fact about the Angkor complex is its location 72 degrees of longitude east of the Pyramids of Giza. The temples of Bakong, Prah Ko and Prei Monli at Roluos, south of the main Angkor complex, are situated in relation to each other in such a way that they mirror the three stars in the Corona Borealis as they appeared at dawn on the spring equinox in 10,500 BC. It is interesting to note that the Corona Borealis would not have been visible from these temples during the tenth and eleventh centuries when they were constructed." [7]
>
> ~ MARTIN GRAY, SACRED EARTH

With the combination of the constellation of Draco, which is shaped like a giant serpent, and the tower of the temple said to represent the North Pole, the milky ocean as the starry cosmos which shifts as the earth rotates through precession, all aligned at the spring equinox, with the dark and light halves of the year on either side as the devas and asuras, and Indra as the sun rising to crown the tower, Angkor Wat brings together the counterparts of the story of the Churning of the Milky Ocean in symphony with the earth and sky.

Even the entrance to Angkor Wat incorporates cosmic symbolism and numbers encoding the cycles of time. Different sections of the entrance to Angkor Wat were designed to represent the great world ages of Hindu cosmology called Yugas.[8]

Angkor also aligns to the winter solstice, and so more information about it is detailed in the previous chapter dedicated to ancient sites that align to the winter solstice. There is also a detailed explanation of the meaning of its symbolism in chapter four "The Spiritual Meaning of the Spring Equinox."

TIKAL ~ GUATEMALA

Tikal is a ruined ancient city with a series of stepped pyramids and temples located deep in the jungle of Guatemala. As with many sites in Central America, some of the structures were successively built over, making their origins much older. The tall pyramid style temples rise majestically above the canopy of the rainforest—a scene made famous by their appearance in the Star Wars film A New Hope.[9]

Temple of the Great Jaguar at Tikal.

The Temple of the Great Jaguar (Temple I) is one of the main stepped pyramid temples of the city, and aligns to the spring equinox. It was built to entomb the Maya king Jasaw Chan K'awiil I,[10] just like many stepped pyramids were for the pharaohs of ancient Egypt. And just as in Egypt, these tombs were intended as "resurrection machines" for the deceased, expressing the fundamental religious beliefs of those who built them. That's why they contain important symbols—the king assumed the spiritual role of the Jaguar, just as the pharaohs assumed the role of Osiris.

On the equinox, the sun rises behind the Temple of the Great Jaguar, causing it to cast a shadow over the much smaller Temple of the Moon in front of it, dedicated to the king's wife.[11] This visual connection between the feminine moon temple and the solar Jaguar temple may have represented how someone becomes one with the Spiritual Mother at spiritual resurrection.

Additionally, when looking towards Temple I from the nearby Temple III (Temple of the Jaguar Priest and tomb of the king Dark Sun), the rising spring equinox sun crowns the pinnacle of Temple I.[12] Temple I has nine levels, symbolizing the nine regions of the underworld in Maya cosmology. The spring equinox sun rises up these nine levels, representing resurrection from the underworld.

Temple I was decorated with a wooden lintel depicting a jaguar with water lilies sprouting from its head, protecting the king.[13] The use of this symbol on the temple, along with its alignment, provides more clues to its meaning.

The jaguar symbol dates to at least 1,500 BC, when it was used by the earliest recorded cultures in Central America (those of the Olmec and Maya). It was considered the night sun (or dark sun)—the form the sun takes in its journey through the underworld.[14] The water-lily jaguar was considered a transformer, and could also be depicted amidst flames.[15] These transformative flames likely represent divine fire.

The symbol of the water lily or lotus has parallels in other remnants of the Religion of the Sun, where it was used as a symbol of the sun. For example, one of the most important symbols in ancient Egypt was the blue water lily, which opens only during the day—closing, and sinking beneath the water at night, and reemerging in the morning—just like the sun. Because of this, it was used to symbolize the resurrection and rebirth of the sun, and passages of ancient Egyptian texts recount how pharaohs would resurrect by being symbolically transformed into water lilies. It was also one of the most important symbols in India, often used to symbolize the rising of the eternal spirit from out of the water/mud of materiality.

> "I am the holy lotus that cometh forth from the light [...]. I have made my way, and I seek after him, that is to say, Horus [the resurrected Son/sun]. I am the pure lotus that cometh forth from the field [of Ra, the sun god]." [16]
> ~ THE CHAPTER OF CHANGING INTO A LOTUS, THE EGYPTIAN BOOK OF THE DEAD

The symbol of the water-lily jaguar that adorns the Jaguar pyramid is a symbol of resurrection, as after being transformed in the fires of the underworld, the night/underworld form of the sun emerges, just as a water lily does from the earth and the spring equinox sun from the horizon—ascending the nine symbolic levels of the pyramid/underworld.

The rising sun was very much associated with resurrection for the Maya, as plates illustrating the resurrection of the Maya maize god were common at Tikal.[17]

Like other Central American sites, Tikal descended into human sacrifice and bloodletting. Graffiti inside the temples depicts scenes of sacrificial victims. Again, this was a horrific distortion of the original spiritual knowledge as has happened so many times in the past, and why it is continually given anew.

CAHOKIA MOUNDS ~ ILLINOIS, UNITED STATES

Cahokia Mounds, located in the U.S. state of Illinois, is considered as being built by the largest and most sophisticated pre-Columbian civilization north of Mexico. It covered an area of 6 square miles or 16 square kilometers, contained 120 man-made earthen mounds, and at one stage became home to around 40,000 inhabitants.

This city contained a woodhenge, which is a sacred circle made of wooden posts (just like the one built near Stonehenge in England). The wood used was red cedar, which was considered sacred. When standing at the center of the circle, where a large "observation post" was located, the sun on the solstices and equinoxes aligned with some of the posts of the circle.

ANCIENT SOLSTICE

The observation post of the Cahokia Woodhenge.

The most visually spectacular of the alignments at the site was sunrise on the equinox. One of the wood posts that aligned with the equinox also aligned with the front of Monks Mound—the largest mound in the entire complex, with a footprint larger than that of the Great Pyramid of Egypt.

On the equinox, Monks Mound is described as appearing to give birth to the rising sun.[18] However, given that the time of the spring equinox was associated with resurrection for the Maya of Central America, perhaps the mound symbolized not the birth of the sun, but its resurrection. As support for this, at the spring equinox the Maya god Hun Hunahpu resurrected as the sun from the earth and underworld symbolized as a turtle, and Monks Mound, from which the sun "resurrects," appears to have been built in the shape of a turtle.

> "Monks mound is prominently situated as the central feature of the Cahokia Mounds group, a group of around 120 mounds in the region. From an aerial and profile view, the mound is composed in the shape of a turtle effigy. These projections may represent the turtle's hind legs on the north side, constructed to indicate movement. The front projections on the first terrace represent legs of the turtle. I suggest the possibility is that this is an effigy of a turtle burying its eggs, or possibly a turtle walking south. Several versions of this account are found throughout North America. I concur with the late Oscar Schneider, 'Monks Mound, that giant earthwork built in four stages with a projecting ramp to the south, is actually a giant turtle figure.' If it was a sacred 'National Monument' for Turtle Island, presently known as North America, [then it] was once held in the highest regards as among the world's most sacred places. Monks Mound was used for ceremonies that relate to the 'big house' ceremony, in which the sky people sat on the north and the earth people sat on the south of the path of the sun. They contemplated the intricate workings of the cosmos, their ancestors, and their descendants." [19]
>
> ~ VINCE BARROWS

Additionally, a carving of a turtle was found at Monks Mound and is described by researcher Vince Barrows as having a trident on its left side, which is symbolic of death and darkness, and a symbol of the sun on its right, which depicts birth.[20] Perhaps this carving symbolizes the dual aspects of creation—of darkness and light, which rotate on the point of balance at the equinox. Incredibly, it contains the same elements of the Churning of the Milky Ocean scene illustrated at Angkor Wat in Cambodia, where the forces of darkness and light are depicted as being on either side of a turtle. And like Angkor Wat, Monks Mound is also aligned to the spring equinox.

CAIRN T ~ IRELAND

Cairn T at the site of Loughcrew.

Cairn T is the name given to an ancient mound with an inner chamber that aligns to the equinoxes, and is believed to be older than Newgrange—dated to between 3,500 to 3,300 BC.[21] It is the main and central mound in a group of Neolithic sites at a place called Loughcrew, which may have originally had fifty to one hundred mounds.[22] It is thirty-five meters in diameter and was once covered in a thick mantle of quartz. The rising sun on the spring equinox enters the mound and travels into its inner chamber which is in the shape of a cross/cruciform, to alight the back stone, called the Equinox Stone, which is covered in sun and other astronomical symbols.[23]

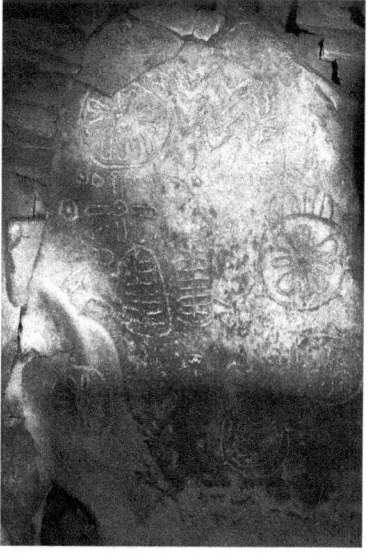

The Equinox Stone within Cairn T. The light of the rising sun on the equinox enters the chamber and illuminates this stone, as in this image, which has been simulated using a torch.

The equinox sun, viewed from Cairn T, rises over the Hill of Slane, which is a sacred hill that is framed by the view looking back out from the chamber of Cairn T.[24] The Hill of Slane formed part of a larger equinox alignment in ancient Ireland as described in the Millmount-Croagh Patrick alignment further on.

KNOWTH ~ IRELAND

Nearby Cairn T at Loughcrew is another ancient Neolithic site called Knowth, believed to have been built around 3,200 BC (around the same time as Newgrange). It is the largest ancient monument in Ireland and contains the largest collection of megalithic artwork in all of Europe. Some believe it could have served as an ancient repository of wisdom that was carved symbolically into its stone (much like the temples of Egypt).[25]

It is a giant man-made mound one acre in size with two inner chambers—one aligned to the east, and the other to the west. The light of the rising sun enters the eastern chamber six days after the equinox, while the light of the setting sun enters the western chamber approximately eighteen days before the equinox. The reason for this offset has been suggested by Charles Scribner: the alignment of these passages could be used to predict the solstices and equinoxes using lunar months. For example, the western passage is aligned to sunset thirteen lunar months before the following spring equinox.[26]

The east chamber (the direction of east is typically associated with the spring equinox) is in a cruciform shape—it is the biggest in Ireland and houses a large stone basin with a sun symbol carved into it, thought to have be placed inside Knowth before the temple mound was built, as it is too large to have been brought in later. It is shaped like a cauldron—an important motif in Irish mythology. The most well-known cauldron in Irish myth belonged to Dagda, the supreme deity and chief of the Tuatha Dé Danann, who is said to have built and owned Newgrange.[27] His cauldron was one of the four treasures the Tuatha Dé Danann are said to have brought to Ireland—the others being the Stone of Destiny at Tara, the Sword of Light, and Spear of Lugh (who became mythologized as a sun god).

Cauldrons became associated with witches; however, they were used as a spiritual symbol in ancient times.

In Irish myth the cauldron was said to have had the power to regenerate life so that dead bodies could be placed into the cauldron and drawn out alive and whole again.[28] This is symbolic of resurrection. The mound and cauldron are symbols of the womb, from which all life comes forth. The symbol of the cross in the east chamber connects this part of the mound with the spring equinox, the time of Jesus' resurrection, thousands of years before he enacted the same spiritual principle.

There are also a pair of large standing stones outside the mound's west entrance—one tall and thin, acting as a phallic symbol representing the masculine force, and the other squat and round, representing the feminine.[29] The presence of these symbols further associates the symbology of the mound with birth and regeneration.

THE MILLMOUNT-CROAGH PATRICK ALIGNMENT ~ IRELAND

The ancient man-made mound at Millmount—once a sacred astronomical observatory, now a fort with canon fire displays.

The Millmount-Croagh Patrick alignment to the equinox is not just to one particular site, but is created from the alignment of a number of sites in relation to each other, which were built from the east to the west coast of Ireland stretching over 135 miles.

The ancient people who created this alignment were aware of how natural land formations aligned at certain times of year, and incorporated them into the design of their sacred sites—again bringing the earthly and celestial together on the ground as was done at many other ancient sites around the world. These types of alignments, which incorporate different sites that stretch for miles, can be found across the British Isles.

This alignment starts at a place called Millmount (near the east coast of Ireland), which is an ancient temple mound that later became used as a fort and has been built over and left unexcavated. In Irish myth it is identified as the burial place of Amergin mac Míled, an ancient Druid warrior and chief.

Standing at Millmount, one can watch the sun, around two days after the spring equinox (around March 23), set directly over the Hill of Slane, which stands 158 meters tall. The Hill of Slane was named after Sláine, the king of the Fir Bolg (an ancient race that used to inhabit Ireland), who is said to have been buried there. The Hill of Slane was also supposed to have been the location of a mythical healing well, which was used by the Tuatha Dé Danann to heal their wounds during battle. Later, it was believed to be the place where Saint Patrick lit the Easter fire on March 23 (coinciding with the solar alignment). There is an artificial mound on the western end of the hilltop, and two Neolithic standing stones in the burial yard of the Christian abbey that stands there today, indicating that this was once an ancient sacred site built over by the Christians, who built atop of so many other ancient sites across the British Isles.[30]

The alignment continues west with the equinox sunset, skirting the hills of Loughcrew (home of Cairn T which aligns to the equinox sunrises) on its way, and traveling directly through Rathcroghan (or Cruachan Aí), one of the largest archeological complexes in the world, with two hundred monuments located in a ten-mile radius.

The alignment ends on the west coast of Ireland at Croagh Patrick, one of Ireland's sacred mountains, intersecting the Christian church built on its summit precisely. Again, this was an ancient sacred site that was taken over by Christians. The mountain's top is shaped like a pyramid, which can be seen from miles around. The old name for the mountain is Croghan Aigle, which might be translated as "the Eagle's Peak." The mountain is ringed by old sites, monuments, and standing stones, revealing that it was a place held sacred from ancient times.

CAIRNPAPPLE AND ARTHUR'S SEAT ALIGNMENT ~ SCOTLAND

Ancient cairn, stone circle, wooden post holes,
and man-made ditch atop of Cairnpapple.

This alignment to the equinox is another created by natural formations that became sacred sites and observation points of the spring equinox sunrise.

Cairnpapple is an ancient megalithic complex set on top of a hill in Scotland, which is said to have been used as a sacred site for around four thousand years, starting around 3,500 BC. It includes a standing stone circle.

From the site of Cairnpapple, the spring equinox sun rises over Arthur's Seat, associated with King Arthur, and also Huly Hill, which is another site of an ancient cairn and standing stones, forming a sacred landscape of alignments to the sun.[31]

PERSEPOLIS ~ IRAN

Although Persepolis has no known alignments to the spring equinox, this ancient city was principally used for celebrations of the autumn and spring equinoxes.[32] Ornate murals at the site depict the powers of light symbolically defeating those of darkness as occurs in nature at the spring equinox.

Relief at Persepolis with a lion representing the sun and summer season, and the bull the winter season.

"In Zoroastrianism, light is the great symbol of God and Goodness, whether in the light of the sun or in the sacred fire. The Spring Equinox and the lengthening of the days is thus a symbol of the victory of Light over the cold and darkness of winter. Zoroastrianism has a rich heritage of mythological and astrological symbolism which illustrates the significance of Noruz [the spring equinox]. This symbolism is especially evident in the great palace and ritual center of Persepolis [...]." [33]

~ HANNAH M. G. SHAPERO, WRITER ON ZOROASTRIAN STUDIES

Persepolis is an ancient city located in Iran. Its remains date back to 515 BC,[34] however, it is built on a line of ancient sites around the world that are all connected to the ancient Religion of the Sun, and so the location for the city may have been chosen because it was already considered a very ancient sacred place. As support for this, medieval Persians had attributed the site to Jamshid[35]—elsewhere known as Yima—who was said to have survived a great global cataclysm, and have been "the first man" to repopulate the human race after it. Like other wisdom bringers, he was known as a "son of the sun" and was learned in the ancient religion that had existed before the catastrophe.[36]

Vestiges of this religion were preserved for thousands of years in Iran, with the solstices and equinoxes forming the most important ceremonial dates. These dates are still celebrated in Iran today—the autumn equinox celebration is called Mehrgan, the winter solstice Yalda, and spring equinox Nowruz.

The celebration of the solstices and equinoxes has very ancient roots in Iran—being celebrated in the ancient Indo-Iranian religion, in Zoroastrianism, and later in Mithraism, all of which were developments of the same ancient tradition, which had derived from the ancient Religion of the Sun. In an old Persian poem, the celebration of the spring equinox is attributed to Jamshid/Yima. Zoroaster, the founder of Zoroastrianism, was said to have highly emphasized the celebration of both the autumn and spring equinoxes.[37] Even today, the symbol of the winged sun disk, called the Faravahar and found engraved at Persepolis, is a national symbol, and the imperial throne of Iran is called The Sun Throne.[38]

The Faravahar sun symbol at Persepolis.

MORE SITES

Here are some more sites that align to the spring equinox:

Anubis Caves in Oklahoma, USA
According to Phillip M. Leonard, "On days of the equinoxes, a group of petroglyphs in a small cave are lighted successively by the sun, much as actors on a stage are spotlighted in an opera. Finally, just at sunset, after the other figures have been eclipsed by the shadow, only what we interpret as Anubis, the Egyptian jackal god, is left in sunshine on the cave wall."[39]

Bryn Celli Ddu in Wales
A white standing stone pillar within the inner chamber of the mound was used to determine the solstices and equinoxes; the entrance stones are positioned so that the sun's light is directed at the pillar and moves up and down it over the course of the year. On the morning of the equinoxes, the sunlight moves onto the wall behind the pillar, splitting in two to light up the sides of the chamber, which are carved with patterns and cup-markings.[40]

Chaco Canyon in New Mexico, USA
There are many alignments to the equinox seen on the glyphs and in the structures at Chaco Canyon, including the sun rising through two doors of the largest isolated kiva called Casa Rinconada.[41][42]

Grianan of Aileach in Ireland
At sunrise on the equinox, a beam of light shines through the entrance of the Grianan, creating a spectacular path of light through the middle of the site.[43]

Kokino Megalithic Observatory & Sacred Site in Macedonia
At Kokino, one can observe the equinox at sunrise on one of the main marker grooves on the observatory wall.[44]

Mamed Canyon Dolmen in Russia
On the morning of the equinox, the sun can be seen rising over the top of the pyramid-shaped Mamed canyon dolmen.[45]

Mnajdra in Malta
On the equinox at the Mnajdra Solar Temple in Malta, the rays of the rising sun pass directly through the temple's main doorway and light up the main axis to the altar at the end.[46]

Dolmens and Megaliths in Montana, USA
Among many alignments at the Montana Megaliths, the "Bird Watches Sky" menhir directly faces the sun at high noon on the equinox.[47]

At the equinox the statue named "Robotic Watcher" faces the sunrise precisely, with the sun illuminating a portion of the statue's face (the inset left eye).[48]

Nebelivka Temple in Ukraine
A huge temple of the Cucuteni-Tripillia people dated to 4,000 BC (the largest ancient temple found in Europe so far) had its main axis aligned to the equinox sunrise, so that "On the equinox day, the sunlight passed through the main gate, through the entrance to the temple and lit the central altar No. 7. In the dark temple, the altar, covered with red clay, shone in the rays of the sun."[49] Other altars within the temple aligned to sunrise on the winter and summer solstices.[50] This temple no longer stands; in 2012 its foundations were unearthed by archeologists.

Picture Canyon in Colorado, USA
On the equinox sunrise at Crack Cave, the sun's rays penetrate the cave entrance, illuminating the hand-pecked lines engraved on a small protrusion on the north cave wall, about ten to fifteen feet from the entrance. The petroglyphs stay illuminated for about ten to twelve minutes before the light fades away.[51]

Punkri Burwadih in India
Punkri Burwadih is reportedly the only site in India where hundreds of people gather at the spring and autumn equinoxes each year to view the stunning sunrise, seen framed by the "V"-shaped notch between two standing stones.[52]

Swansea Petroglyphs in Eastern California, USA
A light serpent heliolithic animation occurs on the morning of the equinox, where an image of a snake with open mouth, made of sunlight, slowly proceeds toward a spiral petroglyph and starts "eating" its inner ring, also referred to as an "egg."[53]

Uaxactún in Guatemala
A number of temples at the ancient Maya city of Uaxactún were built to align with the solstices and equinoxes. Three temples stand opposite the Pyramid of the Masks, which acts as a viewing platform. When viewed from the Pyramid of the Masks the sun rises behind the central temple (Temple II) on the equinox in alignment with the staircase of the Pyramid of the Masks, and can be seen rising from behind the other two temples (Temples I and III) on the winter and summer solstices.[54]

CHAPTER ELEVEN

Ancient Sacred Sites Aligned to the Summer Solstice

Some of the most famous ancient megalithic sites in the world align to the summer solstice. Below are a few examples—there are many others that have not been included.

THE GREAT PYRAMIDS AND SPHINX ~ EGYPT

An artist's rendition of the summer solstice sun setting between the two largest Great Pyramids of Egypt, crowning the Sphinx in the foreground.

At the Great Pyramids of Egypt, when facing the Sphinx, the sun on the summer solstice sets precisely between the two largest of the Great Pyramids. In doing so, the sun forms a halo of light around the head of the Sphinx. It also creates the Egyptian hieroglyph for the word "horizon," which portrays the sun between two mountains.

The original name for the Sphinx is unknown, but by 1,400 BC it was revered as a sun god and referred to as "Horus of the Horizon" (Hor-em-akhet). Horus was an ancient Egyptian sun god, and since the Sphinx gazes precisely at the point on the horizon where the sun rises on the equinox, it's likely the name refers to this alignment. But what if there was another, more hidden meaning intended also—as the Sphinx literally portrays the living sun (Horus) in the glyph of the horizon.

The Great Pyramid was also positioned so that at noon during the months around midsummer the light of the sun illuminated the entire surface of the pyramid.

> "During seven months and a half of each year—namely, for three months and three quarters before and after midsummer—the noon rays of the sun fell on all four faces of the pyramid; or, according to a Peruvian expression [...] the sun shone on the pyramid 'with all his rays.' Such conditions as these might have been regarded as very suitable for a temple devoted to sun-worship." [1]
> ~ RICHARD A. PROCTOR, THE GREAT PYRAMID

THE OSIREION ~ EGYPT

There is an incredibly mysterious temple at the ancient site of Abydos in Egypt. For thousands of years Abydos was believed to be the final resting place of the wisdom bringer and Egyptian god Osiris. Then in AD 1902 the Osireion temple was unearthed, which many speculated could have been Osiris' tomb.[2]

The Osireion temple.

The Osireion shares clear similarities with the Valley Temple, which is located next to the Sphinx. The oldest layer of the Valley Temple is made out of giant limestone blocks that are badly weathered, and so appears to have been renovated at some time later in its history with huge granite blocks. This later granite renovation blockwork looks very similar in style to the Osireion, which has led researchers to speculate that they were built by the same people.[3]

The age of the Osireion is contested. Like the Valley Temple, the Osireion is also so old it was covered in sand and forgotten thousands of years ago, being rediscovered even by the pharaohs of Egypt themselves who renovated them. It was unearthed during the construction of the temple of the Pharaoh Seti I around 1,280 BC, and later again when excavated along with the temple of Seti I in AD 1902, after both had become covered in sand.

Like the Great Pyramids and Sphinx, the Osireion has a summer solstice sunset alignment. On the summer solstice, the light of the setting sun shines through a nearby gap in the Libyan Hills, which intersects the Osireion temple.[4]

The temple was constructed near a natural spring, which was used to feed a pool of water inside the temple to form a moat around its central part. Some believe this was intended to symbolize the mound that rose from the primeval waters at the beginning of creation in ancient Egyptian texts.

Other mysterious aspects of the site include a flower of life symbol found inscribed on some of the pillars of the temple, believed to have been left there by Greeks possibly around 300 BC. Ancient hieroglyphs of what appear to be hovercraft, and various flying machines like helicopters, can be found in the temple of Seti I next door.

THE ESSENE MONASTERY, QUMRAN ~ WEST BANK

The ruins of what is believed to have been the Essene community at Qumran.

The Essene community is believed to have existed between around 200 BC to the first century AD and lived together in various places in the Levant and Egypt.

Qumran is an archeological site located near the shore of the Dead Sea in the West Bank. The ruins of stone buildings there are believed to have been a monastery of the Essenes. The largest room was used for rituals, and is aligned to the summer solstice sunset[5]—there are two altars at the eastern wall of the room which may have been illuminated by the solstice sunlight.

Additionally, a limestone sundial was discovered there, designed to measure the sun throughout the year rather than the day, and could determine the solstices and equinoxes. The historian Josephus Flavius describes how the Essenes addressed prayers to the sun.

"And as for their piety towards God, it is very extraordinary; for before sun-rising they speak not a word about profane matters, but put up

certain prayers which they have received from their forefathers, as if they made a supplication for its rising." [6]
~ JOSEPHUS FLAVIUS

However, there were a number of groups in the region where the Essenes are said to have lived, which have been broadly defined as Essene, but historically had different names.

Two historians, Philo and Epiphanius, describe groups in the area which practiced a form of sun worship. Jesus is believed to have spent time with one or some of these groups, and perhaps even gave rise to them, as the author below describes them as a remnant of the Essenes who accepted a so-called spurious form of Christianity. The author probably sees it as "spurious" because it was based on Jesus' esoteric teachings and is therefore considered unorthodox.

> "Philo relates of the Therapeutes (*Vit. Cont.* II, II. p. 485), that they 'stand with their faces and their whole body toward the East, and when they see that the sun is risen, holding out their hands to heaven they pray for a happy day and for truth and for keen vision of reason.' [...]
>
> Epiphanius (*Hær.* xix. 2, xx. 3, pp. 40 sq., 47) speaks of a sect called the Sampsæans or 'Sun-worshipers,' as existing in his own time in Peræa on the borders of Moab and on the shores of the Dead Sea. He describes them as a remnant of the Ossenes (i.e. Essenes), who have accepted a spurious form of Christianity and are neither Jews nor Christians. [...]
>
> In this heresy we have plainly the dregs of Essenism, which has only been corrupted from its earlier and nobler type by the admixture of a spurious Christianity. But how came the Essenes to be called Sampsæans? What was the original meaning of this outward reverence which they paid to the sun? Did they regard it merely as the symbol of Divine illumination, just as Philo frequently treats it as a type of God, the center of all light (e.g. *de. Somn.* i. 13 sq., I. p. 631 sq.), and even calls the heavenly bodies 'visible and sensible gods' (*de Mund. Op.* 7, I. p. 6)? Or did they honor the light, as the pure ethereal element in contrast to gross terrestrial matter, according to a suggestion of a recent writer (Keim I. p. 289)? [...] We cannot fail therefore to recognize the action of some foreign influence in this Essene practice—whether Greek or Syrian or Persian, it will be time to consider hereafter." [7]
> ~ J. B. LIGHTFOOT, ON SOME POINTS CONNECTED WITH THE ESSENES

This influence may have come from Jesus, or from mystery schools that understood the significance of the spiritual sun.

STONEHENGE ~ ENGLAND

Stonehenge is perhaps the most famous site known to align to the solstice in the world. Evidence shows that it has been a sacred place of the British peoples for thousands of years—as far back as 8,000-7,500 BC.[8] For periods in its history, it was perhaps the most important religious site in Britain, and even became a site of religious pilgrimage for ancient peoples from other parts of Europe. Today it is experiencing a revival, being visited as a sacred site again in the last few decades by tens of thousands every year at the summer solstice.

Stonehenge underwent various stages of building and modification over its long history, which is very roughly summarized as follows. First, wooden posts were erected nearby—on an east-west alignment,[9] which would have marked sunrise and sunset on the equinoxes. These are believed to have been installed by hunter-gatherers. Thousands of years later, the Stonehenge Cursus (next to the site of Stonehenge) was built on an east-west alignment (pointing to sunrise and sunset on the equinoxes). A few hundred years later a circular earthen ditch and bank was constructed on the site of Stonehenge—with its main entrance aligned to midsummer sunrise and winter solstice sunset.[10] These phases are believed to have been built by the "Windmill Hill people"[11] who brought farming and domesticated animals, and came from continental Europe. An inner circle of bluestones was also erected around this time, and is believed to have been brought by people from west Wales where the stones were quarried, as burials of people of Welsh descent have been found at the site dating to the time.[12] Following this, shortly before the arrival of the Bell Beaker Indo-Europeans, it's believed the huge sarsen stones were installed. The Beaker people then made a number of modifications to the site: the bluestones were rearranged, the grand avenue leading from Stonehenge to the nearby river Avon dug out, and a woodhenge built nearby aligned to the winter solstice sunrise.[13] Later, around 1,500 BC, the "Wessex Peoples" (not to be confused with the much later Saxon kingdom of Wessex), who were descended from the Beaker people, made further changes. Remarkably, this indicates that Stonehenge was revered by a number of major ancient populations of Britain.

In 2013, archaeologists discovered the likely reason why the site of Stonehenge was selected as a sacred place and held that way down thousands of years: excavations revealed that natural ridges at the site, formed during the ice age, point to the winter solstice sunset in one direction, and the summer solstice sunrise in the other. Ancient peoples are thought to have noticed this natural alignment, and considering the solstices sacred times, made it a site of religious significance.[14] The avenue leading to Stonehenge, its main entrance, and its axis are all built along this alignment.

Stonehenge appears to have been used to celebrate both the winter and summer solstice.

Evidence shows that at the winter solstice a large portion of the entire population of Britain, including people from Scotland, Wales, and northern England, traveled to Stonehenge for this huge annual event. Today, at midwinter, the sun can still be seen setting directly through the central trilithon.

The summer solstice, however, was also a time of great religious importance. At sunrise on the summer solstice, the sun rises along the middle of the avenue that leads to Stonehenge, and shines into the center of the stone circle. This avenue was flanked by a pair of large upright stones (only one of these remains today, called the Heel Stone), as well as further upright pillars, giving the impression of the sun shining down a corridor towards the altar.[15]

The summer solstice sunrise aligns with the avenue that adjoins Stonehenge. At sunrise the sun shines down the middle of the avenue into the center of the stone circle.

Nearby Stonehenge there is a large area called the Stonehenge Cursus, which is an area of earthen ditches and banks around three kilometers long and 100-150 meters wide. Within this area are two large pits around sixteen feet across and three feet deep that, when viewed from the Heel Stone just outside Stonehenge, align to the summer solstice sunrise and sunset. These were probably used for ceremonial processions on the summer solstice.

> "The perimeter of the Cursus may well have defined a route guiding ceremonial processions which took place on the longest day of the year. [...] It is possible that procession within the Cursus moved from the eastern pit at sunrise, continuing eastwards along the Cursus and, following the path of the sun overhead, and perhaps back to the west, reaching the western pit at sunset to mark the longest day of the year. Observers of the ceremony would have been positioned at the Heel Stone, of which the two pits are aligned." [16]
> ~ PROFESSOR GAFFNEY

> "If you measure the walking distance between the two pits, the procession would reach exactly half-way at midday, when the sun would be directly on top of Stonehenge. This is more than just a coincidence, indicating that the exact length of the Cursus and the positioning of the pits are of significance." [17]
> ~ DR. HENRY CHAPMAN

A carved-out notch in one of the trilithons also marks both the winter solstice sunrise and summer solstice sunset. These two alignments cross over the center of the Altar Stone at an angle of 80 degrees from one another. This angle is also found on the most famous ancient gold artifact in Britain, called the Bush Barrow Lozenge, which was unearthed in a burial within sight of Stonehenge.[18] It reveals the people using Stonehenge were well aware of the rising and setting points of the sun on the solstices, and that these times were extremely important to them.

Yet another ancient site called Durrington Walls lies two miles northeast of Stonehenge. It contains a henge consisting of concentric circles that would have been made out of large timber posts. The circle is aligned to the winter solstice sunrise, and has a paved avenue leading to the River Avon aligned to the summer solstice sunset.[19]

Stonehenge is said to be the site of the largest late Neolithic cemetery.[20] Following this, it became the site of the greatest concentration of round barrow burials in the whole of Britain.[21] Burials analyzed from Stonehenge reveal that from around the time of the sarsen stones, and for at least one thousand years following, people from as far as the Mediterranean and Germany traveled to Stonehenge.[22] It's very likely Stonehenge was sought as a place of healing, as well as used for sun worship, and for burial with a hope in immortality or salvation through the sun in the afterlife. It probably acted, much like other sacred places, as a great religious center—for initiates; for learning and administration; for service and worship; and for the sick, the living, and the dead.

Row of ancient megalithic trilithons in Libya.

Although most see Stonehenge as a completely unique site in the world, there existed other ancient sites that look near identical to Stonehenge, having the same gigantic stone "trilithons." These were/are located in North Africa, in present day Libya, as well as in India,[23] and other ancient megalithic trilithon designs have been noted as being found in the temples of Malta, in predynastic Egypt, and as entrances to the chambered mounds of Ireland.[24]

The connection between the ancient sites in North Africa and Stonehenge is further reinforced by the presence in North Africa of cairns, barrows, dolmens, and standing stone circles, just like those found in Europe and particularly Britain.[25] The Mzora standing stones in Morocco is the largest stone ellipse in the world. Both Mzora and the standing stones of Nabta Playa in Egypt (which is the next site featured below) were built using the same geometrical principles (by using a Pythagorean right-angled triangle) that were also used in the standing stone circles of Britain, as uncovered through the research of Alexander Thom.[26] Researcher Bob Quinn also found numerous similarities between Mzora and Newgrange in Ireland.[27]

Sketch of the Mzora standing stones in Morocco made in 1830.

Thousands of years ago North Africa was a green wilderness, which had been covered in lakes and rivers. These gradually dried up and the area became the desert it is today, forcing its ancient inhabitants to migrate—most likely northward into Europe. The connection between the ancient sites of North Africa and the megalithic sites of Britain may provide clues as to who the builders of the standing stones of Stonehenge were.

Ancient standing stones aligned to the solstices are also located in Armenia, India, South Africa, Brazil, New Zealand, and across Europe—attesting to the presence of the same megalithic culture in other parts of the world.

NABTA PLAYA ~ EGYPT

A replica of the stone circle at Nabta Playa from the Aswan Nubia museum.

In the Sahara Desert at Nabta Playa in southern Egypt, about 800 km south of Cairo, there are a number of very ancient standing stones that have some remarkable alignments to the sun and stars. They consist of a circle of smaller stones, and larger monoliths nearby which are arranged in various outlier positions radiating from a central stone.

The stone circle has an alignment north-south and another to the rising sun on the summer solstice. The astrophysicist Thomas G. Brophy has also proposed that three of its stones align to the three stars of Orion's Belt as they appeared on the meridian before summer solstice sunrise between 6,400 and 4,900 BC. He also proposed that three of its stones marked the three shoulder stars of Orion at around 16,500 BC while on the meridian at winter solstice sunset. The three stones marking the belt aligned when Orion appeared the least tilted in the sky, and those of the shoulders when it appeared tilted the most; the change in tilt being due to the precession of the equinoxes. Brophy believes the stone circle was built during the later period, and that those stones aligned at the earlier date of 16,500 BC were for conceptual purposes.

Brophy also studied the larger stones nearby, which are arranged in radial positions from a central stone. He discovered they align to the same stars in Orion that the circle does, but at their individual heliacal risings (when they rise just before dawn) on the spring equinox, when viewed from the central sighting stone. The date of these alignments falls between 6,400 and 5,200 BC.[28] Another of the stones aligns to the star Vega at around 6,400 BC and another to Sirius at 6,100 BC.[29] Most incredibly of all, however, Brophy discovered that the distance between these stones and the central sighting stone matches the distance of the stars they align to from Earth on a scale of roughly 1 meter to 0.8 light years—within the margin of error found in calculating astronomical distances today.[30]

The dates of the alignments, along with radio carbon dates of campfires at the site, indicate it was built and in use between 6,400 and 4,900 BC. Today the region is an inhospitable desert, but during that time had seasonal lakes and grasslands, which supported large, organized settlements.

Alignments to the summer solstice, spring equinox, Sirius, and Orion were also used in the design of the Great Pyramids and Sphinx—these and other similarities have led some to theorize that the builders of the site at Nabta Playa and the site of the Great Pyramids at Giza are connected.[31] Additionally, the site was built on the Tropic of Cancer, which appears to have been done on purpose so that the vertical stones at the site marked the sun's zenith passage at the summer solstice so that they cast no shadow.[32]

LINN OIR ALIGNMENT, MOUNT SESKIN ~ IRELAND

On Mount Seskin, the tallest of the Tallaght Hills (so called because they are located outside of the town of Tallaght), there are a number of ancient stone ruins including standing stones and passage cairns.[33] While looking from Mount Seskin towards the ocean, the summer solstice sun rises right beside Lambay Island and reflects off a pool of water on the mountain, called Linn Oir meaning golden pond.[34]

EXTERNSTEINE ~ GERMANY

The temple atop of Externsteine. The hole in the shrine aligns to the summer solstice sunrise.

Externsteine is a spectacular formation of naturally occurring rocks in Germany. It was likely used as a sacred place for thousands of years, and became an especially sacred site to Germanic pagans. There are a number of sacred areas carved into the rocks, and surrounding Externsteine are other ancient sacred places—such as megaliths, ancient roads and walls, burial grounds, and what would have been sacred groves.

At the highest point on the rocks is a small shrine carved into the stone. There is a hole carved above an altar which aligns to sunrise on the summer solstice, as well as to the moon at its most northerly extreme.[35] These times of year are when the light of the sun (both direct and reflected) are considered at its greatest, and indicate the prominence of the sun in Germanic paganism.

The rocks of Externsteine naturally align to the summer solstice sunset, which is perhaps one of the reasons it was selected as a sacred place; nearby there is an important historical German monument that lies on this alignment and was likely built over an existing ancient site. Additionally, a line can be drawn from where the moon rises on the day of its most northerly extreme through Externsteine and a number of nearby sacred sites, revealing they were built purposely on this alignment.[36]

Within a cave at Externsteine, there is an ancient runic engraving of two outstretched arms. This same symbol was used by the megalithic civilization of Western Europe, the ancient civilization of Elam near Mesopotamia in what is now Iran, and the predynastic civilization in Egypt[37] (appearing later as the "ka" hieroglyph in ancient Egypt). It's drawn on the most northerly side of the cave—linking it to the northern extremes of the moon and sun. A possible interpretation of this symbol based on its use in Egypt could be the eternal spirit (of a person) worshiping the divine sun.

Interestingly, the design of the shrine at Externsteine shares similarities with an ancient tablet discovered in Sippar (the city of the sun) in Mesopotamia that depicts priests worshiping the sun god Shamash.[38]

Ancient tablet from Mesopotamia depicting priests worshiping the sun god, dated to ca. 888-855 BC.

Externsteine was used by Germanic pagans until around AD 772, when they were ruthlessly Christianized. It is said to have been the location of a symbolic pillar known as the Irminsul—representing the sacred world tree and cosmic axis in Germanic paganism. In 772, King Charlemagne destroyed this pillar, returning ten years later to behead 4,500 Germanic leaders who had continued to practice Germanic paganism despite their forced conversion to Christianity.[39]

There is much evidence that connects the wisdom bringer Odin/Wotan with this site and the ancient religion practiced at it.[40] Odin was said to have sacrificed himself on the world tree, known as the Irminsul, and various carvings and symbols indicate he was perhaps the most important deity worshiped here.

AJANTA CAVES ~ INDIA

The Ajanta Caves are an extraordinary group of around thirty elaborate man-made shrines and temples cut into the side of a sheer cliff face that is naturally U-shaped and located in a remote jungle. The caves are believed to have been built by Buddhist monks who carved them into the cliff face between the second century BC and AD 480-650, as they contain sculptures and artwork centered around the life of Buddha.[41]

Two of the caves align to celestial events.

Cave twenty-six aligns to the summer solstice sunrise. It contains a statue of Buddha seated within a stupa, which is illuminated by the rays of the rising sun on the summer solstice.[42]

ANCIENT SACRED SITES ALIGNED TO THE SUMMER SOLSTICE

Cave twenty-six at Ajanta, which aligns to the summer solstice sunrise. As the sun rises, a beam of light penetrates this cave and illuminates the stupa and the statue of Buddha within.

A stupa is a symbolic monument which is said Buddha uses to ascend and descend.

The summer solstice is a time of ascent. In the cave aligned to the summer solstice, Buddha is seated with his feet on a pedestal. Perhaps this was symbolic of him no longer being on the earth—similarly, ancient Egyptian gods were sometimes portrayed upon pedestals to show their heavenly status.

The creator god Amun being worshiped, seated with his feet raised above the level of the ground similar to the statue of Buddha at Ajanta.

SERPENT MOUND ~ OHIO, UNITED STATES

Serpent Mound is a giant earthwork in the shape of a serpent made by an ancient people who once lived in North America. The head of the serpent faces the summer solstice sunset. It follows the curve of a natural ridge with the same alignment, which is likely why this site was selected as a sacred place.

The mound is around 1,370 feet (420 meters) long. The serpent holds an oval in its mouth, has seven undulating coils along its body, and the tip of its tail is coiled three times. Its coils point to the solstice and equinox sunrises, as well as to lunar phenomena. Researcher Ross Hamilton also discovered that the mound mirrors the constellation of Draco on the ground, and encodes the knowledge of the astronomical phenomenon called the precession of the equinoxes—following the same practice used at other ancient sites aligned to the solstices and equinoxes. According to Hamilton, if archeoastronomy is used to date it, the mound may have been built around 2,750 BC.[43]

It is believed there was an altar inside the oval at the head,[44] in which ceremonies could have been conducted while watching the summer solstice sunset.

Interestingly, there exists another very similar site in a very different part of the world: Scotland. At a place called Loch Nell there is an ancient serpent mound, around three hundred feet long, and which used to have a circle of stones which contained an altar at its head. It too faced west, although not to the summer solstice sunset, but so that looking back east across its body it had a special view of three mountain peaks.[45] Someone who viewed the site in the mid-nineteenth century before much of it was damaged and dismantled wrote:

> "The mound was built in such a manner that the worshiper standing at the altar would naturally look eastward, directly along the whole length of the Great Reptile, and across the dark lake, to the triple peaks of Ben Cruachan. This position must have been carefully selected, as from no other point are the three peaks visible." [46]

A drawing published in 1883 of the Loch Nell serpent mound in Scotland. The altar in the stone circle at the head of the serpent is in the foreground, and the three mountain peaks in the background. The design of this particular serpent mound shares a number of similarities with the one in Ohio.

There are other ancient serpent mounds in the British Isles—in Scotland, Ireland,[47] and England. At least one dated to around 2,000 BC in England used fire burned stones, which also appear to have been used in the building of Serpent Mound in Ohio.[48] The oval at the heads of these serpents may have represented the sun, thus forming the same symbol of a serpent with a sun disk on its head depicted in ancient Egypt.

Could Ohio's Serpent Mound be part of a lineage of people and knowledge that ran from Egypt, through the British Isles and Europe, and is now barely traceable in North America? I think so.

CHACO CANYON ~ NEW MEXICO, UNITED STATES

Chaco Canyon is an ancient city located in the state of New Mexico in the United States, which is attributed to a mysterious people called the "Anasazi." Its buildings have multiple alignments to the solstices and equinoxes, as well as other celestial phenomena. Although dated to between the ninth and twelfth centuries AD, this site and others built by the Anasazi have deeper and much more far reaching roots.

The Anasazi were described in oral tradition as a "peaceful and prosperous people" who had "worshiped the sun" and lived in the region since "time immemorial."[49] In Hopi oral history they were said to have been almost entirely massacred by an invading tribe from the north—the Hopi and Zuni peoples are said to be descended from the survivors.[50]

The researcher Gary A. David discovered that the villages and ruins of the Ancestral Puebloans/Hopi are laid out in the same configuration as the stars in the constellation of Orion, and that Chaco Canyon corresponds to the star Sirius. Additionally, he noticed that lines drawn between the positions of these ruins align to the solstice sunrises and sunsets.[51]

The kiva (ceremonial building) called Casa Rinconada in Chaco Canyon. On the summer solstice one of its windows lets in the light of the rising sun.

Incredibly, this practice of aligning sites to these specific constellations and to the sun is found at the site of the Great Pyramids of Egypt, and other sacred sites around the world. Orion and Sirius were particularly central in ancient Egypt as the representations of the wisdom bringer Osiris and his wife Isis.

But the evidence for an ancient Egyptian connection doesn't end there. Chaco Canyon and another site of the Anasazi, called Mesa Verde in Colorado, encode complex solar and celestial alignments into their designs and incorporated sun temples. They also encoded advanced geometry, such as the golden ratio, Pythagorean triangle, and Golden Rectangle, which were used at ancient sites in Egypt and Europe.[52] They used a standard unit of measurement to build them also used in Europe,[53] and in some cases their buildings were six stories high. The ancient form of writing called Ogham used by the Irish was also found inscribed into the sun temple at the Anazasi site of Mesa Verde; when translated, it describes the natural solar alignment of a nearby cave formation.[54] A study found that the remains of ancient pottery discovered at Anasazi sites shared similarities too close to be coincidence with other far more ancient cultures in Eastern Europe and China. Included among the common symbols were solar symbols like the swastika and double spiral.[55]

Located near the ruins of the ancient city of Chaco Canyon is the famous Sun Dagger. Found high up on the top of the Fajada Butte, a giant volcanic outcrop, is a stone carving of a spiral. Stone slabs especially arranged around it direct the sunlight so that on the summer solstice, a dagger of sunlight pierces the center of the spiral. Daggers of sunlight over different parts of the spiral also mark the winter solstice and the equinoxes.[56]

Down below, the Casa Rinconada, which is one of the five great kivas (temple buildings) of Chaco Canyon, aligns to the summer solstice sunrise. Kivas were sacred circular temples that had thatched ceilings. As the sun rises, a beam of light shines through a lone window and moves across the room until it illuminates one of the five niches on the western wall.[57]

AHU TONGARIKI ~ EASTER ISLAND

The Ahu Tongariki is the largest ahu (or stone platform) on Easter Island. On it stand fifteen moai (giant stone statues). These fifteen statues face the summer solstice sunset, watching it disappear over the ocean.[58] One of them is the heaviest ever erected on the island, weighing eighty-six tons.

EL CASTILLO, TULUM ~ MEXICO

Temple at Tulum that aligns with the rising sun on the summer solstice.

The ancient Maya city of Tulum is dedicated to the Maya "descending god" and consists of a number of ceremonial buildings still held sacred by the Maya today. The ruins of this ancient city stand on a bluff overlooking the ocean. The original name of this site was "Zama" which means "City of Dawn" because it faces sunrise.[59]

The main temple of the city called El Castillo has an opening that allows the summer solstice sunrise to shine through it.[60] The nearby Temple of the Frescoes was used as an observatory for tracking the movements of the sun.[61]

A number of the temples were built over even older structures, and artifacts have been found dated to the first century AD, although many of the buildings were erected around AD 1200.

The descending god carved into a temple at Tulum.

The descending god is portrayed throughout the site descending from heaven, with his legs in the air and his head crowned. He is believed by some to be a representation of the Maya wisdom bringer Kukulcán and is associated with the planet Venus,[62] the "Morning Star," just as Jesus was.

> "I Jesus have sent mine angel to testify unto you these things in the churches. I am the root and the offspring of David, and the bright and morning star." [63]
> ~ REVELATION 22:16

Throughout the site there are frescoes that depict scenes of feathered serpents, the act of creation, and are particularly focused on death and rebirth.

> "There is an architectural expression of rebirth at Tulum. The easternmost structure at Tulum, Structure 45, is a round-based structure. Round structures are associated with Kukulcan. One of Kukulcan's most important manifestations is Venus as Morning Star. According to the widespread pan-Mesoamerican myth, Kukulcan was reborn in the east in the form of Venus as Morning Star after descent and death in the west and a long passage in the Underworld." [64]
> ~ ARTHUR G. MILLER, WEST AND EAST IN MAYA THOUGHT: DEATH AND REBIRTH AT PALENQUE AND TULUM

Again, as at other ancient sites of the Religion of the Sun, there is the same central theme of death, descent into the underworld, and resurrection.

THE PYRAMID OF THE MAGICIAN, UXMAL ~ MEXICO

Uxmal is a Maya city that is said to date between AD 600 and 1000. The city's tallest structure is called The Pyramid of the Magician—so-called because according to one account, it was built by the wisdom bringer Itzamna who was considered a magician.[65] The pyramid's western staircase aligns to sunset on the summer solstice.[66]

This first pyramid temple was successively built upon four times, meaning that the pyramid is now made of five layers in total. This was a common practice amongst the ancient cultures of Central and South America, who often built over or destroyed and rebuilt sacred structures.[67]

Unfortunately, human sacrifice and ritual bloodletting were practiced here, as they were in other Maya cities. However, it's likely the original culture did not practice these rites, but were taken over by those who did as happened at many other Maya sites.

THE LOST WORLD PYRAMID, TIKAL ~ GUATEMALA

The Lost World Pyramid at Tikal. It started as a small platform before 700 BC that faced three structures aligned to the solstices and equinoxes.

The ancient Maya city called Tikal is located in the dense jungles of Guatemala. The oldest part of it is called the Lost World and consists of thirty-eight structures. They are believed to have been set aside entirely for the observance of the cosmos.

The main structure of the Lost World is a great pyramid, which was built in five successive layers over hundreds of years, just like the Pyramid of the Magician at Uxmal. It is believed to be one of the most ancient structures at Tikal. When viewed from the eastern side of the pyramid, three nearby temples align with sunrise on the winter solstice, equinoxes, and summer solstice respectively.[68]

A similar grouping of structures, in which a pyramid is used as a viewing platform to see the sunrise on the solstices and equinoxes over three temples, was also found in Guatemala at Uaxactun. The ancient Mayan name for this site was Siaan K'aan, which means "Born in Heaven."[69]

THE WAY OF VIRACOCHA ~ BOLIVIA AND PERU

In South America, the sites the wisdom bringer Viracocha was said to have been involved in building lie along a straight line stretching over one thousand miles called "The Way of Viracocha," as it is said to correspond to the route he traveled through South America before departing across the Pacific Ocean. This "Way" also mirrors the alignment of the Milky Way on the summer solstice.[70]

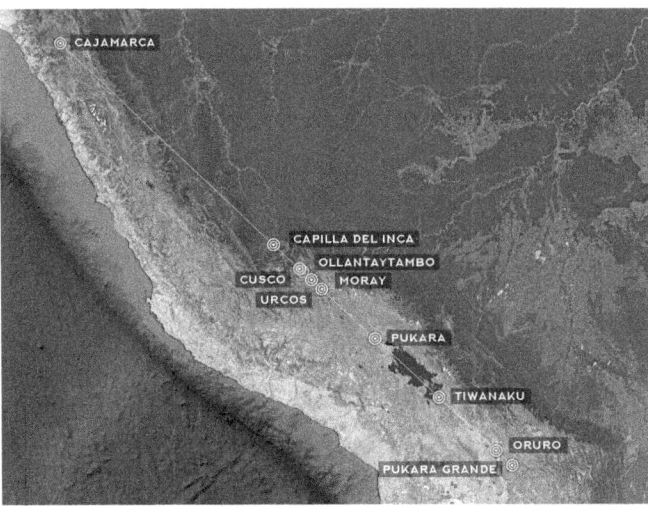

> "The alignment's association with Viracocha, the great Andean creator god, teacher and civilizer of humankind, is a highly significant one. Many legends concerning the feats of Viracocha speak of his undertaking a journey, from the city of Tiwanaku toward

the Northwest, eventually to leave the shores of South America's Pacific coast around the present day border between Peru and Ecuador. Viracocha's legendary journey, Sholten D'Ebneth revealed, corresponded with her own geometrical discovery of the alignment of many of the most ancient and sacred sites in the Andes, including the famous ones at Cusco (Cuzco), Ollantaytambo and, of course, the great and mysterious complex of Tiwanaku (Tiahuanaco). [...] it is perhaps worth pondering the sheer technical challenge of surveying this vast alignment across some of the most rugged, remote and mountainous terrain on earth. Indeed, my own research and that of others, indicate that the alignment could extend beyond Tiwanaku. [...] If my findings are correct, it implies that whoever surveyed the Way of Viracocha, not only had an understanding of the earth's curvature, but also understood the principles of spherical trigonometry. It is equally likely that those who undertook this work knew the dimensions of the earth. The question then arose in my mind: could it be that Viracocha, the great teacher and restorer of civilization in the Andes, in some way embodied the scientific knowledge of a sophisticated, but long forgotten high culture?" [71]

~ DAVE TRUMAN, ANCIENT ALIGNMENT IN THE ANDES HINTS AT A LOST GLOBAL HIGH CULTURE

The sites along The Way of Viracocha include massive polygonal stone blockwork and precision cut stones of enormous weight and proportions, and a number of them incorporate alignments to the sun at the solstices and/or equinoxes.

STEPPED PYRAMIDS ~ VARIOUS ISLANDS AROUND THE WORLD

Identical, and near identical, stepped pyramids aligned to the solstices can be found on a number of islands worldwide, revealing that the ancient Religion of the Sun, along with its style of sacred structures, was spread across the world by a seafaring civilization (which I call the Lost Civilization of the Sun).

These pyramids are found, among other places, on the Canary Islands off the coast of Morocco, in the Azores (which lie along the mid-Atlantic ridge, on what are likely the remnants of the lost islands of Atlantis[72]), on Sicily in the Mediterranean, on Mauritius off the coast of Madagascar (Africa), and in the Maldives off the coast of India. A stepped pyramid also used to stand on Tahiti.

At some of these sites the builders are unknown, however, there exists strong evidence as to who they were likely to have been, based on the people associated with the stepped pyramids of the Canary Islands.

Pyramid on the island of Teneriffe in the Canary Islands. The stairs of a number of pyramids face the winter solstice sunrise. From the top of the largest pyramid a double sunset on the summer solstice can be observed.[73]

For thousands of years, people described as fair skinned, blonde and red haired, and blue eyed, lived with Stone Age technology in the Canary Islands. These people lived in isolation until they were finally discovered by the Spanish, who later invaded and finally wiped them out in 1496. The Spanish recorded their observations of these native people whom they called the Guanches. They wrote how they practiced a solar religion, had a solar theocracy, used to offer prayers to the rising sun, had built stepped pyramids, practiced mummification,[74] and worshiped a trinity of supreme Father God, Mother Goddess, and their Divine Son[75]—characteristics of those who formed part of the Lost Civilization of the Sun.

ZIGGURAT OF UR ~ IRAQ

An illustration of what the Ziggurat of Ur possibly looked like.

Ur was an ancient Sumerian city, the remains of which are now located in Iraq. The Ziggurat of Ur is an ancient ceremonial stepped temple located in Ur, the ruins of which still partially stand; its great entrance staircase was (and still is) aligned to the summer solstice sunrise.[76] Its design is similar to numerous other ancient pyramid sites that are also aligned to solstices and equinoxes around the world.

Like many of these sites, it was built over successively down the ages, and was renovated even in times we would consider ancient today. Its most recent outer layer has been dated to around 2000 BC.[77] However, even older layers have been discovered inside,[78] revealing that this is a site that was considered sacred even before the ziggurat we now see today existed. It is one of the ancient sites that lie on the line that encircles the earth which also intersects the Great Pyramids of Giza, Easter Island, and Machu Picchu.[79]

WURDI YOUANG STONE ARRANGEMENT ~ AUSTRALIA

At Mount Rothwell in the state of Victoria in Australia, there is a stone ovoid-shaped arrangement around fifty meters in diameter. It aligns to the sunsets of the solstices and equinoxes.[80] There are other stone arrangements in Australia, but none of them are known to have astronomical alignments.[81] There are no materials at the site that can be dated, no oral traditions related to the site, and the site is not precise enough for the small changes in solar alignments to indicate when it was most accurate, so Wurdi Youang has been unable to be dated.[82] An Aboriginal people have inhabited the area for the last twenty-five thousand years, and the land first came under the ownership of British settlers in 1835. It has stayed within the same family ever since, who claim never to have built it, so Wurdi Youang could have been built anywhere between twenty-five thousand years ago right up to 1835.[83] Carbon dates obtained at nearby sites indicate it could have been built at around 9,000 BC, but these are only suggestive.[84]

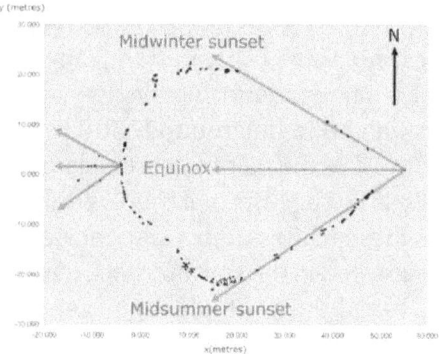

Diagram illustrating the solar alignments of Wurdi Youang.

A few of the stones from the site at Wurdi Youang.

LASCAUX CAVE PAINTINGS ~ FRANCE

Rendition of one of the paintings inside Lascaux cave.

Lascaux Cave is located in France, and is decorated with a vast number of cave paintings and engravings—with over 1,500 engravings and 600 drawings—estimated to be around 17,300 years old.[85]

Most of the paintings are of large animals and geometric shapes, but recent research suggests that there is much more to these paintings than first seems—as these figures depict star constellations, and reveal that their painters were interested in the sun and stars, particularly during summer, and that they seem to have held a spiritual significance.

French researcher Chantal Jègues-Wolkiewiez discovered that the entrance to the cave aligns with the summer solstice sunset—at this time of year, the sun's light enters the cave and illuminates it for almost one hour each day, for a few days surrounding the solstice.[86] She also calculated that the light of the full moon entered the cave on the morning of the winter solstice, and that other painted caves in the area align to the setting sun on the winter solstice.[87]

> "The cave cannot have been chosen at random, quite the contrary in fact. The paintings were made so that every summer an extraordinary illumination show would be performed when the sun came and shone on the walls of the main room. Starting from this observation Chantal Jègues-Wolkiewiez attempted to verify her theory. If the paintings in this room, which has such a striking circular vault shape were designed according to this exceptional event, they could also logically be linked to the structure of the sky over Lascaux on this very summer night as the first stars appeared in the sky."[88]

Jègues-Wolkiewiez went on to discover that the paintings in the main area of the cave represent an extensive star map of the main constellations as they appeared around the end of the last ice age, which is when they were painted—specifically the part of the sky that is perpetually crossed by the sun.[89]

No one knows what the purpose of these caves or paintings were, but it's been suggested that they were possibly ceremonial and sacred places as most of the paintings are located at a distance from the entrance, and many of the chambers are hard to get to.[90] If this was their purpose, Lascaux would be one of the most ancient known sites in the world where spiritual rites took place on the solstice.

MORE SITES

Here are some more sites that align to the summer solstice:

Ales Stenar Megalithic "Stone Ship" in Sweden
On the summer solstice the sun rises between two stones "mid-ship" and sets in alignment with a stone at the "bow" of the ship.[91]

Pyramids on Pico island in the Azores (Portugal)
Pico Island features over 140 pyramids, particularly concentrated in the Madalena area of the island, and most are oriented southeast/northwest, in an alignment with the island's volcano and sunset on the summer solstice.[92]

Big Horn Medicine Wheel in Wyoming, USA
On the summer solstice, the cairn at the center of the circle is aligned with two cairns at the outer edge that mark the sunrise and sunset respectively.[93]

Bryn Celli Ddu in Wales
The light of the rising sun on the summer solstice aligns to the passage of this ancient mound; it enters the passageway and reflects on quartz within the mound to illuminate its inner chamber. It also illuminates a double spiral carved onto a stone within the mound. A lone standing stone outside the mound also aligns to the passage and summer solstice sunrise. Post holes outside the mound would have once been part of the oldest known building in Wales, and the site itself is one of the most important megalithic sites in Wales.[94]

Buzovgrad Megalithic Structure in Bulgaria
On the summer solstice at the Buzovgrad megalithic structure called "The Gate of the Mother Goddess," the last rays of the sun pierce directly through the gate at sunset.[95]

Cahokia Woodhenge in Illinois, USA
Posts at the Cahokia Woodhenge align to sunrise on the summer solstice.[96]

Chankillo Solar Observatory and Temple in Peru
On the summer solstice, the sunrise aligns to the last of the thirteen "towers" and then begins descending along its annual path, climbing down the towers and ending outside of the first tower on the winter solstice.[97]

Gors Fawr Stone Circle in Wales
A pair of outlying standing stones, set 134 meters away from the circle, act like a doorway through which the sun rises on the summer solstice. The circle is located in an area of ancient sites in the foothills of the Preseli Mountains, which is where the bluestones used in the construction of Stonehenge were quarried from.[98]

Harman Kaya Observatory in Bulgaria
The sun can be seen through specific notches in the rock formation on the summer solstice.[99]

Kanayama Megaliths of Japan
At the Senkoku Ishi megalithic group, which is part of the Kanayama megaliths, the inner space underneath one of the seven-meter-high megalithic stones gets illuminated during the summer solstice, and measures the whole period of midsummer.[100]

Kokino Megalithic Observatory & Sacred Site in Macedonia
When viewed from the center of the site, the summer solstice sun rises directly over one of the marking stones on the horizon.[101]

Lepenski Vir Settlement in Serbia
This settlement was positioned so that on the summer solstice, when looking from its northern end, someone could see a "double sunrise" through the shape of the imposing nearby cliff called Treskavac, and from its southern end the sun could be seen rising on the southern part of the top of Treskavac. The settlement has been called the oldest city in Europe, and was established somewhere between 9,500 to 7,200 BC.[102]

Stepped Pyramids in Mauritius
Three pyramids on the island nation of Mauritius align to the summer solstice sunrise.[103]

Mnajdra in Malta
On the summer solstice at the Mnajdra Solar Temple, the rays of the sun pass directly through the temple's main doorway and light up the edge of a megalith to the left of the doorway connecting the first pair of chambers to the inner chambers.[104]

Dolmens and Megaliths in Montana, USA
Tizer Dolmen faces directly south, and exactly at noon on summer solstice day the sun shines between the two pillars of the dolmen, aligning to the other rock structures on a mountain peak behind the dolmen.[105]

Omahk Sacred Landscape and the Majorville Medicine Wheel, Alberta, Canada

On the morning of the summer solstice 5,200 years ago, sunrise corresponded to a valley formed by the bottom edge of the "sun ring" hill and a smaller hill on its west. The valley forms a V-like shape just below the horizon, and creates a highly precise (and obvious) solar marker.[106]

Oyu Stone Circles in Japan

The four-thousand-year-old Oyu stone circles on the left bank of the Oyu river (in the northeastern Akita Prefecture) include a sundial which marks the sunset on the summer solstice.[107]

Punkri Burwadih in India

The summer solstice sunrise is visible through the "V" notch between two menhirs.[108]

Rujm el-Hiri in the Levant

At Rujm el-Hiri, located in the Golan Heights between modern-day Israel and Syria, the northeast entryways marked the summer solstice at approximately 3,000 and 15,000 BC.[109]

Yazilikaya Rock Sanctuary in Turkey

Ancient sites of the Hittites were aligned to the solstices. Within their Yazilikaya rock sanctuary, a statue of the sun goddess of Arinna, probably plated with gold, would have been lit by the rays of the setting sun on the summer solstice. A relief of a great king of the Hittites carved onto one of the walls, with a winged sun disk above him, is also illuminated by the sun on the summer solstice. It's likely that the king and his entourage would have witnessed this display of light, symbolically seeing the power of the sun being invested in the king. One of the walls on the gatehouse leading to the sanctuary also aligns to summer solstice sunset, and is the oldest of the structures built there.[110] Ancient texts of the Hittites reveal that along with the solstices, the equinoxes were also extremely important religious days.[111]

PART III
CEREMONIES

CHAPTER TWELVE

A Guide to Celebrating the Solstices and Equinoxes

The ancient order of the Pythagoreans in Greece, celebrating the rising sun.

Ancient people across the world celebrated the solstices and equinoxes as evident in hundreds if not thousands of ancient sites, myths, and texts, and some of the most famous spiritual figures such as Jesus, Osiris, Hu Gadarn, Mithras, Dionysus, Hun Hunahpu, Quetzalcoatl, etc., experienced major events in their life stories at these times. While some of these traditions were simple and based on an appreciation of the natural world, many celebrated the profound spiritual significance of these special times of year. These celebrations were the most important holy days of the ancient Religion of the Sun, and their continued celebration survived in the many traditions that derived from or were influenced by it, and are still celebrated today.

Many ancient people knew that the natural world and its cycles contain the principles of creation, and that these principles are spiritual in their nature.

This is why some of the world's most famous religious symbols can be found in the natural world, such as the yin and yang, the swastika, cross, spiral, etc., and why the study of science and mathematics ultimately comes upon a fabric of life that is intelligent in its design.

The maxim of wisdom, "as above, so below," indicates how cosmic and natural phenomena are intimately connected to the human being and journey of consciousness. We are undeniably part of the universe, and so too therefore is the process of spiritual awakening. The sun (and stars) is the source of light and life in our universe, just as the spirit is the source of light and life within us. Spiritual figures and texts placed so much emphasis on the journey of the sun, as the path of the sun is symbolic of the path of consciousness/spirit in its journey to awakening, and the solstices and equinoxes are symbolic of this journey's major stages.

WHY CELEBRATE THE SOLSTICES AND EQUINOXES?

Some ancient peoples throughout history were in touch with a different way of gaining knowledge than most are familiar with. This way of learning is timeless, and is gained through individual practice, experience, and observation of the natural world, rather than just reading.

Today, although we have become distant from and even hostile toward our environment, the principles of creation remain eternal. They are there within and all around us for anyone who opens their eyes enough to see.

Although the solstices and equinoxes are celestial events, they are also very personal ones. They communicate not only cosmic principles, but inner ones too, as the inner and outer world are connected.

Each individual can have their own reasons for celebrating the solstices and equinoxes, but the following celebrations I've put together give everyone participating an opportunity to experience spiritual principles directly. The spirit in life teaches—through these celebrations an individual can learn something personal about their own journey of consciousness, and a group celebrating can learn and perceive something together. Some people who celebrated the ceremony for the summer solstice for the first time (as given in an earlier version of this work) felt something so powerfully spiritual and significant from it that they said they would never be the same again.

It's important to note that the ceremonies in this book are not about a worship of the physical sun. Instead they are like plays that enact the individual journey on the path of the spiritual sun, which can be found in the progress of the sun throughout the year.

This style of ceremony was used in the past to celebrate the solstices and equinoxes. For example, the Druids performed a solar drama annually in Wales and likely across other parts of Great Britain and Ireland. They were called the Mabyn Ogion, meaning "Adherents to the Babe Son."[1]

In ancient Egypt the events of the life, death, and resurrection of Osiris were enacted in ceremonies and mystery plays that were held annually.[2] And in the Eleusinian Mysteries of Greece, the goddess Demeter's search for her daughter Persephone, and Persephone's death and rebirth, was ceremoniously enacted on the equinoxes each year.[3]

These same kind of ceremonies can likewise be used today, to assist in the perception of the principles of creation, which are found manifest in nature and can be experienced and understood through celebrations that enact these principles in tune with the cycles of the cosmos.

CONNECT WITH THE HEAVENS AND THE EARTH BY CELEBRATING THE SOLSTICES AND EQUINOXES

Kurds celebrating the ancient, pre-Islamic, Zoroastrian/Indo-Iranian spring equinox rite called Nowruz in Iran.

Solstices and equinoxes are a time of connection between the heavens and the earth, the personal and the divine, the inner and the outer, the material and the spiritual. It is a beautiful time, which unfortunately most people today have lost touch with, as did other civilizations who degenerated in the past and lost their spiritual orientation.

By taking part in ceremonies to celebrate the solstices and equinoxes, one is able to use the event for its higher purpose just as the ancients did—to connect with the cosmos, to understand eternal principles through intuitive experience and the cycles of nature, and to take spiritual nourishment. This is not simply the revival of something past, but the partaking in something eternal that permeates our lives, even if we pay little attention to it.

The whole of creation is imbued with the principles of spirituality, and thus these principles can not only be found all around us, but also within us, allowing us to understand our origins and the purpose of life. This has allowed people throughout the ages to tap into the same spiritual knowledge.

"In everything that is life is the law written. You find it in the grass, in the tree, in the river, in the mountain, in the birds of heaven, in the fishes of the sea; but seek it chiefly in yourselves. For I tell you truly, all living things are nearer to God than the scripture which is without life. God so made life and all living things that they might by the everlasting word teach the laws of the true God to man. God wrote not the laws in the pages of books, but in your heart and in your spirit. They are in your breath, your blood, your bone; in your flesh, your bowels, your eyes, your ears, and in every little part of your body. They are present in the air, in the water, in the earth, in the plants, in the sunbeams, in the depths and in the heights. They all speak to you that you may understand the tongue and the will of the living God. But you shut your eyes that you may not see, and you shut your ears that you may not hear. I tell you truly, that the scripture is the work of man, but life and all its hosts are the work of our God. Wherefore do you not listen to the words of God which are written in His works? And wherefore do you study the dead scriptures which are the work of the hands of men?" [4]

~ JESUS IN THE ESSENE GOSPEL OF PEACE

The message of the spiritual sun transcends both time and culture and forms a cosmic book for all who can read it.

CELEBRATING ACCORDING TO YOUR CIRCUMSTANCES

Your circumstances will really determine how you'll be able to celebrate, but there is still a lot of flexibility and room for creativity. It can be celebrated all the way from a detailed ritual to simply being present for the sunrise/sunset.

IN A GROUP AT A DEDICATED LOCATION

The organization called The Druid Order performing a ceremony at Stonehenge during the summer solstice.

The ideal way to celebrate any solstice and equinox is out in the open air, where the sun is clearly visible, with a large group of people who share the same spiritual intent. Chanting becomes especially moving with lots of voices, and the energy of a focused gathering of people can be really uplifting. It would be great if every city had a place where people could go and celebrate together in large numbers.

The more detailed ceremonies I've created in this book are really tailored for people who have their own dedicated sacred space where they can feel comfortable and relaxed in practicing the Religion of the Sun.

IN A GROUP AT A PUBLIC LOCATION

If you don't have your own sacred space, there are lots of public venues that could be used for holding a ceremony. You may even prefer to use an existing sacred space because of its ancient energy and connection to your tradition. There are many existing ancient sacred sites and places that are open to the public. If there aren't any within reach of you, you could choose a beautiful natural location, like a park.

If you only have venues open to you where people who are not involved in the celebration may be staring or even insulting, you may want to simplify the ceremony to the point where you feel comfortable.

WITH A SMALL NUMBER OF PEOPLE

The example group ceremonies I've created require a certain number of participants to fulfill the different ceremonial roles. If you find that you don't have enough people to fulfill all the roles, just cut the ceremony back until you can fulfill the most crucial ones; or, you could simplify the ceremony so that although not every action is performed, the main essence of the ceremony remains.

Your ceremony may be as simple as chanting or singing songs relevant to the occasion while watching the rising or setting sun—perhaps doing a few readings, lighting a fire or candle, and dressing for the occasion.

ON YOUR OWN

Most reading this book will probably be celebrating on their own. That's why I've included example ceremonies especially for solitary practitioners. If you're celebrating on your own, you could still conduct your ceremony at an ancient site or outdoor location, or you could find a nice private spot in your garden or patio to watch the sunrise or sunset. You could even create a very simple outdoor sacred space with stones and candles. Alternatively, you could also celebrate indoors in a room that lets in the sunlight and make a simple sacred space there by incorporating the symbols related to the ceremony, using statues, images, candles, aromas, and even music.

ANCIENT SOLSTICE

A solitary neo-pagan ritual/prayer being performed at a land feature in Italy held sacred since ancient times.

If you prefer, you could try constructing your own simple ceremony, or chant mantras, or sit in quietness, prayer, or reflection. You could even just watch the rising or setting sun.

However, there is no substitute for attending an actual ceremony with other people, which is why pilgrimages to sacred sites were so important to ancient people at these times of year.

WORKING OUT A CALENDAR AND PREPARING IN ADVANCE

A woman in Iran doing a ritual on Yalda night, which is the night before the winter solstice—the close equivalent of Christmas Eve.

The solar year can be mapped out well in advance, giving plenty of time to prepare the celebration for each solstice and equinox. There are websites that give the upcoming dates for the solstices and equinoxes, which occur more or less on the same days every year.

One thing to be aware of is that the solar calendar in the Northern Hemisphere is opposite to the one in the Southern Hemisphere. So when it's the winter solstice in the Northern Hemisphere in a place like the United States, India or Europe, it is actually the summer solstice in the Southern Hemisphere in a place like South America or Australia. Likewise, the autumn equinox in the north is the spring equinox in the south.

So although the world celebrates Christmas at the time of the winter solstice (around December 21) in the Northern Hemisphere, those in the Southern Hemisphere who wish to celebrate Christmas according to its true meaning should celebrate it at the time of their actual winter solstice, which would instead be around June 21 (the solstice) and the three days following. The same applies to Easter, which is a celebration of the spring equinox.

The precise time of the solstice or equinox is usually given in Universal Time (UT), which you'll need to convert into your local time. Once you do that, you will probably end up with a time that is not exactly sunrise or sunset. To work out when to celebrate the solstice or equinox, simply find the sunrise or sunset closest to the local time you have. So for example, if the time given is 3am in your local time zone and you are celebrating the winter solstice sunrise, then celebrate it the morning of that day a few hours later. If you're celebrating the autumn equinox sunset, then celebrate it at sunset the day before.

Make sure you have your sacred space and things for the ceremony prepared well in advance so you are not rushed beforehand. Take some time leading up the ceremony to practice any songs, chants, or readings you'll be doing, and rehearse your ceremony until you feel confident remembering it. This will help it go smoothly on the day, so that you aren't distracted by trying to remember things and can relax into the ceremony and celebration.

USING A SACRED SPACE

Having a sacred space is very important. As humans wishing to connect with the divine, we've always created them as temples, pyramids, kivas, churches, sacred circles, etc. A dedicated space like this helps us to move from an ordinary state of mind, full of the thoughts of the day, etc., to one of inner quietness, presence in the moment, reverence for divinity, and receptivity to spiritual feelings and learning.

A sacred space can be anything from a huge temple to a room in your house. Whatever the resources, the principle is the same—it becomes an energetically focused place for connecting with the spiritual.

USING AN EXISTING SACRED PLACE

You don't have to create a sacred space of your own, as there are many existing ancient sacred sites where you could conduct your celebration. This could be a man-made site, or a land feature that was held sacred in the past, like a mountain or spring. For example, there are ancient standing stones, mounds, mountains, springs, etc., across Europe that are hardly visited. The Americas are also full of sacred sites and places. You may need to apply for permission to use a site for your ceremony, especially if it might obstruct other visitors to it. Or you might simply be able to turn up, especially if you are going to have a very informal celebration with a small number of people.

Human activity imbues places with energies, which is why some places have a certain vibe. Ancient sites have also been imbued with energy, sometimes over very long periods of time, depending on how they were used. If they were used for ceremonies of light in the ancient Religion of the Sun, they can have an awesome and uplifting power, like the Great Pyramids of Egypt. Unfortunately some sites were used for horrific practices, like human and animal sacrifice, and so the fear and suffering experienced there can be imprinted energetically in them. It's worth bearing this in mind when choosing an ancient site, as you may find that you pick up on this vibe during your ceremony and it affects what you feel and experience there, perhaps even negatively.

It's important, whenever visiting ancient sites, to take care not to damage or alter the site in any way. Make sure not to climb on or walk over things that are fragile and liable to break or move, nor to remove anything from the site as a souvenir, or to show someone, etc., as each stone and plant may form a unique part of the site's character and history. Some of these sites may still be considered sacred by peoples today, so it's important to be respectful and to treat the site as if you wanted it to remain intact and protected as far into the future as possible.

CREATING YOUR OWN SACRED SPACE

When creating your own sacred space, it's best to align it to the moment of either sunrise or sunset of the particular solar event you are celebrating, and to give all the participants a clear view of it. This has the effect of bringing the energies of the cosmos to Earth, which is why so many ancient sites were aligned this way. There's something very special about being in a temple or sacred circle, etc., and having the light of the sun or a star shine into it in alignment. It really is magical, so no wonder ancient practitioners of the Religion of the Sun went to extraordinary lengths in some cases to align their sites to the heavens using sacred geometry, symbols, and significant numbers.

As ancient people did, you could either create one site that has multiple solar alignments, such as the Lost World Pyramid at the ancient city of Tikal in Guatemala, or as they did in the ancient British Isles, create different sites for different alignments, such as Newgrange and Knowth in Ireland.

You can get a lot of ideas of how to create a sacred site from the ancient sites of the world, which are written about in this book (and there are also many others not included). While creating most of these is far beyond most people's resources, it is possible to take the concepts and designs they were based on and replicate them in simple ways.

A modern sacred circle in Lithuania.

One of the simplest site designs that has been used for thousands of years to celebrate the solstice and equinox is a sacred standing stone and/or wood circle. These types of circles are still made by communities today, and can be put together using wooden posts and stones that can be moved into place without machinery.

The circle can be made of wood, stone, or a combination of the two, like the modern example you see in the picture above in Lithuania. It can even be made of or include plants and trees, like the sacred groves of the Druids, of which there are no traces left today.

If you're unable to do it outside due to a lack of privacy or difficult weather conditions, you could always celebrate in a room that lets the light of the sun in at the moment of sunrise or sunset on the solstice or equinox. There are many examples of ancient peoples celebrating in this way. For example, the Pueblo peoples of North America created kivas (which were their temples) that were entirely enclosed except for a window that let in a shaft of light on the solstice.

While it's not within everyone's budget to build a room like this, there are some fairly simple ways of doing it. A cheap do-it-yourself tepee or cabin could be put on a site and its door aligned to the solstice or equinox. Then, only the door need be opened, or perhaps a cabin window could be aligned instead. Or, you may already have rooms in your house which the sun shines into through a window during the solstices and equinoxes. Then, all you need do is to prepare this room for your ceremony.

Ancient peoples often had to adapt to new environments, constructing their sacred places using whatever resources were available. The same applies today; when designing your sacred space, you can adapt it to whatever materials you have on hand—whether they be earth, stones, wood, plants, etc. I recommend always using chemically unprocessed materials wherever possible, as these retain their natural spiritual energies.

GATEWAYS AND PROCESSIONS AS A TRANSITION TO A SPIRITUAL PLACE

The gate to the Ki Monastery in the Himalayas, signifying the entrance to a sacred place.

Entering a sacred place always has its requirements, as the sacredness and energy of the space needs to be preserved for a sacred place to have a sense of presence. The most powerful sacred places are where this energy has been built up and maintained by the people who used it—sometimes over very long periods of time.

A sacred place is always entered by some sort of gate, entrance, or doorway that one has to pass through. This can serve as a reminder of the transition needed before entering the sacred space, bringing one into the present moment, provoking a reverence for the divine, respect for the principles of spirituality, etc. In ancient times and still at many religious sites today, before passing through, a person had to repeat a special phrase, bow, or say a small prayer. Some even ritually cleansed in water and put on white garments as a symbol of purifying oneself inwardly before presenting themselves before the spiritual. This kind of practice was important, for example, to the Buddhist monks in the high places of Tibet.

A gateway to an area which has a sacred space could be a timber arch, two standing stones, or something even simpler, and decorated with special plants and symbols as was done in ancient times. A doorway into a room that is used for spiritual purposes serves in the same way. So if you're looking to create a sacred space of any kind, I'd suggest having a dedicated entrance.

You could also incorporate a sense of journey to your sacred space, so that even before you reach the entrance, you begin to attune yourself to the event.

Pilgrimages and processions have long been a part of sacred ceremonies; there is evidence, for example, that they formed a major part of summer solstice celebrations at Stonehenge in ancient times.

To do this, all the participants could gather at a meeting point some distance from the sacred site where you're going to conduct your ceremony, and then walk together in a procession chanting, or in silence while being in the present moment, or with someone playing an instrument like a wooden flute, bell, drum, or harp, etc. If it is safe and practical to do so, each person could carry a lit candle to the sacred site in a procession symbolizing the spiritual light each person has within; this looks especially beautiful before dawn.

BAD WEATHER

It's a good idea to check the weather forecast in your local area a few days in advance of your ceremony to see what the weather will be like at the time of your ceremony. If there is any chance you won't be able to do your ceremony because of the weather, such as rain, hail, extreme cold, etc., then it's best to have a backup location where you can do the ceremony indoors, or if that's not possible, then to reschedule the ceremony for a clear part of the day or for the next day that is clear. Although the situation might not be ideal, it's better to do whatever you can to still do your ceremony rather than miss out.

Another common issue is that you can't see the sun at the time of the ceremony because of clouds. In this case I recommend still continuing with your ceremony regardless, but basing the timing of it on the time of sunrise or sunset at your location. So for example, if sunrise will occur at 6:35am at your location, then you would perform the ceremonial actions you would have anyway when the sun's light is first due to become visible. Even though you can't see the sun, it's still there, and the event still occurs in nature, so it is still very much worth doing a ceremony.

DOING THINGS IN A SUNWISE DIRECTION

There is evidence that many ancient solstice and equinox celebrations involved walking or dancing in the direction the sun appears to travel through the sky. For example, Andean winter solstice celebrations involve musical dances that move in clockwise and counter-clockwise spirals.[5] A giant earthwork near Stonehenge is believed to have been used for processions on the summer solstice, in which people walked in the direction of the sun from

Dances at the Inca/Andean winter solstice celebration in Peru.

east to west.[6] One of the oldest forms of dance in Russia is called Khorovod, which means "moving around the sun." It was originally part of pagan ceremonies that honoured the sun, and was seen as a way of offering repentance.[7] The dances took different forms; one involved dancing in a circle moving east to west like the path travelled by the sun. The circular dances of Southeastern Europe called kolo/koro, and the dances around the maypole in Northern and Western Europe, are all likely related.

As in traditional solstice and equinox ceremonies, you can choose to walk in procession to your sacred space, dance, or circle objects, in a sunwise direction to symbolize the path of the sun. A number of example ceremonies I have written in the following chapters include performing ceremonial actions in the direction of the sun, so I explain here what a sunwise direction means and how it differs depending on your location.

Sometimes walking the direction of the sun is very straightforward and simply involves walking in a cardinal direction. For example, processions can travel from west (where the sun sets) to east (where it rises) to symbolize the path of the sun through the underworld to rise and "resurrect" in the east. No matter where you are in the world, the sun always rises in an easterly direction and sets in a westerly one, so these directions have the same meaning wherever you are. However, in the Northern Hemisphere, the sun is at its height when it is farthest north (which is the time of summer solstice in the Northern Hemisphere), while in the Southern Hemisphere, the sun's height is when it is farthest south (summer solstice in the Southern Hemisphere). Any directions either toward the north or south have opposite meanings in the two hemispheres.

Sometimes the motion is not linear (in a straight line) but circular. Circling around an object, or dancing in a circle, are examples of this. In these cases, circling in a sunwise direction will differ depending on where you are in the world—being either always clockwise, always counter-clockwise, or clockwise around the December solstice and counter-clockwise around the June solstice.

I've based this on the direction the sun appears to travel each day when viewed from different latitudes on Earth. Someone north of the Tropic of Cancer facing south (the general direction of the sun), always sees the sun rise in the east and set in the west moving in a clockwise direction. Conversely, if they are south of the Tropic of Capricorn facing north (the general direction of the sun), the sun moves from east to west in a counter-clockwise direction.

Now if the sun were to trace a line throughout the course of a year, and you could see this line both above and beneath the horizon, it would trace a spiral that moved away and toward you, expanding and contracting as it did—always clockwise north of the Tropic of Cancer, and counter-clockwise south of the Tropic of Capricorn.[8]

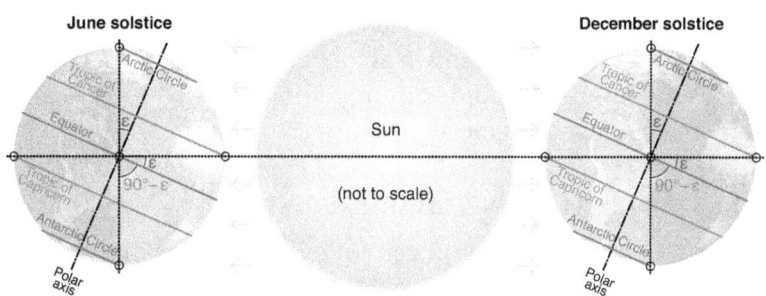

Diagram of Earth's tilt toward and away from the sun at the solstices with the major circles of latitude marked.

Those at latitudes between the Tropic of Cancer and Tropic of Capricorn (e.g. around the equator) will see the sun go clockwise around the December solstice (when facing the general direction of the sun) and counter-clockwise around the June solstice, with the date these directions reverse depending on the latitude.

Therefore, circling or spiralling in a "sunwise" direction in the following chapters always means clockwise north of the Tropic of Cancer, counter-clockwise south of the Tropic of Capricorn, and either clockwise or counter-clockwise at equatorial latitudes, depending on the exact location and time of year.

Depending on what is being symbolized, you could choose to perform an action both in a clockwise and counter-clockwise motion, and in expanding and contracting spirals—representing the dual nature of creation and its expansion from the source and return to it.

WORKING OUT CEREMONIES AND ACTIVITIES

A ritual being performed by the Supreme Council of Ethnikoi Hellenes at an ancient site in Greece, with an image of the sun front and center. Their rituals are mainly conducted on the solstices and equinoxes.

I've put together detailed guides for creating ceremonies in the following chapters. They are based on an understanding of the deeper meaning of the solstices and equinoxes and incorporate symbols and rituals from the ancient Religion of the Sun that were used in actual ceremonies in ancient times.

Before getting into these guides though, here are some general pointers relevant to any solstice or equinox ceremony.

HOW TO USE THE FOLLOWING CHAPTERS

To make your own ceremony, you can follow the guides outlined in the following chapters, which cater for people on their own, or for those who would like to do a ceremony with any number of people.

Depending on your circumstances, you may choose to do something very elaborate or very simple. The guides I've put together cater for each of these extremes and everything in between. Your ceremony could involve numerous people taking roles, with lots of items, special clothing, music, and a dedicated sacred space, or be as simple as chanting, doing readings, singing songs, or sitting and watching the sunrise or sunset on your own or with a few friends.

CELEBRATING ACCORDING TO TRADITION

As soon as anyone begins putting together a ceremony, they'll find that they touch upon culture. Everything past is part of culture, as it was expressed by a particular people at a specific time and place—whether it be a chant, song, instrument, type of clothing, representation of a deity, etc. The Religion of the Sun spread to many parts of the world where it was preserved by peoples to greater and lesser degrees. Thus, many of its principles, though the same, have been given unique expression in different cultures and traditions.

For an authentic experience of the ancient Religion of the Sun, I recommend people celebrate the solstices and equinoxes according to their tradition. If careful and thorough in what they include, participants can feel transported back in time, and at the same time fully in the present, as though the two are one—a very magical experience.

But the Religion of the Sun is not preserved in every culture, and so if it was never part of yours, you could try finding the next most similar culture to yours where it was and celebrate according to that. I suggest researching the oldest roots of your own culture/people first though. Sometimes you just have to brush away the accumulated layers that have built up over it, and set the clock back far enough. You may be surprised at what you find. The way the world is today is not how it was one thousand, two thousand, or five thousand or more years ago.

However, many people are unaware of their cultural roots or are living in countries far from their ancestral homelands. For example, what does someone do if they are of Indian descent living in a country of people who are largely of Celtic and Germanic ancestry and whose oldest surviving native population are Native Americans, as in the United States? In these kinds of circumstances, I recommend celebrating according to the tradition of their ancestral homeland, which in this case (since the person is of Indian descent), would be Vedic/Hindu. However, if they are celebrating among those who are mostly of Celtic descent, then the ceremony would be Celtic themed, but they would attend in Vedic/Hindu clothing. Those who conduct the ceremony should be of Celtic descent themselves and be dressed in traditional Celtic clothing.

If someone is working within an evenly diverse group of people, another option is to rotate the cultural theme of the ceremonies—so if half are of Indian descent and half Celtic, the ceremonies could be rotated between Vedic/Hindu and Celtic.

Native American Pueblo people performing the eagle dance. This same dance is performed by the Pueblo people at Chaco Canyon in the United States on the summer solstice.

Continuing with this example, if someone of Indian descent living in the United States was invited by Native Americans to a solstice or equinox ceremony of theirs, then the ceremony would be according to Native American culture, but they could attend in their own cultural dress (Vedic/Hindu) as a respectful guest. There is a way to maintain integrity toward one's own culture and identity, without having to forgo it or to subordinate it to that of another, while at the same time respecting the culture and identity of others.

In terms of sacred places, there are no ancient Vedic/Hindu sacred sites in the United States. This means that if they wanted to do a ceremony at an ancient site in the country where they live, it would have to be at one that is not in their tradition. In this case, they could do their Vedic/Hindu themed ceremony at one of these sites (as long as they have permission), but in a way that acknowledges the original builders of the site, and is respectful toward them as well as to any surviving custodians of the site who are their descendants.

Having said that, the history of many ancient sites is often misunderstood or wrong. Although current indigenous peoples may have inhabited and/or renovated a lot of them, often the origins of these sites stretch back much further in time and the original builders are no longer acknowledged in academia. It's best that someone educates themselves well on any ancient site they intend to do a ceremony at, and then be respectful toward the original builders (whether credited in mainstream academia or not) and to any other peoples who made a substantial contribution to the site.

A good example of this is the ancient site of Tiwanaku in Bolivia. Histories of the indigenous people record that the site was first established by a race of giants who were destroyed by a great flood, and was later rebuilt by Viracocha and his followers, who were described as fair-skinned with red hair, and as having come from across the ocean. Although the ancestry of these men is unknown, fair skin and red hair is most predominantly found in the British Isles today. It's believed Tiwanaku was most recently inhabited by ancestors of the local indigenous people called the Aymara, who use the site for ceremonies on the solstice today, and have lived in the area for thousands of years—possibly even being present when Viracocha arrived. And so (given that there are no giants around today) those who have some cultural connection to Tiwanaku are indigenous Aymara and Britons.

Ceremonies don't have to be performed at ancient sites though—someone can create their own sacred space according to their tradition anywhere it's appropriate.

In the case of people who are of mixed ancestry, someone could choose to celebrate according to the culture most predominately connected to their ancestry. If it's not clear, or is a close mix, they could celebrate according to any or all of those cultures related to their ancestry, or the one they feel the most affinity toward.

It is possible to create a syncretic ceremony using elements from different cultures. Someone may find, however, that the ceremony itself feels a bit "rootless," and doesn't have the same ancient feel to it that one done according to a sole culture does. One example where I could see a syncretic ceremony working though, is one in which a fairly even spread of people from different cultures participate. In this case, it could be possible to incorporate something from the culture of every person attending.

CEREMONIAL CLOTHING

There's something about wearing special clothing for special occasions. Monks/nuns, priests/priestesses, and yogis/yoginis have worn them for thousands of years, and even today non-religious people still wear traditional garments for special occasions like weddings.

Different colors appear in different places in nature and each affect the way we feel differently. Because they are part of the design of the universe, they represent and symbolize different spiritual principles. White for example has always been used as a color of spirituality, while black has been used to evoke dark forces, which is why I don't suggest using black in any of the ceremonies, unless dark forces are being represented. White is by default the best color for any ceremony. The ancient Druids are believed to have worn white as the color of the sun.[9] The sun's light contains all the colors of the visible spectrum, appearing to our eyes as white, which is why when the sun's light is refracted, we see it split into all its colors, creating a rainbow. The sun photographed from space is white, but we mostly see it as a golden yellow (and sometimes orange, or red) from Earth, as the blue end of the light spectrum is scattered by Earth's atmosphere. The sun is actually sending out most of its photons (packets of light) in the green portion of the light spectrum[10]—the same color as the leaves and grass, which are being nourished by its light through photosynthesis.

The standard clothing used for the ceremonies in this book is white with a yellow or gold trim or sash. The color white symbolizes the sun generally. Yellow or gold is the color of the Spiritual Son, and the golden, yellow light of the spectrum that reaches our eyes on Earth has a symbolic significance. It represents the light of the Spiritual Son as being the mediator between heaven and earth, as it is the color of the sun that we can see from Earth. It is also related to the element of helium, which was discovered as a yellow spectral line in the sun. The element was named after the Greek sun god Helios, and is the second lightest and most abundant element in the universe—having been formed during the first acts of creation in the universe. It then went on to form stars along with hydrogen.[11] As life is multidimensional, these elements and processes have higher, spiritual origins and properties, and this is why aspects like their color are used in the ceremonies.

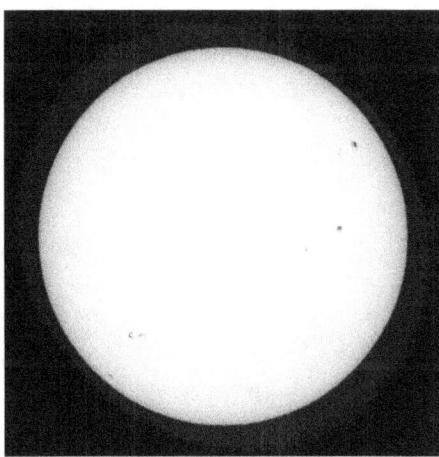

The sun when photographed in space is seen as white.

Depending on your circumstances, the clothing for the ceremonies can range from being whole custom-made garments to colored headbands or scarves worn with normal clothing, or even normal clothing in the desired color (e.g. a yellow t-shirt or red jacket).

Either way, I would recommend garments made of natural fabrics that are elegant and based on traditional designs, as natural fibers have certain properties that synthetic fibers don't. A good example of this can be seen in the clothing worn by the Romuvan community in Lithuania who are reviving the ancient celebrations of the Baltic Indo-Europeans, which include the solstices and equinoxes.

Romuvan ceremony in Lithuania.

READINGS FROM SACRED TEXTS

Sacred texts can be read aloud as part of any ceremony. There are many references in ancient texts and traditions to the themes found in the ceremonies in this book.

If you're looking for extra readings, there is a page on the SakroSawel.com website where there is a list of sacred texts I recommend as being derived from or influenced by the ancient Religion of the Sun, so you could have a look through that list to find readings for the ceremonies if you like.

Crowds climbing toward and congregating at the peak of the Pyramid of the Sun to celebrate the spring equinox, at the ancient site of Teotihuacan in Mexico.

USING SOUND

Sound can be used in ceremonies in a variety of different ways. For example, it can be used for certain parts of the ceremony with a bell that rings to announce the beginning of the ceremony, or drums played during a procession. It could be sung or played in the background to create an ambience. Or it could be a focus of a certain part of the ceremony, with times dedicated to playing music or singing songs.

Sound can be made from just one instrument, like a bell or drum, or it could be a number of instruments played together. Sound can also be made using vocals, with chanting, mantras, and songs. These songs could be existing traditional songs or songs you've composed yourself. Vocals can be combined with instruments or each can be used on their own.

Ideally, sound is used to evoke the mood of the event and its meaning. This is because sound is a powerful communicator. It can help participants to "feel" what's happening in the ceremony, rather than just "think" about it—transforming a simple ceremony into a profoundly moving experience.

If you're inexperienced with music, the simplest way to create sound is to have everyone chant at the same musical note. It can take some practice to get this right and find a note that everyone in the group is comfortable singing, so it's worth rehearsing ahead of the ceremony.

A chant doesn't have to be complex to be effective. What is most important is the tone and harmony it's sung with, even if it's just a vowel that is being chanted. The ancient Egyptians, for example, were well known in ancient times for their sacred chants, which were a series of vowels sung like hymns.[12] Similar chants appear in the texts of the early Christian Gnostics,[13] and the same principle used in Gregorian chanting.

It can be hard to create music and song that is impactful if you are inexperienced or have a small number of people, so an easy option is to play prerecorded songs using speakers during your ceremony. You could choose all the songs and music you want to include as part of your ceremony well ahead and set up a music player, ideally with a remote, so that you can control the music throughout the ceremony. The music could play on its own, or you can use it as backing for people to sing along to.

Ceremonies also often involve saying or reading things aloud. In a ceremony performed by a larger group, it's almost completely necessary to say things aloud as a way of communicating. However, if you're on your own or with a small group of people, in circumstances in which it's not appropriate to say things aloud, such as a public place, you could choose to read or say things to yourself. Verbalizing things does have a power though, so I recommend speaking aloud where you can.

THE MANTRA OM (ALSO KNOWN AS AUM)

One of the easiest and most effective chants to use for any solstice or equinox ceremony is the Vedic mantra Om (written as Aum). If you're looking to do a very simple ceremony, and particularly if you're celebrating on your own, this mantra is a good one to use. Your ceremony could be as simple as watching the rising or setting sun, and chanting the mantra Om. Here is some information about it for those who'd like to use it in their solstice or equinox ritual.

The mantra Om is very ancient; it appears in the texts called the Upanishads, which were written in India. It is considered to be the greatest mantra of all, and is the most popular and famous mantra in the world. It is relevant to any solstice or equinox as it is a mantra of the spiritual sun. This mantra can be used by anyone, and is culturally relevant to those working within an Indo-European tradition.

The following excerpt from the Maitrāyaṇīya Upanishad describes the meaning of the mantra Om. It is said to represent both the source of creation, called Brahman, as well as creation itself. This source is identified as light, which has its origin in the sun. This spiritual source/sun is said to reside both within us and at the same time within the sun. Like the mantra Om which is composed of three letters, Brahman is said to be a trinity of masculine, feminine, and neutral (just like the trinity of Father, Mother, and Son), which everything in creation is woven upon. The text also refers to the path of the sun as the path to emancipation.

Interestingly, the Egyptian supreme creator deity called Atum contains the same letters as this sacred mantra.

> "This (Soul) verily bears a twofold form, Prāṇa [life force/cosmic energy] and yonder Sun. [...] Yonder sun is the external soul, Prāṇa is the internal; hence it is said that from the external soul's motion is inferred the motion of the internal soul. But whosoever is wise, void of sin, the master of his senses, clear-minded, firmly abiding in Him, having his eyes withdrawn (from all external objects), he indeed says that from the internal soul's motion is inferred the motion of the external soul. Now that golden being within the sun who beholds this earth from his golden sphere, is the same who abiding within, in the lotus of the heart, devours food.
>
> 'Now that which dwelling within the lotus of the heart devours food, the same, dwelling as the solar fire in the sky, being called Time, and invisible, devours all beings as its food.' (The Vālakhilyas asked) 'What is its lotus and of what composed?' (Prajāpati answered), 'Its lotus is the same as the ether; the four quarters and the four intermediate points are its petals. These two, Prāṇa and the Sun, revolve near to each other—let him worship them both, by the syllable Om, by the mystical words, and by the Gāyatrī.
>
> There are two forms of the supreme Brahman, the material and the immaterial; the material is unreal, the immaterial is real, is Brahman. That which is Brahman is light; that which is light is the Sun. This Sun was identical with Om; it divided itself into three parts, for Om consists of three mātrās. "By these are woven the warp and woof of all things, and this am I," thus He speaks.' [...]

> 'It hath been also elsewhere said—the sound-endowed form of this (Prāṇa-Āditya Soul) is Om; masculine, feminine, and neuter—this is the gender-endowed form [...].
>
> As the lamp consists of the union of the wick, the vessel, and the oil, so from the union of the individual body and the world exist the Individual Soul and the pure Sun.
>
> Therefore let him devoutly honour the aforesaid (round of ceremonial rites) by repeating the word Om (at their commencement.) Unbounded is its might, and located in three sites—in the fire, the Sun, and in prāṇa. [...]
>
> The syllable Om is verily the essential nature of that ether which abides in the cavity of the heart. By this syllable, Om, that (splendour) germinates, it shoots upward, it expands, it becomes continuously the vehicle of the worship of Brahman. [...]
>
> Endless are the rays of that soul which abides like a lamp in the heart— white and black, brown and blue, tawny and reddish. One of these rises upward which pierces the orb of the sun; by this, having passed beyond the world of Brahman, they attain to the supreme abode. [...]
>
> Therefore yonder adorable Sun is the cause of creation, of heaven, and of emancipation.'" [14]
>
> ~ THE MAITRĀYAṆĪYA UPANISHAD

The mantra OM is really pronounced and most accurately written as AUM as the "au" sound is a subtle intonation that arises when the mantra is pronounced. Each letter of the mantra is said to have its own significance.

> "In Hindu mythology, the letter A also represents the process of creation, when it is said that all existence issued forth from Brahma's golden nucleus; the letter U refers to Vishnu, the god who is said to preserve this world by balancing Brahma on a lotus above himself; the M symbolizes the final part of the cycle of existence, when it is said that Vishnu falls asleep and Brahma has to breathe in so that all existing things have to disintegrate and are reduced to their essence to him. [...] Finally, the silence at the end of the mantra symbolizes the period between death and rebirth. One must not forget that this silence is an important part of the mantra." [15]
>
> ~ AUM, NEW WORLD ENCYCLOPEDIA

THE DAY AND DAYS SURROUNDING THE EVENT

In ancient times, celebrations for the solstices and equinoxes not only consisted of a special ceremony at sunrise or sunset, but carried on throughout the days and nights surrounding them. Depending on the meaning of the occasion, the days surrounding the event can be filled with lots of spiritual practice, singing spiritual songs, pilgrimages to sacred sites, processions by candlelight, readings of sacred texts, spiritual dancing, mantras, music, bonfires, times of prayer, reflection, meditation, etc.

It's especially nice to gather around a fire and sing spiritual songs. Fire itself is living and divine, and very much connected to the sun and its own fire, as well as to the fire of the spirit within. This is why fire has always held a special place in religious rites and places throughout the world.

With that in mind, the ceremonies in this book could form just one part of a much larger and longer celebration. To work out how you'd like to do it, you could look at the meaning of these times of year provided in this book, and put together a program of activities surrounding the ceremony that reflect this spiritual meaning.

BACKGROUND INFORMATION ON THE MEANING BEHIND THE CEREMONIES

It helps to understand the meaning of the event you're celebrating, at least on some level. You could be surprised, however, to find that you feel an understanding during the celebration itself that touches you in a direct way beyond words and thought, and which may even be difficult to explain to somebody else.

In this book I've put together detailed descriptions of the meanings of the solstices and equinoxes based on ancient texts and sites of the Religion of the Sun from all over the world, and even if some things "go over your head" at the moment, it's worth reflecting on them and the ancient texts quoted before your event.

TEN TIPS FOR CREATING YOUR OWN CEREMONY

1. Choose someone to guide the ceremony. It's important to have a sense of order if a ceremony is going to be effective. That's one of the reasons why it's a good idea to have a priest and/or priestess guiding the ceremony who knows it by heart. I'd recommend having a way to clearly signal to all those participating that your ceremony has begun, and likewise that it has closed, and to have the priest/priestess guide the participants through all of the steps—especially if there are going to be people attending who are not familiar with the ceremony. The priest/priestess is also the representative of those attending; as it's not practical for everyone to always perform every ceremonial action, the priest/priestess essentially does this on their behalf, and so should reflect and express what the participants feel, wish to say, want to do, etc., in the ceremony.

2. Assign roles/activities for all those attending. Look at how many people you have available to partake in the ceremony and assign any roles there are between them. Look also at how many people will be watching the ceremony, and what they'll be doing throughout it. I recommend involving them in the ceremonial activities in some way, whether they do symbolic actions, join in chants, repeat certain words, etc., so that everyone has a sense of participating, and also because more people focusing on and enacting the ceremony creates a greater energy and power.

3. As part of the ceremony you may wish to invoke the deity or deities who are represented, and ask them to be present for it, such as Odin, Jesus, etc. You need to be sure however, that these deities were real people who became "sons of the sun" and that they are still risen Beings, and are not purely mythological or are now fallen such as Bael. It's also possible for each to call upon their own Spiritual Mother and/or Father to be present for the ceremony (although our Spiritual Father and Mother are never "away" from us). The Spiritual Father and Mother can also be referred to with the prefix Divine, Sacred, or Holy, etc.—whatever is most comfortable to say in your language or was historically used in your tradition.

This can be very powerful to do as it is really the presence of and the connection and communion with spiritual beings (commonly referred to as gods), as well as each one's own higher Being, that can make a ceremony powerful.

4. Write out the steps of your ceremony. Write down each and every action, song, word, chant, etc., of your ceremony, so that you end up with a final set of instructions. You can use this to rehearse your ceremony so that everyone participating in it knows exactly what they need to do and are able to memorize their part in it for it to go smoothly on the day.

5. Make a list of all the items you'll need. Write down each item you'll use as part of your ceremony—from clothing, to props, instruments, altar items, etc. This will allow you to methodically make sure that you have every item involved in the ceremony well before it.

6. Be discerning. Since many traditions have strayed from the original meaning with time, retelling, and other later introduced influences, I'd recommend only incorporating those things from your tradition that are relevant to the profound and core meaning of the solstice or equinox you are celebrating, as adding other things that are not meaningful can confuse and thus weaken your ceremony. I recommend using this book as a guide, and definitely avoiding anything that involves violence, lust, or the sacrifice of any living thing, as if you include any of these things (even if historically accurate) your ceremony will be under the influence of darkness, not of light.

7. Be flexible and creative. Most traditions that have descended from the ancient Religion of the Sun only survived in remnants. If your tradition doesn't have enough to create a coherent ceremony, then you could choose symbols from within your tradition, but construct your own sequence of events based on the meaning of the solstice or equinox you are celebrating. You'll probably find you need to be very creative and change things around a lot. I don't think there is anything wrong with this, as spirituality is not static, but is living and eternal. Personally, I feel the most important thing is ending up with a ceremony that expresses the deeper meaning of the event rather than rigidly conforming to a tradition that has lost integral parts or has gone astray.

8. Remember, ceremonial formalities are only a means to an end. The most important part of a ceremony is not complex actions and ornate surroundings. If taken seriously, these enable us to focus our attention on the spiritual by keeping our mind concentrated and directing it toward meaningful symbols. However, for the ceremony to really work what will be most important is your inner state—whether you are receptive to the experience of the ceremony, and whether you are respectful in your intentions toward spiritual beings and forces.

9. Think about the purpose(s) of your ceremony. Ceremonies are a great way to bring people together, to create a sense of common purpose and bond, and to express and preserve religion and culture. And so a ceremony can fulfill communal, social, and cultural goals. They can also just be a fun, uplifting, and relaxing thing to do. But they can also have a spiritual purpose. Ceremony can be a formulized way to enable all those participating to gain profound spiritual experience, as a ceremony can facilitate the connection with spiritual forces and beings.

10. Enjoy yourself. If you are preparing for a large or complex ceremony, getting everything together can be stressful and a lot of work, especially under the pressure of time. However large or small your ceremony, things don't always go to plan—key people can get stuck in traffic, items can get lost, unexpected weather come over, etc. I recommend doing your best not to let it get to you, as otherwise your ceremony will be ruined by your own emotional state—feeling anxious or upset will block your sense of enjoyment and spiritual connection. That's why whatever happens, my advice is to push past any negative feelings and not allow external circumstances to throw you off, but to carry on as best you can, even if it is far from what you'd hoped. You might be surprised, as by doing this, you could have a magical experience that you could never have planned for.

THE VALUE OF EXPERIENCE

The aim of this book is not only to rekindle an interest in the Religion of the Sun, but also the experience of it. My hope is that people all over the world will start celebrating the solstices and equinoxes again as major events in their towns and cities, with celebrations based on their true meaning that everyone can enjoy—connecting again with the spirit in nature through bonfires and spiritual music. Creating your own ceremony at home or with friends can connect you to the ancients and make you feel part of the spiritual order of the universe.

The more involved ceremonies, outlined in the following chapters, are best practiced at dedicated locations, and could become part of an annual calendar of events that people take part in and even travel to four times a year.

One of the great things about the solstice and equinox is that a tradition of their celebration exists in many cultures, so it is possible for people to celebrate it according to the culture they are most connected to, while at the same time, connecting with its profound meaning. If enough people took up the principles contained in these celebrations, they could help to give birth to a sense of spiritual harmony while at the same time celebrating the richness of cultural diversity throughout the world.

People celebrating the summer solstice called Kupala in Russia.

Autumn Equinox

CHAPTER THIRTEEN

Ceremonies to Celebrate the Autumn Equinox

This chapter outlines ceremonies for celebrating the autumn equinox, both for people on their own and in a group. I've included example ceremonies, as well as a basic outline of the principles involved for those who'd like to construct their own ceremony or who are already working within an existing tradition.

CEREMONY OVERVIEW

The autumn equinox is symbolized by the death and descent into the underworld of those representing the Spiritual Son. Jesus and Quetzalcoatl on the cross, and Odin on the tree, mirror the sun crossing the celestial equator at the equinox and its descent into the darkness of winter.

At the autumn equinox the sun descends into darkness in its annual journey—it is a time of death, descent, and growing darkness; so too then do autumn equinox ceremonies reflect this in tune with nature's cycles. An autumn equinox ceremony essentially symbolizes the descent into the underworld on the path of the spiritual sun.

This event was portrayed in the lives of many deities in association with the autumn equinox, and appears in numerous cultures. It often involved the self-sacrifice of a sun god on a cross or tree, and subsequent descent into the underworld and subconscious, represented by the growing darkness of winter. Their death is symbolic of the death of their egos and lower self, which they had to pass through before they could spiritually resurrect at the spring equinox. There, within the darkness of the subconscious, one had to symbolically confront a horrible beast or enemy, representing the egos, in order to overcome them, and subsequently acquire knowledge and consciousness. Often this deity was accompanied by and/or aided by a goddess who represents a higher feminine part of each one's Being known as the Spiritual Mother. The underworld is the womb of the Spiritual Mother, which is where she gestates creation, and so she plays an important part of this ritual.

Because of the deathly and difficult nature of the event, the mood of this ceremony is one of somberness and seriousness. If the ceremony involves any songs or readings to the Spiritual Mother, these have a mood of praise and veneration.

A GUIDE TO CREATING AN AUTUMN EQUINOX CEREMONY

Whether you are a solitary practitioner or working with a group of people, this guide can help you to create your own ceremony, or to expand upon or modify the historical remnants of an existing traditional ceremony.

PREPARING FOR YOUR CEREMONY

To start with, I recommend reading the chapters "The Spiritual Meaning of the Autumn Equinox" and "A Guide to Celebrating the Solstices and Equinoxes," as these provide some important background information.

Here is a guide to what information I recommend you gather together first, before creating your ceremony:

1. Autumn equinox traditions (optional). This step is optional—it's if you'd like to do a ceremony according to your tradition.

I recommend doing some research to find out how the autumn equinox was celebrated in your culture (as long as it is connected in some way to the ancient Religion of the Sun). This is not always easy as so many records of the past have been lost or destroyed. If you can't find much, I'd recommend looking for anything in your tradition that is relevant to the profound meaning of the autumn equinox. This could include ancient sites that are aligned to it, and symbols and stories that are relevant to it.

See if there is anything you would like to incorporate into your ceremony.

2. Symbols of the autumn equinox. It's nice to use and wear actual symbols of the equinox in your ceremony, just as ancient peoples did. Look for any symbols of the equinox you can find in your tradition. I've given a number of examples in this book, such as the double spiral, infinity, horns of the solstices, the yin and yang, Hunab Ku, the double-headed axe (labrys), and cross/cruciform. If there isn't a specific equinox symbol in your tradition, then any solar symbol can be used.

Work out how to incorporate these symbols into your ceremony. For example, you could wear a pendant of the symbol, or have a representation of it on an altar, or make it part of your sacred ceremonial space by creating it out of stones on the ground, etc.

3. Central figure. Choose what will represent the figure that descends into the underworld in your ceremony. The sun represents the descent of the Spiritual Son as it sets on the autumn equinox, so you may choose to have nothing else representing this central figure but the sun itself.

For those who would like to do a ceremony according to your tradition, you could also look to symbolize this figure using a deity from your tradition. Look for one that descended into the underworld and/or battled against darkness.

There are many examples of figures who descended into the underworld given in this book, such as the god Wotan/Odin in Germanic/Nordic paganism; Quetzalcoatl of the Aztecs; Kukulkan, the Maize God, and the flaming water-lily jaguar of the Maya; Theseus of the ancient Greeks/Minoans; Persephone of the ancient Greeks; Jesus of the ancient Gnostics; and Osiris of the ancient Egyptians.

The battle of the Hindu deity Rama against Ravana with the aid of Durga is also relevant to the autumn equinox.

Decide how you will incorporate this central figure into your ceremony. You could have a statue, painting, or symbol of them on an altar or somewhere in your sacred space. If you are doing a larger group ceremony, then someone could dress as this figure and represent them.

4. Symbols of descent (optional). This step is optional—it's if you would like to do a ceremony according to your tradition.

Extract the most important and relevant symbols involved in the descent and/or battle against evil of the figure you have chosen in the above step 3. Look specifically for those things that represent the following:

    a. The cross of the autumn equinox (e.g. a sacred tree, cross, or cruciform)

    b. The underworld (e.g. tomb, mound, turtle, labyrinth, water)

    c. The underworld's nine regions (e.g. ninth hour, nine nights, nine years, nine terraces)

    d. The egos (e.g. evil opponent, beast, animal, demon)

    e. The Spiritual Mother

    f. The knowledge and consciousness gained from the descent (e.g. runes, rescued female, treasure)

Work out how you would like to incorporate these symbols into your ceremony and/or sacred space. For example, you might symbolize the underworld as a standing stone circle, a bowl or cauldron of water, a cave, a symbol of a turtle, etc., depending on the tradition.

5. Chants, mantras, songs, prayers, readings, music, etc. As part of your ceremony you could choose to read from sacred texts, or sing songs, etc. These could be traditional songs that are part of autumn equinox celebrations, excerpts from sacred texts that are relevant to the meaning of the autumn equinox, chants that convey the meaning of the autumn equinox, or even just pieces of music played on traditional instruments that suit the mood of the event. You may even like to compose your own. Choose which ones you'd like to incorporate as part of your ceremony.

6. Sacred space location and design. Work out where you will hold your ceremony. It will need to be located where everyone participating can see the autumn equinox sunset. Ideally, it would also be aligned to the autumn equinox sunset in some way, just as many ancient sites are—which can be done simply by lining up stones, candles, an altar, etc., with the sun. Whatever design or location you choose, I recommend having a candle or ceremonial fire you can light as part of your ceremony.

BASIC STRUCTURE

This is a basic outline of an autumn equinox ceremony, which can be adapted to any tradition, or can be done without any specific cultural references. It can also be adapted to be more complex, or steps can be left out to make it simpler.

1. Prepare the sacred space where you will conduct your ceremony well in advance.

2. Hold your ceremony at the sunset closest to the autumn equinox in your time zone (see section "Working out a Calendar and Preparing in Advance" in previous chapter), as this is when the sun itself symbolizes the descent into the underworld. Make sure your ceremony begins before sunset so that the sunset takes place within the ceremony, having worked out how long your ceremony will take so that you are not rushed as the sun sets.

3. Open your ceremony in whatever way you wish—this could be by saying a prayer, a mantra, or chant. Or it could be by playing an instrument or song. I would recommend using any of these as a way to focus your mind and to connect yourself with the spiritual both within and surrounding you. As part of this, you could light a candle or ceremonial fire of some kind and keep it burning throughout the ceremony.

4. Praise the Spiritual Mother (optional). Each person has an aspect of their higher Being known as the Spiritual Mother. She plays an important part in the events symbolized by this ceremony, so it's appropriate to praise and/or petition her. You could do this simply by repeating something like, "Spiritual Mother, please guide me/us," or there may be special phrases in your tradition which you can use. You could use the translation of "Spiritual Mother" into your language, or the name of a mother goddess in your tradition. It may be helpful to have a statue or image of the Spiritual Mother that you can address yourself to.

5. Do a reading (optional). Optionally, you could recite something from a sacred text about a figure in your tradition who descended into the underworld, retell mythology to do with it, or recite something you've written about it. You could have related statues or images incorporated into your sacred space, or on your altar, etc.

6. Symbolize the descent through the nine layers of the underworld (optional). The sun setting beneath the horizon at the autumn equinox symbolizes the descent into the underworld, so you don't have to do anything to symbolize it yourself if you prefer not to. For those who would like to also symbolize it themselves in some way there are many ways you can do this, and it can be based on something existing in your tradition. For example, you can symbolize the nine regions of the underworld using nine candles, nine sounds on an instrument, nine steps or stairs, etc. You could walk sunwise around a symbol of the double spiral or a candle nine times (see section "Doing Things in a Sunwise Direction" in chapter 12).

7. Recite prayers, mantras, songs. You might like to spend some time repeating a prayer or mantra, or singing a song. These could be in praise to the Spiritual Mother.

8. Watch the sunset. The equinox itself is the main event of the ceremony, and in nature it has its own energies, which can be perceived and felt. As an option, you might like to watch the sunset in silence, or watch it while silently praying, or while singing a chant or mantra. Just make sure not to stare into a bright sun as it can harm your eyes.

9. Symbolize the death/defeat of the ego (optional). You could do this, for example, by burning a symbol of the ego from your tradition in your ceremonial fire.

10. Symbolize gaining knowledge (optional). Once the sun has fully set, symbolize gaining knowledge and consciousness in some way. The easiest way to do this is by lighting your own handheld candle from the fire you lit at the beginning of the ceremony. Depending on your tradition, other options include uncovering runes (Germanic/Nordic), a golden treasure (Maya), or a sheaf of wheat (Eleusinian).

11. Close the ceremony. You could do this by saying a prayer of thanks, or by leaving a symbolic offering like flowers.

12. Leave. Walk away from your ceremonial space holding your lit candle, runes, etc., if you have included them.

EXAMPLE THEMES

There are many different examples of ceremonies you could perform based on your particular tradition. Not all of them conform to the basic ceremonial structure outlined above, but that's fine, as they contain enough symbolic elements already to create a coherent ceremony. Here are just a few basic outlines to start with.

ANCIENT EGYPTIAN

The betrayal of Osiris by Seth could be symbolized, and Osiris' subsequent descent into the underworld as the river Nile and Milky Way. Readings could be done from ancient Egyptian texts, such as the Book of the Dead, the Pyramid Texts, and the 42 Negative Confessions.

CELTIC

You could symbolize the bard Taliesun (representing the sun) returning to the womb of the goddess Ceridwen (representing the underworld), where he learns great knowledge. The ancient Celtic tradition of burning a wicker man could also be incorporated, symbolically representing the death of the ego—the false and perishable self.

GERMANIC/NORDIC

See the example ceremony in this chapter.

GNOSTIC CHRISTIAN

The Passion and crucifixion of Jesus and his descent into the underworld could be symbolized. He could be accompanied by a woman playing his mother Mary, representing the Spiritual Mother. Relevant readings could be done from the Gospels, but also from ancient Gnostic texts.

As an alternative to the orthodox rendition of the crucifixion, the descent of Pistis Sophia into the underworld (much like Persephone in the Eleusinian Mysteries) could be symbolized, with readings done from the ancient Gnostic text Pistis Sophia.

GREEK (ELEUSINIAN)

The autumn equinox was when the Greater Eleusinian Mysteries were held: participants had first to be purified and then walk a pilgrimage along a Sacred Way, enacting the goddess Demeter's search for her daughter Persephone.[1]

A woman could take the role of Persephone (symbolizing consciousness), and enact her descent into Hades (the underworld). Persephone could take a sheaf or handful of wheat with her and bury it in the earth, symbolizing the seed of spiritual transformation that must go into the ground to germinate the life of the spirit within.

She could be watched over by a woman playing Demeter, representing the Spiritual Mother, who holds a flaming torch and double-headed axe, and who symbolically searches for her for nine days (representing the nine layers of the underworld) as she does in mythology. Excerpts from the Hymn to Demeter could be read, as this was composed in the seventh century BC and was used for hundreds of years as the canonical hymn of the Eleusinian Mysteries.[2]

HINDU/VEDIC

See the example Hindu ceremony in this chapter.

As another option, a man could take the role of Rama and enact appealing to the goddess Durga for help, then enacting the defeat of Ravana. Alternatively two people playing Rama and Durga could dramatically defeat the buffalo demon Mahishasura. Readings could be done from the ancient texts the Ramayana and the Devi Mahatmyam. There are also many mantras and traditional songs you could incorporate that are specifically related to Durga or Kali destroying the egos.

MAYA

A man could take the role of Kukulkan, the Maize God (Hun Hunahpu), or the water-lily jaguar, and enact the descent through the nine regions of Xibalba (the underworld). He could take with him a sheaf of corn/maize and plant it symbolically in the earth. He could also symbolically battle the Lords of Death/Xibalba, representing the battle against the ego, and win a golden treasure (as in Maya mythology) representing gained knowledge and consciousness.

MINOAN/GREEK

See the example ceremony in this chapter.

EXAMPLE SOLITARY OR SMALL GROUP CEREMONY ~ Vedic/Hindu

This example ceremony is in the Vedic/Hindu tradition, and is based on traditional ceremonies held as part of the celebration of Navratri and Durga Puja around the time of the autumn equinox in India.

A man worshiping the goddess Durga using an aarti lamp, as is done in this ceremony.

THE TIMING OF THE CEREMONY

This ceremony begins before the sunset closest to the autumn equinox in your time zone.

ITEMS NEEDED

- A statue or image of the goddess Durga or Kali either on their own or slaying the buffalo demon Mahishasura.

- A statue or image of Rama. Alternatively, a statue of Rama worshipping Durga could be used (as used traditionally in Durga Puja celebrations in India).

- An altar—ideally square or rectangular in shape, so that it has four sides, representing the four material elements, and physical world.

- Red cloth to place over the altar.

- An aarti lamp with fuel.

- A small handheld bell.

- Incense.

- Flowers—ideally the marigold flower that is traditionally offered on altars in India, or lotuses or waterlilies as were offered by Rama to Durga, but any flowers will do. There should be a handful, bouquet, or wreath of flowers for each participant.

- A ceremonial fire.

- An image or effigy of Mahishasura that can be ceremonially burned in fire. It could be made of straw, wood, paper, or cardboard, etc.

- A spear or replica of one, which ideally is painted golden. This doesn't have to be life size, and is optional.

- A small container of barley seeds for each participant.

- A clay pot filled with soil for each participant.

- A small handheld lamp with fuel for each participant.

- Mats that can be placed on the ground for each participant to sit on.

THE PARTICIPANTS

Ideally each participant dresses in traditional Indian style garments that are yellow and red, just yellow, or yellow and white. The yellow represents the Spiritual Son, and the red the descent of the Son into matter/earth (it's particles in Earth's atmosphere that cause the sun to appear red, particularly at sunset).

One person can conduct this ceremony, but if you have more than one person, then you'll need to assign roles. I suggest that one person have the role of guiding the ceremony. I'll refer to them as the Guide in the ceremony itself.

A painting of the very first Durga Puja. It was said to have been performed by Rama, who offered 107 blue lotus flowers to Durga as seen on the altar in the foreground, and has his bow and arrow pointed at his eye to make up the 108th. The goddess Durga is upon her lion amid the clouds in the background.

THE SETUP OF THE SACRED SPACE

The sacred space consists of an altar and a mat for each person placed on the ground before it. Directly in front of each mat there should be a clay pot with soil.

The altar should be arranged so that the participants look toward the altar and sunset. However, the altar should not obscure the view of the sunset, so it can be slightly offset if need be.

The altar is covered in the red cloth. The statues/images of Rama and Durga/Kali and Mahishasura are placed on it. The aarti lamp and incense are placed on the altar before the statues/images.

The ceremonial fire should be in front of the participants, and ideally align with the sunset. The image/effigy of Mahishasura is placed near the ceremonial fire. The spear is stood erect (using a stand or by burying it partially in the ground) with its tip pointing upward, on the right side of the fire when facing the sun.

A Hindu ceremony being performed in India. The sacred space in this ceremony follows the same basic layout.

INSTRUCTIONS FOR THE CEREMONY

1. The sacred space is ready. The sacred space has been prepared in advance and is ready. The ceremonial fire should already be lit and have enough fuel to burn throughout the entire ceremony. Each participant stands at a distance from the sacred space, and each holds a container of barley seeds, an unlit lamp, and flowers. The Guide also holds the bell (they can wear a bag to carry their other items).

2. Procession to the sacred space and lighting of the altar lamp. The Guide rings the bell, and the participants walk in single file behind them to the sacred space (ideally in a westerly direction to symbolize walking the path of the sun) in silence. The Guide continues to ring the bell at intervals while they walk. Once everyone reaches the sacred space they each place their individual containers of seed, handheld lamps, and flowers in front of their mats, beside their clay pots of soil. While the rest seat themselves, the Guide places the bell on the altar and lights the aarti lamp on the altar, and then sits on their mat also. All sit facing the sunset. If you find it uncomfortable to sit cross-legged, then you could have a cushion or chair, etc., to make sure you are comfortable throughout the duration of the ceremony.

3. Chanting of mantras. The Guide signals for the participants to begin chanting a mantra, and everyone begins. It's best to choose a mantra relevant to the occasion. This could be the mantra Om, the Gayatri mantra of the sun, or mantras praising the Spiritual Mother. When ready, the Guide signals for all participants to stop chanting, and everyone becomes silent.

4. Lighting of incense and praise of the Spiritual Mother. The Guide goes to the altar and kneels before it. They light the incense and say,

> "Jai Devi Maa, Supreme Mother, protector of the universe, who exists in the form of all.
>
> You are the eternal cause of liberation, even as you are the cause of bondage to this transitory existence.
>
> You are Savitri, the source of all purity and protection; you are the supreme mother of the gods.
>
> Armed with sword and spear, and with club and discus, waging war with conch, bow and arrows, sling and iron mace, you inspire dread. Yet, you are pleasing, more pleasing than all else that is pleasing, and exceedingly beautiful. Transcending both highest and lowest, you are indeed the supreme sovereign.
>
> You are this entire, manifold world and you are primordial matter, supreme and untransformed.
>
> O Devi, who are the cause of liberation and great, inconceivable austerities: sages yearning for liberation contemplate you with sense restrained, intent upon truth, with all faults cast off, for you are the blessed, supreme knowledge.
>
> O Devi, who remove the sufferings of those who take refuge in you, be gracious. Be gracious, mother of the entire world. Be gracious, ruler of all. Protect us, O Devi." [3]

5. Ringing of the bell and circling of the lamp. The Guide picks up the lit aarti lamp in their right hand and the bell in their left. They circle the aarti lamp in front of the statue/image of Durga in a clockwise direction, and ring the bell, while praising the Spiritual Mother, saying something like,

> "Jai Devi Maa, salutation be to you, save us from error, Supreme Mother."

The other participants repeat this phrase. This is done a total of nine times.

6. Invocation to the Mother in the four directions. The Guide then stands, facing the sun in front of the fire and says,

> "Oh Devi, protect us with Your spear. O Ambika, protect us with Your sword, protect us by the sound of Your gong and by the twang of Your bow-string. O Candika, guard us in the east, in the west, in the north and in the south by the brandishing of Your spear, O Ishwari." [4]

They return to their mat.

7. Sacred text reading. Any of the participants can then read something relevant aloud, such as the excerpt from the Krittivasa Ramayana in which Rama petitions Durga, or you could simply recite the story in your own words.

8. Circling the fire nine times. The Guide makes a signal and all the participants then stand up and walk slowly in a sunwise direction around the ceremonial fire nine times (see section "Doing Things in a Sunwise Direction" in chapter 12). They say together, during each round, "*Dakshine Kali, protect us.*" The participants then return to their mats and sit down.

9. Mantras, songs, and prayers. Songs, prayers, and mantras relevant to the occasion can be sung. Mantras could include the Mantra of Durga and the Dakshine Kali Beej Mantra. Prayers and traditional songs could include the Devi Aparadha Kshamapana Stotram, the Durga Chalisa, the Mahishasura Mardini Stotra, and Sri Kali Chalisa. Readings can be done from the Hindu text the Devimahatmya and the Devi Sukta from the Rig Veda (10.125.3-10.125.8).

10. The sunset is observed in silence. When the sun first begins to visibly set below the horizon or behind any terrestrial object, the Guide signals for the chanting of songs, reading of texts, etc., to finish. All watch the sun until it has completely set (without looking directly at it if it is too bright), in silence.

11. Flowers are placed on the altar. Once the sun is set, one by one each participant gets up and places their flowers on the altar in front of the statue/image of Durga, and returns to their seat.

12. Petition to the Spiritual Mother. A participant then holds up the representation of Mahishasura.

They say,

> "You are the supreme maya. Deluded, O Devi, is all this universe. In this world, you alone, when pleased, are the cause of liberation.
>
> Where malevolent beings and venomous serpents lurk, where enemies and thieves abound, where forest conflagrations rage, there and even in mid-ocean you stand to protect the universe.
>
> Possessing all power, may your terrible, flaming trident, exceedingly sharp, protect us from dread.
>
> May your bell that fills the world with its ringing protect us from all evils, even as a mother protects her children.
>
> May your sword, blazing as the sun's rays, be for our welfare.
>
> O Devi who removes the afflictions of all. May you subdue all evil within us." [5]

13. The image/effigy of Mahishasura is burned. The participant holding the image/effigy of Mahishasura puts it in the ceremonial fire to burn. They say,

> "O Devi, we bow to you."

All participants watch in silence, and may silently say their own personal prayers if they wish.

14. The seeds are buried. Once the effigy has finished burning, the Guide makes a signal, and one by one, each participant picks up their barley seeds and buries them in the soil within their individual clay pot.

15. Individual lamps are lit. One by one, each participant lights their individual handheld lamp from the ceremonial fire.

16. Closing prayer to the Spiritual Mother. A participant then says:

> "Oh Queen of all,
>
> You who exist in the form of all
> and possess every might
>
> Save us from error, Oh Devi
>
> Salutation be to You, Devi Durga
>
> Mother, I bow to Thee again and again,
> destroyer of worldly sufferings,
> embodiment of bliss,
> dispenser of wisdom and devotion." [6]

The remaining participants repeat after them at each line.

17. All leave holding their lit lamp. One by one each participant stands up, and then all walk away from the sacred space holding their lit lamp, until they have left the ceremonial area. The ceremony has now concluded.

After the ceremony you could gather around a fire, sing songs/chants, or do further readings. Any activities should conclude before midnight.

THE MEANING OF THE CEREMONY

A typical ceremonial fire being used as part of
a traditional Vedic ceremony called yajna.

Ceremonial fires are an important part of ancient Vedic and Hindu rituals. In this ceremony, the fire symbolizes the central fire within the earth, which is also found within us. The spear symbolizes the spear of Durga, which she uses to destroy Mahishasura/the egos—it is the force called Shakti in Hinduism, which is the awakened energy of the divine feminine, also symbolized by the fire.

The red altar cloth symbolizes the color of the earth and underworld, which is the womb of the Spiritual Mother.

The Spiritual Mother is praised as she is traditionally in Hinduism. Lighting incense helps create an atmosphere conducive to the divine, and she is praised nine times to symbolize the nine regions of her underworld realm.

The wording used in steps 4, 5, and 17, is based on the Devimahatmya, which is used in traditional Navratri/Durga Puja celebrations. Feel free to modify it as you wish.

The participants walk around the fire nine times to symbolize the descent through the nine layers of the underworld. They walk in the direction the sun travels across the sky from sunrise to sunset, which is clockwise if in the Northern Hemisphere and facing south, and counter-clockwise if in the Southern Hemisphere and facing north. Dakshine Kali is the name used for the Spiritual Mother, as she is the form of the goddess who is said to face south, the same direction as the sun in its descent across the celestial equator at the autumn equinox (if in the Northern Hemisphere), and the same direction as those descending into the underworld, so that she can save them.

The songs and mantras in step 9 are aimed at putting the participants in touch with the Spiritual Mother and her role.

The flowers offered are like those Rama needed to first offer Durga before she would help him in his battle against the demon king Ravana. They symbolize what we give in return for the Spiritual Mother ridding us of our egos—the repentance, surrender, our self-sacrifice, etc.

Hindu priests tending a heaped pile of flowers that have been offered before a statue of the goddess Durga as part of a Durga Puja ceremony.

The burning of the image/effigy of Mahishasura represents the Spiritual Mother destroying the ego. Sometimes an actual bull is sacrificed in India, however, as explained in chapter 1, the founders and teachers of the Religion of the Sun were profoundly against animal sacrifice, as am I—as it is cruel and unnecessary. The act of making offerings into a fire is an ancient Vedic ritual called yajna, and these offerings can represent one's egos and attachments as described below.

> "The fire represents God or truth. The sacrificial food, the samagri (mixture of seeds, plants, resins, grains, etc.) is offered into the fire. The mixture represents our worldly samskaras such as attachment, greed, violence, etc. that bind us to our lower nature and trap us in egocentric thoughts and desires. We offer the seeds of all future actions into this fire of self-knowledge to be completely consumed. Symbolically we are offering our very lives into the fire of purification and sacrifice. [...] Agni is equally the fire of the sun, of lightning and of the flame that humanity lights for purposes of worship." [7]
>
> ~ SWAMI MUKTANANDA SARASWATI, THE ANCIENT SACRED FIRE OF YAJNA

Burying barley seeds in a clay pot of soil is part of traditional Durga Puja ceremonies. In this ceremony it represents the seeds of each one's individual potential, which are contained in their energies, being buried within matter, with the aim of sprouting the eternal life of the Spiritual Son within.

The lighting of individual lamps represents the consciousness and wisdom gained from the descent into the darkness of one's psyche and subconscious, and the death of the ego.

EXAMPLE SOLITARY OR SMALL GROUP CEREMONY ~ Germanic/Nordic

Statue of Odin/Wotan crowned by the sun. He is one of the foremost gods in Germanic tradition, and is central in this ceremony.

This ceremony is based on a central theme that runs throughout surviving Germanic/Nordic mythology preserved in its primary texts—the Eddas. The author and expert in Old Norse mythology Maria Kvilhaug explains that an ancient path of initiation forms the basis of many of the stories in the Eddas.[8] In particular, this path is said to have first been ventured upon by Odin, one of the most foremost gods of Germanic tradition, and the events he goes through symbolize its stages.[9] The goal of this path was to obtain knowledge and to reach resurrection, immortality, and salvation.[10]

The main events of this path correspond to the major stages on the path of the spiritual sun. In his quest, Odin sacrifices himself and descends into the underworld, just as the sun "dies" and descends into the darkness of the coming winter at the autumn equinox.

After having to pass through many trials, one reached the heart of the underworld where they would bathe or drink from the well/cauldron of the sun goddess, and would be reborn like the sun at the time of greatest darkness, the winter solstice—shining like light.

Odin then resurrects and returns to the world as a great sage and teacher, just as the sun rises from the underworld to shed the dark mortal sheath of winter at the spring equinox.

The final stage was a return/ascent to the three bright heavens of the immortals, that shine like the sun, as an awakened and enlightened being—just as the sun ascends to its pinnacle in the sky at the summer solstice.

The solstices and equinoxes were probably the most important sacred times in ancient Germanic tradition as evidenced in ancient accounts and sacred sites, and so today are the most important ritual times in modern Germanic revivals. With Christianization and the passage of time, their meaning was almost lost... but not completely—as upon close examination echoes of them were preserved in the ancient path of initiation that runs like an undercurrent throughout the Eddas.

> "[...] if one could maintain one's integrity, conquer hatred, fear and emotional turmoil, the quest for knowledge was also a quest that would ultimately lead to immortality and divinity." [11]
>
> ~ MARIA KVILHAUG, THE SEED OF YGGDRASIL

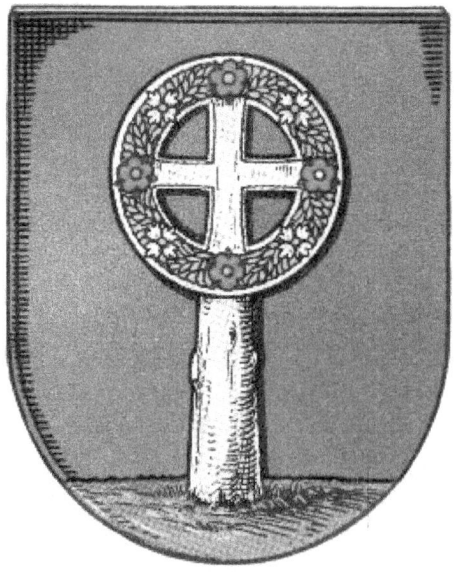

Symbol of the solar cross—one of the most important symbols in Germanic tradition. Its arms correspond to the solstices and equinoxes, and the path of the sun. Here it sits atop the world tree.

THE TIMING OF THE CEREMONY

This ceremony begins before the sunset closest to the autumn equinox in the local time zone.

ITEMS NEEDED

⊕ A statue or image of Odin/Wotan.

⊕ A statue or image of the sacred Yggdrasil tree. Or, you could even use a live tree to represent it.

⊕ As an alternative to the above two items, you could have a statue or image of Odin/Wotan on the world tree.

⊕ Runes within a container of some kind, like a bag or box. There should be a set for each participant.

⊕ A spear—this can be ceremonial and of any size.

⊕ A valknut symbol.

⊕ An empty plate and drinking horn (or cup).

⊕ A jewel, transparent marble, or glass ball—anything that can be used to represent an eye.

Valknut symbol in an ancient stone carving from Gotland, Sweden. It symbolizes the nine worlds described in old Norse texts, and the nine regions of the underworld.

⊕ A candle or ceremonial fire.

⊕ Incense.

⊕ A cauldron (or bowl) made of any natural materials except iron or a part of an animal. This is filled with water.

⊕ A statue of an ancient Germanic/Nordic goddess—ideally Hel or another who is associated with the underworld.

⊕ Symbol of a monstrous/evil looking serpent.

⊕ An ancient style handheld drum.

⊕ Handheld candles for each participant that can be held and carried safely.

THE PARTICIPANTS

Ideally each participant dresses in traditional ancient Germanic garments, wearing Germanic symbols of the sun (as pendants or embroidery, etc.), such as solar crosses and swastikas.

One person can conduct this ceremony, but if you have more than one person, then you'll need to assign roles.

An Asatru priest performing a ceremony in Iceland. Asatru is a name given to the pre-Christian Germanic/Nordic religion.

The Guide/Priest

I suggest that one person have the role of guiding the ceremony. I'll refer to them as the Guide in the ceremony itself. They should be male if possible as they speak as Odin in parts of the ceremony.

Priestess

Ideally a woman would perform the role of priestess in the ceremony, to represent the goddess in the underworld. However, if you don't have a female participating, or not enough people, just replace her with the Guide.

THE SETUP OF THE SACRED SPACE

An Asatru priest performing a ceremony in Iceland. These are often held outdoors in sacred natural locations, as this ceremony is.

The sacred space consists of an altar and seats of some kind for each person, made of natural materials, like tree stumps, rocks, or a mat woven from natural materials, placed before it. The space could also be enclosed within a circle of stones or wood. Directly in front of each seat there should be a container of runes.

The altar should be arranged so that the participants look toward the altar and sunset. However, the altar should not obscure the view of the sunset, so it can be slightly offset if need be.

If you are using a separate representation of the Yggdrasil, then this is placed on the altar. If using an actual tree, then your altar should be set up beneath the tree. If you are using a candle, this is on the altar also. The symbols of the eye, valknut, empty plate, and drinking horn are placed on the altar. The unlit incense is placed before the representation of Odin.

An Asatru priest and priestess in Sweden performing a ceremony at a tree, as this ceremony can be.

If you are using a ceremonial fire, it should be in front of the participants, and ideally align with the sunset.

The spear will be placed upright either on or beside the altar (depending on the size of the spear you use), so there should be some way to do this ready within the sacred space, for example, using a holder/bracket, or standing it in a hole in the ground.

The cauldron is placed on the ground by the altar (and is filled with water), and next to it the statue of the goddess and the representation of the serpent.

If you are doing the ceremony alone, the drum should be within the sacred space. Otherwise, it is brought to the sacred space during the procession to it.

INSTRUCTIONS FOR THE CEREMONY

1. The sacred space is ready. The sacred space has been prepared in advance and is ready. The ceremonial fire/candle is not lit as lighting it is part of the ceremony, but everything needed to light it, and for it to burn throughout the ceremony, should be ready within the sacred space.

2. Bringing of Odin to the sacred space. Each participant stands at a distance from the sacred space and holds an unlit handheld candle. The Guide holds the representation of Odin in their left arm, and the spear in their right. They'll need to carry their unlit candle in a bag or pouch they wear.

The Guide signals that the ceremony will now begin. They say:

> "I/we honor the path that Odin showed, from self-sacrifice to knowledge and the light of wisdom."

The Guide walks in front and the rest of the participants walk slowly and purposefully in single file behind them in silence to the sacred space (ideally in a westerly direction to symbolize walking the path of the sun).

If you have more than one person, then one of the participants could carry and beat the drum during the procession to the sacred space. If you have enough people, this procession could be quite powerful—with everyone holding unlit torches instead, and singing or playing Norse/Germanic music that is relevant to the occasion.

3. Placing of the spear and Odin. The Guide stands by the altar. The rest of the participants take their seats, and place their unlit candle on the ground in front of them. The Guide places the spear upright, either upon or beside the altar. They place the representation of Odin on the altar, facing the participants.

4. Invocation of Odin. The Guide says:

> "Hail Odin [or Wuotan, Woden, Wotan, etc., depending on your specific tradition], You who search for wisdom neverending, enduring every trial for its sake and ours. Lead us, show us, empower us on our journey for truth, light, and wisdom."

The Guide pronounces the following names of Odin, and any other participants repeat each name after them. These names are in Old Norse, but you could alternatively pronounce them in Old High German, or English, etc. The English translation of each name appears next to each name, but these are not said in this version.

"Aldaföðr" (Father of men/the age/world)
"Hávi" (High One)
"Forni" (Ancient One)
"Gangari" (Wanderer or Wayweary)
"Hleifruðr" (Wayfinder)
"Farmagnuðr" (Journey empowerer)
"Sanngetall" (Finder of Truth)
"Vakr" (Wakeful, Awakener)
"Hroptr" (Sage) [12]

5. Lighting the incense. The Guide lights the incense—there should be enough for it to burn throughout the ceremony.

6. Pointing of the spear. The Guide picks up the spear and points it at the representation of Odin.

7. Reading from *Hávamál* (the Sayings of the High One). The Guide reads from *Hávamál*:

> "I know that I hung on a windy tree
> nine long nights,
> wounded with a spear, dedicated to Odin,
> myself to myself,
> on that tree of which no man knows
> from where its roots run.
> No bread did they give me nor a drink from a horn,
> downwards I peered;
> I took up the runes, screaming I took them,
> then I fell back from there." [13]

The Guide puts the spear back in its place and is seated.

8. Watching the sunset and chanting runes. All participants watch the sunset. This can be done in silence, or while chanting the names of relevant runes, such as Uruz, Ansuz, Nauthiz, Eihwaz, and Kenaz, or while singing or playing music relevant to the event.

9. Symbolic yelling. Immediately after the sun has fully set, the Guide stands and picks up the runes (still in their container) from the altar, holds them above their head, and shouts (or says loudly) as if in pain:

"Hagalaz!"

The Guide then puts the container of runes back on the altar and is seated.

10. Reading from *Völuspá*. The Priestess says:

> "A hall I saw,
> far from the sun,
>
> On Nastrond it stands,
> and the doors face north,
>
> Venom drops
> through the smoke-vent down,
>
> For around the walls
> do serpents wind.
>
> I there saw wading
> through rivers wild
> treacherous men
> and murderers too,
>
> And workers of ill
> with the wives of men;
>
> There Nithhogg sucked
> the blood of the slain,
>
> And the wolf tore men;
> would you know yet more?" [14]

11. Nine sounds of the drum. The Priestess, or one of the other participants, makes nine sounds on the drum.

12. Lighting of the fire. The Priestess lights the candle on the altar or the ceremonial fire.

13. Further reading from *Hávamál*. The Priestess says:

> "Knowledge you must find, meaningful knowledge,
> a very great knowledge,
> a very powerful knowledge,
>
> Which the mighty sage stained
>
> And the powerful gods made
>
> And Odin carved out." [15]

14. Opening of the runes. The Guide opens the container of runes on the altar and lays them out. The other participants open their containers of runes but without taking the runes out.

15. The eye in the well. The Guide takes the representation of the eye from the altar, and says:

> "In the depths of the underworld, at the root of the Great Tree Yggdrasill lies Mimir's Well, wherein all wisdom and understanding are stored; it fills those who drink from it with ancient lore. Odin's eye is hidden deep within it, for he laid it there as a pledge to take a drink. Would you know yet more?" [16]

The Guide places the symbolic eye within the cauldron of water, and is then seated.

16. Pointing the spear. The Priestess picks up the spear and points it at each participant (in a nonthreatening/nonmenacing way) while saying the following lines, pointing at the representation of the serpent at the last line. If there are many participants, she points it toward them all generally. If on your own, hold the spear upright and point it at the serpent at the last line.

> "Do you know how to ask?
> Do you know how to search?
> Do you know how to see?
> Do you know how to understand?
> Do you know how to endure the trials?
> Do you know how to give?
> Do you know how to self-sacrifice?
> Do you know how to kill the ego?" [17]

The Priestess puts the spear back in its place.

17. Candles are lit. The Priestess lights each participant's handheld candle from the ceremonial fire or candle on the altar.

18. Chants, songs, readings, music. This can be a time of doing any of these that are relevant to the event.

19. Thanking Odin and ceremony closure. The Guide closes the ceremony by saying something like:

> "Hail to you Odin, Journey Master, for your guidance, wisdom, and inspiration. Hail."

All participants repeat, *"Hail."*

20. Putting out the incense. The Guide extinguishes the incense.

21. Leaving with candles and runes. The Guide takes up their lit handheld candle and runes, as then do all participants. The Guide leaves the sacred space and all other participants follow behind them. The ceremony has ended.

After the ceremony people could gather around a fire, sing songs/chants, or do further readings. Any activities should conclude before midnight.

THE MEANING OF THE CEREMONY

The procession to the sacred space represents walking the path of the sun. The events Odin goes through in his quest for knowledge represents this path, which is why he is carried to the sacred space as if walking with his spear upon it.

All participants walk with an unlit candle to show how they are in the darkness of ignorance—without knowledge or the light of awakened consciousness. This knowledge is yet to be gained from the descent into darkness.

Odin is invoked as he is an awakened Being that exists in higher dimensions who can be called upon. He is called using nine of his names (he was known by many), as nine is a number closely associated with him in Norse texts. Incense is lit to signify his presence.

Illustration of Odin sacrificing himself on his own spear while hanging on the sacred world tree Yggdrasil.

The description of Odin's self-sacrifice from the Old Norse poem called *Hávamál* is read. The spear is pointed at the statue of Odin to enact Odin sacrificing himself on his own spear. It symbolizes how one needs to sacrifice their own lower self in order to reunite with their higher/inner spiritual Being.

Note that this is a self-sacrifice, not a human sacrifice—although it became used as a method of sacrificing people to Odin in ancient times. This is a complete misinterpretation of what was obviously symbolic of an inner, spiritual death and journey, in the same way Jesus' death on the cross is seen as an act of self-sacrifice by Christians, and symbolic death and descent into the underworld was part of ancient initiatory mysteries that flourished in Egypt and Greece.

The empty plate and drinking horn on the altar represent how Odin is given no bread or drink from a horn. This symbolizes the voluntary hardships someone has to put themselves through in life in order to gain knowledge. The bread and drink can also symbolize the substance and energies of the Spiritual Son that nourish us spiritually, and which ultimately sustain life. They are absent because they are withdrawn from the person at this stage on the path, just as the powers of the sun diminish at the autumn equinox, so that they can be tested.

An Asatru altar.

The runes Uruz, Ansuz, Nauthiz, Eihwaz, and Kenaz are chanted. Uruz is associated with the primal being whose body was used to make creation, and also the primeval void from where creation manifested.[18] Ansuz is the rune associated with Odin.[19] Nauthiz means "need"—the old Norwegian Rune Poem associated it with a man in distress. It's known as "a rune of hardship, of stress and challenge that provides growth and evolution," in which "times of hardship are necessary in order to face ourselves, our mistakes and weaknesses."[20] Eihwaz means "yew tree"—it is often associated with the Yggdrasil tree that Odin sacrificed himself on, and with death and traveling to the underworld. In the Anglo-Saxon Rune poem it was called "the guardian of flame,"

Ancient carvings of runes on a stone in Sweden.

the flame possibly symbolizing knowledge.[21] Kenaz in Old Saxon sources means "torch," and may be related to the High German word "kennen," which means "to know"[22]—again associating fire with knowledge, which is what fire is used to symbolize in this ceremony. Chanting these runes signifies the journey Odin portrayed—from nonbeing, chaos, and need, through self-sacrifice and descent into the underworld/subconscious, to reach the light of knowledge and awakened consciousness.

The Guide yells "Hagalaz" as he holds up the runes to symbolize Odin's screaming as he takes up the runes. This yelling represents the pain of having to face opposition and one's egos in order to obtain the knowledge of oneself, and all the inner turmoil this causes within one's psyche. This inner turmoil is like the chaos of creation and the underworld. Hagalaz is the rune known as "hail"; it symbolizes the destructive powers of nature and is associated with Hel/the underworld,[23] where the destructive forces of nature, such as death, are most potent—as the old and inferior must be destroyed before the new and superior can be born. Hagalaz is pronounced just after the sun sets to signify the descent into the underworld.

The Priestess speaks as the Spiritual Mother who is symbolized by the statue of the goddess. Her realm is the underworld (as it is in Norse tradition), as it is her womb. The cauldron also symbolizes her womb, and the wells that exist in the underworld in ancient Norse texts. These wells are the Well of Memory, the Well of Hel, and the Well of Origin. While hanging on Yggdrasil, Odin receives three gifts, which indicates he peers downward into each of these wells.[24] Essentially, these wells are one, revealing three different functions of the underworld, and the womb of the Spiritual Mother.

Odin depicted with one eye, as he sacrificed one into the Well of Memory in order to obtain knowledge.

The Well of Memory is where all the memories of the universe are stored[25]—meaning that it's essentially a store of all experience and thus knowledge, just as our psyche (both conscious and subconscious) is. In mythology, Odin sacrifices one of his eyes into this well in order to obtain a drink from it—illustrating how this knowledge is gained not through worldly vision, but through an inner perception, by looking within oneself, into one's psyche and subconscious, right to its very root. The Guide placing the symbol of the eye in the cauldron during the ceremony represents this.

The Well of Hel is where the souls of the dead are ground into oblivion before joining the streams of life that return them to the world renewed and cleansed.[26] The runes are found by the Well of Origin, "where the secrets of life and fate may be revealed"[27] by the goddess who teaches there; those who bathe in it are said to emerge "bright, shining and transparent – much like a 'light being'"[28] and the immortal light elves (which are those that have attained enlightenment),[29] symbolic of spiritual resurrection.

In this ceremony, the goddess is by the cauldron—symbol of the wells of the underworld. It's later, at the spring equinox, that someone symbolically bathes in the cauldron, to resurrect.

The goddess and cauldron represent central components of Norse initiation ritual, as those who descended into the underworld, and passed the trials put to them, would be given a drink by a priestess from a cauldron in the very heart of the underworld.[30] This initiation ritual was symbolic of the initiations that occur in other dimensions out of the body, and the inner, spiritual transformation someone goes through as a result.

The Priestess reads from *Völuspá*, an Old Norse poem, in which a seeress answers Odin in his quest for knowledge. She describes Hel to him.

The goddess Hel in the underworld. Here she is illustrated at the roots of the world tree, beside her a serpent and bowl, as in this ceremony.

Odin questioning the seeress/volva, as described in *Völuspá*.

The nine beats on the drum symbolizes the nine regions/worlds of the underworld, corresponding to the nine nights Odin hung for, symbolizing the descent through these regions and passing through nine initiations—to reach the runes (the knowledge) carved into the very roots of the world tree. The valknut is another symbol of these nine regions and initiations.

The Priestess lights the candle/fire symbolizing the knowledge and consciousness extracted from the descent into the underworld/subconscious.

Runes are remnants of a very ancient system of writing that probably originated at least thousands of years ago—being used by the ancient megalith builders that inhabited the Mediterranean, North Africa, and Western Europe.[31] The Phoenician alphabet is another remnant of it, from which the modern English alphabet derives. Each letter signifies some principle of creation. Thus in ancient Germanic tradition they represent far more than just letters themselves—but the very knowledge of the forces and principles of creation. In this ceremony, the runes are used to symbolize this knowledge—which not only relates to the outside world, but also to ourselves.

Runes laid out around a ceremonial fire.

The Priestess takes up the spear as the Spiritual Mother is ultimately the one who has the power to destroy our egos. She questions the participants, as in Norse initiation rituals one was often questioned to prove their knowledge.[32] It symbolizes the initiations that take place in the higher dimensions for those who are worthy, and the trials one must face against one's egos, such as hatred, fear, greed, and rage, which were central to Norse initiation.[33] The words she repeats are based on Hávamál, but have been modified so that they are more clearly meaningful.

She finally points the spear at the serpent; in this ceremony it symbolizes the ego that must die/be destroyed before one can obtain knowledge, greater consciousness, and reach to the birth of the spiritual sun within and resurrection. In an Old English/Anglo-Saxon charm, called the "Nine Herbs Charm," Woden (Odin) is said to have used nine herbs to smite a venomous serpent,[34] and in an Old Norse text he throws a monstrous serpent into the ocean.[35] And so the serpent in this ceremony symbolizes the forces of evil and the ego, which Odin fights against.

A serpent formed an important part of Norse initiation ritual. It guarded the gold of divine wisdom in the underworld, and had to be slain to obtain it.[36] It's referred to as the dragon Nithhogg in the ceremony, which corresponds to the dragon/serpent that formed a central part of initiations in the ancient world as I explained in chapter 2. This serpent/dragon became the treasure guarding dragon, and the dragon slain by the hero to free the damsel in distress (symbolizing the ego that is destroyed to free consciousness as explained in chapter 3) in European mythology.

These mysteries were also practiced in ancient Egypt:

> "Behold the serpent it sleeps at the bole of a tree from which hangs the body of man, the tree of his backbone. It is on guard, safeguarding the precious gem of spiritual powers, which lies enwrapped in the threefold covering. To obtain the gem the serpent must be aroused and then overcome." [37]
> ~ THE SACRED REGISTERS - PART 9, THE KOLBRIN

However, the Spiritual Mother is also often symbolized as a serpent, as serpents have been used to represent many things. In the Religion of the Sun there are two types of symbolic serpents—ascending serpents, which represent the risen kundalini, and descending serpents, which represent its opposite, and have been symbolized as the tails of demons. The energy of the Spiritual Mother (symbolized as a serpent), can be used to create either. And so in this ceremony, the monstrous/evil serpent symbolizes the ego and the tail of the demon that descends into the underworld, and which needs to be killed and cut off for someone to spiritually ascend and progress.

Illustration of Odin beneath a tree with carvings of runes.

The Priestess lights the candles of each participant, signifying the light of consciousness and knowledge obtained once the ego is killed. It takes the symbolic place of divine gold, and the sleeping solar goddess who needed to be awakened (who could represent consciousness and the kundalini) in Norse initiation.[38]

All leave with runes and their candle lit to symbolize what they have gained from the descent into darkness.

EXAMPLE GROUP CEREMONY ~ Minoan/Greek

Here is an example of a ceremony based on the Minoan tradition. The Minoans were an ancient civilization on the island of Crete that flourished between around 2,700 BC to 1,450 BC.[39] They aligned a number of their sacred sites to the autumn equinox, and held the sun as supremely spiritually significant.

THE TIMING OF THE CEREMONY

This ceremony begins before the sunset closest to the autumn equinox in the local time zone.

ITEMS NEEDED

⊕ A sword.

⊕ A labrys (the ancient Minoan/Greek symbol of the double-headed axe).

⊕ A long red thread made of natural fibers.

⊕ Minotaur mask that can be ceremonially burned in fire. It can be made of straw, wood, paper, or cardboard, etc.

⊕ The symbol of a double spiral on the end of a pole that can be stood upright in the ground.

⊕ A candle or torch that can be carried and held safely.

⊕ One or a number of handheld drums.

⊕ An outfit of the Greek mythological hero Theseus.

⊕ An outfit of the Greek mythological princess Ariadne.

⊕ An outfit of the Greek mythological figure the Minotaur (which also consists of a Minotaur mask; it is not burnt but worn by the person playing the role of the Minotaur for the duration of the ceremony).

An ancient Minoan artifact decorated with the double spiral, which is a symbol of the equinox. Spirals were used frequently in Minoan artwork.

THE SETUP OF THE SACRED CIRCLE

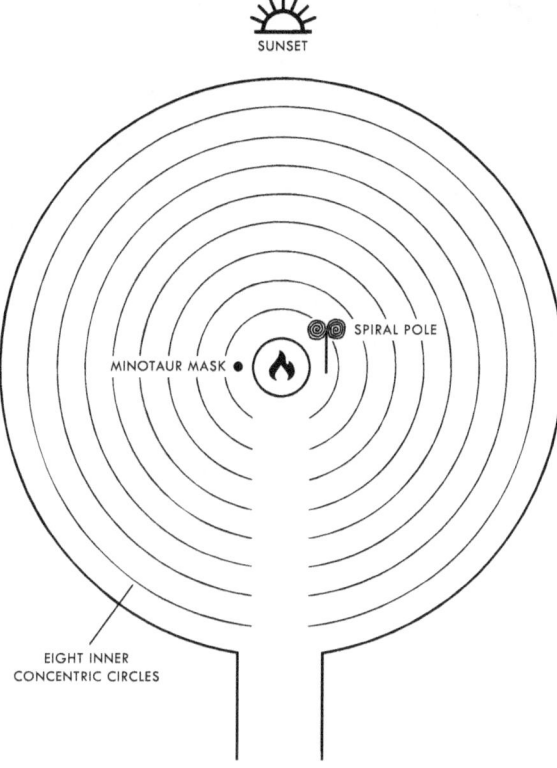

The ceremony takes place in a sacred circle from where you can see the setting sun, with a place for a fire in the middle.

Before the ceremony, the symbol of the double spiral on a pole should be stood up in the ground near the fire, facing toward the participants. The Minotaur mask is placed next to the fire.

The inside of the circle represents the labyrinth and underworld. There should be one entrance to the circle and it should align with the sunset on the equinox—being built on the eastern side of the circle, so that when someone enters the circle they walk toward the direction of west.

The nine regions of the underworld also need to be symbolized in some way. Ideally, if you have a big enough outdoor space, you could create a large sacred circle and mark out eight concentric circles inside it, making the center where the fire is the ninth. You could do this by pegging a string of natural fibers into the ground, by laying out stones, or by using sand sprinkled in circles, etc. Just make sure that however you do it, you leave a walkway from the edge of the sacred circle, through the concentric circles, to the area where the fire is, so that Theseus, the Spiritual Mother, and Minotaur can walk to the bonfire without tripping on anything. If you don't have enough space, you can symbolize the nine layers another way, by stacking nine smooth stones upon each other on the ground by the fire, for example.

A mosaic of the Minoan labyrinth with Theseus slaying the Minotaur at the center dating to the second century AD, located at the ancient site of Paphos in Cyprus. This depiction is used to create the layered sacred circle in the ceremony, representing the regions of the underworld. This mosaic also has eight concentric passageways with a center at the ninth, just as the ceremonial circle does.

THE PARTICIPANTS

Theseus

A man plays the role of Theseus and dresses as he is portrayed in ancient artwork. He carries a sword in his right hand and an unlit candle or torch in his left that can be held safely once lit. He can wear a symbol of the sun from any ancient Greek tradition.

Ariadne

A woman plays the role of Ariadne. She is dressed in red as a traditional Cretan princess, making sure she is dressed in a dignified way (with her chest and legs fully covered). She holds the red thread.

Left: Ancient Greek pottery depicting Theseus slaying the Minotaur. Right: An ancient mosaic of Ariadne.

The Minotaur
A man plays the role of the Minotaur. He dresses in red, and wears a minotaur mask/headdress of a bull.

The Spiritual Mother
A woman plays the role of the Spiritual Mother (and Mistress of the Labyrinth). She is dressed in a traditional Cretan/Greek dress, which is the color red (the same color as Adriane and the Minotaur), making sure she is dressed in a dignified way (with her chest and legs fully covered). She holds the labrys and wears a crown.

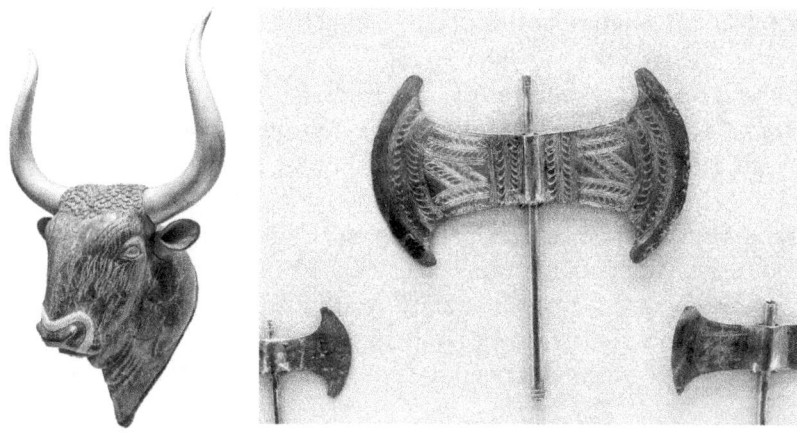

Left: An ancient Minoan rhyton (drinking vessel), which would have been used in ceremonies, housed in a museum in Crete. Right: An ancient ceremonial Minoan labrys.

Seven Men and Seven Women
Ideally seven men and seven women would take these roles, making a total of fourteen people, but because this is impractical for most, the next best option is to just have a mix of seven men and women in total. Another option is to just have one person play the role, dressed with a seven rayed sun symbol. They dress in traditional Cretan/Greek robes colored golden yellow or gold.

General Participants
All the remaining participants dress in traditional Cretan/Greek robes colored white.

Drummers
At least one of the General Participants carries a handheld drum which they will play during the ceremony.

Priest
A man will conduct the ceremony. They dress in white traditional Cretan/Greek robes, but so they are discernable from the General Participants.

INSTRUCTIONS FOR THE CEREMONY

1. The sacred space is ready and all participants take their positions. The fire in the center of the circle should be lit and have enough wood/fuel to burn throughout the entire ceremony. The symbol of the double spiral and the Minotaur mask should be by the fire. The Spiritual Mother stands by the fire, facing the sunset (so her back is to everyone else). The Minotaur stands inside the circle at a distance from the fire, facing Ariadne and Theseus. Theseus and Ariadne stand at a distance from the sacred circle, facing the setting sun, with Ariadne on the left of Theseus. The Seven Men and Women stand behind Ariadne and Theseus, and the General Participants behind them. The Priest stands in front of Ariadne and Theseus, facing the General Participants.

2. The Priest opens the ceremony. The Priest says "*This autumn equinox rite now begins,*" to signal the beginning of the ceremony. He can also sound an instrument. He then says,

> "King Minos has decreed that seven men and seven maidens shall be fed to the Minotaur. It is the King's will that you be tested and found worthy. To save them and yourself, you must face your own inner darkness and destroy the beast that lives within you. Only like this can you gain gnosis and pneuma."

3. Procession to the sacred space. The Drummer(s) begin beating a solemn beat, and the General Participants begin chanting/singing a relevant traditional Greek song. The Priest turns around and walks toward the circle, followed by Ariadne and Theseus who walk together behind him, and then the Seven Men and Maidens, followed by the General Participants—all walking in procession.

4. All take their positions at the sacred space. The Priest walks to the entrance of the sacred circle, stops and turns to face the General Participants. He stands on the right side of the entrance when facing toward the circle. Adriane and Theseus walk to the entrance and stand before the Priest. The General Participants stand outside the circle facing the sunset, positioned so that everyone can see the ceremony taking place inside the circle, as do the Seven Men and Women, but slightly apart from them. However, if you have a big enough sacred circle, then the Seven Men and Women, and all the General Participants, can follow behind Adriane and Theseus, and continue following Theseus for the remainder of the ceremony.

5. Invocation of the Spiritual Mother. The Priest signals for the drumming and chanting to stop. Everyone goes silent.

The Priest says:

> "Mistress of the Labyrinth,
> She of the golden double-axe,[40]
> Holy goddess,
> Lovely delightful queen,
> Universal mother,
> From whom both men and Gods immortal came,
> All-bounteous,
> Prolific,
> Venerable,
> Blessed and divine,
> In verdure flourishing, in glory bright, bearing light,[41]
> Come, O Lady resplendent with gifts.[42]
> Come, much invoked, and to these rites inclined,
> Thy mystic suppliant bless, with favoring mind.[43]
> Hail goddess! Keep us safe, and govern this rite.[44]
> Matere teija."

The General Participants repeat after him, "*Matere teija.*"

The Priest again says, "*Matere teija,*" and the General Participants repeat after him again, so that this is done a total of nine times. Once the nine times are complete, the Spiritual Mother turns to face everyone.

6. Ariadne sends Theseus on his quest. Adriane turns and says to Theseus, "*The light shines in darkness. Go into the darkness and bring back light.*" She attaches one end of the thread to Theseus' garment, and holds the other.

7. Theseus is called to descend. The Priest says, "*It is time to descend,*" to which Theseus raises his sword.

8. Singing/chanting. While waiting for the sun to begin setting, the Priest begins chanting or singing a traditional song relevant to the occasion, and the General Participants join in.

9. The descent into the underworld is enacted. As soon as the sun begins to set (which is as soon as any part of the sun becomes obscured by any terrestrial object) the Priest signals for the chanting to stop and says, "*I descend.*"

And the General Participants repeat after him, "*I descend.*" The Drummers play one beat, and Theseus walks through one layer of the circle (in a straight line to the central fire) or takes one step (depending on how big the circle is), with Adriane unravelling the thread as he goes. All this is done a total of nine times, until Theseus stands at the center of the circle, next to the Spiritual Mother, facing the sunset and the Minotaur. As the drums beat, the Minotaur moves and sways menacingly.

10. The Minotaur mask is displayed. The Spiritual Mother picks up, and holds up the Minotaur mask.

11. Petitions are made to the Spiritual Mother. The Priest says, "*Matere teija, destroy it.*" All the participants (except the Priest, Minotaur, and Spiritual Mother) repeat, "*Matere teija, destroy it.*" This is done three times.

> The Priest says,
>> "Be gracious, O thrice-prayed for, great Queen of goddesses!" [45]

12. The Minotaur mask is burned. The Spiritual Mother throws the Minotaur mask into the fire. The Spiritual Mother says, "*Death to the beast... life to the sun.*" All watch until the mask finishes burning.

13. Lighting of Theseus' candle/torch. The Spiritual Mother turns to Theseus and lights his candle/torch from the fire.

14. Theseus leaves the labyrinth and returns to Ariadne. Theseus turns and walks out of the circle, holding his sword, and lit candle/torch. Ariadne collects the slack of the thread until the two meet.

15. All watch the sunset, with chants, songs, and readings. All watch the sun completely set if it hasn't already, or its afterglow fade. There could be readings done from sacred texts, chants, songs, and music relevant to the occasion.

16. Thanks given to the Spiritual Mother. Once the sun has fully set and the readings have finished, the Priest says,

> "Matere teija,
>> Nurse of all mortals,
>> All flowers are thine,
>> And fruits of lovely green.
>> Earthly, pure, and divine.[46]
>> Hail goddess!"

The participants repeat, "*Hail goddess!*"

17. Ceremony ending. The Priest begins walking away from the ceremonial area. Theseus and Ariadne follow, the Seven Men and Maidens follow them, and then the General Participants. Finally the Minotaur leaves the circle followed by the Spiritual Mother, who follows behind everyone else. Once everyone has left the ceremonial area, the ceremony has ended.

After the ceremony people could gather around a fire, sing songs/chants, or do further readings. Any activities should conclude before midnight.

THE MEANING OF THE CEREMONY

Every stage on the path of the spiritual sun begins with a descent into one's inner darkness and underworld, as to ascend spiritually, we must first descend.

The ceremony symbolizes the descent into one's psychological inner darkness in order to destroy the egos, and to extract the light of knowledge and consciousness. This psychological descent is accompanied by hardship, suffering, and facing opposition in one's life, as this is how we learn and are tested along the path of the spiritual sun.

Many of the items and elements used in this ceremony are evidenced as being used in ancient Minoan rituals.

Painting of a procession during the ancient Greek religious festival called the Thesmophoria, which was held around the autumn equinox.

Processions were part of Minoan ritual, which is why this ceremony begins with one.[47] A solemn processional march was also held at the start of Eleusinian rites in Greece.[48]

In the legend of the Minotaur, King Minos orders seven young men and seven young women to be fed to the Minotaur every nine years; Theseus then sets out to save them. These men and women represent the seven solar bodies (male) and the kundalini risen in each (female) that the walker of the path has created within themselves in preparation for the birth of the Spiritual Son at the winter solstice.

Theseus represents the walker of the path of the spiritual sun. He is dressed as a warrior because he fights psychologically against the egos he carries within. The sword represents his willpower to defeat evil and control his sexual energy.

Ariadne partly represents the Spiritual Mother. In the legend of the Minotaur, it is her thread that allows Theseus to find his way back out of the Labyrinth. In the ceremony, it represents the connection each person has to their Spiritual Mother.

The Spiritual Mother in the ceremony represents the Mother of each one's higher Being who helps us on the path of the spiritual sun. She is within the sacred circle as it represents her womb—the underworld. The labrys she holds symbolizes the equinox—and the rotation from its central axis to either ascend or descend spiritually. They were used ceremonially by priestesses in Minoan rituals. This is also symbolized by the double spiral at the center of the sacred circle, which is another symbol used by the Minoans.

The red color the Spiritual Mother wears represents the sexual energies of a person that are lustful, and thus which all the egos feed from, which is why in the ceremony the Minotaur wears the same red color as the Mother. The red is the color of the womb, of the earth, and the infra-red light of the underworld. Incredibly, it's the energies of the Spiritual Mother that are used to create the egos. These egos are needed for us to be able to acquire the knowledge of both darkness and of light; it's in overcoming the darkness of the egos that we gain knowledge and consciousness, which is light. The energies of the Mother in their lower aspect are ultimately behind the egos, sexual desire, and the underworld, which is why she is referred to as "Maya" by the Hindus, meaning "illusion." However, because her energies create "Maya," she also has the power to free us from it, as symbolized by warrior goddesses in remnants of the Religion of the Sun. The Mother carries a weapon because she destroys our egos. Thus she provides the means for our own salvation by providing the world of darkness, matter, and the egos, which we go into as our place of learning, and then by liberating us from it through her ability to transform our inner energies and destroy our egos. The ceremonial fire is the inner sexual fire in which the egos are destroyed.

The words "Matere teija" were found on ancient Minoan artifacts—it means "Divine Mother."[49] It is used to call upon the Spiritual Mother who destroys the egos. The Divine/Spiritual Mother was worshiped in Minoan rituals. The wording used to praise and invoke her is based on ancient hymns to the goddess Demeter, such as the Homeric and Orphic hymns, some of which were used in the Eleusinian and Orphic Mysteries. Demeter was the goddess central to the Eleusinian Mysteries in Greece, which had been established by Minoans, and thus Demeter is likely a later embodiment of the Minoan Divine Mother.[50]

An ancient tablet inscribed in the Minoan language known as "Linear B."

The circle is divided into nine regions because there are nine regions of the underworld, and Theseus descends through them to reach the center, which is the location of the central fire both within the earth and within each person.

The symbolic underworld of the Minoans was said to be inhabited by the Minotaur, which was a mythological beast that was half man and half bull; this is symbolic of the person turned into an animalistic beast by the egos. The bull or buffalo is often used as a symbol of the ego. The Hindus also used it in this way, as the Hindu mother goddess Durga wages her symbolic war against the buffalo demon. Our egos inhabit our psychological underworld, which is why the labyrinth is the symbolic abode of the Minotaur.

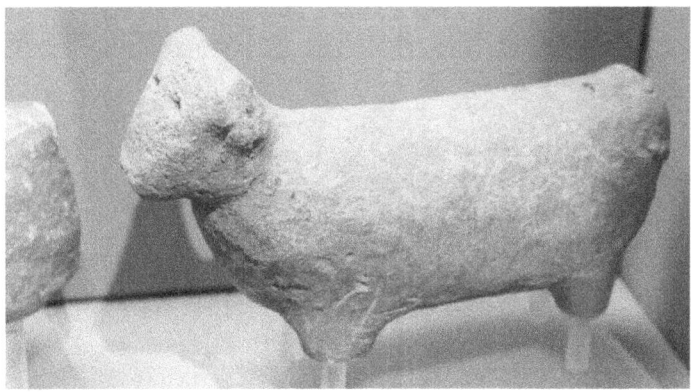

This is an actual Minoan bull effigy that was used as an offering in their rituals. I've used a Minatour mask in the ceremony instead because an animal effigy is getting too close to animal sacrifice and may become a stepping stone to that awful practice for some people.

Bull masks were used in ancient Minoan ceremonies. Bulls were also sacrificed in their rituals.[51] As explained in chapter 1, the founders and teachers of the Religion of the Sun were profoundly against animal sacrifice, as am I, and so a Minotaur/bull mask is used in this ceremony instead. Offering the bull mask into the fire symbolizes the death of the Minotaur and destroying the egos, as the bull is a symbol of the egos. The Spiritual Mother is the one who throws it into the fire, symbolizing how it is she who destroys them.

Theseus enters the circle with his candle/torch unlit, because the walker of the path descends in darkness. The Spiritual Mother lights Theseus's candle/torch in the ceremony because she is the one who releases our consciousness from the egos. The lighting of the candle/torch is symbolic of Theseus gaining knowledge from the depths of the underworld (and psyche).

Song and prayer form part of the ceremony as these were used in Minoan rituals to facilitate communion with the divine.[52]

Winter Solstice

CHAPTER FOURTEEN

Ceremonies to Celebrate the Winter Solstice

This chapter outlines ceremonies for celebrating the winter solstice, both for people on their own and in a group. I've included an example ceremony, as well as a basic outline of the principles involved for those who'd like to construct their own ceremony or who are already working within an existing tradition.

CEREMONY OVERVIEW

Left: The newborn Jesus. Center: Ancient sculpture of Mithras being born from the cosmic egg. Right: Modern illustration of the Celtic trinity of Father (sun), Mother (moon/earth), and their baby Son (or "Son of the Sun").

A winter solstice ceremony essentially celebrates the birth of the Spiritual Son into creation, and the potential each one has for their own Spiritual Son to be born within them.

It symbolizes how masculine and feminine, Father and Mother, create the Spiritual Son—the divine child—on both a macrocosmic (cosmic) and microcosmic (individual) scale. Just as the sun appears to be born out of the darkness of winter, so the light of the sun manifests from out of the dark, primordial chaos of creation, and within the darkness of the human psyche.

There are accounts of winter solstice ceremonies that portrayed this, which were derived from the Religion of the Sun and were practiced across parts of the ancient world—in ancient Egypt, Eleusis in Greece, in Rome, and in Jordan.

All of them, including the celebration of the birth of Jesus, symbolically enact the birth of the Spiritual Son from the dark womb of the Spiritual Mother.

The mood of this ceremony is one of reverence and joy, as they celebrate the birth of the divine savior.

A GUIDE TO CREATING A WINTER SOLSTICE CEREMONY

Whether you are a solitary practitioner or working with a group of people, this guide will help you to create your own ceremony, or to expand upon or modify the historical remnants of an existing traditional ceremony:

PREPARING FOR YOUR CEREMONY

To start with, I recommend reading the chapters "The Spiritual Meaning of the Winter Solstice" and "A Guide to Celebrating the Solstices and Equinoxes," as these provide some important background information.

Here is a guide to what information I recommend you gather together first, before creating your ceremony:

1. Winter solstice traditions (optional). This step is optional—it's if you'd like to do a ceremony according to your tradition.

I recommend doing some research to find out how the winter solstice was celebrated in your culture (as long as it is connected in some way to the ancient Religion of the Sun). This is not always easy as so many records of the past have been lost or destroyed. If you can't find much, I recommend looking for anything in your tradition that is relevant to the profound meaning of the winter solstice. This could include ancient sites that are aligned to it, and symbols and stories that are relevant to it.

See if there is anything you would like to incorporate into your ceremony.

2. Symbols of the winter solstice. It's nice to use and wear actual symbols of the solstice in your ceremony, just as ancient peoples did. Look for any symbols of the winter solstice you can find in your tradition. A common symbol of the winter solstice is the spiral, but any symbol of the sun is relevant to the winter solstice, such as the solar disk, the winged sun disk, the solar cross, swastika, and many others. Particularly relevant is the symbol of the sun held between the cow horns of the goddess Hathor, and the two mountains of the horizon, found in ancient Egypt.

Work out how to incorporate these symbols into your ceremony. For example, you could wear a pendant of the symbol, or have a representation of it on an altar, or make it part of your sacred ceremonial space by creating it out of stones on the ground, etc.

3. The Spiritual Son. Choose what will represent the Spiritual Son in your ceremony. The winter solstice sun represents the birth of the Spiritual Son as it rises, so you may choose to have nothing else representing the Spiritual Son but the sun itself.

For those of you who would like to do a ceremony according to your tradition, you may also want to symbolize the Spiritual Son using a deity from your tradition. Typically, these figures are associated with the sun, and their life events mirror the sun's path and major stages. There are many examples given in this book—Horus in ancient Egypt, Mithra in Iran (later Mithras in Rome), Hu Gadarn and the Mabyn Taliesin of the Druids, Jesus, Inti of the Inca, Kolyada of the Slavs, Baldr of the Germanics/Nordics, and Krishna of the Hindus. The event of their birth is the central part of the ceremony.

Decide how this central figure will be represented in your ceremony. You could have a statue, painting, or symbol of them on an altar or somewhere in your sacred space. If you are doing a larger group ceremony, then someone could dress as and represent this figure.

4. Birth of the Spiritual Son (optional). This step is optional—it's if you'd like to do a ceremony according to your tradition.

Look at the symbolism surrounding the birth of the Spiritual Son in your tradition. To find these symbols, you could look at mythology, sacred texts, as well as the design of sacred sites in your tradition that are aligned to the winter solstice sunrise. For example, often both a father sky god and a mother earth goddess are present as parents of the sun. Symbols you could look to include are:

    a. The womb of the Spiritual Mother.

    b. The Spiritual Mother Goddess.

    c. The Spiritual Father God.

    d. Fire, representing the divine fire of the sun.

Work out how you would like to incorporate these symbols into your ceremony and/or sacred space. For example, you might like to symbolize the womb of the divine feminine as a sacred circle, a bowl or cauldron of water, a cave, symbol of a turtle, or even just the earth itself, depending on the tradition.

Because the winter solstice is to do with creation, I highly recommend having symbols of each of the three fundamental forces of creation present—of Father, Mother, and Son. These could go on your ceremonial altar or form part of your sacred space. If you have a group doing the ceremony, then three people could dress as and represent them.

5. Chants, mantras, songs, prayers, readings, music, etc. As part of your ceremony you could choose to read from sacred texts, or sing songs, etc. These could be traditional songs that are part of winter solstice celebrations, excerpts from sacred texts that are relevant to the meaning of the winter solstice, chants that convey the meaning of the winter solstice, or even just pieces of music played on traditional instruments that suit the mood of the event. You may even like to compose your own. Choose which ones you'd like to incorporate as part of your ceremony.

6. Sacred space location and design. Work out where you will hold your ceremony. It will need to be located where everyone participating can see the winter solstice sunrise. Ideally, it would also be aligned to the winter solstice sunrise in some way, just as many ancient sites are—which can be done simply by lining up stones, candles, an altar, etc., with the sun. Whatever design or location you choose, I recommend having a candle or fire you can light as part of your ceremony.

BASIC STRUCTURE

This is a basic outline of a winter solstice ceremony, which can be adapted to any tradition, or can be done without any specific cultural references. It can also be made more complex, or steps can be left out to make it simpler.

1. Prepare the sacred space where you will conduct your ceremony well in advance. I recommend representing the three forces of creation (Father, Mother, and Son) in some way. However, if you wish, you can have nothing but the sky (Father), earth (Mother), and sun (Son) represent them.

2. Hold your ceremony at sunrise either on the day closest to the actual winter solstice in your time zone, or the third day following it (see section "Working out a Calendar and Preparing in Advance" in previous chapter). Sunrise on the day of the winter solstice symbolically represents the creation of the Spiritual Son, while sunrise on the third day following it, when the sun stops "standing still," represents the birth of the Spiritual Son fully into matter and a human being. Depending on your tradition and what your ceremony symbolizes, you could hold it on either of these days or do a ceremony for both. Whatever you choose, make sure your ceremony begins before sunrise so that the sunrise takes place within the ceremony, having worked out how long your ceremony will take so that you are not rushed as the sun rises.

3. Open your ceremony in whatever way you wish. I recommend saying a short phrase, prayer, mantra, or chant relevant to the winter solstice, or even just playing an instrument, like ringing a bell and lighting some incense. There is no need to spend a lot of time on chants or mantras, etc., here as they form a large part of the ceremony that follows.

4. Praise the Spiritual Father, Mother, and Son (optional). Each person has aspects of their higher Being known as the Spiritual Father, Mother, and Son. They play an important part in the events symbolized by this ceremony, so it's appropriate to praise and/or petition them. You could do this by praising them for their role in creation, or there may be special phrases in your tradition which you can use. You could use the translation of their names into your language, or the name of a trinity of relevant deities in your tradition. It may be helpful to have a statue or image of them that you can address yourself to.

5. Do a reading (optional). You could recite something from a sacred text about a figure in your tradition who represented the Spiritual Son, retell mythology to do with it, or recite something you've written about it. You could also recite sacred verses to do with first creation.

6. Recite prayers, mantras, songs, etc. This step is now about the anticipation of the coming birth of the Son as the rising sun. It should be done before the sun has actually appeared. You could recite prayers, mantras, or songs that are relevant to the winter solstice and the birth of the Spiritual Son.

7. Watch the sun rise. The sunrise itself is the main event of the ceremony, and in nature it has its own energies, which can be perceived and felt. The moments before sunrise on the winter solstice can be especially magical and mystical. If you are alone or in a small group, you might like to watch the sunrise in silence, or while in silent prayer. Silence doesn't work so well for a larger group of people though, so another option is to sing, play music, or chant as it rises. Just make sure not to stare into a bright sun as it can harm your eyes.

8. Light the fire or candle. As the sun first begins to appear, which is the moment it appears over the horizon or any objects like trees that are in the way, light your ceremonial fire. The lighting of the fire as the sun first rises symbolizes the birth of the sacred fire, the Son/sun.

9. Light a handheld candle (optional). Each participant can light their own handheld candle from the fire lit within the ceremony, symbolizing each one's own divine Being coming into existence at the dawn of creation.

10. More readings (optional). You could read more relevant excerpts from sacred texts about the Spiritual Son and/or creation.

11. Recite prayers, mantras, songs, play traditional music, etc. This step is to celebrate the birth of the Spiritual Son as the rising sun, which can be a time of rejoicing.

12. Close the ceremony. You could do this by saying a prayer of thanks, or by leaving a symbolic offering like flowers.

13. Leave. Walk away from your ceremonial space, holding your lit candle if you have one.

EXAMPLE THEMES

There are many different examples of ceremonies you could perform based on your particular tradition. Here are just a few basic outlines to start with:

ANCIENT EGYPTIAN

The birth of Horus as the child of Osiris and Isis (or alternatively Ra and Hathor) could be celebrated. Readings could be done from ancient Egyptian texts, such as the Book of the Dead and the Pyramid Texts.

DRUID/CELTIC

The birth of Hu as the child of Ceridwen and Celu could be celebrated—which could even be done from inside a sacred cave or mound, ideally aligned to the winter solstice sunrise.

GERMANIC/NORDIC

The Germanic winter solstice celebration was called Yule—a name associated with Odin who was called "Yule father." It was celebrated over the three nights of solstice solar standstill at midwinter.[1] Evidence suggests that it was seen as the time of the rebirth of the sun (who in Scandinavia became personified as the goddess Sol). This solar goddess was central to Norse initiation rituals—after their descent into the underworld, the initiate often awoke this sleeping goddess and mystically united with her. Thus, the initiate experienced a spiritual transformation through her, and a kind of spiritual rebirth. The sun goddess was likely used to represent the initiate's higher/

inner spiritual self, which they had to find within the dark depths of their own inner underworld/subconscious and reunite with.[2]

Baldr was also a dying and resurrecting sun god in Germanic mythology, and so a suggested ceremony could center around the birth of Baldr to Odin and his wife Frigg.

As in Yule celebrations, evergreens could be used (symbolizing the immortality of the Spiritual Son) and candles lit (symbolizing the birth of light).

GNOSTIC CHRISTIAN

The celebration of Christmas is well known to many. On the third morning following the solstice, the birth of the Spiritual Son as Jesus could be celebrated.

GREEK (ELEUSINIAN)

There are references in the Eleusinian Mysteries to a "ritual of the divine child," in which it was said that "Mighty Potnia [the great goddess] bore a great son." It involved the symbolic birth of a divine son to a great mother goddess of the earth, and possibly a sky father god.[3] The birth of this child was announced by the high priest during the Great Mystery in the Telesterion, which was one of the main centers of the Eleusinian Mysteries.[4]

HINDU

Krishna is believed to have been born at midnight on the 23rd of June 3,227 BC according to the Gregorian calendar.[5] This is the time of the summer solstice in India, although Krishna's birth is most commonly celebrated in August or September today. Jesus was also said to have been born at midnight on a solstice. Krishna's birth may have been placed at the summer solstice because it was considered as the time of the exit from this world to heaven, and so suited when Krishna would descend from heaven and enter the world to take his birth. However, since Krishna can represent the Spiritual Son, his birthday can be celebrated according to its spiritual meaning at the winter solstice instead.

INCA/ANDEAN

See the following example ceremony.

IRANIAN AND ROMAN

The birth of the sun-god Mithra/Mithras could be celebrated. His birthday was celebrated on the winter solstice both in Persia and Rome, and is still celebrated by Iranians and Zoroastrians in the festival called Yalda. This festival celebrates the victory of the forces of light over darkness, and the renewal of the sun. Historical accounts indicate Mithra was considered at least for a time, the son of the great god Ahura Mazda, and the goddess Anahita (Ishtar in Babylonia and Aditi in the Vedas).[6]

EXAMPLE GROUP CEREMONY ~ Inca (Andean)

The official national celebration of Inti Raymi held every year at Cusco in Peru.

Here is an example of a ceremony based on the Inca winter solstice ceremony called Inti Raymi. The name "Inti Raymi" translates to sun festival. In the times of the Inca it was called "Wawa Inti Raymi," meaning festival of the baby sun. It centers around the celebration of the sun god Inti, who was the supreme god of the Inca.[7]

It is based on the accounts of the actual ancient Inca ceremony, the main source of which comes from the chronicler Garcilaso de la Vega (born in 1539) in his book called *Royal Commentaries of the Incas and General History of Peru*. His father was a Spanish conquistador and his mother a royal Inca woman, who was granddaughter of the last Inca king. Garcilaso was raised listening to the stories and histories of the Inca Empire until he was twenty—moving from Peru to Spain permanently at the age of twenty-one.[8] His unique insight into the traditions of the Incas, combined with his Spanish education, allowed him to record these precious accounts while the memory of them still survived. Other accounts were also recorded by Spanish historians in the sixteenth century, just after the Inca Empire had been conquered by the Spanish.

THE TIMING OF THE CEREMONY

This ceremony begins before sunrise three days following the winter solstice, which generally falls on June 24 in the Southern Hemisphere. The modern reenactment of Inti Raymi in Peru is held on June 24. When this enactment was instigated in 1944 it was believed that the original ceremony had been celebrated on the winter solstice itself (which generally occurs on June 21), only shifting to June 24 after the Spanish conquest in order to coincide with the Catholic festival of John the Baptist.[9] A careful reading of Garcilaso's commentaries indicate, however, that the Inca did indeed celebrate Inti Raymi three days following the solstice, as he states "it took place after the June solstice,"[10] and that they prepared themselves for it over three days.[11] Logically, the three day period of preparation would correspond to the three days of solar standstill following the solstice.

ITEMS NEEDED

⊕ A ceremonial fire.

⊕ A handheld concave metal device (traditionally used by the Incas), that can be used to direct the rays of the sun to light a fire. Alternatively, a magnifying glass can be used.

⊕ A small handful of cotton fibres.

⊕ A golden metal drinking cup—ideally a traditional *keru/aquilla*.

⊕ A large ceramic or golden-colored metal pitcher for pouring water—ideally a traditional *tinajon/aryballos/urpus*.

⊕ An altar covered in white cloth that the pitcher and cup is placed on.

⊕ Cups for every participant in the ceremony—ideally traditional *kerus*.

⊕ Corn bread for every participant in the ceremony.

⊕ Non-alcoholic *chicha* for every participant (or water).

⊕ Baskets to carry the bread in.

⊕ Flowers for every participant.

⊕ Yellow flower petals.

⊕ An outfit of the Inca sun king.

⊕ Costumes of various ugly looking animals for a number of people to wear.

⊕ Traditional musical instruments.

THE SETUP OF THE SACRED SPACE

The sacred space consists of a large platform with stairs leading up to it, which is big enough for the ceremonial fire and altar to be upon, and for at least two people to comfortably move around on. The Quechua and Aymara people used these platforms, called ushnus, to perform ceremonies. They were usually carved or made out of stone, and one like this is still used for the official national winter solstice ceremony in Bolivia held at the ancient site of Tiwanaku, as well as the national celebration of Inti Raymi in Peru at the ancient site of Sacsayhuaman. Ideally it would have four levels. If this is not practical for you, then you could always create a workaround. Ideally it would still be raised, but if this is not possible you could always just mark out a four-sided sacred area with stones.

One of the most well-known ancient Inca ushnus, at a site called Vilcashuaman. It resembles a flat-topped stepped pyramid, which was one of the most common sacred structures in the ancient Religion of the Sun.

Photo of the modern Inti Raymi winter solstice celebration held at the ancient site of Sacsayhuaman in Peru, with an ushnu platform in the center built especially for the ceremony.

Upon the platform, or within the sacred area, the ceremonial fire is prepared with enough wood/fuel to burn throughout the ceremony. It is not lit, as lighting it is part of the ceremony itself. In the times of the Inca, the ceremonial fire was kept within the temple of the sun called the Coricancha, and so in this case the sun temple is treated as being upon the platform (or within the sacred space). You could symbolize this in some way, as long as participants can still see the fire.

The lens/concave device is placed near the fire, along with some cotton, which will be used to light the fire (a backup way to light the fire should also be there, like a lighter or matches, if the concave device doesn't work).

The altar is also set up on the platform with the pitcher and golden cup upon it. The pitcher is full of chicha or water, while the cup is empty. The pitcher should be positioned so that the rays of the rising sun touch it.

THE PARTICIPANTS

Sun King/Sapa Inca
A man plays the role of the Inca Sun King (called the Sapa Inca), who represents Inti as a "Son of the Sun," a title the Sapa Inca historically held. He dresses in traditional garments, ideally mostly colored golden yellow or gold, and wears an image of the sun god Inti on his forehead as part of a traditional golden crown.

High Priest/Villaq Umu
A man performs the role of Priest. The head priest of the Inca Empire who served the sun god Inti was called the Villaq Umu.[12] He dresses in traditional Inca garments.

Virgins of the Sun
Any number of women take the role of the Inca priestesses that were called the Virgins of the Sun.

Yuncas
Any number of men and/or women dress wearing the most repulsive masks possible as the people known as the Yuncas did historically when attending Inti Raymi.[13]

Left: Statue of the Sapa Inca at the city of Cusco in Peru. Center: Illustration of an Inca priestess called a Virgin of the Sun. Right: Participants of the Inti Raymi festival still come dressed in masks and silly costumes today.

Musicians
Any number of people play musical instruments at different times in the ceremony.

Singers
Any number of people can be singers for the ceremony.

General Participants
All the remaining participants dress in traditional Inca clothing. Historically, all those who attended Inti Raymi came as well attired as possible, as it was the most important festival in the Empire.[14]

INSTRUCTIONS FOR THE CEREMONY

1. Virgins of the Sun prepare the ceremonial bread and chicha. The night before the ceremony, the Virgins of the Sun bake the traditional corn bread that was historically prepared the night before Inti Raymi.[15] However, they can prepare anything else for the bread in the days of solar standstill leading up to the ceremony. They make one bread for every person in the ceremony. They also prepare the chicha in the days of solar standstill before the ceremony.

2. The sacred space is ready and all take their positions. Before sunrise, on the third morning following the winter solstice, everything is ready and prepared at the sacred space. The General Participants stand some distance away from the sacred space in two lines, facing one another, with enough room between the lines for the Ceremonial Entourage (all those fulfilling special roles in the ceremony) to walk between. Each General Participant carries flowers in whatever way is practical, as well as a small empty cup. The Ceremonial Entourage stand out of sight of the General Participants, some distance from the sacred space.

3. Traditional music is played for the arrival of the Ceremonial Entourage. The musicians and singers begin playing. Ideally they play traditional Andean music, and can begin by sounding the traditional seashell horns called *pututos*, which are used in the celebration of Inti Raymi today to announce the arrival of the Sapa Inca.

4. The Ceremonial Entourage arrives. One Virgin of the Sun walks in front of the Ceremonial Entourage, spreading yellow flower petals on the ground where they will walk, as is done in Inti Raymi today. The Sapa Inca/Sun King leads the Ceremonial Entourage. He is followed by the Priest and then the remaining Virgins of the Sun. The Virgins of the Sun carry the bread they have baked in handheld baskets. The Yuncas follow behind them, dancing. Finally any special musicians and singers follow the Yuncas, and continue singing and playing their instruments as they walk. The Ceremonial Entourage walks toward the sacred space between the lines of General Participants.

5. Procession to the sacred space. Once the Ceremonial Entourage has passed, the General Participants follow in procession behind them, walking toward the sacred space. During the reign of the Inca, "absolutely everyone" from across the Inca Empire either attended Inti Raymi or was represented if they were unable to attend,[16] with many walking great distances to get there. The walk to the sacred space is a much shorter one that signifies the same kind of pilgrimage people historically made to attend this most important festival.

6. The General Participants take their place for the ceremony. The Ceremonial Entourage stand before the sacred space, but do not enter it yet. The General Participants gather around the sacred space so that they will each have a clear view of the rising sun.

7. The Priest enters the sacred space. The Priest enters the sacred space, and stands by the altar, facing the participants.

8. The Sapa Inca enters the sacred space. The Sapa Inca/Sun King enters the sacred space and stands near the ceremonial fire, facing the place where the sun will rise.

9. The Virgins of the Sun take their place. The Virgins of the Sun enter the sacred space to place the baskets of bread within it. They then leave the sacred space, and walk over to stand with the General Participants, though slightly apart from them, but so all will still have a clear view of the rising sun.

10. The ceremony begins. The Priest signals for the music to stop. The music stops and he signals that the ceremony will now start.

11. The Yuncas take their place. The Priest signals for the music to start again, but the musicians play a different music this time—they purposely play their instruments badly. The Yuncas begin dancing around the ceremonial area in a crazy way, and make gestures and grimaces of crazy people, fools, and silly people. They spend some time circling around the General Participants before taking their place near them but slightly apart, so that all will still have a clear view of the sunrise. Once the Yuncas have taken their place for the ceremony, the Priest signals for the music to stop. The musicians stop playing and the Yuncas become still.

12. All wait for sunrise in silent anticipation. Everyone waits in silence for the sun to rise.

13. The chorus of singing begins. When the sun first appears over the horizon or any terrestrial objects, the Priest signals for the singers to begin singing. They begin singing quietly at first to match the size of the sun, gradually getting louder as it grows and continues to rise. Musicians can also join in, gradually increasing in volume likewise. The songs and music are traditional Andean songs. This singing and music continues ideally until step 16.

14. Traditional Inca worship and prayer to the sun. At the same time, everyone performs the traditional Inca worship of the sun by squatting in the Inca form of prayer. They blow kisses at the sun by opening their arms wide and then folding them to kiss their hands and extend their arms again, as though kissing a newborn child. An alternative or addition to this is to simply raise one's hands so that one's palms face the sun, as is popularly done during solstice and equinox celebrations in Central and South America today. Each person can say prayers to the sun while doing this if they wish.

15. The fire is lit. After some time, the Sapa Inca lights the ceremonial fire. He does this by using the concave device and cotton. The concave device is held so that the sun's light is directed at the cotton and lights it. This cotton is then used to light the ceremonial fire. The Priest can help if necessary. If they're unable to light the fire using the concave device, the Sapa Inca can simply light the cotton using a match.

16. Blessing and eating of the bread. Once the ceremonial fire is burning fully, the Sapa Inca stands and picks up a basket of bread. He holds it up to the sun. He then takes a piece of bread for himself, and then passes the basket to the Priest who also takes a piece for himself. The Priest then passes the basket out of the sacred space to a waiting Virgin of the Sun. The Virgin of the Sun begins distributing the bread to each participant. Every basket of bread is held up by the Sapa Inca and passed around to the participants in this way, but the Sapa Inca and the Priest only take one piece of bread from the first basket. The Virgins of the Sun distribute the bread until everyone has a piece of bread. Then the Sapa Inca eats first, and then all the rest of the participants eat their piece of bread (or as much of it as they wish).

17. Blessing and drinking of the chicha. Once everyone is pretty much finished with their bread, the Sapa Inca walks over to the altar. He takes the pitcher in his right hand and holds it up to the sun. He then pours a small cup of chicha for himself and another for the Priest. The Sapa Inca then passes the pitcher to the Priest who passes it out of the sacred space to a waiting Virgin of the Sun. The Virgin of the Sun then pours a small drink of chicha into the cups of all the participants. If there are lots of participants, the priest could fill a number of pitchers from the main pitcher held by a number of waiting Virgins of the Sun. Once everyone has chicha in their cup, the Sapa Inca drinks first from the cup he holds in his left hand, and then all the rest of the participants drink from their cups.

18. Readings, prayers, songs, music. Optionally the Priest could now recite something, the participants could all do prayers to the sun, traditional Andean songs related to the event could be sung, and traditional music played. This is a time of great celebration, reverence, and joy for the birth of the Spiritual Son/sun.

19. Offerings of flowers to the sun. The Virgins of the Sun collect the flowers from all the General Participants and take them to the Priest, who places them within the sacred space as offerings to the sun.

20. The Sapa Inca leaves. The Priest signals for the Ceremonial Entourage to now leave the sacred space, which can occur while any singing or music continues. The Sapa Inca leaves first, followed by the Priest. They walk away from the ceremonial area as the remaining participants watch.

21. The ceremony concludes though celebrations continue. The ceremony has now finished, though people are free to remain singing, dancing, and celebrating around the fire. The crescendo of singing and music can reach its loudest at midday, and as the sun sets, the music and singing becomes quieter and more solemn and sad until finally going completely quiet at sunset. Any activities should conclude before midnight.

THE MEANING OF THE CEREMONY

This ceremony is based on how the actual celebration of Inti Raymi was conducted in the days of the Inca. As in the ceremony, the priestesses called the Virgins of the Sun would make a traditional corn bread called *zancu* the night before. This type of bread was considered sacred, and was made almost exclusively to be eaten for this celebration.[17]

In this ceremony the platform (or sacred space), which was traditionally used in Inca ceremonies, represents where the earthly and divine meet. On a microcosmic level it represents the human body and psyche that has been purified to become a receptacle for the divine, and on a macrocosmic level it represents the whole of material creation. Its four levels and/or four sides represent the four material elements, the four dimensions of the material world, and the four material bodies—which the Spiritual Son is born into.

In this ceremony, the Sapa Inca symbolizes the sun god Inti and the Spiritual Son, as the Inca King was considered "the firstborn of the sun."[18] His arrival symbolizes his birth into the world and within a person—manifesting into material creation like the light of the sun. The yellow flower petals spread before him signify the path of the spiritual sun he walks.

Standing on the platform, he represents the Spiritual Son upon the foundation of the human body that is fit to receive him.

The priest represents the person whom the Spiritual Son is born within.

The Yuncas attended the Inti Raymi festival in ancient times dressed in horrible looking masks and costumes.[19] In this ceremony they symbolize the egos, the psychological forces of chaos, disorder, darkness, and disharmony that someone still has in their subconscious when the Spiritual Son is born within them. These symbolize the same thing as the animals in the stables where Jesus was born, which is the animalistic ego.

Everyone waits in silence of the sun to rise, as this is how it was anticipated in the ancient Inti Raymi festival, even by the Inca king himself. It creates an atmosphere of great anticipation and reverence. Once the sun begins to rise, just as in the historical celebration, the traditional Inca worship of the sun is done.

> "Everything being prepared, the following day, which was that of the festival, the Inca went out at daybreak accompanied by his whole kin. They departed in due order [...] to the main square of the city called Haucaipata. There they waited for the sun to rise and stood with bare feet, attentively gazing toward the east. When the Sun began to appear, they all squatted (which among the Indians is as though they were to kneel) to worship it. This they did by raising their arms and placing their hands beside their faces, kissing the air, which is the same as kissing one's hand or the garment of a prince as a mark of respect in Spain. They worshipped the Sun with great affection and acknowledgement that he was their god and natural father." [20]
> ~ GARCILASO DE LA VEGA, THE ROYAL COMMENTARIES OF THE INCAS

Modern attendees to the Inti Raymi festival holding up their hands to the sun.

Singing also begins as the sun rises, just as in the time of the Inca, and crescendos at midday, to wane until finally becoming silent at sunset. It represents one's feelings and wishes being in accordance with the divine.

> "Everyone was very silent waiting for the sun to rise and as soon as the sun emerged the choirs started to sing a song in a low voice each one moving one foot as a way of a musical compass with much harmony and order. As the sun rose the song became louder and louder. The Inca King directed with his own voice. [...] When the sun had reached midday the voices were very loud and soon after started to go down as the sun descended. There was a perfect correspondence between the song and the path of the sun. [...] At sunset the song became slow and sad with voices each time more weak until they ceased with the last solar rays, which coincided with their expression of humility and abidance which were the continuous vowing everyone was making." [21]
>
> ~ THE CHRONICLER BARTOLOME DE LAS CASAS (1484-1566), SPANISH HISTORIAN, SOCIAL REFORMER, AND DOMINICAN FRIAR, IN HIS ACCOUNTS OF INTI RAYMI

Once the sun rises, it is a great celebration of the Spiritual Son as savior, his birth into the world, and the potential for him to be born within every person.

Each participant offers flowers to the sun as a symbol of devotion and worship. In ancient times attendees to Inti Raymi would bring many kinds of gifts and offerings to be taken to the sun temple, the Coricancha, where they were consecrated to the sun god Inti.[22] In this ceremony, flowers are used as a simple but meaningful expression of this same offering. As in the Inca celebration, the priest accepts these gifts and places them in the sacred space—representing the sun temple. Flowers are given rather than sacrificial animals in accordance with the wishes of the wisdom bringers like Quetzalcoatl and Viracocha, who brought the Religion of the Sun to the Americas, and who were against animal (and human) sacrifice, saying that only flowers and fruits should be offered.

Illustration of the Inca worshiping the sun god Inti within the Coricancha temple.

The Sapa Inca uses a concave device to light cotton, which is then used to light the ceremonial fire, just as in the original Inca ceremony. The Inca specifically wished to light their sacred fire from the light of the sun itself, which is why this concave device was used to direct the sun's light much like a magnifying glass. In this ceremony, it symbolizes the Spiritual Son manifesting into material creation, like the fire of the sun coming to Earth.

> "The fire [...] had to be new, given by the Sun's hand, as they put it. To this end they used to take a large bracelet called a *chipana*, like those the Incas usually wore on their left wrists. It was kept by the high priest, and was larger than the usual size, and had on its front a highly burnished concave bowl like a half orange. It was placed against the sun and at a certain point where the rays reflected from the bowl came together, they placed a piece of well-carded cotton [...]. The fire was carried to the temple of the Sun and the house of the virgins where it was kept alive throughout the year." [23]
> ~ GARCILASO DE LA VEGA, THE ROYAL COMMENTARIES OF THE INCAS

In the ancient celebration of Inti Raymi, both the sacred bread called *zancu* and a specially brewed corn drink called *chicha* were ritually consumed by the Inca elite. The chicha was offered to the sun, then the Sapa Inca would drink first, followed by the remaining Inca nobility.[24]

> "At intervals the vessel the Inca held was replenished, so that the first liquid which had been sanctified by the hands of the Sun or of the Inca, or both of them, should transmit its virtue to each of the recipients." [25]
> ~ GARCILASO DE LA VEGA, THE ROYAL COMMENTARIES OF THE INCAS

This bears a remarkable similarity to the Christian Communion, in which participants ritually eat a specially consecrated bread and wine said to embody the body and blood of Christ.

In this ceremony, the bread and chicha/water symbolize the substance and energy of the Spiritual Son. The Sapa Inca holds up the bread and chicha to the first rays of the rising winter solstice sun so that they absorb the energy of the sun before being consumed. The corn they were made of symbolizes the sacred seed of the sun. The three days of solar standstill in which the Virgins of the Sun prepare the bread and chicha for the ceremony can symbolize the gestation of the seed before the sun is born. The corn bread and chicha embodied the divine substance of the sun in the times of the Inca, as they do in this ceremony. Consuming them symbolizes how the Spiritual Son can be born within a person, and also acknowledges that it is the energy of the sun which nourishes and sustains us both physically and spiritually.

> "The banquet seemed indeed rather a gift from the Sun to his children than from the children to the Sun, and for that reason the virgins prepared it, as wives of the Sun." [26]
> ~ GARCILASO DE LA VEGA, THE ROYAL COMMENTARIES OF THE INCAS

The Virgins of the Sun prepared the sacred bread because they were considered pure enough, and correlate to the priestesses of the sun in other traditions of the Religion of Sun. They represent the consciousness within each person, which is spiritually undefiled and commits itself to reuniting with its Spiritual Son.

In the times of the Inca Empire, the Virgins of the Sun prepared the bread for the Inca elite—women of the Sun prepared it for everyone else.

> "An infinite number of other women appointed for the purpose kneaded the bread and prepared the meal for the rest of the people. The bread, though it was for the community, was compounded with care and attention that at least the flour should be prepared by damsels; for this bread was regarded as something sacred and not allowed to be eaten during the year, but only at this festivity, which was their feast of feasts." [27]
>
> ~ GARCILASO DE LA VEGA, THE ROYAL COMMENTARIES OF THE INCAS

Women preparing flat corn bread for the Inti Raymi festival, however, the bread used for the festival in ancient times was described as round and the size of an apple.

Every person no matter what their standing in society is nourished by the same sun, and, by taking the path of the spiritual sun, is able to incarnate their Spiritual Son and become a "Son of the Sun." This is why all participants in the ceremony partake of the bread and drink.

WINTER SOLSTICE CEREMONY

Inti Raymi celebrates the Spiritual Son coming into the world and is celebrated on the third day following the solstice. However, in addition to this, you could also hold a ceremony on the winter solstice itself. This would celebrate the birth of the Spiritual Son into creation.

For the winter solstice ceremony, I always recommend having the trinity of Father, Mother, and Son present in some way. In this case, the Spiritual Father and Mother could be represented by the parents of Inti, called Hanaqpacha Inti Tayta and Pachamama.

Hanaqpacha Inti Tayta is the god that represents the divine invisible supreme sun behind the sun[28] and his symbol is the condor.[29] He represents the Spiritual Father—the masculine aspect of the creator, and also of each one's higher

Inti Raymi ceremony held in Argentina.

Being. He is most associated with the sky and heavens as these represent the transcendence of the spirit. The condor was his symbol because it lives in the sky, above all others.

Pachamama is the Andean Mother Earth, and mother of the sun god Inti.[30] She represents the Spiritual Mother—the female aspect of the creator, and also of each one's higher Being. She is most associated with the earth as the element of earth represents substance and form, as well as her womb. She has also been symbolized by the serpent in Mesoamerican cultures.

Together, Hanaqpacha Inti Tayta and Pachamama symbolize the dual masculine and feminine forces that give rise to creation, and give birth to the Spiritual Son, who is symbolized by the sun, called Inti by the Inca.

Hanaqpacha Inti Tayta, Pachamama, and Inti symbolize the three fundamental forces of creation, which were often symbolized as the feathered sun serpent, and can be celebrated on the Inca/Andean winter solstice.

Spring Equinox

CHAPTER FIFTEEN

Ceremonies to Celebrate the Spring Equinox

This chapter outlines ceremonies for celebrating the spring equinox, both for people on their own and in a group. I've included an example ceremony, as well as a basic outline of the principles involved for those who'd like to construct their own ceremony or who are already working within an existing tradition.

CEREMONY OVERVIEW

Left: The resurrected Osiris. Center: The resurrected Jesus. Right: The resurrected Hun Hunahpu.

A spring equinox ceremony essentially celebrates the resurrection of the Spiritual Son.

From out of the underworld, and the darkness of winter, the sun rises to overpower the confines of matter and mortality, and ascends toward eternal light at the summer solstice. It represents the potential each one has to attain spiritual immortality and salvation through the resurrection of their own Spiritual Son within them.

This was portrayed in the lives of many ancient deities who were associated with the sun, and who were celebrated as resurrecting at the spring equinox. This ancient tradition continued into the modern day with the celebration of Jesus' resurrection occurring around the spring equinox in the Northern Hemisphere.

The mood of this ceremony is one of happiness and reverence.

A GUIDE TO CREATING A SPRING EQUINOX CEREMONY

Whether you are a solitary practitioner or working with a group of people, this guide can help you to create your own ceremony, or to expand upon or modify the historical remnants of an existing traditional ceremony.

PREPARING FOR YOUR CEREMONY

To start with, I recommend reading the chapters "The Spiritual Meaning of the Spring Equinox" and "A Guide to Celebrating the Solstices and Equinoxes," as these provide some important background information.

Here is a guide to what information I recommend you gather together first, before creating your ceremony:

1. Spring equinox traditions (optional). This step is optional—it's if you'd like to do a ceremony according to your tradition.

I recommend doing some research to find out how the spring equinox was celebrated in your culture (as long as it is connected in some way to the ancient Religion of the Sun). This is not always easy to do as so many records of the past have been lost or destroyed. If you can't find much, I'd recommend looking for anything in your tradition that is relevant to the profound meaning of the spring equinox. This could include ancient sites that are aligned to it, and symbols and stories that are relevant to it.

See if there is anything you'd like to incorporate into your ceremony.

2. Symbols of the spring equinox. It's nice to use and wear actual symbols of the equinox in your ceremony, just as ancient peoples did. Look for any symbols of the spring equinox you can find in your tradition. The symbols most relevant to the spring equinox are the solar cross and upright cruciform/Latin cross, as they represent the cross of resurrection. If there isn't a specific equinox symbol in your tradition then any solar symbol can be used.

Work out how to incorporate these symbols into your ceremony. For example, you could wear a pendant of the symbol, or have a representation of it on an altar, or make it part of your sacred ceremonial space by creating it out of stones on the ground, etc.

3. The Spiritual Son. Choose what will represent the Spiritual Son in your ceremony. Whatever you choose, the sun represents the resurrection of the Spiritual Son as it rises on the spring equinox, so you may choose to have nothing else representing the Spiritual Son but the sun itself.

For those of you who'd like to do a ceremony according to your tradition, you could also look to symbolize the Spiritual Son using a deity from your tradition. Typically, these figures are associated with the sun, and their life events mirror the sun's path and its major stages. In particular, look for one who resurrected.

Examples include Baldr in Germanic/Nordic paganism, the Maize God/flaming water-lily jaguar of the Maya, Jesus of the ancient Gnostics, and Osiris of the ancient Egyptians.

Decide how you will incorporate this figure into your ceremony. You could have a statue, painting, or symbol of them on an altar or somewhere in your sacred space. If you are doing a larger group ceremony, then someone could dress as and represent this figure.

4. Symbols of resurrection (optional). This step is optional—it's if you'd like to do a ceremony according to your tradition.

Extract the most important and relevant symbols involved in the story of the resurrection of the figure you have chosen above in step 3. Look specifically for those things that represent the following:

- a. The cross of the spring equinox (e.g. a sacred tree, cruciform/Latin cross, cross)
- b. The underworld (e.g. tomb, mound, turtle, water, cauldron)
- c. The underworld's nine regions (e.g. ninth hour, nine nights, nine years, nine terraces)
- d. The Spiritual Mother
- e. The one who resurrects the Spiritual Son (e.g. Anubis)
- f. The breaking of any trappings (e.g. gates opening, tomb opening, chains breaking)
- g. Symbols of resurrection (e.g. sprouting of certain plants, like maize/corn or wheat)

Work out how you would like to incorporate these symbols into your ceremony and/or sacred space. For example, you might symbolize the underworld as a standing stone circle, a bowl or cauldron of water, a cave, sarcophagus, symbol of a turtle, etc., depending on the tradition.

5. Chants, mantras, songs, prayers, readings, music, etc. As part of your ceremony you could choose to read from sacred texts, or sing songs, etc. These could be traditional songs that are part of spring equinox celebrations, excerpts from sacred texts that are relevant to the meaning of the spring equinox, chants that convey the meaning of the spring equinox, or even just pieces of music played on traditional instruments that suit the mood of the event. You may even like to compose your own. Choose which ones you'd like to incorporate as part of your ceremony.

6. Sacred space location and design. Work out where you will hold your ceremony. It will need to be located where everyone participating can see the sunrise. Ideally, it would also be aligned to the spring equinox sunrise in some way, just as many ancient sites are—which can be done simply by lining up stones, candles, an altar, etc., with the sun. Whatever design or location you choose, I recommend having a candle or fire you can light as part of your ceremony.

BASIC STRUCTURE

This is a basic outline of a spring equinox ceremony, which can be adapted to any tradition, or can be done without any specific cultural references. It can also be made more complex, or steps can be left out to make it simpler.

1. Prepare the sacred space where you will conduct your ceremony well in advance.

2. Hold your ceremony at the sunrise closest to the spring equinox in your time zone (see section "Working out a Calendar and Preparing in Advance" in previous chapter), as this is when the sun itself symbolizes resurrection. Make sure your ceremony begins before sunrise so that the sunrise takes place within the ceremony, having worked out how long your ceremony will take so that you are not rushed as the sun rises.

3. Open your ceremony in whatever way you wish—this could be by saying a prayer, a mantra, or chant. Or it could be by playing an instrument, or song. I would recommend using any of these as a way to focus your mind and to connect yourself with the spiritual both within and surrounding you.

4. Praise the Spiritual Mother (optional). Each person has an aspect of their higher Being known as the Spiritual Mother. She plays an important part in the events symbolized by this ceremony, so it's appropriate to praise and/or petition her. You could do this simply by repeating something like, "Spiritual Mother, please guide me/us," or there may be special phrases in your tradition which you can use. You could use the translation of "Spiritual Mother" into your language, or the name of a mother goddess in your tradition. It may be helpful to have a statue or image of the Spiritual Mother that you can address yourself to.

5. Do a reading (optional). Optionally, you could recite something from a sacred text about a figure in your tradition who resurrected, retell mythology to do with it, or recite something you've written about it. You could have related statues or images incorporated into your sacred space, or on your altar, etc.

6. Recite prayers, mantras, songs (optional). You might like to spend some time repeating a prayer or mantra, or singing a song related to the meaning of the spring equinox while waiting for the sun to rise.

7. Watch the sunrise. The equinox sunrise itself is the main event of the ceremony, and in nature it has its own energies, which it's possible to perceive and feel. If you are alone or in a small group, you might like to watch the sunrise in silence, or while in silent prayer. Silence doesn't work so well for a larger group of people though, so another option is to sing, play music, or chant as it rises. Just make sure not to stare into a bright sun as it can harm your eyes.

8. Light a candle or ceremonial fire (optional). As the sun first begins to appear, you can light a ceremonial fire or candle to symbolize the resurrection of the Spiritual Son/sun and his return to earth from the underworld.

9. Symbolize resurrection (optional). The sun rising at the spring equinox symbolizes spiritual resurrection, so you don't have to do anything to symbolize it yourself if you prefer not to. For those who would like to there are many ways you can do this, and it can be based on something existing in your tradition. For example, you could raise up a statue or image of the Spiritual Son from the ground, or from underneath a covering, or from within a symbol of the underworld. If you are doing a ceremony with a group of people, then someone representing the Spiritual Son could act this out rather than raising up a statue or image.

10. Celebrate the resurrected Son. This can be done through songs, chants, mantras, the reading of texts, traditional dance, music, prayer, or quiet contemplation.

11. Close the ceremony. You could do this by saying a prayer of thanks, or by leaving a symbolic offering like flowers.

EXAMPLE THEMES

There are many different examples of ceremonies you could perform based on your particular tradition. Not all of them conform to the basic ceremonial structure I've outlined, but that's fine, as they contain enough symbolic elements already to create a coherent ceremony. Here are just a few basic outlines to start with.

ANCIENT EGYPTIAN

Perhaps the greatest celebration in ancient Egypt was that of the resurrection of Osiris. In ancient times, it re-enacted the events of his life, death, and resurrection. It was said to have been performed across Egypt in many of its largest and most famous temples, not only for the benefit of the dead pharaoh, but for all the worshipers of Osiris who hoped to attain eternal life through him.[1] A spring equinox ceremony could symbolize the resurrection of Osiris either on a small scale or a larger one, with various people taking the roles of Osiris, Anubis, Isis, and Thoth. Readings could be done from texts like the Pyramid Texts and the Book of the Dead.

CELTIC

Spiritual resurrection from a sun cauldron within a mound (symbolizing the womb of the goddess and her underworld realm) aligned to the sun appears to have been a central initiatory rite of the Neolithic mound builders and Druids, as well as among the Norse. A ceremony could recreate the symbolism of this ritual.

GERMANIC/NORDIC

Odin's resurrection following his self-sacrifice on the world tree, and his return from its roots in the underworld, could be symbolized.

Alternatively, the return of the summer sun god Baldr from Hel to Earth following Ragnarok (as narrated in *Völuspá*) could be celebrated, symbolizing his resurrection.

Being resurrected from the underworld by the goddess was central to Norse initiation rituals,[2] and a ceremony could essentially enact and celebrate this spiritual event.

GNOSTIC CHRISTIAN

The resurrection of Jesus could be celebrated. Readings could be done from the four Gospels, but also from many of the lesser known ancient sacred texts of Gnostic Christianity, such as the Odes of Solomon, and those in the Nag Hammadi Library.

HINDU

A ceremony could symbolize or enact in some way the most important parts of the story of the Churning of the Milky Ocean.

MAYA

See the example ceremony in this chapter.

EXAMPLE SOLITARY OR SMALL GROUP CEREMONY ~ Maya

A Maya winter solstice ceremony at the ancient site of Tikal in Guatemala. Similar ceremonies are held at other Maya sites at the equinoxes.

This example ceremony is in the Maya tradition, however, similar mythology is found among some of the pre-Columbian North American tribes and cultures, such as the Mississippian,[3] and other Mesoamerican cultures such as the Aztec. It is based on traditional Maya ceremonies still performed today. Their practice survived in remote parts of Mesoamerica, maintaining a continuity of ancient traditions, and has experienced a public revival in the last three decades.[4] This ceremony is based on these surviving ceremonies as recorded by the ethnographer Jean Molesky-Poz and referred to in ancient Maya sacred texts.

Maya ceremonies are typically conducted on the solstices and equinoxes at sacred natural locations, as this ceremony is.

> "Dawn, dusk, the equinoxes, and the solstices at specific geographical locations were viewed as sacred; these time-spaces provided entrance to the sacred. At these sites, at designated times, people performed rituals interlocking themselves with cosmic cycles." [5]
> ~ JEAN MOLESKY-POZ, CONTEMPORARY MAYA SPIRITUALITY

THE TIMING OF THE CEREMONY

This ceremony begins before the sunrise closest to the spring equinox in the local time zone.

ITEMS NEEDED

- A ceremonial fire with enough wood to burn throughout the ceremony, or a green candle.
- Sugar.
- Representation of the Spiritual Son as either Hun Hunahpu, Kukulkan, or the water-lily jaguar.
- A small black cloth.
- A cob of maize.
- A transparent bowl of water, with a turtle shell or a statue of a turtle placed within the water.
- A representation of the Lords of Xibalba.
- Incense (preferably copal).
- Fresh pine branches, or leaves of any evergreen tree.
- Purple, yellow, red, and white flowers.
- A mat (ideally a handwoven Maya mat made of natural materials) for each participant.
- A traditional Maya whistle for each participant.
- Conch shell trumpet (optional).
- A small red rag to dress the representation of the Spiritual Son in (optional).

THE SETUP OF THE SACRED SPACE

The ceremony is ideally held outdoors in nature either at the mouth of a cave or natural spring, as these are seen as portals to the underworld in Maya religion and Maya ceremonies are traditionally held at them.

The sacred space is mostly constructed during the ceremony as it is traditionally. It can either be partially prepared before the ceremony begins, or entirely once you arrive at the location where you will conduct it.

It consists of a mat for each participant laid out on the ground, facing the sunrise. As part of the ceremony the

Illustration of a Maya ceremony, held at a natural place using materials that are easily carried and constructed.

symbol of the solar cross is marked out on the ground using sugar. This is done in front of the participants—being between them and the sunrise, and so that one axis is aligned east-west and thus with the sunrise.

A ceremonial fire is made where the center of the solar cross will be located, or a green candle is placed there.

Purple flowers are laid at the end of the western arm, yellow at the southern, red at the eastern, and white at the northern.

A representation of the Lords of Xibalba is placed at the end of the western arm of the cross.

A transparent bowl of water with a turtle shell in the water is placed at the end of the eastern arm so that the sun will appear to rise from its back.

A statue or representation of either Hun Hunahpu, Kukulkan, or the water-lily jaguar, is placed lying down by the ceremonial fire/candle in the center of the cross, with his head facing where the sun will rise (east, as this is how ancient Maya burials were laid) and is covered with a black cloth. As an option, it can also be dressed in a red rag. The maize is also placed there.

Pine branches are then laid around the solar cross in a circle in a sunwise direction (see section "Doing Things in a Sunwise Direction" in chapter 12).

Symbol of a solar cross found at a Mississippian mound site in North America. This symbol is central to Mesoamerican religion. This one also incorporates a swastika.

THE PARTICIPANTS

Guide
A man or woman takes the role of guiding the ceremony. They dress in white with a red sash tied around their waist, and wear a red headband as in traditional Maya ceremonies.

General Participants
If there is more than one person doing this ceremony, the remainder of the participants are simply the General Participants. They dress as the Guide does, but without the head band.

INSTRUCTIONS FOR THE CEREMONY

1. The sacred space is prepared. This step is either done before the ceremony begins, or once you arrive at the location where you will do the ceremony (after step 3). The mat or mats are laid out in position facing the sunrise. All the materials to create the solar cross and ceremonial fire are ready at the sacred area: the sugar, maize, bowl of water with turtle shell, incense, pine leaves, flowers, and wood/fuel for the fire or candle. The fire/candle is unlit, as lighting it is part of the ceremony.

2. The ceremony begins. The participants stand at a distance away from the sacred space. The Guide carries the representation of the Spiritual Son upright in their arms, and any other participants stand in single file behind them. Each person carries a whistle. If you are doing your ceremony at a sacred location and you need to walk a distance to get there, you could carry all the materials with you for the ceremony. The Guide says:

> "Xibalba is crowded with trials, for there are many kinds of trials there.[6] The Son must pass through these trials and overcome the Lords of the underworld to attain immortality."

3. Journey through the underworld. The Guide sprinkles some of each of the four colors of flowers on the ground in front of them in separate piles in a row. They step through the purple flowers and begin walking to the sacred space; any remaining participants follow behind. Along the way to the sacred space, the Guide stops nine times—the final time at the sacred space. Each time the Guide stops, all participants (including the Guide), blow once on their whistle, and say "*Uk'u'x Ulew, sacha' la nu mak,*" meaning, "Heart of Earth, take away my sin." Ideally, the journey would be from a westerly to easterly direction.

4. Bringing of the Spiritual Son. The Guide lays the representation of the Spiritual Son on the ground and covers it with the black cloth. Any remaining participants are seated on their mats.

5. Marking of the solar cross. The Guide takes the sugar and marks out a solar cross on the ground (in whatever size is practical), drawing first the arm from west to east, and then from south to north. When in the west, they say, "*In the name of the Heart of the Creator of the Water.*" When in the east, they say, "*In the name of the Heart of the Creator of the Fire.*" When in the south, they say, "*In the name of the Heart of the Creator of the Earth.*" When in the north, they say, "*In the name of the Heart of the Creator of the Wind.*" They then mark the circle in a sunwise direction.

6. Laying of the flowers in the four directions. The Guide takes up the flowers and places the purple flowers at the end of the western arm, white at the northern, red at the eastern, and yellow at the southern.

7. The placement of the Spiritual Son and maize in the center. The Guide takes the representation of the Spiritual Son and moves it so that it is near the center of the solar cross by the fire/candle. They then take the maize and place it there also.

8. The placement of the Lords of Xibalba in the west. The Guide takes the representation of the Lords of Xibalba and places it at the end of the western arm.

9. The placement of the turtle in the east. The Guide takes the bowl of water and turtle, and places it at the end of the eastern arm.

10. The eternal circling of the pine. The Guide takes the pine branches and lays them end to end around the outside of the solar cross in a circle in a sunwise direction.

11. Prayer to the Spiritual Father and Mother. The Guide stands facing the direction of sunrise and lifts their arms, calling to sky and earth, to Father and Mother, saying:

> "Oh Ajaw. Uk'u'x Kaj (Heart of Sky), Uk'u'x Ulew (Heart of Earth)
> Oh you, B'itol, Tz'akol! (Father-Mother)
> Look at me/us! Listen to me/us!
> Do not leave me/us. Do not abandon me/us." [7]

(Note: Use "me" if you are doing this ceremony alone and "us" if there is more than one person.)

12. Incensing the direction of the sun. The Guide takes the incense and incenses the direction of the rising sun. While they do this, any remaining participants kneel on their mats facing the sunrise, as long as they are physically able—otherwise they remain seated. The Guide leaves the incense burning at the end of the eastern arm of the solar cross, and kneels on their mat (if they are physically able, or is otherwise seated).

13. Blowing of the conch. Before the sun appears, but when it is close to appearing, the Guide blows the conch.

14. Lighting of the fire at first light. When the sun first begins to appear over any terrestrial object the Guide lights the ceremonial fire or candle, and says:

> "The child who is born in the light, and the son who is begotten in the light.[8] He overcomes the darkness, he rises again. The ears of maize have sprouted once again. The heart of his mother rejoices for the maize has sprouted a second time.[9]"

15. Rising up of the Spiritual Son. While the fire burns, the Guide uncovers the representation of the Spiritual Son, and holds it and the maize up above their heads toward the sun, and then toward any other participants. They then lower them, and can eventually put them down by the fire, but so the Spiritual Son remains standing and without the black cloth.

16. Traditional Maya prayer, song, dance, readings. Any or all of these are done, celebrating the resurrected Son/sun. Participants can sit or stand, however is comfortable.

17. Returning things to the fire and earth. While prayers, songs, dance, or readings continue, the Guide removes the representation of the Lords of Xibalba from the sacred area and then the bowl of water with turtle shell inside. If you are using a ceremonial fire, the representation of the Spiritual Son and the maize remains by the fire. The flowers are collected—first purple, then white, then red, then yellow, and are thrown into the fire. The pine branches are then collected and are used to sweep away the solar cross of sugar, and are then also thrown into the fire. All participants remain while the fire burns. If you are using a candle only, then everything is gathered in the same order, but instead of burning the natural items, they are given back to the earth by scattering or leaving them on the ground.

18. Giving of thanks to the Spiritual Father and Mother. While the fire still burns, the Guide says something like:

> "Oh Ajaw. Uk'u'x Kaj (Heart of Sky), Uk'u'x Ulew (Heart of Earth)
> Oh, B'itol, Tz'akol (Father-Mother)
> You who created the green earth and blue sky,
> Its four corners and four sides.
> Giver of breath and giver of heart,
> Who gave birth to the son of light.
> You who are compassionate and wise in all things,
> I/We remember you, I/we speak your names,
> I/We call upon you, I/we worship you." [10]

(Note: Use "I" if you are doing this ceremony alone and "we" if there is more than one person.)

19. Conclusion of the ceremony. The Guide walks away from the sacred space, holding the representation of the Spiritual Son and maize. The ceremony has now concluded.

THE MEANING OF THE CEREMONY

This ceremony enacts the resurrection of the Spiritual Son (as symbolized by Hun Hunahpu, Kukulkan, and the water-lily jaguar).

The journey to the sacred space represents the journey of the Spiritual Son through the underworld (the one who has him within). The four colors of flowers sprinkled on the ground represent the four paths Hun Hunahpu had to choose between to reach the underworld. He chose the black path (purple flowers are used in Maya ceremonies as there aren't black flowers), which is the one that takes him there as it is the one associated with the west—the place where the sun sets, and leads to darkness.

> "At length they arrived at a crossroads [...]. One was Red Road and another was Black Road; White Road was one while another was Yellow Road. Thus there were four roads.
>
> Now this, the black road said: "Me! Take me, for I am the lord's road." Thus spoke the road. [...] They started then on the road to Xibalba." [11]
> ~ POPOL VUH

The nine pauses symbolize passing through the nine regions of the underworld. The participants blow on a Maya whistle signifying their journey through the underworld. These whistles have been found in Maya burial sites, as they were thought to guide the dead along this journey.[12]

The walk to the sacred space is done before sunrise in darkness, symbolizing the darkness of the underworld. The Lords of Xibalba are the gods of the underworld whom the Spiritual Son must defeat in order to resurrect. They symbolize the powers of darkness and the egos.

The participants call upon the Heart of Earth—the Spiritual Mother whose womb is the underworld. They ask her to take

Illustration of facing the terrors of Xibalba—the Maya underworld.

away their sins, saying "Sacha' la nu mak," which is a phrase used in traditional Maya ceremonies,[13] as it's one's Spiritual Mother who has the power to do this. Overcoming the egos (the cause of sin) is what allows someone to pass through the trials of the underworld.

If the ceremony is held at the mouth of a cave or at a spring, this symbolizes the mouth of the underworld, which the Spiritual Son emerges from. In Maya cosmology, the portal leading from the underworld into the earthly world is located in the east where the sun rises (resurrects) on the equinox. Walking from west to east represents the journey from death to life, from out of the underworld.

A solar cross marked on the ground with sugar forms a central part of Maya ceremonies. In this ceremony it is drawn from west to east, and then south to north, rather than it is traditionally, which is from east to west (then north to south). This is to symbolize the journey from west to east through the underworld to resurrect.

The solar cross represents creation, with its four directions. It also represents the cross of the solstices and equinoxes, which the Spiritual Son resurrects upon and journeys through.

> "The source of the cross metaphor is variously interpreted as *the cardinal directions, the solstital positions*, or *the sun's path*. Yet Maya attention to astronomy laid the foundation. The sun's movement is the primordial root."[14]
>
> ~ JEAN MOLESKY-POZ, CONTEMPORARY MAYA SPIRITUALITY

An invocation is made to the "Heart of the Creator" in the four elements, and the four colors of flowers are laid at the ends of each arm, as in traditional Maya ceremonies. These four colors are assigned in Maya religion to the four cardinal directions, and represent the four directions of space and time, which the material world exists within. As explained earlier, they were also the four path colors Hun Hunahpu needed to choose between—the black path leading to the underworld. The red path is where he will resurrect. The invocation recognizes the divinity of creation and the creator (called Ajaw in Maya religion) as existing within the natural world, and as being the divine source of it.

The representation of the Lords of Xibalba is placed in the west, symbolizing the forces of darkness and the underworld.

Illustration of one of the Lords of Xibalba.

The turtle shell in water is placed in the east, symbolizing the portal out of the underworld. In Maya religion, the turtle represents the tomb of the earth,[15] which the Spiritual Son/sun resurrects from. It is depicted as floating on water, which represents the earth "floating" through the cosmos.

The Maya maize god Hun Hunahpu resurrecting from a turtle. Illustration is of a plate found at a temple at the ancient Maya city of Palenque in Mexico.

"One Hunahpu [...] is emerging from a split turtle carapace representing the earth's surface. It floats on water, as indicated by the water lily and other symbols below. [...] Hun Hunahpu is thus seen emerging from the Underworld (symbolized by the Akbal skull on the side of the carapace) and through the earth's surface. This was the ultimate metaphor for a people for whom maize was life itself. The descent into Xibalba by Hun Hunahpu and his brother, followed by their sacrificial death, parallels the farmer planting his corn seed in a hole in the ground at the end of the dry season; the resurrection of Hun Hunahpu by the Hero Twins involves the germination of the seed and sprouting of the young corn plant with the arrival of the rains."[16]
~ MICHAEL D. COE, THE HERO TWINS: MYTH AND IMAGE

The Spiritual Son and maize are placed at the center of the cross by the fire, as they symbolize the spiritual sun that is ultimately at the center of and is the source of creation, the elements, and four directions. Traditionally, when a Maya farmer planted their field, they ritually planted a cob of Maize at the center of their field after having marked out the four directions.

"At the center he then places a special kind of maize ear [...]. These cobs are burned and their ashes are buried beneath the ground so that they can come back to life and make more maize (Christenson 2001, 117)."[17]

In Maya religion, the lifecycle of maize is the central theme illustrating the principles of life, death, and resurrection. It is the underlying motif of the main story in the Maya book Popol Vuh. Newly sprouted maize is symbolic of the resurrected Maize God Hun Hunahpu. Maize itself is considered sacred—seen as the substance humans are made from, and which comes from the sun.

> "[...] the Grandmother [mother of Hun Hunahpu] was weeping, crying out before the ears of unripe maize that had been left planted. They had sprouted, but then they dried up when they were burned in the pit oven [the underworld]. Then the ears of maize had sprouted once again, and the Grandmother had burned copal incense before them as a memorial. The heart of their grandmother rejoiced when the maize sprouted a second time. Thus they were deified by their grandmother. She named it Center House, Center Ancestral Plot, Revitalized Maize, and Leveled Earth. She named it Center House and Center Harvest for it was in the very center of the interior of their home where they had planted the ears of maize. She named it Leveled Earth and Revitalized Maize for it was upon level ground that the ears of maize had been planted. She named it Revitalized Maize because the maize had sprouted again [resurrected]." [18]
> ~ POPOL VUH

Pine branches are laid around the solar cross, as they are in traditional Maya ceremonies. In this ceremony, they represent the eternal nature of the Spiritual Son and the path of the spiritual sun. They are laid in a sunwise direction to symbolize the path and movement of the sun.

The Spiritual Father and Mother (the dual masculine and feminine aspects of the creator) are addressed using traditional Maya ceremonial phrases and/or wording from the Popol Vuh.

The direction of the rising sun is incensed, and people kneel in anticipation of its rising, as recorded in the oldest surviving written records of Maya ceremony, Popol Vuh.

> "Then they unwrapped their copal incense, for the sun was to come forth. They unwrapped it with victory in their hearts. [...] These three were the copal incenses that they burned, waving their censers toward the rising sun. They wept bitterly as they waved their censers, burning the sacred copal incense before they saw and witnessed the birth of the sun.
>
> And when the sun came forth, all the small animals and great animals rejoiced. They came up from the rivers and from the canyons. They were there on the mountain peak. As one they turned their faces toward the coming forth of the sun. Then the pumas and the jaguars

cried out. The first bird to sing was the parrot, as it is called. All the animals truly rejoiced. The eagles and the white vultures, all the small and great birds, spread their wings." [19]

~ POPOL VUH

Quetzalcoatl was said to have blown a conch shell trumpet in the underworld to herald the creation of humankind.[20] Conch trumpets are often used in Maya ceremonies. It signals the coming of the Spiritual Son from within the underworld.

Illustration of a conch trumpet from an Aztec codex.

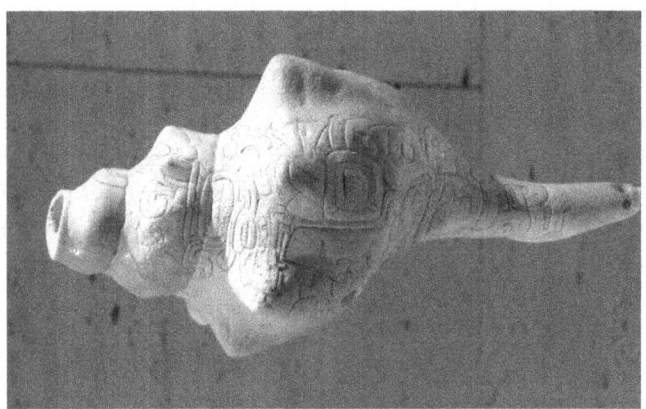

Ancient Maya conch trumpet.

The fire is lit at sunrise to symbolize the resurrection of the Spiritual Son, who is divine fire. Only after they were burned in fire did the sons of Hun Hunahpu resurrect, representing the spiritual purification and transformation through inner fire. The wording used at this step is based on excerpts from Popol Vuh.

In Maya ceremonies a green and blue candle are lit at the center of the cross, representing "Heart of the Earth" (Mother Earth) and "Heart of the Sky" (Father Sky) respectively. In this ceremony only a green candle is used to symbolize how the Spiritual Son has returned to and become one with the Spiritual Mother, but not yet with his Spiritual Father (which occurs at the summer solstice). Green is the color of new vegetation, representing life sprung from the earth and underworld.

The black cloth covering the Spiritual Son represents the underworld he is within. Removing him from beneath the cloth and holding him up is symbolic of his resurrection from it.

He is clothed in red, as this is the color of rebirth and resurrection in Maya tradition, which is why graves were often covered in red cinnabar.[21] It is a rag, as in Popol Vuh the sons of Hun Hunahpu appear in rags after they resurrect, because these are all they had to clothe themselves in after their ordeal in the underworld. However, their appearance is deceiving, as now they have great powers.

> "And on the very next day [after they resurrected], they appeared again as two poor orphans. They wore rags in front and rags on their backs. Rags were thus all they had to cover themselves. But they did not act according to their appearance [...] for many marvels they did then." [22]
> ~ POPOL VUH

The rags symbolize the personality and the weak state of someone who has been through the trials of the underworld, which mask the true nature of the resurrected Spiritual Son they have within. Even though they seem weak/poor in the world after going through such hardships, in reality the Spiritual Son within them has great spiritual powers.

Many of the natural materials, such as the pine and flowers, are burned in the fire, as these are traditionally offered and burned in Maya ritual. It symbolizes creation returning to its source. However, the Spiritual Son and maize are not burned, symbolizing how they remain immortal/eternal.

Summer Solstice

CHAPTER SIXTEEN

Ceremonies to Celebrate the Summer Solstice

This chapter outlines ceremonies for celebrating the summer solstice, both for people on their own or in a group. I've included an example ceremony, as well as a basic outline of the principles involved for those who'd like to construct their own ceremony or who are already working within an existing tradition.

CEREMONY OVERVIEW

The summer solstice represents spiritual ascension. Left: Although ascension is most often associated with Jesus, it is also a central theme in Hinduism. Image is a Hindu portrayal of the ascent to heaven. Center: The ascension of Jesus. Right: Mithras sitting on a cloud beside the sun god Sol after his ascension.

A summer solstice ceremony essentially symbolizes the ascent of the Spiritual Son within a person's consciousness into the higher realms of light, and his return to the Spiritual Father.

The summer solstice is the completion of the path of the spiritual sun, when light is at its height. It is when the trinity of one's Being—of Father, Mother, and Son—becomes whole again, and one can return to the unmanifest source of creation.

It recognizes the light of the sun (and stars) as being of the same essential spiritual nature as the light of consciousness within ourselves, and within all beings, and celebrates the potential each person has to awaken.

As with the winter solstice, the summer solstice has a number of solar events around it that can be celebrated. This is partly due to the phenomenon of the sun appearing to stand still for three days, which occurs at both solstices.

Sunrise on the summer solstice represents the ascent into heaven.

Midday (or more precisely "solar noon") on the summer solstice represents enlightenment and the return to the Spiritual Father. Solar noon is when the sun reaches its highest position in the sky during the day, which in most cases does not occur at twelve o'clock. There are websites that can calculate solar noon for your location.

The three days of solar standstill represent the return to source, which culminates at sunset on the third day—symbolizing the return to the unmanifest source of creation. Sunset on the day of the summer solstice can also be celebrated with the same meaning.

Ceremonies can be conducted at any or all of these times. Their mood is one of happiness and joy.

A GUIDE TO CREATING A SUMMER SOLSTICE CEREMONY

Whether you are a solitary practitioner or working with a group of people, this guide can help you to create your own ceremony, or to expand upon or modify the historical remnants of an existing traditional ceremony.

PREPARING FOR YOUR CEREMONY

To start with, I recommend reading the chapters "The Spiritual Meaning of the Summer Solstice" and "A Guide to Celebrating the Solstices and Equinoxes," as these provide some important background information.

Here is a guide to what information I recommend you gather together first, before creating your ceremony:

1. Summer solstice traditions (optional). This step is optional—it's if you'd like to do a ceremony according to your tradition.

I recommend doing some research to find out how the summer solstice was celebrated in your culture (as long as it is connected in some way to the ancient Religion of the Sun). This is not always easy as so many records of the past have been lost or destroyed. If you can't find much, I'd recommend looking for anything in your tradition that is relevant to the profound meaning of the summer solstice. This could include ancient sites that are aligned to it, and symbols and stories that are relevant to it.

See if there is anything you would like to incorporate into your ceremony.

2. Symbols of the summer solstice. It's nice to use and wear actual symbols of the solstice in your ceremony, just as ancient peoples did. Any symbol of the sun is relevant to the summer solstice, such as the solar cross, swastika, sun wheel, winged sun-disk, Faravahar, etc.

Work out how to incorporate these symbols into your ceremony. For example, you could wear a pendant of the symbol, or have a representation of it on an altar, or make it part of your sacred ceremonial space by creating it out of stones on the ground, etc.

3. Central figure. Choose what will represent the figure that ascends into the higher/heavenly realms in your ceremony. The sun represents the ascent of the Spiritual Son as it rises on the summer solstice, its return to the Spiritual Father at solar noon, and return in wholeness to the source of creation over the three days of solar standstill ending with sunset on the third day, so you may choose to have nothing else representing this central figure but the sun itself.

For those of you who would like to do a ceremony according to your tradition, you could also look to symbolize this figure using a deity from your tradition. Look for one that was associated with the sun and that symbolized the Spiritual Son. There are many examples given in this book, such as Horus, Jesus, Krishna, Baldr, Mithra/Mithras, Viracocha, Quetzalcoatl/Kukulkan, Svarog, Dazhbog, Hu, Lugh, etc.

Decide how you will incorporate this central figure into your ceremony. You could have a statue, painting, or symbol of them on an altar or somewhere in your sacred space. If you are doing a larger group ceremony, then someone could dress as this figure and represent them.

4. Symbols of ascent (optional). This step is optional—it's if you would like to do a ceremony according to your tradition.

Look for any symbols of ascent into higher realms related to the figure you have chosen in the above step 3. Look specifically for those things that represent the following:

    a. The Spiritual Son

    b. The Spiritual Father

    c. Ascension

    d. Higher/heavenly realms

    e. The source of creation and the return to it

Work out how you would like to incorporate these symbols into your ceremony and/or sacred space.

5. Chants, mantras, songs, prayers, readings, music, etc. As part of your ceremony you could choose to read from sacred texts, or sing songs, etc. These could be traditional songs that are part of summer solstice celebrations, excerpts from sacred texts that are relevant to the meaning of the summer solstice, chants that convey the meaning of the summer solstice, or even just pieces of music played on traditional instruments that suit the mood of the event. You may even like to compose your own. Choose which ones you'd like to incorporate as part of your ceremony.

6. Sacred space location and design. Work out where you will hold your ceremony. It will need to be located where everyone participating can see the sun. Ideally, it would also be aligned to the sun (either at sunrise, solar noon, or sunset) in some way, just as many ancient sites are—which can be done simply by lining up stones, candles, an altar, etc., between the viewers and the sun. Whatever design or location you choose, I recommend having a candle or fire you can light as part of your ceremony.

BASIC STRUCTURE

This is a basic outline of a summer solstice ceremony, which can be adapted to any tradition, or can be done without any specific cultural references. It can also be adapted to be more complex, or steps can be left out to make it simpler.

1. Prepare the sacred space where you will conduct your ceremony well in advance.

2. Hold your ceremony at sunrise, and/or solar noon, and/or sunset nearest the summer solstice or on the third day following it (see section "Working out a Calendar and Preparing in Advance" in previous chapter), as this is when the sun itself symbolizes the ascent into heaven and return to source. Make sure any ceremony you choose to do begins before these times so that the particular sunrise, solar noon, or sunset takes place within the ceremony, having worked out how long your ceremony will take so that you are not rushed.

3. Open your ceremony in whatever way you wish—this could be by saying a prayer, a mantra, or chant. Or it could be by playing an instrument or song. I would recommend using any of these as a way to focus your mind and to connect yourself with the spiritual both within and surrounding you.

4. Light a candle or ceremonial fire. The flame of the candle represents the divine inner fire, the Spiritual Son. You can symbolize his journey on the path of the sun by carrying a lit handheld candle to your sacred space, and using it to light your ceremonial fire if you have one. Or you can simply light your candle and ceremonial fire while within your sacred space.

5. Praise your Spiritual Father (optional). Each person has an aspect of their higher Being known as the Spiritual Father. He plays an important part in the events symbolized by this ceremony, so it's appropriate to praise and/or petition him. You could do this simply by repeating something like, "Spiritual Father, please guide me/us," or there may be special phrases in your tradition which you can use. You could use the translation of "Spiritual Father" into your language, or the name of a father god in your tradition. It may be helpful to have a statue or image of the Spiritual Father that you can address yourself to.

6. Do a reading (optional). Optionally, you could recite something from a sacred text about the Spiritual Son in your tradition who ascended to heaven (or returned to source, attained immortality/salvation/enlightenment), retell mythology to do with it, or recite something you've written about it. You could have related statues or images incorporated into your sacred space, or on your altar, etc.

7. Symbolize the ascent to heaven and the Spiritual Father, and/or return to source (optional). The rising sun on the summer solstice symbolizes the ascent to heaven (fully returning at solar noon, and returning to source at sunset), so you don't have to do anything to symbolize it yourself if you prefer not to. For those who would like to also symbolize it themselves in some way there are many ways you can do this, and it can be based on something existing in your tradition. For example, you can raise a symbol of the sun, or float yellow flowers and/or candles on water.

8. Recite prayers, mantras, songs. You might like to spend some time repeating a prayer or mantra, or singing a song. These could be in praise to the Spiritual Father.

9. Watch or be present for the solar event (whether sunrise, solar noon, or sunset). The particular solar event you are celebrating is the main event of the ceremony, and in nature it has its own energies, which it's possible to sense and feel. As an option, you might like to be present for it in silence, or while silently praying, or while singing a chant or mantra. Just be careful though not to look directly at a bright sun, as it can damage your eyes.

10. Close the ceremony. You could do this by saying a prayer of thanks, or by leaving a symbolic offering, such as flowers.

EXAMPLE THEMES

There are many different examples of ceremonies you could perform based on your particular tradition. Not all of them conform to the basic ceremonial structure I've outlined, but that's fine, as they contain enough symbolic elements already to create a coherent ceremony. Here are just a few basic outlines to start with.

ANCIENT EGYPTIAN

A ceremony could symbolize Osiris returning to his father Atum in the region of the circumpolar stars. Readings could be done from the Pyramid Texts and Book of the Dead.

CELTIC

The crowning of the sun god (or Oak King) could be celebrated, and his return to the region of the circumpolar stars, symbolizing his ascent to the eternal realms of light.

GERMANIC/NORDIC

A ceremony could symbolize obtaining salvation by returning to the eternal land of the three bright, heavenly realms of the light elves (those who have attained immortality),[1] which correspond to the three rings of the Absolute and three days of solar standstill at the summer solstice. These are the last three of the twelve cosmic dimensions described in Norse texts.[2]

GNOSTIC CHRISTIAN

The ascension of Jesus could be celebrated, with readings taken from Pistis Sophia, the Odes of Solomon, the Essene Gospel of Peace, and the Nag Hammadi Library.

MAYA

A ceremony could symbolize the ascent through the thirteen heavens of Maya tradition (consisting of nine heavens of the realm of creation, three corresponding to the three rings of the Absolute, and the final unmanifest source). In Gnostic Christianity, they are known as the thirteen aeons. It could also symbolize the Spiritual Son uniting with the world tree, which was represented by the Maya King Pacal in his famous tomb, which is aligned to the summer solstice.

ROMAN

The ascent of Mithras to heaven in the chariot of the sun, and his reunion with the creator and Spiritual Father as Sol, could form the central part of a ceremony.

SLAVIC

See the following example ceremony.

EXAMPLE GROUP CEREMONY ~ Slavic

Slavic summer solstice ceremony in Russia.

This example ceremony is in the Slavic tradition, and is based on traditional ceremonies held as part of the celebration of the summer solstice in Slavic countries still today, such as Russia, Ukraine, Poland, and Belarus. The summer solstice is considered by many Slavs as the most important festival of the year and is perhaps the most celebrated of the four solstices and equinoxes by pagans across Europe and Russia. It is called Kupalo Rodnover.

While many different European traditions celebrate the summer solstice—such as the Celts/Druids, Hellenes/Greeks, Romuvans/Lithuanians, etc.—these celebrations all derive from the same ancient Indo-European source, and many of these groups recognize that they share a common cultural and spiritual heritage.

Little written information about the ancient Slavic tradition survived the introduction of Christianity. Therefore, today many Slavs are reviving their ancient traditions by tracing parallels between other Indo-European traditions and their own, particularly the Vedic tradition preserved in India and the Germanic/Nordic tradition, which share clear and documented similarities.

Likewise, this ceremony is based largely on surviving Slavic religious customs, but also draws upon other Indo-European traditions.

The names of Slavic deities differ according to region, but share similarities, often now being used interchangeably. If working within an existing regional Slavic tradition, feel free to modify the names of deities accordingly.

THE TIMING OF THE CEREMONY

This ceremony begins just before the sunrise closest to the summer solstice in the local time zone.

ITEMS NEEDED

- An archway, which can be made of wood and/or greenery.

- A ceremonial fire.

- A table/altar covered in white linen.

- A large bowl of water (left outside the night before).

- A golden crown.

- A maypole topped with a wreath and/or a symbol of the sacred world tree from any Indo-European tradition, such as the Yggdrasil or Irminsul (Nordic/Germanic). These can be any size, depending on your resources.

- Three wooden statues carved in the image of Svarog (or Rod), Hors Dazhbog, and Lada (or Ziva). These can either be large poles in the ground, or small statues, depending on your resources.

- A Slavic symbol of the sun, such as a solar cross, swastika, hands of god/Svarog, or sun wheel. This can be on a flag, cloth, made of metal (except iron), carved in wood, or made as a wreath out of the leaves of an evergreen tree. It can be any color except black.

- A handheld torch or candle that can be carried safely.

- A marigold flower (or any other flower that looks like the sun) for every participant, which they carry however is practical.

- Optional: wreaths of flowers to be worn by female participants.

- Optional: wreaths of leaves to be worn by male participants. Choose a tree which is deciduous (which means it drops its leaves in autumn and winter, and has leaves which come into their full growth at summer) if possible.

THE PARTICIPANTS

Slavic priests conducting a ceremony at a shrine in Russia.

Priest/Volkhv
A man takes the role of Priest. He dresses in white traditional Slavic clothing, with a blue belt, and wears either a wreath of evergreen leaves, a golden headband, or a traditional Slavic headband with a symbol of the sun embroidered on it. He symbolically enacts the role of Svarog. Ideally he should be old enough to be the father of the man playing the role of Hors Dazhbog.

Priestess/Zhritsa
A woman takes the role of Priestess. Ideally she is the wife of the Priest. She dresses in white traditional Slavic clothing, with a red belt, and wears a wreath of yellow flowers. She symbolically enacts the role of Lada.

Hors Dazhbog
A man plays the role of Hors Dazhbog. He should be a mature man, but ideally young enough to be the son of the Priest. He dresses in white traditional Slavic clothing with a yellow belt, and either wears a large pendant of a symbol of the sun or has it embroidered on the front of his shirt/tunic. He will also carry a symbol of the sun and the handheld torch or candle.

General Participants
The remaining participants dress in white traditional Slavic clothing, and will optionally put on a wreath of leaves (men) or flowers (women) during the ceremony. They each carry a yellow flower.

THE SETUP OF THE SACRED SPACE

A shrine in Russia dedicated to the Slavic god of the sun and fire.
It's a good example of the kind of sacred space that is used in this ceremony.

The sacred space is constructed outside in traditional Slavic style. It can be made of a wooden circular enclosure with an entrance facing the rising summer solstice sun, with a ceremonial fire in the center, or have no enclosure with just the fire. The altar is placed near the fire, and the bowl of water and golden crown are placed on the altar.

Ideally there would be three traditional carved poles in the image of Svarog, Hors Dazhbog, and Lada erected within the sacred space facing the sunrise, with Svarog on the left (when facing the statues, which is to the right of Dazhbog), Dazhbog in the center, and Lada on the right. If you don't have the resources for large poles, then wooden statues of any size are fine to use.

The symbol of the sun will be erected during the ceremony, above Dazhbog, facing the sunrise.

The maypole and/or symbol of the world tree stands within the sacred space.

At a distance from the sacred space, there is a wooden entrance/arch that aligns with the summer solstice sunrise, so that from within the sacred space the sun rises in alignment with the arch.

INSTRUCTIONS FOR THE CEREMONY

1. The sacred space is ready. The sacred space has been prepared in advance and is ready. The ceremonial fire should not be lit yet, as lighting it is part of the ceremony, but it should have enough wood/fuel to burn throughout the entire ceremony.

2. Purification in water. Sometime before sunrise, each participant goes out to a nearby water source, like a stream or lake, and washes their hands and face in water. If there is no natural water source nearby, then they leave a bowl of water outside the night before, and wash in it the morning before the ceremony.

3. Gathering for the ceremony. The Priest stands by the ceremonial fire on the side of Svarog, facing where the sun will rise. Dazhbog stands some distance away from the sacred space so that he will walk from a southerly to northerly direction (if in the Northern Hemisphere, and vice versa if in the Southern) if possible. He holds the symbol of the sun and the handheld torch or candle, which is lit. The Priestess stands behind Dazhbog, and all the General Participants gather behind them in a procession. The General Participants do not yet wear their wreaths, but carry them.

4. Bringing of the sun symbol to the sacred space. Dazhbog begins chanting a song or mantra to the sun, and starts walking to the sacred space. The Priestess and General Participants follow behind him, singing also. Dazhbog and the Priestess enter the sacred space, and Dazhbog places the symbol of the sun on the ground and the torch or candle anywhere it can continue burning safely. They then stand facing where the sun will rise—the Priest on the side of Svarog, the Priestess on that of Lada, and Dazhbog between them. If there is enough room within the sacred space, the General Participants enter it, and stand around the edge of the sacred space in a semicircle, facing the direction of sunrise. If there is not enough room within the sacred space, they do the same, but around the outside of the circle.

5. Chanting in honor of the sun. All chant and sing songs in anticipation of the sun rising.

6. The ceremonial fire is lit. When the sun first begins to appear above the horizon or any terrestrial object, Dazhbog lights the ceremonial fire.

7. Raising of the sun symbol. Dazhbog picks up the symbol of the sun, and erects it above the statue of Dazhbog. It should be as high as possible—at least above head height, so all participants can see it.

8. Crowning of Dazhbog. The Priest picks up the golden crown. Dazhbog kneels before him, and the Priest places it ceremoniously upon his head. Dazhbog stands, and he and the Priest face the sunrise. The General Participants sing a chant/song in celebration. As an option, women can also throw flower petals.

9. Wreathing of the participants. The participants all place their wreaths upon their heads.

10. Reading of sacred writings. The Priest can read or recite any sacred writings relevant to the occasion.

11. Floating flowers upon the water. The General Participants line up in single file, and approach the bowl of water one by one. Each may spend a short time saying a prayer aloud or silently if they wish. They take the marigold flower they've been carrying, and float it in the bowl of water.

12. Circling of the maypole and fire. The General Participants form two circles around the maypole and fire, by holding hands (the Priest, Priestess, and Dazhbog, remain within the circle by the maypole and fire, being seated on ceremonial chairs if they need to). The inner circle should be the men, and the outer the women. The men circle around the maypole in a sunwise direction, and the women counter-sunwise. After this, one circle is made, again by holding hands, with men and women alternating between each other, circling in a sunwise direction (see section "Doing Things in a Sunwise Direction" in chapter 12). Dances should be based on the traditional circular sun dances. If you don't have enough participants, just the one circle of men and women can be done. Songs, mantras, or chants relevant to the occasion can be sung while this is happening.

13. Leaving by the gate of the sun. The Priest, Dazhbog, and Priestess join hands and leave the sacred space, walking through the wooden arch as the General Participants watch. The General Participants also then all walk through the wooden arch. The ceremony has now ended.

As an alternative to step 11 or in addition to it, participants can have prepared wreaths of flowers with lit candles in the center, and float these on lakes and streams, symbolizing the same thing.

Celebrations can continue after the ceremony, but any activities should conclude before midnight.

THE MEANING OF THE CEREMONY

This ceremony symbolizes the ascension of Dazhbog, the Spiritual Son/sun, and his return to heavenly Svarga—the realm of his father Svarog.

The three fundamental forces of creation—of Father, Mother, and Son—are represented by Svarog, Lada, and Dazhbog. They also represent the three parts of each one's higher Being.

In some Serbian folk songs, a trinity of Slavic deities is associated with the Christian Trinity. The Slavic trinity given in these songs is of Vishnji, Ziva, and Branjanj, which correlates to the trinity of Vishnu, Shiva, and Brahma in India. This is no coincidence, as incredibly, these folk tales say that the Slavic trinity was brought from India when the ancestors of the Serbian people had once lived there, but had been forced to flee and find new lands.[3] In India, all three deities of the trinity are male, but in this Serbian Slavic trinity Ziva is female, which corresponds to the role the feminine has in creation. This may have been based on another creative trinity in India—of Vishnu, Lakshmi, and Brahma—in which Lakshmi is a goddess.

> "May our cattle be healthy
> All the cows and all the sheep
> All the kids and all the lambs
> All the great big horses
> Which carry our heroes
> Dear soldiers of the god Triglav
> god Triglav the holy trinity
> Vishnji god, the creator
> Strong Ziva the destroyer
> and Branjanj the protector" [4]

Ziva is a Slavic mother goddess associated with water (Lada with earth), and Svarog a god associated with fire and heaven (and Rod with heaven). These elements are both present in the ceremony, representing the dual feminine and masculine forces of creation, and the corresponding aspects of each one's higher Being. Slavic summer solstice festivals celebrated the union of water and fire, and the marriage of earth and heaven.[5] This is symbolic of the female and male aspects of one's higher Being reuniting as one, and are also represented in the ceremony by the sacred world tree with its roots in the earthly/underworld realm (feminine) and branches reaching into the heavenly realm (masculine) united as one through the trunk—the Spiritual Son. The maypole also symbolizes this spiritual union.

Men in Belarus erect a pole for Kupala.

The trinity of Father, Mother, and Son corresponds to the realms of heaven, underworld/earth, and middle/intermediary plane, which in Slavic traditions are called Prav, Nav, and Yav, and in Vedic tradition Svah, Bhu, and Bhuvah.[6] Slavic statues of the Triglav or trinity were carved as pillars with three or four faces. The pillar is said to represent the axis that connects the three realms of underworld, earth, and heaven, like the world tree[7] and maypole.

The purification in water before the ceremony begins is based on a Slavic custom of washing in a natural water source before sunrise on the morning of the summer solstice. The word for the summer solstice—Kupala—actually means "to bathe," and was so named because of this custom.[8] It represents the inner purification one must go through before being able to spiritually ascend; this energetic purification is done with the aid of one's Spiritual Mother (the mother goddess associated with water). After bathing, the sun was honored,[9] as it is in this ceremony.

White is worn, as this is the color of the sun symbolizing completion, where all colors return to their source, which is white light. It is also the color of purity, symbolizing inner spiritual purity. The priest wears a blue belt, as blue is that of the heavens/Svarga and the sky. The priestess wears a red belt, as red is the color of the earth. Dazhbog wears yellow, and this is the color of the sun as seen from Earth.

Dazhbog brings the symbol of the sun to the sacred space, symbolizing the journey on the path of the spiritual sun, and its raising as the sun rises symbolizes the ascension of the Spiritual Son. He walks in the direction of south to north to symbolize ascending on the path of the sun to where the sun is at its height at the summer solstice in the Northern Hemisphere, which is in the north. These directions are reversed if doing the ceremony in the Southern Hemisphere (for an explanation see section "Doing Things in a Sunwise Direction" in chapter 12).

Dazhbog also carries the fire to the ceremony, symbolizing the divine fire of the Spiritual Son ascending to Svarga/heaven represented by his walk with it to the sacred space. It is used to light the ceremonial fire symbolizing the return of the Spiritual Son to the realm of the Spiritual Father. To follow Slavic custom, this fire can then be used to light all other celebratory fires.

The Priest crowns Dazhbog with the crown of Nav (heaven),[10] symbolizing the Spiritual Son becoming one with the Spiritual Father and being made king of the three realms, symbolized by the powerful ruler Svetovid who is the form of the sun god celebrated in Slavic tradition at the summer solstice.[11] A statue of Triglav—ruler of the three realms—was said to have had its heads covered with a tiara or hat of gold,[12] and likewise a golden crown is used in this ceremony, symbolizing the full power of the sun.

Kupala by Viktor Kryzhanivskyi Solceslav. It depicts the solar god rising as fire from water, as one with the world tree, and crowned as king at summer.

The wreaths placed upon the heads of the participants symbolize the union of the human with the divine, of earth being crowned by the heavenly sun, as in Slavic tradition flower wreaths symbolize the sun during the spring and summer months[13] when vegetation reaches its full bloom.

Slavic ceremony in Poland—women wear wreaths of flowers and men wreaths of oak leaves.

The participants carry a yellow flower each, which represents their own divine Being. At summer, this Being has symbolically come into full bloom, reaching its potential. Placing it in the bowl of water symbolizes its return to heaven. This echoes Slavic summer solstice customs, in which flowers are floated on lakes and rivers.

A girl in Russia floats a candle and wreath of flowers on a river at Kupala.

The circular dances around the maypole and fire are very ancient dances that are still part of Slavic summer solstice festivals today. In Montenegro, young people danced the ancient circular sun dance called Koro wearing wreaths of flowers on the Christian "Feast of Ascension" (celebrating the ascension of Jesus),[14] which would have replaced an earlier summer pagan festival likely symbolizing the ascension of the pre-Christian Slavic sun god.

The circle of men and women around the fire creates the symbol of the sun, and the three rings of the Absolute that correspond to the three days of summer solstice solar standstill, when viewed from above. They circle in opposite directions to symbolize the dual nature of masculine and feminine. The circle of women and men join to become one, symbolizing the last ring of the Absolute where the masculine and feminine halves of one's Being become one.

Circle dances at the summer solstice in Russia.

The participants all leave by the arch, symbolizing the northern gate of the sun that those who reach salvation are said to leave the material world by. This gate is spoken of in the ancient Hindu texts the Upanishads, and by Krishna in the famous Bhagavad Gita.

An archway made of wood and/or greenery used for midsummer celebrations in Lithuania—similar ones are used in Slavic summer solstice celebrations.

CHAPTER SEVENTEEN

Conclusion

I hope this book contributes to the rekindling of the celebration of the path of the spiritual sun and the spiritual knowledge contained within it. This knowledge is helpful to anyone wishing to undertake the path of the spiritual sun that ancient people once read in creation, and to anyone who wishes to practice the principles contained in the Religion of the Sun, which was once humanity's most prolific religion.

APPLYING THE PRINCIPLES OF THE SUN

The great cycle of the sun and the earth reflects the principles that are the very keys to this path. The west and the autumn equinox, which the Maya associated with the color black, is symbolic of inner death. The winter solstice, associated with the color yellow, is symbolic of inner birth and creation. The east and spring equinox, associated with red, is symbolic of self-sacrifice. And the summer solstice, associated with the color white, is symbolic of ascension and the completion of the path of the sun, as the color of the sun and its light beyond the atmosphere of the earth.

> "The red wild bees are in the east. A large red blossom is their cup. The red Plumeria is their flower.
>
> The white wild bees are in the north. The white pachca is their flower. A large white blossom is their cup.
>
> The black wild bees are in the west. The black laurel flower is their flower. A large black blossom is their cup.

The yellow wild bees are in the south. A large yellow blossom is their cup ... is their flower."[1]
~ THE BOOK OF CHILAM BALAM OF CHUMAYEL

The three principles of inner death, birth, and self-sacrifice signify the basis of the practice that leads someone to ascend on the path of the sun, to reach its completion—thereby returning to their Being and the divine source, symbolized by the sun at the summer solstice and the circumpolar region of the stars.

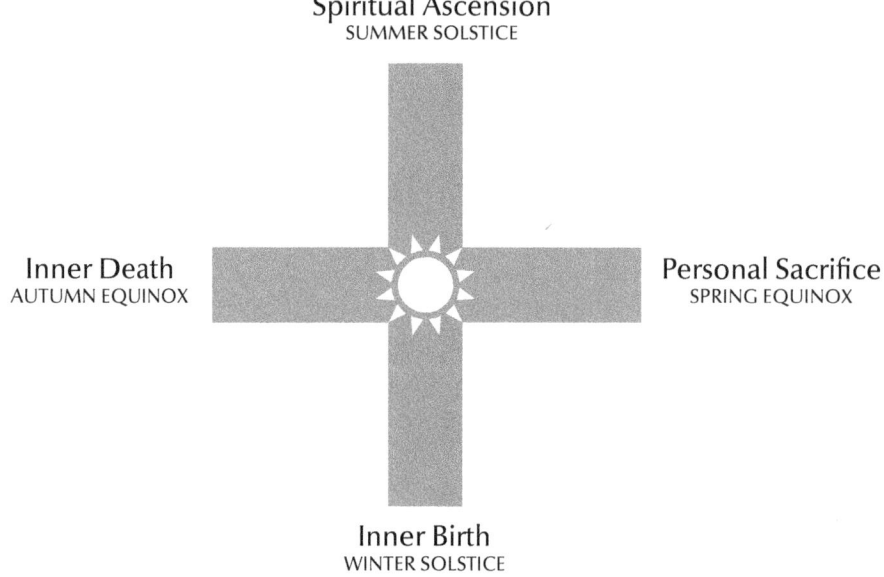

These principles are those of creation and are immutable, naturally observable, and timeless.

This kind of knowledge today may be largely derided as fantasy by some, but it wasn't in the past—it was greatly valued. The solstices and equinoxes, and the spiritual principles reflected in them, held significant meaning for many ancient peoples. Humanity's rich heritage of spiritual, mythological, and religious texts, art, and artefacts is a testimony to the central role this knowledge played in their lives.

Although the key components of this ancient knowledge are timeless, this is a different humanity and a different world today. It is a time when the material dominates the spiritual, where humanity has lost the understanding of natural principles, and where the majority of people think a lot, but seldom perceive spiritual truths.

Until now, the ancient knowledge of the spiritual sun has been all but lost to humanity. Yet I hope this book will contribute to its lasting re-emergence; moreover, that the wisdom of the sun will once again serve as a guiding light for all those seeking the return to their higher Being.

I also hope that in time, people in many cities and towns throughout the world will come together to celebrate the solstices and equinoxes, and that sites will be created where four times a year people go to celebrate these ancient and wondrous festivals, keeping alive the awareness of the spiritual sun and the incredible knowledge it conveys.

MORE INFORMATION

For more information about the history of the ancient Religion of the Sun, see the book *The Ancient Religion of the Sun* by Lara Atwood, and the website SakroSawel.com

PUBLISHER'S NOTE

The authors have worked very hard over nine years to put together this book, and the utmost has been done to ensure all sources are fully referenced and credited. It contains unique and original work, which is breaking new ground in its field, and the authors should be properly credited if this work is used elsewhere.

In academia, there are rigorous standards and expectations requiring proper attribution when drawing upon the work of others. Outside this field, however, there often seems to be a "free for all" kind of attitude and plagiarism is rife.

Yet stealing is not ok, whether it is of physical items, a passage of writing, or something more intangible like an idea or a body of research—all of these things have cost their owner in time and effort. It's unethical and intellectually dishonest to present the ideas and research of another as if it were one's own.

If you have seen any work from this book that has been used without proper attribution, please let us know by contacting us, the publisher, through our website suraondrunar.org

HOW TO CITE THIS WORK

If you would like to use this book as a source in your own work, at a minimum please include a reference to the authors' names, the book title, and where applicable, the relevant page number(s) for any content or ideas referred to. In informal internet mediums like blog posts and online videos, a hyperlink back to the original source should also be provided where possible.

In formal publications, full citations should be used that follow any industry-recognized style guide. Here is an example of a formal citation of this book:

Atwood, Mark with Lara Atwood. *Ancient Solstice: Uncovering the Spiritual Meaning of the Solstices and Equinoxes*. Updated 4th ed. Sura Ondrunar Publishing, 2021, p. [Insert page number(s) where applicable].

References

TEXTUAL REFERENCES

PREFACE

1. "Gurdjieff's Search for Esoteric Knowledge." Learning Institute for Growth, Healing and Transformation. http://gurdjiefffourthway.org/pdf/search.pdf, 5.
2. Note that resellers of our books set their own prices; neither we or our publisher have any control over the prices they set, nor receive any money from their sale. Reseller prices are sometimes determined by a book's availability—a rare book may cost hundreds of dollars on Amazon for example. We receive no money from the sale of our books at all—no matter who is selling them and at what price they are sold.

CHAPTER ONE: THE SPIRITUAL MEANING OF THE SOLSTICES AND EQUINOXES

1. Prabhavananda, Swami, and Frederick Manchester, trans. *The Upanishads: Breath from the Eternal*. New York: New American Library, 2002, p. 74.
2. Giles, Lionel, trans. *The Sayings of Lao-Tzŭ*. Edited by L. Cranmer-Byng and Dr. S. A. Kapadia. New York: E. P. Dutton and Company, Inc., 1905, p. 21.
3. Hall, Manly P. *The Secret Teachings of All Ages*. San Francisco: H.S. Crocker Company, 1928, p. 85.
4. For some example theories, see https://en.wikipedia.org/wiki/Extra_dimensions.
5. Szekely, Edmond Bordeaux, trans. *The Essene Gospel of Peace: Book Four*. USA: International Biogenic Society, 1981, p. 38.
6. Lambdin, Thomas O., trans. "The Gospel of Thomas." In *The Nag Hammadi Library in English*, edited by James M. Robinson. San Francisco: HarperCollins, 1990, p. 126.
7. Prabhavananda and Manchester, trans., *Upanishads*, 21.
8. Mead, G. R. S., trans. *Pistis Sophia*. London: J. M. Watkins, 1921, p. 155-156.
9. Hall, *Secret Teachings*, 51.
10. Walker, Brian Browne, trans. *Hua Hu Ching: The Unknown Teachings of Lao Tzu*. San Francisco: HarperCollins, 1995, p. 43.
11. Hall, *Secret Teachings*, 39.
12. Giles, trans., *Sayings of Lao-Tzŭ*, 19.
13. Hall, *Secret Teachings*, 40.
14. Hume, Robert Ernest, trans. *The Thirteen Principal Upanishads*. Oxford University Press, 1921, p. 435.
15. Hall, *Secret Teachings*, 51.
16. "Sun worship." Britannica. https://www.britannica.com/topic/sun-worship.

17. Drower, E. S. *The Mandaeans of Iraq and Iran: Their Cults, Customs, Magic, Legends, and Folklore*. Leiden: Brill, 1962. The Gnostic Society Library. http://gnosis.org/library/manda-dower-1937.html.
18. Smith, William Benjamin. "Meaning of the Epithet Nazorean (Nazarene)." *The Monist* 15, no. 1 (January 1905): 25-45. https://www.jstor.org/stable/27899560.
19. Budge, E. A. Wallis, trans. *The Book of the Dead: The Papyrus of Ani*. London: The British Museum, 1895, p. liii.
20. *The Kolbrin*. The Culdian Trust, 2014, p. 111. eBook.
21. Lambdin, trans., *"The Gospel of Thomas,"* 135.
22. *The Holy Bible*. New International Version (NIV). Biblica, 2011.
23. Swarupananda, Swami, trans. *Srimad-Bhagavad-Gita*. Almora: Advaita Ashrama, 1909, p. 330.
24. Heyerdahl, Thor. *American Indians in the Pacific*. London: Allen & Unwin, 1952, p. 251.
25. Ibid.
26. Budge, E. A. Wallis. *Osiris and the Egyptian Resurrection, Vol. 1*. London: Philip Lee Warner, 1911, p. 2-22.
27. "Helena Blavatsky." Wikipedia. https://en.wikipedia.org/wiki/Helena_Blavatsky#Tibet.
28. *Stanzas of Dzyan*. Theosophy Wiki. https://theosophy.wiki/en/Stanzas_of_Dzyan.
29. Müller, F. Max, trans. *Vedic Hymns: Part 1, Hymns to the Maruts, Rudra, Vâyu, and Vâta*. Clarendon: Oxford University Press, 1891, p. 1.
30. *Stanzas of Dzyan*.
31. Atwood, Lara. *The Ancient Religion of the Sun: The Wisdom Bringers and The Lost Civilization of the Sun*. 2nd ed. Sura Ondrunar Publishing, 2021, p. 145-146.
32. Peel, Malcolm L., and Jan Zandee, trans. "The Teachings of Silvanus." In *The Nag Hammadi Library in English*, edited by James M. Robinson. San Francisco: HarperCollins, 1990, p. 387.
33. *The Gospel of the Kailedy*. The Culdian Trust, 1998, p. 7.
34. Chand, Devi, trans. *The Yajur Veda*. Hoshiarpur: All India Dayanand Salvation Mission, 1959, p. 54.
35. Worrall, Simon. "How 40,000 Tons of Cosmic Dust Falling to Earth Affects You and Me." National Geographic, January 28, 2015. https://www.nationalgeographic.com/news/2015/01/150128-big-bang-universe-supernova-astrophysics-health-space-ngbooktalk/.
36. Jayawardhana, Ray. "Our Cosmic Selves." The New York Times, April 3, 2015. https://www.nytimes.com/2015/04/05/opinion/sunday/our-cosmic-selves.html.
37. "Electric Sun Theory." Electric Universe Theory Project. https://www.electricuniverse.info/electric-sun-theory/.
38. "Sun, Thunder, Fire." Old European Culture, June 17, 2017. http://oldeuropeanculture.blogspot.com/2017/06/sun-thunder-fire.html.
39. Molesky-Poz, Jean. *Contemporary Maya Spirituality: The Ancient Ways Are Not Lost*. Austin: University of Texas Press, 2006, location 2939. Kindle edition.
40. Griffith, Ralph T. H., trans. *The Hymns of the Rigveda*. 1896, book 1, hymn 59.
41. Srivastava, V. C., trans. *Samba-Purana*. Parimal Publication Pvt. Ltd., 2013, p. 3.
42. Purohit Swami, Shri, trans. *The Bhagavad Gita*. Circa 1935.
43. Griffith, trans., *Hymns of the Rigveda*, book 1, hymn 1.
44. "The Sacred Fire and Agni." American Institute of Vedic Studies, June 13, 2012. https://vedanet.com/2012/06/13/the-sacred-fire-and-agni/.
45. Humbach, Helmut, and Pallan Ichaporia, trans. *The Heritage of Zarathushtra: A New Translation of His Gathas*. Heidelberg: Universitätsverlag Winter, 1994; Yasna Haptanhaiti 36.6 translation by Helmut Humbach and Pallan Ichaporia from Shapero, Hannah. "Zoroastrian Mysticism I: The Mysticism of the Gathas." Pyracantha Studios, March 3, 1996. http://www.pyracantha.com/Z/mysticz4.html.
46. Mills, L. H., trans. *The Zend Avesta, Part III, Sacred Books of the East, Vol. 31*. Oxford University Press, 1887, p. 255, 346.
47. Hall, *Secret Teachings*, 39.
48. Budge, trans., *Book of the Dead*, 317.
49. Lambdin, trans., "The Gospel of Thomas," 135.

50. Purohit, trans., *The Bhagavad Gita*.
51. Ibid.
52. Krishnananda, Swami, trans. "Narayana Sukta." In *Daily Invocations*. Rishikesh: The Divine Life Trust Society, 67-70.
53. Chand, trans., *The Yajur Veda*, 38.
54. Hume, trans., *The Thirteen Principal Upanishads*, 373-374.
55. Alexander, Eben. "My Experience in Coma." http://ebenalexander.com/about/my-experience-in-coma/; Eben Alexander in Tsakiris, Alex. "Neurosurgeon Dr. Eben Alexander's Near-death experience defies medical model of consciousness." Skeptiko, November 22, 2011. https://skeptiko.com/154-neurosurgeon-dr-eben-alexander-near-death-experience/; Alexander, Eben, M.D. *Proof of Heaven*. Simon & Schuster: New York, 2012, p. 45, 46.
56. *The Kolbrin*, 239-240.
57. Ibid., 160.
58. Easwaran, Eknath, trans. *The Upanishads*. Tomales: Nilgiri Press, 2007, p. 188.
59. Purohit, trans., *The Bhagavad Gita*.
60. Cowell, E. B., trans. *The Maitri or Maitrāyanīya Upanishad*. Calcutta: Asiatic Society of Bengal, 1870, p. 258, 276-7.
61. Easwaran, trans., *The Upanishads*, 226-227.
62. Lundy, John P. *Monumental Christianity*. New York: J W Bouton, 1876, p. 165.
63. Hancock, Graham, and Robert Bauval. *The Message of the Sphinx: A Quest for the Hidden Legacy of Mankind*. New York: Three Rivers Press, 1996, p. 208-209.
64. Ibid., 213.
65. *Stanzas of Dzyan*.
66. See article by Allen Tsai http://www.chinesefortunecalendar.com/YinYang.htm for more information.
67. "Yin and Yang." Old European Culture, February 5, 2018. http://oldeuropeanculture.blogspot.com/2018/02/yin-and-yang.html.
68. Image attribution: "What is the Design of the UMass Sunwheel?" University of Massachusetts Amherst. https://www.umass.edu/sunwheel/pages/design.html.
69. "Awen." Wikipedia. https://en.wikipedia.org/wiki/Awen; Orr, Emma Restall. *Living Druidry*. Piatkus Books, 2004.
70. Atwood, *Ancient Religion of the Sun*, 345-348.
71. O'Connell, Cathal. "What Shape Are Photons? Quantum Holography Sheds Light." Cosmos, July 20, 2016. https://cosmosmagazine.com/physics/what-shape-is-a-photon.
72. "Mezine." Wikipedia. https://en.wikipedia.org/wiki/Mezine.
73. See article by Sergey Smelyakov found at http://www.astrotheos.com/Page8.htm for a more detailed explanation.
74. "Analemma." Wikipedia. https://en.wikipedia.org/wiki/Analemma.
75. Brennan, Martin. *The Stones of Time: Calendars, Sundials, and Stone Chambers of Ancient Ireland*. Rochester: Inner Traditions International, 1994, p. 190.
76. "Biography." Charles Ross. http://charlesrossstudio.com/biography.
77. "Tarim mummies." Wikipedia. https://en.wikipedia.org/wiki/Tarim_mummies.
78. Doutré, Martin. "Megalithic New Zealand." Ancient Celtic New Zealand, 2000. http://www.celticnz.co.nz/mnz_pt1.html.
79. "NASA's IBEX Provides First View of the Solar System's Tail." NASA, July 11, 2013. https://www.nasa.gov/content/nasa-s-ibex-provides-first-view-of-the-solar-system-s-tail.
80. "Venus." Wikipedia. https://en.wikipedia.org/wiki/Venus#Pentagram_of_Venus.
81. Mannikka, Eleanor. *Angkor Wat: Time, Space, and Kingship*. University of Hawaii Press, 2000, p. 49-58.
82. Greer, Stephen M. "Exopolitics or Xenopolitics?" Sirius Disclosure, March 2013. https://siriusdisclosure.com/cseti-papers/exopolitics-or-xenopolitics/; Greer, Stephen M. *Hidden Truth, Forbidden Knowledge*. Crossing Point, Inc., 2006; "Evidence." Sirius Disclosure. https://siriusdisclosure.com/evidence/.

83. "Two crosses." Old European Culture, July 25, 2016. https://oldeuropeanculture.blogspot.com/2016/07/two-crosses.html.
84. Ibid.
85. Angel, Paul Tudor. "Who Built New England's Megalithic Monuments?" *The Barnes Review* (November 1997). Planet Vermont Quarterly. http://planetvermont.com/pvq/v9n2/megaliths.html.
86. Eccott, David J. "The Ogams of the Sun Temple." Old News. http://www.onter.net/biblio/eccott.pdf.
87. "How Old Is Crom Dubh." Old European Culture, April 16, 2015. https://oldeuropeanculture.blogspot.com/2015/04/how-old-is-crom-dubh.html.
88. "Grange Circle." Old European Culture, September 11, 2014. https://oldeuropeanculture.blogspot.com/2014/09/grange-circle.html.
89. "How old is Crom Dubh," Old European Culture.
90. "Yalda Night." Wikipedia. https://en.wikipedia.org/wiki/Yalda_Night.
91. Betham, Sir William. "The Celtæ." Chap. 7 in *The Gael and Cymbri*. Dublin: William Curry, Jun. and Co., 1834.
92. Smith, Thomas, trans. *Ante-Nicene Christian Library, Vol. XVII: The Clementine Homilies*. Edited by Alexander Roberts and James Donaldson. Edinburgh: T. & T. Clark, 1870, p. 2.
93. Ibid., 1-2.
94. Ibid., 5.
95. Christenson, Allen J., trans. *Popol Vuh: Sacred Book of the Quiché Maya People*. Norman: University of Oklahoma Press, 2003. Electronic version, Mesoweb, 2007, p. 218. http://www.mesoweb.com/publications/Christenson/PopolVuh.pdf.
96. Ibid., 236, 248.
97. *The Kolbrin*, chap. 12.
98. Ibid., chap. 14.
99. Heyerdahl, Thor. "The Bearded Gods Speak." In *The Quest for America*, by Geoffrey Ashe. New York: Praeger, 1971.
100. James, M. R., trans. *The Apocryphal New Testament*. Oxford University Press, 1983, p. 10.
101. Smith, trans., *Clementine Homilies*, 81.
102. *The Kolbrin*, 57.
103. Ibid., 712.
104. Ibid., 133.
105. Szekely, Edmond Bordeaux, trans. *The Essene Gospel of Peace: Book One*. USA: International Biogenic Society, 1981, p. 13.

CHAPTER TWO: THE SPIRITUAL MEANING OF THE AUTUMN EQUINOX

1. Nicols, Mike. "The Death of Llew, a Seasonal Interpretation." 1999. Internet Sacred Text Archive. https://www.sacred-texts.com/bos/bos052.htm.
2. Mackenzie, Donald A. *Teutonic Myth and Legend*. London: Gresham Publications, 1912, p. 146.
3. Nicols, "The Death of Llew."
4. "St. Michael the Archangel." Catholic Online. https://www.catholic.org/encyclopedia/view.php?id=7948.
5. "Michaelmas." People of Goda, the Clan of Tubal Cain, September 25, 2014. https://www.clantubalcain.com/2014/09/25/michaelmas-3/.
6. New American Standard Bible (NASB). The Lockman Foundation, 1995.
7. Nichols, Mike. "Harvest Home." 1999. Internet Sacred Text Archive. https://www.sacred-texts.com/bos/bos051.htm.
8. *The Holy Bible*, New International Version (NIV). Biblica, 2011.
9. Ibid.
10. Easwaran, Eknath, trans. *The Upanishads*. Tomales: Nilgiri Press, 2007, p. 127.
11. Whiteman, Yvonne. "Guide to the Kolbrin." GrahamHanock.com, October 17, 2015. https://grahamhancock.com/whitemany1/.

12. *The Kolbrin*. The Culdian Trust, 2014, p. 421. eBook.
13. Ibid., 229.
14. Ibid., 203.
15. "When Was the Giza Complex Constructed." Ancient-Wisdom, February 10, 2009. http://www.ancient-wisdom.com/Ghizawhen.htm.
16. "Draco (constellation)." Wikipedia. https://en.wikipedia.org/wiki/Draco_(constellation).
17. Ibid.
18. "Typhon." Wikipedia. https://en.wikipedia.org/wiki/Typhon.
19. "Duat." Wikipedia. https://en.wikipedia.org/wiki/Duat.
20. "Apep." Wikipedia. https://en.wikipedia.org/wiki/Apep.
21. Kvilhaug, Maria. *The Seed of Yggdrasill: Deciphering the Hidden Messages in Old Norse Myths*. Whyte Tracks, 2016, section 5.2 The Peace of Wisdom and the Song of the Millstone: The Chains That Bound Fenrir. Kindle edition.
22. Ibid., section 3.14 Soma and Haoma, Ambrosia, Kykeon, Cerridwen's Cauldron and the Indo-European Connection: The Book of Taliesin.
23. "When was the Giza Complex Constructed," Ancient-Wisdom.
24. Sparavigna, Amelia. "The Pleiades: the celestial herd of ancient timekeepers." Politecnico di Torino, 2008. https://arxiv.org/ftp/arxiv/papers/0810/0810.1592.pdf.
25. "The Pleiades in Mythology." Pleiade Associates. http://www.pleiade.org/pleiades_02.html.
26. "Neith." Wikipedia. https://en.wikipedia.org/wiki/Neith.
27. Dungen, Wim van den. "The Book of : The Hidden Chamber ca. 1426 BCE or : the Twelve Hours of the Night and the Midnight Mystery, Section 3, The Summary of the Amduat, The Twelve Hours : A Commentary." MAAT.sofiatopia.org, December 7, 2010. http://www.sofiatopia.org/maat/hidden_chamber03.htm.
28. Ibid.
29. Ancient Architects. "Secrets of the Subterranean Chamber of the Great Pyramid." YouTube, March 31, 2020. https://youtu.be/g8gRR44PiPQ.
30. Dungen, "The Book of : The Hidden Chamber."
31. Proctor, Richard A. *The Great Pyramid: Observatory, Tomb, and Temple*. London: Longmans, Green, and Co., 1888, p. 71-77. Note that Smyth's measurements of the entrance passage to the Great Pyramid have been criticized as irrelevant as different areas of the passages have slightly differing dimensions (see https://en.wikipedia.org/wiki/Charles_Piazzi_Smyth note 5). However, this is likely due to subsidence (see Davidson and Aldersmith, *The Great Pyramid: Its Divine Message*, 118-119). Also, Smyth's interpretation of these particular measurements have been viewed as far-fetched. Yet given the stellar and solar alignments of the Great Pyramid and their correlation with Egyptian religion, which itself correlates to the design of the Great Pyramid, I can't help but feel there is something to them.
32. Davidson, D., and H. Aldersmith. *The Great Pyramid: Its Divine Message, Vol. I. Pyramid Records*. London: William Rider and Son Limited, 1961, p. 129-137.
33. Dungen, "The Book of : The Hidden Chamber."
34. Ibid.
35. Young, John K. *Sacred Sites of the Knights Templar*. Gloucester: Fair Winds Press, 2003, p. 185.
36. *The Gospel of the Kailedy*. The Culdian Trust, 1998, p. 16-17.
37. Panikkar, Raimon, trans. "The Hymn of the Origins." In *The Vedic Experience: Mantramanjari*. Maryknoll: Orbis Books, 2016.
38. Grant, Evan. "Evan Grant: Making Sound Visible through Cymatics." YouTube, September 9, 2009. https://youtu.be/CsjV1gjBMbQ?t=94.
39. Emmel, Stephen, trans. "The Dialogue of the Savior." In *The Nag Hammadi Library in English*, edited by James M. Robinson. San Francisco: HarperCollins, 1990, p. 250.
40. Isenberg, Wesley W., trans. "The Gospel of Philip." In *The Nag Hammadi Library in English*, edited by James M. Robinson. San Francisco: HarperCollins, 1990, p. 142.
41. "Eleusinian Mysteries." Wikipedia. https://en.wikipedia.org/wiki/Eleusinian_Mysteries.
42. Szekely, Edmond Bordeaux, trans. *The Essene Gospel of Peace: Book Three*. USA: International Biogenic Society, 1981, p. 93.

43. Purohit Swami, Shri, trans. *The Bhagavad Gita*. Circa 1935.
44. Easwaran, trans., *The Upanishads*, 227.
45. *The Holy Bible*, NIV.
46. See examples of this in Chapter Three.
47. Donaldson, James, trans. *Ante-Nicene Christian Library, Vol. XVII: The Clementine Homilies*. Edited by Alexander Roberts and James Donaldson. Edinburgh: T. & T. Clark, 1870, p. 269-270.
48. *The Holy Bible*, NIV.
49. Salaman, Clement, Dorine Van Oyen, William D. Wharton, and Jean-Pierre Mahe, trans. *The Way of Hermes: New Translations of The Corpus Hermeticum and The Definitions of Hermes Trismegistus to Asclepius*. Rochester: Inner Traditions, 2004, book 13:14.
50. Zandee, J. *Death as an Enemy: According to Ancient Egyptian Conceptions*. Translated by W. F. Klasens. Leiden: E. J. Brill, 1960, p. 58.
51. Mercer, Samuel A. B., trans. *The Pyramid Texts*. New York: Longmans, Green & Co., 1952, p. 302.
52. Wilhelm, Richard, trans. *The Secret of the Golden Flower*. Translated from German to English by Cary F. Baynes. San Diego: Harcourt Brace & Company, 1962, p. 23.
53. James, M. R., trans. "The Acts of Thomas." In *The Apocryphal New Testament*. Oxford: Clarendon Press, 1924. The Gnostic Society Library. http://gnosis.org/library/actthom.htm.
54. Wile, Douglas, trans. *True Transmission of the Golden Elixir*. Albany: State University of New York Press, 1992.
55. Nabaraz, Payam. *The Mysteries of Mithras*. Rochester: Inner Traditions, 2005, p. 30.
56. James, trans., "The Acts of Thomas."
57. Edwards, Edmundo R., and Juan Antonio Belmonte. "Megalithic Astronomy of Easter Island: A Reassessment." *Journal for the History of Astronomy* 35, part 4, no. 121 (November 2004): 427. http://articles.adsabs.harvard.edu/cgi-bin/nph-iarticle_query?bibcode=2004JHA....35..421E.
58. James, trans., "The Acts of Thomas."
59. Szekely, Edmond Bordeaux, trans. *The Essene Gospel of Peace: Book Four*. USA: International Biogenic Society, 1981, p. 16.
60. Mackenzie, *Teutonic Myth and Legend*, 14, 18.
61. Budge, E. A. Wallis, trans. *The Book of the Dead: The Papyrus of Ani*. London: The British Museum, 1895, p. 308, 331-332.
62. Kvilhaug, *Seed of Yggdrasill*, section 3.17 Not Quite the Christian Poem After All. Sólarljóð (The Song of the Sun); chap. 3: Introduction: A Path of Initiation.
63. Parrott, Douglas M., and R. McL. Wilson, trans. "The Acts of Peter and the Twelve Apostles." In *The Nag Hammadi Library in English*, edited by James M. Robinson. San Francisco: HarperCollins, 1990, p. 291.
64. Easwaran, trans., *The Upanishads*, 168.
65. Purohit, trans., *The Bhagavad Gita*.
66. Roys, Ralph L., trans. *The Book of Chilam Balam of Chumayel*. Washington D.C.: Carnegie Institution, 1933, p. 104. Internet Sacred Text Archive. https://www.sacred-texts.com/nam/maya/cbc/cbc15.htm.
67. Wile, trans., *True Transmission*.
68. "Nabapatrika: A Puja Ritual." The Statesman, October 10, 2016. https://www.thestatesman.com/supplements/nabapatrika-a-puja-ritual-170016.html.
69. Ganguli, Kisari Mohan, trans. *The Mahabharata*. Circa 1883-1896.
70. "Durga Chalisa" (lyrics traditional). English translation found here: http://www.indif.com/nri/chalisas/durgachalisa/durgachalisa_meaning.asp.
71. Sharma, Pt. Atma Ram, trans. *Maha Calisa Samgraha*, edited by Dr. R. C. Prasad, revised by Dr. G. P. Bhatt. Dehli: Motilal Banarsidass, 1994, p. 202.
72. V, Jayaram. "Symbolic Significance of Ramayana." Hinduwebsite.com. https://www.hinduwebsite.com/symbolism/ramayana.asp.
73. Das, Subhamoy. "The History and Origin of the Durga Puja Festival." Learn Religions, September 3, 2018. https://www.thoughtco.com/the-history-and-origin-of-durga-puja-1770159. Note that this story is found in the version of the Ramayana known as the Krittivasi Ramayana composed by Bengali poets in the fifteenth century.

74. "Durga." Wikipedia. https://en.wikipedia.org/wiki/Durga. Devi Sukta, Rigveda 10.125.3-10.125.8, based on Griffith, Ralph T. H. (trans.). "The Rig Veda/Mandala 10/Hymn 125." Wikisource. https://en.wikisource.org/wiki/The_Rig_Veda/Mandala_10/Hymn_125; McDaniel, June. *Offering Flowers, Feeding Skulls: Popular Goddess Worship in West Bengal*. Oxford University Press, 2004, p. 90.
75. Kali, Devadatta, trans. *In Praise of the Goddess: The Devimahatmya and Its Meaning*. Berwick: Nicolas-Hays, 2003, p. 65, 66-67.
76. "Kali." Wikipedia. https://en.wikipedia.org/wiki/Kali.
77. Hall, Linda B. "Visions of the Feminine: The Dual Goddesses of Ancient Mexico." *Southwest Review* 63, no. 2 (Spring 1978): 134. https://www.jstor.org/stable/43469052.
78. "Sekhmet." Wikipedia. https://en.wikipedia.org/wiki/Sekhmet.
79. Hill, J. "Sekhmet." Ancient Egypt Online, 2008. https://ancientegyptonline.co.uk/sekhmet/.
80. Srivastava, V. C., trans. *Samba-Purana*. Parimal Publication Pvt. Ltd., 2013., p. 85.
81. Lord, Daniel A. *Mount Carmel Novena*. St. Louis: The Queen's Work, 1947.
82. Prabhavananda, Swami, and Frederick Manchester, trans. *The Upanishads: Breath from the Eternal*. New York: New American Library, 2002, p. 121, 125, 127.
83. Kali, trans., *In Praise of the Goddess*, 1.56-1.58, 1.74-1.76, 1.80-1.81, 4.7, 4.9, 11.3-11.5, 11.26, 11.27, 11.33.
84. Mark, Joshua J. "Labyrinth." Ancient History Encyclopedia, April 16, 2018. https://www.ancient.eu/Labyrinth/.
85. "Potnia." Wikipedia. https://en.wikipedia.org/wiki/Potnia.
86. Ibid.
87. Waters, Frank. *The Book of the Hopi*. New York: Penguin Books, 1977, p. 23-24.
88. Fell, Barry. *America B.C.: Ancient Settlers in the New World*. New York: Pocket Books, 1976, p. 287.
89. "The Riddle of the Minoans – Solved?" Cogniarchae, July 11, 2018. https://cogniarchae.com/2018/07/11/the-riddle-of-the-minoans-solved/.
90. Kvilhaug, *Seed of Yggdrasill*, chap. 3: Introduction: A Path of Initiation.
91. Ibid., section 7.5 Salvation - The Old Norse Elysium: Apuleius' Initiation and the Old Norse Mysteries.
92. Ibid., chap. 3, Introduction: A Path of Initiation.
93. Ibid., chap. 3, Introduction: A Path of Initiation; section 7.5 Salvation - The Old Norse Elysium: Apuleius' Initiation and the Old Norse Mysteries.
94. Ibid., section 7.5 Salvation - The Old Norse Elysium: Apuleius' Initiation and the Old Norse Mysteries.
95. Ibid., section 7.5 Salvation - The Old Norse Elysium: Apuleius' Initiation and the Old Norse Mysteries; section 10.2 The Ritual Behind the Myth.
96. Ibid., section 10.2 The Ritual Behind the Myth.
97. Ibid., section 5.8 Lost in Illusion: When Freyia Became Many.
98. Ibid., section 7.5 Salvation – The Old Norse Elysium.
99. Apuleius. *The Golden Ass*. Translated by E. J. Kenney. London: Penguin Books, 2004, p. 207, 209-210.

CHAPTER THREE: THE SPIRITUAL MEANING OF THE WINTER SOLSTICE

1. Price, Massoume. "Festival of Zayeshmehr (Yalda)." The Circle of Ancient Iranian Studies, 2010. https://www.cais-soas.com/CAIS/Celebrations/yalda.htm.
2. "Makar Sankranti." Wikipedia. https://en.wikipedia.org/wiki/Makar_Sankranti.
3. "Lascaux Cave: (Palaeolithic Cave-art)." Ancient-Wisdom. http://ancient-wisdom.com/francelascaux.htm.
4. Mead, G. R. S. *Did Jesus Live 100 B.C.?* London: Theosophical Publishing Society, 1903. The Gnostic Society Library. http://gnosis.org/library/grs-mead/jesus_live_100/ch19.html.
5. *Stanzas of Dzyan*. Theosophy Wiki. https://theosophy.wiki/en/Stanzas_of_Dzyan.
6. *Magical Egypt*. Episode 1, "The Invisible Science." Directed by Chance Gardner, featuring John Anthony West. 2001.
7. Lambdin, Thomas O., trans. "The Gospel of Thomas." In *The Nag Hammadi Library in English*, edited by James M. Robinson. San Francisco: HarperCollins, 1990, p. 126.

8. Hall, Manly P. *The Secret Teachings of All Ages*. San Francisco: H.S. Crocker Company, 1928, p. 40.
9. Vega, Garcilaso de la. *Royal Commentaries of the Incas and General History of Peru, Vol. 1 and Vol. 2*. Translated by Harold V. Livermore. University of Texas Press, 1989, location 7509. Kindle edition.
10. *The Holy Bible*. New International Version (NIV). Biblica, 2011.
11. Mead, G. R. S., trans. *Echoes from the Gnosis, Vol. X: The Hymn of the Robe of Glory*. London: Theosophical Publishing Society, 1908, p. 15, 16-17.
12. *The Holy Bible*, NIV.
13. Hall, *Secret Teachings*, 29.
14. Translation found in Wile, Douglas. *The Ethos of Chinese Sexual Practices*. Albany: State University of New York Press, 1992.
15. Walker, Brian Browne, trans. *Hua Hu Ching: The Unknown Teachings of Lao Tzu*. San Francisco: HarperCollins, 1995, p. 47.
16. Prabhavananda, Swami, and Frederick Manchester, trans. *The Upanishads: Breath from the Eternal*. New York: New American Library, 2002, p. 35.
17. Morgan, Morien O. *The Mabin of the Mabionogion*. London: Research into Lost Knowledge Organization, 1984, p. ii-iv. First published as *The Royal Winged Son of Stonehenge and Avebury*.
18. Suckling, Nigel. "The Chinese Creation." Unicorn Garden. http://www.unicorngarden.com/creation.htm.
19. Christenson, Allen J., trans. *Popol Vuh: Sacred Book of the Quiché Maya People*. Norman: University of Oklahoma Press, 2003. Electronic version, Mesoweb, 2007, p. 54-55. http://www.mesoweb.com/publications/Christenson/PopolVuh.pdf.
20. Szekely, Edmond Bordeaux, trans. *The Essene Gospel of Peace: Book One*. USA: International Biogenic Society, 1981, p. 19; Szekely, Edmond Bordeaux, trans. *The Essene Gospel of Peace: Book Four*. USA: International Biogenic Society, 1981, p. 14.
21. Müller, F. Max, trans. *The Upanishads, Part II, Sacred Books of the East, Vol. XV*. Oxford: Clarendon Press, 1884, p. 85-86.
22. Legge, James, trans. *The Yî King, Sacred Books of the East, Vol. 16, The Sacred Books of China, Vol. 2*. Oxford: Clarendon Press, 1882, p. 358, 395, 435.
23. Waite, A. E., trans. *The Alchemical Writings of Edward Kelly*. London: James Elliott and Co., 1893, p. 35.
24. Bacstrom, Sigismund, trans. "The Emerald Tablet of Hermes." In Hall, *Secret Teachings*.
25. Copenhaver, Brian P., trans. *Hermetica*. Cambridge University Press, 2002, p. 40. Kindle edition.
26. Paracelsus. *Paracelsus: Selected Writings*. Translated by Norbert Guterman. Edited by Jolande Jacobi. New Jersey: Princeton University Press, 1995, p. 21.
27. Szekely, trans., *Gospel of Peace: Book Four*, 13.
28. Wile, Douglas, trans. *True Transmission of the Golden Elixir*. Albany: State University of New York Press, 1992.
29. Isenberg, Wesley W., trans. "The Gospel of Philip." In *The Nag Hammadi Library in English*, edited by James M. Robinson. San Francisco: HarperCollins, 1990, p. 148, 150-151, 158.
30. Walker, trans., *Hua Hu Ching*, 84.
31. Wilhelm, Richard, trans. *The Secret of the Golden Flower*. Translated from German to English by Cary F. Baynes. San Diego: Harcourt Brace & Company, 1962, p. 31.
32. *The Holy Bible*. King James Version (KJV).
33. Wilhelm, trans., *Secret of the Golden Flower*, 71.
34. *The Holy Bible*, NIV.
35. Mead, G. R. S., trans. *Pistis Sophia*. London: J. M. Watkins, 1921, p. 148, 149-150.
36. Cumont, Franz. *The Mysteries of Mithra*. Translated by Thomas J. McCormack. Chicago: Open Court, 1903. Internet Sacred Text Archive. https://www.sacred-texts.com/cla/mom/mom07.htm.
37. Ibid., 127-128.
38. Smith, Thomas, trans. *Ante-Nicene Christian Library, Vol. XVII: The Clementine Homilies*. Edited by Alexander Roberts and James Donaldson. Edinburgh: T. & T. Clark, 1870, p. 34.
39. Easwaran, Eknath, trans. *The Upanishads*. Tomales: Nilgiri Press, 2007, p. 76-77.

40. Purohit Swami, Shri, trans. *The Bhagavad Gita*. Circa 1935.
41. "Viracocha." Wikipedia. https://en.wikipedia.org/wiki/Viracocha.
42. Ibid.
43. Tapasyananda, Swami, trans. *Shrimad Bhagavad Gita*. Mylapore: Sri Ramakrishna Math, 2003, p. 239.
44. Parrott, Douglas M., and R. McL. Wilson, trans. "The Acts of Peter and the Twelve Apostles." In *The Nag Hammadi Library in English*, edited by James M. Robinson. San Francisco: HarperCollins, 1990, p. 290.
45. Morgan, *Mabin of the Mabinogion*, 60.
46. Murphy, Anthony. "101 Facts about Newgrange." Mythical Ireland, November 8, 2017. https://mythicalireland.com/ancient-sites/101-facts-about-newgrange/; Shaw, Judith. "Boann, Celtic Goddess of Inspiration and Creativity." Feminism & Religion, July 27, 2016. https://feminismandreligion.com/2016/07/27/boann-celtic-goddess-of-inspiration-and-creativity-by-judith-shaw/.
47. Murphy, "101 Facts about Newgrange."
48. "Passage Mounds: (Form and Function)." Ancient-Wisdom. http://www.ancient-wisdom.com/passagemounds.htm.
49. Waters, Frank. *The Book of the Hopi*. New York: Penguin Books, 1977, p. 23-24.
50. "Callanish Stones." Wikipedia. https://en.wikipedia.org/wiki/Callanish_Stones.
51. Waters, *Book of the Hopi*, 24.
52. "Mithras." Hellenic Faith, October 12, 2017. https://hellenicfaith.com/mithras/.
53. Ibid.
54. Ibid.
55. Timesofindia.com. "When is Krishna Janmashtami 2020? Date, Puja Muhurat, Vrat Vidhi, Fasting & Significance of Gokulashtami." ETimes, August 9, 2020. https://timesofindia.indiatimes.com/life-style/events/when-is-krishna-janmashtami-2020-date-puja-muhurat-vrat-vidhi-fasting-significance-of-gokulashtami/articleshow/77435465.cms.
56. "El Castillo." World-Mysteries.com. https://old.world-mysteries.com/chichen_kukulcan.htm.
57. Mann, Nicholas. "Nicholas Mann: Avebury Cosmos: Our Ancestors and the Stars." YouTube, April 4, 2014. https://youtu.be/6uixeGHmK4g?t=406.
58. "Labyrinths." Ancient-Wisdom. http://www.ancient-wisdom.com/labyrinths.htm.
59. At the winter solstice the Druids would gather in Wales to watch the sun rise over the sacred mountain of Mynydd Dinas, and believed the sun represented the birth of a divine baby Son who grew as the year progressed toward the summer solstice.
60. "Vishnu." Wikipedia. https://en.wikipedia.org/wiki/Vishnu#Trivikrama:_The_Three_Steps_of_Vishnu.
61. Giles, Lionel, trans. *The Sayings of Lao-Tzŭ*. Edited by L. Cranmer-Byng and Dr. S. A. Kapadia. New York: E. P. Dutton and Company, Inc., 1905, p. 22.
62. Parrott, Douglas M., trans. "Eugnostos the Blessed and The Sophia of Jesus Christ." In *The Nag Hammadi Library in English*, edited by James M. Robinson. San Francisco: HarperCollins, 1990, p. 229-230.
63. Wisse, Frederik, trans. "The Apocryphon of John." In *The Nag Hammadi Library in English*, edited by James M. Robinson. San Francisco: HarperCollins, 1990, p. 122.
64. "Biblical Magi." Wikipedia. https://www.en.wikipedia.org/wiki/Biblical_Magi.
65. Roys, Ralph L., trans. *The Book of Chilam Balam of Chumayel*. Washington D.C.: Carnegie Institution, 1933, p. 105. Internet Sacred Text Archive. https://www.sacred-texts.com/nam/maya/cbc/cbc15.htm.
66. Cowell, E. B., trans. *The Maitri or Maitrāyanīya Upanishad*. Calcutta: Asiatic Society of Bengal, 1870, p. 257-258.

CHAPTER FOUR: THE SPIRITUAL MEANING OF THE SPRING EQUINOX

1. Mannikka, Eleanor. *Angkor Wat: Time, Space, and Kingship*. University of Hawaii Press, 2000, p. 37, 39.

2. "108: The Significance of the Number." Stephen Knapp and His Books on Vedic Culture, Eastern Philosophy, and Spirituality. https://www.stephen-knapp.com/108_the_significance_of_the_number.htm.
3. Mead, G. R. S., trans. *Pistis Sophia*. London: J. M. Watkins, 1921, p. 262.
4. *The Holy Bible*. New International Version (NIV). Biblica, 2011.
5. Ibid.
6. Ibid.
7. Snyder, G. W. "To George Washington from G. W. Snyder." August 22, 1798. Founders Online. https://founders.archives.gov/documents/Washington/06-02-02-0435.
8. *The Holy Bible*, NIV.
9. Morgan, Owen. *The Light of Britannia*. Cardiff: D. Owen & Company, 1893, p. 22-23.
10. *The Holy Bible*, NIV.
11. Ibid.
12. Ibid.
13. Ibid.
14. Charlesworth, James H., trans. *The Earliest Christian Hymnbook: The Odes of Solomon*. Eugene: Wipf and Stock, 2009, p. 32-33.
15. Purohit Swami, Shri, trans. *The Bhagavad Gita*. Circa 1935.
16. Lambdin, Thomas O., trans. "The Gospel of Thomas." In *The Nag Hammadi Library in English*, edited by James M. Robinson. San Francisco: HarperCollins, 1990, p. 130.
17. Larrington, Carolyne, trans. *The Poetic Edda*. Oxford University Press, 1999, p. 34.
18. Purohit, trans., *The Bhagavad Gita*.
19. Chand, Devi, trans. *The Yajur Veda*. Hoshiarpur: All India Dayanand Salvation Mission, 1959, p. 23.
20. Easwaran, Eknath, trans. *The Upanishads*. Tomales: Nilgiri Press, 2007, p. 76.
21. Kasser, Rodolphe, Marvin Meyer, and Gregor Wurst, trans., in collaboration with François Gaudard. *The Gospel of Judas*. Washington: National Geographic Society, 2006, p. 43.
22. *The Holy Bible*, NIV.
23. Easwaran, trans., *The Upanishads*, 91.
24. Budge, E. A. Wallis. "Hathor and the Hathor-Goddesses." Chap. 14 in *The Gods of the Egyptians Vol 1*. 1904. Wisdom Library. https://www.wisdomlib.org/egypt/book/the-gods-of-the-egyptians-vol-1/d/doc6831.html.
25. Ibid.
26. Ibid.
27. Ibid.
28. Ibid.
29. Allen, James P. "Why a Pyramid? Pyramid Religion." In *The Treasures of the Pyramids*, edited by Zahi Hawass. Italy: White Star, 2003, p. 26. http://gizamedia.rc.fas.harvard.edu/documents/allen_treasures_022-027.pdf.
30. Ibid., 24.
31. Ibid.
32. Ibid., 26.
33. Ibid., 27.
34. Murphy, Anthony. "The Milky Way in Irish Mythology and Folklore." Mythical Ireland, October 10, 2016. https://blog.mythicalireland.com/2016/10/the-milky-way-in-irish-mythology-and_10.html.
35. Macbain, Gillies. "Finding Easter at Knowth." Mythical Ireland, November 7, 2017. https://www.mythicalireland.com/ancient-sites/knowth-cnogba/.
36. Byrne, Martin. "The East Passage and Chamber at Knowth." The Sacred Island, October 15, 2016. http://www.carrowkeel.com/sites/boyne/knowth3.html.
37. Ibid.
38. Ibid.
39. Ibid.

40. Morgan, *The Light of Britannia*, chap. 11.
41. Kvilhaug, Maria. *The Seed of Yggdrasill: Deciphering the Hidden Messages in Old Norse Myths*. Whyte Tracks, 2016, section 3.14 Soma and Haoma, Ambrosia, Kykeon, Cerridwen's Cauldron and the Indo-European Connection: The Book of Taliesin. Kindle edition.
42. Williams, Rowan, and Gwyneth Lewis. *The Book of Taliesin*. Penguin Books Ltd., 2019, p. 53. Kindle edition.
43. Kvilhaug, *Seed of Yggdrasill*, section 2.12, Nornir, Fylgjur – and the Runes of Fate: Óðinn – Uprooting the Runes; section 3.1 The Mead of Poetry (Hávamál – The High One's Speech); section 3.12 Bright Rune, The Mead-Producer Above Valhǫll: Grímnismál (The Song of the Masked One) and Valkyriur Ready to Ride the Earth; section 3.16 The Mead and the Sun Goddess.
44. Ibid., section 3.17: Not Quite the Christian Poem After All. Sólarljóð (The Song of the Sun).
45. *The Mabinogion*. Translated by Siogned Davies. Oxford: Oxford University Press, 2018, p. 413. Kindle edition.
46. "The Gundestrup Cauldron - The Cauldron of Fate?". National Museum of Denmark. https://en.natmus.dk/historical-knowledge/denmark/prehistoric-period-until-1050-ad/the-early-iron-age/the-gundestrup-cauldron/the-gundestrup-cauldron-the-caldron-of-fate/.
47. Wirth, Diane E. "Quetzalcoatl, the Maya Maize God and Jesus Christ." *Journal of Book of Mormon Studies*. Provo, Utah: Maxwell Institute, 2002, p. 11.
48. Barrows, Vince. "A History of Monks Mound." 2007. https://www.freewebs.com/historyofmonksmound/.
49. *The Holy Bible*. King James Version (KJV).
50. Parrott, Douglas M., trans. "Eugnostos the Blessed and The Sophia of Jesus Christ." In *The Nag Hammadi Library in English*, edited by James M. Robinson. San Francisco: HarperCollins, 1990, p. 226.
51. Szekely, Edmond Bordeaux, trans. *The Essene Gospel of Peace: Book Four*. USA: International Biogenic Society, 1981, p. 37-38.
52. *Stanzas of Dzyan*. Theosophy Wiki. https://theosophy.wiki/en/Stanzas_of_Dzyan.
53. Szekely, trans., *Gospel of Peace: Book Four*, 18.
54. David, Rosalie. *Religion and Magic in Ancient Egypt*. Penguin UK, 2002, p. 95.
55. Mercer, Samuel A. B., trans. *The Pyramid Texts*. New York: Longmans, Green & Co., 1952, p. 289.

CHAPTER FIVE: DECODING THE ANCIENT MEANING OF THE SPHINX AND ITS ORIGIN AS ANUBIS

1. Temple, Robert, with Olivia Temple. *The Sphinx Mystery*. Inner Traditions, 2009, p. 244.
2. Hancock, Graham. *America Before: The Key to Earth's Lost Civilization*. St. Martin's Press, 2019, location 5508 (Judgment section). Kindle edition.
3. Temple with Temple, *The Sphinx Mystery*, 220-223.
4. Kaulins, Andis. "The Ark of the Covenant." LexiLine – History of Civilization. http://www.lexiline.com/lexiline/lexi222.htm.
5. Collins, Andrew. *Gods of Eden*. Rochester, Vermont: Bear & Company, 2002, p. 171.
6. Based on translations by Faulkner, R. O. *The Ancient Egyptian Pyramid Texts*. Oxford University Press, 1969; Piankoff, Alexandre. *The Pyramid of Unas*. Princeton University Press, 1968; Speleers, Louis. *Les Textes des Pyramides Egyptiennes*. Gand: I. Vanderpoorten, 1923. Pyramid Texts Online. http://www.pyramidtextsonline.com/translation.html.
7. Translation in DuQuesne, Terence. *Jackal at the Shaman's Gate*. Thame Oxon: Darengo Publications, 1991, p. 13.
8. Temple, Robert. *Egyptian Dawn*. London: Random House, 2010, p. 43-44.
9. Temple with Temple, *The Sphinx Mystery*, 250, 298.
10. Ibid., 261.
11. Ibid., 275, 284.
12. DuQuesne, Terence. *The Jackal Divinities of Egypt*. London: Darengo Publications, 2005. Quoted in Temple with Temple, *The Sphinx Mystery*, 299.
13. Faulkner, R. O., trans. *The Ancient Egyptian Pyramid Texts*. Oxford: Clarendon Press, 1998, p. 291.
14. Ibid.

15. Hill, J. "Atum." Ancient Egypt Online, 2008. https://ancientegyptonline.co.uk/atum/.
16. Clark, R. T. Rundle, trans. *Myth and Symbol in Ancient Egypt*. London: Thames & Hudson, 1959, p. 130-140.
17. Temple with Temple, *The Sphinx Mystery*, 289-290.
18. Mercer, Samuel A. B., trans. *The Pyramid Texts*. New York: Longmans, Green & Co., 1952, p. 58.
19. Based on translations by Faulkner, Piankoff, and Speleers. Pyramid Texts Online.
20. Faulkner, trans., *Ancient Egyptian Pyramid Texts*.
21. Mercer, trans., *The Pyramid Texts*, 239.
22. Temple with Temple, *The Sphinx Mystery*, 222.
23. Based on translations by Faulkner, Piankoff, and Speleers. Pyramid Texts Online.
24. Faulkner, trans., *Ancient Egyptian Pyramid Texts*.
25. Hancock, Graham, and Robert Bauval. *The Message of the Sphinx: A Quest for the Hidden Legacy of Mankind*. New York: Three Rivers Press, 1996, p. 71-75.
26. Ibid., 249.
27. Ibid., 75.
28. Sweatman, Martin. *Prehistory Decoded*. Troubador Publishing, 2018, location 2596. Kindle edition.
29. Hill, J. "Wepwawet." Ancient Egypt Online, 2016. https://ancientegyptonline.co.uk/wepwawet/.
30. Hancock, Graham. *Magicians of the Gods*. London: Hodder & Stoughton, 2016, p. 203.
31. Bridges, Vincent. "Abydos, the Osireion and Egyptian Sacred Science." Vincent Bridges Archive, September 1, 2000. http://vincentbridges.com/post/145759129272/abydosthe-osireion-and-egyptian-sacred-science.
32. Ibid.
33. Ibid.
34. Hancock, *Magicians of the Gods*, 197.
35. Ibid.
36. Hancock and Bauval, *Message of the Sphinx*, 66-70.
37. Ibid., 70-78.
38. Mercer, trans., *The Pyramid Texts*, 153.
39. Temple with Temple, *The Sphinx Mystery*, 141.
40. Ibid., 379.
41. Ibid., 381.
42. Temple, Robert. "Lost Technology of the Ancients: The Crystal Sun." New Dawn Magazine. No. 65, 2001. https://www.newdawnmagazine.com/articles/lost-technology-of-the-ancients-the-crystal-sun.
43. Temple with Temple, *The Sphinx Mystery*, 367.
44. Ibid., 393.
45. Ibid., 299.
46. Budge, E. A. Wallis. *The Gods of the Egyptians Vol II*. Chicago: The Open Court Publishing Company, 1904, p. 262.
47. Faulkner, trans., *Ancient Egyptian Pyramid Texts*.
48. Temple with Temple, *The Sphinx Mystery*, 388.
49. Schoch, Robert M. "Robert M. Schoch: Research Highlights. The Great Sphinx." The Official Website of Robert M. Schoch. https://www.robertschoch.com/sphinx.html.
50. Carlson, Randall. "Sphinx Quarry Erosion from Floods? / Durable Civilization? -Cosmography101-32.5 Randall Carlson '08." YouTube, August 3, 2019. https://youtu.be/IwVcNIykoVs?t=1183.
51. Ibid., 11:02.
52. Ibid.
53. Ibid., 13:34.
54. Temple, *Egyptian Dawn*, 365.
55. Carlson, "Sphinx Quarry Erosion from Floods?" 21:12.
56. "Great Sphinx of Giza." Wikipedia. https://en.wikipedia.org/wiki/Great_Sphinx_of_Giza.

57. Temple with Temple, *The Sphinx Mystery*, 310.
58. Ibid.
59. Ibid.
60. Ibid., 188-195, 310.
61. Temple, *Egyptian Dawn*, 282.
62. Ibid. See chap. 6 "The 'Lost Kings' and a Pyramid of the First Dynasty" for some early examples of this in Egyptian history.
63. Geggel, Laura. "Eight Million Dog Mummies Found in Egyptian Mass Grave." CBS News, June 19, 2015. https://www.cbsnews.com/news/8-million-dog-mummies-found-in-egyptian-mass-grave/.
64. Piankoff, Alexandre, trans. *The Wandering of the Soul*. Princeton University Press, 1974.
65. "Nymphaea Caerulea." Wikipedia. https://en.wikipedia.org/wiki/Nymphaea_caerulea.
66. Hall, Manly P. *The Secret Teachings of All Ages*. San Francisco: H.S. Crocker Company, 1928, p. 44.
67. David, Rosalie. *Religion and Magic in Ancient Egypt*. Penguin UK, 2002, p. 97.
68. Copenhaver, Brian P., trans. *Hermetica*. Cambridge University Press, 2002, p. 81. Kindle edition.

CHAPTER SIX: THE SPIRITUAL MEANING OF THE SUMMER SOLSTICE

1. Morgan, Owen. *The Light of Britannia*. Cardiff: D. Owen & Company, 1893, chap. 2.
2. *Stanzas of Dzyan*. Theosophy Wiki. https://theosophy.wiki/en/Stanzas_of_Dzyan.
3. Szekely, Edmond Bordeaux, trans. *The Essene Gospel of Peace: Book One*. USA: International Biogenic Society, 1981, p. 19.
4. Parrott, Douglas M., trans. "Eugnostos the Blessed and The Sophia of Jesus Christ." In *The Nag Hammadi Library in English*, edited by James M. Robinson. San Francisco: HarperCollins, 1990, p. 241.
5. *The Holy Bible*. New International Version (NIV). Biblica, 2011.
6. Srivastava, V. C., trans. *Samba-Purana*. Parimal Publication Pvt. Ltd., 2013, p. 86.
7. Walker, Brian Browne, trans. *The Tao Te Ching of Lao Tzu*. New York: St. Martin's Griffin, 1996, p. 14.
8. Easwaran, Eknath, trans. *The Upanishads*. Tomales: Nilgiri Press, 2007, p. 76.
9. Prabhavananda, Swami, and Frederick Manchester, trans. *The Upanishads: Breath from the Eternal*. New York: New American Library, 2002, p. 80-81.
10. Easwaran, Eknath, trans. *The Bhagavad Gita*. Tomales: Nilgiri Press, 2007, p. 232-233.
11. Wisse, Frederik, trans. "The Apocryphon of John." In *The Nag Hammadi Library in English*, edited by James M. Robinson. San Francisco: HarperCollins, 1990, p. 105.
12. Wile, Douglas, trans. *True Transmission of the Golden Elixir*. Albany: State University of New York Press, 1992.
13. Alighieri, Dante. *The Divine Comedy: Paradiso*. Translated by Allen Mandelbaum. Everyman's Library, 1995, p. 540.
14. See https://youtu.be/Yw13EAX3cZk or do a search for "Cymatic imagery of the Om chant."
15. Study by Penrose and Gurzadyan; see more here: http://arxiv.org/ftp/arxiv/papers/1011/1011.3706.pdf.
16. Plato. *Critias*. Translated by Benjamin Jowett. Available from: http://classics.mit.edu/Plato/critias.html.
17. Kvilhaug, Maria. *The Seed of Yggdrasill: Deciphering the Hidden Messages in Old Norse Myths*. Whyte Tracks, 2016, section 2.12 Vanir, Seiðr, and The Sacred Mead: Chart: The Three Upper Heavens of Immortality; section 7.1 Elves, Souls and Reincarnation; section 12.6 Óðinn – The Universal Spirit. Kindle edition.
18. *The Holy Bible*, NIV.
19. "Atmospheric escape." Wikipedia. https://en.wikipedia.org/wiki/Atmospheric_escape.
20. "Ascension of Jesus." Wikipedia. https://en.wikipedia.org/wiki/Ascension_of_Jesus.
21. Mead, G. R. S., trans. *Pistis Sophia*. London: J. M. Watkins, 1921, p. 12-13.
22. "Tulum." Wikipedia. https://en.wikipedia.org/wiki/Tulum.
23. Mead, trans., *Pistis Sophia*, 5-6.
24. Ibid., 190.

25. Patterson, Stephen, and Marvin Meyer, trans. "Gospel of Thomas." In *The Complete Gospels: Annotated Scholars Version*, edited by Robert J. Miller. Polebridge Press, 1992.
26. Isenberg, Wesley W., trans. "The Gospel of Philip." In *The Nag Hammadi Library in English*, edited by James M. Robinson. San Francisco: HarperCollins, 1990, p. 160.
27. Patterson and Meyer, trans., "Gospel of Thomas."
28. Mead, trans., *Pistis Sophia*, 191, 192.
29. Wile, trans., *True Transmission*.
30. Easwaran, trans., *The Upanishads*, 143-144.
31. Mead, trans. *Pistis Sophia*, 1.
32. "Summer Solstice." The Druid Order. http://thedruidorder.org/ceremonies/summer-solstice.html.
33. Wigington, Patti. "Introduction to Slavic Mythology." ThoughtCo. https://www.thoughtco.com/slavic-mythology-4768524.
34. Bellows, Henry Adams, trans. *The Poetic Edda: The Mythological Poems*. Mineola: Dover Publications, 2004, p.3. Found in "Norse Cosmology." Wikipedia. https://en.wikipedia.org/wiki/Norse_cosmology.
35. "The Irminsul." Real Rune Magick, December 25, 2017. http://realrunemagick.blogspot.com/2017/12/the-irminsul.html.
36. Maestri, Nicoletta. "Ceiba Pentandra: The Sacred Tree of the Maya." ThoughtCo. https://www.thoughtco.com/ceiba-pentandra-sacred-tree-maya-171615.
37. "K'inich Janaab' Pakal." Wikipedia. https://en.wikipedia.org/wiki/K'inich_Janaab'_Pakal.
38. "The Palenque Sarcophagus Lid of King Pakal." FringePop321. https://www.fringepop321.com/the-palenque-sarcophagus-lid-of-king-pakal.htm.
39. Blankenbehler, Benjamin. "Palenque: Ritual Architecture of Ancient Mayans." Architecture Revived, October 21, 2015. http://www.architecturerevived.com/palenque-ritual-architecture-of-ancient-mayans/.
40. "Votan." Wikipedia. https://en.wikipedia.org/wiki/Votan.
41. Atwood, Lara. *The Ancient Religion of the Sun: The Wisdom Bringers and The Lost Civilization of the Sun*. 2nd ed. Sura Ondrunar Publishing, 2021, p. 117-136.
42. Blankenbehler, "Palenque: Ritual Architecture of Ancient Mayans."
43. Szekely, Edmond Bordeaux, trans. *Essene Gospel of Peace: Book Two*. USA: International Biogenic Society, 1981, p. 34.
44. Szekely, Edmond Bordeaux, trans. *The Essene Gospel of Peace: Book Four*. USA: International Biogenic Society, 1981, p. 11.
45. Mead, trans., *Pistis Sophia*, 313.
46. Lambdin, Thomas O., trans. "The Gospel of Thomas." In *The Nag Hammadi Library in English*, edited by James M. Robinson. San Francisco: HarperCollins, 1990, p. 129.
47. Hall, Manly P. *The Secret Teachings of All Ages*. San Francisco: H.S. Crocker Company, 1928, p. 39.
48. Parrott, Douglas M., trans. "Eugnostos the Blessed and The Sophia of Jesus Christ." In *The Nag Hammadi Library in English*, edited by James M. Robinson. San Francisco: HarperCollins, 1990, p. 228.
49. Hülsen, Christian. "XXXII. The Temple of Vesta." In *The Roman Forum – Its History and Its Monuments*. Ermanno Loescher & Co, Publishers to H. M. the Queen of Italy, 1906. http://penelope.uchicago.edu/Thayer/E/Gazetteer/Places/Europe/Italy/Lazio/Roma/Rome/Forum_Romanum/_Texts/Huelsen*/2/32.html; Goux, Jean-Joseph. "Vesta, or the Place of Being." *Representations* 1, no. 1 (February 1983): 91-107. https://doi.org/10.2307/3043761.
50. NicGrioghair, Branfionn. "Who is Brigid?" Mythical Ireland, 1997. https://www.mythicalireland.com/myths-and-legends/brigid-bright-goddess-of-the-gael/.
51. Ibid.
52. Ibid.
53. Vega, Garcilaso de la. *Royal Commentaries of the Incas and General History of Peru, Vol. 1 and Vol. 2*. Translated by Harold V. Livermore. University of Texas Press, 1989, location 4652. Kindle edition.
54. Kennedy, Gordon. *The White Indians of Nivaria*. Mecca, California: Nivaria Press, 2010, p. 46.

55. Robinson, William C., Jr., trans. "The Exegesis on the Soul." In *The Nag Hammadi Library in English*, edited by James M. Robinson. San Francisco: HarperCollins, 1990, p. 192.
56. Parrott, trans., "Sophia of Jesus Christ," 234-235.
57. Robinson, trans., "Exegesis on the Soul," 195-196.
58. Wigington, Patti. "What Was the Vestalia?" Learn Religions. https://www.learnreligions.com/the-roman-vestalia-festival-2562247.
59. Iles, Linda. "St. Brigid of the Wells." Mirror of Isis, 2010. https://mirrorofisis.freeyellow.com/id536.html.
60. Morgan, Morien O. *The Mabin of the Mabionogion*. London: Research into Lost Knowledge Organization, 1984, p. ii-iv. First published as *The Royal Winged Son of Stonehenge and Avebury*.
61. Ibid., 48.
62. Ibid.
63. Morgan, *The Light of Britannia*, chap 3.
64. Mercer, Samuel A. B., trans. *The Pyramid Texts*. New York: Longmans, Green & Co., 1952, p. 59.
65. Morgan, *The Light of Britannia*, chap. 10.
66. Roys, Ralph L., trans. *The Book of Chilam Balam of Chumayel*. Washington D.C.: Carnegie Institution, 1933, p. 131. Internet Sacred Text Archive. https://www.sacred-texts.com/nam/maya/cbc/cbc15.htm.
67. Charlesworth, James H., trans. *The Earliest Christian Hymnbook: The Odes of Solomon*. Eugene: Wipf and Stock, 2009, p. 32-33.
68. Morgan, *Mabin of the Mabionogion*.
69. Isenberg, trans., "The Gospel of Philip," 142.
70. "Triglav, Trojan, Trinity, Trimurti, Agni." Old European Culture, July 26, 2014. http://oldeuropeanculture.blogspot.com/2014/07/triglav-trojan-trinity-trimurti-agni.html.
71. "Summer Solstice - Alban Hefin." The Order of Bards, Ovates, and Druids. https://www.druidry.org/druid-way/teaching-and-practice/druid-festivals/summer-solstice-alban-hefin.
72. "Grange Circle." Old European Culture, September 11, 2014. https://oldeuropeanculture.blogspot.com/2014/09/grange-circle.html.
73. Mead, trans., *Pistis Sophia*, 117.
74. Charlesworth, trans., *Odes of Solomon*, I.
75. Carlson, Randall. "Stonehenge and The Squaring of the Circle." YouTube, August 27, 2018. https://youtu.be/cKXDWy_zXzI?t=371.
76. Morgan, *Mabin of the Mabionogion*, 274.
77. George, Arthur. "Summer Solstice Mythology: Midsummer Night." Mythology Matters, June 19, 2015. https://mythologymatters.wordpress.com/2015/06/19/summer-solstice-mythology-midsummer-night/.
78. Morgan, *The Light of Britannia*, chap. 2.
79. Mercer, trans., *The Pyramid Texts*, 186-187.
80. Ibid., 240.
81. Based on translations by Faulkner, R. O. *The Ancient Egyptian Pyramid Texts*. Oxford University Press, 1969; Piankoff, Alexandre. *The Pyramid of Unas*. Princeton University Press, 1968; Speleers, Louis. *Les Textes des Pyramides Egyptiennes*. Gand: I. Vanderpoorten, 1923. Pyramid Texts Online. http://www.pyramidtextsonline.com/translation.html.
82. Kasser, Rodolphe, Marvin Meyer, and Gregor Wurst, trans., in collaboration with François Gaudard. *The Gospel of Judas*. Washington: National Geographic Society, 2006, p. 43.
83. Hall, *Secret Teachings*, 40.
84. *Rigveda*. Translation from the American Institute of Vedic Studies. https://www.vedanet.com/the-ancient-yoga-of-the-sun/.

CHAPTER SEVEN: INTRODUCTION

1. Alison, Jim. "Exploring Geographic and Geometric Relationships along a Line of Ancient Sites around the World." GrahamHancock.com, May 1, 2001. https://grahamhancock.com/geographic-geometric-relationships-alisonj/.

CHAPTER EIGHT: ANCIENT SACRED SITES ALIGNED TO THE AUTUMN EQUINOX

1. Proctor, Richard A. *The Great Pyramid: Observatory, Tomb, and Temple*. London: Longmans, Green, and Co., 1888, p. 100.
2. "When Was the Giza Complex Constructed." Ancient-Wisdom, February 10, 2009. http://www.ancient-wisdom.com/Ghizawhen.htm.
3. Sickleharvest. "Time Features of the Great Pyramid, Part 30." Sickle of Truth, May 5, 2018. https://www.sickleoftruthblog.com/2018/05/05/time-features-of-the-great-pyramid-part-30/.
4. "When Was the Giza Complex Constructed." Ancient-Wisdom.
5. Katz, Brigit. "Is the Fall Equinox the Secret to the Pyramids' Near-Perfect Alignment?" Smithsonian Magazine, February 22, 2018. https://www.smithsonianmag.com/smart-news/fall-equinox-secret-pyramids-near-perfect-alignment-180968223/.
6. Proctor, *The Great Pyramid*, 82-126.
7. "When was the Giza Complex Constructed." Ancient-Wisdom. http://www.ancient-wisdom.com/Ghizawhen.htm#6.4.
8. Davidson, D., and H. Aldersmith. *The Great Pyramid: Its Divine Message, Vol. I. Pyramid Records*. London: William Rider and Son Limited, 1961, p. 174-175.
9. Creighton, Simon, and Gary Osborn. "The Great Pyramid and the Axis of the Earth – Part 2." GrahamHancock.com, December 5, 2008. https://grahamhancock.com/creightons4/.
10. "El Castillo, Chichen Itza." Wikipedia. https://en.wikipedia.org/wiki/El_Castillo,_Chichen_Itza#Construction.
11. Heyerdahl, Thor. *American Indians in the Pacific*. London: Allen & Unwin, 1952, p. 278-279. Cites: Brinton, Daniel G. *American Hero-Myths*. Philadelphia: H. C. Watts & Co., 1882.
12. Šprajc, Ivan. "Astronomical Alignments at Teotihuacan, Mexico." *Latin American Antiquity* 11, no. 4 (2000): 403-415. https://doi.org/10.2307/972004.
13. Jones, Tom. "Calendars in Mesoamerica." In *Encyclopaedia of the History of Science, Technology, and Medicine in Non-Western Cultures*, edited by H. Selin. Dordrecht: Springer, 2008. https://doi.org/10.1007/978-1-4020-4425-0_9402.
14. Heyworth, Robin. "Teotihuacan: Pyramid of the Sun & The Orion Mystery." Uncovered History, November 11, 2014. http://uncoveredhistory.com/mexico/teotihuacan/teotihuacan-pyramid-of-the-sun/.
15. "Teotihuacan." Wikipedia. https://en.wikipedia.org/wiki/Teotihuacan.
16. "Pyramid of the Sun." Britannica. https://www.britannica.com/place/Pyramid-of-the-Sun.
17. Heyworth, "Teotihuacan."
18. "Great Goddess of Teotihuacan." Wikipedia. https://en.wikipedia.org/wiki/Great_Goddess_of_Teotihuacan.
19. Heyworth, "Teotihuacan."
20. "Teotihuacan." Wikipedia.
21. Heyworth, "Teotihuacan."
22. Truman, Dave. "Teotihuacan: Model of a Very Different Cosmos." GrahamHancock.com, July 16, 2019. https://grahamhancock.com/trumand5/.
23. Hancock, Graham, and Santha Faiia. *Heaven's Mirror: Quest for the Lost Civilization*. Three Rivers Press, 1998, p. 11.
24. "Quinametzin." Wikipedia. https://en.wikipedia.org/wiki/Quinametzin.
25. Hancock and Faiia, *Heaven's Mirror*, 11-19.
26. Gray, Martin. "Machu Picchu." Places of Peace and Power. https://sacredsites.com/americas/peru/machu_picchu.html.
27. Ibid.
28. Ibid.
29. Edwards, Edmundo R., and Juan Antonio Belmonte. "Megalithic Astronomy of Easter Island: A Reassessment." *Journal for the History of Astronomy* 35, part 4, no. 121 (November 2004): 427. http://articles.adsabs.harvard.edu/cgi-bin/nph-iarticle_query?bibcode=2004JHA....35..421E.
30. Grant-Peterkin, James. "Vernal (Spring) Equinox at Ahu Akivi." Easter Island News, September 24, 2012. https://easterislandnews.blogspot.com/2012/09/vernal-spring-equinox-at-ahu-akivi.html.

31. Atwood, Lara. *The Ancient Religion of the Sun: The Wisdom Bringers and The Lost Civilization of the Sun*. 2nd ed. Sura Ondrunar Publishing, 2021, p. 105-107.
32. Heyerdahl, Thor. *Aku-Aku: The Secret of Easter Island*. Chicago: Rand McNally & Company, 1958, p. 357-359.
33. "Rongorongo and the Indus Script." Boloji, October 27, 2012. https://www.boloji.com/articles/13273/rongorongo-and-the-indus-script.
34. Martin Doutré, archeoastronomer and author of www.celticnz.co.nz.
35. Atwood, *Ancient Religion of the Sun*, 103, 106.
36. "Labyrinth." Wikipedia. https://en.wikipedia.org/wiki/Labyrinth#Cretan_labyrinth.
37. Henriksson, G., and M. Blomberg. "The Evidence from Knossos on the Minoan Calendar." *Mediterranean Archaeology and Archaeometry* 11, no. 1 (2011): 63.
38. Ibid., 65.
39. Ibid., 64. Cites: Blomberg, M., G. Henriksson, and M. Papathanassiou. "The Calendaric Relationship between the Minoan Peak Sanctuary on Juktas and the Palace at Knossos." In *Proceedings of the Conference "Astronomy of ancient Civilizations" of the European society for Astronomy in Culture (SEAC) and National Astronomical Meeting (JENAM), Moscow, May 23-27, 2000*, edited by T. M. Potyomkina and V. N. Obridko. Moscow, 2002, p. 81-92; Henriksson, G., and M. Blomberg. "Evidence for Minoan astronomical observations from the peak sanctuaries on Petsophas and Traostalos." *Opuscula Atheniensia* 21, (1996): 99-114.
40. "Potnia." Wikipedia. https://en.wikipedia.org/wiki/Potnia.
41. Mörner, Nils-Axel, and Bob G. Lind. "Stonehenge Has Got a Younger Sister – Ales Stones in Sweden Decoded." *International Journal of Astronomy and Astrophysics* 2, no. 1 (2012): 23-27. http://doi.org/10.4236/ijaa.2012.21004.
42. Stoev, Alexey, and Penka Muglova. "Harman Kaya." The Rock-Cut Sacred Places of the Thracians and Other Palaeo-Balkan and Other Ancient Anatolian Peoples, June 21, 2005. http://rock-cut.thracians.org/en/s_m_harman.php.
43. Freeman, Dr. Gordon R. *Hidden Stonehenge: Ancient Temple in North America Reveals the Key to Ancient Wonders*. Watkins Publishing, 2012.
44. Gillespie, Alan. "A Precise Petroglyph Equinox Marker in Eastern California." The Equinox Project. http://www.equinox-project.com/v23071.htm.

CHAPTER NINE: ANCIENT SACRED SITES ALIGNED TO THE WINTER SOLSTICE

1. Mann, Nicholas. "Nicholas Mann: Avebury Cosmos: Our Ancestors and the Stars." YouTube, April 4, 2014. https://youtu.be/6uixeGHmK4g?t=420.
2. "Stonehenge – the Age of the Megaliths." Bradshaw Foundation, May 2, 2007. http://www.bradshawfoundation.com/stonehenge/stonehenge.php.
3. "El Castillo." World-Mysteries.com. https://old.world-mysteries.com/chichen_kukulcan.htm.
4. Haughton, Brian. "The Nebra Sky Disk - Ancient Map of the Stars." Ancient History Encyclopedia, May 10, 2011. https://www.ancient.eu/article/235/the-nebra-sky-disk---ancient-map-of-the-stars/.
5. "Nebra Sky Disc — Bronze Age representation of the sky, Germany." UNESCO Astronomy and World Heritage Webportal, August 27, 2018. https://www3.astronomicalheritage.net/index.php/show-entity?identity=96&idsubentity=1.
6. Morgan, Morien O. *The Mabin of the Mabionogion*. London: Research into Lost Knowledge Organization, 1984. First published as *The Royal Winged Son of Stonehenge and Avebury*.
7. Ibid., 60.
8. "The Temple of Amun at Karnak, Egypt." UNESCO Astronomy and World Heritage Webportal. https://www3.astronomicalheritage.net/index.php/show-entity?identity=22&idsubentity=1.
9. See diagram by Bannister, Fletcher. "Temple of Amun Plan, Karnak." Ancient History Encyclopedia, September 16, 2016. https://www.ancient.eu/image/5682/.
10. Murphy, Anthony. "101 Facts about Newgrange." Mythical Ireland, November 8, 2017. https://mythicalireland.com/ancient-sites/101-facts-about-newgrange/.
11. "Megalithic Malta." MegalithomaniaUK, November 23, 2018. https://youtu.be/2N1K_AJdueQ?t=300.
12. "Four Treasures of the Tuatha Dé Danann." Wikipedia. https://en.wikipedia.org/wiki/Four_Treasures_of_the_Tuatha_Dé_Danann.

13. Scranton, Laird. "The Druids and Other Pieces of the Puzzle." In *The Mystery of Skara Brae: Neolithic Scotland and the Origins of Ancient Egypt*. Rochester: Inner Traditions, 2016.
14. Halpin, David. "Thoth's Storm: New Evidence for Ancient Egyptians in Ireland." Humans Are Free, 2016. http://humansarefree.com/2016/07/thoths-storm-new-evidence-for-ancient.html.
15. "Designing Your Own Newgrange Tomb!" Space Math @ NASA, October 7, 2010. http://spacemath.gsfc.nasa.gov/SED11/P8Newgrange.pdf.
16. Murphy, "101 Facts about Newgrange"; Shaw, Judith. "Boann, Celtic Goddess of Inspiration and Creativity." Feminism & Religion, July 27, 2016. https://feminismandreligion.com/2016/07/27/boann-celtic-goddess-of-inspiration-and-creativity-by-judith-shaw/.
17. Murphy, "101 Facts about Newgrange."
18. "Ring of Brodgar: (Henge-Circle)." Ancient-Wisdom, January 8, 2009. http://www.ancient-wisdom.com/scotlandbrodgar.htm.
19. Tompkins, Peter. *Secrets of the Great Pyramid*. Harper & Row, 1971, p. 130-133.
20. Scranton, Laird, *The Mystery of Skara Brae*, chap. 3.
21. Doutré, Martin. "Ring O' Brodgar, Orkney Islands: Gateway to the Americas." Ancient Celtic New Zealand, 2000. http://www.celticnz.co.nz/Brodgar/Brodgar1.htm.
22. Fell, Barry. *America B.C.: Ancient Settlers in the New World*. New York: Pocket Books, 1976.
23. "Six Mysterious Stone Structures of New England." New England Historical Society, 2020. https://www.newenglandhistoricalsociety.com/6-mysterious-stone-structures-new-england/.
24. Fell, *America B.C.*
25. Ibid.
26. Ibid.
27. "Natural Winter Solstice Alignment Cave in Clay Co. Kentucky USA." Facebook, February 22, 2014. https://www.facebook.com/Natural-Winter-Solstice-Alignment-Cave-in-Clay-Co-Kentucky-USA-669035706473619/.
28. "Arqueoastronomía en Rapa Nui." Moe Varua, August 15, 2010. https://moevarua.com/en/archaeoastronomy-0n-rapa-nui/.
29. Liller, William, and Julio D. Duarte. "Easter Island's 'Solar Ranging Device,' Ahu Huri A Urenga, and Vicinity." *Archaeoastronomy* 9, (1986): 52.
30. Temple, Robert. "Lost Technology of the Ancients: The Crystal Sun." New Dawn Magazine. No. 65, 2001. https://www.newdawnmagazine.com/articles/lost-technology-of-the-ancients-the-crystal-sun.
31. "Ancient Time Keepers, Part 3: Archaeoastronomy." World-Mysteries Blog, September 23, 2011. https://blog.world-mysteries.com/science/ancient-time-keepers-archaeoastronomy/.
32. "Tiahuanaco." Anselm Pi Rambla, December 15, 2016. http://www.pirambla.com/en/works/tiahuanaco.html.
33. Heyerdahl, Thor. *American Indians in the Pacific*. London: Allen & Unwin, 1952, p. 234-236, 247, 251.
34. Ibid., 230-231, 258.
35. Heyerdahl, Thor. "The Bearded Gods Speak." In *The Quest for America*, by Geoffrey Ashe. New York: Praeger, 1971.
36. Heyerdahl, Thor. *Aku-Aku: The Secret of Easter Island*. Chicago: Rand McNally & Company, 1958, p. 357-359.
37. Asheshov, Nicholas. "Ancient Inca Sun Pillars Still Mark June Solstice." Kim MacQuarrie, July 1, 2009. http://www.kimmacquarrie.com/ancient-inca-sun-pillars-still-mark-june-solstice/.
38. Hancock, Graham. *Magicians of the Gods*. London: Hodder & Stoughton, 2016, p. 384.
39. "Viracocha." Wikipedia. https://en.wikipedia.org/wiki/Viracocha.
40. "Tiwanaku." Crystalinks. https://www.crystalinks.com/tiahuanaco.html.
41. "Viracocha." Wikipedia.
42. Ibid.
43. "The Fascinating Story behind the Ancient Rock-Cut Ajanta Caves." Curiosmos, May 6, 2019. https://curiosmos.com/the-fascinating-story-behind-the-ancient-rock-cut-ajanta-caves/.
44. Gayre of Gayre, R. *The Origin of the Zimbabwean Civilisation*. Salisbury: Galaxie Press, 1972, preface.
45. Hall, R. N., and W. G. Neal. *The Ancient Ruins of Rhodesia*. 2nd ed. London: Methuen & Co., 1904, p. xxxiv, 37-39.

46. Azize, Joseph. *The Phoenician Solar Theology: An Investigation into the Phoenician Opinion of the Sun Found in Julian's Hymn to King Helios.* Gorgias Press, 2005. https://b-ok.cc/book/2474368/4bdf0f.
47. Clark, Stuart, and Damian Carrington. "Eclipse Brings Claim of Medieval African Observatory." New Scientist, December 4, 2002. https://www.newscientist.com/article/dn3137-eclipse-brings-claim-of-medieval-african-observatory/.
48. "The Spider Geoglyph & the Stars of Orion." The Morien Institute. http://www.morien-institute.org/nazca8.html.
49. "Nazca Lines." Wikipedia. https://en.wikipedia.org/wiki/Nazca_Lines.
50. Olsen, Dee. "New DNA Results Released from the Paracas Elongated Skulls." Megalithic Marvels, February 3, 2018. https://megalithicmarvels.com/2018/02/03/new-dna-results-released-from-the-paracas-elongated-skulls/.
51. "Paracas Culture." Wikipedia. https://en.wikipedia.org/wiki/Paracas_culture.
52. Doutré, Martin. "The Nazca Lines of Peru." Ancient Celtic New Zealand, 2000. http://www.celticnz.co.nz/Nazca/Nazca1.htm.
53. Golomb, Jason. "Nasca Lines." National Geographic. https://www.nationalgeographic.com/history/archaeology/nasca-lines/.
54. Belmonte, Juan Antonio., A. César González–García, and Andrea Polcaro. "Light and Shadows over Petra: Astronomy and Landscape in Nabataean Lands." *Nexus Network Journal* 15, no. 3 (2013): 487-501. https://doi.org/10.1007/s00004-013-0164-6.
55. Ibid., 496.
56. Mead, G. R. S. *Did Jesus Live 100 B.C.?* London: Theosophical Publishing Society, 1903. The Gnostic Society Library. http://gnosis.org/library/grs-mead/jesus_live_100/ch19.html.
57. Mannikka, Eleanor. *Angkor Wat: Time, Space, and Kingship.* University of Hawaii Press, 2000, p. 215.
58. Mannikka, Eleanor. "Angkor Secrets to Be Lost in a Sound and Light Show 'Insult.'" The Phnom Penh Post, December 1, 1995. https://www.phnompenhpost.com/national/angkor-secrets-be-lost-sound-and-light-show-insult.
59. Hancock, Graham, and Santha Faiia. *Heaven's Mirror: Quest for the Lost Civilization.* Three Rivers Press, 1998.
60. "Suryavarman II." Wikipedia. https://en.wikipedia.org/wiki/Suryavarman_II.
61. Mannikka, *Angkor Wat,* 51.
62. Russkaya Imperia. "Vedas and Human DNA." YouTube, April 10, 2010. https://youtu.be/QK_R1BmkzmY?t=205.
63. "Arkaim." Wikipedia. https://en.wikipedia.org/wiki/Arkaim.
64. "Goseck Henge: (The 'German Stonehenge')." Ancient-Wisdom, September 27, 2011. http://www.ancient-wisdom.com/germanygoseck.htm. Cites: Heath, Robin. *Sun, Moon & Stonehenge.* Blue Stone Press, 1998.
65. "Goseck Henge," Ancient-Wisdom.
66. Sudakov, Dmitry. "Arkaim, Russia's Strongest Anomaly Zone." Pravda.Ru, June 7, 2010. http://www.pravdareport.com/science/113680-arkaim/.
67. "Arkaim." Wikipedia.
68. Ibid. Quotes: Shnirelman, V. A. "Archaeology and Ethnic Politics: The Discovery of Arkaim." *Museum International* 50, no.2 (1998): 33-39. https://doi.org/10.1111/1468-0033.00146.
69. LePage, Victoria. "Arkaim: Russia's Ancient City & the Arctic Origin of Civilisation." *New Dawn Magazine* 111 (2008).
70. Grigoryev, Stanislav. "The Urals Intends to Develop Pilgrimage to the 'Russian Stonehenge.'" Interfax, May 8, 2008. http://www.interfax-religion.com/?act=news&div=4653.
71. Mörner, Nils-Axel, and Bob G. Lind. "Stonehenge Has Got a Younger Sister – Ales Stones in Sweden Decoded." *International Journal of Astronomy and Astrophysics* 2, no. 1 (2012): 23-27. http://doi.org/10.4236/ijaa.2012.21004.
72. "Bryn Celli Ddu: (Passage-Mound, Henge)." Ancient-Wisdom, June 18, 2006. http://www.ancient-wisdom.com/walesbryncelliddu.htm.
73. Seppa, Nathan. "Metropolitan Life on the Mississippi." The Washington Post, March 12, 1997. http://www.washingtonpost.com/wp-srv/national/daily/march/12/cahokia.htm.

74. Sofaer, Anna, Volker Zinser, and Rolf M Sinclair. "A Unique Solar Marking Construct." *Science* 206, no. 4416 (October, 1979): 283-291. https://solsticeproject.org/images/pdfs/19-uniquesolar%2520%25281979%2529.pdf.
75. Stoev, Alexey, and Penka Muglova. "Harman Kaya." The Rock-Cut Sacred Places of the Thracians and Other Palaeo-Balkan and Other Ancient Anatolian Peoples, June 21, 2005. http://rock-cut.thracians.org/en/s_m_harman.php.
76. "Location of the Kanayama Megaliths." The Kanayama Megaliths and Archaeoastronomy in Japan: The Ancient Solar Calendar, April 8, 2017. http://www.seiryu.ne.jp/~kankou-kanayama/megaliths/index2.html.
77. "Winter Solstice Sunrise at Higashinoyama." Iwaya-Iwakage of Kanayama Megaliths: Megaliths for an Ancient Solar Calendar, December 26, 2017. https://iwakage.wordpress.com/2017/12/26/winter-solstice-sunrise-at-higashinoyama/.
78. Cenev, Gjore. "Megalithic Observatory Kokino." *Publications of the Astronomical Observatory of Belgrade* 80 (May 2006): 313-317. http://articles.adsabs.harvard.edu//full/2006POBeo..80..313C/0000316.000.html.
79. "Mesa Verde National Park." Wikipedia. https://en.wikipedia.org/wiki/Mesa_Verde_National_Park#Astronomy.
80. Freeman, Dr. Gordon R. *Hidden Stonehenge: Ancient Temple in North America Reveals the Key to Ancient Wonders*. Watkins Publishing, 2012.
81. "Oyu Stone Circles." Jomon Archaeological Sites in Hokkaido and Northern Tohoku, November 29, 2013. http://jomon-japan.jp/en/jomon-sites/oyu/.
82. "The Restoration of the Fallen Menhir of Punkri Burwadih." The Heritage Trust, September 16, 2012. https://theheritagetrust.wordpress.com/2012/09/12/the-restoration-of-the-fallen-menhir-of-punkri-burwadih/.
83. "Parque Arqueológico do Solstício." Wikipedia. https://en.wikipedia.org/wiki/Parque_Arqueológico_do_Solstício.
84. Lorenzi, Rossella. "Ancient Stonehenge-Like 'Calendar Rock' Aligns with Winter Solstice." Seeker, January 5, 2017. https://www.seeker.com/ancient-stonehenge-like-calendar-rock-aligned-with-winter-solstice-2180344326.html.
85. "Archaeoastronomy and Dolmens." Publications. http://terra-xx.narod.ru/pb8.htm.
86. Zangger, Eberhard. "The Hidden Celestial Sanctuary of the Hittites." Popular Archaeology, June 19, 2019. https://popular-archaeology.com/article/the-hidden-celestial-sanctuary-of-the-hittites/.
87. "A History of Calendars: An Ancient Hittite Metonic Calendar?". Druidcraft Calendar, February 4, 2020. https://druidcraftcalendar.co.uk/calendar-history/a-history-of-calendars-an-ancient-hittite-metonic-calendar/.

CHAPTER TEN: ANCIENT SACRED SITES ALIGNED TO THE SPRING EQUINOX

1. Hancock, Graham, and Robert Bauval. *The Message of the Sphinx: A Quest for the Hidden Legacy of Mankind*. New York: Three Rivers Press, 1996, p. 71-75.
2. "Mapping the Sphinx." Ancient Egypt Research Associates, November 1, 2005. http://www.aeraweb.org/sphinx-project/mapping-the-sphinx/.
3. Mannikka, Eleanor. *Angkor Wat: Time, Space, and Kingship*. University of Hawaii Press, 2000, p. 44.
4. Hancock, Graham, and Santha Faiia. *Heaven's Mirror: Quest for the Lost Civilization*. Three Rivers Press, 1998, p. 133.
5. Rod-ari, Dr. Melody. "Angkor Wat." Khan Academy. https://www.khanacademy.org/humanities/ap-art-history/south-east-se-asia/cambodia-art/a/angkor-wat.
6. Mannikka, *Angkor Wat*, 37.
7. Gray, Martin. *Sacred Earth*. New York: Sterling, 2011, p. 168.
8. Mannikka, *Angkor Wat*, 49-51.
9. "Tikal." Wikipedia. https://en.wikipedia.org/wiki/Tikal.
10. "Tikal Temple I." Wikipedia. https://en.wikipedia.org/wiki/Tikal_Temple_I.
11. Haiken, Melanie. "Tikal Rediscovered: The Greatest Mayan City Just Got a Lot Grander." AFAR, March 14, 2019. https://www.afar.com/magazine/tikal-rediscovered-the-greatest-mayan-city-just-got-a-lot-grander.

12. Šprajc, Ivan. "Equinoxes in Mesoamerican Architectural Alignments: Prehispanic Reality or Modern Myth?" Research Gate, January, 2013. https://www.researchgate.net/figure/Tikal-Peten-Guatemala-rising-Sun-above-the-roof-comb-of-Temple-I-obser-ved-from_fig4_264220189.
13. "Maya Jaguar Gods." Wikipedia. https://en.wikipedia.org/wiki/Maya_jaguar_gods.
14. Ibid.
15. Ibid.
16. Budge, E. A. Wallis, trans. "The Chapter of Changing into a Lotus." In *The Book of the Dead: Papyrus of Ani, Vol. II*. New York: G. P. Putnam's Sons, 1913, p. 557.
17. "Plate with Maize God Resurrection Scene, A.D. 600–800." Princeton University Art Museum. https://artmuseum.princeton.edu/collections/objects/8905.
18. "Woodhenge." Cahokia Mounds, July 14, 2015. https://cahokiamounds.org/explore/#tab-id-4.
19. Barrows, Vince. "A History of Monks Mound." 2007. https://www.freewebs.com/historyofmonksmound/.
20. Ibid.
21. Murphy, Anthony. "Loughcrew – Sliabh Na Calliagh." Mythical Ireland, September 5, 2019. https://www.mythicalireland.com/ancient-sites/loughcrew-sliabh-na-calliagh/.
22. Ibid.
23. Byrne, Martin. "Megalithic Art at Cairn T." The Sacred Island, December 30, 2017. http://www.carrowkeel.com/sites/loughcrew/cairnt2.html.
24. Murphy, Anthony. "Ancient Astronomers of the Stone Age." Mythical Ireland, January 21, 2019. https://www.mythicalireland.com/astronomy/ancient-astronomers-of-the-stone-age/.
25. Byrne, Martin. "Knowth's Engraved Stones." The Sacred Island, April 10, 2010. http://www.carrowkeel.com/sites/boyne/knowth5.html.
26. Macbain, Gillies. "Finding Easter at Knowth." Mythical Ireland, November 7, 2017. https://www.mythicalireland.com/ancient-sites/knowth-cnogba/.
27. Ibid.
28. Byrne, Martin. "The East Passage and Chamber at Knowth." The Sacred Island, October 15, 2016. http://www.carrowkeel.com/sites/boyne/knowth3.html.
29. Byrne, Martin. "The West Passage." The Sacred Island, April 30, 2016. http://www.carrowkeel.com/sites/boyne/knowth4.html.
30. "The Hill of Slane – Sláine." Mythical Ireland, November 2, 2017. https://www.mythicalireland.com/ancient-sites/the-hill-of-slane-slaine/.
31. Coppens, Philip. *Land of the Gods: How a Scottish Landscape Was Sanctified to Become Arthur's Camelot*. Enkhuizen: Frontier Publishing, 2007, p. 91.
32. "Persepolis." Wikipedia. https://en.wikipedia.org/wiki/Persepolis.
33. "Novruz, The Fire of Spring." English Zoroastrian. http://www.zoroastrian.org.uk/vohuman/Article/Noruz The Fire of Spring.htm.
34. "Persepolis." Wikipedia. https://en.wikipedia.org/wiki/Persepolis.
35. Ibid.
36. Atwood, Lara. *The Ancient Religion of the Sun: The Wisdom Bringers and The Lost Civilization of the Sun*. 2nd ed. Sura Ondrunar Publishing, 2021, p. 97-99.
37. "Nowruz." Wikipedia. https://en.wikipedia.org/wiki/Nowruz.
38. "Faravahar." Wikipedia. https://en.wikipedia.org/wiki/Faravahar.
39. Leonard, Phillip M. *A Monument to Mithras*. 2013. Quoted in Lehrburger, Carl. *Secrets of Ancient America: Archaeoastronomy and the Legacy of the Phoenicians, Celts, and Other Forgotten Explorers*. Bear & Company, 2015, location 136. Kindle edition.
40. "Bryn Celli Ddu: (Passage-Mound, Henge)." Ancient-Wisdom, June 18, 2006. http://www.ancient-wisdom.com/walesbryncelliddu.htm.
41. "Chaco Culture National Historical Park." Wikipedia. https://en.wikipedia.org/wiki/Chaco_Culture_National_Historical_Park.
42. Meghan. "Chaco Canyon, Part 3: Casa Rinconada, The Autumnal Equinox, and Petroglyphs." Another Walk in the Park, October 9, 2013. https://anotherwalkinthepark.com/2013/10/09/chaco-canyon-part-3-casa-rinconada-the-autumnal-equinox-and-petroglyphs/.

43. "Spring Equinox 2012." Guarding Grianán Aileach, March 21, 2012. https://unknownswilly.wordpress.com/2012/03/21/spring-equinox/.
44. Cenev, Gjore. *Ancient Secrets of Kokino Observatory*. Amazon Digital Services LLC., 2012, location 131. Kindle edition.
45. "Archaeoastronomy and Dolmens." Publications. http://terra-xx.narod.ru/pb8.htm.
46. "Mnajdra Prehistoric Temples." World Monuments Fund, August 10, 2011. https://www.wmf.org/project/mnajdra-prehistoric-temples.
47. Ryder, Julie. "Megaliths in Montana, USA." Galacticfacets. https://www.galacticfacets.com/megaliths-in-montana-usa.html.
48. Ibid.
49. Tarnovski, Griandr. "Trypilian Temple - Observatory at Nebelivka." Bezvodovka, August 31, 2018. http://www.bezvodovka.com/en/pysmena/nebelivka.html.
50. Ibid.
51. Everett, Laneha. "Equinox at Crack Cave." Canyon Journeys, March 18, 2019. https://canyon-journeys.com/equinox-solar-alighments/equinox-at-crack-cave/.
52. Das, Subhashis. "Government Mute on the Destruction of a Few Megalithic Sites in Hazaribagh. Jharkhand. East India." Megaliths of India, June 29, 2017. http://subhashisdas.com/government-mute-on-the-destruction-of-a-few-megalithic-sites-in-hazaribagh-jharkhand-east-india/.
53. Schmidt, Roderick L. "An Analysis of the Inyo Equinox Display." The Equinox Project. http://www.equinox-project.com/analy.htm.
54. "Beyond Tikal – Uaxactun Archaeological Site, Guatemala." Trans-Americas Journey, November 28, 2011. https://trans-americas.com/uaxactun-archaeological-site-equinox-guatemala/.

CHAPTER ELEVEN: ANCIENT SACRED SITES ALIGNED TO THE SUMMER SOLSTICE

1. Proctor, Richard A. *The Great Pyramid: Observatory, Tomb, and Temple*. London: Longmans, Green, and Co., 1888, p. 18.
2. "Abydos." Our Egypt, May 6, 2012. http://www.our-egypt.com/en/travel-guide/upper-egypt/abydos/.
3. "Abydoss (Abjou): (The Osireion)." Ancient-Wisdom. http://www.ancient-wisdom.com/egyptabydoss.htm#valleytemple.
4. Bridges, Vincent. "Abydos, the Osireion and Egyptian Sacred Science." Vincent Bridges Archive, September 1, 2000. http://vincentbridges.com/post/145759129272/abydosthe-osireion-and-egyptian-sacred-science.
5. Lönnqvist, Kenneth, and Minna Lönnqvist. "Spatial Approach to the Ruins of Khirbet Qumran at the Dead Sea." *XXth ISPRS Congress Technical Commission V* (July 12-23, 2004): 558-563. https://www.isprs.org/proceedings/XXXV/congress/comm5/papers/616.pdf.
6. Josephus, Flavius. *The Jewish War*, book 2, chap. 8. Wikiquote. https://en.wikiquote.org/wiki/Josephus_on_the_Essenes.
7. Lightfoot, J. B. "On Some Points Connected with the Essenes." In *Saint Paul's Epistles to the Colossians and Philemon*. London: MacMillan and Co., 1875.
8. Greaney, Susan. "History of Stonehenge." English Heritage, December 18, 2013. https://www.english-heritage.org.uk/visit/places/stonehenge/history-and-stories/history/.
9. "Stonehenge." Wikipedia. https://en.wikipedia.org/wiki/Stonehenge.
10. Ibid.
11. "Stonehenge – the Age of the Megaliths." Bradshaw Foundation, May 2, 2007. http://www.bradshawfoundation.com/stonehenge/stonehenge.php.
12. Snoeck, Christophe, John Pouncett, Philippe Claeys, Steven Goderis, Nadine Mattielli, Mike Parker Pearson, Christie Willis, et al. "Strontium Isotope Analysis on Cremated Human Remains from Stonehenge Support Links with West Wales." *Scientific Reports* 8 (August 2, 2018). https://doi.org/10.1038/s41598-018-28969-8.
13. "Stonehenge." Wikipedia.
14. Alberge, Dalya. "Stonehenge Was Built on Solstice Axis, Dig Confirms." The Guardian, September 8, 2013. https://www.theguardian.com/culture/2013/sep/08/stonehenge-ice-age-solstice-axis.

15. Ruggles, Clive, Bill Burton, David Hughes, Andrew Lawson, and Derek McNally. "Stonehenge and Ancient Astronomy." Royal Astronomical Society, 2009. http://www.stonehengeandaveburywhs.org/assets/Stonehenge.LowRes.pdf.
16. "Discoveries Provide Evidence of a Celestial Procession at Stonehenge." University of Birmingham, Nov 26, 2011. https://www.birmingham.ac.uk/news/latest/2011/11/25Nov-Discoveries-provide-evidence-of-a-celestial-procession-at-Stonehenge.aspx.
17. Ibid.
18. Banton, Simon. "Astronomical Alignments at Stonehenge." Salisbury and Stonehenge Guided Tours, January 6, 2017. http://www.stonehenge-tours.com/blog.Astronomical-Alignments-at-Stonehenge.html.
19. "Durrington Walls." Wikipedia. https://en.wikipedia.org/wiki/Durrington_Walls.
20. Greaney, "History of Stonehenge."
21. Ibid.
22. Ravilious, Kate. "Bejeweled Stonehenge Boy Came from Mediterranean?" National Geographic, October 14, 2010. https://www.nationalgeographic.com/news/2010/10/101013-stonehenge-burials-boy-science-mediterranean/.
23. Temple, Robert. *Egyptian Dawn*. London: Random House, 2010, p. 409.
24. "Trilithons: (Ancient Constructions)." Ancient-Wisdom, August 28, 2011. http://www.ancient-wisdom.com/trilithons.htm.
25. "Ancient Libya." Wikipedia. https://en.wikipedia.org/wiki/Ancient_Libya.
26. Lloyd, Ellen. "Was Megalithic Stone Circle of Mzoura the Tomb of Giant Antaeus?" Ancient Pages, September 5, 2015. http://www.ancientpages.com/2015/09/05/was-megalithic-stone-circle-of-mzoura-the-tomb-of-giant-antaeus/.
27. O'Connell, Tony. "Mzora Stone Circle." Atlantipedia, February 14, 2014. http://atlantipedia.ie/samples/mzora-stone-circle-n/.
28. *Magical Egypt*. Directed by Chance Gardner, featuring John Anthony West. 2001. Interview with Thomas G. Brophy. https://youtu.be/T42nRhpOHBg.
29. Brophy, Thomas G., and Paul Rosen. "Satellite Imagery Measures of the Astronomically Aligned Megalithis at Nabta Playa." *Mediterranean Archaeology and Archaeometry* 5, no. 1 (2005): 15-24.
30. Brophy, Thomas G. *The Origin Map: Discovery of a Prehistoric, Megalithic, Astrophysical Map and Sculpture of the Universe*. Lincoln: Writers Club Press, 2002.
31. Ibid.
32. "Nabta Playa: (Stone Circle)." Ancient-Wisdom. http://www.ancient-wisdom.com/egyptnabta.htm.
33. "Tallaght." Wikipedia. https://en.wikipedia.org/wiki/Tallaght.
34. Niamh and Con. "Celtic Druid's Summer Solstice." Celtic Druid Temple, June 17, 2017. https://www.celticdruidtemple.com/blog/celtic-druids-summer-solstice.
35. Gray, Martin. "Externsteine." Places of Peace and Power, July 30, 2013. https://sacredsites.com/europe/germany/externsteine.html.
36. Teudt, Wilhelm. *Germanische Heiligtümer*. Eugen Diedlichs in Jena, 1929.
37. Ibid.
38. Ibid.
39. Gorgani, Cyrus. "The Irminsul." Real Rune Magick, December 25, 2017. http://realrunemagick.blogspot.com/2017/12/the-irminsul.html.
40. Ibid.
41. "Ajanta Caves." Wikipedia. https://en.wikipedia.org/wiki/Ajanta_Caves.
42. Singh, Manager, and Babasaheb Ramrao Arbad. "Architectural History and Painting Art at Ajanta: Some Salient Features." *Arts* 2, no. 3 (2013): 134-150. https://doi.org/10.3390/arts2030134.
43. Hamilton, Ross. *The Mystery of the Serpent Mound: In Search of the Alphabet of the Gods*. Berkeley: Frog Books, 2001, xxiv-xxvi.
44. Putnam, F. W. "The Serpent Mound of Ohio." *The Century Illustrated Monthly Magazine* 39 (November 1889 - April 1890). ScienceViews.com. http://scienceviews.com/indian/the_serpent_mound_of_ohio.html.

45. Collins, Andrew. "Britain's First Prehistoric Serpent Mound to Be Buried beneath Bypass." AndrewCollins.com, July 7, 2007. https://www.andrewcollins.com/page/news/Rotherwas.htm.
46. Ibid.
47. Bonwick, James. "Serpent Faith." In *Irish Druids and Old Irish Religions*. 1894. Library Ireland. https://www.libraryireland.com/Druids/Serpent-Faith-4.php.
48. Collins, "Britain's First Prehistoric Serpent Mound."
49. Kuckelman, Kristin A. "Oral History." The Archaeology of Castle Rock Pueblo, 2000. http://www.crowcanyon.org/researchreports/castlerock/text/crpw_oralhistory.asp.
50. Ibid.
51. David, Gary A. "The Orion Zone: Ancient Star Cities of the American Southwest." GrahamHancock.com, February 17, 2006. https://grahamhancock.com/davidga1/.
52. Gannon, Megan. "Ancient Pueblo Used Golden Ratio to Build the Sun Temple." Live Science, February 13, 2017. https://www.livescience.com/57862-sun-temple-golden-ratio-found.html.
53. De Pastino, Blake. "Mesa Verde's Sun Temple Reveals Geometrical 'Genius,' Physicist Says." Western Digs, January 26, 2017. http://westerndigs.org/mesa-verdes-sun-temple-reveals-geometrical-genius-physicist-says/.
54. Eccott, David J. "The Ogams of the Sun Temple." *Migration & Diffusion Periodical* 6, no. 23 (2005). http://www.onter.net/biblio/eccott.pdf.
55. Klyosov, Anatole A., and Elena A. Mironova. "A DNA Genealogy Solution to the Puzzle of Ancient Look-Alike Ceramics across the World." *Advances in Anthropology* 3, no. 3 (2013): 164-172. https://doi.org/10.4236/aa.2013.33022.
56. "Fajada Butte." Wikipedia. https://en.wikipedia.org/wiki/Fajada_Butte#Sun_Dagger_site.
57. "Casa Rinconada." Space Math @ NASA, October 5, 2010. https://spacemath.gsfc.nasa.gov/SED11/P2CasaRinconada.pdf.
58. "Ahu Tongariki." Wikipedia. https://en.wikipedia.org/wiki/Ahu_Tongariki.
59. "Tulum." Wikipedia. https://en.wikipedia.org/wiki/Tulum.
60. Grace. "World Ending in 2012?" Grace's Mosaic Moments, February 16, 2012. http://mosaicmoments.blogspot.com/2012/02/world-ending-in-2012.html.
61. "Tulum." Wikipedia.
62. Sutherland, A. "Ancient Maya Ruins of Tulum: Sea Port and Sacred Site for Worshiping of Descending God." Ancient Pages, August 10, 2016. http://www.ancientpages.com/2016/08/10/ancient-maya-ruins-of-tulum-sea-port-and-sacred-site-for-worshiping-of-descending-god/.
63. *The Holy Bible*. King James Version (KJV).
64. Miller, Arthur G. "West and East in Maya Thought: Death and Rebirth at Palenque and Tulum." *First Palenque Round Table* (1974): 45-49. https://pdfs.semanticscholar.org/3518/e572c4be4bcd4a8219a257f8496ceacec5ca.pdf.
65. "Pyramid of the Magician." Wikipedia. https://en.wikipedia.org/wiki/Pyramid_of_the_Magician.
66. Ibid., https://en.wikipedia.org/wiki/Pyramid_of_the_Magician#Description.
67. "Pyramids in Latin America." History, October 29, 2009. https://www.history.com/topics/ancient-history/pyramids-in-latin-america.
68. "Mundo Perdido, Tikal." Wikipedia. https://en.wikipedia.org/wiki/Mundo_Perdido,_Tikal.
69. Bokor, Matt. "Uaxactún Ancient Mayan Observatory." The Antigua Guide, June 2, 2017. https://www.theantiguaguide.com/uaxactun-ancient-mayan-observatory/.
70. Truman, Dave. "Ancient Alignment in the Andes Hints at a Lost Global High Culture." GrahamHancock.com, January 2, 2016. https://grahamhancock.com/truman d1/.
71. Ibid.
72. Atwood, Lara. *The Ancient Religion of the Sun: The Wisdom Bringers and The Lost Civilization of the Sun*. 2nd ed. Sura Ondrunar Publishing, 2021, p. 78-83.
73. "Pyramids of Güímar." Wikipedia. https://en.wikipedia.org/wiki/Pyramids_of_Guimar.
74. Kennedy, Gordon. *The White Indians of Nivaria*. Mecca, California: Nivaria Press, 2010, p. 46.
75. "Guanches." Wikipedia. https://en.wikipedia.org/wiki/Guanches.
76. Penprase, Bryan E. *The Power of Stars: How Celestial Observations Have Shaped Civilization*. Springer Science & Business Media, 2010, p. 205-206.

77. "Ur." In *The Oxford Companion to Archaeology*. 2nd ed., edited by Neil Asher Silberman. Oxford University Press, 2012. http://www.oxfordreference.com/view/10.1093/acref/9780199735785.001.0001/acref-9780199735785-e-0468.

78. Woolley, Leonard. *Ur Excavations, Vol. V: The Ziggurat and Its Surroundings*. London: The British Museum, 1939, p. 1.

79. Alison, Jim. "Exploring Geographic and Geometric Relationships along a Line of Ancient Sites around the World." GrahamHancock.com, May 1, 2001. https://grahamhancock.com/geographic-geometric-relationships-alisonj/.

80. Norris, Ray P., Cilla Norris, Duane W. Hamacher, and Reg Abrahams. "Wurdi Youang: An Australian Aboriginal Stone Arrangement with Possible Solar Indications." *Rock Art Research* 30, no. 1 (2013): 55-65. https://www.atnf.csiro.au/people/Ray.Norris/papers/n258.pdf.

81. Ibid.

82. Ibid.

83. Hamacher, Dr. Duane. "Wurdi Youang - an Aboriginal Stone Arrangement with Possible Solar Alignments." Australian Indigenous Astronomy, March 11, 2011. http://aboriginalastronomy.blogspot.com/2011/03/wurdi-youang-aboriginal-stone.html.

84. "Wurdi Youang." Wikipedia. https://en.wikipedia.org/wiki/Wurdi_Youang.

85. "Lascaux Cave: (Palaeolithic Cave-art)." Ancient-Wisdom. http://ancient-wisdom.com/francelascaux.htm.

86. Ibid.

87. Ibid.

88. Lima, Pedro, and Stephane Begoin-Pascal Goetgheluck. "The Lascaux Cave: A Prehistoric Sky-Map..." Issuu, September 25, 2008. https://issuu.com/lightmediation/docs/the_lascaux_cave___a_prehistoric_sky-map_3390.

89. Ibid.

90. Tedesco, Laura Anne. "Lascaux (ca. 15,000 B.C.)." In *Heilbrunn Timeline of Art History*. New York: The Metropolitan Museum of Art, 2000. http://www.metmuseum.org/toah/hd/lasc/hd_lasc.htm.

91. Lind, Bob G. "The Summer Solstice." Ales Stenar, January 1, 2009. http://www.alesstenar.com/eng/SummerSolstice.htm.

92. Azevedo, Virgílio. "Arqueólogos Revelam Segredos das Pirâmides da Ilha do Pico." Expresso, August 27, 2013. https://expresso.pt/sociedade/arqueologos-revelam-segredos-das-piramides-da-ilha-do-pico=f827624.

93. Eddy, J. A. "Astronomical Alignment of the Big Horn Medicine Wheel." *Science* 184, no. 4141 (1974): 1035-1043. https://doi.org/10.1126/science.184.4141.1035.

94. "Bryn Celli Ddu: (Passage-Mound, Henge)." Ancient-Wisdom, June 18, 2006. http://www.ancient-wisdom.com/walesbryncelliddu.htm.

95. "The Bulgarian Stonehenge - the Gate of Mother Goddess: The Megalith near the Village of Buzovgrad." Park Hotel Stara Zagora, June 21, 2019. http://хотелстаразагора.com/en/landmarks/the-bulgarian-stonehenge-the-gate-of-mother-goddess-the-megalith-near-the-village-of-buzovgrad/.

96. Seppa, Nathan. "Metropolitan Life on the Mississippi." The Washington Post, March 12, 1997. http://www.washingtonpost.com/wp-srv/national/daily/march/12/cahokia.htm.

97. "The Puzzle of the Thirteen Solar Towers of Chankillo." MIT Technology Review, August 21, 2012. https://www.technologyreview.com/s/428951/the-puzzle-of-the-13-solar-towers-of-chankillo/.

98. "Gors Fawr: (Stone Circle, Avenue)." Ancient-Wisdom, August 30, 2010. http://www.ancient-wisdom.com/walesgorsfawr.htm.

99. Stoev, Alexey, and Penka Muglova. "Harman Kaya." The Rock-Cut Sacred Places of the Thracians and Other Palaeo-Balkan and Other Ancient Anatolian Peoples, June 21, 2005. http://rock-cut.thracians.org/en/s_m_harman.php.

100. "Relations with the Sun's Track - The Megaliths with a Marked Stone - Midsummer." The Kanayama Megaliths and Archaeoastronomy in Japan: The Ancient Solar Calendar. http://www.seiryu.ne.jp/~kankou-kanayama/megaliths/senkoku/1_2.htm.

101. Cenev, Gjore. "Megalithic Observatory Kokino." *Publications of the Astronomical Observatory of Belgrade* 80 (May 2006): 313-317. http://articles.adsabs.harvard.edu//full/2006POBeo..80..313C/0000316.000.html.

102. "Lepenski Vir." Wikipedia. https://en.wikipedia.org/wiki/Lepenski_Vir.
103. Osmanagich, Semir Sam. "Pyramids in Mauritius: 'Sweet News from the Sugar Cane Fields in Mauritius.'" August 18, 2009. http://static1.1.sqspcdn.com/static/f/291652/11290596/1300459802400/Pyramids+in+Mauritus+-+August+2009.pdf.
104. "Mnajdra." Wikipedia. https://en.wikipedia.org/wiki/Mnajdra.
105. Ryder, Julie. "Megaliths in Montana, USA." Galacticfacets. https://www.galacticfacets.com/megaliths-in-montana-usa.html.
106. Freeman, Dr. Gordon R. *Hidden Stonehenge: Ancient Temple in North America Reveals the Key to Ancient Wonders*. Watkins Publishing, 2012.
107. "Oyu Stone Circles." Jomon Archaeological Sites in Hokkaido and Northern Tohoku, November 29, 2013. http://jomon-japan.jp/en/jomon-sites/oyu/.
108. "The Restoration of the Fallen Menhir of Punkri Burwadih." The Heritage Trust, September 16, 2012. https://theheritagetrust.wordpress.com/2012/09/12/the-restoration-of-the-fallen-menhir-of-punkri-burwadih/.
109. Aveni, Anthony, and Yonathan Mizrachi. "The Geometry and Astronomy of Rujm El-Hiri, a Megalithic Site in the Southern Levant." *Journal of Field Archaeology* 25, no. 4 (1998): 475–496.
110. Zangger, Eberhard. "The Hidden Celestial Sanctuary of the Hittites." Popular Archaeology, June 19, 2019. https://popular-archaeology.com/article/the-hidden-celestial-sanctuary-of-the-hittites/.
111. "A History of Calendars: An Ancient Hittite Metonic Calendar?". Druidcraft Calendar, February 4, 2020. https://druidcraftcalendar.co.uk/calendar-history/a-history-of-calendars-an-ancient-hittite-metonic-calendar/.

CHAPTER TWELVE: A GUIDE TO CELEBRATING THE SOLSTICES AND EQUINOXES

1. Morgan, Morien O. *The Mabin of the Mabionogion*. London: Research into Lost Knowledge Organization, 1984, p. ii-iv. First published as *The Royal Winged Son of Stonehenge and Avebury*.
2. David, Rosalie. *Religious Ritual at Abydos*. Warminster: Aris and Phillips, 1973, p. 266-267.
3. Mark, Joshua J. "The Eleusinian Mysteries: The Rites of Demeter." Ancient History Encyclopedia, January 18, 2012. https://www.ancient.eu/article/32/the-eleusinian-mysteries-the-rites-of-demeter/.
4. Szekely, Edmond Bordeaux, trans. *The Essene Gospel of Peace: Book One*. USA: International Biogenic Society, 1981, p. 13.
5. Vallejo, Jessie M., and Jorge G. F. Moreno Soto. "Andean Solstice Celebrations Capture the Wondrous Churn of Spacetime." Smithsonian Magazine, June 21, 2018. https://www.smithsonianmag.com/smithsonian-institution/andean-solstice-celebrations-capture-spacetime-180969426/.
6. "Discoveries Provide Evidence of a Celestial Procession at Stonehenge." University of Birmingham, Nov 26, 2011. https://www.birmingham.ac.uk/news/latest/2011/11/25Nov-Discoveries-provide-evidence-of-a-celestial-procession-at-Stonehenge.aspx.
7. Krylova, Daria. "Eight Facts about the Khorovod, Russia's Oldest Dance." Russia Beyond, January 5, 2017. https://www.rbth.com/arts/2016/12/07/8-facts-about-the-khorovod-russias-oldest-dance_654295.
8. Türler, Marc. "Calendrical Interpretation of Spirals in Irish Megalithic Art," 2. https://arxiv.org/ftp/arxiv/papers/1903/1903.07393.pdf
9. Hall, Manly P. *The Secret Teachings of All Ages*. San Francisco: H.S. Crocker Company, 1928, p. 22.
10. "What Color is the Sun?" Stanford SOLAR Center. http://solar-center.stanford.edu/SID/activities/GreenSun.html.
11. "Helium." Wikipedia. https://en.wikipedia.org/wiki/Helium.
12. Demetrius. *On Style*, II, 71. Translated by W. Rhys Roberts. Loeb edition, 347. In Godwin, Joscelyn. *The Mystery of the Seven Vowels*. Grand Rapids: Phanes Press, 1991, p. 22.
13. See the collection of ancient Gnostic texts called the Nag Hammadi Library.
14. Cowell, E. B., trans. *The Maitri or Maitrāyanīya Upanishad*. Calcutta: Asiatic Society of Bengal, 1870, p. 256-259, 277, 283-284, 289.
15. "AUM." New World Encyclopedia. https://www.newworldencyclopedia.org/entry/AUM.

CHAPTER THIRTEEN: CEREMONIES TO CELEBRATE THE AUTUMN EQUINOX

1. Mark, Joshua J. "The Eleusinian Mysteries: The Rites of Demeter." Ancient History Encyclopedia, January 18, 2012. https://www.ancient.eu/article/32/the-eleusinian-mysteries-the-rites-of-demeter/.
2. Evelyn-White, Hugh G., trans. *Hymn to Demeter*. Loeb Classical Library, 1914. Internet Sacred Text Archive. https://www.sacred-texts.com/cla/demeter.htm.
3. Based on Kali, Devadatta, trans. *In Praise of the Goddess: The Devimahatmya and Its Meaning*. Berwick: Nicolas-Hays, 2003.
4. Based on *Devi Mahatmyam*, translated by Swami Jagadiswarananda. Chennai: Sri Ramakrishna Math, 1953.
5. Based on *Devi Mahatmyam*, translated by Devadatta Kali.
6. Based on *Devi Mahatmyam*, translated by Swami Jagadiswarananda.
7. Saraswati, Swami Muktananda. "The Ancient Sacred Fire of Yajna." YOGA, 2004. http://www.yogamag.net/archives/2004/bmar04/ancient.shtml.
8. Kvilhaug, Maria. *The Seed of Yggdrasill: Deciphering the Hidden Messages in Old Norse Myths*. Whyte Tracks, 2016, chap. 3: Introduction: A Path of Initiation. Kindle edition.
9. Ibid., section 9.2 The Sacred Marriage.
10. Ibid., section 2.12 Nornir, Fylgjur – and the Runes of Fate: The Fylgjur – "Followers;" section 3.9 The Maidens of the Wind Shielded Island, Oddrúnargrátr (The Lament of Oddrún); section 10.2 The Ritual Behind the Myth.
11. Ibid., section 5.3 Out of Eden (Paradise Lost).
12. "List of names of Odin." Wikipedia. https://en.wikipedia.org/wiki/List_of_names_of_Odin.
13. Larrington, Carolyne, trans. *The Poetic Edda*. Oxford University Press, 1999, p. 34.
14. Bellows, Henry Adams, trans. *The Poetic Edda*. Princeton University Press, 1936, p. 17. Internet Sacred Text Archive. https://www.sacred-texts.com/neu/poe/poe03.htm.
15. Based on the translation of *Hávamál* by Carolyne Larrington.
16. Based on Sturluson, Snorri. *The Prose Edda*. Translated by Arthur Gilchrist Brodeur, 1916, p. 27. Internet Sacred Text Archive. http://www.sacred-texts.com/neu/pre/pre04.htm; Bellows, trans. *The Poetic Edda*, 13.
17. Based on the translation of *Hávamál* by Carolyne Larrington.
18. "Uruz Rune Meaning." The Wicked Griffin, March 23, 2018. https://thewickedgriffin.com/uruz-rune-meaning.
19. "Ansuz Rune Meaning." The Wicked Griffin, March 23, 2018. https://thewickedgriffin.com/ansuz-rune-meaning.
20. "Nauthiz Rune Meaning." The Wicked Griffin, March 23, 2018. https://thewickedgriffin.com/nauthiz-rune-meaning.
21. "Eihwaz Rune Meaning." The Wicked Griffin, March 23, 2018. https://thewickedgriffin.com/eihwaz-rune-meaning.
22. "Kenaz Rune Meaning." The Wicked Griffin, March 23, 2018. https://thewickedgriffin.com/kenaz-rune-meaning.
23. "Hagalaz Rune Meaning." The Wicked Griffin, March 23, 2018. https://thewickedgriffin.com/hagalaz-rune-meaning.
24. Kvilhaug, *Seed of Yggdrasill*, section 2.12 Nornir, Fylgjur – and the Runes of Fate: Óðinn – Uprooting the Runes.
25. Ibid.
26. Ibid.
27. Ibid.
28. Ibid.
29. Ibid.
30. Ibid., section 3.14 Soma and Haoma, Ambrosia, Kykeon, Cerridwen's Cauldron and the Indo-European Connection: The Book of Taliesin.

31. Temple, Robert. *Egyptian Dawn*. London: Random House, 2010, p. 422.
32. Kvilhaug, *Seed of Yggdrasill*, chap. 3: Introduction: A Path of Initiation.
33. Ibid.
34. "Nine Herbs Charm." Wikipedia. https://en.wikipedia.org/wiki/Nine_Herbs_Charm.
35. "Jörmungandr." Wikipedia. https://en.wikipedia.org/wiki/Jormungandr.
36. Kvilhaug, *Seed of Yggdrasill*, section 5.2 The Peace of Wisdom and the Song of the Millstone: The Chains That Bound Fenrir.
37. *The Kolbrin*. The Culdian Trust, 2014, p. 179-180. eBook.
38. Kvilhaug, *Seed of Yggdrasill*, section 2.11 Yggdrasill – The World Tree: The Serpent, the Squirrel and the Eagle; section 2.12 Vanir, Seiðr, and The Sacred Mead: Restoring Gullveigr to Cultural Memory – How and Why the Burned Witch of the Edda Has Been Misintepreted; section 3.12 Bright Rune, The Mead-Producer Above Valhǫll: Grímnismál (The Song of the Masked One) and Valkyriur Ready to Ride the Earth; section 3.16 The Mead and the Sun Goddess.
39. "Minoan civilization." Wikipedia. https://en.wikipedia.org/wiki/Minoan_civilization.
40. Nagy, Gregory, trans. "Homeric Hymn to Demeter." The Center for Hellenic Studies, December 12, 2018. https://chs.harvard.edu/CHS/article/display/5292.
41. Based on Orphic Hymn 39 to Demeter, translated by Thomas Taylor, 1792. Theoi Project. https://www.theoi.com/Text/OrphicHymns1.html#39.
42. Nagy, trans., "Homeric Hymn to Demeter."
43. From Orphic Hymn 40 to Demeter, translated by Thomas Taylor. Theoi Project. https://www.theoi.com/Text/OrphicHymns1.html#40.
44. Based on Homeric Hymn 13 to Demeter, translated by Hugh G. Evelyn-White, 1914. Theoi Project. https://www.theoi.com/Olympios/Demeter.html.
45. From Callimachus, Hymn 6 to Demeter, translated by A. W. Mair, 1921. Theoi Project. https://www.theoi.com/Olympios/Demeter.html.
46. Based on Orphic Hymn 39 to Demeter, translated by Taylor.
47. Sakoulas, Thomas. "Minoan Culture." Ancient-Greece.org. https://www.ancient-greece.org/culture/minoan-cult.html.
48. "Eleusinian Mysteries." Britannica. https://www.britannica.com/topic/Eleusinian-Mysteries.
49. *KE-RA-ME-JA: Studies Presented to Cynthia W. Shelmerdine*. Edited by Dimitri Nakassis, Joann Gulizio, and Sarah A. James. Philadelphia: INSTAP Academic Press, 2014, p. 120. http://sites.utexas.edu/scripts/files/2017/05/gulizio_nakassis_2014_kerameja.pdf.
50. "Demeter." Wikipedia. https://en.wikipedia.org/wiki/Demeter.
51. Sakoulas, "Minoan Culture."
52. Ibid.

CHAPTER FOURTEEN: CEREMONIES TO CELEBRATE THE WINTER SOLSTICE

1. "Yule." Wikipedia. https://en.wikipedia.org/wiki/Yule.
2. Kvilhaug, Maria. "The Old Norse Yule Celebration – Myth and Ritual." Freyia Völundarhúsins, December 21, 2012. http://freya.theladyofthelabyrinth.com/?page_id=397.
3. "Eleusinian Mysteries." Wikipedia. https://en.wikipedia.org/wiki/Eleusinian_Mysteries.
4. Taylor, Kelly B. "Paganism in the Roman World." December 4, 1995. http://www.crowdog.net/demeter.html.
5. "Krishna Date of Birth." Drik Panchang, May 26, 2012. https://www.drikpanchang.com/dashavatara/lord-krishna/krishna-date-of-birth.html.
6. "Mithraism (Zoroastrian perspective)." Mithras and Mithraism. https://mithras.webs.com/mithraismzoroastrian.htm.
7. "Inti Raymi." Wikipedia. https://es.wikipedia.org/wiki/Inti_Raymi.
8. "Inca Garcilaso de la Vega." Wikipedia. https://en.wikipedia.org/wiki/Inca_Garcilaso_de_la_Vega.
9. "Inti Raymi History." Peru Hop. https://www.peruhop.com/history-of-inti-raymi/.
10. Vega, Garcilaso de la. *Royal Commentaries of the Incas and General History of Peru, Vol. 1 and Vol. 2*. Translated by Harold V. Livermore. University of Texas Press, 1989, location 7509. Kindle edition.
11. Ibid., location 7540.

12. Cartwright, Mark. "Inca Religion." Ancient History Encyclopedia, February 15, 2016. https://www.ancient.eu/Inca_Religion/.
13. Vega, *Commentaries of the Incas*, location 7529.
14. Ibid., location 7540.
15. Ibid.
16. Ibid., location 7519.
17. Ibid., location 7540.
18. Ibid., location 7519.
19. Ibid., location 7529.
20. Ibid., location 7561.
21. Found in Vega, Juan José, and Luis Guzmán Palomino. "El Inti Raymi Inkaico: La Verdadera Historia de la Gran Fiesta Del Sol." Museo de Arqueología y Antropología, 2005, p. 37-71. http://sisbib.unmsm.edu.pe/bibvirtual/publicaciones/antropologia/2003_N01/a05.htm.
22. Vega, *Commentaries of the Incas*, location 8766.
23. Ibid., location 7621.
24. Ibid., location 7571.
25. Ibid.
26. Ibid., location 7550.
27. Ibid.
28. O'Neill, Patt. "K." Glossary of Terminology of the Shamanic & Ceremonial Traditions of the Inca Medicine Lineage, 2014. http://incaglossary.org/k.html#kinsaintikuna.
29. O'Neill, Patt. "H." Glossary of Terminology of the Shamanic & Ceremonial Traditions of the Inca Medicine Lineage, 2014. http://www.incaglossary.org/h.html#hanaqpacha.
30. "Pachamama." Wikipedia. https://www.en.wikipedia.org/wiki/Pachamama.

CHAPTER FIFTEEN: CEREMONIES TO CELEBRATE THE SPRING EQUINOX

1. David, Rosalie. *Religious Ritual at Abydos*. Warminster: Aris and Phillips, 1973, p. 263-265.
2. Kvilhaug, Maria. *The Seed of Yggdrasill: Deciphering the Hidden Messages in Old Norse Myths*. Whyte Tracks, 2016, chap. 3: Introduction: A Path of Initiation; section 12.1 An Old Norse Mystery School?: Isis in Germany – or a Northern Mystery Religion. Kindle edition.
3. "Maya Hero Twins." Wikipedia. https://en.wikipedia.org/wiki/Maya_Hero_Twins.
4. Molesky-Poz, Jean. *Contemporary Maya Spirituality: The Ancient Ways Are Not Lost*. Austin: University of Texas Press, 2006, location 252. Kindle edition.
5. Ibid., location 1968.
6. Christenson, Allen J., trans. *Popol Vuh: Sacred Book of the Quiché Maya People*. Norman: University of Oklahoma Press, 2003. Electronic version, Mesoweb, 2007, p. 110. http://www.mesoweb.com/publications/Christenson/PopolVuh.pdf.
7. Molesky-Poz, *Contemporary Maya Spirituality*, location 1019.
8. Christenson, trans., *Popol Vuh*, 177.
9. Ibid., 175.
10. Based on *Popol Vuh*, translated by Allen Christenson.
11. Christenson, trans., *Popol Vuh*, 107-108.
12. "Maya Civilization: What is it??" Brookings School District. https://local-brookings.k12.sd.us/6Red/Social Studies/Maya/Maya Artifacts (What is it).pdf, 14; "Mayan Terracotta Whistle in the Form of a Shaman." Barakat Gallery. http://store.barakatgallery.com/product/mayan-terracotta-whistle-in-the-form-of-a-shaman/; "Maya death rituals." Wikipedia. https://en.wikipedia.org/wiki/Maya_death_rituals.
13. Christenson, *Popol Vuh*, 122.
14. Molesky-Poz, *Contemporary Maya Spirituality,* location 2311.
15. Coe, Michael D. "The Hero Twins: Myth and Image." In *The Maya Vase Book: A Corpus of Rollout Photographs of Maya Vases, Vol. 1*. New York: Kerr Associates, 1989, p. 177. http://www.mesoweb.com/publications/MayaVase/Coe1989-OCR.pdf.

16. Ibid., 177-178.
17. Christenson, *Popol Vuh*, 175.
18. Christenson, trans., *Popol Vuh*, 175-176.
19. Ibid., 212.
20. Mursell, Ian. "The Conch Trumpet." Mexicolore, July 14, 2013. https://www.mexicolore.co.uk/aztecs/music/conch-trumpet.
21. "Maya death rituals." Wikipedia.
22. Christenson, trans., *Popol Vuh*, 167.

CHAPTER SIXTEEN: CEREMONIES TO CELEBRATE THE SUMMER SOLSTICE

1. Kvilhaug, Maria. *The Seed of Yggdrasill: Deciphering the Hidden Messages in Old Norse Myths*. Whyte Tracks, 2016, section 2.12 Vanir, Seiðr, and The Sacred Mead: Freyr – The Lord of Elves. Kindle edition.
2. Ibid.
3. "Triglav, Trojan, Trinity, Trimurti, Agni." Old European Culture, July 26, 2014. http://oldeuropeanculture.blogspot.com/2014/07/triglav-trojan-trinity-trimurti-agni.html.
4. Ibid.
5. The World Tree. "KUPALA - Slavic Summer Solstice Traditions." YouTube, June 7, 2019. https://youtu.be/IhH9444XI5Q.
6. Saranathan, Jayasree. "Migration of Aryan Gods from India to Europe – Triglav, a case in point." Jayasree Saranathan, May 15, 2018. https://jayasreesaranathan.blogspot.com/2018/05/migration-of-aryan-gods-from-india-to.html.
7. "Slavic paganism." Wikipedia. https://en.wikipedia.org/wiki/Slavic_paganism.
8. The World Tree. "KUPALA - Slavic Summer Solstice Traditions."
9. Ibid.
10. V, Boris. "Slavic Creation Myth: How Our World Was Created According to Slavs." Slavorum, November 9, 2011. https://www.slavorum.org/slavic-creation-myth/.
11. "Bogovo Gumno - God's Threshing Floor." Old European Culture, August 12, 2014. http://oldeuropeanculture.blogspot.com/2014/08/bogovo-gumno-gods-threshing-floor.html.
12. "Triglav, Trojan, Trinity, Trimurti, Agni." Old European Culture.
13. Ibid.
14. "Bogovo Gumno." Old European Culture.

CHAPTER SEVENTEEN: CONCLUSION

1. Roys, Ralph L., trans. *The Book of Chilam Balam of Chumayel*. Washington D.C.: Carnegie Institution, 1933, p. 65. Internet Sacred Text Archive. https://www.sacred-texts.com/nam/maya/cbc/cbc15.htm.

IMAGE REFERENCES

All Creative Commons works in this book are derivatives which have been processed with cropping, rotation, and/or other image adjustments.

Image credits are listed by page number.

MISC

Chapter Headings: Solar Cross, symbol re-created by Sura Ondrunar Publishing based on petroglyph at the Three Rivers Petroglyph Site in New Mexico, USA.

11, 277, 367. Illustration of an Aztec sun calendar by Antonio de Leon y Gama, 1792. Public domain.

81, 127, 167, 243, 395, 439, 461, 481. "Yin Yang motifs" © Sura Ondrunar Publishing.

PREFACE

6. Left: Varma, Raja Ravi. *Kali,* before 1906. Wikimedia Commons, 2012. https://en.wikipedia.org/wiki/File:Kali_by_Raja_Ravi_Varma.jpg. Public domain.
6. Right: Luidger, Photographer. *Statue of Coatlicue.* National Anthropology Museum, Mexico City, Wikimedia Commons, 2004. https://commons.wikimedia.org/wiki/File:20041229-Coatlicue (Museo Nacional de Antropología) MQ-3.jpg. CC BY-SA 3.0.

CHAPTER ONE

13. Dunn, Andrew, photographer. *Summer Solstice 2005 Sunrise over Stonehenge 01.* Wikimedia Commons, 2005. https://commons.wikimedia.org/wiki/File:Summer_Solstice_2005_Sunrise_over_Stonehenge_01.jpg. CC BY-SA 2.0.
14. Image based on Divad. *Equinoxes-Solstice-EN.* Wikimedia Commons, 2005. https://commons.wikimedia.org/wiki/File:Equinoxes-solstice_EN.svg. Public domain.
15. Merian, Matthias. *Emblem 21.* In *Atalanta Fugiens* by Michael Maier, Johann Theodor de Bry in Oppenheim, 1617, p. 93. Wikimedia Commons, 2008. https://en.wikipedia.org/wiki/File:Michael_Maier_Atalanta_Fugiens_Emblem_21.jpeg. Public domain.
17. Anonymous. *Anch and Sunwheel.* In *Book of the Dead of Ani,* frame 2, Vignette of sunrise, circa 19th Dynasty (1292 to 1189 BC). British Museum, Wikimedia Commons, 2006. https://commons.wikimedia.org/wiki/File:Totenbuch.jpg. Public domain.
24. Upper collage image 1: Egorov, Valery, photographer. *View of West Facade of Chartres Cathedral.* Shutterstock.com. https://www.shutterstock.com/image-photo/view-west-facade-chartres-cathedral-1076537756. Licensed from Shutterstock.com.
24. Upper collage image 2: HelloRF Zcool, photographer. *Guangzhou Shushe Sacred Heart Cathedral.* Shutterstock.com. https://www.shutterstock.com/image-photo/guangzhou-shushe-sacred-heart-cathedral-1173463153. Licensed from Shutterstock.com.
24. Upper collage image 3: F11photo, photographer. *St. John the Baptist Cathedral in Savannah Georgia USA,* Shutterstock.com. https://www.shutterstock.com/image-photo/st-john-baptist-cathedral-savannah-georgia-493931884. Licensed from Shutterstock.com.
24. Upper collage image 4: Ravi, Joe, photographer. *St. Philomena's Church Is a Catholic Church Built in Honour of St. Philomena in Mysore.* Shutterstock.com. https://www.shutterstock.com/image-photo/guangzhou-shushe-sacred-heart-cathedral-1173463153. Licensed from Shutterstock.com.
24. Center collage, image 1: Hendrikse, Boyd, photographer. *Cristo de la Concordia (Christ of Peace) Is a Statue of Jesus Christ Located atop San Pedro Hill, to the East of Cochabamba, Bolivia.* Shutterstock.com. https://www.shutterstock.com/image-photo/cristo-de-la-concordia-christ-peace-192340583. Licensed from Shutterstock.com.

24. Center collage, image 2: Petrova, Maria, photographer. *Famous Statue of the Christ the Reedemer, Lubango Angola.* Shutterstock.com. https://www.shutterstock.com/image-photo/famous-statue-christ-reedemer-lubango-angola-21157789. Licensed from Shutterstock.com.
24. Center collage, image 3: Catay, photographer. *Jesus Statue in Beirut 4 February 2018.* Shutterstock.com. https://www.shutterstock.com/image-photo/jesus-statue-beirut-4-february-2018-1041517408. Licensed from Shutterstock.com.
24. Center collage, image 4: Lashkov, Fedor, photographer. *The Christian Park in Essentuki.* Shutterstock.com. https://www.shutterstock.com/image-photo/christian-park-essentuki-669164776. Licensed from Shutterstock.com.
24. Lower collage, top left: Bon, Jerome, photographer. *Great Pyramid of Giza.* Wikimedia Commons, 2015. https://commons.wikimedia.org/wiki/File:Great_Pyramid_of_Giza_(2427530661).jpg. CC BY 2.0.
24. Lower collage, top center: Skubasteve834, photographer. *Monks Mound.* Wikimedia Commons, 2013. https://commons.wikimedia.org/wiki/File:Monks_Mound_in_July.JPG. CC BY-SA-3.0.
24. Lower collage, top right: Brücke-Osteuropa, photographer. *Pingling,* Wikimedia Commons, 2011. https://de.wikipedia.org/wiki/Datei:Pingling_1.jpg. Public domain.
24. Lower collage, second left: Schwen, Daniel, photographer. *Chichen Itza.* Wikimedia Commons, 2009. https://commons.wikimedia.org/wiki/File:Chichen_Itza_3.jpg. CC BY-SA 4.0.
24. Lower collage, second center: Peaceofangkor, photographer. *Prang (Behind Prasat Thom).* Wikimedia Commons, 2006. https://commons.wikimedia.org/wiki/File:0505280017PThompyramid.jpg. Public domain.
24. Lower collage, second right: Ximenez, Pedro, photographer. *Pyramid Güimar.* Wikimedia Commons, 2009. https://commons.wikimedia.org/wiki/File:Pyramide Güimar.jpg. CC BY-SA 2.0.
24. Lower collage, third left: Wilson, Captain W. *Marae Mahaiatea on Tahiti Island,* 1799. British Museum, Wikimedia Commons, 2017. https://commons.wikimedia.org/wiki/File:Oc,G.T.1663,_Mana_Expedition_to_Easter_Island,_British_Museum.jpg. Public domain.
24. Lower collage, third center: Jagadeesan, Madhuranthakan, photographer. *Sri Kanteshwara Temple Gopuram.* Wikimedia Commons, 2016. https://commons.wikimedia.org/wiki/File:N-KA-B159_Srikanteshwara_Temple_Gopuram_Nanjangud.jpg. CC BY-SA 4.0.
24. Lower collage, third right: Duffell, Marjorie V. *The Ziggurat of Nabonidus Restored,* plate 88, in Ur excavations. Vol. 5, Ziggurat and its surroundings by Leonard Woolley, publications of the Joint expedition of the British Museum and of the University Museum, University of Pennsylvania, Philadelphia, to Mesopotamia, published for the trustees of the two museums by aid of a grant made by the Carnegie corporation of New York, 1939, p. 255. Internet Archive, 2019. https://archive.org/details/urexcavations5/page/n3. Public domain.
25. Upper collage, top left: Saamiblog: http://saamiblog.blogspot.com, photographer. *Buckle from Oseberg Vikingship Buddha 3.* Wikimedia Commons, 2009. https://commons.wikimedia.org/wiki/File:Buckle_from_Oseberg_Vikingship_Buddha_3.JPG. CC BY-SA 3.0.
25. Upper collage, top center: Chirita, Cristian, photographer. *Archeological Artefacts in Sozopol Museum.* Sozopol Museum, Wikimedia Commons, 2011. https://commons.wikimedia.org/wiki/File:Sozopol_Archaeological_Museum_IMG_4214.JPG. GNU Free Documentation License, Version 1.2. https://commons.wikimedia.org/wiki/Commons:GNU_Free_Documentation_License,_version_1.2.
25. Upper collage, top right: Dbachmann, photographer. *Samarra Bowl.* Pergamonmuseum, Berlin, Wikimedia Commons, 2010. https://en.wikipedia.org/wiki/File:Samarra_bowl.jpg. CC BY-SA 4.0.
25. Upper collage, center left: Haylli, photographer. *Sican Vessel in the Huaca Rajada Site Museum.* Huaca Rajada Site Museum, Wikimedia Commons, 2009. https://commons.wikimedia.org/wiki/File:Sican-Vessel-in-the-Huaca-Rajada-Site-Museum-001.JPG. Public domain.
25. Upper collage, center: PHGCOM, photographer. *Etruscan Pendant with Swastika Symbols Bolsena Italy 700 BCE to 650 BCE.* Louvre Museum, Wikimedia Commons, 2010. https://commons.wikimedia.org/wiki/File:Etruscan_pendant_with_swastika_symbols_Bolsena_Italy_700_BCE_to_650_BCE.jpg. CC BY-SA 3.0.
25. Upper collage, center right: BabelStone, photographer. *Early Anglo-Saxon Cinerary Urn from North Elmham, Norfolk.* British Museum, Wikimedia Commons, 2010. https://commons.wikimedia.org/wiki/File:British_Museum_cinerary_urn_with_swastika_motifs.jpg. Public domain.

IMAGE REFERENCES

25. Upper collage, bottom left: Шнапс, photographer. Скоба для стрел (*Bracket for Arrows*). Wikimedia Commons, 2012. https://commons.wikimedia.org/wiki/File:Скоба_для_стрел.JPG. CC BY-SA 3.0.
25. Upper collage, bottom center: Tylas at English Wikipedia, photographer. *Zionpictographs*. Zion National Park, Wikimedia Commons, 2006. https://commons.wikimedia.org/wiki/File:Zionpictographs.jpg. CC BY-SA 3.0.
25. Upper collage, bottom right: Before My Ken, photographer. *Indus Valley Civilization Seals*. British Museum, Wikimedia Commons, 2009. https://commons.wikimedia.org/wiki/File:IndusValleySeals_swastikas.JPG. CC BY-SA 3.0.
25. Lower collage, top left: Pattych at English Wikipedia, photographer. *MocheBeardedMen*. Wikimedia Commons, 2010. https://en.wikipedia.org/wiki/File:MocheBeardedMen.jpg. CC BY-SA 3.0.
25. Lower collage, top right: Anonymous. *Pashupati Seal* from Mohenjo-daro, 2600–1900 BC. Wikimedia Commons, 2010. https://commons.wikimedia.org/wiki/File:Shiva_Pashupati.jpg. Public domain.
25. Lower collage, bottom left: Fortuna, Roberto, and Kira Ursem, photographers. *Gundestrup Cauldron*. Nationalmuseet, Wikimedia Commons, 2016. https://en.wikipedia.org/wiki/File:Gundestrupkedlen-_00054_(cropped).jpg. CC BY-SA 3.0.
25. Lower collage, bottom right: Ober, Frederick A. *Quetzalcoatl*. In *Travels in Mexico and Life Among the Mexicans,* San Francisco: J. Dewing and Co., 1884, p. 508. Wikimedia Commons, 2017. https://commons.wikimedia.org/wiki/File:TLM_D516_Quetzalcoatl.jpg. Public domain.
26. Vasnetsov, Viktor M. *Christ Pantocrator (Christ the Savior),* circa 1885-1896. The Anthenaeum, 2016. https://www.the-athenaeum.org/art/detail.php?ID=222902. Public domain.
31. Lyokin, photographer. *Fire Temple Ateshgah in Azerbaijan*. https://www.shutterstock.com/image-photo/fire-temple-ateshgah-azerbaijan-1220800237. Licensed from Shutterstock.com.
33. Srkris at English Wikipedia, photographer. *Hindu Priest from the Nambudiri Caste Performs a Yajna*, Kerala, India. Wikimedia Commons, 2008. https://commons.wikimedia.org/wiki/File:Yajna1.jpg. Public domain.
34. Masalskis, Mantas, photographer. *Romuvan Ceremony (6)*. Wikimedia Commons, 2009. https://commons.wikimedia.org/wiki/File:Romuvan ceremony (6).PNG. CC BY 2.0.
35. Sommers, Johanni Domino, illustrator. In *Veterum Persarum Et Parthorum Et Medorum Religionis Historia* by Thomas Hyde, 1790, pg 307. Internet Archive, 2016. https://archive.org/details/bub_gb_Uv5mAAAAcAAJ/page/n369/mode/2up. Public domain.
38. Julius, Albert Stephen, artist. *Set of color dispersion through prism*. Shutterstock.com. https://www.shutterstock.com/image-vector/set-color-dispersion-through-prism-triangular-1950923059. Licensed from Shutterstock.com
41. Rama, photographer. *Taperet Stele E52,* between 1065 and 664 BC. Department of Egyptian Antiquities of the Louvre, Wikimedia Commons, 2007. https://commons.wikimedia.org/wiki/File:Taperet_stele_E52_mp3h9201.jpg. CC BY-SA 3.0 France.
46. Than217 at English Wikipedia, photographer. *Khafre's Pyramid and the Great Sphinx*. Wikimedia Commons, 2008. https://commons.wikimedia.org/wiki/File:Khafre.jpg. Public domain.
49. Top-left: Klem. *Yin and Yang*. Wikimedia Commons, 2007. https://commons.wikimedia.org/wiki/File:Yin_and_Yang.svg. Public domain.
49. Top-right: Image created for book based on web article by Tsai, Allen. *The Origin of Chinese Yin Yang Symbol*. https://www.chinesefortunecalendar.com/YinYang.htm.
49. Bottom: Spinden, Herbert Joseph. *Mexican Blanket with Design Representing Sand and Water*. In *Ancient Civilizations of Mexico and Central America,* New York American Museum Press, 1922, p. 220. Wikimedia Commons, 2015. https://commons.wikimedia.org/wiki/File:Ancient_civilizations_of_Mexico_and_Central_America_(1922)_(18007507938).jpg. Public domain.
50. Top: Collinson, James. *The Holy Family,* 1878. Wikimedia Commons, 2007. https://commons.wikimedia.org/wiki/File:Collinson,_Holy_Family.jpg. Public domain.
50. Bottom: *Daily Path of the Sun in the Sky* image created for the book, based on image from https://www.umass.edu/sunwheel/pages/design.html.
51. Top: Wikimedia user: MithrandirMage, artist, based on work of Wikimedia user BD2412. *A symbol representing the Awen from Celtic mythology*. Wikimedia Commons, 2007. https://en.wikipedia.org/wiki/File:Awen_symbol_final.svg. Public domain.

51. Center: Ttog. *Fadenkreuz*. Wikimedia Commons, 2006. https://commons.wikimedia.org/wiki/File:Fadenkreuz.svg. Public domain.
51. Bottom: Roe, Herb. *Mound 72 Woodhenge Diagram HRoe 2013*. Wikimedia Commons, 2013. https://commons.wikimedia.org/wiki/File:Mound_72_Woodhenge_diagram_HRoe_2013.jpg. CC BY-SA 3.0
52. Top-left: Anonymous. *Nimrud Stele Winged Sun*, 9th century BC, Stele to Assurnasiripal II at Nimrud. Wikimedia Commons, 2007. https://commons.wikimedia.org/wiki/File:Nimrud_stele_winged_sun.jpg. Public domain.
52. Top-right: Helix84. *Knights Templar Cross*. Wikimedia Commons, 2007. https://commons.wikimedia.org/wiki/File:Knights_Templar_Cross.svg. Public domain.
52. Bottom left: Bjoertvedt, photographer. *Nordens Ark in Sotenäs, Sweden*, 2013. Wikimedia Commons, 2013. https://commons.wikimedia.org/wiki/File:Soten%C3%A4s_Tossene_73-1_Aaby_ID_10161200730001_IMG_8005.JPG. CC BY-SA 3.0.
52. Bottom right: OsgoodeLawyer. *Earth Symbol*. Wikimedia Commons, 2013. https://commons.wikimedia.org/wiki/File:Earth_symbol.svg. Public domain.
53. Top: Image based on Divad, *Equinoxes-Solstice-EN*. Wikimedia Commons, 2005. https://commons.wikimedia.org/wiki/File:Equinoxes-solstice_EN.svg. Public domain.
53. Bottom: Diagram illustrating solar cross based on Colivine, *Orbital Relations of the Solstice, Equinox & Intervening Seasons*. Wikimedia Commons, 2011. https://commons.wikimedia.org/wiki/File:Orbital relations of the Solstice, Equinox & Intervening Seasons.svg. Public domain.
54. Top: Geralt. *Cross Christ Faith*. Pixabay. https://pixabay.com/photos/cross-christ-faith-god-jesus-2713354. Used with permission.
54. Center: Diagram based on Gothika. *The Seasons and Some of Earth's Orbit's Characteristics*. Wikimedia Commons, 2010. https://en.wikipedia.org/wiki/File:Seasons1.svg. CC BY-SA 3.0.
54. Bottom: Scoyle17, photographer. *Celtic Cross Letterkenny*. Wikimedia Commons, 2006. https://commons.wikimedia.org/wiki/File:Celtic_Cross_Letterkenny.jpg. Public domain.
55. Top: Hale, Susan. *Tablet of Cross at Palenque*. In *The Story of Mexico*, New York: G. P. Putnam's sons, 1889, p. 75. Wikimedia Commons, 2014. https://commons.wikimedia.org/wiki/File:TSOM_D107_Tablet_of_cross_at_Palenque.png. Public domain.
55. Bottom: Kane, Saint. *Swastika with the Sun*. Wikimedia Commons, 2008. https://commons.wikimedia.org/wiki/File:Swastika_With_The_Sun.jpg. Public domain.
56. Top: Wilkowski, Ratomir. *ReceBogaSwargi*. Wikimedia Commons, 2010. https://commons.wikimedia.org/wiki/File:ReceBogaSwargi.svg. CC BY 3.0.
56. Bottom left: Dbachmann, photographer. *Samarra Bowl*. Pergamonmuseum, Berlin, Wikimedia Commons, 2010. https://en.wikipedia.org/wiki/File:Samarra_bowl.jpg. CC BY-SA 4.0.
56. Bottom right: Roe, Herb. *Chromesun 4 Uktenas Design*. Wikimedia Commons, 2008. https://commons.wikimedia.org/wiki/File:Chromesun_4_uktenas_design.jpg. CC BY-SA 3.0.
57. Top: Image created for book based on illustration in article by Smelyakov, Sergey. *Crucifying the Earth on the Galactic Cross*. http://www.astrotheos.com/Page8.htm.
57. Bottom: Infinity symbol created with unicode U+236.
58. Top: JLP Horizons. *Analemma Earth*. Wikimedia Commons, 2007. https://commons.wikimedia.org/wiki/File:Analemma_Earth.png. Public domain.
58. Bottom: Sura Ondrunar Publishing. *Double Spiral*. 2016.
59. Top: Brennan, Martin. Double spiral illustration in *The Stones of Time*, Vermont: Inner Traditions International, 1994, p. 190.
59. Bottom Left: Sura Ondrunar Publishing. *Artist's Impression of Tarim Mummy Full Facial Painting*. 2018.
59. Bottom right: Robley, Major-General G. 1820 illustration of Maori chief Hongi Hika in *Maori Wars of the Nineteenth Century* by S. Percy Smith, Whitcombe & Tombs Limited, 1910. The New Zealand Electronic Text Collection, http://www.nzetc.org/etexts/SmiMaor/SmiMaorP001a.jpg. CC BY-SA 3.0 NZ.
60. Top: Nomadtales, photographer. *Newgrange Entrance Stone*. Newgrange, Ireland, Wikimedia Commons, 2005. https://commons.wikimedia.org/wiki/File:Newgrange_Entrance_Stone.jpg. CC BY-SA 3.0.

IMAGE REFERENCES

60. Bottom: DjSadhu. Spiraling rotation of the planets in *Solar System 2.0 – the Helical Model*. Youtube.com, 2015. https://youtu.be/mvgaxQGPg7I. Used with permission.
61. Top: Krishnavedala. *Golden-Triangles-Pentagram*. Wikimedia Commons, 2012. https://commons.wikimedia.org/wiki/File:Golden-triangles-pentagram.svg. Public domain.
61. Bottom: CWitte. *Venus Pentagram*. Wikimedia Commons, 2007. https://commons.wikimedia.org/wiki/File:Venus_pentagramm.svg. CC BY-SA 3.0.
62. Top: Image created for book based on cobaltduck. *Is There Anything Significant about the Cross-Quarter Days, in Terms of a Sinusoid?* Math.Stockechange. com, 2016. https://math.stackexchange.com/questions/1603545/is-there-anything-significant-about-the-cross-quarter-days-in-terms-of-a-sinuso.
62. Bottom: Anonymous. *Oroboros*. Fol. 279 of Codex *Parisinus Graecus* 2327, a copy (made by Theodoros Pelecanos (Pelekanos) of Corfu in Khandak, Iraklio, Crete in 1478) of a lost manuscript of an early medieval tract which was attributed to Synosius (Synesius) of Cyrene (d. 412). Wikimedia Commons, 2005. Original image https://commons.wikimedia.org/wiki/File:Serpiente_alquimica.jpg, variation used in the book https://commons.wikimedia.org/wiki/File:Ouroboros.png. Public domain.
63. Top left: Anonymous. *Horus-Harpocrates in the Sun*. In *Papyrus of Dama-Heroub*, 21st Dynasty, 11th-10th century BC. Wikimedia Commons, 2013. https://commons.wikimedia.org/wiki/File:Horus-Harpocrates_in_the_Sun.jpg. Public domain.
63. Top right: De Leon y Gama, Antonio. Illustration of an Aztec sun calendar in *Historical and Chronological Description of the Two Stones Found during the New Paving of the Mexico's Main Plaza*, 1792. Wikimedia Commons, 2009. https://commons.wikimedia.org/wiki/File:Descripción histórica y cronológica de las dos piedras que con ocasión del nuevo empedrado que se está formando en la plaza principal de México, se hallaron en ella el año de 1790-1b.jpg. Public domain.
63. Center: DiegoAma. *Romuva Flag*. Wikimedia Commons, 2019. https://commons.wikimedia.org/wiki/File:Romuva_Flag.png. CC BY-SA 4.0.
63. Bottom: Anonymous. *The Churning of the Ocean of Milk*, circa 1800. British Museum, Wikimedia Commons, 2010. https://commons.wikimedia.org/wiki/File:Samudramanthan.jpg. Public domain.
64. Top: Luiluilui, photographer. *Kuelap Steine*, Kuelap Fortress, Peru. Wikimedia Commons, 2010. https://commons.wikimedia.org/wiki/File:Kuelap_Steine.JPG. CC BY-SA 3.0.
64. Bottom: Gnomon image created for book based on illustration by Martin Brennan in *The Stones of Time*, Vermont: Inner Traditions International, 1994, p. 190.
65. Top: Sauber, Wolfgang, photographer. *AMI - Goldene Doppelax*, golden Minoan labrys. Archaeological Museum in Herakleion, Wikimedia Commons, 2009. https://en.wikipedia.org/wiki/File:AMI_-_Goldene_Doppelaxt.jpg . CC BY-SA 3.0.
65. Bottom: Champollion, Jean-François. *Api or Hapi*, 1823-25. Brooklyn Museum, Wikipedia Commons, 2014. https://en.wikipedia.org/wiki/File:Api or Hapi (Apis, Taureau Consacré a la Lune), N372.2.jpg. Public domain.
66. Top: Lang Antonsen, Kenny Arne. *Cucuteni-Trypillian Temple*. Wikimedia Commons, 2019. https://commons.wikimedia.org/wiki/File:Cucuteni-trypillian_temple.jpg. CC BY-SA 4.0.
66. Bottom: Pringle, Lucy, photographer. *Crop circle 21st June 2001, East Field, Wiltshire, 2001*. https://cropcircles.lucypringle.co.uk/photos/2001/uk2001ar.shtml#pic2. © Lucy Pringle, used by permission.
68. Top: *Cross of the Sun* diagram created for book based on Old European Culture. *Two Crosses*. 2016. https://oldeuropeanculture.blogspot.com/2016/07/two-crosses.html.
68. Bottom: *Cross of the Earth* diagram created for book based on Old European Culture. *Two Crosses*. 2016. https://oldeuropeanculture.blogspot.com/2016/07/two-crosses.html.
78. © Sura Ondrunar Publishing.

CHAPTER TWO

84. Michaelica. Libra sign, *Set of Zodiac Symbol Icons*. Shutterstock.com. https://www.shutterstock.com/image-vector/set-zodiac-symbol-icons-vector-illustration-231315553. Licensed from Shutterstock.com.
85. Parrot, A., photographer. *Horus and Seth Crowning Ramesses III*. Wikimedia Commons, 2016. https://commons.wikimedia.org/wiki/File:Horus_and_Seth_crowning_Ramesses_III.JPG. Public domain.

86. Gehrts, Johannes. *Baldur*. In *Walhall: Germanische Götter- und Heldensagen für Alt und Jung am Deutsche Herd Erzählt* by Felix Dahn, Kreuznach: R. Voigtländer, 1888, p. 125. Wikimedia Commons, 2008. https://commons.wikimedia.org/wiki/File:Baldur_by_Johannes_Gehrts.jpg. Public domain.
87. Lieferinxe, Josse. *St. Michael Killing the Dragon*, 1493-1505. Musée du Petit Palais, Avignon, Wikimedia Commons, 2011. https://commons.wikimedia.org/wiki/File:Titelbild Engel, Dämonen und phantastische Wesen.jpg. Public domain.
88. Top: Doepler, Carl Emil. *Odin, der Göttervater*. In *Nordisch-Germanische Götter und Helden* by Wilhelm Wägner and Otto Spamer, Leipzig, 1882, p. 7. Wikimedia Commons, 2008. https://commons.wikimedia.org/wiki/File:Odin, der Göttervater.jpg. Public domain.
88. Bottom: Smith, Elmer Boyd, *Each Arrow Overshot His Head* in *In the Days of Giants: A Book of Norse Tales* by Abbie Farwell, Houghton, Mifflin & Co., 1902, p. 232. Wikimedia Commons, 2008. https://commons.wikimedia.org/wiki/File:Each_arrow_overshot_his_head_by_Elmer_Boyd_Smith.jpg. Public domain.
89. Brooke, Simon, photographer. *The Wicker Man Burns - Geograph.org.uk*. Wikimedia Commons, 2010. https://commons.wikimedia.org/wiki/File:The_Wicker_Man_burns_-_geograph.org.uk_-_50168.jpg. CC BY-SA 2.0.
91. Underwood & Underwood. *Khufu's Sarcophagus, Broken by Robbers, in the Sepulchre-Chamber of the Great Pyramid, Egypt*, 1904. Travelers in the Middle East Archive (TIMEA), Wikimedia Commons, 2010. https://commons.wikimedia.org/wiki/File:Khufu's sarcophagus, broken by robbers, in the sepulchre-chamber of the Great Pyramid, Egypt. View two men by sarcophagus. (25) (1904) - front - TIMEA.jpg. CC BY-SA 2.5.
92. Bodsworth, Jon, photographer. *Descendant-Grande-Pyramide*. Wikimedia Commons, 2007. https://commons.wikimedia.org/wiki/File:Descendant-grande-pyramide.jpg. © Jon Bodsworth, used by permission.
94. Top left: Anonymous. *Set killing the demon snake Apep*, Egyptian Museum, Cairo. Wikimedia Commons, 2012. https://commons.wikimedia.org/wiki/File:Set_speared_Apep.jpg. Public domain.
94. Top center: Frølich, Lorentz, artist. *Thor and Jörmungandr*. In *Den ældre Eddas Gudesange* by Karl Gjellerup, 1895. Wikimedia Commons, 2008. https://commons.wikimedia.org/wiki/File:Thor_and_J%C3%B6rmungandr_by_Fr%C3%B8lich.jpg. Public domain.
94. Top right: Anonymous. *Saint Michel emblème de Bruxelles*, circa 17th century. Wikimedia Commons, 2007. https://commons.wikimedia.org/wiki/File:Saint_Michel_embl%C3%A8me_de_Bruxelles.jpg. Public domain.
94. Bottom: Anonymous. *Battle of Zeus against Typhon*. In *Galerie Mythologique* by Aubin Louis Millin, 1811. Based on Chalcidian pottery circa 540-530 BC. Image enhanced by Wikimedia user: Shakko. Wikimedia Commons, 2011. https://commons.wikimedia.org/wiki/File:Combat_de_Zeus_contre_Typhon.jpg. Public domain.
95. Eichmann, Gerd, photographer. *Valley of the Kings in Egypt*, Grave 34, 1982. Wikimedia Commons, 2020. https://commons.wikimedia.org/wiki/File:Tal_der_Koenige-48-Grab_34-Fluss_durch_4_Register-1982-gje.jpg. CC BY-SA 4.0.
98. Sura Ondrunar Publishing. *Double Spiral*. 2016.
99. Left: Klem. *Yin and Yang*. Wikimedia Commons, 2007. https://commons.wikimedia.org/wiki/File:Yin_and_Yang.svg. Public domain.
99. Right: Image created for book based on web article by Tsai, Allen. *The Origin of Chinese Yin Yang Symbol*. https://www.chinesefortunecalendar.com/YinYang.htm.
101. Saint-Pol, Bibi, photographer. Anonymous. *Demeter and Metanira*, circa 340 BC. Altes Museum, Wikimedia Commons, 2008. https://commons.wikimedia.org/wiki/File:Eleusinian_hydria_Antikensammlung_Berlin_1984.46_n2.jpg. Public domain.
102. Anonymous. *Young Corn God*, 8th century. The Michael C. Rockefeller Memorial Collection, Bequest of Nelson A. Rockefeller, 1979, Metropolitan Museum of Art, Wikimedia Commons, 2017. https://commons.wikimedia.org/wiki/File:Young_Corn_God_MET_1979.206.728_b.jpeg. Public domain.
105. Anonymous. *Illustration of the Celestial Spheres*. In *Le livre du Ciel et du Monde* by Nicole Oresme, 1377. Wikimedia Commons, 2007. https://commons.wikimedia.org/wiki/File:Oresme_Spheres.jpg. Public domain.

IMAGE REFERENCES

106. Top: Sewell, Ian, photographer. *Ahu-Akivi-1*. Wikimedia Commons, 2006. https://commons.wikimedia.org/wiki/File:Ahu-Akivi-1.JPG. CC BY-SA 3.0.

106. Bottom: Weinstein, Brett, photographer. *Golden Mask of Psusennes I*. Wikimedia Commons, 2009. https://commons.wikimedia.org/wiki/File:Golden_Mask_of_Psusennes_I.jpg. CC BY-SA 2.5.

107. Left: Anonymous. *Egyptian God Sokar-Osiris*, from the Papyrus of Ani, circa 1300 BC, facsimile made by E. A. Wallis Budge, 1890. British Museum, Wikimedia Commons, 2010. https://commons.wikimedia.org/wiki/File:BD_Sokar-Osiris.jpg. Public domain.

107. Center: D_odin, photographer. *Mahavishnu Settles on the Serpent Anantasheesh and Lakshmi Massages His Feet. Sculpture of the Supreme God Vishnu in Hinduism*. Shutterstock.com. https://www.shutterstock.com/image-photo/mahavishnu-settles-on-serpent-anantasheesh-lakshmi-754817707. Licensed from Shutterstock.com.

107. Right: Anonymous. *Cambodian Crowned Naga-Protected Buddha*, circa 1150-1190. Bequest of A. B. Griswold, 1992, Walters Art Museum. Wikimedia Commons, 2012. https://commons.wikimedia.org/wiki/File:Cambodian_-_Crowned_Naga-Protected_Buddha_-_Walters_25171.jpg. Public domain.

108. Anonymous. *Sri Surya Bhagvan, Bazaar Art,* circa 1940s. Wikimedia Commons, 2015. https://commons.wikimedia.org/wiki/File:Shri Surya Bhagvan bazaar art, c.1940's.jpg. Public domain.

109. Left: Woelber, Paxson, photographer. *The El Castillo Pyramid at Chichen Itza, Mexico*. Wikimedia Commons, 2014. https://commons.wikimedia.org/wiki/File:The_El_Castillo_Pyramid_at_Chichen_Itza,_Mexico.jpg. CC BY-SA 3.0.

109. Right: Spence, Lewis. *The Descent of Quetzalcoatl*. In *The Myths of Mexico and Peru,* New York: T. Y. Crowell company, 1913, p. xiv. Wikimedia Commons, 2013. https://commons.wikimedia.org/wiki/File:Xiv-The_Descent_of_Quetzalcoatl.jpg. Public domain.

110. Top: Klopacka, Jozef. *A Beautiful Oil Painting on Canvas of a Woman Goddess Lada as a Mighty Loving Guardian and Protective Spirit upon the Earth Portrait*. Shutterstock.com. https://www.shutterstock.com/image-illustration/beautiful-oil-painting-on-canvas-woman-244690525. Licensed from Shutterstock.

110. Bottom: TStein. Edited by Geek3. *Earth's Magnetic Field Confusion*. Wikimedia Commons, 2008, 2019. https://commons.wikimedia.org/wiki/File:Earths_Magnetic_Field_Confusion.svg. CC BY-SA 3.0.

111. Infinity symbol created with unicode U+236.

113. Anonymous. *Durga Mahisasuramardini*, early 18th century. Wikimedia Commons, 2008. https://commons.wikimedia.org/wiki/File:Durga_Mahisasuramardini.JPG. Public domain.

116. Top: Anonymous. *Kali Poster*, circa 1940s. Wikimedia Commons, 2010. https://commons.wikimedia.org/wiki/File:Kaliposter1940s.jpg. Public domain.

116. Bottom left: Luidger, photographer. *Statue of Coatlicue*. National Anthropology Museum, Mexico City, Wikimedia Commons, 2010. https://commons.wikimedia.org/wiki/File:20041229-Coatlicue (Museo Nacional de Antropología) MQ-3.jpg. CC BY-SA 3.0.

116. Bottom right: Stormnight, photographer. *Sekhmet (British Museum)*. British Museum, Wikimedia Commons, 2008. https://commons.wikimedia.org/wiki/File:Sekhmet (British Museum).jpg. CC BY-SA 4.0.

117. Sailko, photographer. *Akkadian Period, Black Limestone Seal with Ishtar with Foot on a Lion's Back and a Devout, 2350-2150 ac*. Oriental Institute Museum, Wikimedia Commons, 2018. https://commons.wikimedia.org/wiki/File:Periodo_accadico,_sigillo_in_calcare_nero_con_ishtar_con_piede_su_schiena_di_leone_e_una_devota,_2350-2150_ac_ca.jpg. CC BY 3.0.

118. Left: Anonymous. *Kali Kangra Painting*, circa 19th century. Wikimedia Commons, 2012. https://commons.wikimedia.org/wiki/File:Kali_Kangra_Painting.jpg. Public domain.

118. Right: Pagani, Giovanni. *Vierge du Secours*, 1506. Musée du Petit Palais, Wikimedia Commons, 2016. https://commons.wikimedia.org/wiki/File:Giovanni_Pagani_-_Vierge_du_secours.jpg. Public domain.

121. Maffei, P.A. *Minotaurus* from *Gemmae Antiche*, 1709. Wikimedia Commons, 2006. https://tl.wikipedia.org/wiki/Talaksan:Minotaurus.gif. Public domain.

122. Top: AnonMoos, artist. *Cretan labyrinth*. Wikimedia Commons, 2009. https://commons.wikimedia.org/wiki/File:Cretan-labyrinth-round2.svg. Public Domain.

122. Bottom: Guerber, H.A. *Theseus and the Minotaur*. In *The Story of the Greeks*, American Book Company, 1896. Wikimedia Commons, 2014. https://commons.wikimedia.org/wiki/File:Theseus_and_the_Minotaur.gif. Public domain.

123. Anonymous. *Isiac Priest*, circa 62-79 AD. National Archaeological Museum of Naples, Wikimedia Commons, 2013. https://en.wikipedia.org/wiki/File:Isiac_water_ceremony.jpg. Public domain.

CHAPTER THREE

129. Shira, photographer. *Newgrange*. Wikimedia Commons, 2006. https://commons.wikimedia.org/wiki/File:Newgrange.JPG. CC BY-SA 3.0.

130. Prabhat Kumar Verma, photographer. *Makar Sankranti Day during the Kumbh Mela, or Pitcher Festival in Allahabad (Prayagraj), Uttar Pradesh*. Shutterstock.com https://www.shutterstock.com/image-photo/allahabad-naga-sadhus-take-holy-dip-1285519654. Licensed from Shutterstock.com.

132. Top: Aziz1005, phototgrapher. *Dhushara*. National Museum of Damascus, Wikimedia Commons, 2007. https://en.wikipedia.org/wiki/File:Dhushara.JPG. Public domain.

132. Bottom: Angelico, Fra. *Christ the Judge*, 1447. Cappella di San Brizio, Wikimedia Commons, 2011. https://commons.wikimedia.org/wiki/File:Fra_Angelico_-_Christ_the_Judge_-_WGA00679.jpg. Public domain.

134. Top: Sura Ondrunar Publishing, composite image. *Winter Solstice Sunrise at Karnak*. Includes images from: moonfish8, *Ram-headed sphinxes, Karnak Temple, Luxor, Egypt*, https://www.shutterstock.com/image-photo/ramheaded-sphinxes-karnak-temple-luxor-egypt-179121524, Manish Upadhyay, *silhouette of bird flying in sunrise*, https://unsplash.com/photos/r4VJBODbMC8, Pagie page, *sunrise view*, https://unsplash.com/photos/vq-2SRf9fE8, Robert Thiemann, *Alaska Sunset*, https://unsplash.com/photos/3k0cTsHhQeE, zaie, *golden light*, https://www.freepik.com/free-vector/golden-light-shining-particles-bokeh-sparks-glare-with-highlight-effect_10817226.htm. Images licensed from shutterstock, unsplash, freepik.

134. Bottom: Illustration of *Statue of Isis and Horus*. In *Meyers Konversationslexikon* by Joesph Meyers, 4th edition, 1885-1890. Wikimedia Commons, 2005. https://commons.wikimedia.org/wiki/File:Egypt.IsisHorus.01.png. Public domain.

136. Sharpe, Samuel. *Luxor Nativity*, 1879. Wikimedia Commons, 2007. https://commons.wikimedia.org/wiki/File:Luxor_Nativity_Sharpe.JPG. Public domain.

142. Anonymous. *Tibetan Thanka of Guhyasamaja Akshobhyavajra*, 17th century. Rubin Museum of Art, Wikimedia Commons, 2014. https://commons.wikimedia.org/wiki/File:17th_century_Central_Tibeten_thanka_of_Guhyasamaja_Akshobhyavajra,_Rubin_Museum_of_Art.jpg. Public domain.

145. Anonymous. Illustration from *The Donum Dei*, 17th century. Wikimedia Commons, 2013. https://commons.wikimedia.org/wiki/File:Alchemische_Vereinigung_aus_dem_Donum_Dei.jpg. Public domain.

148. Anonymous. *Depiction of Viracocha*. Wikimedia Commons, 2016. https://commons.wikimedia.org/wiki/File:Viracocha.jpg. Public domain.

149. Uccello, Paolo. *St George and the Dragon*, circa 1458-1460. Musée Jacquemart-André, Wikimedia Commons, 2009. https://commons.wikimedia.org/wiki/File:Saint_George_and_the_Dragon_by_Paolo_Uccello_(Paris)_01.jpg. Public domain.

153. Deror avi, photographer. *Church of the Saviour on the Blood*. Wikimedia Commons, 2009. https://commons.wikimedia.org/wiki/File:Church_of_the_Saviour_on_the_Blood_IMG_7407.JPG. CC BY-SA 3.0.

155. Left: AnonMoos, artist. *Cretan labyrinth*. Wikimedia Commons, 2009. https://commons.wikimedia.org/wiki/File:Cretan-labyrinth-round2.svg. Public Domain.

155. Right: Leask, H.G., artist. *The Stone Circle*. In *Newgrange, Co. Meath - Brŭjna bóinne* by R. A. S. Macalister, Dublin : Published by the Stationery Office, 1929.

155. Bottom: White, Ethan Doyle, photographer. *Model of Mnajdra*, Ħaġar Qim/Mnajdra visitor's centre, southern Malta, 2017. Wikimedia Commons, 2017. https://commons.wikimedia.org/wiki/File:Model_of_Mnajdra.jpg. CC BY-SA 4.0.

156. Left: Branley, Stephen, photographer. *Calanais Stones*, 2008. Wikimedia Commons, 2011. https://commons.wikimedia.org/wiki/File:Calanais_Stones_-_geograph.org.uk_-_1236575.jpg. CC BY-SA 2.0.

156. Right: James, Henry, artist, Pasicles, derivative work. *Plan of the Callanish Stones*. In *Rude Stone Monuments in All Countries: Their Age and Uses* by James Fergusson, London: J. Murray, 1872. Wikimedia Commons, 2014. https://en.wikipedia.org/wiki/File:Plan_of_the_Callanish_Stones.png. Public domain.

IMAGE REFERENCES

157. Nguyen, Marie-Lan, photographer. *Mithras Petra Genetrix Terme*, 180-192 AD, Baths of Diocletian. Epigraphical Museum, Wikimedia Commons, 2007. https://commons.wikimedia.org/wiki/File:Mithras_petra_genetrix_Terme.jpg. Public domain.

158. Top: Renalias, Josep, photographer. *Torre de Glastonbury*. Wikimedia Commons, 2008. https://commons.wikimedia.org/wiki/File:Torre_de_Glastonbury.JPG. CC-BY-SA 3.0.

158. Bottom: Von Deschwanden, Melchior Paul. *Das Christuskind*, 1881. Wikimedia Commons, 2013. https://commons.wikimedia.org/wiki/File:Melchior_Paul_von_Deschwander_Das_Christuskind.jpg. Public domain.

159. Dalbéra, Jean-Pierre, photographer. *Le Temple de Changu Narayan (Bhaktapur)*, Nepal. Wikimedia Commons, 2014. https://en.wikipedia.org/wiki/File:Le_temple_de_Changu_Narayan_(Bhaktapur)_(8567815983).jpg. CC BY 2.0

160. Liberato, Ricardo. *All Gizah Pyramids*. Wikimedia Commons, 2008. https://commons.wikimedia.org/wiki/File:Pyramids_at_Gizah.jpg. CC BY-SA 2.0.

162. Van Honthorst, Gerard. *The Adoration of the Shepherds*, 1622. Wallraf–Richartz Museum, Wikimedia Commons, 2011. https://commons.wikimedia.org/wiki/File:Gerard_van_Honthorst_-_Adoration_of_the_Shepherds_-_WGA11657.jpg. Public domain.

163. Hofmann, Heinrich. *The Visit of the Wise-Men*, 1887. Wikimedia Commons, 2004. https://commons.wikimedia.org/wiki/File:The_visit_of_the_wise-men.jpg. Public domain.

164. Gallet, Herve. *Kin Soleil*. Wikimedia Commons, 2017. https://commons.wikimedia.org/wiki/File:KIN_Soleil.jpg. CC BY-SA 4.0.

165. Left: Anonymous. *A Roundel of Brahma*, 19th century, India. Wikimedia Commons, 2012. https://en.wikipedia.org/wiki/File:A_roundel_of_Brahma.jpg. Public domain.

165. Right: Hunefer. *The Judgement of the Dead in the Presence of Osiris*. In *the Book of the Dead of Hunefer*, 1275 BC. British Museum, Wikimedia Commons, 2012. https://commons.wikimedia.org/wiki/File:The_judgement_of_the_dead_in_the_presence_of_Osiris.jpg. Public domain.

CHAPTER FOUR

170. Anonymous. *The Churning of the Ocean of Milk*, circa 1800. British Museum, Wikimedia Commons, 2010. https://commons.wikimedia.org/wiki/File:Samudramanthan.jpg. Public domain.

171. Markalexander100, photographer. *The Churning of the Ocean of Milk*, bas-relief on the south of the east wall of Angkor Wat's third enclosure. Wikimedia Commons, 2005. https://commons.wikimedia.org/wiki/File:Awatoceanofmilk01_-_color_corrected.JPG. CC BY-SA 3.0.

172. Heng, Kim, photographer. *Equinox at Angkor 21st March 2012*, Wikimedia Commons, 2012. https://commons.wikimedia.org/wiki/File:Equinox_at_Angkor_21st_March_2012.JPG. CC BY-SA 3.0.

174. Bgabel at wikivoyage, photographer. *TIB lhasa Sera Lebensrad*. Sera Monastery, Wikimedia Commons, 2010. https://commons.wikimedia.org/wiki/File:TIB-lhasa-sera-lebensrad.jpg. CC BY-SA 3.0.

175. Elishams, photographer. *Samudr Manthan*, Temple de Shri Krishna Pranami, Haridwar, India. Wikimedia Commons, 2006. https://commons.wikimedia.org/wiki/File:Samudr_manthan.jpg. CC BY 2.5.

178. Tissot, James. *The Jews Took up Rocks to Stone Jesus*, circa 1886-1896. Brooklyn Museum, Wikimedia Commons, 2010. https://commons.wikimedia.org/wiki/File:Brooklyn Museum - The Jews Took Up Rocks to Stone Jesus (Les juifs prirent des pierres pour lapider Jésus) - James Tissot.jpg. Public domain.

179. Bloch, Carl Heinrich. *The Last Supper*, circa late 19th century. Wikimedia Commons, 2013. https://commons.wikimedia.org/wiki/File:The-Last-Supper-large.jpg. Public domain.

180. Di Bondone, Giotto. *No. 31 Scenes from the Life of Christ: 15. The Arrest of Christ (Kiss of Judas)*, circa 1304-1306. Scrovegni Chapel, Wikimedia Commons, 2013. https://commons.wikimedia.org/wiki/File:Giotto_di_Bondone_-_No._31_Scenes_from_the_Life_of_Christ_-_15._The_Arrest_of_Christ_(Kiss_of_Judas)_-_WGA09216_adj.jpg. Public domain.

181. Delaroche, Paul. *Joan of Arc Is Interrogated by the Cardinal of Winchester in Her Prison*, 1824. Musée des Beaux-Arts de Rouen, Wikimedia Commons, 2009. https://commons.wikimedia.org/wiki/File:Joan_of_arc_interrogation.jpg. Public domain.

182. Munkácsy, Mihály. *Christ in front of Pilate*, 1881. Hungarian National Gallery, Wikimedia Commons, 2015. https://commons.wikimedia.org/wiki/File:Munkacsy_-_Christ_in_front_of_Pilate.jpg. Public domain.

183. Left: Collingwood, W. G. *Odin's Self-Sacrifice*. In *The Elder or Poetic Edda, Commonly Known as Sæmund's Edda*, edited and translated by Olive Bray, 1908, p. 61. Wikimedia Commons, 2008. https://commons.wikimedia.org/wiki/File:Odin's Self-sacrifice by Collingwood.jpg. Public domain.

183. Center: Barber, John Warner. *The Crucifixion*. In *The life of Our Lord and Savior Jesus Christ* by John Fleetwood, New Haven: Nathan Whiting, 1830, p. 426. Wikimedia Commons, 2015. https://commons.wikimedia.org/wiki/File:The_life_of_our_Lord_and_Savior_Jesus_Christ_-_containing_a_full,_accurate,_and_universal_history_from_his_taking_upon_himself_our_nature_to_his_crucifixion,_resurrection,_and_ascension-_together_with_(14592569250).jpg. Public domain.

183. Right: Anonymous. *Xolotl*. In *The Codex Fejervary-Mayer,* circa 15th century. Wikimedia Commons, 2006. https://commons.wikimedia.org/wiki/File:Xolotl_1.jpg. Public domain.

184. Top: Sura Ondrunar Publishing. *Cross of the Sun.* 2019.

184. Bottom: Image based on Divad. *Equinoxes-Solstice-EN*. Wikimedia Commons, 2005. https://commons.wikimedia.org/wiki/File:Equinoxes-solstice_EN.svg. Public domain.

187. De Tovar, Juan. *The Aztec Tonalpohualli Calendar*, circa 1546-1626. John Carter Brown Library, Wikimedia Commons, 2014. https://commons.wikimedia.org/wiki/File:The_Aztec_Tonalpohualli_Calendar_WDL6732.png. Public domain.

188. Bkwillwm, photographer. *Knowth Entrance to Second Passage 2010*, Ireland. Wikimedia Commons, 2010. https://commons.wikimedia.org/wiki/File:Knowth_entrance_to_second_passage_2010.JPG. CC BY-SA 3.0.

189. Bramantino. *Crocifissione*, circa 1510s. Pinacoteca di Brera, Wikimedia Commons, 2012. https://commons.wikimedia.org/wiki/File:Bramantino,_crocifissione.jpg. Public domain.

190. Mantegna, Andrea. *La Résurrection*, circa 1457-1459. Musée des beaux-arts de Tours, Wikimedia Commons, 2009. https://commons.wikimedia.org/wiki/File:Mantegna, Andrea - La Résurrection - 1457-1459.jpg. Public domain.

191. Collingwood, W. G. *Odin's Self-Sacrifice*. In *The Elder or Poetic Edda, Commonly Known as Sæmund's Edda*, edited and translated by Olive Bray, 1908, p. 61. Wikimedia Commons, 2008. https://commons.wikimedia.org/wiki/File:Odin's Self-sacrifice by Collingwood.jpg. Public domain.

194. Anonymous. *Anubis Attending the Mummy of Sennedjem*, from a wall painting in the tomb of Sennedjem. Wikimedia Commons, 2007. https://commons.wikimedia.org/wiki/File:Anubis_attending_the_mummy_of_Sennedjem.jpg. Public domain.

195. Sura Ondrunar Publishing. *Sphinx as Anubis*. 2012.

197. Top: Bloch, Carl. *Burial of Christ*, circa 1800s. Wikimedia Commons, 2013. https://commons.wikimedia.org/wiki/File:BurialofChrist_CarlBloch.jpg. Public domain.

197. Bottom: Néfermaât, photographer. Edited by JMCC1. *Statues of Hathor*. Luxor Museum, Wikimedia Commons, 2011. https://commons.wikimedia.org/wiki/File:GD-EG-Louxor-111-b.jpg. CC BY-SA 2.5.

198. World History Archive, photographer. *Goddess Nut Bending to Form the sky,* papyrus copy based on late Egyptian temple at Denderah. Alamy Stock Photo. https://www.alamy.com/stock-photo-egyptian-cosmos-goddess-nut-bending-to-form-the-sky-papyrus-copy-based-57303488.html. Licensed from Alamy Stock Photo.

199. Stroup, Kevin, photographer. *Knowth, Co. Meath, Ireland*. Wikimedia Commons, 2017. https://commons.wikimedia.org/wiki/File:Knowth,_Co._Meath,_Ireland_-_panoramio_(32).jpg. CC BY 3.0.

201. Top: Rosemania, photographer. *Silver Cauldron*, circa 150-0 BC, Gundestrup, Denmark. Historic Museum of Bern, Wikimedia Commons, 2009. https://commons.wikimedia.org/wiki/File:Silver_cauldron.jpg. CC BY 2.0.

201. Bottom: Thyssen, Malene, photographer, http://commons.wikimedia.org/wiki/User:Malene. *Gundestrup Cauldron*, Nationalmuseet, Denmark, 2004. Wikimedia Commons, 2005. https://commons.wikimedia.org/wiki/File:Gundestrupkarret3.jpg. CC BY-SA 3.0.

202. Schele, Linda. *Drawing of Plate Interior Showing the Rebirth of the Maize God from a Turtle Shell SD-5505*. In *Maya Cosmos: Three Thousand Years on the Shaman's Path*, by David A. Freidel, Linda Schele, and Joy Parker, New York: W. Morrow, 1993, p. 371, fig. 8:25b. Ancient Americas at LACMA, http://ancientamericas.org/collection/aa010550. © David Schele, used by permission on behalf of LACMA.

203. Follower of Hieronymus Bosch. *Christ in Limbo*, circa 1575. Indianapolis Museum of Art, Wikimedia Commons, 2015. https://commons.wikimedia.org/wiki/File:Follower_of_Jheronimus_Bosch_Christ_in_Limbo.jpg. Public domain.

IMAGE REFERENCES

204. Laslovarga, photographer. *Tikal, Guatemala*. Wikimedia Commons, 2013. https://commons.wikimedia.org/wiki/File:Tikal,_Guatemala_Laslovarga14.JPG. CC BY-SA 30.
205. ShillukinUSA, photographer. *Anubis, Isis, Nephthys in the Theban Tomb 335 (Nakhtamun), from the Reign of Ramesses II*. Wikimedia Commons, 2013. https://commons.wikimedia.org/wiki/File:ThebanTomb335.png. Public domain.
207. Budge, E. A. Wallis. *Osiris Philae*. In *Osiris and the Egyptian Resurrection*, London: P. L. Warner, 1911, p. 58. Wikimedia Commons, 2008. https://commons.wikimedia.org/wiki/File:Osiris_Philae.jpg. Public domain.
208. Tausch, Olaf. *Philae 13*, relief in the Isis Temple of Philae on the island of Agilkia, Egypt. Wikimedia Commons, 2014. https://commons.wikimedia.org/wiki/File:Philae_13.jpg. CC BY 3.0.

CHAPTER FIVE

209. Sura Ondrunar Publishing. *Sphinx as Anubis*. 2012.
210. Bonfils, Maison, *Le Sphynx apres les Déblaiements et les Deux Grandes Pyramides*, between 1867-1899. Wikimedia Commons, 2009. https://en.wikipedia.org/wiki/File:Sphinx_partially_excavated2.jpg. Public domain.
211. Profberger at English Wikipedia, photographer. *Golden Wolf Small*. Wikimedia Commons, 2012. https://en.wikipedia.org/wiki/File:Golden_wolf_small.jpg. CC BY-SA 3.0.
212. Kocjan, Marek, photographer. *Great Sphinx of Giza 2*. Wikimedia Commons, 2009. https://commons.wikimedia.org/wiki/File:Great_Sphinx_of_Giza_2.jpg. CC BY-SA 3.0.
213. Anonymous. *Anubis Attending the Mummy of Sennedjem*, from a wall painting in the tomb of Sennedjem. Wikimedia Commons, 2007. https://commons.wikimedia.org/wiki/File:Anubis_attending_the_mummy_of_Sennedjem.jpg. Public domain.
214. Hunefer. *The Judgement of the Dead in the Presence of Osiris*. In *The Book of the Dead of Hunefer*, 1275 BC. British Museum, Wikimedia Commons, 2012. https://commons.wikimedia.org/wiki/File:The_judgement_of_the_dead_in_the_presence_of_Osiris.jpg. Public domain.
215. Horemweb. *Diagram of Khafre's Valley Area with the Temples and the Sphinx, Based on Lehner's and Verner's Works*. Wikimedia Commons, 2009. https://commons.wikimedia.org/wiki/File:Kahfre_valley_sphinx.svg. Public domain.
216. Left: Bodsworth, Jon, photographer. *Tutankhamun Jackal*. Wikimedia Commons, 2008. https://commons.wikimedia.org/wiki/File:Tutanhkamun_jackal.jpg. © Jon Bodsworth, used by permission.
216. Right: Anonymous. *Pyramidion of Iufaa*, 664–525 BC. Rogers Fund, 1921, Metropolitan Museum of Art, Wikimedia Commons, 2017. https://en.wikipedia.org/wiki/File:Pyramidion_of_Iufaa_MET_21.2.66_01.jpg. Public domain.
219. Top: Anonymous. *A Complete Set of Canopic Jars*, circa 900-800 BC. Walters Art Museum, Wikimedia Commons, 2012. https://commons.wikimedia.org/wiki/File:Egyptian_-_A_Complete_Set_of_Canopic_Jars_-_Walters_41171,_41172,_41173,_41174_-_Group.jpg. Public domain.
219. Bottom: Andre, photographer. *Kist uit de 27- 31e Dynastie*. Flickr.com, 2009. https://www.flickr.com/photos/9987501@N08/3643941456. CC BY-NC-SA 2.0.
220. Gnuckx, photographer. *Italy Vatican*. Flickr.com, 2018. https://www.flickr.com/photos/34409164@N06/3492615876. CC BY 2.0.
221. Based on Wykis. *Explained Atom*. Wikimedia Commons, 2006. https://commons.wikimedia.org/wiki/File:Explained_Atom.svg. Public domain.
222. Anonymous. Illustration from *The Book of the Dead of Khensumose*. Wikimedia Commons, 2015. https://commons.wikimedia.org/wiki/File:Sunrise_at_Creation.jpg. Public domain.
224. Chipdawes, photographer. *Pyramid Texts from Pyramid of Teti I in Saqqara*. Wikimedia Commons, 2006. https://commons.wikimedia.org/wiki/File:Hieroglyph_Text_from_Teti_I_pyramid.jpg. Public domain.
226. Bronger, Torsten. *Leo Constellation Map*. Wikimeda Commons, 2003. https://commons.wikimedia.org/wiki/File:Leo_constellation_map.png. CC BY-SA 3.0.
227. Left: RsAzevedo, photographer. *Osireion at Abydos*. Wikimeda Commons, 2008. https://commons.wikimedia.org/wiki/File:Osireion_at_Abydos.jpg. CC BY-SA 3.0.
227. Right: Mayer, Daniel, photographer. *Giza Plateau - Great Sphinx - inside Temple*. Wikimeda Commons, 2008. https://commons.wikimedia.org/wiki/File:Giza_Plateau_-_Great_Sphinx_-_inside_temple.JPG. CC BY-SA 4.0.

229. English Wikipedia user Davkal, photographer. *Orion – Pyramids*. Wikimedia Commons, 2009. https://commons.wikimedia.org/wiki/File:Orion_-_pyramids.jpg. CC BY-SA 3.0.

230. Budge, E. A. Wallace. *The Great Pyramid, Showing Passages and Mummy Chambers.* In *The Nile: Notes for Travellers in Egypt*, London: Harrison and Sons, 1902, p. 100. Travelers in the Middle East Archive (TIMEA), Wikimedia Commons, 2010. https://commons.wikimedia.org/wiki/File:The_Great_Pyramid,_showing_passages_and_mummy_chambers._(1902)_-_TIMEA.jpg. Licensed from Travelers in the Middle East Archive (TIMEA). CC BY-SA 2.5.

231. Left: Storch, Hedwig, photographer. *Karnak Temple 9456*. Wikimedia Commons, 2009. https://commons.wikimedia.org/wiki/File:Karnak_temple_9456.JPG. Creative Commons BY-SA 3.0.

231. Right: Pal1983, photographer. *Small Sphinx with the Head of a Jackal*. Shutterstock.com https://www.shutterstock.com/image-photo/small-sphinx-head-jackal-ramesseum-memorial-422367220. Licensed from Shutterstock.com.

234. Anonymous. *Giza. Pyramid of Khafre and Sphinx*, circa 1865-1899. Cornell University Library, Wikimedia Commons, 2012. https://commons.wikimedia.org/wiki/File:Giza._Pyramid_of_Khafre_and_Sphinx.jpg. Public domain.

235. Hajor, photographer. *Egypt.LuxorTemple.03*. Wikimedia Commons, 2005. https://commons.wikimedia.org/wiki/File:Egypt.LuxorTemple.03.jpg. CC BY-SA 3.0.

237. Top: Ollermann, Hans, photographer. *Akhenaten as a Sphinx*. Kestner Museum, Germany, Wikimedia Commons, 2008. https://commons.wikimedia.org/wiki/File:Akhenaten_as_a_Sphinx_(Kestner_Museum).jpg. CC BY 2.0.

238. Bottom: Hajor, photographer. *Egypt.Saqqara.Panorama.01*. Wikimedia Commons, 2005. https://commons.wikimedia.org/wiki/File:Egypt.Saqqara.Panorama.01.jpg. CC BY-SA 3.0.

241. Parrot, A., derivative work of photograph by Nina Aldin Thune. *Sun over Pyramid*. Wikimedia Commons, 2009. https://commons.wikimedia.org/wiki/File:Sun_Over_Pyramid.jpg. CC BY-SA 3.0.

CHAPTER SIX

246. Top: Simonwakefield, photographer. *Stonehenge (Sun)*. Wikimedia Commons, 2009. https://commons.wikimedia.org/wiki/File:Stonehenge (sun).jpg. CC BY 2.0.

246. Bottom: Varma, Raja Ravi. *Lord Garuda*, 18th century. Wikimedia Commons, 2012. https://commons.wikimedia.org/wiki/File:Raja_Ravi_Varma,_Lord_Garuda.jpg. Public domain.

248. Top Left: Cook, Arthur Bernard. *Illustration of a First Century AD Marble Relief in the Estense Museum in Modena, Italy*. In *Zeus: A Study in Ancient Religion*, Cambridge: The University Press, 1914. Wikimedia Commons, 2015. https://commons.wikimedia.org/wiki/File:Zeus_-_a_study_in_ancient_religion_(1914)_(14780178984).jpg. Public domain.

248. Top Right: Sailko, photographer. *Messico, Aztechi, Serpente Piumato Quetzalcoatl, Pietra Periodo Postclassico Recente, 1400-1510 ca. 02*, circa 15th-16th century. Musée du quai Branly, Wikimedia Commons, 2015. https://commons.wikimedia.org/wiki/File:Messico,_aztechi,_serpente_piumato_quetzalcoatl,_pietra_periodo_postclassico_recente,_1400-1510_ca._02.JPG. CC BY 3.0.

248. Bottom: Hajor, photographer. *Tomb KV34 (Thutmose III) 11.th hour Amduat,* Valley of the Kings, Luxor, Egypt. Wikimedia Commons, 2005. https://commons.wikimedia.org/wiki/File:Egypt.KV34.07.jpg. CC BY-SA 3.0.

252. Doré, Gustave. *Rosa Celeste: Dante and Beatrice Gaze upon the Highest Heaven, The Empyrean*, 19th century. In *The Divine Comedy by Dante, Illustrated, Complete,* by Dante Alighieri, edited by Henry Francis, *London: Cassell & Company,* 1892. Wikimedia Commons, 2006. https://commons.wikimedia.org/wiki/File:Paradiso_Canto_31.jpg. Public domain.

253. Left: Image based on the research by Roger Penrose and Vahe Gurzadyan, 2010. https://arxiv.org/ftp/arxiv/papers/1011/1011.3706.pdf. Background is a public domain image from NASA / WMAP Science Team.

253. Right: Aldorado, photographer. *May Pole (Maibaum) Top - Blue Sky*. Shutterstock.com. https://www.shutterstock.com/image-photo/may-pole-maibaum-top-blue-sky-433964464. Licensed from Shutterstock.com.

254. West, Benjamin. *The Ascension*, 1801. Denver Art Museum, Wikimedia Commons, 2009. https://commons.wikimedia.org/wiki/File:The_Ascension)_by_Benjamin_West,_PRA.jpg. Public domain.

258. Sura Ondrunar Publishing. *Sphinx Summer Solstice Sunset*. 2013.

259. Anonymous. Illustration from *The Book of the Dead of Khensumose*. Wikimedia Commons, 2015. https://commons.wikimedia.org/wiki/File:Sunrise_at_Creation.jpg. Public domain.

IMAGE REFERENCES

260. Left: Süßen, Matthias, photographer. *Maibaum Ostfriesland967*, Maypole in Aurich, East Frisia. Wikimedia Commons, 2010. https://commons.wikimedia.org/wiki/File:Maibaum_Ostfriesland967.jpg. CC BY 3.0.
260. Right: Sura Ondrunar Publishing. *Ancient Symbol of the Sun Illustration*. 2016.
261. Budge, E. A. Wallis. *Tet with the Head of Osiris*. In *Osiris and the Egyptian Resurrection*, London: P. L. Warner, 1911, p. 52. Internet Archive, 2008. https://archive.org/details/osirisegyptianre00budg/page/52. Public domain.
262. Left top: OsgoodeLawyer. *Earth Symbol*, unicode U+2295. Wikimedia Commons, 2013. https://commons.wikimedia.org/wiki/File:Earth_symbol.svg. Public domain.
262. Left bottom: Nyo. *Irminsul*. Wikimedia Commons, 2007. https://commons.wikimedia.org/wiki/File:Irminsul_pillar_black.PNG. CC BY 2.0.
262. Center: Le Plongeon, Augustus. Illustration in *Sacred Mysteries Among the Mayas and the Quiches*, 1886. Third edition, New York: Macoy Publishing and Masonic Supply Company, 1909, p. 134. Internet Archive, 2017. https://archive.org/details/PlongeonALeSacredMysteriesAmongTheMayansQuiches1909/page/n179. Public domain.
262. Right: Larry-Rains. *Caduceus Illustration*. Shutterstock.com. https://www.shutterstock.com/image-vector/caduceus-illustration-566291899?src=-1-39. Licensed from Shutterstock.com.
264. Lalupa, photographer. *Palazzo Braschi - Vestale 1020774*. Wikimedia Commons, 2007. https://commons.wikimedia.org/wiki/File:Palazzo_Braschi_-_Vestale_1020774.JPG. CC BY-SA 3.0.
267. Leighton, Frederic. *Invocation*. Wikimedia Commons, 2015. https://commons.wikimedia.org/wiki/File:Leighton,_Frederic_-_Invocation.jpg. Public domain.
269. De Montfaucon, Bernard. *Two Druids*, 18th century engraving based on a bas-relief found at Autun, France. In *History of British Costume*, by J. R. Planché, 1836. Wikimedia Commons, 2007. https://en.wikipedia.org/wiki/File:Two_Druids.PNG. Public domain.
271. Nyman, Bengt, photographer. *Midsummer Crown*. Wikimedia Commons, 2012. https://commons.wikimedia.org/wiki/File:Midsummer_Crown.jpg. CC BY 2.0.
272. Left: Käyttäjä:Kompak. Edited by Perhelion. *Ra-Horakhty Based on Nefertari's Tomb*. Wikimedia Commons, 2016. https://commons.wikimedia.org/wiki/File:Sun_god_Ra.svg. CC BY-SA 3.0.
272. Center: Ellis, Edward S., and Charles F. Horne. *Woden*. In *The Story of the Greatest Nations, from the Dawn of History to the Twentieth Century*, 1900, p. 247. Flickr.com. https://flic.kr/p/oxEEja. Public domain.
272. Right: Mahamuni. *Lord of Gods Vishnu*. Shrimad Bhagavata Mahapurana, Gorakhpur: Gita Press. Wikimedia Commons, 2018. https://commons.wikimedia.org/wiki/File:Lord_of_Gods_Vishnu.jpg. Public domain.

CHAPTER SEVEN

280. Sura Ondrunar Publishing. *Great line*. 2018. Made with Google Earth, 2018. © Google, Data SIO, NOAA, U.S. Navy, NGA, GEBCO, Image Landsat / Copernicus, Image IBCAO.

CHAPTER EIGHT

282. Bodsworth, Jon, photographer. *Descendant-Grande-Pyramide*. Wikimedia Commons, 2007. https://commons.wikimedia.org/wiki/File:Descendant-grande-pyramide.jpg. © Jon Bodsworth, used by permission.
283. ATSZ56, photographer. *Chichen Itza Equinox*, March equinox 2009. Wikimedia Commons, 2009. https://commons.wikimedia.org/wiki/File:ChichenItzaEquinox.jpg. Public domain.
285. Nateirma~commonswiki, photographer. *Teonate*. Wikimedia Commons, 2006. https://commons.wikimedia.org/wiki/File:Teonate.JPG. CC BY-SA 3.0.
286. Klein, Jordan, photographer. *Intihuatana Solar Clock*, Machu Picchu, Peru. Wikimedia Commons, 2006. https://commons.wikimedia.org/wiki/File:Intihuatana_Solar_Clock.jpg. CC BY 2.0.
287. Sewell, Ian, photographer. *Ahu-Akivi-1*, Easter Island. Wikimedia Commons, 2006. https://commons.wikimedia.org/wiki/File:Ahu-Akivi-1.JPG. CC BY-SA 3.0.
288. Collage, top left: Gybas DigiPhoto, photographer. *Moai from Ahu Tongariki on Easter Island*. Shutterstock.com. https://www.shutterstock.com/image-photo/moai-ahu-tongariki-on-easter-island-10886431. Licensed from Shutterstock.com.

288. Collage, top center: Ndede, photographer. *Archaeological Work Gobeklitepe Turkey*. Shutterstock.com. https://www.shutterstock.com/image-photo/archaeological-work-gobeklitepe-turkey-1087902086. Licensed from Shutterstock.com.

288. Collage, top right: Kaiser, Jennifer, photographer. *Statue from Gobeklitepe,* Urfa Museum. Flickr.com, 2015. https://www.flickr.com/photos/kaiserjennifer/20263074231. CC BY 2.0.

288. Collage, bottom left: TheWanderingScot.com, photographer. *Kabul Museum: Kafiristan Statue.* 2009. http://thewanderingscot.com/photos/2009 Stans/Afghanistan/midis/IMG_7902.jpg. © TheWanderingsScot.com, used with permission.

288. Collage, bottom center: Anonymous. *Two European Ladies and a Man Are Standing in front of a Statue in Napu, Menado*, before 1937. Tropenmuseum, part of the National Museum of World Cultures. Wikimedia Commons, 2009. https://en.wikipedia.org/wiki/File:COLLECTIE_TROPENMUSEUM_Twee_Europese_dames_en_een_man_staan_voor_een_afgodsbeeld_te_Napu_Menado_TMnr_10000852.jpg. CC BY-SA 3.0.

288. Collage, bottom right: Damsea, photographer. *French Polynesia Tahiti Island Carved Stone Tiki Statue on the Marae Arahurahu, South Pacific, Oceania*. Shutterstock.com. https://www.shutterstock.com/image-photo/french-polynesia-tahiti-island-carved-stone-784904116. Licensed from Shutterstock.com.

288. Image right: Papiermond, photographer. *Karajia1*. Wikimedia Commons, 2006. https://en.wikipedia.org/wiki/File:Karajia1.jpg. CC BY-SA 3.0.

289. -Luyten-, photographer. *Dzibilchaltun*, Temple of the Seven Dolls. Dzibilchaltún, Yucatan, Mexico. Wikimedia Commons, 2007. https://commons.wikimedia.org/wiki/File:Dzibilchaltun.jpg. Public domain.

290. Gagnon, Bernard, photographer. *Knossos - North Portico 02*, The North Portico in Knossos, Crete, Greece. Wikimedia Commons, 2012. https://en.wikipedia.org/wiki/File:Knossos_-_North_Portico_02.jpg. CC BY-SA 3.0.

291. Sauber, Wolfgang, photographer. *AMI - Goldene Doppelaxt*, golden Minoan labrys. Archaeological Museum in Herakleion, Wikimedia Commons, 2009. https://en.wikipedia.org/wiki/File:AMI_-_Goldene_Doppelaxt.jpg. CC BY-SA 3.0.

CHAPTER NINE

294. Top: Graham, Edwin, photographer. *Street and Glastonbury Tor from Walton Hill*. Wikimedia Commons, 2010. https://commons.wikimedia.org/wiki/File:Street_and_Glastonbury_Tor.jpg. CC BY-SA 2.0.

294. Bottom: Comvaser, photographer. *Chichen Itza CB*. Wikimedia Commons, 2009. https://commons.wikimedia.org/wiki/File:Chichen_Itza_CB.jpg. CC BY-SA 4.0.

295. Top: Antonsen, Kenny Arne Lang. *Goseck Circle, Germany 4900 - 4700 BC*. In *Old Europe - First Civilization 7000-3000 BC*. Wikimedia Commons, 2019. https://commons.wikimedia.org/wiki/File:Goseck_circle,_Germany_4900_-_4700_BC.jpg. CC BY-SA 4.0.

295. Bottom: Zenz, Rainer. *Goseck-2,* drawing based on plans from Instituts für Prähistorische Archäologie Martin-Luther-Universität Halle-Wittenberg. Wikimedia Commons, 2004. https://commons.wikimedia.org/wiki/File:Goseck-2.jpg. Public domain.

296. Anagoria, photographer. *1600 Himmelsscheibe von Nebra Sky Disk Anagoria*. Pergamon Museum, Wikimedia Commons, 2012. https://commons.wikimedia.org/wiki/File:1600_Himmelsscheibe_von_Nebra_sky_disk_anagoria.jpg. CC BY 3.0.

297. Ceridwen, photographer. *Mynydd Dinas under Snow - Geograph.org.uk*. Wikimedia Commons, 2011. https://commons.wikimedia.org/wiki/File:Mynydd_Dinas_under_snow_-_geograph.org.uk_-_1151816.jpg. CC BY-SA 2.0.

298. Mountains Hunter, photographer. *Karnak Temple Sphinxes Alley*. Shutterstock.com. https://www.shutterstock.com/image-photo/karnak-temple-sphinxes-alley-ruins-1034827522. Licensed from Shutterstock.com.

299. Top left: F-E-Cameron, Steve, photographer. *S F-E-CAMERON EGYPT 2006 FEB 00289,* Temple of Horus at Edfu. Wikimedia Commons, 2007. https://commons.wikimedia.org/wiki/File:S_F-E-CAMERON_EGYPT_2006_FEB_00289.JPG. CC BY-SA 3.0.

299. Top right: Storch, Hedwig, photographer. *Karnak Temple 9456*. Wikimedia Commons, 2009. https://commons.wikimedia.org/wiki/File:Karnak_temple_9456.JPG. CC BY-SA 3.0.

299. Bottom: Shira, photographer. *Newgrange*. Wikimedia Commons, 2006. https://commons.wikimedia.org/wiki/File:Newgrange.JPG. CC BY-SA 3.0.

IMAGE REFERENCES

300. Wakeman, William Frederick. *Sketch of a Cross Section of the Newgrange Passage Grave*, circa 1900. In *Wakeman's Handbook of Irish Antiquities*, Dublin: Hodges, Figgis, 1903, p. 85. Wikimedia Commons, 2010. https://commons.wikimedia.org/wiki/File:Wakeman_Newgrange_tumulus_chamber_cross_section.png. Public domain.

301. Johnbraid, photographer. *Ring of Brodgar, Orkney, Scotland*. Shutterstock.com. https://www.shutterstock.com/image-photo/ring-brodgar-orkney-scotland-neolithic-stone-134528468. Licensed from Shutterstock.com.

302. Burke, Rob, photographer. *Maes Howe Entrance Passage*. Wikimedia Commons, 2010. https://commons.wikimedia.org/wiki/File:Maes_Howe_entrance_passage_-_geograph.org.uk_-_33791.jpg. CC BY-SA 2.0.

304. RPBaiao, photographer. *Statue of Moai at the Sacred Site of Ahu Kuri a Urenga, Easter Island*. Shutterstock.com. https://www.shutterstock.com/image-photo/state-moai-sacred-site-ahu-kuri-714630817. Licensed from Shutterstock.com.

305. Budge, E. A. Wallace. *The Great Pyramid, Showing Passages and Mummy Chambers*. In *The Nile: Notes for Travellers in Egypt*, London: Harrison and Sons, 1902, p. 100. Travelers in the Middle East Archive (TIMEA), Wikimedia Commons, 2010. https://commons.wikimedia.org/wiki/File:The_Great_Pyramid,_showing_passages_and_mummy_chambers._(1902)_-_TIMEA.jpg. CC BY-SA 2.5.

306. Mhwater, photographer. *The Gateway of the Sun from the Tiwanaku Civilization in Bolivia*. Wikimedia Commons, 2006. https://commons.wikimedia.org/wiki/File:Zonnepoort_tiwanaku.jpg. Public domain.

309. Guzmán, Fabricio, photographer. *Machupicchu Intihuatana*, Temple of the Sun at Machu Picchu, Peru. Wikimedia Commons, 2006. https://commons.wikimedia.org/wiki/File:Machupicchu_intihuatana.JPG. Public domain.

310. Top: Robertson, D. Gordon E., photographer. *Ollantaytambo, Tunupa Monument*. Wikimedia Commons, 2011. https://commons.wikimedia.org/wiki/File:Ollantaytambo,_Tunupa_monument.jpg. CC BY-SA 3.0.

310. Bottom: Abhishek Bansal, Ekta, photographer. *Another Stupa of Ajanta*, Ajanta Caves. Wikimedia Commons, 2010. https://commons.wikimedia.org/wiki/File:Another_Stupa_of_Ajanta.JPG. CC BY-SA 3.0.

311. Derk, Jan, photographer. *The Great Enclosure, Which Is Part of the Great Zimbabwe Ruins*. Wikimedia Commons, 2006. https://commons.wikimedia.org/wiki/File:Great-Zimbabwe.jpg. Public domain.

312. Ostertag, Raymond, photographer. *Nasca Astronaut 2007 08*, Nasca, Peru. Wikimedia Commons, 2007. https://commons.wikimedia.org/wiki/File:Nasca_Astronaut_2007_08.JPG. CC BY-SA 3.0.

315. Top: Azurfrog, photographer. *Al Deir Petra*. Wikimedia Commons, 2013. https://en.wikipedia.org/wiki/File:Al_Deir_Petra.JPG. CC BY-SA 3.0.

315. Bottom: Heron, photographer. *Model by Dy Proeung, in Siem Reap, Cambodia, of Angkor Wat Central Structure*. Wikimedia Commons, 2011. https://en.wikipedia.org/wiki/File:Angkor-wat-central.jpg. CC BY-SA 3.0.

317. Jvtrplzz. *Arkaim Infographic*. Wikimedia Commons, 2018. https://en.wikipedia.org/wiki/File:Arkaim_Infographic.jpg. Public domain.

319. Grigoriev, S., photographer. *Vera Island, Megalyth 2*. Wikimedia Commons, 2011. https://commons.wikimedia.org/wiki/File:OV-M2.jpg. CC BY-SA 3.0.

CHAPTER TEN

324. Hajor, photographer. *Great Sphinx of Giza and Khafre's Pyramid*, Giza Plateau, Cairo. Wikimedia Commons, 2011. https://commons.wikimedia.org/wiki/File:Egypt.Giza.Sphinx.01.jpg. CC BY-SA 3.0.

325. Top: Heng, Kim (សុគីមហេង), photographer. *Equinox at Angkor 21st March 2012*. Wikimedia Commons, 2012. https://commons.wikimedia.org/wiki/File:Equinox_at_Angkor_21st_March_2012.JPG. CC BY-SA 3.0.

325. Bottom: Markalexander100, photographer. *The Churning of the Ocean of Milk*, bas-relief on the south of the east wall of Angkor Wat's third enclosure. Wikimedia Commons, 2005. https://commons.wikimedia.org/wiki/File:Awatoceanofmilk01_-_color_corrected.JPG. CC BY-SA 3.0.

326. Tau'olunga. *Precession N, the Path of the North Celestial Pole among the Stars due to the Precession*. Wikimedia Commons, 2006. https://en.wikipedia.org/wiki/File:Precession_N.gif. CC BY-SA 2.5.

328. Ostertag, Raymond, photographer. *Tikal Temple1 2006 08 11,* Guatemala. Wikimedia Commons, 2011. https://commons.wikimedia.org/wiki/File:Tikal_Temple1_2006_08_11.JPG. CC-BY-SA 2.5.

330. QuartierLatin1968, photographer. *The Central Column of Cahokia's Woodhenge.* Wikimedia Commons, 2013. https://commons.wikimedia.org/wiki/File:Woodhenge_Cahokia_3998.jpg. CC BY-SA 3.0.

331. Top: Whyte, William, photographer. *Cairn T Loughcrew.* Wikimedia Commons, 2008. https://commons.wikimedia.org/wiki/File:Cairn_T_Loughcrew.jpg. CC BY-SA 2.0.

331. Bottom: Hurson, Rob, photographer. *Sun Wall, Loughcrew.* Wikimedia Commons, 2014. https://commons.wikimedia.org/wiki/File:Sun_wall,_Loughcrew.jpg. CC BY-SA 4.0.

332. Sitoman, photographer. *Knowth01,* Knowth, Ireland. Wikimedia Commons, 2007. https://commons.wikimedia.org/wiki/File:Knowth01.jpg. Public domain.

333. Campbell, Kieran, photographer. *Cannon Fire at Millmount, Drogheda.* Wikimedia Commons, 2011. https://commons.wikimedia.org/wiki/File:Cannon_fire_at_Millmount,_Drogheda_-_geograph.org.uk_-_1079077.jpg. CC BY-SA 2.0.

334. Allen, James, photographer. *Summit of Cairnpapple.* Wikimedia Commons, 2011. https://commons.wikimedia.org/wiki/File:Summit_of_Cairnpapple_-_geograph.org.uk_-_1062278.jpg. CC BY-SA 2.0.

335. Top: Alborzagros, photographer. *Gate of All Nations, Persepolis.* Wikimedia Commons, 2015. https://en.wikipedia.org/wiki/File:Gate_of_All_Nations,_Persepolis.jpg. CC BY-SA 3.0.

335. Bottom: Pentocelo, photographer. Edited by JMCC1. *Persepolis Apadana Eastern Stairway Triangle.* Wikimedia Commons, 2006, 2012. https://en.wikipedia.org/wiki/File:Persepolis_Apadana_Eastern_Stairway_Triangle.jpg. Public domain.

336. Sahand Ace, photograph. *Faravahar Symbol in Persepolis.* Wikimedia Commons, 2013. https://commons.wikimedia.org/wiki/File:Farvahar1.JPG. CC BY-SA 3.0.

CHAPTER ELEVEN

339. Sura Ondrunar Publishing. *Sphinx Summer Solstice Sunset.* 2013.

340. Markh, photographer. *Osireion at Abydos.* Wikimedia Commons, 2008. https://commons.wikimedia.org/wiki/File:Osireion_at_Abydos.jpg. CC BY-SA 3.0.

341. Bukvoed, photographer. *Qumran National Park,* Israel. Wikimedia Commons, 2010. https://commons.wikimedia.org/wiki/File:Kumran-1-84.jpg. CC BY 3.0.

343. GailJohnson, photographer. *Stonehenge an Ancient Prehistoric Stone Monument near Salisbury Wiltshire UK.* Bigstock.com. https://www.bigstockphoto.com/fi/image-6771320/stock-photo-stonehenge. Used under license from GailJohnson / Bigstock.com.

344. Anonymous. *Stonehenge on Midsummer, 1700 BC.* In *Nordisk Familjebok,* vol. 27, 1918, p. 115. Wikimedia Commons, 2006. https://commons.wikimedia.org/wiki/File:Stonehenge_vid_midsommar_1700_f_Kr,_Nordisk_familjebok.png. Public domain.

346. Top: Weld-Blundell, Mr. H., photographer. *Megalithic Group at Messa in the Cyrenaica.* In *The Hill of the Graces: A Record of Investigation among the Trilithons and Megalithic Sites of Tripoli,* by H. S. Cowper, London: Methuen & Co., 1897, p. 169. Internet Archive, 2009. https://archive.org/details/hillgracesareco01cowpgoog/page/n199. Public domain.

346. Bottom: De Capell Brooke, Sir Arthur. *L'Uted.* In *Sketches in Spain and Morocco,* London: Henry Colburn and Richard Bentley, 1831, p. 39. Internet Archive, 2009. https://archive.org/details/sketchesinspainm02brok/page/n53. Public domain.

347. Collage, top left: Heghnaraghpour, photographer. *Karahounch,* Zorats Karer, Armenia. Wikimedia Commons, 2017. https://commons.wikimedia.org/wiki/File:Karahounch.jpg. CC BY-SA 4.0.

347. Collage, top center: Haimann, Giuseppe. *Hana Segal.* In *Cirenaica (Tripolitania) Disegni Presi da Schizzi Dell'autore,* Milano U. Hoepli, 1886, p. 59. Internet Archive, 2010. https://archive.org/details/cirenaicatripoli00haim/page/59. Public domain.

347. Collage, top right: Leandroisola, photographer. *The Calzoene's "Stonehenge,"* Calçoene, Brazil, 2008. Wikimedia Commons, 2008. https://commons.wikimedia.org/wiki/File:Calçoene,_Stonehenge brasileira, Amapá.jpg. CC BY 4.0.

347. Collage, bottom left: Boychou, photographer. *Stone Erections of Willong Khullen,* Manipur, India. Wikimedia Commons, 2010. https://commons.wikimedia.org/wiki/File:Stone_Erections_of_Willong_Khullen.jpg. CC BY-SA 3.0.

IMAGE REFERENCES

347. Collage, bottom center: Woods, David, photographer. *A Portion of the Orkney Neolithic Site, the Ring of Brodgar*. Shutterstock.com. https://www.shutterstock.com/image-photo/portion-orkney-neolithic-site-ring-brodgar-4674436. Licensed from Shutterstock.com.

347. Collage, bottom right: Adwo, photographer. *South Africa's Adam's Calendar Stone Replica – Argentina*. Shutterstock.com. https://www.shutterstock.com/image-photo/south-africas-adams-calendar-stone-replica-630489557. Licensed from Shutterstock.com.

347. Image bottom: Raymbetz, photographer. *Calendar Aswan*, Nabta Playa Calendar Circle, reconstructed at Aswan Nubia museum. Wikimedia Commons, 2009. https://commons.wikimedia.org/wiki/File:Calendar_aswan.JPG. CC BY-SA 3.0.

349. Engelhardt, R., photographer. *2007-06-06-Externsteine-33*, Horn-Bad Meinberg, Germany. Wikimedia Commons, 2009. https://commons.wikimedia.org/wiki/File:2007-06-06-Externsteine-33.jpg. CC BY-SA 3.0.

350. Natritmeyer, photographer. *Tablet of Shamash*. Wikimedia Commons, 2018. https://en.wikipedia.org/wiki/File:Tablet_of_Shamash.jpg. CC BY-SA 4.0.

351. Top: Dola.das85, photographer. *Ajanta Cave*, an inside view of cave 19 of Ajanta Caves. Wikimedia Commons, 2012. https://commons.wikimedia.org/wiki/File:Ajanta_Cave.jpg. CC BY-SA 3.0.

351. Bottom: Naville, Henry Edouard, photographer. *Hathor Chapel at the Temple of Thutmosis III*, Deir el-Bahari, Eqypt, 1907. In *The XIth Dynasty Temple at Deir el-Bahari*, London, 1907, p. xxviii-d. Wikimedia Commons, 2010. https://commons.wikimedia.org/wiki/File:Hathor-shrine-D.JPG. Public domain.

352. Price, Timothy and Nichole I. Stump. *View from Above*. In *A digital GIS Map of Ohio's Great Serpent Mound*. Wikimedia Commons, 2005. https://commons.wikimedia.org/wiki/File:Serpent_Mound.jpg. CC BY-SA 3.0.

353. Gordon-Cumming, Constance. *Loch Nell Serpent Mound*. In *In the Hebrides*, London: Chatto and Windus, 1883, p. 74. Public domain.

354. HJPD, photographer. *Casa Rinconada*, Chaco Canyon, New Mexico, U.S.A. Wikimedia Commons, 2010. https://commons.wikimedia.org/wiki/File:Casa_Rinconada.jpg. CC BY 3.0.

355. Top: Hooper, Honey, photographer. *Easter Island Ahu (2006)*. Wikimedia Commons, 2009. https://commons.wikimedia.org/wiki/File:Easter Island Ahu (2006).jpg. CC BY 2.5.

355. Bottom: Sverzel, photographer. *Tulum Sverzel*, view toward the main temple in Tulum, Mexico. Wikimedia Commons, 2008. https://en.wikipedia.org/wiki/File:Tulum_sverzel.jpg. CC BY-SA 3.0.

356. El Comandante, photographer. *Descending God (Tulum)*. Wikimedia Commons, 2012. https://commons.wikimedia.org/wiki/File:Descending God (Tulum).JPG. CC BY-SA 3.0.

357. Top: Tato grasso, photographer. *0073 Uxmal*, Mexico. Wikimedia Commons, 2007. https://commons.wikimedia.org/wiki/File:0073_Uxmal.JPG. CC BY-SA 2.5.

357. Bottom: Jarvis, Dennis, photographer. *Guatemala-1520*, The Lost World Pyramid, Tikal, Guatemala. Wikimedia Commons, 2012. https://commons.wikimedia.org/wiki/File:Flickr_-_archer10_(Dennis)_-_Guatemala-1520.jpg. CC BY-SA 2.0.

358. Image created for book, based on Truman, Dave. "Ancient Alignment in the Andes Hints at a Lost Global High Culture." GrahamHancock.com, January 2, 2016. https://grahamhancock.com/truman1. Background © Google Earth, image Landsat / Copernicus, Data SIO, NOAA, U.S. Navy, NGA, GEBCO, Data LDEO-Columbia, NSF, NOAA.

360. Top: Ximenez, Pedro, photographer. *Pyramide Güimar*. Wikimedia Commons, 2009. https://commons.wikimedia.org/wiki/File:Pyramide Güimar.jpg. CC BY-SA 2.0.

360. Bottom: Wikiwikiyarou. Edited by Daniele Pugliesi. *Ziggurat of Ur*, based on a 1939 drawing by Leonard Woolley, *Ur Excavations*, Vol. V. *The Ziggurat and Its Surroundings*, fig. 1.4. Wikimedia Commons, 2014. https://commons.wikimedia.org/wiki/File:Ziggurat_of_ur.jpg. Public domain.

361. Top: Norris, Ray P. *Wurdi Younag Alignments*. Aboriginal Indigenous Astronomy, 2011. http://aboriginalastronomy.blogspot.com/2011/03/wurdi-youang-aboriginal-stone.html. © Ray P. Norris, http://www.emudreaming.com. Reproduced with permission.

361. Bottom: Norris, Ray P, photographer. *Wurdi Younag*, Victoria, Australia. Wikimedia Commons, 2016. https://commons.wikimedia.org/wiki/File:Wurdi_Youang.jpg. CC BY-SA 2.5.

362. Bandarin, Francesco. *Lascaux Cave*. © UNESCO, UNESCO.org, 2006. http://whc.unesco.org/en/list/85/gallery. CC BY-SA 3.0 IGO.

CHAPTER TWELVE

369. Bronnikov, Fyodor. *Pythagoreans Anthem to the Rising Sun*. 1869. Wikimedia Commons, 2007. https://commons.wikimedia.org/wiki/File:Bronnikov_gimnpifagoreizev.jpg. Public domain.

371. Azarian, Dana, photographer. *Celebrating Nowruz in Mariwan*. Tasnim News Agency, 2016, Wikimedia Commons, 2017. https://commons.wikimedia.org/wiki/File:Celebrating_Nowruz_in_Mariwan.jpg. CC BY 4.0.

372. Sandyraidy, photographer. *Druids Celebrating at Stonehenge (1)*. Wikimedia Commons, 2009. https://commons.wikimedia.org/wiki/File:Druids_celebrating_at_Stonehenge_(1).png. CC BY-SA 2.0.

374. Top: Dedda71, photographer. *Pagan Meditation*. Wikimedia Commons, 2009. https://commons.wikimedia.org/wiki/File:Pagan_meditation.jpg. CC BY 3.0.

374. Bottom: PersianDutchNetwork, photographer. *Persian Lady Recites Hafez Poems in Yalda Night*. Wikimedia Commons, 2014. https://commons.wikimedia.org/wiki/File:Persian_Lady_recites_Hafez_Poems_in_Yalda_Night.jpg. CC BY-SA 3.0.

377. GiW, photographer. *Stebykla 01*, reconstruction of ancient Lithuanian "Sky Lighthouse Observation" (Kulionys, Molėtai district). Wikimedia Commons, 2012. https://commons.wikimedia.org/wiki/File:Stebykla_01.jpg. CC BY-SA 3.0.

378. Smit, photographer. *Gate to Ki Monastery*. Shutterstock.com. https://www.shutterstock.com/image-photo/gates-ki-monastery-himalayas-mountain-125246675. Licensed from Shutterstock.com.

379. Cleveland, Jeff, photographer. *Inti Raymi Ceremony*. Shutterstock.com. https://www.shutterstock.com/image-photo/cusco-peru-june-24-2015-men-1414113587. Licensed from Shutterstock.com.

381. Top: NASA. *Axial Tilt vs Tropical and Polar Circles*. Wikimedia Commons, 2015. https://en.wikipedia.org/wiki/File:Axial_tilt_vs_tropical_and_polar_circles.svg. Public domain.

381. Bottom: YSEE. *Hellen ritual (3)*. Supreme Council of Ethnikoi Hellenes, Wikimedia Commons, 2009. https://commons.wikimedia.org/wiki/File:Hellen_ritual_(3).jpg. CC BY 2.0.

383. Harvey, Fred. *An Indian Dance in Front of the Hopi House, Grand Canyon National Park*, circa 1910s. Detroit Publishing Company Collection, Wikimedia Commons, 2018. https://commons.wikimedia.org/wiki/File:"An Indian Dance in Front of the Hopi House, Grand Canyon National Park, Eagle Dance, Fred Harvey" (NBY 18962).jpg. Public domain.

385. Elston, Geoff, photographer. *Sun White*. Society for Popular Astronomy, Wikimedia Commons, 2014. https://commons.wikimedia.org/wiki/File:Sun_white.jpg. CC BY 4.0.

386. Top: Masalskis, Mantas, photographer. *Romuvan ceremony (10)*. Wikimedia Commons, 2009. https://commons.wikimedia.org/wiki/File:Romuvan ceremony (10).PNG. CC BY 2.0.

386. Bottom: Thelmadatter, photographer. *PyramidSunEquinox1*. Wikimedia Commons, 2010. https://commons.wikimedia.org/wiki/File:PyramidSunEquinox1.JPG. CC BY-SA 3.0.

393. Lobachev, Vladimir, photographer. *Ivan Kupala Day in 2011 08*, Belgorod region. Wikimedia Commons, 2014. https://commons.wikimedia.org/wiki/File:Ivan_Kupala_Day_in_2011_08.JPG. CC BY-SA 3.0.

CHAPTER THIRTEEN

397. Left: Collingwood, W. G. *Odin's Self-Sacrifice*. In *The Elder or Poetic Edda, Commonly Known as Sæmund's Edda*, edited and translated by Olive Bray, 1908, p. 61. Wikimedia Commons, 2008. https://commons.wikimedia.org/wiki/File:Odin's Self-sacrifice by Collingwood.jpg. Public domain.

397. Center: Barber, John Warner. *The Crucifixion*. In *The life of Our Lord and Savior Jesus Christ* by John Fleetwood, New Haven: Nathan Whiting, 1830, page 426. Wikimedia Commons, 2015. https://commons.wikimedia.org/wiki/File:The_life_of_our_Lord_and_Savior_Jesus_Christ_-_containing_a_full,_accurate,_and_universal_history_from_his_taking_upon_himself_our_nature_to_his_crucifixion,_resurrection,_and_ascension-_together_with_(14592569250).jpg. Public domain.

397. Right: Anonymous. *Xolotl*. In *Codex Fejervary-Mayer,* circa 15th century. Wikimedia Commons, 2006. https://commons.wikimedia.org/wiki/File:Xolotl_1.jpg. Public domain.

404. Mukerjee, photographer. *D01944 Arati Rakshitbari Giridih*, at a puja in Giridih, Jharkhand. Wikimedia Commons, 2008. https://commons.wikimedia.org/wiki/File:D01944_Arati_Rakshitbari_giridih.jpg. CC BY-SA 4.0.

IMAGE REFERENCES

406. Chore Bagan Art Studio. *Rama is Shown about to Offer His Eyes to Make up the Full Number - 108 - of Lotus Blossoms Needed in the Puja That He Must Offer to the Goddess Durga to Gain Her Blessing*. Album of popular prints mounted on cloth pages, circa 1895. Wikimedia Commons, 2012. https://commons.wikimedia.org/wiki/File:Rama_is_shown_about_to_offer_his_eyes_to_make_up_the_full_number_-_108_-_of_lotus_blossoms_needed_in_the_puja_that_he_must_offer_to_the_goddess_Durga_to_gain_her_blessing..jpg. Public domain.

407. Royan, Jorge, photographer. *India - Varanasi Sun Greet – 0270*, Ganges Varanasi Benares, India. Wikimedia Commons, 2012. https://commons.wikimedia.org/wiki/File:India_-_Varanasi_sun_greet_-_0270.jpg. CC BY-SA 3.0.

411. Srkris at English Wikipedia, photographer. *Hindu Priest from the Nambudiri Caste Performs a Yajna*, Kerala, India. Wikimedia Commons, 2008. https://commons.wikimedia.org/wiki/File:Yajna1.jpg. Public domain.

412. Ministry of Tourism (GODL-India). *The Priest in the Final Rituals of Immersing the Darpan to Mark the Completion of the Five Durga Puja Festival on the Maha Dashami at Kolkata on October 21, 2007*. Wikimedia Commons, 2018. https://commons.wikimedia.org/wiki/File:The_Priest_in_the_final_rituals_of_immersing_the_Darpan_to_mark_the_completion_of_the_five_Durga_Puja_Festival_on_the_Maha_Dashami_at_Kolkata_on_October_21,_2007.jpg. © Government of India, used with permission.

413. Maison, Rudolf. *Der Schlafende Wotan* (marble). 1900. Photograph from *Plastiken und Ölgemälde moderner Meister*, edited by Hugo Helbing, 1913. Wikimedia Commons, 2017. https://commons.wikimedia.org/wiki/File:Rudolf_Maison_-_Wotan_(marble).png. Public domain.

414. Anonymous. *Wappen von Irmenseul*. Coat of arms of Irmenseul, 1938. Wikimedia Commons, 2009. https://commons.wikimedia.org/wiki/File:Wappen_Irmenseul.png. Public domain.

415. Berig, photographer. Edits by Nils von Barth and The Man in Question. *Sacrificial Scene on Hammars – Valknut*, Stora Hammar stone, Sweden. Wikimedia Commons, 2009. https://commons.wikimedia.org/wiki/File:Sacrificial_scene_on_Hammars_-_Valknut.png. CC BY-SA 3.0.

416. Top: Berg, Jónína K., photographer. Edited by Haukur Þorgeirsson. *Jörmundur Ingi 1994*, Jörmundur Ingi Hansen being sworn in as allsherjargoði ("common chieftain" or "high priest") at Þingvellir. Wikimedia Commons, 2009. https://commons.wikimedia.org/wiki/File:Jörmundur Ingi 1994.jpg. CC BY-SA 3.0.

416. Bottom: Þorgeirsson, Haukur, photographer. *Sigurblót 2009*, Iceland. Wikimedia Commons, 2009. https://commons.wikimedia.org/wiki/File:Sigurblót 2009.JPG. CC BY-SA 3.0.

417. Creutz, Gunnar, photographer. *Forn Sed Sverige Tingsblot 2011 Rådsgydja o Rådsgode*, Sweden. Wikimedia Commons, 2011. https://commons.wikimedia.org/wiki/File:Forn Sed Sverige Tingsblot 2011 Rådsgydja o Rådsgode.jpg. Public domain.

422. Collingwood, W. G. *Odin's Self-Sacrifice*. In *The Elder or Poetic Edda, Commonly Known as Sæmund's Edda*, edited and translated by Olive Bray, 1908, p. 61. Wikimedia Commons, 2008. https://commons.wikimedia.org/wiki/File:Odin's Self-sacrifice by Collingwood.jpg. Public domain.

423. Top: Radcliff, Rebecca, photographer. *Heathen Altar*. Wikimedia Commons, 2009. https://commons.wikimedia.org/wiki/File:Heathen_altar.png. CC BY-SA 2.0.

423. Bottom: Novikov, Alexei, photographer. *Runic Inscriptions*. Shutterstock.com. https://www.shutterstock.com/image-photo/runic-inscriptions-on-runestone-ljungby-sweden-286417871. Licensed from Shutterstock.com.

424. Rosen, Georg von. *Oden som Vandringsman*. 1886. Wikimedia Commons, 2005. https://commons.wikimedia.org/wiki/File:Georg_von_Rosen_-_Oden_som_vandringsman,_1886_(Odin,_the_Wanderer).jpg. Public domain.

425. Top: Gehrts, Johannes. *Hel, the Goddess of the Nether World*. In *The Open Court*, Vol. XI., no. 488 (January 1897), p. 179. Wikimedia Commons, 2015. https://commons.wikimedia.org/wiki/File:The_Open_court_(1897)_(14779072661).jpg. Public domain.

425. Bottom: Frølich, Lorenz. *Odin og Völven*. In *Den ældre Eddas Gudesange*, by Karl Gjellerup, 1895. Wikimedia Commons, 2008. https://commons.wikimedia.org/wiki/File:Odin og Völven by Frølich.jpg. Public domain.

426. Runologe, photographer. *Runensteinkreis - Rune Stone Circle – 02*, Bavaria. Wikimedia Commons, 2015. https://commons.wikimedia.org/wiki/File:Runensteinkreis_-_Rune_Stone_Circle_-_02.jpg. Public domain.

427. Sander, Fredrik. *Odin*. In *Eddan: De Nordiska Guda- och Hjältesångerna*, by Fredrik Sander translated by Erik Brate, 1913. Wikimedia Commons, 2006. https://commons.wikimedia.org/wiki/File:Ed0004.jpg. Public domain.

428. Sauber, Wolfgang, photographer. *AMI - Kamaresvase 1*. Archaeological Museum of Herakleion, Wikimedia Commons, 2009. https://commons.wikimedia.org/wiki/File:AMI_-_Kamaresvase_1.jpg. CC BY-SA 3.0.

429. *Autumn Equinox Ceremony Diagram*. © Sura Ondrunar Publishing.

430. Top: Shonagon, photographer. *Labyrinth - House of Theseus – Paphos*, Crete. Wikimedia Commons, 2013. https://commons.wikimedia.org/wiki/File:Labyrinth_-_House_of_Theseus_-_Paphos.jpg. Public domain.

430. Bottom left: Nguyen, Marie-Lan, photographer. *Theseus Minotaur Louvre F33 n2*, Canino Collection; purchase, 1840. Wikimedia Commons, 2007. https://commons.wikimedia.org/wiki/File:Theseus_Minotaur_Louvre_F33_n2.jpg. Public domain.

430. Bottom right: Osseman, Dick, photographer. *Antakya Dionysus and Ariadne Mosaic 7507*. Antakya Archaeological Museum, Wikimedia Commons, 2019. https://commons.wikimedia.org/wiki/File:Antakya_Dionysus_and_Ariadne_mosaic_7507.jpg. CC BY-SA 4.0.

431. Left: Gilmanshin, photographer. *Head of Minoan Bull*. Shutterstock.com. https://www.shutterstock.com/image-photo/head-minoan-bull-sacred-animal-ancient-257368639. Licensed from Shutterstock.com.

431. Right: Sauber, Wolfgang, photographer. *AMI - Goldene Doppelaxt*, golden Minoan labrys. Archaeological Museum in Herakleion, Wikimedia Commons, 2009. https://en.wikipedia.org/wiki/File:AMI_-_Goldene_Doppelaxt.jpg. CC BY-SA 3.0.

435. Millet, Francis Davis. *Thesmophoria*. Between 1894 and 1897. Brigham Young University Museum of Art, Wikimedia Commons, 2015. https://commons.wikimedia.org/wiki/File:'Thesmophoria' by Francis Davis Millet, 1894-1897.jpg. Public domain.

437. Top: Mollerus, Sharon, photographer. *NAMA Linear B Tablet of Pylos*. National Archaeological Museum of Athens, Wikimedia Commons, 2009. https://commons.wikimedia.org/wiki/File:NAMA_Linear_B_tablet_of_Pylos.jpg. CC BY 2.0.

437. Bottom: Todd, Gary, photographer. *Ancient Greece Minoan Clay Figurine Votive Offering (28509610536)*. Museum of Cycladic Art, Athens, Wikimedia Commons, 2019. https://commons.wikimedia.org/wiki/File:Ancient_Greece_Minoan_Clay_Figurine_Votive_Offering_(28509610536).jpg. Public domain.

CHAPTER FOURTEEN

441. Left: Moroder, Wolfgang, photographer. *Geburt Christi Pescoller Senior 1923*. Chapel of Saint Mary, San Ciascian, Italy, Wikimedia Commons, 2013. https://commons.wikimedia.org/wiki/File:Geburt_Christi_Pescoller_senior_1923.jpg. CC BY-SA 3.0.

441. Center: Raddato, Carole, photographer. *Stone Relief with Mithras Emerging from the Cosmic Egg, from Housesteads, CIMRM 860, Great North Museum, Newcastle (24455529177)*. Great North Museum, Newcastle, Wikimedia Commons, 2018. https://commons.wikimedia.org/wiki/File:Stone_relief_with_Mithras_emerging_from_the_cosmic_egg,_from_Housesteads,_CIMRM_860,_Great_North_Museum,_Newcastle_(24455529177).jpg. CC BY-SA 2.0.

441. Right: Camocon. *Wiccan Syzygy*. Wikimedia Commons, 2011. https://commons.wikimedia.org/wiki/File:Wiccan_Syzygy.png. Public domain.

448. Motta, Cyntia, photographer. *Inti Raymi*, Cusco, Peru. Wikimedia Commons, 2008. https://commons.wikimedia.org/wiki/File:Inti_Raymi.jpg. CC BY-SA 3.0.

450. Top: Martínez, Marco Antonio Ochante, photographer. *Vilcashuamán 03 - Ayacucho – Perú*. Wikimedia Commons, 2017. https://commons.wikimedia.org/wiki/File:Vilcashuamán 03 - Ayacucho - Perú.jpg. CC BY-SA 4.0.

450. Bottom: Green, Mark, photographer. *Inti Raymi*. Shutterstock.com. https://www.shutterstock.com/image-photo/june-24-2010-cusco-peru-inca-1088104811?src=TmK_Pa6tS59Jj1t9AIsqUQ-1-23. Licensed from Shutterstock.com.

451. Left: ECP Photography, photographer. *Incan Statue*. Shutterstock.com. https://www.shutterstock.com/image-photo/incan-statue-standing-high-square-cusco-683532586?src=I_vXvQlgRglDU5rWrejdkw-1-64. Licensed from Shutterstock.com.

451. Center: Wellcome Collection. *Virgin of the Sun*. In *The Costume of the Inhabitants of Peru*, London: J. Edington, circa 1810. Wikimedia Commons, 2014. https://commons.wikimedia.org/wiki/File:Virgin_of_the_Sun_Wellcome_L0042050.jpg. CC BY 4.0.

IMAGE REFERENCES

451. Right: Karenmcoboss, photographer. *Inyi Raymi 02*, Equador. Wikimedia Commons, 2019. https://commons.wikimedia.org/wiki/File:Inyi_Raymi_02.jpg. CC BY-SA 4.0.

456. Jisa39, photographer. *Celebración del Inti Raymi en el Museo Nacional de Historia Natural*, at the National Museum of Natural History of Chile. Wikimedia Commons, 2017. https://commons.wikimedia.org/wiki/File:Celebración del Inti Raymi en el Museo Nacional de Historia Natural.jpg. CC BY-SA 4.0.

457. Murúa, Martín de. *Inca Pachacútec in the Coricancha*. In *Historia General del Piru*, circa 1580-1616. Wikimedia Commons, 2008. https://commons.wikimedia.org/wiki/File:Pachacuteckoricancha.jpg. Public domain.

459. Tanko, Barna, photographer. *Quechua Women Preparing Flat Bread*. Shutterstock.com. https://www.shutterstock.com/image-photo/june-25-2017-cotacachi-ecuador-quechua-695547583. Licensed from Shutterstock.com.

460. Raele, P., photographer. *Inti Raymi 2018*. Wikimedia Commons, 2019. https://commons.wikimedia.org/wiki/File:Inti_Raymi_2018.jpg. CC BY-SA 4.0.

CHAPTER FIFTEEN

463. Left: Ignati, photographer. *Detail aus dem Grab des Sennudjem*, detail from the tomb of Sennedjem. Wikimedia Commons, 2011. https://commons.wikimedia.org/wiki/File:Detail_aus_dem_Grab_des_Sennudjem.jpg. Public domain.

463. Center: Bloch, Carl Heinrich. *The Resurrection*. 1881. Frederiksborg Palace, Copenhagen, Wikimedia Commons, 2012. https://commons.wikimedia.org/wiki/File:Carl_Heinrich_Bloch_-_The_Resserection.jpg. Public domain.

463. Right: Schele, Linda. *Drawing of Plate Interior Showing the Rebirth of the Maize God from a Turtle Shell* SD-5505. In *Maya Cosmos: Three Thousand Years on the Shaman's Path*, by David A. Freidel, Linda Schele, and Joy Parker, New York: W. Morrow, 1993, p. 371, fig. 8:25b. Ancient Americas at LACMA, http://ancientamericas.org/collection/aa010550. © David Schele, used by permission on behalf of LACMA.

469. Todorovic, Aleksandar, photographer. *Maya Fire Ceremony*. Shutterstock.com. https://www.shutterstock.com/image-photo/tikal-guatemala-dec-21-2015-unidentified-540351640. Licensed from Shutterstock.com.

470. James, Gilbert. *How the Sun Appeared Like the Moon*. In *The Myths of Mexico and Peru*, by Lewis Spence, New York: Thomas Y. Crowell Company Publishers, 1913, p. 330. Wikimedia Commons, 2015. https://commons.wikimedia.org/wiki/File:The_myths_of_Mexico_and_Peru_(1913)_(14783779812).jpg. Public domain.

471. Roe, Herb, photographer. *Cox Style Gorget HRoe 2012*. Wikimedia Commons, 2012. https://commons.wikimedia.org/wiki/File:Cox_style_gorget_HRoe_2012.jpg. CC BY-SA 3.0.

475. Sewell, William. *In the House of Bats*. In *The Myths of Mexico and Peru* by Lewis Spence, New York: Thomas Y. Crowell Company Publishers, 1913, p. 226. Wikimedia Commons, 2015. https://commons.wikimedia.org/wiki/File:The_myths_of_Mexico_and_Peru_(1913)_(14783778402).jpg. Public domain.

476. Anonymous. *Ah Puch*. In *Dresden Codex*, circa 13th-14th century. Vectorized by Drini. Wikimedia Commons, 2009. https://commons.wikimedia.org/wiki/File:Ah_Puch.svg. Public domain.

477. Schele, Linda. *Drawing of Plate Interior Showing the Rebirth of the Maize God from a Turtle Shell* SD-5505. In *Maya Cosmos: Three Thousand Years on the Shaman's Path*, by David A. Freidel, Linda Schele, and Joy Parker, New York: W. Morrow, 1993, p. 371, fig. 8:25b. Ancient Americas at LACMA, http://ancientamericas.org/collection/aa010550. © David Schele, used by permission on behalf of LACMA.

478. Top: Anonymous. *Codex Magliabecchi Aztec Conch Shell Trumpeter*. Circa 1550. In *The Book of the Life of the Ancient Mexicans Part I*, by Zelia Nuttall, Berkeley: University of California, 1903, p. 23. Wikimedia Commons, 2012. https://commons.wikimedia.org/wiki/File:Codex_Magliabecchi_Aztec_conch_shell_trumpeter_quiquizoani.png. Public domain.

478. Bottom: FA2010, photographer. *Maya Conch Shell Trumpet Kimbell*. Kimbell Art Museum, Fort Worth, Wikimedia Commons, 2011. https://commons.wikimedia.org/wiki/File:Maya_Conch_Shell_Trumpet_Kimbell.jpg. Public domain.

CHAPTER SIXTEEN

483. Left: *Yayati Ascend to Heaven*. In *Mahabharata*, by Ramanarayanadatta Astri, Gorakhpur: Geeta Press. Wikimedia Commons, 2013. https://commons.wikimedia.org/wiki/File:Yayati_ascend_to_Heaven.jpg. Public domain.

483. Center: *Jesus Ascends into Heaven*. In *The Bible Panorama, or The Holy Scriptures in Picture and Story*, Philadelphia: Charles Foster Publishing Co., 1891, p. 289. Wikimedia Commons, 2015. https://commons.wikimedia.org/wiki/File:The_Bible_panorama,_or_The_Holy_Scriptures_in_picture_and_story_(1891)_(14804899633).jpg. Public domain.

483. Right: Nguyen, Marie-Lan, photographer. *Mithras Banquet Louvre Ma3441*. Wikimedia Commons, 2007. https://commons.wikimedia.org/wiki/File:Mithras_banquet_Louvre_Ma3441.jpg. Public domain.

489. Salman, Venera, photographer. *Kupala*. Shutterstock.com. https://www.shutterstock.com/image-photo/on-june-22-2016-kupala-festivalholiday-1446752678. Licensed from Shutterstock.com.

491. Javir, Boryslaw, photographer. *Rodnover Shrine in Kaluga, Russia*. Wikimedia Commons, 2013. https://commons.wikimedia.org/wiki/File:Rodnover_shrine_in_Kaluga,_Russia.png. GNU Free Documentation License, Version 1.2. https://commons.wikimedia.org/wiki/Commons:GNU_Free_Documentation_License,_version_1.2.

492. Union of Slavic Rodnover Communities / Союз Славянских Общин Славянской Родной Веры, ССО СРВ. *Shrine of the Temple of Svarozhich's Fire in Krasotinka, Kaluga on Earth Day 2017*, Krasotinka, Kaluga, Russia. Wikimedia Commons, 2018. https://commons.wikimedia.org/wiki/File:Shrine_of_the_Temple_of_Svarozhich's_Fire_in_Krasotinka,_Kaluga_on_Earth_Day_2017.jpg. CC BY-SA 4.0.

496. Lazarenka, Svetlana, photographer. *Men with a Kupala Post*. Shutterstock.com. https://www.shutterstock.com/image-photo/belarus-city-gomel-july-07-2018-1431659099. Licensed from Shutterstock.com.

497. Kryzhanivskyi, Viktor Solceslav (1950-2016). *Kupala*.

498. Top: Members of the Polish Rodnover Association. *Polish Rodnover Veche congregation (0)*, Poland. Wikimedia Commons, 2009. https://commons.wikimedia.org/wiki/File:Polish_Rodnover_Veche_congregation_(0).PNG. CC BY 2.0.

498. Bottom: Belova, Julia, photographer. *Girl Launching Flower Wreath*. Shutterstock.com. https://www.shutterstock.com/image-photo/blonde-girl-traditional-slave-dress-launching-789863320. Licensed from Shutterstock.com.

499. Top: Rak, Irina, photographer. *Festival Ringing Cedars 2014 June 22 Ирина 53*, Ustinka, Belgorod, Russia. Wikimedia Commons, 2014. https://commons.wikimedia.org/wiki/File:Festival Ringing Cedars 2014 June 22 Ирина 53.jpg. CC BY-SA 3.0.

499. Bottom: Loz, Lilija, photographer. *Dew Holiday Festival*. Shutterstock.com. https://www.shutterstock.com/image-photo/vilnius-lithuania-23-june-2018-saint-1406289098. Licensed from Shutterstock.com.

CHAPTER SEVENTEEN

502. Sura Ondrunar Publishing. *Symbolic Cross*. 2019.

503. © Sura Ondrunar Publishing.

Copyright Acknowledgments

Every reasonable effort has been made by the publisher to locate and acknowledge copyright owners, and obtain any necessary clearances. If any works requiring clearance have unwittingly been included, or any corrections need to be made, the publisher will be pleased to do so at the earliest opportunity.

Where works under a Creative Commons license have been used, an abbreviated form of the license name is listed. Full details of the Creative Commons (CC) licenses may be viewed here https://creativecommons.org licenses.

TEXTUAL ACKNOWLEDGMENTS

Copyrighted texts quoted in this book are listed alphabetically by title of work.

"A History of Monks Mound," © 2008 Vince Barrows.

"Abydos, the Osireion and Egyptian Sacred Science," © 2000 Vincent Bridges, https://vincentbridges.com/post/145759129272/abydos-the-osireion-and-egyptian-sacred-science.

Aku-Aku: The Secret of Easter Island, © 1957 Thor Heyerdahl, Chicago: Rand McNally & Company, English edition © 1958 George Allen & Unwin Ltd.

American Indians in the Pacific, © 1952 Thor Heyerdahl, London: George Allen & Unwin.

"Ancient Alignment in the Andes Hints at a Lost Global High Culture," © 2016 Dave Truman, GrahamHancock.com, http://grahamhancock.com/trumand1/.

The Ancient Egyptian Pyramid Texts, © 1969 R. O. Faulkner, Oxford University Press.

"The Ancient Sacred Fire of Yajna," © 2004 Swami Muktananda Saraswati, YOGA, http://www.yog-amag.net/archives/2004/bmar04/ancient.shtml.

"Angkor Secrets to Be Lost in a Sound and Light Show 'Insult,'" ©1995 Eleanor Mannikka, The Phnom Penh Post, https://www.phnompenhpost.com/national/angkor-secrets-be-lost-sound-and-light-show-insult.

Angkor Wat: Time, Space, and Kingship, © 1996 Eleanor Mannikka, Honolulu: University of Hawaii Press 1996, 2000.

"Arkaim: Russia's Ancient City & the Arctic Origin of Civilisation," © 2008 Victoria LePage, New Dawn Magazine, https://www.newdawnmagazine.com/articles/arkaim-russias-ancient-city-the-arctic-origin-of-civilisation.

"AUM," New World Encyclopedia contributors and contributors of the Wikimedia Foundation, 2019, https://www.newworldencyclopedia.org/entry/AUM, under Creative Commons license CC BY-SA 3.0.

"The Bearded Gods Speak," © 1971 Thor Heyerdahl, in *The Quest for America*, Geoffrey Ashe, New York: Praeger Publishers.

Bhagavad Gita: The Scripture of Mankinda, translation © 1984 Swami Tapasyananda, Chennai: Sri Ramakrishna Math.

"Biography," © 2011 Charles Ross, Charles Ross Studio, http://charlesrossstudio.com/biography/.

The Book of Chilam Balam of Chumayel, translation © 1933 Ralph L. Roys, Washington D.C.: Carnegie Institution.

"The Book of: The Hidden Chamber ca. 1426 BCE or : the Twelve Hours of the Night and the Midnight Mystery, Section 3, The Summary of the Amduat, The Twelve Hours : A Commentary." © 2010 Wim van den Dungen, MAAT.sofiatopia.org, December 7, 2010. http://www.sofiatopia.org/maat/hidden_chamber03.htm.

The Book of Taliesin. © 2019 Rowan Williams and Gwyneth Lewis, London: Penguin Books Ltd., 2019.

"Ceiba Pentandra: The Sacred Tree of the Maya," © 2019 Nicoletta Maestri, ThoughtCo, https://www.thoughtco.com/ceiba-pentandra-sacred-tree-maya-171615.

Contemporary Maya Spirituality: The Ancient Ways Are Not Lost, © 2006 Jean Molesky-Poz, Austin: University of Texas Press.

The Crystal Sun: Rediscovering a Lost Technology of the Ancient World, © 2000 Robert K. G. Temple, London: Random House/Century.

Daily Invocations, © 2008 Swami Krishnananda, Risikesh: The Divine Life Trust Society, www.swami-krishnananda.org. Reproduced with permission.

Death as an Enemy: According to Ancient Egyptian Conceptions, © 1960 J. Zandee, translated by W. F. Klasens, Leiden: E.J. Brill.

The Devi Gita: The Song of the Goddess: A Translation, Annotation, and Commentary, © 1998 Cheever Mackenzie Brown, Albany: State University of New York Press.

Devi Mahatmyam, translation © 1953 Swami Jagadiswarananda, Chennai: Sri Ramakrishna Math.

"Discoveries provide evidence of a celestial procession at Stonehenge," © 2011 Vince Gaffney and Henry Chapman, University of Birmingham, https://www.birmingham.ac.uk/news/latest/2011/11/25Nov-Discoveries-provide-evidence-of-a-celestial-procession-at-Stonehenge.aspx.

The Divine Comedy: Paradiso, translation © 1984 Allen Mandelbaum, Everyman's Library 1995.

"Durga," Wikipedia contributors, https://en.wikipedia.org/wiki/Durga, under Creative Commons license CC BY-SA 3.0.

"Durga Chalisa" (lyrics traditional), English translation © 2018 INDIF.COM, http://www.indif.com/nri/chalisas/durgachalisa/durgachalisa_meaning.asp.

The Earliest Christian Hymnbook: The Odes of Solomon, translation © 2009 James H. Charlesworth, Oregon: Wipf and Stock. Used by permission of Wipf and Stock Publishers. www.wipfandstock.com.

"The East Passage and Chamber at Knowth," © 2016 Martin Byrne, The Sacred Island, http://www.carrowkeel.com/sites/boyne/knowth3.html.

"El Inti Raymi Inkaico: La Verdadera Historia de la Gran Fiesta Del Sol," © 2005 Juan José Vega and Luis Guzmán Palomino, Museo de Arqueología y Antropología, http://sisbib.unmsm.edu.pe/bibvirtual/publicaciones/antropologia/2003_N01/a05.htm.

The Essene Gospel of Peace: Book Four, translation © 1981 Edmond Bordeaux Szekely, International Biogenic Society.

The Essene Gospel of Peace: Book One, translation © 1981 Edmond Bordeaux Szekely, International Biogenic Society.

The Essene Gospel of Peace: Book Three, translation © 1981 Edmond Bordeaux Szekely, International Biogenic Society.

The Essene Gospel of Peace: Book Two, translation © 1981 Edmond Bordeaux Szekely, International Biogenic Society.

"The Evidence from Knossos on the Minoan Calendar," G. Henriksson and M. Blomberg, Mediterranean Archaeology and Archaeometry, 2011, http://maajournal.com/Issues/2011/Vol11-1/7_Blomberg.pdf, under Creative Commons license CC BY 4.0.

"Exploring Geographic and Geometric Relationships Along a Line of Ancient Sites Around the World," © 2001 Jim Alison, GrahamHancock.com, https://grahamhancock.com/geographic-geometric-relationships-alisonj/.

The Golden Ass or Metamorphoses, translation © 1998, 2004 E. J. Kenny, London: Penguin Books.

The Gospel of Judas, translation © 2006 Rodolphe Kasser, Marvin Meyer, and Gregor Wurst, in collaboration with François Gaudard, Washington D.C.: National Geographic Society.

The Gospel of the Kailedy, © 1998 The Hope Trust, © 2014 The Culdian Trust, New Zealand: The Culdain Trust, 2014.

"Gurdjieff's Search for Esoteric Knowledge," © 2010 Learning Institute for Growth, Healing and Transformation, http://gurdjiefffourthway.org/pdf/search.pdf.

Heaven's Mirror: Quest for the Lost Civilization. © 1998 Graham Hancock and Santha Faiia. New York: Three Rivers Press, 1998.

Hermetica, translated by Brian P. Copenhaver, © 1992 Cambridge University Press, Kindle Edition.

The Hero Twins: Myth and Image, © 1989 Michael D. Coe, in *The Maya Vase Book A Corpus of Rollout Photographs of Maya Vases (Maya Vase Book) Vol. 1*, Justin Kerr, New York: Kerr Associates.

Hua Hu Ching: The Unknown Teachings of Lao Tzu, translation © 1992 Brian Browne Walker, New York: HarperCollins, 1995.

In Praise of the Goddess: The Devimahatmya and Its Meaning, translation © 2003 David Nelson, Berwick: Nicolas-Hays.

Jackal at the Shaman's Gate, © 1991 Terrence DuQuesne, London: Darengo Publications.

The Jackal Divinities of Egypt, © 2005 Terrence DuQuesne, London: Darengo Publications.

The Kolbrin, © 1998 The Hope Trust, © 2014 The Culdian Trust, New Zealand: The Culdian Trust, 2014. Reproduced with permission.

"The Lascaux Cave: A Prehistoric Sky-Map..." © 2008 Chantal Jègues-Wolkiewiez, Pedro Lima and Stephane Begoin-Pascal Goetgheluck, https://issuu.com/lightmediation/docs/the_lascaux_cave___a_prehistoric_sky-map_3390.

Maha Calisa Samgraha, translated by Pt. Atma Ram Sharma, edited by Dr. R. C. Prasad, revised by Dr. G. P. Bhatt, © 1994 Motilal Banarsidass Publishers Private Limited, Dehli: Motilal Banarsidass, 1994.

"Mapping the Sphinx," © 2005 Ancient Egypt Research Associates, http://www.aeraweb.org/sphinx-project/mapping-the-sphinx/.

"Megalithic New Zealand," © 2000 Martin Doutré, Ancient Celtic New Zealand, http://www.celticnz.co.nz/mnz_pt1.html. Reproduced with permission.

Mount Carmel Novena, © 1947 Daniel A. Lord, St Louis: Queen's Work.

"My Experience in Coma," © 2017 Dr. Eben Alexander, http://ebenalexander.com/about/my-experience-in-coma.

The Mysteries of Mithras, © 2005 Payam Nabaraz, Rochester: Inner Traditions.

Myth and Symbol in Ancient Egypt, © 1959 R. T. Rundle Clark, London: Thames and Hudson.

The Nag Hammadi Library in English, edited by James M. Robinson, San Francisco: HarperCollins, 1990. Copyright © 1978, 1988 by E. J. Brill, Leiden, The Netherlands. Reproduced with permission.

"The Nazca Lines of Peru," © 2000 Martin Doutré, Ancient Celtic New Zealand, http://www.celticnz.co.nz/Nazca/Nazca1.htm. Reproduced with permission.

"Neurosurgeon Dr. Eben Alexander's Near-death experience defies medical model of consciousness," © 2011 Skeptiko, Dr. Eben Alexander, https://skeptiko.com/154-neurosurgeon-dr-eben-alexander-near-death-experience.

"Novruz, The Fire of Spring." © English Zoroastrian, http://www.zoroastrian.org.uk/vohuman/Article/Noruz The Fire of Spring.htm.

Offering Flowers, Feeding Skulls: Popular Goddess Worship in West Bengal, © 2004 June McDaniel, Oxford University Press.

The Orion Zone, © 2007 Gary A. David, Kempton: Adventures Unlimited Press.

Paracelsus: Selected Writings, translated by Norbert Guterman, edited by Jolande Jacobi, Princeton: Princeton University Press, 1995. © 1951 Bollingen Foundation Inc., © 1979 renewed by Princeton University Press.

The Phoenician Solar Theology: An Investigation into the Phoenician Opinion of the Sun Found in Julian's Hymn to King Helios by Joseph Azize. © 2005 Gorgias Press LLC, New Jersey: Gorgias Press, 2005. https://b-ok.cc/book/2474368/4bdf0f.

The Poetic Edda, translation © 1996 Carolyne Larrington, Oxford University Press, 1999.

Popol Vuh: Sacred Book of the Quiché Maya People, translation © 2003 Allen J. Christenson, Norman: University of Oklahoma Press.

Proof of Heaven: A Neurosurgeon's Journey into the Afterlife, © 2012 Eben Alexander, M.D., New York: Simon & Schuster 2012.

The Pyramid Texts, translation © 1952 Samuel A. B. Mercer, New York: Longmans, Green & Co.

Religion and Magic in Ancient Egypt, © 2002 Rosalie David, London: Penguin Group.

"Ring O' Brodgar, Orkney Islands: Gateway to the Americas," © 2000 Martin Doutré, Ancient Celtic New Zealand, http://www.celticnz.co.nz/Brodgar/Brodgar 1.htm. Reproduced with permission.

The Royal Commentaries of the Incas and General History of Peru, translated by Harold V. Livermore, Indianapolis: Hackett Publishing Company, 2006. © General Secretariat of the Organization of American States, © 2006 Hackett Publishing Company.

Sacred Earth: Places of Peace and Power, © 2007 Martin Gray, New York: Sterling Publishing Co.

"The Sacred Fire and Agni," © 2012 American Institute of Vedic Studies. https://vedanet.com/2012/06/13/the-sacred-fire-and-agni/.

Samba-Purana, translation © 2013 V. C. Srivastava, Delhi: Parimal Publications.

Scripture quotations taken from *The Holy Bible*, New International Version® NIV® Copyright © 1973 1978 1984 2011 by Biblica, Inc.™ Used by permission. All rights reserved worldwide.

Scripture quotations taken from the New American Standard Bible® (NASB), Copyright © 1960, 1962, 1963, 1968, 1971, 1972, 1973, 1975, 1977, 1995 by The Lockman Foundation. Used by permission. www.Lockman.org.

The Secret of the Golden Flower, translated by Richard Wilhelm, translated from German to English by Cary F. Baynes, San Diego: Harcourt Brace & Company, 1962. © 1931, 1962.

The Secret Teachings of All Ages, © 1928 Manly P. Hall, San Francisco: H.S. Crocker Company.

The Seed of Yggdrasill: Deciphering the Hidden Messages in Old Norse Myths Heritage edition, © 2016 Maria Kvilhaug, Denmark: Whyte Tracks.

The Stones of Time: Calendars, Sundials, and Stone Chambers of Ancient Ireland by Martin Brennan published by Inner Traditions International and Bear & Company, ©1994. All rights reserved. http://www.Innertraditions.com. Reprinted with permission of publisher.

"Sun worship," © 2019 Encyclopædia Britannica, Inc., https://www.britannica.com/topic/sun-worship.

Translation of the Unas Pyramid Texts by R. O. Faulkner, Alexandre Piankoff, and Louis Speleers, Pyramid Texts Online, Vincent Brown, https://www.pyramidtextsonline.com/translation.html. © 2002-2019 Vincent Brown.

"Triglav, Trojan, Trinity, Trimurti, Agni," © 2014 Old European Culture, http://oldeuropeanculture.blogspot.com/2014/07/triglav-trojan-trinity-trimurti-agni.html.

True Transmission of the Golden Elixir, translation © 1992 Douglas Wile, Albany: State University of New York Press.

The Upanishads, 2nd ed., translated by Eknath Easwaran, Tomales: Nilgiri Press, 2007. © 1987, 2007 by The Blue Mountain Center of Meditation. Reprinted by permission of Nilgiri Press, P. O. Box 256, Tomales, Ca 94971, www.easwaran.org.

The Upanishads: Breath from the Eternal, translated by Swami Prabhavanada Frederick Manchester, New York: Signet Classic, 2002. © 1948, 1957; copyright renewed The Vedanta Society of Southern California.

"Urals intends to develop pilgrimage to the 'Russian Stonehenge,'" © 2008 Stanislav Grigoryev, Interfax, http://www.interfax-religion.com/?act=news&div=4653.

The Vedic Experience Mantramanjari: Anthology of the Vedas for Modern Man and Contemporary Celebration, © 1977 Raimundo Panikkar, Delhi: Motilal Banarsidass Publishers, 2001.

The Wandering of the Soul, translation by Alexandre Piankoff, Princeton University Press, 1974. © Bollingen Foundation.

The Way of Hermes: New Translations of The Corpus Hermeticum and The Definitions of Hermes Trismegistus to Asclepius, translation © 2004 Clement Salaman, Dorine van Oyen, William D. Wharton, Jean-Pierre Mahé, Rochester: Inner Traditions, 2004.

"West and East in Maya Thought: Death and Rebirth at Palenque and Tulum," © 1974 Arthur G. Miller, in *Primera Mesa Redonda de Palenque, Part II*, edited by Merle Greene Robertson, Pebble Beach, California: Robert Louis Stevenson School, Pre-Columbian Art Research.

The White Indians of Nivaria, © 2010 Gordon Kennedy, Mecca: Nivaria Press.

"Why a Pyramid? Pyramid Religion," © 2003 James P. Allen, in *The Treasures of the Pyramids*, edited by Zahi Hawass, Italy: White Star.

The Yajur Veda, translation © 1959 Devi Chand, Hoshiarpur: All India Dayanand Salvation Mission.

"Yasna Haptanhaiti," in *The Heritage of Zarathushtra: A New Translation of His Gathas*, translation © 1994 Helmut Humbach, Pallan Ichaporia, Heidelberg: Universitätsverlag Winter, 1994.

IMAGE ACKNOWLEDGMENTS

Copyrighted images used in this book are listed by page number.

All Creative Commons (CC) works in this book are derivatives which have been processed with various image adjustments.

PREFACE

6. Right: Luidger, photographer. *Statue of Coatlicue*. National Anthropology Museum, Mexico City, Wikimedia Commons, 2004. https://commons.wikimedia.org/wiki/File:20041229-Coatlicue (Museo Nacional de Antropología) MQ-3.jpg. CC BY-SA 3.0.

CHAPTER ONE

13. Dunn, Andrew, photographer. *Summer Solstice 2005 Sunrise over Stonehenge 01*. Wikimedia Commons, 2005. https://commons.wikimedia.org/wiki/File:Summer_Solstice_2005_Sunrise_over_Stonehenge_01.jpg. CC BY-SA 2.0.

24. Upper collage image 1: Egorov, Valery, photographer. *View of West Facade of Chartres Cathedral*. Shutterstock.com. https://www.shutterstock.com/image-photo/view-west-facade-chartres-cathedral-1076537756. Licensed from Shutterstock.com.

24. Upper collage image 2: HelloRF Zcool, photographer. *Guangzhou Shushe Sacred Heart Cathedral*. Shutterstock.com. https://www.shutterstock.com/image-photo/guangzhou-shushe-sacred-heart-cathedral-1173463153. Licensed from Shutterstock.com.

24. Upper collage image 3: F11photo, photographer. *St. John the Baptist Cathedral in Savannah Georgia USA*, Shutterstock.com. https://www.shutterstock.com/image-photo/st-john-baptist-cathedral-savannah-georgia-493931884. Licensed from Shutterstock.com.

24. Upper collage image 4: Ravi, Joe, photographer. *St. Philomena's Church Is a Catholic Church Built in Honour of St. Philomena in Mysore*. Shutterstock.com. https://www.shutterstock.com/image-photo/guangzhou-shushe-sacred-heart-cathedral-1173463153. Licensed from Shutterstock.com.

24. Center collage, image 1: Hendrikse, Boyd, photographer. *Cristo de la Concordia (Christ of Peace) Is a Statue of Jesus Christ Located atop San Pedro Hill, to the East of Cochabamba, Bolivia*. Shutterstock.com. https://www.shutterstock.com/image-photo/cristo-de-la-concordia-christ-peace-192340583. Licensed from Shutterstock.com.

24. Center collage, image 2: Petrova, Maria, photographer. *Famous Statue of the Christ the Reedemer, Lubango Angola*. Shutterstock.com. https://www.shutterstock.com/image-photo/famous-statue-christ-reedemer-lubango-angola-21157789. Licensed from Shutterstock.com.

24. Center collage, image 3: Catay, photographer. *Jesus Statue in Beirut 4 February 2018*. Shutterstock.com. https://www.shutterstock.com/image-photo/jesus-statue-beirut-4-february-2018-1041517408. Licensed from Shutterstock.com.

24. Center collage, image 4: Lashkov, Fedor, photographer. *The Christian Park in Essentuki*. Shutterstock.com. https://www.shutterstock.com/image-photo/christian-park-essentuki-669164776. Licensed from Shutterstock.com.

24. Lower collage, top left: Bon, Jerome, photographer. *Great Pyramid of Giza*. Wikimedia Commons, 2015. https://commons.wikimedia.org/wiki/File:Great_Pyramid_of_Giza_(2427530661).jpg. CC BY 2.0.

24. Lower collage, top center: Skubasteve834, photographer. *Monks Mound*. Wikimedia Commons, 2013. https://commons.wikimedia.org/wiki/File:Monks_Mound_in_July.JPG. CC BY-SA-3.0.

24. Lower collage, second left: Schwen, Daniel, photographer. *Chichen Itza*. Wikimedia Commons, 2009. https://commons.wikimedia.org/wiki/File:Chichen_Itza_3.jpg. CC BY-SA 4.0.

24. Lower collage, second right: Ximenez, Pedro, photographer. *Pyramid Güimar*. Wikimedia Commons, 2009. https://commons.wikimedia.org/wiki/File:Pyramide Güimar.jpg. CC BY-SA 2.0.

24. Lower collage, third center: Jagadeesan, Madhuranthakan, photographer. *Sri Kanteshwara Temple Gopuram*. Wikimedia Commons, 2016. https://commons.wikimedia.org/wiki/File:N-KA-B159_Srikanteshwara_Temple_Gopuram_Nanjangud.jpg. CC BY-SA 4.0.

25. Upper collage, top left: Saamiblog: http://saamiblog.blogspot.com, photographer. *Buckle from Oseberg Vikingship Buddha 3*. Wikimedia Commons, 2009. https://commons.wikimedia.org/wiki/File:Buckle_from_Oseberg_Vikingship_Buddha_3.JPG. CC BY-SA 3.0.

25. Upper collage, top center: Chirita, Cristian, photographer. *Archeological Artefacts in Sozopol Museum*. Sozopol Museum, Wikimedia Commons, 2011. https://commons.wikimedia.org/wiki/File:Sozopol_Archaeological_Museum_IMG_4214.JPG. GNU Free Documentation License, Version 1.2. https://commons.wikimedia.org/wiki/Commons:GNU_Free_Documentation_License,_version_1.2.

25. Upper collage, top right: Dbachmann, photographer. *Samarra Bowl*. Pergamonmuseum, Berlin, Wikimedia Commons, 2010. https://en.wikipedia.org/wiki/File:Samarra_bowl.jpg. CC BY-SA 4.0.

25. Upper collage, center: PHGCOM, photographer. *Etruscan Pendant with Swastika Symbols Bolsena Italy 700 BCE to 650 BCE*. Louvre Museum, Wikimedia Commons, 2010. https://commons.wikimedia.org/wiki/File:Etruscan_pendant_with_swastika_symbols_Bolsena_Italy_700_BCE_to_650_BCE.jpg. CC BY-SA 3.0.

25. Upper collage, bottom left: Шнапс, photographer. Скоба для стрел (*Bracket for Arrows*). Wikimedia Commons, 2012. https://commons.wikimedia.org/wiki/File:Скоба_для_стрел.JPG. CC BY-SA 3.0.

25. Upper collage, bottom center: Tylas at English Wikipedia, photographer. *Zionpictographs*. Zion National Park, Wikimedia Commons, 2006. https://commons.wikimedia.org/wiki/File:Zionpictographs.jpg. CC BY-SA 3.0.

25. Upper collage, bottom right: Before My Ken, photographer. *Indus Valley Civilization Seals*. British Museum, Wikimedia Commons, 2009. https://commons.wikimedia.org/wiki/File:IndusValleySeals_swastikas.JPG. CC BY-SA 3.0.

25. Lower collage, top left: Pattych at English Wikipedia, photographer. *MocheBeardedMen*. Wikimedia Commons, 2010. https://en.wikipedia.org/wiki/File:MocheBeardedMen.jpg. CC BY-SA 3.0.

25. Lower collage, bottom left: Fortuna, Roberto, and Kira Ursem, photographers. *Gundestrup Cauldron*. Nationalmuseet, Wikimedia Commons, 2016. https://en.wikipedia.org/wiki/File:Gundestrupkedlen-_00054_(cropped).jpg. CC BY-SA 3.0.

31. Lyokin, photographer. *Fire Temple Ateshgah in Azerbaijan*. https://www.shutterstock.com/image-photo/fire-temple-ateshgah-azerbaijan-1220800237. Licensed from Shutterstock.com.

34. Masalskis, Mantas, photographer. *Romuvan Ceremony (6)*. Wikimedia Commons, 2009. https://commons.wikimedia.org/wiki/File:Romuvan ceremony (6).PNG. CC BY 2.0.

38. Julius, Albert Stephen, artist. *Set of color dispersion through prism*. Shutterstock.com. https://www.shutterstock.com/image-vector/set-color-dispersion-through-prism-triangular-1950923059. Licensed from Shutterstock.com

41. Rama, photographer. *Taperet Stele E52*, between 1065 and 664 BC. Department of Egyptian Antiquities of the Louvre, Wikimedia Commons, 2007. https://commons.wikimedia.org/wiki/File:Taperet_stele_E52_mp3h9201.jpg. CC BY-SA 3.0 France.

49. Top-right: Image created for book based on web article by Tsai, Allen. *The Origin of Chinese Yin Yang Symbol*. https://www.chinesefortunecalendar.com/YinYang.htm.

50. Bottom: *Daily Path of the Sun in the Sky* image created for the book, based on image from https://www.umass.edu/sunwheel/pages/design.html.

51. Bottom: Roe, Herb. *Mound 72 Woodhenge Diagram HRoe 2013*. Wikimedia Commons, 2013. https://commons.wikimedia.org/wiki/File:Mound_72_Woodhenge_diagram_HRoe_2013.jpg. CC BY-SA 3.0

52. Bottom left: Bjoertvedt, photographer. *Nordens Ark in Sotenäs, Sweden*, 2013. Wikimedia Commons, 2013. https://commons.wikimedia.org/wiki/File:Soten%C3%A4s_Tossene_73-1_Aaby_ID_10161200730001_IMG_8005.JPG. CC BY-SA 3.0.

54. Top: Geralt. *Cross Christ Faith*. Pixabay. https://pixabay.com/photos/cross-christ-faith-god-jesus-2713354. Used with permission.

54. Center: Diagram based on Gothika. *The Seasons and Some of Earth's Orbit's Characteristics*. Wikimedia Commons, 2010. https://en.wikipedia.org/wiki/File:Seasons1.svg. CC BY-SA 3.0.

56. Top: Wilkowski, Ratomir. *ReceBogaSwargi*. Wikimedia Commons, 2010. https://commons.wikimedia.org/wiki/File:ReceBogaSwargi.svg. CC BY 3.0.

56. Bottom left: Dbachmann, photographer. *Samarra Bowl*. Pergamonmuseum, Berlin, Wikimedia Commons, 2010. https://en.wikipedia.org/wiki/File:Samarra_bowl.jpg. CC BY-SA 4.0.
56. Bottom right: Roe, Herb. *Chromesun 4 Uktenas Design*. Wikimedia Commons, 2008. https://commons.wikimedia.org/wiki/File:Chromesun_4_uktenas_design.jpg. CC BY-SA 3.0.
57. Top: Image created for book based on illustration in article by Smelyakov, Sergey. *Crucifying the Earth on the Galactic Cross*. http://www.astrotheos.com/Page8.htm.
57. Bottom: Infinity symbol created with unicode U+236.
58. Bottom: Sura Ondrunar Publishing. *Double Spiral*. 2016.
59. Top: Brennan, Martin. Double spiral illustration in *The Stones of Time*, Vermont: Inner Traditions International, 1994, p. 190.
59. Bottom Left: Sura Ondrunar Publishing. *Artist's Impression of Tarim Mummy Full Facial Painting*. 2018.
59. Bottom right: Robley, Major-General G. 1820 illustration of Maori chief Hongi Hika in *Maori Wars of the Nineteenth Century* by S. Percy Smith, Whitcombe & Tombs Limited, 1910. The New Zealand Electronic Text Collection, http://www.nzetc.org/etexts/SmiMaor/SmiMaorP001a.jpg. CC BY-SA 3.0 NZ.
60. Top: Nomadtales, photographer. *Newgrange Entrance Stone*. Newgrange, Ireland, Wikimedia Commons, 2005. https://commons.wikimedia.org/wiki/File:Newgrange_Entrance_Stone.jpg. CC BY-SA 3.0.
60. Bottom: DjSadhu. Spiraling rotation of the planets in *Solar System 2.0 – the Helical Model*. Youtube.com, 2015. https://youtu.be/mvgaxQGPg7I. Used by permission.
61. Bottom: CWitte. *Venus Pentagram*. Wikimedia Commons, 2007. https://commons.wikimedia.org/wiki/File:Venus_pentagramm.svg. CC BY-SA 3.0.
62. Top: Image created for book based on cobaltduck. *Is There Anything Significant about the Cross-Quarter Days, in Terms of a Sinusoid?* Math.Stockechange. com, 2016. https://math.stackexchange.com/questions/1603545/is-there-anything-significant-about-the-cross-quarter-days-in-terms-of-a-sinuso.
63. Center: DiegoAma. *Romuva Flag*. Wikimedia Commons, 2019. https://commons.wikimedia.org/wiki/File:Romuva_Flag.png. CC BY-SA 4.0.
64. Top: Luiluilui, photographer. *Kuelap Steine*, Kuelap Fortress, Peru. Wikimedia Commons, 2010. https://commons.wikimedia.org/wiki/File:Kuelap_Steine.JPG. CC BY-SA 3.0.
64. Bottom: Gnomon image created for book based on illustration by Martin Brennan in *The Stones of Time*, Vermont: Inner Traditions International, 1994, p. 190.
65. Top: Sauber, Wolfgang, photographer. *AMI - Goldene Doppelax*, golden Minoan labrys. Archaeological Museum in Herakleion, Wikimedia Commons, 2009. https://en.wikipedia.org/wiki/File:AMI_-_Goldene_Doppelaxt.jpg . CC BY-SA 3.0.
66. Top: Lang Antonsen, Kenny Arne. *Cucuteni-Trypillian Temple*. Wikimedia Commons, 2019. https://commons.wikimedia.org/wiki/File:Cucuteni-trypillian_temple.jpg. CC BY-SA 4.0.
66. Bottom: Pringle, Lucy, photographer. *Crop circle 21st June 2001, East Field, Wiltshire, 2001*. https://cropcircles.lucypringle.co.uk/photos/2001/uk2001ar.shtml#pic2. © Lucy Pringle, used by permission.
68. Top: *Cross of the Sun* diagram created for book based on Old European Culture. *Two Crosses*. 2016. https://oldeuropeanculture.blogspot.com/2016/07/two-crosses.html.
68. Bottom: *Cross of the Earth* diagram created for book based on Old European Culture. *Two Crosses*. 2016. https://oldeuropeanculture.blogspot.com/2016/07/two-crosses.html.
78. © Sura Ondrunar Publishing.

CHAPTER TWO

84. Michaelica. Libra sign, *Set of Zodiac Symbol Icons*. Shutterstock.com. https://www.shutterstock.com/image-vector/set-zodiac-symbol-icons-vector-illustration-231315553. Licensed from Shutterstock.com.
89. Brooke, Simon, photographer. *The Wicker Man Burns - Geograph.org.uk*. Wikimedia Commons, 2010. https://commons.wikimedia.org/wiki/File:The_Wicker_Man_burns_-_geograph.org.uk_-_50168.jpg. CC BY-SA 2.0.

91. Underwood & Underwood. *Khufu's Sarcophagus, Broken by Robbers, in the Sepulchre-Chamber of the Great Pyramid, Egypt*, 1904. Travelers in the Middle East Archive (TIMEA), Wikimedia Commons, 2010. https://commons.wikimedia.org/wiki/File:Khufu's sarcophagus, broken by robbers, in the sepulchre-chamber of the Great Pyramid, Egypt. View two men by sarcophagus. (25) (1904) - front - TIMEA.jpg. CC BY-SA 2.5.

92. Bodsworth, Jon, photographer. *Descendant-Grande-Pyramide*. Wikimedia Commons, 2007. https://commons.wikimedia.org/wiki/File:Descendant-grande-pyramide.jpg. © Jon Bodsworth, used by permission.

95. Eichmann, Gerd, photographer. *Valley of the Kings in Egypt*, Grave 34, 1982. Wikimedia Commons, 2020. https://commons.wikimedia.org/wiki/File:Tal_der_Koenige-48-Grab_34-Fluss_durch_4_Register-1982-gje.jpg. CC BY-SA 4.0.

98. Sura Ondrunar Publishing. *Double Spiral*. 2016.

99. Right: Image created for book based on web article by Tsai, Allen. *The Origin of Chinese Yin Yang Symbol.* https://www.chinesefortunecalendar.com/YinYang.htm.

106. Top: Sewell, Ian, photographer. *Ahu-Akivi-1*. Wikimedia Commons, 2006. https://commons.wikimedia.org/wiki/File:Ahu-Akivi-1.JPG. CC BY-SA 3.0.

106. Bottom: Weinstein, Brett, photographer. *Golden Mask of Psusennes I*. Wikimedia Commons, 2009. https://commons.wikimedia.org/wiki/File:Golden_Mask_of_Psusennes_I.jpg. CC BY-SA 2.5.

107. Center: D_odin, photographer. *Mahavishnu Settles on the Serpent Anantasheesh and Lakshmi Massages His Feet. Sculpture of the Supreme God Vishnu in Hinduism*. Shutterstock.com. https://www.shutterstock.com/image-photo/mahavishnu-settles-on-serpent-anantasheesh-lakshmi-754817707. Licensed from Shutterstock.com.

109. Left: Woelber, Paxson, photographer. *The El Castillo Pyramid at Chichen Itza, Mexico*. Wikimedia Commons, 2014. https://commons.wikimedia.org/wiki/File:The_El_Castillo_Pyramid_at_Chichen_Itza,_Mexico.jpg. CC BY-SA 3.0.

110. Top: Klopacka, Jozef. *A Beautiful Oil Painting on Canvas of a Woman Goddess Lada as a Mighty Loving Guardian and Protective Spirit upon the Earth Portrait*. Shutterstock.com. https://www.shutterstock.com/image-illustration/beautiful-oil-painting-on-canvas-woman-244690525. Licensed from Shutterstock.

110. Bottom: TStein. Edited by Geek3. *Earth's Magnetic Field Confusion*. Wikimedia Commons, 2008, 2019. https://commons.wikimedia.org/wiki/File:Earths_Magnetic_Field_Confusion.svg. CC BY-SA 3.0.

116. Bottom left: Luidger, photographer. *Statue of Coatlicue.* National Anthropology Museum, Mexico City, Wikimedia Commons, 2010. https://commons.wikimedia.org/wiki/File:20041229-Coatlicue (Museo Nacional de Antropología) MQ-3.jpg. CC BY-SA 3.0.

116. Bottom right: Stormnight, photographer. *Sekhmet (British Museum)*. British Museum, Wikimedia Commons, 2008. https://commons.wikimedia.org/wiki/File:Sekhmet (British Museum).jpg. CC BY-SA 4.0.

117. Sailko, photographer. *Akkadian Period, Black Limestone Seal with Ishtar with Foot on a Lion's Back and a Devout, 2350-2150 ac*. Oriental Institute Museum, Wikimedia Commons, 2018. https://commons.wikimedia.org/wiki/File:Periodo_accadico,_sigillo_in_calcare_nero_con_ishtar_con_piede_su_schiena_di_leone_e_una_devota,_2350-2150_ac_ca.jpg. CC BY 3.0.

CHAPTER THREE

129. Shira, photographer. *Newgrange*. Wikimedia Commons, 2006. https://commons.wikimedia.org/wiki/File:Newgrange.JPG. CC BY-SA 3.0.

130. Prabhat Kumar Verma, photographer. *Makar Sankranti Day during the Kumbh Mela, or Pitcher Festival in Allahabad (Prayagraj), Uttar Pradesh*. Shutterstock.com https://www.shutterstock.com/image-photo/allahabad-naga-sadhus-take-holy-dip-1285519654. Licensed from Shutterstock.com.

134. Top: Sura Ondrunar Publishing, composite image. *Winter Solstice Sunrise at Karnak*. Includes images from: moonfish8, *Ram-headed sphinxes, Karnak Temple, Luxor, Egypt*, https://www.shutterstock.com/image-photo/ramheaded-sphinxes-karnak-temple-luxor-egypt-179121524, Manish Upadhyay, *silhouette of bird flying in sunrise*, https://unsplash.com/photos/r4VJBODbMC8, Pagie page, *sunrise view*, https://unsplash.com/photos/vq-2SRf9fE8, Robert Thiemann, *Alaska Sunset*, https://unsplash.com/photos/3k0cTsHhQeE, zaie, *golden light*, https://www.freepik.com/free-vector/golden-light-shining-particles-bokeh-sparks-glare-with-highlight-effect_10817226.htm. Images licensed from shutterstock, unsplash, freepik.

COPYRIGHT ACKNOWLEDGMENTS

153. Deror avi, photographer. *Church of the Saviour on the Blood*. Wikimedia Commons, 2009. https://commons.wikimedia.org/wiki/File:Church_of_the_Saviour_on_the_Blood_IMG_7407.JPG. CC BY-SA 3.0.

155. Right: Leask, H.G., artist. *The Stone Circle*. In *Newgrange, Co. Meath - Brújna bóinne* by R. A. S. Macalister, Dublin : Published by the Stationery Office, 1929.

155. Bottom: White, Ethan Doyle, photographer. *Model of Mnajdra*, Ħaġar Qim/Mnajdra visitor's centre, southern Malta, 2017. Wikimedia Commons, 2017. https://commons.wikimedia.org/wiki/File:Model_of_Mnajdra.jpg. CC BY-SA 4.0.

156. Left: Branley, Stephen, photographer. *Calanais Stones*, 2008. Wikimedia Commons, 2011. https://commons.wikimedia.org/wiki/File:Calanais_Stones_-_geograph.org.uk_-_1236575.jpg. CC BY-SA 2.0.

158. Top: Renalias, Josep, photographer. *Torre de Glastonbury*. Wikimedia Commons, 2008. https://commons.wikimedia.org/wiki/File:Torre_de_Glastonbury.JPG. CC-BY-SA 3.0.

159. Dalbéra, Jean-Pierre, photographer. *Le Temple de Changu Narayan (Bhaktapur)*, Nepal. Wikimedia Commons, 2014. https://en.wikipedia.org/wiki/File:Le_temple_de_Changu_Narayan_(Bhaktapur)_(8567815983).jpg. CC BY 2.0

160. Liberato, Ricardo. *All Gizah Pyramids*. Wikimedia Commons, 2008. https://commons.wikimedia.org/wiki/File:Pyramids_at_Gizah.jpg. CC BY-SA 2.0.

164. Gallet, Herve. *Kin Soleil*. Wikimedia Commons, 2017. https://commons.wikimedia.org/wiki/File:KIN_Soleil.jpg. CC BY-SA 4.0.

CHAPTER FOUR

171. Markalexander100, photographer. *The Churning of the Ocean of Milk*, bas-relief on the south of the east wall of Angkor Wat's third enclosure. Wikimedia Commons, 2005. https://commons.wikimedia.org/wiki/File:Awatoceanofmilk01_-_color_corrected.JPG. CC BY-SA 3.0.

172. Heng, Kim, photographer. *Equinox at Angkor 21st March 2012*, Wikimedia Commons, 2012. https://commons.wikimedia.org/wiki/File:Equinox_at_Angkor_21st_March_2012.JPG. CC BY-SA 3.0.

174. Bgabel at wikivoyage, photographer. *TIB lhasa Sera Lebensrad*. Sera Monastery, Wikimedia Commons, 2010. https://commons.wikimedia.org/wiki/File:TIB-lhasa-sera-lebensrad.jpg. CC BY-SA 3.0.

175. Elishams, photographer. *Samudr Manthan*, Temple de Shri Krishna Pranami, Haridwar, India Wikimedia Commons, 2006. https://commons.wikimedia.org/wiki/File:Samudr_manthan.jpg. CC BY 2.5.

184. Top: Sura Ondrunar Publishing. *Cross of the Sun*. 2019.

188. Bkwillwm, photographer. *Knowth Entrance to Second Passage 2010*, Ireland. Wikimedia Commons, 2010. https://commons.wikimedia.org/wiki/File:Knowth_entrance_to_second_passage_2010.JPG. CC BY-SA 3.0.

195. Sura Ondrunar Publishing. *Sphinx as Anubis*. 2012.

197. Bottom: Néfermaât, photographer. Edited by JMCC1. *Statues of Hathor*. Luxor Museum, Wikimedia Commons, 2011. https://commons.wikimedia.org/wiki/File:GD-EG-Louxor-111-b.jpg. CC BY-SA 2.5.

198. World History Archive, photographer. *Goddess Nut Bending to Form the sky,* papyrus copy based on late Egyptian temple at Denderah. Alamy Stock Photo. https://www.alamy.com/stock-photo-egyptian-cosmos-goddess-nut-bending-to-form-the-sky-papyrus-copy-based-57303488.html. Licensed from Alamy Stock Photo.

199. Stroup, Kevin, photographer. *Knowth, Co. Meath, Ireland*. Wikimedia Commons, 2017. https://commons.wikimedia.org/wiki/File:Knowth,_Co._Meath,_Ireland_-_panoramio_(32).jpg. CC BY 3.0.

201. Top: Rosemania, photographer. *Silver Cauldron*, circa 150-0 BC, Gundestrup, Denmark. Historic Museum of Bern, Wikimedia Commons, 2009. https://commons.wikimedia.org/wiki/File:Silver_cauldron.jpg. CC BY 2.0.

201. Bottom: Thyssen, Malene, photographer, http://commons.wikimedia.org/wiki/User:Malene. *Gundestrup Cauldron*, Nationalmuseet, Denmark, 2004. Wikimedia Commons, 2005. https://commons.wikimedia.org/wiki/File:Gundestrupkarret3.jpg. CC BY-SA 3.0.

202. Schele, Linda. *Drawing of Plate Interior Showing the Rebirth of the Maize God from a Turtle Shell* SD-5505. *In Maya Cosmos: Three Thousand Years on the Shaman's Path*, by David A. Freidel, Linda Schele, and Joy Parker, New York: W. Morrow, 1993, p. 371, fig. 8:25b. Ancient Americas at LACMA, http://ancientamericas.org/collection/aa010550. © David Schele, used by permission on behalf of LACMA.

204. Laslovarga, photographer. *Tikal, Guatemala*. Wikimedia Commons, 2013. https://commons.wikimedia.org/wiki/File:Tikal,_Guatemala_Laslovarga14.JPG. CC BY-SA 30.

208. Tausch, Olaf. *Philae 13*, relief in the Isis Temple of Philae on the island of Agilkia, Egypt. Wikimedia Commons, 2014. https://commons.wikimedia.org/wiki/File:Philae_13.jpg. CC BY 3.0.

CHAPTER FIVE

209. Sura Ondrunar Publishing. *Sphinx as Anubis*. 2012.

211. Profberger at English Wikipedia, photographer. *Golden Wolf Small*. Wikimedia Commons, 2012. https://en.wikipedia.org/wiki/File:Golden_wolf_small.jpg. CC BY-SA 3.0.

212. Kocjan, Marek, photographer. *Great Sphinx of Giza 2*. Wikimedia Commons, 2009. https://commons.wikimedia.org/wiki/File:Great_Sphinx_of_Giza_2.jpg. CC BY-SA 3.0.

216. Left: Bodsworth, Jon, photographer. *Tutankhamun Jackal*. Wikimedia Commons, 2008. https://commons.wikimedia.org/wiki/File:Tutanhkamun_jackal.jpg. © Jon Bodsworth, used by permission.

219. Bottom: Andre, photographer. *Kist uit de 27- 31e Dynastie*. Flickr.com, 2009. https://www.flickr.com/photos/9987501@N08/3643941456. CC BY-NC-SA 2.0.

220. Gnuckx, photographer. *Italy Vatican*. Flickr.com, 2018. https://www.flickr.com/photos/34409164@N06/3492615876. CC BY 2.0.

226. Bronger, Torsten. *Leo Constellation Map*. Wikimeda Commons, 2003. https://commons.wikimedia.org/wiki/File:Leo_constellation_map.png. CC BY-SA 3.0.

227. Left: RsAzevedo, photographer. *Osireion at Abydos*. Wikimeda Commons, 2008. https://commons.wikimedia.org/wiki/File:Osireion_at_Abydos.jpg. CC BY-SA 3.0.

227. Right: Mayer, Daniel, photographer. *Giza Plateau - Great Sphinx - inside Temple*. Wikimeda Commons, 2008. https://commons.wikimedia.org/wiki/File:Giza_Plateau_-_Great_Sphinx_-_inside_temple.JPG. CC BY-SA 4.0.

229. English Wikipedia user Davkal, photographer. *Orion – Pyramids*. Wikimedia Commons, 2009. https://commons.wikimedia.org/wiki/File:Orion_-_pyramids.jpg. CC BY-SA 3.0.

230. Budge, E. A. Wallace. *The Great Pyramid, Showing Passages and Mummy Chambers*. In *The Nile: Notes for Travellers in Egypt*, London: Harrison and Sons, 1902, p. 100. Travelers in the Middle East Archive (TIMEA), Wikimedia Commons, 2010. https://commons.wikimedia.org/wiki/File:The_Great_Pyramid,_showing_passages_and_mummy_chambers._(1902)_-_TIMEA.jpg. Licensed from Travelers in the Middle East Archive (TIMEA). CC BY-SA 2.5.

231. Left: Storch, Hedwig, photographer. *Karnak Temple 9456*. Wikimedia Commons, 2009. https://commons.wikimedia.org/wiki/File:Karnak_temple_9456.JPG. Creative Commons BY-SA 3.0.

231. Right: Pal1983, photographer. *Small Sphinx with the Head of a Jackal*. Shutterstock.com https://www.shutterstock.com/image-photo/small-sphinx-head-jackal-ramesseum-memorial-422367220. Licensed from Shutterstock.com.

235. Hajor, photographer. *Egypt.LuxorTemple.03*. Wikimedia Commons, 2005. https://commons.wikimedia.org/wiki/File:Egypt.LuxorTemple.03.jpg. CC BY-SA 3.0.

237. Top: Ollermann, Hans, photographer. *Akhenaten as a Sphinx*. Kestner Museum, Germany, Wikimedia Commons, 2008. https://commons.wikimedia.org/wiki/File:Akhenaten_as_a_Sphinx_(Kestner_Museum).jpg. CC BY 2.0.

238. Bottom: Hajor, photographer. *Egypt.Saqqara.Panorama.01*. Wikimedia Commons, 2005. https://commons.wikimedia.org/wiki/File:Egypt.Saqqara.Panorama.01.jpg. CC BY-SA 3.0.

241. Parrot, A., derivative work of photograph by Nina Aldin Thune. *Sun over Pyramid*. Wikimedia Commons, 2009. https://commons.wikimedia.org/wiki/File:Sun_Over_Pyramid.jpg. CC BY-SA 3.0.

CHAPTER SIX

246. Top: Simonwakefield, photographer. *Stonehenge (Sun)*. Wikimedia Commons, 2009. https://commons.wikimedia.org/wiki/File:Stonehenge (sun).jpg. CC BY 2.0.

COPYRIGHT ACKNOWLEDGMENTS

248. Top Right: Sailko, photographer. *Messico, Aztechi, Serpente Piumato Quetzalcoatl, Pietra Periodo Postclassico Recente, 1400-1510 ca. 02*, circa 15th-16th century. Musée du quai Branly, Wikimedia Commons, 2015. https://commons.wikimedia.org/wiki/File:Messico,_aztechi,_serpente_piumato_quetzalcoatl,_pietra_periodo_postclassico_recente,_1400-1510_ca._02.JPG. CC BY 3.0.

248. Bottom: Hajor, photographer. *Tomb KV34 (Thutmose III) 11.th hour Amduat,* Valley of the Kings, Luxor, Egypt. Wikimedia Commons, 2005. https://commons.wikimedia.org/wiki/File:Egypt.KV34.07.jpg. CC BY-SA 3.0.

253. Left: Image based on the research by Roger Penrose and Vahe Gurzadyan, 2010. https://arxiv.org/ftp/arxiv/papers/1011/1011.3706.pdf. Background is a public domain image from NASA / WMAP Science Team.

253. Right: Aldorado, photographer. *May Pole (Maibaum) Top - Blue Sky.* Shutterstock.com. https://www.shutterstock.com/image-photo/may-pole-maibaum-top-blue-sky-433964464. Licensed from Shutterstock.com.

258. Sura Ondrunar Publishing. *Sphinx Summer Solstice Sunset*. 2013.

260. Left: Süßen, Matthias, photographer. *Maibaum Ostfriesland967*, Maypole in Aurich, East Frisia. Wikimedia Commons, 2010. https://commons.wikimedia.org/wiki/File:Maibaum_Ostfriesland967.jpg. CC BY 3.0.

260. Right: Sura Ondrunar Publishing. *Ancient Symbol of the Sun Illustration*. 2016.

262. Left bottom: Nyo. *Irminsul*. Wikimedia Commons, 2007. https://commons.wikimedia.org/wiki/File:Irminsul_pillar_black.PNG. CC BY 2.0.

.262. Right: Larry-Rains. *Caduceus Illustration*. Shutterstock.com. https://www.shutterstock.com/image-vector/caduceus-illustration-566291899?src=-1-39. Licensed from Shutterstock.com.

264. Lalupa, photographer. *Palazzo Braschi - Vestale 1020774*. Wikimedia Commons, 2007. https://commons.wikimedia.org/wiki/File:Palazzo_Braschi_-_Vestale_1020774.JPG. CC BY-SA 3.0.

271. Nyman, Bengt, photographer. *Midsummer Crown*. Wikimedia Commons, 2012. https://commons.wikimedia.org/wiki/File:Midsummer_Crown.jpg. CC BY 2.0.

272. Left: Käyttäjä:Kompak. Edited by Perhelion. *Ra-Horakhty Based on Nefertari's Tomb*. Wikimedia Commons, 2016. https://commons.wikimedia.org/wiki/File:Sun_god_Ra.svg. CC BY-SA 3.0.

CHAPTER SEVEN

280. Sura Ondrunar Publishing. *Great line*. 2010. Made with Google Earth, 2018. © Google, Data SIO, NOAA, U.S. Navy, NGA, GEBCO, Image Landsat / Copernicus, Image IBCAO.

CHAPTER EIGHT

282. Bodsworth, Jon, photographer. *Descendant-Grande-Pyramide*. Wikimedia Commons, 2007. https://commons.wikimedia.org/wiki/File:Descendant-grande-pyramide.jpg. © Jon Bodsworth, used by permission.

285. Nateirma~commonswiki, photographer. *Teonate*. Wikimedia Commons, 2006. https://commons.wikimedia.org/wiki/File:Teonate.JPG. CC BY-SA 3.0.

286. Klein, Jordan, photographer. *Intihuatana Solar Clock*, Machu Picchu, Peru. Wikimedia Commons, 2006. https://commons.wikimedia.org/wiki/File:Intihuatana_Solar_Clock.jpg. CC BY 2.0.

287. Sewell, Ian, photographer. *Ahu-Akivi-1,* Easter Island. Wikimedia Commons, 2006. https://commons.wikimedia.org/wiki/File:Ahu-Akivi-1.JPG. CC BY-SA 3.0.

288. Collage, top left: Gybas DigiPhoto, photographer. *Moai from Ahu Tongariki on Easter Island*. Shutterstock.com. https://www.shutterstock.com/image-photo/moai-ahu-tongariki-on-easter-island-10886431. Licensed from Shutterstock.com.

288. Collage, top center: Ndede, photographer. *Archaeological Work Gobeklitepe Turkey*. Shutterstock.com. https://www.shutterstock.com/image-photo/archaeological-work-gobeklitepe-turkey-1087902086. Licensed from Shutterstock.com.

288. Collage, top right: Kaiser, Jennifer, photographer. *Statue from Gobeklitepe,* Urfa Museum. Flickr.com, 2015. https://www.flickr.com/photos/kaiserjennifer/20263074231. CC BY 2.0.

288. Collage, bottom left: TheWanderingScot.com, photographer. *Kabul Museum: Kafiristan Statue.* 2009. http://thewanderingscot.com/photos/2009 Stans/Afghanistan/midis/IMG_7902.jpg. © TheWanderingsScot.com, used with permission.

288. Collage, bottom center: Anonymous. *Two European Ladies and a Man Are Standing in front of a Statue in Napu, Menado*, before 1937. Tropenmuseum, part of the National Museum of World Cultures. Wikimedia Commons, 2009. https://en.wikipedia.org/wiki/File:COLLECTIE_TROPENMUSEUM_Twee_Europese_dames_en_een_man_staan_voor_een_afgodsbeeld_te_Napu_Menado_TMnr_10000852.jpg. CC BY-SA 3.0.

288. Collage, bottom right: Damsea, photographer. *French Polynesia Tahiti Island Carved Stone Tiki Statue on the Marae Arahurahu, South Pacific, Oceania*. Shutterstock.com. https://www.shutterstock.com/image-photo/french-polynesia-tahiti-island-carved-stone-784904116. Licensed from Shutterstock.com.

288. Image right: Papiermond, photographer. *Karajia1*. Wikimedia Commons, 2006. https://en.wikipedia.org/wiki/File:Karajia1.jpg. CC BY-SA 3.0.

290. Gagnon, Bernard, photographer. *Knossos - North Portico 02*, The North Portico in Knossos, Crete, Greece. Wikimedia Commons, 2012. https://en.wikipedia.org/wiki/File:Knossos_-_North_Portico_02.jpg. CC BY-SA 3.0.

291. Sauber, Wolfgang, photographer. *AMI - Goldene Doppelaxt*, golden Minoan labrys. Archaeological Museum in Herakleion, Wikimedia Commons, 2009. https://en.wikipedia.org/wiki/File:AMI_-_Goldene_Doppelaxt.jpg. CC BY-SA 3.0.

CHAPTER NINE

294. Top: Graham, Edwin, photographer. *Street and Glastonbury Tor from Walton Hill*. Wikimedia Commons, 2010. https://commons.wikimedia.org/wiki/File:Street_and_Glastonbury_Tor.jpg. CC BY-SA 2.0.

294. Bottom: Comvaser, photographer. *Chichen Itza CB*. Wikimedia Commons, 2009. https://commons.wikimedia.org/wiki/File:Chichen_Itza_CB.jpg. CC BY-SA 4.0.

295. Top: Antonsen, Kenny Arne Lang. *Goseck Circle, Germany 4900 - 4700 BC*. In *Old Europe - First Civilization 7000-3000 BC*. Wikimedia Commons, 2019. https://commons.wikimedia.org/wiki/File:Goseck_circle,_Germany_4900_-_4700_BC.jpg. CC BY-SA 4.0.

296. Anagoria, photographer. *1600 Himmelsscheibe von Nebra Sky Disk Anagoria*. Pergamon Museum, Wikimedia Commons, 2012. https://commons.wikimedia.org/wiki/File:1600_Himmelsscheibe_von_Nebra_sky_disk_anagoria.jpg. CC BY 3.0.

297. Ceridwen, photographer. *Mynydd Dinas under Snow - Geograph.org.uk*. Wikimedia Commons, 2011. https://commons.wikimedia.org/wiki/File:Mynydd_Dinas_under_snow_-_geograph.org.uk_-_1151816.jpg. CC BY-SA 2.0.

298. Mountains Hunter, photographer. *Karnak Temple Sphinxes Alley*. Shutterstock.com. https://www.shutterstock.com/image-photo/karnak-temple-sphinxes-alley-ruins-1034827522. Licensed from Shutterstock.com.

299. Top left: F-E-Cameron, Steve, photographer. *S F-E-CAMERON EGYPT 2006 FEB 00289*, Temple of Horus at Edfu. Wikimedia Commons, 2007. https://commons.wikimedia.org/wiki/File:S_F-E-CAMERON_EGYPT_2006_FEB_00289.JPG. CC BY-SA 3.0.

299. Top right: Storch, Hedwig, photographer. *Karnak Temple 9456*. Wikimedia Commons, 2009. https://commons.wikimedia.org/wiki/File:Karnak_temple_9456.JPG. CC BY-SA 3.0.

299. Bottom: Shira, photographer. *Newgrange*. Wikimedia Commons, 2006. https://commons.wikimedia.org/wiki/File:Newgrange.JPG. CC BY-SA 3.0.

301. Johnbraid, photographer. *Ring of Brodgar, Orkney, Scotland*. Shutterstock.com. https://www.shutterstock.com/image-photo/ring-brodgar-orkney-scotland-neolithic-stone-134528468. Licensed from Shutterstock.com.

302. Burke, Rob, photographer. *Maes Howe Entrance Passage*. Wikimedia Commons, 2010. https://commons.wikimedia.org/wiki/File:Maes_Howe_entrance_passage_-_geograph.org.uk_-_33791.jpg. CC BY-SA 2.0.

304. RPBaiao, photographer. *Statue of Moai at the Sacred Site of Ahu Kuri a Urenga, Easter Island*. Shutterstock.com. https://www.shutterstock.com/image-photo/state-moai-sacred-site-ahu-kuri-714630817. Licensed from Shutterstock.com.

305. Budge, E. A. Wallace. *The Great Pyramid, Showing Passages and Mummy Chambers*. In *The Nile: Notes for Travellers in Egypt*, London: Harrison and Sons, 1902, p. 100. Travelers in the Middle East Archive (TIMEA), Wikimedia Commons, 2010. https://commons.wikimedia.org/wiki/File:The_Great_Pyramid,_showing_passages_and_mummy_chambers._(1902)_-_TIMEA.jpg. CC BY-SA 2.5.

COPYRIGHT ACKNOWLEDGMENTS

310. Top: Robertson, D. Gordon E., photographer. *Ollantaytambo, Tunupa Monument*. Wikimedia Commons, 2011. https://commons.wikimedia.org/wiki/File:Ollantaytambo,_Tunupa_monument.jpg. CC BY-SA 3.0.
310. Bottom: Abhishek Bansal, Ekta, photographer. *Another Stupa of Ajanta*, Ajanta Caves. Wikimedia Commons, 2010. https://commons.wikimedia.org/wiki/File:Another_Stupa_of_Ajanta.JPG. CC BY-SA 3.0.
312. Ostertag, Raymond, photographer. *Nasca Astronaut 2007 08*, Nasca, Peru. Wikimedia Commons, 2007. https://commons.wikimedia.org/wiki/File:Nasca_Astronaut_2007_08.JPG. CC BY-SA 3.0.
315. Top: Azurfrog, photographer. *Al Deir Petra*. Wikimedia Commons, 2013. https://en.wikipedia.org/wiki/File:Al_Deir_Petra.JPG. CC BY-SA 3.0.
315. Bottom: Heron, photographer. *Model by Dy Proeung, in Siem Reap, Cambodia, of Angkor Wat Central Structure*. Wikimedia Commons, 2011. https://en.wikipedia.org/wiki/File:Angkor-wat-central.jpg. CC BY-SA 3.0.
319. Grigoriev, S., photographer. *Vera Island, Megalyth 2*. Wikimedia Commons, 2011. https://commons.wikimedia.org/wiki/File:OV-M2.jpg. CC BY-SA 3.0.

CHAPTER TEN

324. Hajor, photographer. *Great Sphinx of Giza and Khafre's Pyramid*, Giza Plateau, Cairo. Wikimedia Commons, 2011. https://commons.wikimedia.org/wiki/File:Egypt.Giza.Sphinx.01.jpg. CC BY-SA 3.0.
325. Top: Heng, Kim (សុខគីមហេង), photographer. *Equinox at Angkor 21st March 2012*. Wikimedia Commons, 2012. https://commons.wikimedia.org/wiki/File:Equinox_at_Angkor_21st_March_2012.JPG. CC BY-SA 3.0.
325. Bottom: Markalexander100, photographer. *The Churning of the Ocean of Milk*, bas-relief on the south of the east wall of Angkor Wat's third enclosure. Wikimedia Commons, 2005. https://commons.wikimedia.org/wiki/File:Awatoceanofmilk01_-_color_corrected.JPG. CC BY-SA 3.0.
326. Tau'olunga. *Precession N, the Path of the North Celestial Pole among the Stars due to the Precession*. Wikimedia Commons, 2006. https://en.wikipedia.org/wiki/File:Precession_N.gif. CC BY-SA 2.5.
328. Ostertag, Raymond, photographer. *Tikal Temple1 2006 08 11*, Guatemala. Wikimedia Commons, 2011. https://commons.wikimedia.org/wiki/File:Tikal_Temple1_2006_08_11.JPG. CC-BY-SA 2.5.
330. QuartierLatin1968, photographer. *The Central Column of Cahokia's Woodhenge*. Wikimedia Commons, 2013. https://commons.wikimedia.org/wiki/File:Woodhenge_Cahokia_3990.jpg. CC BY-SA 3.0.
331. Top: Whyte, William, photographer. *Cairn T Loughcrew*. Wikimedia Commons, 2008. https://commons.wikimedia.org/wiki/File:Cairn_T_Loughcrew.jpg. CC BY-SA 2.0.
331. Bottom: Hurson, Rob, photographer. *Sun Wall, Loughcrew*. Wikimedia Commons, 2014. https://commons.wikimedia.org/wiki/File:Sun_wall,_Loughcrew.jpg. CC BY-SA 4.0.
333. Campbell, Kieran, photographer. *Cannon Fire at Millmount, Drogheda*. Wikimedia Commons, 2011. https://commons.wikimedia.org/wiki/File:Cannon_fire_at_Millmount,_Drogheda_-_geograph.org.uk_-_1079077.jpg. CC BY-SA 2.0.
334. Allen, James, photographer. *Summit of Cairnpapple*. Wikimedia Commons, 2011. https://commons.wikimedia.org/wiki/File:Summit_of_Cairnpapple_-_geograph.org.uk_-_1062278.jpg. CC BY-SA 2.0.
335. Top: Alborzagros, photographer. *Gate of All Nations, Persepolis*. Wikimedia Commons, 2015. https://en.wikipedia.org/wiki/File:Gate_of_All_Nations,_Persepolis.jpg. CC BY-SA 3.0.
336. Sahand Ace, photograph. *Faravahar Symbol in Persepolis*. Wikimedia Commons, 2013. https://commons.wikimedia.org/wiki/File:Farvahar1.JPG. CC BY-SA 3.0.

CHAPTER ELEVEN

339. Sura Ondrunar Publishing. *Sphinx Summer Solstice Sunset*. 2013.
340. Markh, photographer. *Osireion at Abydos*. Wikimedia Commons, 2008. https://commons.wikimedia.org/wiki/File:Osireion_at_Abydos.jpg. CC BY-SA 3.0.
341. Bukvoed, photographer. *Qumran National Park*, Israel. Wikimedia Commons, 2010. https://commons.wikimedia.org/wiki/File:Kumran-1-84.jpg. CC BY 3.0.

ANCIENT SOLSTICE

343. GailJohnson, photographer. *Stonehenge an Ancient Prehistoric Stone Monument near Salisbury Wiltshire UK*. Bigstock.com. https://www.bigstockphoto.com/fi/image-6771320/stock-photo-stonehenge. Used under license from GailJohnson / Bigstock.com.

347. Collage, top left: Heghnaraghpour, photographer. *Karahounch*, Zorats Karer, Armenia. Wikimedia Commons, 2017. https://commons.wikimedia.org/wiki/File:Karahounch.jpg. CC BY-SA 4.0.

347. Collage, top right: Leandroisola, photographer. *The Calzoene's "Stonehenge,"* Calçoene, Brazil, 2008. Wikimedia Commons, 2008. https://commons.wikimedia.org/wiki/File:Calçoene, Stonehenge brasileira, Amapá.jpg. CC BY 4.0.

347. Collage, bottom left: Boychou, photographer. *Stone Erections of Willong Khullen,* Manipur, India. Wikimedia Commons, 2010. https://commons.wikimedia.org/wiki/File:Stone_Erections_of_Willong_Khullen.jpg. CC BY-SA 3.0.

347. Collage, bottom center: Woods, David, photographer. *A Portion of the Orkney Neolithic Site, the Ring of Brodgar*. Shutterstock.com. https://www.shutterstock.com/image-photo/portion-orkney-neolithic-site-ring-brodgar-4674436. Licensed from Shutterstock.com.

347. Collage, bottom right: Adwo, photographer. *South Africa's Adam's Calendar Stone Replica – Argentina*. Shutterstock.com. https://www.shutterstock.com/image-photo/south-africas-adams-calendar-stone-replica-630489557. Licensed from Shutterstock.com.

347. Image bottom: Raymbetz, photographer. *Calendar Aswan*, Nabta Playa Calendar Circle, reconstructed at Aswan Nubia museum. Wikimedia Commons, 2009. https://commons.wikimedia.org/wiki/File:Calendar_aswan.JPG. CC BY-SA 3.0.

349. Engelhardt, R., photographer. *2007-06-06-Externsteine-33*, Horn-Bad Meinberg, Germany. Wikimedia Commons, 2009. https://commons.wikimedia.org/wiki/File:2007-06-06-Externsteine-33.jpg. CC BY-SA 3.0.

350. Natritmeyer, photographer. *Tablet of Shamash*. Wikimedia Commons, 2018. https://en.wikipedia.org/wiki/File:Tablet_of_Shamash.jpg. CC BY-SA 4.0.

351. Top: Dola.das85, photographer. *Ajanta Cave,* an inside view of cave 19 of Ajanta Caves. Wikimedia Commons, 2012. https://commons.wikimedia.org/wiki/File:Ajanta_Cave.jpg. CC BY-SA 3.0.

352. Price, Timothy and Nichole I. Stump. *View from Above*. In *A digital GIS Map of Ohio's Great Serpent Mound*. Wikimedia Commons, 2005. https://commons.wikimedia.org/wiki/File:Serpent_Mound.jpg. CC BY-SA 3.0.

354. HJPD, photographer. *Casa Rinconada*, Chaco Canyon, New Mexico, U.S.A. Wikimedia Commons, 2010. https://commons.wikimedia.org/wiki/File:Casa_Rinconada.jpg. CC BY 3.0.

355. Top: Hooper, Honey, photographer. *Easter Island Ahu (2006)*. Wikimedia Commons, 2009. https://commons.wikimedia.org/wiki/File:Easter Island Ahu (2006).jpg. CC BY 2.5.

355. Bottom: Sverzel, photographer. *Tulum Sverzel*, view toward the main temple in Tulum, Mexico. Wikimedia Commons, 2008. https://en.wikipedia.org/wiki/File:Tulum_sverzel.jpg. CC BY-SA 3.0.

356. El Comandante, photographer. *Descending God (Tulum)*. Wikimedia Commons, 2012. https://commons.wikimedia.org/wiki/File:Descending God (Tulum).JPG. CC BY-SA 3.0.

357. Top: Tato grasso, photographer. *0073 Uxmal*, Mexico. Wikimedia Commons, 2007. https://commons.wikimedia.org/wiki/File:0073_Uxmal.JPG. CC BY-SA 2.5.

357. Bottom: Jarvis, Dennis, photographer. *Guatemala-1520*, The Lost World Pyramid, Tikal, Guatemala. Wikimedia Commons, 2012. https://commons.wikimedia.org/wiki/File:Flickr_-_archer10_(Dennis)_-_Guatemala-1520.jpg. CC BY-SA 2.0.

358. Image created for book, based on Truman, Dave. "Ancient Alignment in the Andes Hints at a Lost Global High Culture." GrahamHancock.com, January 2, 2016. https://grahamhancock.com/truman d1. Background © Google Earth, image Landsat / Copernicus, Data SIO, NOAA, U.S. Navy, NGA, GEBCO, Data LDEO-Columbia, NSF, NOAA.

360. Top: Ximenez, Pedro, photographer. *Pyramide Güimar*. Wikimedia Commons, 2009. https://commons.wikimedia.org/wiki/File:Pyramide Güimar.jpg. CC BY-SA 2.0.

361. Top: Norris, Ray P. *Wurdi Younag Alignments*. Aboriginal Indigenous Astronomy, 2011. http://aboriginalastronomy.blogspot.com/2011/03/wurdi-youang-aboriginal-stone.html. © Ray P. Norris, http://www.emudreaming.com. Reproduced with permission.

361. Bottom: Norris, Ray P, photographer. *Wurdi Younag*, Victoria, Australia. Wikimedia Commons, 2016. https://commons.wikimedia.org/wiki/File:Wurdi_Youang.jpg. CC BY-SA 2.5.

362. Bandarin, Francesco. *Lascaux Cave*. © UNESCO, UNESCO.org, 2006. http://whc.unesco.org/en/list/85/gallery. CC BY-SA 3.0 IGO.

COPYRIGHT ACKNOWLEDGMENTS

CHAPTER TWELVE

369. Bronnikov, Fyodor. *Pythagoreans Anthem to the Rising Sun*. 1869. Wikimedia Commons, 2007. https://commons.wikimedia.org/wiki/File:Bronnikov_gimnpifagoreizev.jpg. Public domain.

371. Azarian, Dana, photographer. *Celebrating Nowruz in Mariwan*. Tasnim News Agency, 2016, Wikimedia Commons, 2017. https://commons.wikimedia.org/wiki/File:Celebrating_Nowruz_in_Mariwan.jpg. CC BY 4.0.

372. Sandyraidy, photographer. *Druids Celebrating at Stonehenge (1)*. Wikimedia Commons, 2009. https://commons.wikimedia.org/wiki/File:Druids_celebrating_at_Stonehenge_(1).png. CC BY-SA 2.0.

374. Top: Dedda71, photographer. *Pagan Meditation*. Wikimedia Commons, 2009. https://commons.wikimedia.org/wiki/File:Pagan_meditation.jpg. CC BY 3.0.

374. Bottom: PersianDutchNetwork, photographer. *Persian Lady Recites Hafez Poems in Yalda Night*. Wikimedia Commons, 2014. https://commons.wikimedia.org/wiki/File:Persian_Lady_recites_Hafez_Poems_in_Yalda_Night.jpg. CC BY-SA 3.0.

377. GiW, photographer. *Stebykla 01*, reconstruction of ancient Lithuanian "Sky Lighthouse Observation" (Kulionys, Molėtai district). Wikimedia Commons, 2012. https://commons.wikimedia.org/wiki/File:Stebykla_01.jpg. CC BY-SA 3.0.

378. Smit, photographer. *Gate to Ki Monastery*. Shutterstock.com. https://www.shutterstock.com/image-photo/gates-ki-monastery-himalayas-mountain-125246675. Licensed from Shutterstock.com.

379. Cleveland, Jeff, photographer. *Inti Raymi Ceremony*. Shutterstock.com. https://www.shutterstock.com/image-photo/cusco-peru-june-24-2015-men-1414113587. Licensed from Shutterstock.com.

381. Bottom: YSEE. *Hellen ritual (3)*. Supreme Council of Ethnikoi Hellenes, Wikimedia Commons, 2009. https://commons.wikimedia.org/wiki/File:Hellen_ritual_(3).jpg. CC BY 2.0.

385. Elston, Geoff, photographer. *Sun White*. Society for Popular Astronomy, Wikimedia Commons, 2014. https://commons.wikimedia.org/wiki/File:Sun_white.jpg. CC BY 4.0.

386. Top: Masalskis, Mantas, photographer. *Romuvan ceremony (10)*. Wikimedia Commons, 2009. https://commons.wikimedia.org/wiki/File:Romuvan ceremony (10).PNG. CC BY 2.0.

386. Bottom: Thelmadatter, photographer. *PyramidSunEquinox1*. Wikimedia Commons, 2010. https://commons.wikimedia.org/wiki/File:PyramidSunEquinox1.JPG. CC BY-SA 3.0.

393. Lobachev, Vladimir, photographer. *Ivan Kupala Day in 2011 08*, Belgorod region. Wikimedia Commons, 2014. https://commons.wikimedia.org/wiki/File:Ivan_Kupala_Day_in_2011_08.JPG. CC BY-SA 3.0.

CHAPTER THIRTEEN

404. Mukerjee, photographer. *D01944 Arati Rakshitbari Giridih*, at a puja in Giridih, Jharkhand. Wikimedia Commons, 2008. https://commons.wikimedia.org/wiki/File:D01944_Arati_Rakshitbari_giridih.jpg. CC BY-SA 4.0.

407. Royan, Jorge, photographer. *India - Varanasi Sun Greet - 0270*, Ganges Varanasi Benares, India. Wikimedia Commons, 2012. https://commons.wikimedia.org/wiki/File:India_-_Varanasi_sun_greet_-_0270.jpg. CC BY-SA 3.0.

412. Ministry of Tourism (GODL-India). *The Priest in the Final Rituals of Immersing the Darpan to Mark the Completion of the Five Durga Puja Festival on the Maha Dashami at Kolkata on October 21, 2007*. Wikimedia Commons, 2018. https://commons.wikimedia.org/wiki/File:The_Priest_in_the_final_rituals_of_immersing_the_Darpan_to_mark_the_completion_of_the_five_Durga_Puja_Festival_on_the_Maha_Dashami_at_Kolkata_on_October_21,_2007.jpg. © Government of India, used with permission.

415. Berig, photographer. Edits by Nils von Barth and The Man in Question. *Sacrificial Scene on Hammars – Valknut*, Stora Hammar stone, Sweden. Wikimedia Commons, 2009. https://commons.wikimedia.org/wiki/File:Sacrificial_scene_on_Hammars_-_Valknut.png. CC BY-SA 3.0.

416. Top: Berg, Jónína K., photographer. Edited by Haukur Þorgeirsson. *Jörmundur Ingi 1994*, Jörmundur Ingi Hansen being sworn in as allsherjargoði ("common chieftain" or "high priest") at Þingvellir. Wikimedia Commons, 2009. https://commons.wikimedia.org/wiki/File:Jörmundur Ingi 1994.jpg. CC BY-SA 3.0.

416. Bottom: Þorgeirsson, Haukur, photographer. *Sigurblót 2009*, Iceland. Wikimedia Commons, 2009. https://commons.wikimedia.org/wiki/File:Sigurblót 2009.JPG. CC BY-SA 3.0.

423. Top: Radcliff, Rebecca, photographer. *Heathen Altar*. Wikimedia Commons, 2009. https://commons.wikimedia.org/wiki/File:Heathen_altar.png. CC BY-SA 2.0.

423. Bottom: Novikov, Alexei, photographer. *Runic Inscriptions*. Shutterstock.com. https://www.shutterstock.com/image-photo/runic-inscriptions-on-runestone-ljungby-sweden-286417871. Licensed from Shutterstock.com.

428. Sauber, Wolfgang, photographer. *AMI - Kamaresvase 1*. Archaeological Museum of Herakleion, Wikimedia Commons, 2009. https://commons.wikimedia.org/wiki/File:AMI_-_Kamaresvase_1.jpg. CC BY-SA 3.0.

429. *Autumn Equinox Ceremony Diagram*. © Sura Ondrunar Publishing.

430. Bottom right: Osseman, Dick, photographer. *Antakya Dionysus and Ariadne Mosaic 7507*. Antakya Archaeological Museum, Wikimedia Commons, 2019. https://commons.wikimedia.org/wiki/File:Antakya_Dionysus_and_Ariadne_mosaic_7507.jpg. CC BY-SA 4.0.

431. Left: Gilmanshin, photographer. *Head of Minoan Bull*. Shutterstock.com. https://www.shutterstock.com/image-photo/head-minoan-bull-sacred-animal-ancient-257368639. Licensed from Shutterstock.com.

431. Right: Sauber, Wolfgang, photographer. *AMI - Goldene Doppelaxt*, golden Minoan labrys. Archaeological Museum in Herakleion, Wikimedia Commons, 2009. https://en.wikipedia.org/wiki/File:AMI_-_Goldene_Doppelaxt.jpg. CC BY-SA 3.0.

437. Top: Mollerus, Sharon, photographer. *NAMA Linear B Tablet of Pylos*. National Archaeological Museum of Athens, Wikimedia Commons, 2009. https://commons.wikimedia.org/wiki/File:NAMA_Linear_B_tablet_of_Pylos.jpg. CC BY 2.0.

CHAPTER FOURTEEN

441. Left: Moroder, Wolfgang, photographer. *Geburt Christi Pescoller Senior 1923*. Chapel of Saint Mary, San Ciascian, Italy, Wikimedia Commons, 2013. https://commons.wikimedia.org/wiki/File:Geburt_Christi_Pescoller_senior_1923.jpg. CC BY-SA 3.0.

441. Center: Raddato, Carole, photographer. *Stone Relief with Mithras Emerging from the Cosmic Egg, from Housesteads, CIMRM 860, Great North Museum, Newcastle (24455529177)*. Great North Museum, Newcastle, Wikimedia Commons, 2018. https://commons.wikimedia.org/wiki/File:Stone_relief_with_Mithras_emerging_from_the_cosmic_egg,_from_Housesteads,_CIMRM_860,_Great_North_Museum,_Newcastle_(24455529177).jpg. CC BY-SA 2.0.

448. Motta, Cyntia, photographer. *Inti Raymi*, Cusco, Peru. Wikimedia Commons, 2008. https://commons.wikimedia.org/wiki/File:Inti_Raymi.jpg. CC BY-SA 3.0.

450. Top: Martínez, Marco Antonio Ochante, photographer. *Vilcashuamán 03 - Ayacucho – Perú*. Wikimedia Commons, 2017. https://commons.wikimedia.org/wiki/File:Vilcashuamán 03 - Ayacucho - Perú.jpg. CC BY-SA 4.0.

450. Bottom: Green, Mark, photographer. *Inti Raymi*. Shutterstock.com. https://www.shutterstock.com/image-photo/june-24-2010-cusco-peru-inca-1088104811?src=TmK_Pa6tS59Jj1t9AIsqUQ-1-23. Licensed from Shutterstock.com.

451. Left: ECP Photography, photographer. *Incan Statue*. Shutterstock.com. https://www.shutterstock.com/image-photo/incan-statue-standing-high-square-cusco-683532586?src=I_vXvQlgRglDU5rWrejdkw-1-64. Licensed from Shutterstock.com.

451. Center: Wellcome Collection. *Virgin of the Sun*. In *The Costume of the Inhabitants of Peru*, London: J. Edington, circa 1810. Wikimedia Commons, 2014. https://commons.wikimedia.org/wiki/File:Virgin_of_the_Sun_Wellcome_L0042050.jpg. CC BY 4.0.

451. Right: Karenmcoboss, photographer. *Inyi Raymi 02*, Equador. Wikimedia Commons, 2019. https://commons.wikimedia.org/wiki/File:Inyi_Raymi_02.jpg. CC BY-SA 4.0.

456. Jisa39, photographer. *Celebración del Inti Raymi en el Museo Nacional de Historia Natural*, at the National Museum of Natural History of Chile. Wikimedia Commons, 2017. https://commons.wikimedia.org/wiki/File:Celebración del Inti Raymi en el Museo Nacional de Historia Natural.jpg. CC BY-SA 4.0.

459. Tanko, Barna, photographer. *Quechua Women Preparing Flat Bread*. Shutterstock.com. https://www.shutterstock.com/image-photo/june-25-2017-cotacachi-ecuador-quechua-695547583. Licensed from Shutterstock.com.

460. Raele, P., photographer. *Inti Raymi 2018*. Wikimedia Commons, 2019. https://commons.wikimedia.org/wiki/File:Inti_Raymi_2018.jpg. CC BY-SA 4.0.

CHAPTER FIFTEEN

463. Right: Schele, Linda. *Drawing of Plate Interior Showing the Rebirth of the Maize God from a Turtle Shell* SD-5505. In *Maya Cosmos: Three Thousand Years on the Shaman's Path*, by David A. Freidel, Linda Schele, and Joy Parker, New York: W. Morrow, 1993, p. 371, fig. 8:25b. Ancient Americas at LACMA, http://ancientamericas.org/collection/aa010550. © David Schele, used by permission on behalf of LACMA.

469. Todorovic, Aleksandar, photographer. *Maya Fire Ceremony*. Shutterstock.com. https://www.shutterstock.com/image-photo/tikal-guatemala-dec-21-2015-unidentified-540351640. Licensed from Shutterstock.com.

471. Roe, Herb, photographer. *Cox Style Gorget HRoe 2012*. Wikimedia Commons, 2012. https://commons.wikimedia.org/wiki/File:Cox_style_gorget_HRoe_2012.jpg. CC BY-SA 3.0.

477. Schele, Linda. *Drawing of Plate Interior Showing the Rebirth of the Maize God from a Turtle Shell* SD-5505. In *Maya Cosmos: Three Thousand Years on the Shaman's Path*, by David A. Freidel, Linda Schele, and Joy Parker, New York: W. Morrow, 1993, p. 371, fig. 8:25b. Ancient Americas at LACMA, http://ancientamericas.org/collection/aa010550. © David Schele, used by permission on behalf of LACMA.

CHAPTER SIXTEEN

489. Salman, Venera, photographer. *Kupala*. Shutterstock.com. https://www.shutterstock.com/image-photo/on-june-22-2016-kupala-festivalholiday-1446752678. Licensed from Shutterstock.com.

491. Javir, Boryslaw, photographer. *Rodnover Shrine in Kaluga, Russia*. Wikimedia Commons, 2013. https://commons.wikimedia.org/wiki/File:Rodnover_shrine_in_Kaluga,_Russia.png. GNU Free Documentation License, Version 1.2. https://commons.wikimedia.org/wiki/Commons:GNU_Free_Documentation_License,_version_1.2.

492. Union of Slavic Rodnover Communities / Союз Славянских Общин Славянской Родной Веры, ССО СРВ. *Shrine of the Temple of Svarozhich's Fire in Krasotinka, Kaluga on Earth Day 2017*, Krasotinka, Kaluga, Russia. Wikimedia Commons, 2018. https://commons.wikimedia.org/wiki/File:Shrine_of_the_Temple_of_Svarozhich's_Fire_in_Krasotinka,_Kaluga_on_Earth_Day_2017.jpg. CC BY-SA 4.0.

496. Lazarenka, Svetlana, photographer. *Men with a Kupala Post*. Shutterstock.com. https://www.shutterstock.com/image-photo/belarus-city-gomel-july-07-2018-1431659099. Licensed from Shutterstock.com.

497. Kryzhanivskyi, Viktor Solceslav (1950-2016). *Kupala*.

498. Top: Members of the Polish Rodnover Association. *Polish Rodnover Veche congregation (0)*, Poland. Wikimedia Commons, 2009. https://commons.wikimedia.org/wiki/File:Polish_Rodnover_Veche_congregation_(0).PNG. CC BY 2.0.

498. Bottom: Belova, Julia, photographer. *Girl Launching Flower Wreath*. Shutterstock.com. https://www.shutterstock.com/image-photo/blonde-girl-traditional-slave-dress-launching-789863320. Licensed from Shutterstock.com.

499. Top: Rak, Irina, photographer. *Festival Ringing Cedars 2014 June 22 Ирина 53*, Ustinka, Belgorod, Russia. Wikimedia Commons, 2014. https://commons.wikimedia.org/wiki/File:Festival Ringing Cedars 2014 June 22 Ирина 53.jpg. CC BY-SA 3.0.

499. Bottom: Loz, Lilija, photographer. *Dew Holiday Festival*. Shutterstock.com. https://www.shutterstock.com/image-photo/vilnius-lithuania-23-june-2018-saint-1406289098. Licensed from Shutterstock.com.

CHAPTER SEVENTEEN

502. Sura Ondrunar Publishing. *Symbolic Cross*. 2019.
503. © Sura Ondrunar Publishing.

SŪRA ONDRÚNAR
PUBLISHING

suraondrunar.org

For More Information Visit

SAKROSAWEL.COM

www.ingramcontent.com/pod-product-compliance
Lightning Source LLC
Chambersburg PA
CBHW080405230426
43662CB00016B/2321